SER
ON SEVER

BY THE

REV. JOHN WESLEY, A.M.

SOMETIME FELLOW OF LINCOLN COLLEGE, OXFORD

First Series

CONSISTING OF FORTY-FOUR DISCOURSES, PUBLISHED IN FOUR VOLUMES, IN THE
YEARS 1746, 1748, 1750 AND 1760 (FOURTH EDITION, 1787); TO WHICH
REFERENCE IS MADE IN THE TRUST-DEEDS OF THE METHODIST CHAPELS, AS
CONSTITUTING, WITH MR. WESLEY'S NOTES ON THE NEW TESTAMENT, THE
STANDARD DOCTRINES OF THE METHODIST CONNEXION.

THE EPWORTH PRESS

Published by
Epworth Press

4 John Wesley Road
Werrington
Peterborough PE4 6ZP

This edition first published 1944
Twenty-second impression 2005

Printed and bound in Great Britain by Biddles Ltd
King's Lynn, Norfolk

PREFACE

1. THE following Sermons contain the substance of what I have been preaching for between eight and nine years last past.[1] During that time I have frequently spoken in public, on every subject in the ensuing collection; and I am not conscious that there is any one point of doctrine, on which I am accustomed to speak in public, which is not here, incidentally, if not professedly, laid before every Christian reader.   Every serious man who peruses these will therefore see, in the clearest manner, what these doctrines are which I embrace and teach as the essentials of true religion.

2. But I am throughly sensible, these are not proposed in such a manner as some may expect. Nothing here appears in an elaborate, elegant, or oratorical dress. If it had been my desire or design to write thus, my leisure would not permit. But, in truth, I, at present, designed nothing less; for I now write, as I generally speak, *ad populum*—to the bulk of mankind, to those who neither relish nor understand the art of speaking; but who, notwithstanding, are competent judges of those truths which are necessary to present and future happiness. I mention this, that curious readers may spare themselves the labour of seeking for what they will not find.

3. I design plain truth for plain people: therefore, of set purpose, I abstain from all nice and philosophical speculations; from all perplexed and intricate reasonings; and, as far as possible, from even the show of learning, unless in sometimes citing the original Scripture. I labour to avoid all words which are not easy to be understood, all which are not used in common life; and, in particular, those kinds of technical terms that so frequently occur in Bodies of Divinity; those modes of speaking which men of reading are intimately acquainted with, but which to common people are an unknown tongue. Yet, I am not assured, that I do not sometimes slide into them unawares; it is so extremely natural to imagine, that a word which is familiar to ourselves is so to all the world.

4. Nay, my design is, in some sense, to forget all that ever I have read in my life. I mean to speak, in the general, as if I had never read one author, ancient or modern (always excepting the inspired). I am persuaded, that, on the one hand, this may be a means of enabling me more clearly to express the sentiments of my heart, while I simply follow the chain of my own thoughts, without entangling myself with those of

In the year 1746.

other men; and that, on the other, I shall come with fewer weights upon my mind, with less of prejudice and prepossession, either to search for myself, or to deliver to others, the naked truths of the gospel.

5. To candid, reasonable men, I am not afraid to lay open what have been the inmost thoughts of my heart. I have thought, I am a creature of a day, passing through life as an arrow through the air. I am a spirit come from God, and returning to God: just hovering over the great gulf; till, a few moments hence, I am no more seen; I drop into an unchangeable eternity! I want to know one thing—the way to heaven; how to land safe on that happy shore. God Himself has condescended to teach the way; for this very end He came from heaven. He hath written it down in a book. O give me that book! At any price, give me the book of God! I have it: here is knowledge enough for me. Let me be *homo unius libri*.[1] Here then I am, far from the busy ways of men. I sit down alone: only God is here. In His presence I open, I read His book; for this end, to find the way to heaven. Is there a doubt concerning the meaning of what I read? Does anything appear dark or intricate? I lift up my heart to the Father of Lights: 'Lord, is it not Thy word, "If any man lack wisdom, let him ask of God"? Thou "givest liberally, and upbraidest not." Thou hast said, "If any be willing to do Thy will, he shall know." I am willing to do, let me know, Thy will.' I then search after and consider parallel passages of Scripture, 'comparing spiritual things with spiritual.' I meditate thereon with all the attention and earnestness of which my mind is capable. If any doubt still remains, I consult those who are experienced in the things of God; and then the writings whereby, being dead, they yet speak. And what I thus learn, that I teach.

6. I have accordingly set down in the following sermons what I find in the Bible concerning the way to heaven; with a view to distinguish this way of God from all those which are the inventions of men. I have endeavoured to describe the true, the scriptural, experimental religion, so as to omit nothing which is a real part thereof, and to add nothing thereto which is not. And herein it is more especially my desire, first, to guard those who are just setting their faces toward heaven (and who, having little acquaintance with the things of God, are the more liable to be turned out of the way), from formality, from mere outside religion, which has almost driven heart-religion out of the world; and, secondly, to warn those who know the religion of the heart, the faith which worketh by love, lest at any time they make void the law through faith, and so fall back into the snare of the devil.

7. By the advice and at the request of some of my friends, I have

[1] A man of one book.

prefixed to the other sermons contained in this volume, three sermons of my own, and one of my brother's, preached before the University of Oxford. My design required some discourses on those heads; and I preferred these before any others, as being a stronger answer than any which can be drawn up now, to those who have frequently asserted that we have changed our doctrine of late, and do not preach now what we did some years ago. Any man of understanding may now judge for himself, when he has compared the latter with the former sermons.

8. But some may say, I have mistaken the way myself, although I take upon me to teach it to others. It is probable many will think this; and it is very possible that I have. But I trust, whereinsoever I have mistaken, my mind is open to conviction. I sincerely desire to be better informed. I say to God and man, 'What I know not, teach thou me!'

9. Are you persuaded you see more clearly than me? It is not unlikely that you may. Then treat me as you would desire to be treated yourself upon a change of circumstances. Point me out a better way than I have yet known. Show me it is so, by plain proof of Scripture. And if I linger in the path I have been accustomed to tread, and am therefore unwilling to leave it, labour with me a little; take me by the hand, and lead me as I am able to bear. But be not displeased if I entreat you not to beat me down in order to quicken my pace: I can go but feebly and slowly at best; then, I should not be able to go at all. May I not request of you, further, not to give me hard names, in order to bring me into the right way? Suppose I were ever so much in the wrong, I doubt this would not set me right. Rather, it would make me run so much the farther from you, and so get more and more out of the way.

10. Nay, perhaps, if you are angry, so shall I be too; and then there will be small hopes of finding the truth. If once anger arise, ἠΰτε καπνός (as Homer somewhere expresses it), this smoke will so dim the eyes of my soul, that I shall be able to see nothing clearly. For God's sake, if it be possible to avoid it, let us not provoke one another to wrath Let us not kindle in each other this fire of hell; much less blow it up into a flame. If we could discern truth by that dreadful light, would it not be loss, rather than gain? For, how far is love, even with many wrong opinions, to be preferred before truth itself without love! We may die without the knowledge of many truths, and yet be carried into Abraham's bosom. But, if we die without love, what will knowledge avail? Just as much as it avails the devil and his angels.

The God of love forbid we should ever make the trial! May He prepare us for the knowledge of all truth, by filling our hearts with all His love, and with all joy and peace in believing!

CONTENTS

SERMON I

SALVATION BY FAITH

PREACHED AT

ST. MARY'S OXFORD, BEFORE THE UNIVERSITY,
ON JUNE 18, 1738.[1]

By grace are ye saved through faith.—EPH. ii. 8.

ALL the blessings which God hath bestowed upon man are of His mere grace, bounty, or favour; His free, undeserved favour; favour altogether undeserved; man having no claim to the least of His mercies. It was free grace that 'formed man of the dust of the ground, and breathed into him a living soul,' and stamped on that soul the image of God, and 'put all things under his feet.' The same free grace continues to us, at this day, life, and breath, and all things. For there is nothing we are, or have, or do, which can deserve the least thing at God's hand. 'All our works, Thou, O God, hast wrought in us.' These, therefore, are so many more instances of free mercy: and whatever righteousness may be found in man, this is also the gift of God.

2. Wherewithal then shall a sinful man atone for any the least of his sins? With his own works? No. Were they ever so many or holy, they are not his own, but God's. But indeed they are all unholy and sinful themselves, so that every one of them needs a fresh atonement. Only corrupt fruit grows on a corrupt tree. And his heart is altogether corrupt and abominable; being 'come short of the glory of God,' the glorious righteousness at first impressed on his soul, after the image of his great Creator. Therefore, having nothing, neither righteousness nor works, to plead, his mouth is utterly stopped before God.

[1] Wesley put June 18; but he was then in Holland. See *Journal.* It was delivered on June 11.

1

3. If then sinful men find favour with God, it is 'grace upon grace!' If God vouchsafe still to pour fresh blessings upon us, yea, the greatest of all blessings, salvation; what can we say to these things, but, 'Thanks be unto God for His unspeakable gift!' And thus it is. Herein 'God commendeth His love toward us, in that, while we were yet sinners, Christ died' to save us. 'By grace' then 'are ye saved through faith.' Grace is the source, faith the condition, of salvation.

Now, that we fall not short of the grace of God, it concerns us carefully to inquire,—
I.   WHAT FAITH IT IS THROUGH WHICH WE ARE SAVED.
II. WHAT IS THE SALVATION WHICH IS THROUGH FAITH.
III. HOW WE MAY ANSWER SOME OBJECTIONS.

I.   What faith it is through which we are saved.
1.   And, first, it is not barely the faith of a Heathen.
Now, God requireth of a Heathen to believe, 'that God is; that He is a rewarder of them that diligently seek Him'; and that He is to be sought by glorifying Him as God, by giving Him thanks for all things, and by a careful practice of moral virtue, of justice, mercy, and truth, toward their fellow creatures. A Greek or Roman, therefore, yea, a Scythian or Indian, was without excuse if he did not believe thus much: the being and attributes of God, a future state of reward and punishment, and the obligatory nature of moral virtue. For this is barely the faith of a Heathen.

2.   Nor, secondly, is it the faith of a devil, though this goes much farther than that of a Heathen. For the devil believes, not only that there is a wise and powerful God, gracious to reward, and just to punish; but also, that Jesus is the Son of God, the Christ, the Saviour of the world. So we find him declaring, in express terms, 'I know Thee who Thou art; the Holy One of God' (Luke iv. 34). Nor can we doubt but that unhappy spirit believes all those words which came out of the mouth of the Holy One; yea, and whatsoever else was written by those holy men of old, of two of whom he was compelled to give that glorious testimony, 'These men are the servants of the most high

God, who show unto you the way of salvation.' Thus much, then, the great enemy of God and man believes, and trembles in believing,—that God was made manifest in the flesh; that He will 'tread all enemies under His feet'; and that 'all Scripture was given by inspiration of God.' Thus far goeth the faith of a devil.

3. Thirdly. The faith through which we are saved, in that sense of the word which will hereafter be explained, is not barely that which the Apostles themselves had while Christ was yet upon earth; though they so believed on Him as to 'leave all and follow Him'; although they had then power to work miracles, to 'heal all manner of sickness, and all manner of disease'; yea, they had then 'power and authority over all devils'; and, which is beyond all this, were sent by their Master to 'preach the kingdom of God.'

4. What faith is it then through which we are saved? It may be answered, first, in general, it is a faith in Christ: Christ, and God through Christ, are the proper objects of it. Herein, therefore, it is sufficiently, absolutely distinguished from the faith either of ancient or modern Heathens. And from the faith of a devil it is fully distinguished by this: it is not barely a speculative, rational thing, a cold, lifeless assent, a train of ideas in the head; but also a disposition of the heart. For thus saith the Scripture, 'With the heart man believeth unto righteousness'; and, 'If thou shalt confess with thy mouth the Lord Jesus, and shalt believe in thy heart that God hath raised Him from the dead, thou shalt be saved.'

5. And herein does it differ from that faith which the Apostles themselves had while our Lord was on earth, that it acknowledges the necessity and merit of His death, and the power of His resurrection. It acknowledges His death as the only sufficient means of redeeming man from death eternal, and His resurrection as the restoration of us all to life and immortality; inasmuch as He 'was delivered for our sins, and rose again for our justification.' Christian faith is then, not only an assent to the whole gospel of Christ, but also a full reliance on the blood of Christ; a trust in the merits of His life, death, and resurrection; a recumbency upon Him as our atonement and our life, *as given for us*, and *living in us*; and, in consequence hereof, a closing with Him, and

cleaving to Him, as our 'wisdom, righteousness, sanctification, and redemption,' or, in one word, our salvation.

II. What salvation it is, which is through this faith, is the second thing to be considered.

1. And, first, whatsoever else it imply, it is a present salvation. It is something attainable, yea, actually attained, on earth, by those who are partakers of this faith. For thus saith the Apostle to the believers at Ephesus, and in them to the believers of all ages, not, *Ye shall be* (though that also is true), but, '*Ye are saved through faith.*'

2. *Ye are saved* (to comprise all in one word) from sin. This is the salvation which is through faith. This is that great salvation foretold by the angel, before God brought His First-begotten into the world: 'Thou shalt call His name JESUS; for He shall save His people from their sins.' And neither here, nor in other parts of holy writ, is there any limitation or restriction. All His people, or, as it is elsewhere expressed, 'all that believe in Him,' He will save from all their sins; from original and actual, past and present sin, 'of the flesh and of the spirit.' Through faith that is in Him, they are saved both from the guilt and from the power of it.

3. First, from the guilt of all past sin: for, whereas all the world is guilty before God, insomuch that should He 'be extreme to mark what is done amiss, there is none that could abide it'; and whereas, 'by the law is' only 'the knowledge of sin,' but no deliverance from it, so that, 'by' fulfilling 'the deeds of the law, no flesh can be justified in His sight': now, 'the righteousness of God, which is by faith of Jesus Christ, is manifested unto all that believe.' Now, 'they are justified freely by His grace, through the redemption that is in Jesus Christ.' 'Him God hath set forth to be a propitiation through faith in His blood, to declare His righteousness for (or by) the remission of the sins that are past.' Now hath Christ taken away 'the curse of the law, being made a curse for us.' He hath 'blotted out the handwriting that was against us, taking it out of the way, nailing it to His cross.' 'There is therefore no condemnation now to them which' believe 'in Christ Jesus.'

4. And being saved from guilt, they are saved from fear. Not indeed from a filial fear of offending; but from all servile fear; from that fear which hath torment; from fear of punishment; from fear of the wrath of God, whom they now no longer regard as a severe Master, but as an indulgent Father. 'They have not received again the spirit of bondage, but the Spirit of adoption, whereby they cry, Abba, Father: the Spirit itself also bearing witness with their spirits, that they are the children of God.' They are also saved from the fear, though not from the possibility, of falling away from the grace of God, and coming short of the great and precious promises. Thus have they 'peace with God through our Lord Jesus Christ. They rejoice in hope of the glory of God. And the love of God is shed abroad in their hearts, through the Holy Ghost, which is given unto them.' And hereby they are persuaded (though perhaps not at all times, nor with the same fullness of persuasion), that 'neither death, nor life, nor things present, nor things to come, nor height, nor depth, nor any other creature, shall be able to separate them from the love of God, which is in Christ Jesus our Lord.'

5. Again: through this faith they are saved from the power of sin, as well as from the guilt of it. So the Apostle declares, 'Ye know that He was manifested to take away our sins; and in Him is no sin. Whosoever abideth in Him sinneth not' (1 John iii. 5, &c.). Again: 'Little children, let no man deceive you. He that committeth sin is of the devil. Whosoever believeth is born of God. And whosoever is born of God doth not commit sin; for His seed remaineth in him: and he cannot sin, because he is born of God.' Once more: 'We know that whosoever is born of God sinneth not; but he that is begotten of God keepeth himself, and that wicked one toucheth him not' (1 John v. 18).

6. He that is, by faith, born of God sinneth not (1) by any habitual sin; for all habitual sin is sin reigning: but sin cannot reign in any that believeth. Nor (2) by any wilful sin: for his will, while he abideth in the faith, is utterly set against all sin, and abhorreth it as deadly poison. Nor (3) by any sinful desire; for he continually desireth the holy and perfect will of God; and any tendency to an unholy desire, he by the grace of God, stifleth in the birth. Nor (4) doth he sin by infirmities, whether in act.

2

word, or thought; for his infirmities have no concurrence of his will; and without this they are not properly sins. Thus, 'he that is born of God doth not commit sin': and though he cannot say he hath not sinned, yet now 'he sinneth not.'

7. This then is the salvation which is through faith, even in the present world: a salvation from sin, and the consequences of sin, both often expressed in the word *justification*; which, taken in the largest sense, implies a deliverance from guilt and punishment, by the atonement of Christ actually applied to the soul of the sinner now believing on Him, and a deliverance from the power of sin, through Christ *formed in his heart*. So that he who is thus justified, or saved by faith, is indeed *born again*. He is *born again of the Spirit* unto a new life, which 'is hid with Christ in God.' And as a new-born babe he gladly receives the ἄδολον, '*sincere* milk of the word, and grows thereby'; going on in the might of the Lord his God, from faith to faith, from grace to grace, until at length, he come unto 'a perfect man, unto the measure of the stature of the fullness of Christ.'

III. The first usual objection to this is,

1. That to preach salvation, or justification, by faith only, is to preach against holiness and good works. To which a short answer might be given: 'It would be so, if we spake, as some do, of a faith which was separate from these; but we speak of a faith which is not so, but productive of all good works, and all holiness.'

2. But it may be of use to consider it more at large; especially since it is no new objection, but as old as St. Paul's time: for even then it was asked, 'Do we not make void the law through faith?' We answer, first, all who preach not faith do manifestly make void the law; either directly and grossly, by limitations and comments that eat out all the spirit of the text; or indirectly, by not pointing out the only means whereby it is possible to perform it. Whereas, secondly, 'we establish the law,' both by showing its full extent and spiritual meaning; and by calling all to that living way, whereby 'the righteousness of the law may be fulfilled in them.' These, while they trust in the blood of Christ alone, use all the ordinances which He hath appointed, do

all the 'good works which He had before prepared that they should walk therein,' and enjoy and manifest all holy and heavenly tempers, even the same mind that was in Christ Jesus.

3. But does not preaching this faith lead men into pride? We answer, Accidentally it may: therefore ought every believer to be earnestly cautioned, in the words of the great Apostle, 'Because of unbelief,' the first branches 'were broken off: and thou standest by faith. Be not high-minded, but fear. If God spared not the natural branches, take heed lest He spare not thee. Behold therefore the goodness and severity of God! On them which fell, severity; but towards thee, goodness, if thou continue in His goodness; otherwise thou also shalt be cut off.' And while he continues therein, he will remember those words of St. Paul, foreseeing and answering this very objection (Rom. iii. 27), 'Where is boasting then? It is excluded. By what law? of works? Nay: but by the law of faith.' If a man were justified by his works, he would have whereof to glory. But there is no glorying for him 'that worketh not, but believeth on Him that justifieth the ungodly' (Rom. iv. 5). To the same effect are the words both preceding and following the text (Eph. ii. 4, &c.): 'God, who is rich in mercy, even when we were dead in sins, hath quickened us together with Christ (by grace ye are saved), that He might show the exceeding riches of His grace in His kindness toward us through Christ Jesus. For by grace are ye saved through faith; and that not of yourselves.' Of yourselves cometh neither your faith nor your salvation: 'it is the gift of God'; the free, undeserved gift; the faith through which ye are saved, as well as the salvation which He of His own good pleasure, His mere favour, annexes thereto. That ye believe, is one instance of His grace; that believing ye are saved, another. 'Not of works, lest any man should boast.' For all our works, all our righteousness, which were before our believing, merited nothing of God but condemnation; so far were they from deserving faith, which therefore, whenever given, is not of works. Neither is salvation of the works we do when we believe; for it is then God that worketh in us: and, therefore, that He giveth us a reward for what He Himself worketh, only commendeth the riches of His mercy, but leaveth us nothing whereof to glory.

4. However, may not the speaking thus of the mercy of God, as saving or justifying freely by faith only, encourage men in sin? Indeed, it may and will: many will 'continue in sin that grace may abound'; but their blood is upon their own head. The goodness of God ought to lead them to repentance; and so it will those who are sincere of heart. When they know there is yet forgiveness with Him, they will cry aloud that He would blot out their sins also, through faith which is in Jesus. And if they earnestly cry, and faint not; if they seek Him in all the means He hath appointed; if they refuse to be comforted till He come; 'He will come, and will not tarry.' And He can do much work in a short time. Many are the examples, in the Acts of the Apostles, of God's working this faith in men's hearts, even like lightning falling from heaven. So in the same hour that Paul and Silas began to preach, the jailer repented, believed, and was baptized; as were three thousand, by St. Peter, on the day of Pentecost, who all repented and believed at his first preaching. And, blessed be God, there are now many living proofs that He is still 'mighty to save.'

5. Yet to the same truth, placed in another view, a quite contrary objection is made: 'If a man cannot be saved by all that he can do, this will drive men to despair.' True, to despair of being saved by their own works, their own merits, or righteousness. And so it ought; for none can trust in the merits of Christ, till he has utterly renounced his own. He that 'goeth about to establish his own righteousness' cannot receive the righteousness of God. The righteousness which is of faith cannot be given him while he trusteth in that which is of the law.

6. But this, it is said, is an uncomfortable doctrine. The devil spoke like himself, that is, without either truth or shame, when he dared to suggest to men that it is such. It is the only comfortable one, it is 'very full of comfort,' to all self-destroyed, self-condemned sinners. That 'whosoever believeth on Him shall not be ashamed: that the same Lord over all is rich unto all that call upon Him': here is comfort, high as heaven, stronger than death! What! Mercy for all? For Zacchaeus, a public robber? For Mary Magdalene, a common harlot? Methinks I hear one say, 'Then I, even I, may hope for mercy!' And so thou mayest, thou

afflicted one, whom none hath comforted! God will not cast out thy prayer. Nay, perhaps He may say the next hour, 'Be of good cheer, thy sins are forgiven thee'; so forgiven, that they shall reign over thee no more; yea, and that 'the Holy Spirit shall bear witness with thy spirit that thou art a child of God.' O glad tidings! tidings of great joy, which are sent unto all people! 'Ho every one that thirsteth, come ye to the waters: come ye, and buy, without money and without price.' Whatsoever your sins be, 'though red like crimson,' though more than the hairs of your head, 'return ye unto the Lord, and He will have mercy upon you; and to our God, for He will abundantly pardon.'

7. When no more objections occur, then we are simply told that salvation by faith only ought not to be preached as the first doctrine, or, at least, not to be preached at all. But what saith the Holy Ghost? 'Other foundation can no man lay than that which is laid, even Jesus Christ.' So then, that 'whosoever believeth on Him shall be saved,' is, and must be, the foundation of all our preaching; that is, must be preached first. 'Well, but not to all.' To whom then are we not to preach it? Whom shall we except? The poor? Nay; they have a peculiar right to have the gospel preached unto them. The unlearned? No. God hath revealed these things unto unlearned and ignorant men from the beginning. The young? By no means. 'Suffer these,' in any wise, to come unto Christ, 'and forbid them not.' The sinners? Least of all. 'He came not to call the righteous, but sinners to repentance.' Why then, if any, we are to except the rich, the learned, the reputable, the moral men. And, it is true, they too often except themselves from hearing; yet we must speak the words of our Lord. For thus the tenor of our commission runs, 'Go and preach the gospel to every creature.' If any man wrest it, or any part of it, to his destruction, he must bear his own burden. But still, 'as the Lord liveth, whatsoever the Lord saith unto us, that we will speak.'

8. At this time, more especially, will we speak, that 'by grace are ye saved through faith': because, never was the maintaining this doctrine more seasonable than it is at this day. Nothing but this can effectually prevent the increase of the Romish delusion among us. It is endless to attack, one by one, all the errors of that

Church. But salvation by faith strikes at the root, and all fall at once where this is established. It was this doctrine, which our · Church justly calls *the strong rock and foundation of the Christian religion,* that first drove Popery out of these kingdoms; and it is this alone can keep it out. Nothing but this can give a check to that immorality which hath 'overspread the land as a flood.' Can you empty the great deep, drop by drop? Then you may reform us by dissuasives from particular vices. But let the 'righteousness which is of God by faith' be brought in, and so shall its proud waves be stayed. Nothing but this can stop the mouths of those who 'glory in their shame, and openly deny the Lord that bought them.' They can talk as sublimely of the law, as he that hath it written by God in his heart. To hear them speak on this head might incline one to think they were not far from the kingdom of God: but take them out of the law into the gospel; begin with the righteousness of faith; with Christ, 'the end of the law to every one that believeth'; and those who but now appeared almost, if not altogether, Christians, stand confessed the sons of perdition; as far from life and salvation (God be merciful unto them!) as the depth of hell from the height of heaven.

9. For this reason the adversary so rages whenever 'salvation by faith' is declared to the world: for this reason did he stir up earth and hell, to destroy those who first preached it. And for the same reason, knowing that faith alone could overturn the foundations of his kingdom, did he call forth all his forces, and employ all his arts of lies and calumny, to affright Martin Luther from reviving it. Nor can we wonder thereat; for, as that man of God observes, 'How would it enrage a proud, strong man armed, to be stopped and set at nought by a little child coming against him with a reed in his hand!' especially when he knew that little child would surely overthrow him, and tread him under foot. Even so, Lord Jesus! Thus hath Thy strength been ever 'made perfect in weakness'! Go forth then, thou little child that believest in Him, and His 'right hand shall teach thee terrible things!' Though thou art helpless and weak as an infant of days, the strong man shall not be able to stand before thee. Thou shalt prevail over him, and subdue him, and overthrow him, and

trample him under thy feet. Thou shalt march on, under the great Captain of thy salvation, 'conquering and to conquer,' until all thine enemies are destroyed, and 'death is swallowed up in victory.'

Now, thanks be to God, which giveth us the victory through our Lord Jesus Christ; to whom, with the Father and the Holy Ghost, be blessing, and glory, and wisdom, and thanksgiving, and honour, and power, and might, for ever and ever. Amen

SERMON II

THE ALMOST CHRISTIAN

PREACHED AT
ST. MARY'S, OXFORD, BEFORE THE UNIVERSITY,
ON JULY 25, 1741.

Almost thou persuadest me to be a Christian.—ACTS xxvi. 28.

AND many there are who go thus far: ever since the Christian religion was in the world, there have been many in every age and nation who were almost persuaded to be Christians. But seeing it avails nothing before God to go *only thus far*, it highly imports us to consider,—

    I.   WHAT IS IMPLIED IN BEING ALMOST,
    II.   WHAT IN BEING ALTOGETHER, A CHRISTIAN.

    I. (i.) 1. Now, in the being *almost a Christian* is implied, first, heathen honesty. No one, I suppose, will make any question of this; especially, since by heathen honesty here, I mean, not that which is recommended in the writings of their philosophers only, but such as the common Heathens expected one of another, and many of them actually practised. By the rules of this they were taught that they ought not to be unjust; not to take away their neighbour's goods, either by robbery or theft; not to oppress the poor, neither to use extortion toward any; not to cheat or over-reach either the poor or rich, in whatsoever commerce they had with them; to defraud no man of his right; and, if it were possible, to owe no man anything.

2. Again: the common Heathens allowed, that some regard was to be paid to truth, as well as to justice. And, accordingly, they not only held him in abomination who was forsworn, who called God to witness to a lie; but him also who was known to be a slanderer of his neighbour, who falsely accused any man. And, indeed, little better did they esteem wilful liars of any sort, accounting them the disgrace of human kind, and the pests of society.

3. Yet again: there was a sort of love and assistance which they expected one from another. They expected whatever assistance any one could give another, without prejudice to himself. And this they extended not only to those little offices of humanity which are performed without any expense or labour, but like-wise to the feeding the hungry, if they had food to spare; the clothing the naked with their own superfluous raiment; and, in general, the giving, to any that needed, such things as they needed not themselves. Thus far, in the lowest account of it, heathen honesty went; the first thing implied in the being *almost a Christian*.

(ii.) 4. A second thing implied in the being *almost a Christian* is, the having a form of godliness; of that godliness which is prescribed in the gospel of Christ; the having the *outside of a real Christian*. Accordingly, the *almost Christian* does nothing which the gospel forbids. He taketh not the name of God in vain; he blesseth, and curseth not; he sweareth not at all, but his communication is, yea, yea; nay, nay. He profanes not the day of the Lord, nor suffers it to be profaned, even by the stranger that is within his gates. He not only avoids all actual adultery, fornication, and uncleanness, but every word or look that either directly or indirectly tends thereto; nay, and all idle words, abstaining both from detraction, backbiting, talebearing, evil speaking, and from 'all foolish talking and jesting'—εὐτραπελία, a kind of virtue in the heathen moralist's account—briefly, from all conversation that is not 'good to the use of edifying,' and that, consequently, 'grieves the Holy Spirit of God, whereby we are sealed to the day of redemption.'

5. He abstains from 'wine wherein is excess'; from revellings and gluttony. He avoids, as much as in him lies, all strife and contention, continually endeavouring to live peaceably with all men. And, if he suffer wrong, he avengeth not himself, neither returns evil for evil. He is no railer, no brawler, no scoffer, either at the faults or infirmities of his neighbour. He does not willingly wrong, hurt, or grieve any man; but in all things acts and speaks by that plain rule, 'Whatsoever thou wouldest not he should do unto thee, that do not thou to another.'

6. And in doing good, he does not confine himself to cheap and easy offices of kindness, but labours and suffers for the profit of many, that by all means he may help some. In spite of toil or pain, 'whatsoever his hand findeth to do, he doeth it with his might'; whether it be for his friends, or for his enemies; for the evil, or for the good. For being 'not slothful' in this, or in any 'business,' as he 'hath opportunity' he doeth 'good,' all manner of good, 'to all men'; and to their souls as well as their bodies. He reproves the wicked, instructs the ignorant, confirms the wavering, quickens the good, and comforts the afflicted. He labours to awaken those that sleep; to lead those whom God hath already awakened to the 'Fountain opened for sin and for uncleanness,' that they may wash therein and be clean; and to stir up those who are saved through faith, to adorn the gospel of Christ in all things.

7. He that hath the form of godliness uses also the means of grace; yea, all of them, and at all opportunities. He constantly frequents the house of God; and that, not as the manner of some is, who come into the presence of the Most High, either loaded with gold and costly apparel, or in all the gaudy vanity of dress, and either by their unseasonable civilities to each other, or the impertinent gaiety of their behaviour, disclaim all pretensions to the form as well as to the power of godliness. Would to God there were none even among ourselves who fall under the same condemnation! who come into this house, it may be, gazing about, or with all the signs of the most listless, careless indiffer-

ence, though sometimes they may *seem* to use a prayer to God for His blessing on what they are entering upon; who, during that awful service, are either asleep, or reclined in the most convenient posture for it; or, as though they supposed God was asleep, talking with one another, or looking round, as utterly void of employment. Neither let these be accused of the form of godliness. No; he who has even this, behaves with seriousness and attention, in every part of that solemn service. More especially, when he approaches the table of the Lord, it is not with a light or careless behaviour, but with an air, gesture, and deportment which speaks nothing else but 'God be merciful to me a sinner!'

8. To this, if we add the constant use of family prayer, by those who are masters of families, and the setting times apart for private addresses to God, with a daily seriousness of behaviour; he who uniformly practises this outward religion, has the form of godliness. There needs but one thing more in order to his being *almost a Christian*, and that is, sincerity.

(iii.) 9. By sincerity I mean, a real, inward principle of religion, from whence these outward actions flow. And, indeed, if we have not this, we have not heathen honesty; no, not so much of it as will answer the demand of a heathen Epicurean poet. Even this poor wretch, in his sober intervals, is able to testify,

> *Oderunt peccare boni, virtutis amore;*
> *Oderunt peccare mali, formidine poenae.*[1]

So that, if a man only abstains from doing evil in order to avoid punishment, *Non pasces in cruce corvos:*[2] saith the Pagan; there, 'thou hast thy reward.' But even he will not allow such a harmless man as this to be so much as a *good Heathen.* If, then, any man, from the same motive, viz. to avoid punishment, to avoid the loss of his friends, or his gain, or his reputation, should not only abstain from doing evil, but also do ever so much good;

[1] Good men avoid sin from the love of virtue;
Wicked men avoid sin from a fear of punishment.

[2] Thou shalt not be hanged.

yea, and use all the means of grace; yet we could not with any propriety say, this man is even *almost a Christian*! If he has no better principle in his heart, he is only a hypocrite altogether.

10. Sincerity, therefore, is necessarily implied in the being *almost a Christian;* a real design to serve God, a hearty desire to do His will. It is necessarily implied, that a man have a sincere view of pleasing God in all things; in all his conversation; in all his actions; in all he does or leaves undone. This design, if any man be *almost a Christian*, runs through the whole tenor of his life. This is the moving principle, both in his doing good, his abstaining from evil, and his using the ordinances of God.

11. But here it will probably be inquired, 'Is it possible that any man living should go so far as this, and, nevertheless, be *only almost a Christian*? What more than this, can be implied in the being a *Christian altogether?* I answer, first, that it is possible to go thus far, and yet be but *almost a Christian:* I learn, not only from the oracles of God, but also from the sure testimony of experience.

12. Brethren, great is 'my boldness towards you in this behalf.' And 'forgive me this wrong,' if I declare my own folly upon the house-top, for yours and the gospel's sake.—Suffer me, then, to speak freely of myself, even as of another man. I am content to be abased, so ye may be exalted, and to be yet more vile for the glory of my Lord.

13. I did go thus far for many years, as many of this place can testify; using diligence to eschew all evil, and to have a conscience void of offence; redeeming the time; buying up every opportunity of doing all good to all men; constantly and carefully using all the public and all the private means of grace; endeavouring after a steady seriousness of behaviour, at all times, and in all places; and, God is my record, before whom I stand, doing all this in sincerity; having a real design to serve God; a hearty desire to do His will in all things; to please Him who had called me to 'fight the good fight,' and to 'lay hold of eternal life.' Yet my own conscience beareth me witness in the Holy Ghost, that all this time I was but *almost a Christian*.

II. If it be inquired, 'What more than this is implied in the being *altogether a Christian?*' I answer, (i.) 1. First, The love of God. For thus saith His word, 'Thou shalt love the Lord thy God with all thy heart, and with all thy soul, and with all thy mind, and with all thy strength.' Such a love is this, as engrosses the whole heart, as takes up all the affections, as fills the entire capacity of the soul, and employs the utmost extent of all its faculties. He that thus loves the Lord his God, his spirit continually 'rejoiceth in God his Saviour.' His delight is in the Lord, his Lord and his All, to whom 'in everything he giveth thanks. All his desire is unto God, and to the remembrance of His name.' His heart is ever crying out, 'Whom have I in heaven but Thee? and there is none upon earth that I desire beside Thee.' Indeed, what can he desire beside God? Not the world, or the things of the world: for he is 'crucified to the world, and the world crucified to him.' He is crucified to 'the desire of the flesh, the desire of the eye, and the pride of life.' Yea, he is dead to pride of every kind: for 'love is not puffed up' but 'he that dwelling in love, dwelleth in God, and God in him,' is less than nothing in his own eyes.

(ii.) 2. The second thing implied in the being *altogether a Christian* is, the love of our neighbour. For thus said our Lord, in the following words, 'Thou shalt love thy neighbour as thyself.' If any man ask, 'Who is my neighbour?' we reply, Every man in the world; every child of His who is the Father of the spirits of all flesh. Nor may we in any wise except our enemies, or the enemies of God and their own souls. But every Christian loveth these also as himself, yea, 'as Christ loved us.' He that would more fully understand what manner of love this is, may consider St. Paul's description of it. It is 'long-suffering and kind.' It 'envieth not.' It is not rash or hasty in judging. It 'is not puffed up'; but maketh him that loves, the least, the servant of all. Love 'doth not behave itself unseemly'; but becometh 'all things to all men.' She 'seeketh not her own'; but only the good of others, that they may be saved. 'Love is not provoked.' It casteth out wrath, which he who hath is wanting in love. 'It thinketh no evil. It rejoiceth not in iniquity, but rejoiceth in the truth. It covereth all things, believeth all things, hopeth all things, endureth all things.'

(iii.) 3. There is yet one thing more that may be separately considered, though it cannot actually be separate from the preceding, which is implied in the being *altogether a Christian*; and that is the ground of all, even faith. Very excellent things are spoken of this throughout the oracles of God. 'Every one,' saith the beloved disciple, 'that believeth is born of God.' 'To as many as received Him, gave He power to become the sons of God, even to them that believe on His name.' And 'this is the victory that overcometh the world, even our faith.' Yea, our Lord Himself declares, 'He that believeth in the Son hath everlasting life; and cometh not into condemnation, but is passed from death unto life.'

4. But here let no man deceive his own soul. 'It is diligently to be noted, the faith which bringeth not forth repentance, and love, and all good works, is not that right living faith, but a dead and devilish one. For, even the devils believe that Christ was born of a virgin: that He wrought all kinds of miracles, declaring Himself very God; that, for our sakes, He suffered a most painful death, to redeem us from death everlasting; that He rose again the third day; that He ascended into heaven, and sitteth at the right hand of the Father, and at the end of the world shall come again to judge both the quick and dead. These articles of our faith the devils believe, and so they believe all that is written in the Old and New Testament. And yet for all this faith, they be but devils. They remain still in their damnable estate, lacking the very true Christian faith.'[1]

5. 'The right and true Christian faith is' (to go on in the words of our own Church), 'not only to believe that Holy Scripture and the Articles of our Faith are true, but also to have a sure trust and confidence to be saved from everlasting damnation by Christ. It is a sure trust and confidence which a man hath in God, that, by the merits of Christ, his sins are forgiven, and he reconciled to the favour of God; whereof doth follow a loving heart, to obey His commandments.'

6. Now, whosoever has this faith, which 'purifies the heart' (by the power of God, who dwelleth therein) from pride, anger, desire, 'from all unrighteousness,' from 'all filthiness of flesh and spirit'; which fills it with love stronger than death, both to God

[1] Homily on the Salvation of Man

and to all mankind; love that doeth the works of God, glorying to spend and to be spent for all men, and that endureth with joy, not only the reproach of Christ, the being mocked, despised, and hated of all men, but whatsoever the wisdom of God permits the malice of men or devils to inflict,—whosoever has this faith, thus working by love, is not almost only, but altogether, a Christian.

7. But who are the living witnesses of these things? I beseech you, brethren, as in the presence of that God before whom 'hell and destruction are without a covering—how much more the hearts of the children of men?'—that each of you would ask his own heart, 'Am I of that number? Do I so far practise justice, mercy, and truth, as even the rules of heathen honesty require? If so, have I the very *outside* of a Christian? the form of godliness? Do I abstain from evil—from whatsoever is forbidden in the written Word of God? Do I, whatever good my hand findeth to do, do it with my might? Do I seriously use all the ordinances of God at all opportunities? And is all this done with a sincere design and desire to please God in all things?'

8. Are not many of you conscious, that you never came thus far; that you have not been even *almost a Christian*; that you have not come up to the standard of heathen honesty; at least, not to the form of Christian godliness?—much less hath God seen sincerity in you, a real design of pleasing Him in all things. You never so much as intended to devote all your words and works, your business, studies, diversions, to His glory. You never even designed or desired, that whatsoever you did should be done 'in the name of the Lord Jesus,' and as such should be 'a spiritual sacrifice, acceptable to God through Christ.'

9. But, supposing you had, do good designs and good desires make a Christian? By no means, unless they are brought to good effect. 'Hell is paved,' saith one, 'with good intentions.' The great question of all, then, still remains. Is the love of God shed abroad in your heart? Can you cry out, 'My God, and my All'? Do you desire nothing but Him? Are you happy in God? Is He your glory, your delight, your crown of rejoicing? And is this commandment written in your heart, 'That he who loveth God love his brother also'? Do you then love your neighbour as

yourself? Do you love every man, even your enemies, even the enemies of God, as your own soul? as Christ loved you? Yea, dost thou believe that Christ loved thee, and gave Himself for thee? Hast thou faith in His blood? Believest thou the Lamb of God hath taken away thy sins, and cast them as a stone into the depth of the sea? that He hath blotted out the handwriting that was against thee, taking it out of the way, nailing it to His cross? Hast thou indeed redemption through His blood, even the remission of thy sins? And doth His Spirit bear witness with thy spirit, that thou art a child of God?

10. The God and Father of our Lord Jesus Christ, who now standeth in the midst of us, knoweth, that if any man die without this faith and this love, good it were for him that he had never been born. Awake, then, thou that sleepest, and call upon thy God: call in the day when He may be found. Let Him not rest, till He make His 'goodness to pass before thee'; till He proclaim unto thee the name of the Lord, 'The Lord, the Lord God, merciful and gracious, long-suffering, and abundant in goodness and truth, keeping mercy for thousands, forgiving iniquity, and transgression, and sin.' Let no man persuade thee, by vain words, to rest short of this prize of thy high calling. But cry unto Him day and night, who, 'while we were without strength, died for the ungodly,' until thou knowest in whom thou hast believed, and canst say, 'My Lord, and my God!' Remember, 'always to pray, and not to faint,' till thou also canst lift up thy hand unto heaven, and declare to Him that liveth for ever and ever, 'Lord, Thou knowest all things, Thou knowest that I love Thee.'

11. May we all thus experience what it is to be, not almost only, but altogether Christians; being justified freely by His grace, through the redemption that is in Jesus; knowing we have peace with God through Jesus Christ; rejoicing in hope of the glory of God; and having the love of God shed abroad in our hearts, by the Holy Ghost given unto us!

SERMON III

AWAKE, THOU THAT SLEEPEST

PREACHED ON

SUNDAY, APRIL 4, 1742, BEFORE THE UNIVERSITY OF OXFORD,

BY THE REV. CHARLES WESLEY, M.A.

STUDENT OF CHRIST-CHURCH.

Awake, thou that sleepest, and arise from the dead, and Christ shall give thee light.—EPH. v. 14.

In discoursing on these words, I shall, with the help of God,—

    I. DESCRIBE THE SLEEPERS, TO WHOM THEY ARE SPOKEN:
    II. ENFORCE THE EXHORTATION, 'AWAKE, THOU THAT SLEEPEST, AND ARISE FROM THE DEAD': AND,
    III. EXPLAIN THE PROMISE MADE TO SUCH AS DO AWAKE AND ARISE: 'CHRIST SHALL GIVE THEE LIGHT.'

I. 1. And first, as to the sleepers here spoken to. By sleep is signified the natural state of man; that deep sleep of the soul, into which the sin of Adam hath cast all who spring from his loins: that supineness, indolence, and stupidity, that insensibility of his real condition, wherein every man comes into the world, and continues till the voice of God awakes him.

2. Now, 'they that sleep, sleep in the night.' The state of nature is a state of utter darkness; a state wherein 'darkness covers the earth, and gross darkness the people.' The poor unawakened sinner, how much knowledge soever he may have as to other things, has no knowledge of himself: in this respect 'he knoweth nothing yet as he ought to know.' He knows not that he is a fallen spirit, whose only business in the present world, is to recover from his fall, to regain that image of God wherein he was created. He sees *no necessity* for the *one thing needful:* even that

inward universal change, that 'birth from above,' figured out by baptism, which is the beginning of that total renovation. that sanctification of spirit, soul, and body, 'without which no man shall see the Lord'

3. Full of all diseases as he is, he fancies himself in perfect health. Fast bound in misery and iron, he dreams that he is at liberty. He says, 'Peace! Peace!' while the devil, as 'a strong, man armed,' is in full possession of his soul. He sleeps on still, and takes his rest, though hell is moved from beneath to meet him; though the pit from whence there is no return hath opened its mouth to swallow him up. A fire is kindled around him, yet he knoweth it not; yea, it burns him, yet he lays it not to heart.

4. By one who sleeps, we are, therefore, to understand (and would to God we might all understand it!) a sinner satisfied in his sins; contented to remain in his fallen state, to live and die without the image of God; one who is ignorant both of his disease, and of the only remedy for it; one who never was warned, or never regarded the warning voice of God, 'to flee from the wrath to come'; one that never yet saw he was in danger of hell-fire, or cried out in the earnestness of his soul, 'What must I do to be saved?'

5. If this sleeper be not outwardly vicious, his sleep is usually the deepest of all: whether he be of the Laodicean spirit, 'neither cold nor hot,' but a quiet, rational, inoffensive, good-natured professor of the religion of his fathers; or whether he be zealous and orthodox, and, 'after the most straitest sect of our religion,' live 'a Pharisee'; that is, according to the scriptural account, one that justifies himself; one that labours to establish his own righteousness, as the ground of his acceptance with God.

6. This is he, who, 'having a form of godliness, denies the power thereof'; yea, and probably reviles it, wheresoever it is found, as mere extravagance and delusion. Meanwhile, the wretched self-deceiver thanks God, that he is 'not as other men are; adulterers, unjust, extortioners': no, he doeth no wrong to any man. He 'fasts twice in a week,' uses all the means of grace, is constant at church and sacrament; yea, and 'gives tithes of all that he has'; does all the good that he can 'touching the righteous-

3

ness of the law,' he is 'blameless': he wants nothing of godliness, but the power; nothing of religion, but the spirit; nothing of Christianity, but the truth and the life.

7. But know ye not, that, however highly esteemed among men such a Christian as this may be, he is an abomination in the sight of God, and an heir of every woe which the Son of God, yesterday, to-day, and for ever, denounces against 'scribes and Pharisees, hypocrites'? He hath 'made clean the outside of the cup and the platter,' but within is full of all filthiness. 'An evil disease cleaveth still unto him, so that his inward parts are very wickedness.' Our Lord fitly compares him to a 'painted sepulchre,' which 'appears beautiful without'; but, nevertheless, is 'full of dead men's bones, and of all uncleanness.' The bones indeed are no longer dry; the sinews and flesh are come upon them, and the skin covers them above: but there is no breath in them, no Spirit of the living God. And, 'if any man have not the Spirit of Christ, he is none of His.' 'Ye are Christ's, if so be that the Spirit of God dwell in you': but, if not, God knoweth that ye abide in death, even until now.

8. This is another character of the sleeper here spoken to. He abides in death, though he knows it not. He is dead unto God, 'dead in trespasses and sins.' For, 'to be carnally minded is death.' Even as it is written, 'By one man sin entered into the world, and death by sin; and so death passed upon all men'; not only temporal death, but likewise spiritual and eternal. 'In that day that thou eatest,' said God to Adam, 'thou shalt surely die'; not bodily (unless as he then became mortal), but spiritually: thou shalt lose the life of thy soul; thou shalt die to God; shalt be separated from Him, thy essential life and happiness.

9. Thus first was dissolved the vital union of our soul with God; insomuch that 'in the midst of' natural 'life, we are' now in spiritual 'death.' And herein we remain till the Second Adam becomes a quickening Spirit to s; till He raises the dead, the dead in sin, in pleasure, riches, or honours. But, before any dead soul can live, he 'hears' (hearkens to) 'the voice of the Son of God': he is made sensible of his lost estate, and receives the sentence of death in himself. He knows himself to be 'dead while he liveth'; dead to God, and all the things of God; having no more power to

perform the actions of a living Christian, than a dead body to perform the functions of a living man.

10. And most certain it is, that one dead in sin has not 'senses exercised to discern spiritual good and evil.' 'Having eyes, he sees not; he hath ears, and hears not.' He doth not 'taste and see that the Lord is gracious.' He 'hath not seen God at any time,' nor 'heard His voice,' nor 'handled the word of life.' In vain is the name of Jesus 'like ointment poured forth, and all His garments smell of myrrh, aloes, and cassia.' The soul that sleepeth in death hath no perception of any objects of this kind. His heart is 'past feeling,' and understandeth none of these things.

11. And hence, having no spiritual senses, no inlets of spiritual knowledge, the natural man receiveth not the things of the Spirit of God; nay, he is so far from receiving them, that whatsoever is spiritually discerned is mere foolishness unto him. He is not content with being utterly ignorant of spiritual things, but he denies the very existence of them. And spiritual sensation itself is to him the foolishness of folly. 'How,' saith he, 'can these things be? How can any man *know* that he is alive to God?' Even as you know that your body is now alive. Faith is the life of the soul; and if ye have this life abiding in you, ye want no marks to evidence it *to yourself:* but ἔλεγχος Πνεύματος, that divine consciousness, that *witness of* God, which is more and greater than ten thousand human witnesses.

12. If He doth not now bear witness with thy spirit, that thou art a child of God, O that He might convince thee, thou poor unawakened sinner, by His demonstration and power, that thou art a child of the devil! O that, as I prophesy, there might now be 'a noise and a shaking'; and may 'the bones come together, bone to his bone!' Then 'come from the four winds, O Breath! and breathe on these slain, that they may live!' And do not ye harden your hearts, and resist the Holy Ghost, who even now is come to convince you of sin, 'because you believe not on the name of the only begotten Son of God.'

II. 1. Wherefore, 'awake, thou that sleepest, and arise from the dead.' God calleth thee now by my mouth; and bids thee know thyself, thou fallen spirit, thy true state and only concern below. 'What meanest thou, O sleeper? Arise! Call upon thy God, if so be thy God will think upon thee, that thou perish not.' A mighty tempest is stirred up round about thee, and thou art sinking into the depths of perdition, the gulf of God's judgements. If thou wouldest escape them, cast thyself into them. 'Judge thyself, and thou shalt not be judged of the Lord.'

2. Awake, awake! Stand up this moment, lest thou 'drink at the Lord's hand the cup of His fury.' Stir up thyself to lay hold on the Lord, the Lord thy Righteousness, mighty to save! 'Shake thyself from the dust.' At least, let the earthquake of God's threatenings shake thee. Awake, and cry out with the trembling jailer, 'What must I do to be saved?' And never rest till thou believest on the Lord Jesus, with a faith which is His gift, by the operation of His Spirit.

3. If I speak to any one of you, more than to another, it is to thee, who thinkest thyself unconcerned in this exhortation. 'I have a message from God unto thee.' In His name, I warn thee 'to flee from the wrath to come.' Thou unholy soul, see thy picture in condemned Peter, lying in the dark dungeon, between the soldiers, bound with two chains, the keepers before the door keeping the prison. The night is far spent, the morning is at hand, when thou art to be brought forth to execution. And in these dreadful circumstances, thou art fast asleep; thou art fast asleep in the devil's arms, on the brink of the pit, in the jaws of everlasting destruction!

4. O may the Angel of the Lord come upon thee, and the light shine into thy prison! And mayest thou feel the stroke of an Almighty Hand, raising thee, with, 'Arise up quickly, gird thyself, and bind on thy sandals, cast thy garment about thee, and follow Me.'

5. Awake, thou everlasting spirit, out of thy dream of worldly happiness! Did not God create thee for Himself? Then thou canst not rest till thou restest in Him. Return, thou wanderer! Fly back to thy ark, This is not thy home. Think not of building tabernacles here. Thou art but a stranger, a sojourner upon earth; a creature of a day, but just launching out into an unchangeable state. Make haste. Eternity is at hand. Eternity depends on this moment. An eternity of happiness, or an eternity of misery!

6. In what state is thy soul? Was God, while I am yet speaking, to require it of thee, art thou ready to meet death and judgement? Canst thou stand in His sight, who is of 'purer eyes than to behold iniquity'? Art thou 'meet to be partaker of the inheritance of the saints in light'? Hast thou 'fought a good fight, and kept the faith'? Hast thou secured the one thing needful? Hast thou recovered the image of God, even righteousness and true holiness? Hast thou put off the old man, and put on the new? Art thou clothed upon with Christ?

7. Hast thou oil in thy lamp? grace in thy heart? Dost thou 'love the Lord thy God with all thy heart, and with all thy mind, and with all thy soul, and with all thy strength'? Is that mind in thee, which was also in Christ Jesus? Art thou a Christian indeed; that is, a new creature? Are old things passed away, and all things become new?

8. Art thou a 'partaker of the divine nature'? Knowest thou not, that 'Christ is in thee, except thou be reprobate'? Knowest thou, that God 'dwelleth in thee, and thou in God, by His Spirit, which He hath given thee'? Knowest thou not that 'thy body is a temple of the Holy Ghost, which thou hast of God'? Hast thou the witness in thyself? the earnest of thine inheritance? Hast thou 'received the Holy Ghost'? Or dost thou start at the question, not knowing 'whether there be any Holy Ghost'?

9. If it offends thee, be thou assured, that thou neither art a Christian, nor desirest to be one. Nay, thy very prayer is turned into sin; and thou hast solemnly mocked God this very day, by praying for the inspiration of His Holy Spirit, when thou didst not believe there was any such thing to be received.

10. Yet, on the authority of God's Word, and our own Church, I must repeat the question, 'Hast thou received the Holy Ghost?' If thou hast not, thou art not yet a Christian. For a Christian is a man that is 'anointed with the Holy Ghost and with power.' Thou art not yet made a partaker of pure religion and undefiled. Dost thou know what religion is?—that it is a participation of the divine nature; the life of God in the soul of man; Christ formed in the heart; 'Christ in thee, the hope of glory'; happiness and holiness; heaven begun upon earth; 'a kingdom of God within thee; not meat and drink,' no outward

thing; 'but righteousness, and peace, and joy in the Holy Ghost'; an everlasting kingdom brought into thy soul; a 'peace of God, that passeth all understanding; 'a 'joy unspeakable, and full of glory'?

11. Knowest thou, that 'in Jesus Christ, neither circumcision availeth anything, nor uncircumcision; but faith that worketh by love'; but a new creation? Seest thou the necessity of that inward change, that spiritual birth, that life from the dead, that holiness? And art thou throughly convinced, that without it no man shall see the Lord? Art thou labouring after it?—'giving all diligence to make thy calling and election sure,' 'working out thy salvation with fear and trembling,' 'agonizing to enter in at the strait gate'? Art thou in earnest about thy soul? And canst thou tell the Searcher of hearts, 'Thou, O God, art the thing that I long for! Lord, Thou knowest all things; Thou knowest that I *would* love Thee!'

12. Thou hopest to be saved; but what reason hast thou to give of the hope that is in thee? Is it because thou hast done no harm? or, because thou hast done much good? or, because thou art not like other men; but wise, or learned, or honest, and morally good; esteemed of men, and of a fair reputation? Alas! all this will never bring thee to God. It is in His account lighter than vanity. Dost thou know Jesus Christ, whom He hath sent? Hath He taught thee, that 'by grace we are saved through faith; and that not of ourselves: it is the gift of God: not of works, lest any man should boast'? Hast thou received the faithful saying, as the whole foundation of thy hope, 'that Jesus Christ came into the world to save sinners'? Hast thou learned what that meaneth, 'I came not to call the righteous, but sinners to repentance? I am not sent, but unto the lost sheep'? Art thou (he that heareth, let him understand!) lost, dead, *damned already*? Dost thou know thy deserts? Dost thou feel thy wants? Art thou 'poor in spirit'? mourning for God, and refusing to be comforted? Is the prodigal 'come to himself,' and well content to be therefore thought beside himself' by those who are still feeding upon the husks which he hath left? Art thou willing to live godly in Christ Jesus? And dost thou therefore suffer persecution? Do men say all manner of evil against thee falsely, for the Son of Man's sake?

13. O that in all these questions ye may hear the voice that wakes the dead; and feel that hammer of the Word, which breaketh the rocks in pieces! 'If ye will hear His voice to-day, while it is called to-day, harden not your hearts.' Now, 'awake, thou that sleepest' in spiritual death, that thou sleep not in death eternal! Feel thy lost estate, and 'arise from the dead.' Leave thine old companions in sin and death. Follow thou Jesus, and let the dead bury their dead. 'Save thyself from this untoward generation.' 'Come out from among them, and be thou separate, and touch not the unclean thing, and the Lord shall receive thee.' 'Christ shall give thee light.'

III. 1. This promise, I come, lastly, to explain. And how encouraging a consideration is this, that whosoever thou art, who obeyest His call, thou canst not seek His face in vain! If thou even now 'awakest, and arisest from the dead,' He hath bound Himself to 'give thee light.' 'The Lord shall give thee grace and glory'; the light of His grace here, and the light of His glory when thou receivest the crown that fadeth not away. 'Thy light shall break forth as the morning, and thy darkness be as the noon-day.' 'God, who commanded the light to shine out of darkness, shall shine in thy heart; to give the knowledge of the glory of God in the face of Jesus Christ.' On them that fear the Lord shall the Sun of Righteousness arise with healing in His wings.' And in that day it shall be said unto thee, 'Arise, shine; for thy light is come, and the glory of the Lord is risen upon thee.' For Christ shall reveal Himself in thee: and He is the true Light.

2. God is light, and will give Himself to every awakened sinner that waiteth for Him; and thou shalt then be a temple of the living God, and Christ shall 'dwell in thy heart by faith'; and, 'being rooted and grounded in love, thou shalt be able to comprehend with all saints, what is the breadth, and length, and depth, and height of that love of Christ which passeth knowledge.'

3. Ye see your calling, brethren. We are called to be 'an habitation of God through His Spirit'; and, through His Spirit dwelling in us, to be saints here, and partakers of the inheritance

of the saints in light. So exceeding great are the promises which are given unto us, actually given unto us who believe! For by faith 'we receive, not the spirit of the world, but the Spirit which is of God'—the sum of all the promises—'that we may know the things that are freely given to us of God.'

4. The Spirit of Christ is that great gift of God, which at sundry times, and in divers manners, He hath promised to man, and hath fully bestowed since the time that Christ was glorified. Those promises, before made to the fathers, He hath thus fulfilled: 'I will put My spirit within you, and cause you to walk in My statutes' (Ezek. xxxvi. 27). 'I will pour water upon him that is thirsty, and floods upon the dry ground; I will pour My Spirit upon thy seed, and My blessing upon thine offspring' (Isa. xliv. 3).

5. Ye may all be living witnesses of these things; of remission of sins, and the gift of the Holy Ghost. 'If thou canst believe, all things are possible to him that believeth.' 'Who among you is there that feareth the Lord, and' yet walketh on 'in darkness, and hath no light?' I ask thee, in the name of Jesus, Believest thou that His arm is not shortened at all? that He is still mighty to save? that He is the same yesterday, to-day, and for ever? that He hath now power on earth to forgive sins? 'Son, be of good cheer; thy sins are forgiven.' God, for Christ's sake, hath forgiven thee. Receive this, 'not as the word of man; but as it is indeed, the word of God'; and thou art justified freely through faith. Thou shalt be sanctified also through faith which is in Jesus, and shalt set to thy seal, even thine, that 'God hath given unto us eternal life, and this life is in His Son.'

6. Men and brethren, let me freely speak unto you; and suffer ye the word of exhortation, even from one the least esteemed in the Church. Your conscience beareth you witness in the Holy Ghost, that these things are so, if so be ye have tasted that the Lord is gracious. 'This is eternal life, to know the only true God, and Jesus Christ, whom He hath sent.' This experimental knowledge, and this alone, is true Christianity. He is a Christian who hath received the Spirit of Christ. He is not a Christian who hath not received Him. Neither is it possible to have received Him, and not know it. 'For, at that day' (when He

cometh, saith our Lord), 'ye shall know that I am in My Father, and you in Me, and I in you.' This is that 'Spirit of Truth, whom the world cannot receive, because it seeth Him not, neither knoweth Him: but ye know Him; for He dwelleth with you, and shall be in you' (John xiv. 17).

7. The world cannot receive Him, but utterly reject the Promise of the Father, contradicting and blaspheming. But every spirit which confesseth not this is not of God. Yea, 'this is that spirit of Antichrist, whereof ye have heard that it should come into the world; and even now it is in the world.' He is Antichrist whosoever denies the inspiration of the Holy Ghost, or that the indwelling Spirit of God is the common privilege of all believers, the blessing of the gospel, the unspeakable gift, the universal promise, the criterion of a real Christian.

8. It nothing helps them to say, 'We do not deny the *assistance* of God's Spirit; but only this *inspiration:* this *receiving the Holy Ghost:* and being *sensible* of it. It is only this *feeling* of the Spirit, this being *moved* by the Spirit, or *filled* with it, which we deny to have any place in sound religion.' But, in *only denying this:* you deny the whole Scriptures; the whole truth, and promise, and testimony of God.

9. Our own excellent Church knows nothing of this devilish distinction; but speaks plainly of 'feeling the Spirit of Christ';[1] of being 'moved by the Holy Ghost'[2] and knowing and 'feeling there is no other name than that of Jesus,'[3] whereby we can receive life and salvation. She teaches us all to pray for the 'inspiration of the Holy Spirit';[4] yea, that we may be 'filled with the Holy Ghost.'[5] Nay, and every Presbyter of hers professes to receive the Holy Ghost by the imposition of hands. Therefore, to deny any of these, is, in effect, to renounce the Church of England, as well as the whole Christian revelation.

10. But 'the wisdom of God' was always 'foolishness with men.' No marvel, then, that the great mystery of the gospel should be now also 'hid from the wise and prudent,' as well as in the days of old; that it should be almost universally denied,

---

[1] Art. 17.   [3] Visitation of the sick.
[2] Office of consecrating Priests.   [4] Collect before the Holy Communion.
                    [5] Order of Confirmation.

ridiculed, and exploded, as mere frenzy; and that all who dare
avow it still are branded with the names of madmen and enthusiasts! This is 'that falling away' which was to come; that
general apostasy of all orders and degrees of men, which we even
now find to have overspread the earth. 'Run to and fro in the
streets of Jerusalem, and see if ye can find a man,' a man that
loveth the Lord his God with all his heart, and serveth Him with
all his strength. How does our own land mourn (that we look
no farther) under the overflowings of ungodliness! What
villanies of every kind are committed day by day; yea, too often
with impunity, by those who sin with a high hand, and glory in
their shame! Who can reckon up the oaths, curses, profaneness
blasphemies; the lying, slandering, evil-speaking; the Sabbath-
breaking, gluttony, drunkenness, revenge; the whoredoms,
adulteries, and various uncleanness; the frauds, injustice, oppression, extortion, which overspread our land as a flood?

11. And even among those who have kept themselves pure
from those grosser abominations; how much anger and pride
how much sloth and idleness, how much softness and effeminacy
how much luxury and self-indulgence, how much covetousnes
and ambition, how much thirst of praise, how much love of the
world, how much fear of man, is to be found! Meanwhile, how
little of true religion! For, where is he that loveth either God or
his neighbour, as He hath given us commandment? On the one
hand, are those who have not so much as the form of godliness:
on the other, those who have the form only: there stands the
open, there the *painted*, sepulchre. So that in very deed, whosoever were earnestly to behold any public gathering together of
the people (I fear those in our churches are not to be excepted)
might easily perceive, 'that the one part were Sadducees, and the
other Pharisees': the one having almost as little concern about
religion, as if there were 'no resurrection, neither angel nor
spirit'; and the other making it a mere lifeless form, a dull round
of external performances, without either true faith, or the love of
God, or joy in the Holy Ghost!

12. Would to God I could except *us* of this place! 'Brethren
my heart's desire, and prayer to God, for you is, that ye may be
saved' from this overflowing of ungodliness; and that here may

its proud waves be stayed! But is it so indeed? God knoweth, yea, and our own consciences, it is not. Ye have not kept yourselves pure. Corrupt are we also and abominable; and few are there that understand any more; few that worship God in spirit and in truth. We, too, are 'a generation that set not our hearts aright, and whose spirit cleaveth not steadfastly unto God.' He hath appointed us indeed to be 'the salt of the earth: but if the salt hath lost its savour, it is thenceforth good for nothing; but to be cast out, and to be trodden underfoot of men.'

13. And 'shall I not visit for these things, saith the Lord? Shall not My soul be avenged on such a nation as this?' Yea, we know not how soon He may say to the sword, 'Sword, go through this land!' He hath given us long space to repent. He lets us alone this year also: but He warns and awakens us by thunder. His judgements are abroad in the earth; and we have all reason to expect the heaviest of all, even that He 'should come unto us quickly, and remove our candlestick out of its place, except we repent and do the first works'; unless we return to the principles of the Reformation, the truth and simplicity of the gospel. Perhaps we are now resisting the last effort of divine grace to save us. Perhaps we have wellnigh 'filled up the measure of our iniquities,' by rejecting the counsel of God against ourselves, and casting out His messengers.

14. O God, 'in the midst of wrath, remember mercy'! Be glorified in our reformation, not in our destruction! Let us 'hear the rod, and Him that appointed it'! Now that Thy 'judgements are abroad in the earth,' let the inhabitants of the world 'learn righteousness'!

15. My brethren, it is high time for us to awake out of sleep before the 'great trumpet of the Lord be blown,' and our land become a field of blood. O may we speedily see the things that make for our peace, before they are hid from our eyes! 'Turn Thou us, O good Lord, and let Thine anger cease from us. O Lord, look down from heaven, behold and visit this vine'; and cause us to know 'the time of our visitation.' 'Help us, O God of our salvation, for the glory of Thy name! O deliver us, and be merciful to our sins, for Thy name's sake! And so we will not go back from Thee. O let us live, and we shall call upon Thy

name. Turn us again, O Lord God of Hosts! Show the light of Thy countenance, and we shall be whole.'

'Now unto Him that is able to do exceeding abundantly above all that we can ask or think, according to the power that worketh in us, unto Him be glory in the church by Christ Jesus throughout all ages, world without end. Amen!'

SERMON IV

SCRIPTURAL CHRISTIANITY[1]

PREACHED AT

ST. MARY'S, OXFORD, BEFORE THE UNIVERSITY,

AUGUST 24, 1744.

'Whosoever heareth the sound of the trumpet, and taketh not warning; if the sword come, and take him away, his blood shall be upon his own head.'—EZEK. xxxiii. 4.

And they were all filled with the Holy Ghost.—ACTS iv. 31.

THE same expression occurs in the second chapter, where we read, 'When the day of Pentecost was fully come, they were all' (the Apostles, with the women, and the mother of Jesus, and His brethren) 'with one accord in one place. And suddenly there came a sound from heaven as of a rushing mighty wind. And there appeared unto them cloven tongues like as of fire, and it sat upon each of them. And they were all filled with the Holy Ghost': one immediate effect whereof was, they 'began to speak

---

[1] This sermon was originally published in a separate pamphlet, accompanied by the following address 'to the reader,' to which was affixed the author's signature: 'It was not my design, when I wrote, ever to print the latter part of the following sermon: but the false and scurrilous accounts of it which have been published, almost in every corner of the nation, constrain me to publish the whole, just as it was preached: that men of reason may judge for themselves.'—ED.

with other tongues'; insomuch that both the Parthians, Medes, Elamites, and the other strangers who 'came together, when this was noised abroad, heard them speak, in their several tongues, the wonderful works of God' (Acts ii. 1-6).

2. In this chapter we read, that when the Apostles and brethren had been praying, and praising God, 'the place was shaken where they were assembled together, and they were all filled with the Holy Ghost.' Not that we find any visible appearance here, such as had been in the former instance: nor are we informed that the *extraordinary gifts* of the Holy Ghost were then given to all or any of them; such as the gifts of 'healing, of working' other 'miracles, of prophecy, of discerning spirits, the speaking with divers kinds of tongues, and the interpretation of tongues' (1 Cor. xii. 9, 10).

3. Whether these gifts of the Holy Ghost were designed to remain in the church throughout all ages, and whether or no they will be restored at the nearer approach of the 'restitution of all things,' are questions which it is not needful to decide. But it is needful to observe this, that, even in the infancy of the church, God divided them with a sparing hand. Were all even then prophets? Were all workers of miracles? Had all the gifts of healing? Did all speak with tongues? No, in no wise. Perhaps not one in a thousand. Probably none but the teachers in the church, and only some of them (1 Cor. xii. 28-30). It was, therefore, for a more excellent purpose than this, that 'they were all filled with the Holy Ghost.'

4. It was, to give them (what none can deny to be essential to all Christians in all ages) the mind which was in Christ, those holy fruits of the Spirit, which whosoever hath not, is none of His; to fill them with 'love, joy, peace, long-suffering, gentleness, goodness' (Gal. v. 22-24); to endue them with faith (perhaps it might be rendered, *fidelity*), with meekness and temperance; to enable them to crucify the flesh, with its affections and lusts, its passions and desires; and in consequence of that inward change, to fulfil all outward righteousness; to 'walk as Christ also walked,' in 'the work of faith, in the patience of hope, the labour of love' (1 Thess. i. 3).

5. Without busying ourselves, then, in curious, needless inquiries, touching those *extraordinary* gifts of the Spirit, let us

take a nearer view of these His *ordinary* fruits, which we are assured will remain throughout all ages;—of that great work of God among the children of men, which we are used to express by one word, 'Christianity'; not as it implies a set of opinions, a system of doctrines, but as it refers to men's hearts and lives. And this Christianity it may be useful to consider under three distinct views:

   I. As beginning to exist in individuals:
   II. As spreading from one to another:
   III. As covering the earth.

I design to close these considerations with a plain, practical application.

I. 1. And, first, let us consider Christianity in its rise, as beginning to exist in individuals.

Suppose, then, one of those who heard the Apostle Peter preaching repentance and remission of sins, was pricked to the heart, was convinced of sin, repented, and then believed in Jesus. By this faith of the operation of God, which was the very substance, or subsistence, of things hoped for (Heb. xi. 1), the demonstrative evidence of invisible things, he instantly received the Spirit of adoption, whereby he now cried, 'Abba, Father' (Rom. viii. 15). Now first it was that he could call Jesus Lord, by the Holy Ghost (1 Cor. xii. 3), the Spirit itself bearing witness with his spirit, that he was a child of God (Rom. viii. 16). Now it was that he could truly say, 'I live not, but Christ liveth in me; and the life which I now live in the flesh, I live by faith in the Son of God, who loved me, and gave Himself for me' (Gal. ii. 20).

2. This, then, was the very essence of his faith, a divine ἔλεγχος (*evidence* or *conviction*) of the love of God the Father, through the Son of His love, to him a sinner, now accepted in the Beloved. And, 'being justified by faith, he had peace with God' (Rom. v. 1), yea, 'the peace of God ruling in his heart'; a peace, which passing all understanding (πάντα νοῦν, all barely rational conception), kept his heart and mind from all doubt and

fear, through the knowledge of Him in whom he had believed. He could not, therefore, 'be afraid of any evil tidings'; for his 'heart stood fast, believing in the Lord.' He feared not what man could do unto him, knowing the very hairs of his head were all numbered. He feared not all the powers of darkness, whom God was daily bruising under his feet. Least of all was he afraid to die; nay, he desired to 'depart, and to be with Christ' (Phil. i. 23); who, 'through death, had destroyed him that had the power of death, even the devil; and delivered them who, through fear of death, were all their life-time,' till then, 'subject to bondage' (Heb. ii. 15).

3. His soul, therefore, magnified the Lord, and his spirit rejoiced in God his Saviour. 'He rejoiced in Him with joy unspeakable,' who had reconciled him to God, even the Father; 'in whom he had redemption through His blood, the forgiveness of sins.' He rejoiced in that witness of God's Spirit with his spirit, that he was a child of God; and more abundantly, 'in hope of the glory of God'; in hope of the glorious image of God, and full renewal of his soul in righteousness and true holiness and in hope of that crown of glory, that 'inheritance, incorruptible, undefiled, and that fadeth not away.'

4. 'The love of God was also shed abroad in his heart by the Holy Ghost which was given unto him' (Rom. v. 5). 'Because he was a son, God had sent forth the Spirit of His Son into his heart, crying, Abba, Father!' (Gal. iv. 6). And that filial love of God was continually increased by the witness he had in himself (1 John v. 10) of God's pardoning love to him; by 'beholding what manner of love it was which the Father had bestowed upon him, that he should be called a child of God' (1 John iii. 1). So that God was the desire of his eyes, and the joy of his heart; his portion in time and in eternity.

5. He that thus *loved* God could not but love his brother also; and 'not in word only, but in deed and in truth.' If God,' said he, 'so loved us, we ought also to love one another' (1 John iv. 11); yea, every soul of man, as 'the mercy of God is over all His works' (Ps. cxlv. 9). Agreeably hereto, the affection of this lover of God embraced all mankind for His sake; not excepting those whom he had never seen in the flesh, or those of whom he knew

nothing more than that they were 'the offspring of God,' for whose souls His Son had died; not excepting the 'evil' and 'unthankful,' and least of all his enemies, those who hated, or persecuted, or despitefully used him for his Master's sake. These had a peculiar place, both in his heart and in his prayers. He loved them 'even as Christ loved us.'

6. And 'love is not puffed up' (1 Cor. xiii. 4). It abases to the dust every soul wherein it dwells. Accordingly, he was lowly of heart, little, mean, and vile in his own eyes. He neither sought nor received the praise of men, but that which cometh of God only. He was meek and long-suffering, gentle to all, and easy to be entreated. Faithfulness and truth never forsook him: they were 'bound about his neck, and wrote on the table of his heart.' By the same spirit he was enabled to be temperate in all things, refraining his soul even as a weaned child. He was 'crucified to the world, and the world crucified to him'; superior to 'the desire of the flesh, the desire of the eye, and the pride of life.' By the same almighty love was he saved, both from passion and pride; from lust and vanity; from ambition and covetousness; and from every temper which was not in Christ.

7. It may be easily believed, he who had this love in his heart would work no evil to his neighbour. It was impossible for him, knowingly and designedly, to do harm to any man. He was at the greatest distance from cruelty and wrong, from any unjust or unkind action. With the same care did he 'set a watch before his mouth, and keep the door of his lips,' lest he should offend in tongue, either against justice, or against mercy or truth. He put away all lying, falsehood, and fraud; neither was guile found in his mouth. He spake evil of no man; nor did an unkind word ever come out of his lips.

8. And as he was deeply sensible of the truth of that word, 'Without Me ye can do nothing,' and, consequently, of the need he had to be watered of God every moment; so he continued daily in all the ordinances of God, the stated channels of His grace to man: 'in the Apostles' doctrine,' or teaching, receiving that food of the soul with all readiness of heart; in 'the breaking of bread,' which he found to be the communion of the body of Christ; and 'in the prayers' and praises offered up by the great

congregation. And thus, he daily 'grew in grace,' increasing in strength, in the knowledge and love of God.

9. But it did not satisfy him, barely to abstain from doing evil. His soul was athirst to do good. The language of his heart continually was, ' "My Father worketh hitherto, and I work." My Lord went about doing good; and shall not I tread in His steps?' As he had opportunity, therefore, if he could do no good of a higher kind, he fed the hungry, clothed the naked, helped the fatherless or stranger, visited and assisted them that were sick or in prison. He gave all his goods to feed the poor. He rejoiced to labour or to suffer for them; and whereinsoever he might profit another, there especially to 'deny himself.' He counted nothing too dear to part with for them, as well remembering the word of his Lord, 'Inasmuch as ye have done it unto one of the least of these My brethren, ye have done it unto Me' (Matt. xxv. 40).

10. Such was Christianity in its rise. Such was a Christian in ancient days. Such was every one of those who, when they heard the threatenings of the chief priests and elders, 'lifted up their voice to God with one accord, and were all filled with the Holy Ghost. The multitude of them that believed were of one heart and of one soul': so did the love of Him in whom they had believed constrain them to love one another! 'Neither said any of them that aught of the things which he possessed was his own; but they had all things common': so fully were they crucified to the world, and the world crucified to them! 'And they continued steadfastly with one accord in the Apostles' doctrine, and in the breaking of bread, and in prayers' (Acts ii. 42). 'And great grace was upon them all: neither was there any among them that lacked: for as many as were possessors of lands or houses sold them, and brought the prices of the things that were sold, and laid them down at the Apostles' feet: and distribution was made unto every man according as he had need' (Acts iv. 31-35).

II. 1. Let us take a view, in the second place, of this Christianity, as spreading from one to another, and so gradually making its way into the world: for such was the will of God concerning it, who did not 'light a candle to put it under a bushel, but that it might give light to all that were in the house.' And this our

4

Lord had declared to His first disciples, 'Ye are the salt of the earth,' 'the light of the world'; at the same time that He gave that general command, 'Let your light so shine before men, that they may see your good works, and glorify your Father which is in heaven' (Matt. v. 13-16).

2. And, indeed, supposing a few of these lovers of mankind to see 'the whole world lying in wickedness,' can we believe they would be unconcerned at the sight, at the misery of those for whom their Lord died? Would not their bowels yearn over them, and their hearts melt away for very trouble? Could they then stand idle all the day long, even were there no command from Him whom they loved? Rather, would they not labour, by all possible means, to pluck some of these brands out of the burning? Undoubtedly they would: they would spare no pains to bring back whomsoever they could of those poor 'sheep that had gone astray, to the great Shepherd and Bishop of their souls' (1 Pet. ii. 25).

3. So the Christians of old did. They laboured, having opportunity, 'to do good unto all men' (Gal. vi. 10), warning them to flee from the wrath to come; now, now to escape the damnation of hell. They declared, 'The times of ignorance God winked at; but now He calleth all men everywhere to repent' (Acts xvii. 30). They cried aloud, Turn ye, turn ye, from your evil ways: 'so iniquity shall not be your ruin' (Ezek. xviii. 30). They 'reasoned' with them of 'temperance, and righteousness,' or justice—of the virtues opposite to their reigning sins; 'and of judgement to come'—of the wrath of God which would surely be executed on evil-doers in that day when He should judge the world (Acts xxiv. 25).

4. They endeavoured herein to speak to every man severally as he had need. To the careless, to those who lay unconcerned in darkness and in the shadow of death, they thundered, 'Awake, thou that sleepest; arise from the dead, and Christ shall give thee light.' But to those who were already awakened out of sleep, and groaning under a sense of the wrath of God, their language was, 'We have an Advocate with the Father; He is the propitiation for our sins.' Meantime, those who had believed, they provoked to love and to good works; to patient continuance in well-doing;

and to abound more and more in that holiness without which no man can see the Lord (Heb. xii. 14).

5. And their labour was not in vain in the Lord. His word ran and was glorified. It grew mightily and prevailed. But so much the more did offences prevail also. The world in general were offended, 'because they testified of it, that the works thereof were evil' (John vii. 7). The men of pleasure were offended, not only because these men were made, as it were, to reprove their thoughts ('He professeth,' said they, 'to have the knowledge of God; he calleth himself the child of the Lord; his life is not like other men's; his ways are of another fashion; he abstaineth from our ways, as from filthiness; he maketh his boast, that God is his Father' (Wis. ii. 13-16); but much more, because so many of their companions were taken away, and would no more 'run with them to the same excess of riot' (1 Pet. iv. 4). The men of reputation were offended, because, as the gospel spread, they declined in the esteem of the people; and because many no longer dared to give them flattering titles, or to pay man the homage due to God only. The men of trade called one another together, and said, 'Sirs, ye know that by this craft we have our wealth: but ye see and hear that these men have persuaded and turned away much people; so that this our craft is in danger to be set at nought' (Acts xix. 25, &c.). Above all, the men of religion, so called, the men of *outside* religion, 'the saints of the world,' were offended, and ready at every opportunity to cry out, 'Men of Israel, help! We have found these men pestilent fellows, movers of sedition throughout the world' (Acts xxiv. 5). 'These are the men that teach all men everywhere against the people, and against this place' (Acts xxi. 28).

6. Thus it was that the heavens grew black with clouds, and the storm gathered amain. For the more Christianity spread, the more hurt was done, in the account of those who received it not; and the number increased of those who were more and more enraged at these men who thus 'turned the world upside down' (Acts xvii. 6); insomuch that more and more cried out, 'Away with such fellows from the earth; it is not fit that they should live'; yea, and sincerely believed, that whosoever should kill them would do God service

7. Meanwhile they did not fail to 'cast out their name as evil' (Luke vi. 22); so that 'this sect was everywhere spoken against' (Acts xxviii. 22). Men said all manner of evil of them, even as had been done of the prophets that were before them(Matt. v. 12). And whatsoever any would affirm, others would believe; so that offences grew as the stars of heaven for multitude. And hence arose, at the time fore-ordained of the Father, persecution in all its forms. Some, for a season, suffered only shame and reproach; some, 'the spoiling of their goods'; 'some had trial of mocking and scourging; some of bonds and imprisonment'; and others 'resisted unto blood' (Heb. x. 34; xi. 36, &c.)'

8. Now it was that the pillars of hell were shaken, and the kingdom of God spread more and more. Sinners were everywhere 'turned from darkness to light, and from the power of Satan unto God.' He gave His children 'such a mouth, and such wisdom, as all their adversaries could not resist'; and their lives were of equal force with their words. But above all, their sufferings spake to all the world. They 'approved themselves the servants of God, in afflictions, in necessities, in distresses, in stripes, in imprisonments, in tumults, in labours; in perils in the sea, in perils in the wilderness, in weariness and painfulness, in hunger and thirst, in cold and nakedness' (2 Cor. vi. 4, &c.). And when, having fought the good fight, they were led as sheep to the slaughter, and offered up on the sacrifice and service of their faith, then the blood of each found a voice, and the Heathen owned, 'He being dead, yet speaketh.'

9. Thus did Christianity spread itself in the earth. But how soon did the tares appear with the wheat, and the *mystery of iniquity* work, as well as the *mystery of godliness*! How soon did Satan find a seat, even *in the temple of God:* 'till the woman fled into the wilderness,' and 'the faithful were again minished from the children of men'! Here we tread a beaten path: the still increasing corruptions of the succeeding generations have been largely described, from time to time, by those witnesses God raised up, to show that He had 'built His church upon a rock, and the gates of hell should not' wholly 'prevail against her' (Matt. xvi. 18).

III. 1. But shall we not see greater things than these? Yea, greater than have been yet from the beginning of the world. Can Satan cause the truth of God to fail, or His promises to be of none effect? If not, the time will come when Christianity will prevail over all, and cover the earth. Let us stand a little, and survey (the third thing which was proposed) this strange sight, a *Christian world*. Of this the prophets of old inquired and searched diligently (1 Pet. i. 10, 11, &c.): of this the Spirit which was in them testified: 'It shall come to pass in the last days, that the mountain of the Lord's house shall be established in the top of the mountains, and shall be exalted above the hills; and all nations shall flow unto it. . . . And they shall beat their swords into ploughshares, and their spears into pruning-hooks: nation shall not lift up sword against nation, neither shall they learn war any more' (Isa. ii. 2, 4). 'In that day there shall be a Root of Jesse, which shall stand for an Ensign of the people; to it shall the Gentiles seek: and His rest shall be glorious. And it shall come to pass in that day, that the Lord shall set His hand again to recover the remnant of His people; and He shall set up an Ensign for the nations, and shall assemble the outcasts of Israel, and gather together the dispersed of Judah from the four corners of the earth' (Isa. xi. 10-12). 'The wolf shall then dwell with the lamb, and the leopard shall lie down with the kid; and the calf and the young lion and the fatling together; and a little child shall lead them. They shall not hurt nor destroy, saith the Lord, in all My holy mountain: for the earth shall be full of the knowledge of the Lord, as the waters cover the sea' (Isa. xi. 6-9).

2. To the same effect are the words of the great Apostle, which it is evident have never yet been fulfilled. 'Hath God cast away His people? God forbid. But through their fall salvation is come to the Gentiles. And if the diminishing of them be the riches of the Gentiles; how much more their fullness? For I would not, brethren, that ye should be ignorant of this mystery; that blindness in part is happened to Israel, until the fullness of the Gentiles be come in: and so all Israel shall be saved' (Rom. xi. 1, 11, 12, 25, 26).

3. Suppose now the fullness of time to be come, and the prophecies to be accomplished. What a prospect is this! All is

peace, 'quietness, and assurance for ever.' Here is no din of arms,
no confused noise,' no 'garments rolled in blood.' 'Destructions
are come to a perpetual end': wars are ceased from the earth.
Neither are there any intestine jars remaining; no brother rising
up against brother; no country or city divided against itself, and
tearing out its own bowels. Civil discord is at an end for evermore, and none is left either to destroy or hurt his neighbour.
Here is no oppression to 'make' even 'the wise man mad'; no
extortion to 'grind the face of the poor'; no robbery or wrong;
no rapine or injustice; for all are 'content with such things as
they possess.' Thus 'righteousness and peace have kissed each
other' (Ps. lxxxv. 10); they have 'taken root and filled the land';
'righteousness flourishing out of the earth'; and 'peace looking
down from heaven.'

4. And with righteousness or justice, mercy is also found.
The earth is no longer full of cruel habitations. The Lord hath
destroyed both the blood-thirsty and malicious, the envious and
revengeful man. Were there any provocation, there is none that
now knoweth to return evil for evil; but indeed there is none
that doeth evil, no, not one; for all are harmless as doves. And
being filled with peace and joy in believing, and united in one
body, by one Spirit, they all love as brethren, they are all of one
heart and of one soul. 'Neither saith any of them, that aught of
the things which he possesseth is his own.' There is none among
them that lacketh: for every man loveth his neighbour as himself.
And all walk by one rule: 'Whatever ye would that men should
do unto you, even so do unto them.'

5. It follows, that no unkind word can ever be heard among
them, no strife of tongues, no contention of any kind, no railing
or evil-speaking, but every one 'opens his mouth with wisdom,
and in his tongue there is the law of kindness.' Equally incapable
are they of fraud or guile: their love is without dissimulation:
their words are always the just expression of their thoughts,
opening a window into their breast, that whosoever desires may
look into their hearts, and see that only love and God are there.

6. Thus, where the Lord Omnipotent taketh to Himself His
mighty power and reigneth, doth He 'subdue all things to Himself,' cause every heart to overflow with love, and fill every

mouth with praise. 'Happy are the people that are in such a case: yea, blessed are the people who have the Lord for their God' (Ps. cxliv. 15). 'Arise, shine,' saith the Lord; 'for thy light is come, and the glory of the Lord is risen upon thee. Thou hast known that I the Lord am thy Saviour and thy Redeemer, the mighty God of Jacob. I have made thy officers peace, and thy exactors righteousness. Violence shall no more be heard in thy land, wasting nor destruction within thy borders; but thou shalt call thy walls Salvation and thy gates Praise. Thy people are all righteous; they shall inherit the land for ever, the branch of My planting, the work of My hands, that I may be glorified. The sun shall be no more thy light by day; neither for brightness shall the moon give light unto thee: but the Lord shall be unto thee an everlasting light, and thy God thy glory' (Isa. lx. 1, 16-19, 21).

IV. Having thus briefly considered Christianity, as beginning, as going on, and as covering the earth, it remains only that I should close the whole with a plain, practical application.

1. And, first, I would ask, Where does this Christianity now exist? Where, I pray, do the Christians live? Which is the country, the inhabitants whereof are all thus filled with the Holy Ghost?—are all of one heart and of one soul; cannot suffer one among them to lack anything, but continually give to every man as he hath need; who, one and all, have the love of God filling their hearts, and constraining them to love their neighbour as themselves; who have all 'put on bowels of mercy, humbleness of mind, gentleness, long-suffering'—who offend not in any kind, either by word or deed, against justice, mercy, or truth; but in every point do unto all men, as they would these should do unto them? With what propriety can we term any a Christian country, which does not answer this description? Why then, let us confess we have never yet seen a Christian country upon earth.

2. I beseech you, brethren, by the mercies of God, if ye do account me a madman or a fool, yet, *as a fool bear with me.* It is utterly needful that some one should use great plainness of speech towards you. It is more especially needful at *this* time; for who knoweth but it is the *last*? Who knoweth how soon the righteous

Judge may say, 'I will no more be entreated for this people'?
'Though Noah, Daniel, and Job were in this land, they should
but deliver their own souls.' And who will use this plainness, if I
do not? Therefore I, even I, will speak. And I adjure you, by the
living God, that ye steel not your breasts against receiving a
blessing at *my* hands. Do not say in your hearts, *Non persuadebis,
etiamsi persuaseris*[1]; or, in other words, Lord, Thou shalt not *send
by whom Thou wilt send*; let me rather perish in my blood, than be
saved by this man!

3. Brethren, 'I am persuaded better things of you, though I
thus speak.' Let me ask you then, in tender love, and in the
spirit of meekness, Is this city a Christian city? Is Christianity,
scriptural Christianity, found here? Are we, considered as a
community of men, so 'filled with the Holy Ghost,' as to enjoy
in our hearts, and show forth in our lives, the genuine fruits of
that Spirit? Are all the Magistrates, all Heads and Governors of
Colleges and Halls, and their respective Societies (not to speak of
the inhabitants of the town), 'of one heart and one soul'? Is 'the
love of God shed abroad in our hearts'? Are our tempers the
same that were in Him? And are our lives agreeable thereto?
Are we 'holy as He who hath called us is holy in all manner of
conversation'?

4. I entreat you to observe, that here are no peculiar notions
now under consideration; that the question moved is not concerning *doubtful opinions* of one kind or another, but concerning
the undoubted, fundamental branches (if there be any such) of
our common Christianity. And for the decision thereof, I appeal
to your own conscience, guided by the Word of God. He therefore that is not condemned by his own heart, let him go free.

5. In the fear, then, and in the presence of the great God,
before whom both you and I shall shortly appear, I pray you
that are in authority over us, whom I reverence for your office
sake, to consider (and not after the manner of dissemblers with
God), are you 'filled with the Holy Ghost'? Are you lively
portraitures of Him whom ye are appointed to represent among
men? 'I have said, Ye are gods,' ye magistrates and rulers; ye are

[1] Your persuasions shall not prevail with us even though they should
really convince us.—ED.

by office so nearly allied to the God of heaven! In your several stations and degrees, ye are to show forth unto us 'the Lord our Governor.' Are all the thoughts of your hearts, all your tempers and desires, suitable to your high calling? Are all your words like unto those which come out of the mouth of God? Is there in all your actions dignity and love?—a greatness which words cannot express, which can flow only from a heart 'full of God'; and yet consistent with the character of 'man that is a worm, and the son of man that is a worm'?

6. Ye venerable men, who are more especially called to form the tender minds of youth, to dispel thence the shades of ignorance and error, and train them up to be wise unto salvation, are you 'filled with the Holy Ghost'? with all those 'fruits of the Spirit,' which your important office so indispensably requires? Is your heart whole with God? full of love and zeal to set up His kingdom on earth? Do you continually remind those under your care, that the one rational end of all our studies, is to know, love, and serve 'the only true God, and Jesus Christ whom He hath sent'? Do you inculcate upon them day by day, that love alone never faileth (whereas, whether there be tongues, they shall fail, or philosophical knowledge, it shall vanish away); and that without love, all learning is but splendid ignorance, pompous folly, vexation of spirit? Has all you teach an actual tendency to the love of God, and of all mankind for His sake? Have you an eye to this end in whatever you prescribe, touching the kind, the manner, and the measure of their studies; desiring and labouring that, wherever the lot of these young soldiers of Christ is cast, they may be so many burning and shining lights, adorning the gospel of Christ in all things? And permit me to ask, Do you put forth all your strength in the vast work you have undertaken? Do you labour herein with all your might? exerting every faculty of your soul, using every talent which God hath lent you and that to the uttermost of your power?

7. Let it not be said, that I speak here, as if all under your care were intended to be clergymen. Not so; I only speak as if they were all intended to be Christians. But what example is set them by us who enjoy the beneficence of our forefathers? by Fellows, Students, Scholars; more especially those who are of

some rank and eminence? Do ye, brethren, abound in the fruits
of the Spirit, in lowliness of mind, in self-denial and mortification,
in seriousness and composure of spirit, in patience, meekness,
sobriety, temperance; and in unwearied, restless endeavours to
do good in every kind unto all men, to relieve their outward
wants, and to bring their souls to the true knowledge and love
of God? Is this the general character of Fellows of Colleges?
I fear it is not. Rather, have not pride and haughtiness of spirit,
impatience and peevishness, sloth and indolence, gluttony and
sensuality, and even a proverbial uselessness, been objected to
us, perhaps not always by our enemies, nor wholly without
ground? O that God would roll away this reproach from us,
that the very memory of it might perish for ever!

8. Many of us are more immediately consecrated to God,
called to minister in holy things. Are we then patterns to the
rest, 'in word, in conversation, in charity, in spirit, in faith, in
purity' (1 Tim. iv. 12)? Is there written on our forehead and on
our heart, 'Holiness to the Lord'? From what motives did we
enter upon this office? Was it indeed with a single eye 'to serve
God, trusting that we were inwardly moved by the Holy Ghost
to take upon us this ministration, for the promoting of His
glory, and the edifying of His people'? And have we 'clearly
determined, by God's grace, to give ourselves wholly to this
office'? Do we forsake and set aside, as much as in us lies, all
worldly cares and studies? Do we apply ourselves wholly to this
one thing, and draw all our cares and studies this way? Are we
apt to teach? Are we taught of God, that we may be able to
teach others also? Do we know God? Do we know Jesus
Christ? Hath 'God revealed His Son in us'? And hath He 'made
us able ministers of the new covenant'? Where then are the
'seals of our apostleship'? Who, that were dead in trespasses and
sins, have been quickened by our word? Have we a burning
zeal to save souls from death, so that for their sake we often
forget even to eat our bread? Do we speak plain, 'by manifestation of the truth commending ourselves to every man's conscience in the sight of God' (2 Cor iv 2)? Are we dead to the
world, and the things of the world, 'laying up all our treasure in
heaven'? Do we lord over God's heritage? Or are we the least,

the servants of all? When we bear the reproach of Christ, does it sit heavy upon us? Or do we rejoice therein? When we are smitten on the one cheek, do we resent it? Are we impatient of affronts? Or do we turn the other also; not resisting the evil, but overcoming evil with good? Have we a bitter zeal, inciting us to strive sharply and passionately with them that are out of the way? Or is our zeal the flame of love, so as to direct all our words with sweetness, lowliness, and meekness of wisdom?

9. Once more: what shall we say concerning the youth of this place? Have you either the form or the power of Christian godliness? Are you humble, teachable, advisable; or stubborn, self-willed, heady, and high-minded? Are you obedient to your superiors as to parents? Or do you despise those to whom you owe the tenderest reverence? Are you diligent in your easy business, pursuing your studies with all your strength? Do you redeem the time, crowding as much work into every day as it can contain? Rather, are ye not conscious to yourselves, that you waste away day after day, either in reading what has no tendency to Christianity, or in gaming, or in—you know not what? Are you better managers of your fortune than of your time? Do you, out of principle, take care to owe no man anything? Do you 'remember the Sabbbath-day, to keep it holy'; to spend it in the more immediate worship of God? When you are in His house, do you consider that God is there? Do you behave 'as seeing Him that is invisible'? Do you know how to 'possess your bodies in sanctification and honour'? Are not drunkenness and uncleanness found among you? Yea, are there not of you who 'glory in their shame'? Do not many of you 'take the name of God in vain,' perhaps habitually, without either remorse or fear? Yea, are there not a multitude of you that are forsworn? I fear, a swiftly-increasing multitude. Be not surprised, brethren. Before God and this congregation, I own myself to have been of the number, solemnly swearing to observe all those customs, which I then knew nothing of; and those statutes, which I did not so much as read over, either then, or for some years after. What is perjury, if this is not? But if it be, O what a weight of sin, yea, sin of no common dye, lieth upon us! And doth not the Most High regard it?

10. May it not be one of the consequences of this, that so many of you are a generation of triflers; triflers with God, with one another, and with your own souls? For, how few of you spend, from one week to another, a single hour in private prayer! How few have any thought of God in the general tenor of your conversation! Who of you is in any degree acquainted with the work of His Spirit, His supernatural work in the souls of men? Can you bear, unless now and then in a church, any talk of the Holy Ghost? Would you not take it for granted, if one began such a conversation, that it was either hypocrisy or enthusiasm? In the name of the Lord God Almighty, I ask, what religion are you of? Even the talk of Christianity, ye cannot, will not bear. O my brethren, what a Christian city is this! 'It is time for Thee, Lord, to lay to Thine hand!'

11. For, indeed, what probability, what possibility, rather (speaking after the manner of men), is there that Christianity, scriptural Christianity, should be again the religion of this place? that all orders of men among us should speak and live as men 'filled with the Holy Ghost'? By whom should this Christianity be restored? By those of you that are in authority? Are you convinced then that this is scriptural Christianity? Are you desirous it should be restored? And do ye not count your fortune, liberty, life, dear unto yourselves, so ye may be instrumental in the restoring of it? But suppose ye have this desire, who hath any power proportioned to the effect? Perhaps some of you have made a few faint attempts, but with how small success! Shall Christianity then be restored by young, unknown, inconsiderable men? I know not whether ye yourselves could suffer it. Would not some of you cry out, 'Young man, in so doing thou reproachest us'? But there is no danger of your being put to the proof; so hath iniquity overspread us like a flood. Whom then shall God send?—the famine, the pestilence (the last messengers of God to a guilty land), or the sword, 'the armies of the' Romish 'aliens,' to reform us into our first love? Nay, 'rather let us fall into Thy hand, O Lord, and let us not fall into the hand of man.'

Lord, save, or we perish! Take us out of the mire, that we sink not! O help us against these enemies! for vain is the help of man. Unto Thee all things are possible. According to the greatness of Thy power, preserve Thou those that are appointed to die; and preserve us in the manner that seemeth to Thee good: not as we will, but as Thou wilt!

SERMON V

JUSTIFICATION BY FAITH

To him that worketh not, but believeth on Him that justifieth the ungodly, his faith is counted for righteousness.—ROM. iv. 5.

How a sinner may be justified before God, the Lord and Judge of all, is a question of no common importance to every child of man. It contains the foundation of all our hope, inasmuch as while we are at enmity with God there can be no true peace, no solid joy, either in time or in eternity. What peace can there be, while our own heart condemns us; and much more, He that is greater than our heart, and knoweth all things'? What solid joy either in this world or that to come, while 'the wrath of God abideth on us'?

2. And yet how little hath this important question been understood? What confused notions have many had concerning it! Indeed, not only confused, but often utterly false; contrary to the truth, as light to darkness; notions absolutely inconsistent with the oracles of God, and with the whole analogy of faith. And hence, erring concerning the very foundation, they could not possibly build thereon; at least, not 'gold, silver, or precious stones,' which would endure when tried as by fire; but only 'hay and stubble,' neither acceptable to God, nor profitable to man.

3. In order to do justice, as far as in me lies, to the vast importance of the subject, to save those that seek the truth in sincerity from 'vain jangling and strife of words,' to clear the confusedness of thought into which so many have already been led thereby, and to give them true and just conceptions of this great mystery of godliness, I shall endeavour to show,—

I. WHAT IS THE GENERAL GROUND OF THIS WHOLE DOCTRINE
   OF JUSTIFICATION;
II. WHAT JUSTIFICATION IS;
III. WHO THEY ARE THAT ARE JUSTIFIED; AND,
IV. ON WHAT TERMS THEY ARE JUSTIFIED.

I. I am first to show, what is the general ground of this whole doctrine of justification.

1. In the image of God was man made; holy as He that created him is holy; merciful as the Author of all is merciful; perfect as his Father in heaven is perfect. As God is love, so man, dwelling in love, dwelt in God, and God in him. God made him to be an 'image of His own eternity,' an incorruptible picture of the God of glory. He was accordingly pure, as God is pure, from every spot of sin. He knew not evil in any kind or degree, but was inwardly and outwardly sinless and undefiled. He 'loved the Lord his God with all his heart, and with all his mind, and soul, and strength.'

2. To man, thus upright and perfect, God gave a perfect law, to which He required full and perfect obedience. He required full obedience in every point, and this to be performed without any intermission, from the moment man became a living soul, till the time of his trial should be ended. No allowance was made for any falling short. As, indeed, there was no need of any; man being altogether equal to the task assigned, and thoroughly furnished for every good word and work.

3. To the entire law of love which was written in his heart (against which, perhaps, he could not sin directly), it seemed good to the sovereign wisdom of God to superadd one positive law: 'Thou shalt not eat of the fruit of the tree that groweth in the midst of the garden'; annexing that penalty thereto, 'In the day that thou eatest thereof thou shalt surely die.'

4. Such then was the state of man in Paradise. By the free, unmerited love of God, he was holy and happy: he knew, loved, enjoyed God, which is, in substance, life everlasting. And in this life of love he was to continue for ever, if he continued to obey God in all things; but if he disobeyed Him in any, he was to forfeit all. 'In that day,' said God, 'thou shalt surely die.'

5. Man did disobey God. He 'ate of the tree, of which God commanded him, saying, Thou shalt not eat of it.' And in that day he was condemned by the righteous judgement of God. Then also the sentence, whereof he was warned before, began to take place upon him. For the moment he tasted that fruit, he died. His soul died, was separated from God; separate from whom the soul has no more life than the body has when separate from the soul. His body, likewise, became corruptible and mortal, so that death then took hold on this also. And being already dead in spirit, dead to God, dead in sin, he hastened on to death everlasting; to the destruction both of body and soul, in the fire never to be quenched.

6. Thus 'by one man sin entered into the world, and death by sin. And so death passed upon all men,' as being contained in him who was the common father and representative of us all. Thus, 'through the offence of one,' all are dead, dead to God, dead in sin, dwelling in a corruptible, mortal body, shortly to be dissolved, and under the sentence of death eternal. For as 'by one man's disobedience' all 'were made sinners'; so, by that offence of one 'judgement came upon all men to condemnation' (Rom. v. 12, &c.).

7. In this state we were, even all mankind, when 'God so loved the world, that He gave His only begotten Son, to the end we might not perish, but have everlasting live.' In the fullness of time He was made man, another common Head of mankind, a second general Parent and Representative of the whole human race. And as such it was that 'He bore our griefs,' 'the Lord laying upon Him the iniquities of us all.' Then was He 'wounded for our transgressions, and bruised for our iniquities.' 'He made His soul an offering for sin': He poured out His blood for the transgressors: He 'bare our sins in His own body on the tree,' that by His stripes we might be healed: and by that one oblation of Himself, once offered, He hath redeemed me and all mankind; having thereby 'made a full, perfect, and sufficient sacrifice and satisfaction for the sins of the whole world.'

8. In consideration of this, that the Son of God hath 'tasted death for every man,' God hath now 'reconciled the world to Himself, not imputing to them their' former 'trespasses.' And

thus, 'as by the offence of one judgement came upon all men to
condemnation; even so by the righteousness of one the free gift
came upon all men unto justification.' So that, for the sake of
His well-beloved Son, of what He hath done and suffered for us,
God now vouchsafes, on one only condition (which Himself
also enables us to perform), both to remit the punishment due
to our sins, to reinstate us in His favour, and to restore our dead
souls to spiritual life, as the earnest of life eternal.

9. This, therefore, is the general ground of the whole doctrine
of justification. By the sin of the first Adam, who was not only
the father, but likewise the representative, of us all, we all fell
short of the favour of God; we all became children of wrath;
or, as the Apostle expresses it, 'judgement came upon all men to
condemnation.' Even so, by the sacrifice for sin made by the
second Adam, as the Representative of us all, God is so far
reconciled to all the world, that He hath given them a new covenant; the plain condition whereof being once fulfilled, 'there
is no more condemnation' for us, but 'we are justified freely by
His grace, through the redemption that is in Jesus Christ.'

II. 1. But what is it to be *justified*? What is *justification*? This
was the second thing which I proposed to show. And it is
evident, from what has been already observed, that it is not the
being made actually just and righteous. This is *sanctification*;
which is, indeed, in some degree, the immediate fruit of justification, but, nevertheless, is a distinct gift of God, and of a totally
different nature. The one implies, what God does for us through
His Son; the other, what He works in us by His Spirit. So that,
although some rare instances may be found, wherein the term
justified or *justification* is used in so wide a sense as to include
sanctification also; yet, in general use, they are sufficiently distinguished from each other, both by St. Paul and the other inspired writers.

2. Neither is that far-fetched conceit, that justification is the
clearing us from accusation, particularly that of Satan, easily
proveable from any clear text of holy writ. In the whole
scriptural account of this matter, as above laid down, neither that
accuser nor his accusation appears to be at all taken in. It cannot

indeed be denied, that he is the 'accuser' of men, emphatically so called. But it does in no wise appear, that the great Apostle hath any reference to this, more or less, in all that he hath written touching justification, either to the Romans or the Galatians.

3. It is also far easier to take for granted, than to prove from any clear scripture testimony, that justification is the clearing us from the accusation brought against us by the law: at least, if this forced, unnatural way of speaking mean either more or less than this, that whereas we have transgressed the law of God, and thereby deserved the damnation of hell, God does not inflict on those who are justified the punishment which they had deserved.

4. Least of all does justification imply, that God is deceived in those whom He justifies; that He thinks them to be what, in fact, they are not; that He accounts them to be otherwise than they are. It does by no means imply, that God judges concerning us contrary to the real nature of things; that He esteems us better than we really are, or believes us righteous when we are un-righteous. Surely no. The judgement of the all-wise God is always according to truth. Neither can it ever consist with His unerring wisdom, to think that I am innocent, to judge that I am righteous or holy, because another is so. He can no more, in this manner, confound me with Christ, than with David or Abraham. Let any man, to whom God hath given understanding weigh this without prejudice; and he cannot but perceive, that such a notion of justification is neither reconcileable to reason nor Scripture.

5. The plain scriptural notion of justification is pardon, the forgiveness of sins. It is that act of God the Father, whereby, for the sake of the propitiation made by the blood of His Son, He 'showeth forth His righteousness' (or mercy) 'by the remission of the sins that are past.' This is the easy, natural account of it given by St. Paul, throughout this whole epistle. So he explains it himself, more particularly in this, and in the following chapter. Thus, in the next verses but one to the text, 'Blessed are they,' saith he, 'whose iniquities are forgiven, and whose sins are covered: blessed is the man to whom the Lord will not impute sin.' To him that is justified or forgiven, God 'will not impute sin' to his condemnation He will not condemn him on tha

account, either in this world or in that which is to come. His sins, all his past sins, in thought, word, and deed, are covered, are blotted out, shall not be remembered or mentioned against him, any more than if they had not been. God will not inflict on that sinner what he deserved to suffer, because the Son of His love hath suffered for him. And from the time we are 'accepted through the Beloved,' 'reconciled to God through His blood,' He loves, and blesses, and watches over us for good, even as if we had never sinned.

Indeed the Apostle in one place seems to extend the meaning of the word much farther, where he says, 'Not the hearers of the law, but the doers of the law, shall be justified.' Here he appears to refer our justification to the sentence of the great day. And so our Lord Himself unquestionably doth, when He says, 'By thy words thou shalt be justified': proving thereby that 'for every idle word men shall speak, they shall give an account in the day of judgement'; but perhaps we can hardly produce another instance of St. Paul's using the word in that distant sense. In the general tenor of his writings, it is evident he doth not; and least of all in the text before us, which undeniably speaks, not of those who have already 'finished their course,' but of those who are now just *setting out,* just beginning to 'run the race which is set before them.'

III. 1. But this is the third thing which was to be considered, namely, Who are they that are justified? And the Apostle tells us expressly, the ungodly: 'He' (that is, God) 'justifieth the ungodly' the ungodly of every kind and degree; and none but the ungodly. As 'they that are righteous need no repentance,' so they need no forgiveness. It is only sinners that have any occasion for pardon: it is sin alone which admits of being forgiven. Forgiveness, therefore, has an immediate reference to sin, and, in this respect, to nothing else. It is our *unrighteousness* to which the pardoning God is *merciful*: it is our *iniquity* which He 'remembereth no more.'

2. This seems not to be at all considered by those who so vehemently contend that a man must be sanctified, that is, holy, before he can be justified; especially by such of them as affirm,

that universal holiness or obedience must precede justification. (Unless they mean that justification at the last day, which is wholly out of the present question.) So far from it, that the very supposition is not only flatly impossible (for where there is no love of God, there is no holiness, and there is no love of God but from a sense of His loving us), but also grossly, intrinsically absurd, contradictory to itself. For it is not a saint but a sinner that is forgiven, and under the notion of a sinner. God justifieth not the godly, but the ungodly; not those that are holy already, but the unholy. Upon what condition He doeth this, will be considered quickly: but whatever it is, it cannot be holiness. To assert this, is to say the Lamb of God takes away only those sins which were taken away before.

3. Does then the Good Shepherd seek and save only those that are found already? No. He seeks and saves that which is lost. He pardons those who need His pardoning mercy. He saves from the guilt of sin (and, at the same time, from the power) sinners of every kind, of every degree; men who, till then, were altogether ungodly; in whom the love of the Father was not; and, consequently, in whom dwelt no good thing, no good or truly Christian temper; but all such as were evil and abominable—pride, anger, love of the world, the genuine fruits of that *carnal mind* which is 'enmity against God.'

4. These who are sick, the burden of whose sins is intolerable, are they that need a Physician; these who are guilty, who groan under the wrath of God, are they that need a pardon. These who are *condemned already*, not only by God, but also by their own conscience, as by a thousand witnesses, of all their ungodliness, both in thought, and word and work, cry aloud for him that 'justifieth the ungodly,' through the redemption that is in Jesus, —the ungodly, and 'him that worketh not'; that worketh not, before he is justified, any thing that is good, that is truly virtuous or holy, but only evil continually. For his heart is necessarily, essentially evil, till the love of God is shed abroad therein. And while the tree is corrupt, so are the fruits; 'for an evil tree cannot bring forth good fruit.'

5. If it be objected, 'Nay, but a man, before he is justified, may feed the hungry, or clothe the naked; and these are good

works,'—the answer is easy: He may do these, even before he is justified; and these are, in one sense, 'good works'—they are 'good and profitable to men.' But it does not follow, that they are, strictly speaking, good in themselves, or good in the sight of God. All truly *good works* (to use the words of our Church) *follow after justification*; and they are therefore good and 'acceptable to God in Christ,' because they 'spring out of a true and living faith.' By a parity of reason, all *works done before justification are not good:* in the Christian sense, *forasmuch as they spring not of faith in Jesus Christ* (though from some kind of faith in God they may spring); 'yea rather, for that they are not done as God hath willed and commanded them to be done, we doubt not' (how strange soever it may appear to some) 'but they have the nature of sin.'

6. Perhaps those who doubt of this have not duly considered the weighty reason which is here assigned, why no works done before justification can be truly and properly good. The argument plainly runs thus:—

No works are good, which are not done as God hath willed and commanded them to be done:

But no works done before justification are done as God hath willed and commanded them to be done:

Therefore, no works done before justification are good.

The first proposition is self-evident; and the second—that no works done before justification are done as God hath willed and commanded them to be done—will appear equally plain and undeniable, if we only consider, God hath willed and commanded, that *all our works* should be *done in charity* (ἐν ἀγάπῃ), in love, in that love to God which produces love to all mankind. But none of our works can be done in this love, while the love of the Father (of God as our Father) is not in us; and this love cannot be in us till we receive the 'Spirit of adoption, crying in our hearts, Abba, Father.' If, therefore, God doth not *justify the ungodly:* and him that (in this sense) *worketh not:* then hath Christ died in vain; then, notwithstanding His death, can no flesh living be justified.

IV. 1. But on what terms, then, is he justified, who is

altogether *ungodly:* and till that time *worketh not?* On one alone, which is faith: he 'believeth in Him that justifieth the ungodly.' And 'he that believeth is not condemned'; yea, he is 'passed from death unto life.' 'For the righteousness' (or mercy), 'of God is by faith of Jesus Christ unto all and upon all them that believe: whom God hath set forth for a propitiation, through faith in His blood; that He might be just, and' (consistently with His justice) 'the justifier of him which believeth in Jesus'; 'therefore, we conclude, that a man is justified by faith, without the deeds of the law'; without previous obedience to the moral law, which, indeed, he could not, till now, perform. That it is the moral law, and that alone, which is here intended, appears evidently from the words that follow: 'Do we then make void the law through faith? God forbid! Yea, we establish the law.' What law do we establish by faith? Not the ritual law: not the ceremonial law of Moses. In no wise; but the great, unchangeable law of love, the holy love of God and of our neighbour.

2. Faith in general is a divine, supernatural ἔλεγχος, *evidence* or *conviction:* 'of things not seen,' not discoverable by our bodily senses, as being either past, future, or spiritual. Justifying faith implies, not only a divine evidence or conviction that 'God was in Christ, reconciling the world unto Himself,' but a sure trust and confidence that Christ died for *my* sins, that He loved *me*, and gave Himself for *me.* And at what time soever a sinner thus believes, be it in early childhood, in the strength of his years, or when he is old and hoary-headed, God justifieth that ungodly one: God, for the sake of His Son, pardoneth and absolveth him who had in him, till then, no good thing. Repentance, indeed, God had given him before; but that repentance was neither more nor less than a deep sense of the want of all good, and the presence of all evil. And whatever good he hath, or doeth, from that hour, when he first believes in God through Christ, faith does not *find*, but *bring*. This is the fruit of faith. First the tree is good, and then the fruit is good also.

3. I cannot describe the nature of this faith better than in the words of our own Church: 'The only instrument of salvation' (whereof justification is one branch) 'is faith; that is, a sure trust and confidence that God both hath and will forgive our

sins, that He hath accepted us again into His favour, for the merits of Christ's death and passion. But here we must take heed that we do not halt with God through an inconstant, wavering faith: Peter, coming to Christ upon the water, because he fainted in faith, was in danger of drowning; so we, if we begin to waver or doubt, it is to be feared that we shall sink as Peter did, not into the water, but into the bottomless pit of hell-fire' (*Second Sermon on the Passion*).

'Therefore, have a sure and constant faith, not only that the death of Christ is available for all the world, but that He hath made a full and sufficient sacrifice for *thee*, a perfect cleansing of *thy* sins, so that thou mayest say, with the Apostle, He loved *thee*, and gave Himself for *thee*. For this is to make Christ *thine own*, and to apply His merits unto *thyself*' (*Sermon on the Sacrament: First Part*).

4. By affirming that this faith is the term or *condition of justification* I mean, first, that there is no justification without it. 'He that believeth not is condemned already'; and so long as he believeth not, that condemnation cannot be removed, but 'the wrath of God abideth on him.' As 'there is no other name given under heaven' than that of Jesus of Nazareth, no other merit whereby a condemned sinner can ever be saved from the guilt of sin, so there is no other way of obtaining a share in His merit, than *by faith in His name*. So that as long as we are without this faith, we are 'strangers to the covenant of promise,' we are 'aliens from the commonwealth of Israel, and without God in the world.' Whatsoever virtues (so called) a man may have—I speak of those unto whom the gospel is preached: for 'what have I to do to judge them that are without?'—whatsoever good works (so accounted) he may do, it profiteth not; he is still a *child of wrath:* still under the curse, till he believes in Jesus.

5. Faith, therefore, is the *necessary* condition of justification; yea, and the *only necessary* condition thereof. This is the second point carefully to be observed; that, the very moment God giveth faith (for *it is the gift of God*) to the 'ungodly' that 'worketh not,' that 'faith is counted to him for righteousness.' He hath no righteousness at all, antecedent to this; not so much as negative righteousness, or innocence. But 'faith is imputed to him for

righteousness' the very moment that he believeth. Not that God (as was observed before) thinketh him to be what he is not. But as 'He made Christ to be sin for us,' that is, treated Him as a sinner, punishing Him for our sins, so He counteth us righteous, from the time we believe in Him: that is, He doth not punish us for our sins; yea, treats us as though we were guiltless and righteous.

6. Surely the difficulty of assenting to this proposition, that 'faith is the *only condition* of justification,' must arise from not understanding it. We mean thereby thus much, that it is the only thing without which none is justified; the only thing that is immediately, indispensably, absolutely requisite in order to pardon. As, on the one hand, though a man should have everything else without faith, yet he cannot be justified; so, on the other, though he be supposed to want everything else, yet if he hath faith, he cannot but be justified. For suppose a sinner of any kind or degree, in a full sense of his total ungodliness, of his utter inability to think, speak, or do good, and his absolute meetness for hell-fire; suppose, I say, this sinner, helpless and hopeless, casts himself wholly on the mercy of God in Christ (which indeed he cannot do but by the grace of God), who can doubt but he is forgiven in that moment? Who will affirm that any more is *indispensably required:* before that sinner can be justified?

Now, if there ever was one such instance from the beginning of the world (and have there not been, and are there not, ten thousand times ten thousand?), it plainly follows, that faith is, in the above sense, the sole condition of justification.

7. It does not become poor, guilty, sinful worms, who receive whatsoever blessings they enjoy (from the least drop of water that cools our tongue, to the immense riches of glory in eternity), of grace, of mere favour, and not of debt, to ask of God the reasons of His conduct. It is not meet for us to call Him in question, 'who giveth account to none of His ways'; to demand, Why didst Thou make faith the condition, the only condition, of justification? Wherefore didst Thou decree, *He that believeth:* and he only, *shall be saved?* This is the very point on which St. Paul so strongly insists in the ninth chapter of this Epistle, viz.

that the terms of pardon and acceptance must depend, not on us,
but *on Him that calleth us*: that there is no *unrighteousness with God:*
in fixing His own terms, not according to ours, but His own
good pleasure; who may justly say, 'I will have mercy on whom
I will have mercy,' namely, on him who believeth in Jesus. 'So
then it is not of him that willeth, nor of him that runneth,' to
choose the condition on which he shall find acceptance, 'but of
God that showeth mercy'; that accepteth none at all, but of His
own free love, His unmerited goodness. 'Therefore hath He
mercy on whom He will have mercy,' viz. on those who believe
on the Son of His love; 'and whom He will,' that is, those who
believe not, 'He hardeneth,' leaves at last to the hardness of their
hearts.

8. One reason, however, we may humbly conceive, of God's
fixing this condition of justification, 'If thou believest in the
Lord Jesus Christ, thou shalt be saved,' was to *hide pride from
man.* Pride had already destroyed the very angels of God, had
cast down 'a third part of the stars of heaven.' It was likewise in
great measure owing to this, when the tempter said, 'Ye shall be
as gods,' that Adam fell from his own steadfastness, and brought
sin and death into the world. It was therefore an instance of
wisdom worthy of God, to appoint such a condition of reconciliation for him and all his posterity, as might effectually humble,
might abase them to the dust. And such is faith. It is peculiarly
fitted for this end: for he that cometh unto God by this faith,
must fix his eye singly on his own wickedness, on his guilt and
helplessness, without having the least regard to any supposed
good in himself, to any virtue or righteousness whatsoever. He
must come as a *mere sinner*, inwardly and outwardly, self-
destroyed and self-condemned, bringing nothing to God but
ungodliness only, pleading nothing of his own but sin and misery.
Thus it is, and thus alone, when his *mouth is stopped:* and he stands
utterly *guilty before* God, that he can *look unto Jesus:* as the whole
and sole *propitiation for his sins.* Thus only can he be *found in Him:*
and receive the 'righteousness which is of God by faith.'

9. Thou ungodly one, who hearest or readest these words!
thou vile, helpless, miserable sinner! I charge thee before God
the Judge of all, go straight unto Him, with all thy ungodliness.

Take heed thou destroy not thy own soul by pleading thy righteousness, more or less. Go as altogether ungodly, guilty, lost, destroyed, deserving and dropping into hell; and thou shalt then find favour in His sight, and know that He justifieth the ungodly. As such thou shalt be brought unto the *blood of sprinkling:* as an undone, helpless, damned sinner. Thus *look unto Jesus!* There is *the Lamb of God:* who *taketh away* thy *sins!* Plead thou no works, no righteousness of thine own! no humility, contrition, sincerity! In no wise. That were, in very deed, to deny the Lord that bought thee. No: plead thou singly the blood of the covenant, the ransom paid for thy proud, stubborn, sinful soul. Who art thou, that now seest and feelest both thine inward and outward ungodliness? Thou art the man! I want thee for my Lord! I challenge *thee* for a child of God by faith! The Lord hath need of thee. Thou who feelest thou art just fit for hell, art just fit to advance His glory; the glory of His free grace, justifying the ungodly and him that worketh not. O come quickly! Believe in the Lord Jesus, and thou, even thou, art reconciled to God.

SERMON VI

THE RIGHTEOUSNESS OF FAITH

Moses describeth the righteousness which is of the law, That the man which doeth those things shall live by them.

But the righteousness which is of faith speaketh on this wise, Say not in thine heart, Who shall ascend into heaven (that is, to bring Christ down from above)?

Or, Who shall descend into the deep (that is, to bring up Christ again from the dead)?

But what saith it? The word is nigh thee, even in thy mouth, and in thy heart: that is, the word of faith, which we preach.—ROM. x. 5-8.

THE Apostle does not here oppose the covenant given by Moses, to the covenant given by Christ. If we ever imagined this, it was for want of observing, that the latter as well as the former part of these words were spoken by Moses himself to the people of Israel, and that concerning the covenant which then was (Deut. xxx. 11, 12, 14). But it is the covenant of grace, which God, through Christ, hath established with men in all ages (as well before and under the Jewish dispensation, as since God was manifest in the flesh), which St. Paul here opposes to the covenant of works, made with Adam while in paradise, but commonly supposed to be the only covenant which God had made with man, particularly by those Jews of whom the Apostle writes.

2. Of these it was that he so affectionately speaks in the beginning of this chapter: 'My heart's desire and prayer to God for Israel is, that they may be saved. For I bear them record, that they have a zeal for God, but not according to knowledge. For they being ignorant of God's righteousness' (of the justification that flows from His mere grace and mercy, freely forgiving our sins through the Son of His love, through the redemption which is in Jesus) 'and seeking to establish their own righteousness' (their own holiness, antecedent to faith in 'Him that justifieth the ungodly,' as the ground of their pardon and acceptance), 'have not submitted themselves unto the righteousness of God,' and consequently, seek death in the error of their life.

3. They were ignorant that 'Christ is the end of the law for righteousness to every one that believeth,'—that, by the oblation of Himself once offered, He had put an end to the first law or covenant (which, indeed, was not given by God to Moses, but to Adam in his state of innocence), the strict tenor whereof, without any abatement, was, 'Do this, and live'; and, at the same time, purchased for us that better covenant, 'Believe, and live'; believe, and thou shalt be saved; now saved, both from the guilt and power of sin, and, of consequence, from the wages of it.

4. And how many are equally ignorant now, even among those who are called by the name of Christ! How many who have now 'a zeal for God,' yet have it not 'according to knowledge'; but are still seeking 'to establish their own righteousness' as the ground of their pardon and acceptance; and therefore vehemently refuse to 'submit themselves unto the righteousness of God'! Surely my heart's desire, and prayer to God for you

brethren, is, that ye may be saved. And, in order to remove this grand stumbling-block out of your way, I will endeavour to show, first, what the righteousness *is* which is of the law, and what 'the righteousness which is of faith'; secondly, the folly of trusting in the righteousness of the law, and the wisdom of submitting to that which is of faith.

I. 1. And, first, 'the righteousness which is of the law saith, The man which doeth these things shall live by them.' Constantly and perfectly observe all these things to do them, and then thou shalt live for ever. This law, or covenant (usually called the covenant of works), given by God to man in paradise, required an obedience perfect in all its parts, entire and wanting nothing, as the condition of his eternal continuance in the holiness and happiness wherein he was created.

2. It required that man should fulfil all righteousness, inward and outward, negative and positive: that he should not only abstain from every idle word, and avoid every evil work, but should keep every affection, every desire, every thought, in obedience to the will of God; that he should continue holy as He which had created him was holy, both in heart, and in all manner of conversation; that he should be pure in heart, even as God is pure; perfect as his Father in heaven was perfect: that he should love the Lord his God with all his heart, with all his soul, with all his mind, and with all his strength; that he should love every soul which God had made, even as God had loved him: that by this universal benevolence, he should dwell in God (who is love), and God in him: that he should serve the Lord his God with all his strength, and in all things singly aim at His glory.

3. These were the things which the righteousness of the law required, that he who did them might live thereby. But it farther required, that this entire obedience to God, this inward and outward holiness, this conformity both of heart and life to His will, should be perfect in *degree*. No abatement, no allowance could possibly be made, for falling short in any degree, as to any jot or tittle, either of the outward or the inward law. If every commandment relating to outward things was obeyed, yet that was not sufficient, unless every one was obeyed with all the strength, in the highest measure, and most perfect manner. Nor

did it answer the demand of this covenant to love God with every power and faculty, unless He were loved with the full capacity of each, with the whole possibility of the soul.

4. One thing more was indispensably required by the righteousness of the law, namely, that this universal obedience, this perfect holiness both of heart and life, should be perfectly uninterrupted also, should continue without any intermission, from the moment wherein God created man, and breathed into his nostrils the breath of life, until the days of his trial should be ended, and he should be confirmed in life everlasting.

5. The righteousness, then, which is the of law, speaketh on this wise: 'Thou, O man of God, stand fast in love, in the image of God wherein thou art made. If thou wilt remain in life, keep the commandments, which are now written in thy heart. Love the Lord thy God with all thy heart. Love, as thyself, every soul that He hath made. Desire nothing but God. Aim at God in every thought, in every word and work. Swerve not in one motion of body or soul, from Him, thy mark, and the prize of thy high calling; and let all that is in thee praise His holy name, every power and faculty of thy soul, in every kind, in every degree, and at every moment of thine existence. "This do, and thou shalt live": thy light shall shine, thy love shall flame, more and more, till thou art received up into the house of God in the heavens, to reign with Him for ever and ever.'

6. 'But the righteousness which is of faith speaketh on this wise, Say not in thine heart, Who shall ascend into heaven? that is, to bring down Christ from above' (as though it were some impossible task which God required thee previously to perform, in order to thine acceptance); 'or, Who shall descend into the deep? that is, to bring up Christ from the dead' (as though that were still remaining to be done, for the sake of which thou wert to be accepted); 'but what saith it? The word,' according to the tenor of which thou mayest now be accepted as an heir of life eternal, 'is nigh thee, even in thy mouth, and in thy heart: that is, the word of faith, which we preach'—the new covenant which God hath now established with sinful man through Christ Jesus.

7. By 'the righteousness which is of faith' is meant, that condition of justification (and, in consequence, of present and final

salvation, if we endure therein unto the end) which was given by God to *fallen man*, through the merits and mediation of His only-begotten Son. This was in part revealed to Adam, soon after his fall; being contained in the original promise, made to him, and his seed, concerning the Seed of the woman, who should bruise the serpent's head' (Gen. iii. 15). It was a little more clearly revealed to Abraham, by the Angel of God from heaven, saying, 'By Myself have I sworn, saith the Lord, that in thy Seed shall all the nations of the world be blessed' (Gen. xxii. 16, 18). It was yet more fully made known to Moses, to David, and to the prophets that followed; and, through them, to many of the people of God in their respective generations. But still the bulk even of these were ignorant of it; and very few understood it clearly. Still 'life and immortality' were not so 'brought to light' to the Jews of old, as they are now unto us 'by the gospel.'

8. Now this covenant saith not to sinful man, 'Perform un-sinning obedience, and live.' If this were the term, he would have no more benefit by all which Christ hath done and suffered for him, than if he was required, in order to life, to 'ascend into heaven, and bring down Christ from above'; or to 'descend into the deep,' into the invisible world, and 'bring up Christ from the dead.' It doth not require any impossibility to be done (although, to mere man, what it requires would be impossible; but not to man assisted by the Spirit of God): this were only to mock human weakness. Indeed, strictly speaking, the covenant of *grace* doth not require us to *do* anything at all, as absolutely and indispensably necessary in order to our justification; but only to *believe* in Him who, for the sake of His Son, and the propitiation which He hath made, 'justifieth the ungodly that worketh not, and imputes his faith to him for righteousness. Even so Abraham 'believed in the Lord, and He counted it to him for righteousness' (Gen. xv. 6). 'And he received the sign of circumcision, a seal of the righteousness of faith . . . that he might be the father of all theol that believe . . . that righteousness might be imputed unto them also' (Rom. iv. 11). 'Now it was not written for his sake name, that it,' i. e. faith, 'was imputed to him; but for us also, to whom it shall be imputed,' to whom faith shall be imputed for righteousness, shall stand in the stead of perfect obedience, in

order to our acceptance with God, 'if we believe on Him who raised up Jesus our Lord from the dead: who was delivered' to death 'for our offences, and was raised again for our justification' (Rom. iv. 23-25): for the assurance of the remission of our sins, and of a second life to come, to them that believe.

9. What saith then the covenant of forgiveness, of unmerited love, of pardoning mercy? 'Believe in the Lord Jesus Christ, and thou shalt be saved.' In the day thou believest, thou shalt surely live. Thou shalt be restored to the favour of God; and in His pleasure is life. Thou shalt be saved from the curse, and from the wrath, of God. Thou shalt be quickened from the death of sin into the life of righteousness. And if thou endure to the end, believing in Jesus, thou shalt never taste the second death; but, having suffered with thy Lord, shalt also live and reign with Him for ever and ever.

10. Now 'this word is nigh thee.' This condition of life is plain, easy, always at hand. 'It is in thy mouth, and in thy heart, through the operation of the Spirit of God. The moment 'thou believest in thine heart' in Him whom God 'hath raised from the dead,' and 'confessest with thy mouth the Lord Jesus,' as *thy* Lord and *thy* God, 'thou shalt be saved' from condemnation, from the guilt and punishment of thy former sins, and shalt have power to serve God in true holiness all the remaining days of thy life.

11. What is the difference then between the 'righteousness which is of the law,' and the 'righteousness which is of faith'? between the first covenant, or the covenant of works, and the second, the covenant of grace? The essential, unchangeable difference is this: the one supposes him to whom it is given, to be already holy and happy, created in the image and enjoying the favour of God; and prescribes the condition whereon he may continue therein, in love and joy, life and immortality: the other supposes him to whom it is given, to be now unholy and unhappy, fallen short of the glorious image of God, having the wrath of God abiding on him, and hastening, through sin, whereby his soul is dead, to bodily death, and death everlasting; and to man in this state it prescribes the condition whereon he may regain the pearl he has lost, may recover the favour and image of God, may retrieve the life of God in his soul, and be

restored to the knowledge and the love of God, which is the beginning of life eternal.

12. Again: the covenant of works, in order to man's *continuance* in the favour of God, in His knowledge and love, in holiness and happiness, required of perfect man a *perfect* and uninterrupted *obedience* to every point of the law of God. Whereas, the covenant of grace, in order to man's *recovery* of the favour and the life of God, requires only *faith*; living faith in Him who, through God, justifies him that obeyed not.

13. Yet, again: the covenant of works required of Adam, and all his children, to pay the price themselves, in consideration of which they were to receive all the future blessings of God. But in the covenant of grace, seeing we have nothing to pay, God 'frankly forgives us all': provided only, that we believe in Him who hath paid the price for us; who hath given Himself a 'propitiation for our sins, for the sins of the whole world.'

14. Thus the first covenant required what is now *afar off* from all the children of men; namely, unsinning obedience, which is far from those who are 'conceived and born in sin.' Whereas, the second requires what is nigh at hand; as though it should say, 'Thou art sin! God is love! Thou by sin art fallen short of the glory of God; yet there is mercy with Him. Bring then all thy sins to the pardoning God, and they shall vanish away as a cloud. If thou wert not ungodly, there would be no room for Him to justify thee as ungodly. But now draw near, in full assurance of faith. He speaketh, and it is done. Fear not, only believe; for even the just God justifieth all that believe in Jesus.'

II. 1. These things considered, it will be easy to show, as I proposed to do in the second place, the folly of trusting in the 'righteousness which is of the law,' and the wisdom of submitting to the 'righteousness which is of faith.'

The folly of those who still trust in the 'righteousness which is of the law,' the terms of which are, 'Do this, and live,' may abundantly appear from hence: they set out wrong; their very first step is a fundamental mistake: for, before they can ever think of claiming any blessing on the terms of this covenant, they must suppose themselves to be in His state with whom this covenant

was made. But how vain a supposition is this; since it was made
with Adam in a state of innocence! How weak, therefore, must
that whole building be, which stands on such a foundation! And
how foolish are they who thus build on the sand; who seem
never to have considered, that the covenant of works was not
given to man when he was 'dead in trespasses and sins,' but when
he was alive to God, when he knew no sin, but was holy as God
is holy; who forget that it was never designed for the *recovery*
of the favour and life of God once lost, but only for the *continuance* and increase thereof, till it should be complete in life
everlasting.

2. Neither do they consider, who are thus seeking to establish
their 'own righteousness, which is of the law,' what manner of
obedience or righteousness that is which the law indispensably
requires. It must be perfect and entire in every point, or it
answers not the demand of the law. But which of you is able to
perform such obedience? or, consequently, to live thereby?
Who among you fulfils every jot and tittle even of the outward
commandments of God? doing nothing, great or small, which
God forbids? leaving nothing undone which He enjoins? speaking no *idle word*? having your conversation always 'meet to
minister grace to the hearers'? and, 'whether you eat or drink,
or whatever you do, doing all to the glory of God'? And how
much less are you able to fulfil all the inward commandments of
God; those which require, that every temper and motion of your
soul should be holiness unto the Lord! Are you able to 'love
God with all your heart'? to love all mankind as your own soul?
to 'pray without ceasing? in everything to give thanks'? to have
God always before you? and to keep every affection, desire, and
thought, in obedience to His law?

3. You should farther consider, that the righteousness of the
law requires, not only the obeying every command of God,
negative and positive, internal and external, but likewise in the
perfect degree. In every instance whatever, the voice of the law
is, 'Thou shalt serve the Lord thy God with all thy strength.' It
allows no abatement of any kind: it excuses no defect: it condemns every coming short of the full measure of obedience, and
immediately pronounces a curse on the offender: it regards only

the invariable rules of justice, and saith, 'I know not to show mercy.'

4. Who then can appear before such a Judge, who is 'extreme to mark what is done amiss'? How weak are they who desire to be tried at the bar where 'no flesh living can be justified'!—none of the offspring of Adam. For, suppose we did now keep every commandment with all our strength; yet one single breach, which ever was, utterly destroys our whole claim to life. If we have ever offended in any one point, this righteousness is at an end. For the law condemns all who do not perform uninterrupted as well as perfect obedience. So that, according to the sentence of this, for him who hath once sinned, in any degree, 'there remaineth only a fearful looking for of fiery indignation, which shall devour the adversaries' of God.

5. Is it not then the very foolishness of folly, for fallen man to seek life by this righteousness? for man, who was 'shapen in wickedness, and in sin did his mother conceive him'? man, who is, by nature, all 'earthly, sensual, devilish'; altogether 'corrupt and abominable'; in whom, till he find grace, 'dwelleth no good thing'; nay, who cannot of himself think one good thought; who is indeed all sin, a mere lump of ungodliness, and who commits sin in every breath he draws; whose actual transgressions, in word and deed, are more in number than the hairs of his head? What stupidity, what senselessness, must it be for such an unclean, guilty, helpless worm as this, to dream of seeking acceptance by his own righteousness, of living by 'the righteousness which is of the law'!

6. Now, whatsoever considerations prove the folly of trusting in the 'righteousness which is of the law,' prove equally the wisdom of submitting to the 'righteousness which is of God by faith.' This were easy to be shown with regard to each of the preceding considerations. But, to waive this, the wisdom of the first step hereto, the disclaiming our own righteousness, plainly appears from hence, that it is acting according to truth, to the real nature of things. For, what is it more, than to acknowledge with our heart as well as lips, the true state wherein we are? to acknowledge, that we bring with us into the world a corrupt, sinful nature; more corrupt, indeed, than we can easily con-

ceive, or find words to express? that hereby we are prone to all that is evil, and averse from all that is good: that we are full of pride, self-will, unruly passions, foolish desires, vile and in-ordinate affections; lovers of the world, lovers of pleasure more than lovers of God; that our lives have been no better than our hearts, but many ways ungodly and unholy; insomuch that our actual sins, both in word and deed, have been as the stars of heaven for multitude; that, on all these accounts, we are dis-pleasing to Him who is of purer eyes than to behold iniquity, and deserve nothing from Him but indignation and wrath and death, the due wages of sin? that we cannot, by any of our righteousness (for indeed we have none at all), nor by any of our works (for they are as the tree upon which they grow), appease the wrath of God, or avert the punishment we have justly deserved; yea, that, if left to ourselves, we shall only wax worse and worse, sink deeper and deeper into sin, offend God more and more, both with our evil works, and with the evil tempers of our carnal mind, till we fill up the measure of our iniquities, and bring upon ourselves swift destruction? And is not this the very state wherein by nature we are? To acknowledge this, then, both with our heart and lips, that is, to disclaim our own right-eousness, 'the righteousness which is of the law,' is to act accord-ing to the real nature of things, and, consequently, is an instance of true wisdom.

7. The wisdom of submitting to 'the righteousness of faith' appears, farther, from this consideration, that it is the righteous-ness of God: I mean here, it is that method of reconciliation with God which hath been chosen and established by God Him-self, not only as He is the God of wisdom, but as He is the sover-eign Lord of heaven and earth, and of every creature which He hath made. Now, as it is not meet for man to say unto God, 'What doest Thou?'—as none, who is not utterly void of under-standing, will contend with One that is mightier than he, with Him whose kingdom ruleth over all: so it is true wisdom, it is a mark of sound understanding, to acquiesce in whatever He hath chosen; to say in this, as in all things, 'It is the Lord: let Him do what seemeth Him good.'

8. It may be farther considered, that it was of mere grace, of

free love, of undeserved mercy, that God hath vouchsafed to sinful man any way of reconciliation with Himself; that we were not cut away from His hand, and utterly blotted out of His remembrance. Therefore, whatever method He is pleased to appoint, of His tender mercy, of His unmerited goodness, whereby His enemies, who have so deeply revolted from Him, so long and obstinately rebelled against Him, may still find favour in His sight, it is doubtless our wisdom to accept it with all thankfulness.

9. To mention but one consideration more. It is wisdom to aim at the best end by the best means. Now the best end which any creature can pursue is, happiness in God. And the best end a fallen creature can pursue is, the recovery of the favour and image of God. But the best, indeed the only means under heaven given to a man, whereby he may regain the favour of God, which is better than life itself, or the image of God, which is the true life of the soul, is the submitting to the 'righteousness which is of faith,' the believing in the only-begotten Son of God.

III. 1. Whosoever therefore thou art, who desirest to be forgiven and reconciled to the favour of God, do not say in thy heart, 'I must *first do this*; I must *first* conquer every sin; break off every evil word and work, and do all good to all men; or, I must *first* go to church, receive the Lord's supper, hear more sermons, and say more prayers.' Alas, my brother! thou art clean gone out of the way. Thou art still 'ignorant of the righteousness of God,' and art 'seeking to establish thy own righteousness' as the ground of thy reconciliation. Knowest thou not, that thou canst do nothing but sin, till thou art reconciled to God? Wherefore, then, dost thou say, 'I must do this and this *first*, and then I shall believe'? Nay, but *first believe*! Believe in the Lord Jesus Christ, the propitiation for thy sins. Let this good foundation first be laid, and then thou shalt do all things well.

2. Neither say in thy heart, 'I cannot be accepted yet, because I am not *good enough*.' Who is *good enough*? who ever was, to merit acceptance at God's hands? Was ever any child of Adam *good enough* for this? or will any till the consummation of all things? And, as for thee, thou art not good at all: there dwelleth

in thee no good thing. And thou never wilt be, till thou believe in Jesus. Rather thou wilt find thyself worse and worse. But is there any need of being worse, in order to be accepted? Art thou not *bad enough* already? Indeed thou art; and that God knoweth. And thou thyself canst not deny it. Then delay not. All things are now ready. 'Arise, and wash away thy sins.' The fountain is open. Now is the time to wash thee white in the blood of the Lamb. Now He shall 'purge' thee as 'with hyssop,' and thou shalt 'be clean': He shall 'wash' thee, and thou shalt 'be whiter than snow.'

3. Do not say, 'But I am not *contrite enough*: I am not *sensible enough* of my sins.' I know it. I would to God thou wert more *sensible* of them, more *contrite* a thousand fold than thou art. But do not stay for this. It may be, God will make thee so, not before thou believest, but by believing. It may be, thou wilt not weep much, till thou lovest much because thou hast had much forgiven. In the meantime look unto Jesus. Behold, how He loveth thee! What could He have done more for thee which He hath not done?

> O Lamb of God, was ever pain,
> Was ever love like Thine?

Look steadily upon Him, till He looks on thee, and breaks thy hard heart. Then shall thy 'head' be 'waters' and thy 'eyes fountains of tears.'

4. Nor yet do thou say, 'I must *do* something more *before* I come to Christ.' I grant, supposing thy Lord should delay His coming, it were meet and right to wait for His appearing, in doing, so far as thou hast power, whatsoever He hath commanded thee. But there is no necessity for making such a supposition. How knowest thou that He will delay? Perhaps He will appear, as the dayspring from on high, before the morning light. O do not set Him a time! Expect Him every hour. Now He is nigh! even at the door!

5. And to what end wouldest thou wait for *more sincerity before* thy sins are blotted out? To make thee more worthy of the grace of God? Alas, thou art still 'establishing thy own right-

eousness.' He will have mercy, not because thou art worthy of it, but because His compassions fail not; not because thou art righteous, but because Jesus Christ hath atoned for thy sins.

Again, if there be anything good in *sincerity:* why dost thou expect it *before* thou hast faith?—seeing faith itself is the only root of whatever is really good and holy.

Above all, how long wilt thou forget, that whatsoever thou doest, or whatsoever thou hast, before thy sins are forgiven thee, it avails nothing with God toward the procuring of thy forgiveness! yea, and that it must all be cast behind thy back, trampled under foot, made no account of, or thou wilt never find favour in God's sight; because, until then, thou canst not ask it as a mere sinner, guilty, lost, undone, having nothing to plead, nothing to offer to God, but only the merits of His well-beloved Son, 'who loved *thee*, and gave Himself for *thee*'!

6. To conclude. Whosoever thou art, O man, who hast the sentence of death in thyself, who feelest thyself a condemned sinner, and hast the wrath of God abiding on thee: unto thee saith the Lord, not, 'Do this'—perfectly obey all my commands— 'and live'; but, 'Believe in the Lord Jesus Christ, and thou shalt be saved.' 'The word of faith is nigh unto thee'; now, at this instant, in the present moment, and in thy present state, sinner as thou art, just as thou art, believe the gospel; and 'I will be merciful unto *thy* unrighteousness, and *thy* iniquities will I remember no more.'

SERMON VII

THE WAY TO THE KINGDOM

The kingdom of God is at hand: repent, ye and believe the gospel.—MARK I. 15.

THESE words naturally lead us to consider, first, the nature of true religion, here termed by our Lord 'the kingdom of God,' which, saith He, 'is at hand'; and, secondly, the way thereto, which He points out in those words, 'Repent ye, and believe the gospel.'

I. 1. We are, first, to consider the nature of true religion, here termed by our Lord 'the kindgom of God.' The same expression the great Apostle uses in his Epistle to the Romans, where he likewise explains his Lord's words, saying, 'The kingdom of God is not meat and drink; but righteousness, and peace, and joy in the Holy Ghost' (Rom. xiv. 17).

2. 'The kingdom of God,' or true religion, 'is not meat and drink.' It is well known, that not only the unconverted Jews, but great numbers of those who had received the faith of Christ, were, notwithstanding, 'zealous of the law' (Acts xxi. 20), even the ceremonial law of Moses. Whatsoever, therefore, they found written therein, either concerning meat and drink offerings, or the distinction between clean and unclean meats, they not only observed themselves, but vehemently pressed the same, even on those 'among the Gentiles' (or Heathens) 'who were turned to God'; yea, to such a degree, that some of them taught, wheresoever they came among them, 'Except ye be circumcised, and keep the law' (the whole ritual law), 'ye cannot be saved' (Acts xv. 1, 24).

3. In opposition to these, the Apostle declares, both here and in many other places, that true religion does not consist in *meat* and *drink:* or in any ritual observances; nor, indeed, in any outward thing whatever; in anything exterior to the heart; the whole substance thereof lying in 'righteousness, peace, and joy in the Holy Ghost.'

4. Not in any *outward thing*; such as *forms* or *ceremonies:* even of the most excellent kind. Supposing these to be ever so decent and significant, ever so expressive of inward things: supposing them ever so helpful, not only to the vulgar, whose thought reaches little farther than their sight; but even to men of understanding, men of stronger capacities, as doubtless they may sometimes be; yea, supposing them, as in the case of the Jews, to be appointed by God Himself; yet even 'during the period of time wherein that appointment remains in force, true religion does not principally consist therein; nay, strictly speaking, not

at all. How much more must this hold concerning such rites and forms as are only of human appointment! The religion of Christ rises infinitely higher, and lies immensely deeper, than all these. These are good in their place; just so far as they are in fact subservient to true religion. And it were superstition to object against them, while they are applied only as occasional helps to human weakness. But let no man carry them farther. Let no man dream that they have any intrinsic worth; or that religion cannot subsist without them. This were to make them an abomination to the Lord.

5. The nature of religion is so far from consisting in these, in forms of worship, or rites and ceremonies, that it does not properly consist in any outward actions, of what kind soever. It is true, a man cannot have any religion who is guilty of vicious, immoral actions; or who does to others what he would not they should do unto him, if he were in the same circumstances. And it is also true, that he can have no real religion who 'knows to do good, and doeth it not.' Yet may a man both abstain from outward evil, and do good, and still have no religion. Yea, two persons may do the same outward work; suppose feeding the hungry, or clothing the naked; and, in the meantime, one of these may be truly religious, and the other have no religion at all: for the one may act from the love of God, and the other from the love of praise. So manifest it is, that although true religion naturally leads to every good word and work, yet the real nature thereof lies deeper still, even in 'the hidden man of the heart.'

6. I say of *the heart*. For neither does religion consist in orthodoxy, or right opinions; which, although they are not properly outward things, are not in the heart, but the understanding. A man may be orthodox in every point; he may not only espouse right opinions, but zealously defend them against all opposers; he may think justly concerning the incarnation of our Lord, concerning the ever-blessed Trinity, and every other doctrine contained in the oracles of God; he may assent to all the three creeds—that called the Apostles', the Nicene, and the Athanasian; and yet it is possible he may have no religion at all, no more than a Jew, Turk, or Pagan. He may be almost as

orthodox—as the devil (though indeed not altogether; for every man errs in something; whereas we cannot well conceive him to hold any erroneous opinion), and may, all the while, be as great a stranger as he to the religion of the heart.

7. This alone is religion, truly so called: this alone is in the sight of God of great price. The Apostle sums it all up in three particulars, 'righteousness, and peace, and joy in the Holy Ghost.' And, first, *righteousness.* We cannot be at a loss concerning this, if we remember the words of our Lord, describing the two grand branches thereof, on which 'hang all the Law and the Prophets': 'Thou shalt love the Lord thy God with all thy heart, and with all thy mind, and with all thy soul, and with all thy strength: this is the first and great commandment' (Mark xii. 30); the first and great branch of Christian righteousness. Thou shalt delight thyself in the Lord thy God; thou shalt seek and find all happiness in Him. He shall be 'thy shield, and thy exceeding great reward, in time and in eternity. All thy bones shall say, 'Whom have I in heaven but Thee? And there is none upon earth that I desire beside Thee.' Thou shalt hear and fulfil His word, who saith, 'My son, give me thy heart.' And, having given Him thy heart, thy inmost soul, to reign there without a rival, thou mayest well cry out, in the fullness of thy heart, 'I will love Thee, O Lord, my strength. The Lord is my strong rock, and my defence; my Saviour, my God, and my might, in whom I will trust; my buckler, the horn also of my salvation, and my refuge.'

8. And the second commandment is like unto this; the second great branch of Christian righteousness is closely and inseparably connected therewith; even, 'Thou shalt love thy neighbour as thyself.' *Thou shalt love*—thou shalt embrace with the most tender good-will, the most earnest and cordial affection, the most inflamed desires of preventing or removing all evil, and of procuring for him every possible good. *Thy neighbour*—that is, not only thy friend, thy kinsman, or thy acquaintance; not only the virtuous, the friendly, him that loves thee, that prevents or returns thy kindness; but every child of man, every human creature, every soul which God hath made; not excepting him whom thou never hast seen in the flesh, whom thou knowest

not, either by face or name; not excepting him whom thou knowest to be evil and unthankful, him that still despitefully uses and persecutes thee: him thou shalt love *as thyself*; with the same invariable thirst after his happiness in every kind; the same unwearied care to screen him from whatever might grieve or hurt either his soul or body.

9. Now is not this love 'the fulfilling of the law'? the sum of all Christian righteousness? of all inward righteousness,—for it necessarily implies 'bowels of mercies, humbleness of mind' (seeing 'love is not puffed up'), 'gentleness, meekness, long-suffering' (for love 'is not provoked,' but 'believeth, hopeth, endureth all things'): and of all outward righteousness,—for 'love worketh no evil to his neighbour,' either by word or deed. It cannot willingly hurt or grieve any one. And it is zealous of good works. Every lover of mankind, as he hath opportunity, 'doeth good unto all men' being (without partiality, and without hypocrisy) 'full of mercy and good fruits.'

10. But true religion, or a heart right toward God and man, implies happiness as well as holiness. For it is not only 'righteousness,' but also 'peace and joy in the Holy Ghost.' What peace? 'The peace of God,' which God only can give, and the world cannot take away; the peace which 'passeth all understanding,' all barely rational conception; being a supernatural sensation, a divine taste, of 'the powers of the world to come' such as the natural man knoweth not, how wise soever in the things of this world; nor, indeed, can he know it, in his present state, 'because it is spiritually discerned.' It is a peace that banishes all doubt, all painful uncertainty; the Spirit of God bearing witness with the spirit of a Christian, that he is 'a child of God.' And it banishes fear, all such fear as hath torment: the fear of the wrath of God; the fear of hell; the fear of the devil; and, in particular, the fear of death: he that hath the peace of God, desiring, if it were the will of God, 'to depart, and to be with Christ.'

11. With this peace of God, wherever it is fixed in the soul, there is also 'joy in the Holy Ghost'; joy wrought in the heart by the Holy Ghost, by the ever-blessed Spirit of God. He it is that worketh in us that calm, humble rejoicing in God, through

Christ Jesus, 'by whom we have now received the atonement,' καταλλαγήν, the reconciliation with God; and that enables us boldy to confirm the truth of the royal Psalmist's declaration, 'Blessed is the man' (or rather, *happy*) 'whose unrighteousness is forgiven, and whose sin is covered.' He it is that inspires the Christian soul with that even, solid joy, which arises from the testimony of the Spirit that he is a child of God; and that gives him to 'rejoice with joy unspeakable, in hope of the glory of God'; hope both of the glorious image of God, which is in part, and shall be fully, 'revealed in him'; and of that crown of glory which fadeth not away, reserved in heaven for him.

12. This holiness and happiness, joined in one, are sometimes styled, in the inspired writings, 'the kingdom of God' (as by our Lord in the text), and sometimes, 'the kingdom of heaven.' It is termed, 'the kingdom of God,' because it is the immediate fruit of God's reigning in the soul. So soon as ever He takes unto Himself His mighty power, and sets up His throne in our hearts, they are instantly filled with this 'righteousness, and peace, and joy in the Holy Ghost.' It is called 'the kindgom of heaven,' because it is (in a degree) heaven opened in the soul. For whosoever they are that experience this, they can aver before angels and men,

> Everlasting life is won,
> Glory is on earth begun;

according to the constant tenor of Scripture, which everywhere bears record, God 'hath given unto us eternal life, and this life is in His Son. He that hath the Son' (reigning in his heart) 'hath life,' even life everlasting (1 John v. 11, 12). For 'this is life eternal, to know Thee the only true God, and Jesus Christ, whom Thou hast sent' (John xvii. 3). And they to whom this is given may confidently address God, though they were in the midst of a fiery furnace,—

> Thee, Lord, safe shielded by Thy power,
> Thee, Son of God, JEHOVAH, we adore;

In form of man descending to appear:
To Thee be ceaseless hallelujahs given,
Praise, as in heaven Thy throne, we offer here;
For where Thy presence is display'd, is heaven.

13. And this 'kingdom of God,' or of heaven, is at hand.'
As these words were originally spoken, they implied that 'the
time' was then fulfilled, God being 'made manifest in the flesh,'
when He would set up His kingdom among men, and reign in
the hearts of His people. And is not the time now fulfilled?
For, 'Lo,' (saith He), 'I am with you always,' you who preach
remission of sins in My name, 'even unto the end of the world'
(Matt. xxviii. 20). Wheresoever, therefore, the gospel of Christ
is preached, this His 'kingdom is nigh at hand.' It is not far from
every one of you. Ye may this hour enter thereinto, if so be ye
hearken to His voice, 'Repent ye, and believe the gospel.'

II. 1. This is the way; walk ye in it. And, first, 'repent'; that
is, know yourselves. This is the first repentance, previous to
faith; even conviction, or self-knowledge. Awake, then, thou
that sleepest. Know thyself to be a sinner, and what manner of
sinner thou art. Know that corruption of thy inmost nature,
whereby thou art very far gone from original righteousness,
whereby 'the flesh lusteth' always 'contrary to the Spirit,'
through that 'carnal mind' which 'is enmity against God,'
which 'is not subject to the law of God, neither indeed can be.'
Know that thou art corrupted in every power, in every faculty
of thy soul; that thou art totally corrupted in every one of these,
all the foundations being out of course. The eyes of thine understanding are darkened, so that they cannot discern God, or the
things of God. The clouds of ignorance and error rest upon thee,
and cover thee with the shadow of death. Thou knowest
nothing yet as thou oughtest to know, neither God, nor the
world, nor thyself. Thy will is no longer the will of God, but
is utterly perverse and distorted, averse from all good, from all
which God loves, and prone to all evil, to every abomination
which God hateth. Thy affections are alienated from God, and
scattered abroad over all the earth. All thy passions, both thy

desires and aversions, thy joys and sorrows, thy hopes and fears, are out of frame, are either undue in their degree, or placed on undue objects. So that there is no soundness in thy soul; but 'from the crown of the head, to the sole of the foot' (to use the strong expression of the prophet), there are only 'wounds, and bruises, and putrefying sores.'

2. Such is the inbred corruption of thy heart, of thy very inmost nature. And what manner of branches canst thou expect to grow from such an evil root? Hence springs unbelief; ever departing from the living God; saying, 'Who is the Lord, that I should serve Him? Tush! Thou God carest not for it.' Hence independence; affecting to be like the Most High. Hence pride, in all its forms; teaching thee to say, 'I am rich, and increased in goods, and have need of nothing.' From this evil fountain flow forth the bitter streams of vanity, thirst of praise, ambition, covetousness, the lust of the flesh, the lust of the eye, and the pride of life. From this arise anger, hatred, malice, revenge, envy, jealousy, evil surmisings: from this, all the foolish and hurtful lusts that now 'pierce thee through with many sorrows, and, if not timely prevented, will at length drown thy soul in everlasting perdition.

3. And what fruits can grow on such branches as these? Only such as are bitter and evil continually. Of pride cometh contention, vain boasting, seeking and receiving praise of men, and so robbing God of that glory which He cannot give unto another. Of the lust of the flesh come gluttony or drunkenness, luxury or sensuality, fornication, uncleanness; variously defiling that body which was designed for a temple of the Holy Ghost: of unbelief, every evil word and work. But the time would fail, shouldest thou reckon up all; all the idle words thou hast spoken, provoking the Most High, grieving the Holy One of Israel; all the evil works thou hast done, either wholly evil in themselves, or, at least, not done to the glory of God. For thy actual sins are more than thou art able to express, more than the hairs of thy head. Who can number the sands of the sea, or the drops of rain, or thy iniquities?

4. And knowest thou not that 'the wages of sin is death'?—death, not only temporal, but eternal. 'The soul that sinneth,

it shall die'; for the mouth of the Lord hath spoken it. It shall die the second death. This is the sentence, to 'be punished' with never-ending death, 'with everlasting destruction from the presence of the Lord, and from the glory of His power.' Knowest thou not that every sinner ἔνοχος ἐστι τῇ γεέννῃ τοῦ πυρός, not properly 'is in danger of hell-fire'; that expression is far too weak; but rather 'is under the sentence of hell-fire'; doomed already, just dragging to execution. Thou are guilty of ever-lasting death. It is the just reward of thy inward and outward wickedness. It is just that the sentence should now take place. Dost thou see, dost thou feel this? Art thou throughly convinced that thou deservest God's wrath, and everlasting damnation? Would God do thee no wrong, if He now commanded the earth to open, and swallow thee up?—if thou wert now to go down quick into the pit, into the fire that never shall be quenched? If God hath given thee truly to repent, thou hast a deep sense that these things are so; and that it is of His mere mercy thou art not consumed, swept away from the face of the earth.

5. And what wilt thou do to appease the wrath of God, to atone for all thy sins, and to escape the punishment thou hast so justly deserved? Alas, thou canst do nothing: nothing that will in any wise make amends to God for one evil work, or word, or thought. If thou couldest now do all things well, if from this very hour till thy soul should return to God thou couldest perform perfect, uninterrupted obedience, even this would not atone for what is past. The not increasing thy debt would not discharge it. It would still remain as great as ever. Yea, the present and future obedience of all the men upon earth, and all the angels in heaven, would never make satisfaction to the justice of God for one single sin. How vain, then, was the thought of atoning for thy own sins, by anything thou couldest do! It costeth far more to redeem one soul, than all mankind is able to pay. So that were there no other help for a guilty sinner, without doubt he must have perished everlastingly.

6. But suppose perfect obedience, for the time to come, could atone for the sins that are past, this would profit thee nothing; for thou art not able to perform it; no, not in any one point.

Begin now: make the trial. Shake off that outward sin that so easily besetteth thee. Thou canst not. How then wilt thou change thy life from all evil to all good? Indeed, it is impossible to be done, unless first thy heart be changed. For, so long as the tree remains evil, it cannot bring forth good fruit. But art thou able to change thy own heart, from all sin to all holiness? to quicken a soul that is dead in sin—dead to God, and alive only to the world? No more than thou art able to quicken a dead body, to raise to life him that lieth in the grave. Yea, thou art not able to quicken thy soul in any degree, no more than to give any degree of life to the dead body. Thou canst do nothing, more or less, in this matter; thou art utterly without strength. To be deeply sensible of this, how helpless thou art, as well as how guilty and how sinful,—this is that 'repentance not to be repented of,' which is the forerunner of the kingdom of God.

7. If to this lively conviction of thy inward and outward sins, of thy utter guiltiness and helplessness, there be added suitable affections,—sorrow of heart, for having despised thy own mercies; remorse, and self-condemnation, having thy mouth stopped; shame to lift up thine eyes to heaven; fear of the wrath of God abiding on thee, of His curse hanging over thy head, and of the fiery indignation ready to devour those who forget God, and obey not our Lord Jesus Christ; earnest desire to escape from that indignation, to cease from evil, and learn to do well,—then I say unto thee, in the name of the Lord, 'Thou art not far from the kingdom of God.' One step more, and thou shalt enter in. Thou dost 'repent.' Now, 'believe the gospel.'

8. *The gospel* (that is, good tidings, good news for guilty, helpless sinners), in the largest sense of the word, means, the whole revelation made to men by Jesus Christ; and sometimes the whole account of what our Lord did and suffered while He tabernacled among men. The substance of all is, 'Jesus Christ came into the world to save sinners'; or, 'God so loved the world, that He gave His only-begotten Son, to the end we might not perish, but have everlasting life'; or, 'He was bruised for our transgressions, He was wounded for our iniquities; the chastise-

ment of our peace was upon Him; and with His stripes we are healed.'

9. *Believe* this, and the kingdom of God is thine. By faith thou attainest the promise. 'He pardoneth and absolveth all that truly repent, and unfeignedly believe His holy gospel.' As soon as ever God hath spoken to thy heart, 'Be of good cheer, thy sins are forgiven thee,' His kingdom comes: thou hast 'righteousness, and peace, and joy in the Holy Ghost.'

10. Only beware thou do not deceive thy own soul, with regard to the nature of this faith. It is not, as some have fondly conceived, a bare assent to the truth of the Bible, of the articles of our Creed, or of all that is contained in the Old and New Testament. The devils believe this, as well as I or thou! And yet they are devils still. But it is, over and above this, a sure trust in the mercy of God, through Christ Jesus. It is a confidence in a pardoning God. It is a divine evidence or conviction that 'God was in Christ, reconciling the world to Himself, not imputing to them their' former 'trespasses'; and in particular, that the Son of God hath loved *me*, and given Himself for *me*; and that I, even I, am now reconciled to God by the blood of the cross.

11. Dost thou thus believe? Then the peace of God is in thy heart, and sorrow and sighing flee away. Thou art no longer in doubt of the love of God; it is clear as the noon-day sun. Thou criest out, 'My song shall be always of the loving-kindness of the Lord: with my mouth will I ever be telling of Thy truth, from one generation to another.' Thou art no longer afraid of hell, or death, or him that had once the power of death, the devil; no, nor painfully afraid of God Himself; only thou hast a tender, filial fear of offending Him. Dost thou believe? Then thy 'soul doth magnify the Lord,' and thy 'spirit rejoiceth in God thy Saviour.' Thou rejoicest in that thou hast 'redemption through His blood, even the forgiveness of sins.' Thou rejoicest in that 'Spirit of adoption,' which crieth in thy heart, 'Abba, Father!' Thou rejoicest in a 'hope full of immortality'; in reaching forth unto the 'mark for the prize of thy high calling'; in an earnest expectation of all the good things which God hath prepared for them that love Him.

12. Dost thou now believe? Then 'the love of God is' now 'shed abroad in thy heart.' Thou lovest Him, because He first loved us. And, because thou lovest God, thou lovest thy brother also. And being filled with 'love, peace, joy,' thou art also filled with long-suffering, gentleness, fidelity, goodness, meekness, temperance,' and all the other fruits of the same Spirit; in a word, with whatever dispositions are holy, are heavenly, or divine. For while thou 'beholdest with open,' uncovered 'face' (the veil now being taken away) 'the glory of the Lord,' His glorious love, and the glorious image wherein thou wast created, thou art 'changed into the same image from glory to glory, by the Spirit of the Lord.'

13. This repentance, this faith, this peace, joy, love; this change from glory to glory, is what the wisdom of the world has voted to be madness, mere enthusiasm, utter distraction. But thou, O man of God, regard them not; be thou moved by none of these things. Thou knowest in whom thou hast believed. See that no man take thy crown. Whereunto thou hast already attained, hold fast, and follow, till thou attain all the great and precious promises. And thou who hast not yet known Him, let not vain men make thee ashamed of the gospel of Christ. Be thou in nothing terrified by those who speak evil of the things which they know not. God will soon turn thy heaviness into joy. O let not thy hands hang down! Yet a little longer, and He will take away thy fears, and give thee the spirit of a sound mind. He is nigh 'that justifieth: who is he that condemneth? It is Christ that died, yea rather, that rose again, who is even now at the right hand of God, making intercession' for thee.

Now cast thyself on the Lamb of God, with all thy sins, how many soever they be; and 'an entrance shall' now 'be ministered unto thee into the kingdom of our Lord and Saviour Jesus Christ'!

SERMON VIII

THE FIRST-FRUITS OF THE SPIRIT

There is therefore now no condemnation to them which are in Christ Jesus, who walk not after the flesh, but after the Spirit.—ROM. viii. 1.

BY 'them which are in Christ Jesus,' St. Paul evidently means, those who truly believe in Him; those who, 'being justified by faith, have peace with God through our Lord Jesus Christ.' They who thus believe do no longer 'walk after the flesh,' no longer follow the motions of corrupt nature, but 'after the Spirit'; both their thoughts, words, and works are under the direction of the blessed Spirit of God.

2. 'There is therefore now no condemnation to' these. There is no condemnation to them from God; for He hath *justified* them 'freely by His grace through the redemption that is in Jesus.' He hath forgiven all their iniquities, and blotted out all their sins. And there is no condemnation to them from within; for they' have received, not the spirit of the world, but the Spirit which is of God; that they might know the things which are freely given to them of God' (1 Cor. ii. 12); which Spirit 'beareth witness with their spirits, that they are the children of God.' And to this is added the testimony of their conscience, 'that in simplicity and godly sincerity, not with fleshly wisdom, but by the grace of God, they have had their conversation in the world' (2 Cor. i. 12).

3. But because this scripture has been so frequently misunderstood, and that in so dangerous a manner; because such multitudes of 'unlearned and unstable men' (οἱ ἀμαθεῖς καὶ ἀστήρικτοι, men untaught of God, and consequently unestablished in the truth which is after godliness) have wrested it to their own destruction; I propose to show, as clearly as I can, first, who those are 'which are in Christ Jesus,' and 'walk not after the flesh, but after the Spirit'; and, secondly, how 'there is no condemnation to' these. I shall conclude with some practical inferences

7

I. 1. First, I am to show, who those are that 'are in Christ Jesus.' And are they not those who believe in His name? those who are 'found in Him, not having their own righteousness, but the righteousness which is of God by faith'? These, 'who have redemption through His blood,' are properly said to be *in Him*; for they dwell in Christ, and Christ in them. They are joined unto the Lord in one Spirit. They are ingrafted into Him as branches into the vine. They are united, as members to their head, in a manner which words cannot express, nor could it before enter into their hearts to conceive.

2. Now 'whosoever abideth in Him, sinneth not'; 'walketh not after the flesh.' The flesh, in the usual language of St. Paul, signifies corrupt ntaure. In this sense he uses the word, writing to the Galatians, 'The works of the flesh are manifest' (Gal. v. 19); and a little before, 'Walk in the Spirit, and ye shall not fulfil the lust' (or desire) 'of the flesh' (ver. 16). To prove which, namely, that those who 'walk by the Spirit' do not 'fulfil the lusts of the flesh,' he immediately adds, 'For the flesh lusteth against the Spirit, and the Spirit lusteth against the flesh (for these are contrary to each other); that ye may not do the things which ye would.' So the words are literally translated (ἵνα μὴ ἃ ἂν θέλητε, ταῦτα ποιῆτε), not, 'So that ye cannot do the things that ye would'; as if the flesh overcame the Spirit: a translation which hath not only nothing to do with the original text of the Apostle, but likewise makes his whole argument nothing worth; yea, asserts just the reverse of what he is proving.

3. They who are of Christ, who abide in Him, 'have crucified the flesh with its affections and lusts.' They abstain from all those works of the flesh; from 'adultery and fornication'; from 'uncleanness and lasciviousness'; from 'idolatry, witchcraft, hatred, variance'; from 'emulations, wrath, strife, sedition, heresies, envyings, murders, drunkenness, revellings'; from every design, and word, and work, to which the corruption of nature leads. Although they feel the root of bitterness in themselves, yet are they endued with power from on high to trample it continually under foot, so that it cannot 'spring up to trouble them'; insomuch that every fresh assault which they undergo only gives them fresh occasion of praise, of crying out, 'Thanks

be unto God, who giveth us the victory through Jesus Christ our Lord.'

4. They now 'walk after the Spirit,' both in their hearts and lives. They are taught of Him to love God and their neighbour, with a love which is as 'a well of water, springing up into ever-lasting life.' And by Him they are led into every holy desire, into every divine and heavenly temper, till every thought which arises in their heart is holiness unto the Lord.

5. They who 'walk after the Spirit' are also led by Him into all holiness of conversation. Their 'speech is always in grace, seasoned with salt'; with the love and fear of God. 'No corrupt communication comes out of their mouth: but only that which is good,' that which is 'to the use of edifying,' which is 'meet to minister grace to the hearers.' And herein likewise do they exercise themselves day and night, to do only the things which please God; in all their outward behaviour to follow Him 'who left us an example that we might tread in His steps'; in all their intercourse with their neighbour, to walk in justice, mercy, and truth; and 'whatsoever they do,' in every circumstance of life, to 'do all to the glory of God.'

6. These are they who indeed 'walk after the Spirit.' Being filled with faith and with the Holy Ghost, they possess in their hearts, and show forth in their lives, in the whole course of their words and actions, the genuine fruits of the Spirit of God. namely, 'love, joy, peace, long-suffering, gentleness, goodness, fidelity, meekness, temperance,' and whatsoever else is lovely or praiseworthy. 'They adorn in all things the gospel of God our Saviour'; and give full proof to all mankind, that they are indeed actuated by the same Spirit 'which raised up Jesus from the dead.'

II. 1. I proposed to show, in the second place, how 'there is no condemnation to them which are' thus 'in Christ Jesus,' and thus 'walk not after the flesh, but after the Spirit.'

And, first, to believers in Christ, walking thus, 'there is no condemnation' on account of their past sins. God condemneth them not for any of these: they are as though they had never been; they are cast 'as a stone into the depth of the sea,' and He remembereth them no more. God, having 'set forth His Son to be a propitiation' for them 'through faith in His blood,' hath declared unto them 'His righteousness for the remission of the sins that are past.' He layeth therefore none of these to their charge; their memorial is perished with them.

2. And there is no condemnation in their own breast; no sense of guilt, or dread of the wrath of God. They 'have the witness in themselves': they are conscious of their interest in the blood of sprinkling. 'They have not received again the spirit of bondage unto fear,' unto doubt and racking uncertainty; but they 'have received the Spirit of adoption,' crying in their heart, 'Abba, Father.' Thus, being 'justified by faith,' they have the peace of God ruling in their hearts; flowing from a continual sense of His pardoning mercy, and the 'answer of a good conscience toward God.'

3. If it be said, 'But sometimes a believer in Christ may lose his sight of the mercy of God; sometimes such darkness may fall upon him that he no longer sees Him that is invisible, no longer feels that witness in himself of his part in the atoning blood; and then he is inwardly condemned, he hath again "the sentence of death in himself" ': I answer, supposing it so to be, supposing him not to see the mercy of God, then he is not a believer: for faith implies light, the light of God shining upon the soul. So far, therefore, as any one loses this light, he, for the time, loses his faith. And, no doubt, a true believer in Christ may lose the light of faith; and so far as this is lost, he may, for a time, fall again into condemnation. But this is not the case of them who now 'are in Christ Jesus,' who now believe in His name. For so long as they believe, and walk after the Spirit, neither God condemns them, nor their own heart.

4. They are not condemned, secondly, for any present sins, for now transgressing the commandments of God. For they do not transgress them: they do not 'walk after the flesh, but after the Spirit.' This is the continual proof of their 'love of God, that they keep His commandments'; even as St. John bears witness. 'Whosoever is born of God doth not commit sin. For His seed remaineth in him, and he cannot sin, because he is born of God': he cannot, so long as that seed of God, that

loving, holy faith remaineth in him. So long as 'he keepeth himself' herein, 'that wicked one toucheth him not.' Now it is evident, he is not condemned for the sins which he doth not commit at all. They, therefore, who are thus 'led by the Spirit are not under the law' (Gal. v. 18): not under the curse or condemnation of it; for it condemns none but those who break it. Thus, that law of God, 'Thou shalt not steal,' condemns none but those who do steal. Thus, 'Remember the Sabbath-day to keep it holy,' condemns those only who do not keep it holy. But against the fruits of the Spirit 'there is no law' (ver. 23); as the Apostle more largely declares in those memorable words of his former Epistle to Timothy: 'We know that the law is good, if a man use it lawfully; knowing this' (if, while he uses the law of God, in order either to convince or direct, he know and remember this), ὅτι δικαίῳ νόμος οὐ κεῖται, (not 'that the law is not made for a righteous man,' but) 'that the law does not lie against a righteous man': it has no force against him, no power to condemn him; 'but against the lawless and disobedient, against the ungodly and sinners, against the unholy and profane; according to the glorious gospel of the blessed God' (1 Tim. i. 8, 9, 11).

5. They are not condemned, thirdly, for inward sin, even though it does now remain. That the corruption of nature does still remain, even in those who are the children of God by faith; that they have in them the seeds of pride and vanity, of anger, lust, and evil desire, yea, sin of every kind; is too plain to be denied, being matter of daily experience. And on this account it is, that St. Paul, speaking to those whom he had just before witnessed to be 'in Christ Jesus' (1 Cor. i. 2, 9), to have been 'called of God into the fellowship' (or participation) 'of His Son Jesus Christ'; yet declares, 'Brethren, I could not speak unto you as unto spiritual, but as unto carnal, even as unto babes in Christ' (1 Cor. iii. 1): 'babes in Christ'; so we see they were 'in Christ'; they were believers in a low degree. And yet how much of sin remained in them! of that 'carnal mind, which is not subject to the law of God'!

6. And yet, for all this, they are not condemned. Although they feel the flesh, the evil nature, in them; although they are

more sensible, day by day, that their 'heart is deceitful and desperately wicked'; yet, so long as they do not yield thereto; so long as they give no place to the devil; so long as they maintain a continual war with all sin, with pride, anger, desire, so that the flesh hath not dominion over them, but they still 'walk after the Spirit'; 'there is no condemnation to them which are in Christ Jesus.' God is well pleased with their sincere, though imperfect obedience; and they 'have confidence toward God,' knowing they are His, 'by the Spirit which He hath given' them (1 John iii. 24).

7. Nay, fourthly, although they are continually convinced of sin cleaving to all they do; although they are conscious of not fulfilling the perfect law, either in their thoughts, or words, or works; although they know they do not love the Lord their God with all their heart, and mind, and soul, and strength; although they feel more or less of pride, or self-will, stealing in and mixing with their best duties; although even in their more immediate intercourse with God, when they assemble themselves with the great congregation, and when they pour out their souls in secret to Him who seeth all the thoughts and intents of the heart, they are continually ashamed of their wandering thoughts, or of the deadness and dullness of their affections; yet there is no condemnation to them still, either from God or from their own heart. The consideration of these manifold defects only gives them a deeper sense, that they have always need of that blood of sprinkling which speaks for them in the ears of God, and that Advocate with the Father 'who ever liveth to make intercession for them.' So far are these from driving them away from Him in whom they have believed, that they rather drive them the closer to Him whom they feel the want of every moment. And, at the same time, the deeper sense they have of this want, the more earnest desire do they feel, and the more diligent they are, as they 'have received the Lord Jesus, so to walk in Him.'

8. They are not condemned, fifthly, for sins of infirmity, as they are usually called. Perhaps it were advisable rather to call them *infirmities:* that we may not seem to give any countenance to sin, or to extenuate it in any degree, by thus coupling it with

infirmity. But (if we must retain so ambiguous and dangerous an expression), by sins of infirmity I would mean, such involuntary failings as the saying a thing we believe true, though, in fact, it prove to be false; or, the hurting our neighbour without knowing or designing it, perhaps when we designed to do him good. Though these are deviations from the holy, and acceptable, and perfect will of God, yet they are not properly sins, nor do they bring any guilt on the conscience of 'them which are in Christ Jesus.' They separate not between God and them, neither intercept the light of His countenance; as being no ways inconsistent with their general character of 'walking not after the flesh, but after the Spirit.'

9. Lastly. 'There is no condemnation' to them for anything whatever which it is not in their power to help; whether it be of an inward or outward nature, and whether it be doing something or leaving something undone. For instance, the Lord's supper is to be administered; but you do not partake thereof. Why do you not? You are confined by sickness; therefore you cannot help omitting it; and for the same reason you are not condemned. There is no guilt, because there is no choice. As there 'is a willing mind, it is accepted according to that a man hath, not according to that he hath not.'

10. A believer, indeed, may sometimes be *grieved:* because he cannot do what his soul longs for. He may cry out when he is detained from worshipping God in the great congregation, 'Like as the hart panteth after the water-brooks, so panteth my soul after Thee, O God. My soul is athirst for God, yea, even for the living God: when shall I come to appear in the presence of God?' He may earnestly desire (only still saying in his heart, 'Not as I will, but as Thou wilt') to 'go again with the multitude, and bring them forth into the house of God.' But still, if he cannot go, he feels no condemnation, no guilt, no sense of God's displeasure; but can cheerfully yield up those desires with, 'O my soul, put thy trust in God! for I will yet give Him thanks, who is the help of my countenance and my God.'

11. It is more difficult to determine concerning those which are usually styled sins of surprise: as when one who commonly

in patience possesses his soul, on a sudden and violent temptation, speaks or acts in a manner not consistent with the royal law, 'Thou shalt love thy neighbour as thyself.' Perhaps it is not easy to fix a general rule concerning transgressions of this nature. We cannot say, either that men are, or that they are not, condemned for sins of surprise in general: but it seems, whenever a believer is by surprise overtaken in a fault, there is more or less condemnation, as there is more or less concurrence of his will. In proportion as a sinful desire, or word, or action is more or less voluntary, so we may conceive God is more or less displeased, and there is more or less guilt upon the soul.

12. But if so, then there may be some sins of surprise which bring much guilt and condemnation. For, in some instances, our being surprised is owing to some wilful and culpable neglect; or to a sleepiness of soul which might have been prevented, or shaken off before the temptation came. A man may be previously warned either of God or man, that trials and dangers are at hand; and yet may say in his heart, 'A little more slumber, a little more folding of the hands to rest.' Now, if such an one afterwards fall,though unawares, into the snare which he might have avoided,—that he fell unawares is no excuse; he might have foreseen and have shunned the danger. The falling, even by surprise, in such an instance as this, is, in effect, a wilful sin; and, as such, must expose the sinner to condemnation, both from God and his own conscience.

13. On the other hand, there may be sudden assaults, either from the world, or the god of this world, and frequently from our own evil hearts, which we did not, and hardly could, foresee. And by these even a believer, while weak in faith, may possibly be borne down, suppose into a degree of anger, or thinking evil of another, with scarce any concurrence of his will. Now, in such a case, the jealous God would undoubtedly show him that he had done foolishly. He would be convinced of having swerved from the perfect law, from the mind which was in Christ, and consequently, *grieved* with a godly sorrow, and lovingly *ashamed* before God. Yet need he not come into condemnation. God layeth not folly to his charge, but hath compassion upon him, 'even as a father pitieth his own children.'

And his heart condemneth him not: in the midst of that sorrow and shame he can still say, 'I will trust and not be afraid; for the Lord Jehovah is my strength and my song; He also is become my salvation.'

III. 1. It remains only to draw some practical inferences from the preceding considerations.

And, first, if there be 'no condemnation to them·which are in Christ Jesus,' and 'walk not after the flesh, but after the Spirit,' on account of their past sin; then why art thou fearful, O thou of little faith? Though thy sins were once more in number than the sand, what is that to thee, now thou art in Christ Jesus? 'Who shall lay anything to the charge of God's elect? It is God that justifieth: who is he that condemneth?' All the sins thou hast committed from thy youth up, until the hour when thou wast 'accepted in the Beloved,' are driven away as chaff, are gone, are lost, swallowed up, remembered no more. Thou art now 'born of the Spirit': wilt thou be troubled or afraid of what is done before thou wert born? Away with thy fears! Thou art not called to fear, but to the 'spirit of love and of a sound mind.' Know thy calling! Rejoice in God thy Saviour, and give thanks to God thy Father through Him.

2. Wilt thou say, 'But I have again committed sin, since I had redemption through His blood? And therefore it is, that "I abhor myself, and repent in dust and ashes."' It is meet thou shouldest abhor thyself; and it is God who hath wrought thee to this self-same thing. But, dost thou now believe? Hath He again enabled thee to say, 'I know that my Redeemer liveth'; 'and the life which I now live, I live by faith in the Son of God'? Then that faith again cancels all that is past, and there is no condemnation to thee. At whatsoever time thou truly believest in the name of the Son of God, all thy sins, antecedent to that hour, vanish away as the morning dew. Now then, 'stand thou fast in the liberty wherewith Christ hath made thee free.' He hath once more made thee free from the power of sin, as well as from the guilt and punishment of it. O 'be not entangled again with the yoke of bondage!'—neither the vile, devilish bondage of sin, of evil desires, evil tempers, or words, or works, the most

grievous yoke on this side hell; nor the bondage of slavish, tormenting fear, of guilt and self-condemnation.

3. But secondly, do all they which abide 'in Christ Jesus, walk not after the flesh, but after the Spirit'? Then we cannot but infer, that whosoever now committeth sin, hath no part or lot in this matter. He is even now condemned by his own heart. But, 'if our heart condemn us,' if our own conscience beareth witness that we are guilty, undoubtedly God doth; for 'He is greater than our heart, and knoweth all things'; so that we cannot deceive Him, if we can ourselves. And think not to say, 'I was justified once; my sins were once forgiven me': I know not that; neither will I dispute whether they were or no. Perhaps at this distance of time, it is next to impossible to know, with any tolerable degree of certainty, whether that was a true, genuine work of God, or whether thou didst only deceive thy own soul. But this I know, with the utmost degree of certainty, 'he that committeth sin is of the devil.' Therefore, thou art of thy father the devil. It cannot be denied: for the works of thy father thou doest. O flatter not thyself with vain hopes! Say not to thy soul, 'Peace, peace'! For there is no peace. Cry aloud! Cry unto God out of the deep; if haply He may hear thy voice. Come unto Him as at first, as wretched and poor, as sinful, miserable, blind and naked! And beware thou suffer thy soul to take no rest, till His pardoning love be again revealed; till He heal thy backslidings,' and fill thee again with the 'faith that worketh by love.'

4. Thirdly. Is there no condemnation to them which 'walk after the Spirit,' by reason of *inward sin* still remaining, so long as they do not give way thereto; nor by reason of *sin cleaving* to all they do? Then fret not thyself because of ungodliness, though it still remain in thy heart. Repine not, because thou still comest short of the glorious image of God; nor yet because pride, self-will, or unbelief, cleave to all thy words and works. And be not afraid to know all this evil of thy heart, to know thyself as also thou art known. Yea, desire of God, that thou mayest not think of thyself more highly than thou oughtest to think. Let thy continual prayer be,

> Show me, as my soul can bear,
>   The depth of inbred sin;
> All the unbelief declare,
>   The pride that lurks within.

But when He heareth thy prayer, and unveils thy heart; when He shows thee throughly what spirit thou art of; then beware that thy faith fail thee not, that thou suffer not thy shield to be torn from thee. Be abased. Be humbled in the dust. See thyself nothing, less than nothing, and vanity. But still, 'let not thy heart be troubled, neither let it be afraid.' Still hold fast, 'I, even I, have an Advocate with the Father, Jesus Christ the righteous.' 'And as the heavens are higher than the earth, so is His love higher than even my sins.' Therefore God is merciful to thee a sinner! such a sinner as thou art! God is love; and Christ hath died! Therefore the Father Himself loveth thee! Thou art His child! Therefore He will withhold from thee no manner of thing that is good. Is it good, that the whole body of sin, which is now crucified in thee, should be destroyed? It shall be done! Thou shalt be 'cleansed from all filthiness both of flesh and spirit.' Is it good, that nothing should remain in thy heart but the pure love of God alone? Be of good cheer! 'Thou shalt love the Lord thy God with all thy heart, and mind, and soul, and strength.' 'Faithful is He that hath promised, who also will do it.' It is thy part, patiently to continue in the work of faith, and in the labour of love; and in cheerful peace, in humble confidence, with calm and resigned and yet earnest expectation, to wait till the zeal of the Lord of hosts shall perform this.

5. Fourthly. If they that 'are in Christ,' and 'walk after the Spirit,' are not condemned for *sins of infirmity:* as neither for *involuntary failings*, nor for anything whatever which they are not able to help; then beware, O thou that hast faith in His blood, that Satan herein gain no advantage over thee. Thou art still foolish and weak, blind and ignorant; more weak than any words can express; more foolish than it can yet enter into thy heart to conceive; knowing nothing yet as thou oughtest to know. Yet, let not all thy weakness and folly, or any fruit thereof, which thou art not yet able to avoid, shake thy faith,

thy filial trust in God, or disturb thy peace or joy in the Lord. The rule which some give, as to wilful sins, and which, in that case, may perhaps be dangerous, is undoubtedly wise and safe if it be applied only to the case of weakness and infirmities. Art thou fallen, O man of God? Yet, do not lie there, fretting thyself and bemoaning thy weakness; but meekly say, 'Lord, I shall fall thus every moment, unless Thou uphold me with Thy hand.' And then arise! Leap and walk! Go on thy way! 'Run with patience the race that is set before thee.'

6. Lastly. Since a believer need not come into condemnation, even though he be *surprised* into what his soul abhors (suppose his being surprised is not owing to any carelessness or wilful neglect of his own); if thou who believest art thus overtaken in a fault, then grieve unto the Lord: it shall be a precious balm. Pour out thy heart before Him, and show Him of thy trouble, and pray with all thy might to Him who is 'touched with the feeling of thy infirmities,' that He would establish, and strengthen and settle thy soul, and suffer thee to fall no more. But still He condemneth thee not. Wherefore shouldest thou fear? Thou hast no need of any 'fear that hath torment.' Thou shalt love Him that loveth thee, and it sufficeth: more love will bring more strength. And, as soon as thou lovest Him with all thy heart, thou shalt be 'perfect and entire, lacking nothing.' Wait in peace for that hour, when 'the God of peace shall sanctify thee wholly, so that thy whole spirit and soul and body may be preserved blameless unto the coming of our Lord Jesus Christ'!

SERMON IX

THE SPIRIT OF BONDAGE AND OF ADOPTION

Ye have not received the spirit of bondage again unto fear; but ye have received the Spirit of adoption, whereby we cry, Abba, Father.—ROM. viii. 15.

ST. PAUL here speaks to those who are the children of God by faith. 'Ye,' saith he, who are indeed His children, have drank into His Spirit; 'ye have not received the spirit of bondage again unto fear'; but, 'because ye are sons, God hath sent forth the Spirit of His Son into your hearts.' 'Ye have received the Spirit of adoption, whereby we cry, Abba, Father.'

2. The spirit of bondage and fear is widely distant from this loving Spirit of adoption: those who are influenced only by slavish fear cannot be termed 'the sons of God'; yet some of them may be styled His servants, and are 'not far from the kingdom of heaven.'

3. But it is to be feared, the bulk of mankind, yea, of what is called the Christian world, have not attained even this; but are still afar off, 'neither is God in all their thoughts.' A few names may be found of those who love God; a few more there are that fear Him; but the greater part have neither the fear of God before their eyes, nor the love of God in their hearts.

4. Perhaps most of you, who, by the mercy of God, now partake of a better spirit, may remember the time when ye were as they, when ye were under the same condemnation. But at first ye knew it not, though ye were wallowing daily in your sins and in your blood; till, in due time, ye 'received the spirit of fear' (*ye received*, for this also is the gift of God); and afterwards, fear vanished away, and the Spirit of love filled your hearts.

5. One who is in the first state of mind, without fear or love, is in Scripture termed a 'natural man': one who is under the spirit of bondage and fear, is sometimes said to be 'under the law' (although that expression more frequently signifies one who is under the Jewish dispensation, or who thinks himself obliged to observe all the rites and ceremonies of the Jewish law): but one who has exchanged the spirit of fear for the Spirit of love is properly said to be 'under grace.'

Now, because it highly imports us to know what spirit we are of, I shall endeavour to point out distinctly, first, the state of a 'natural man'; secondly, that of one who is 'under the law'; and, thirdly, of one who is 'under grace.'

I. 1. And, first, the state of a *natural man*. This the Scripture represents as a state of sleep: the voice of God to him is, 'Awake, thou that sleepest.' For his soul is in a deep sleep: his spiritual senses are not awake: they discern neither spiritual good nor evil. The eyes of his understanding are closed; they are sealed together, and see not. Clouds and darkness continually rest upon them; for he lies in the valley of the shadow of death. Hence, having no inlets for the knowledge of spiritual things, all the avenues of his soul being shut up, he is in gross, stupid ignorance of whatever he is most concerned to know. He is utterly ignorant of God, knowing nothing concerning Him as he ought to know. He is totally a stranger to the law of God, as to its true, inward, spiritual meaning. He has no conception of that evangelical holiness, without which no man shall see the Lord; nor of the happiness which they only find whose 'life is hid with Christ in God.'

2. And, for this very reason, because he is fast asleep, he is, in some sense, at rest. Because he is blind, he is also secure: he saith, 'Tush, there shall no harm happen unto me.' The darkness which covers him on every side, keeps him in a kind of peace; so far as peace can consist with the works of the devil, and with an earthly, devilish mind. He *sees* not that he stands on the edge of the pit; therefore he *fears* it not. He cannot *tremble* at the danger he does not *know*. He has not understanding enough to fear. Why is it that he is in no dread of God? Because he is totally ignorant of Him: if not saying in his heart, 'There is no God'; or, that 'He sitteth on the circle of the heavens, and humbleth' not 'Himself to behold the things which are done on earth'; yet satisfying himself as well, to all Epicurean intents and purposes, by saying, 'God is merciful'; confounding and swallowing up all at once in that unwieldy idea of mercy all His holiness and essential hatred of sin; all His justice, wisdom, and truth. He is in no dread of the vengeance denounced against those who obey not the blessed law of God, because he understands it not. He imagines the main point is, to *do thus*, to be *outwardly* blameless; and sees not that it extends to every temper, desire, thought, motion of the heart. Or he fancies that the obligation hereto is ceased; that Christ came to 'destroy the Law and the Prophets'; to save His people *in*, not *from*, their sins; to bring them to heaven without holiness—notwithstanding His own words, 'Not one

jot or tittle of the law shall pass away, till all things are fulfilled';
and, 'Not every one that saith unto Me, Lord, Lord! shall enter
into the kingdom of heaven; but he that doeth the will of My
Father which is in heaven.'

3. He is secure, because he is utterly ignorant of himself.
Hence he talks of 'repenting by-and-by'; he does not indeed
exactly know when, but some time or other before he dies;
taking it for granted, that this is quite in his own power. For
what should hinder his doing it, if he will? If he does but once
set a resolution, no fear but he will make it good!

4. But this ignorance never so strongly glares, as in those who
are termed *men of learning*. If a natural man be one of these, he
can talk at large of his rational faculties, of the freedom of his
will, and the absolute necessity of such freedom, in order to
constitute man a moral agent. He reads, and argues, and proves
to a demonstration, that every man may do as he will: may
dispose his own heart to evil or good, as it seems best in his
own eyes. Thus the god of this world spreads a double veil of
blindness over his heart, lest, by any means, 'the light of the
glorious gospel of Christ should shine' upon it.

5. From the same ignorance of himself and God, there may
sometimes arise, in the natural man, a kind of *joy*, in congratu-
lating himself upon his own wisdom and goodness; and what
the world calls joy, he may often possess. He may have pleasure
in various kinds; either in gratifying the desires of the flesh, or
the desire of the eye, or the pride of life; particularly if he has
large possessions; if he enjoy an affluent fortune; then he may
'clothe' himself 'in purple and fine linen, and fare sumptuously
every day.' And so long as he thus doeth well unto himself,
men will doubtless speak good of him. They will say, 'He is a
happy man.' For, indeed, this is the sum of worldly happiness; to
dress, and visit, and talk, and eat, and drink, and rise up to play.

6. It is not surprising, if one in such circumstances as these,
dosed with the opiates of flattery and sin, should imagine, among
his other waking dreams, that he walks in great *liberty*. How
easily may he persuade himself, that he is at liberty from all
vulgar errors: and from the *prejudice* of education; judging exactly
right, and keeping clear of all extremes. 'I am free,' may he say,

from all the *enthusiasm* of weak and narrow souls; from *super-stition:* the disease of fools and cowards, always righteous over-much; and from *bigotry*, continually incident to those who have not a free and generous way of thinking.' And too sure it is' that he is altogether free from the 'wisdom which cometh from above,' from holiness, from the religion of the heart, from the whole mind which was in Christ.

7. For all this time he is the servant of sin. He commits sin, more or less, day by day. Yet he is not troubled: he 'is in no bondage,' as some speak; he feels no condemnation. He contents himself (even though he should profess to believe that the Christian revelation is of God) with, 'Man is frail. We are all weak. Every man has his infirmity.' Perhaps he quotes Scripture: 'Why, does not Solomon say, The righteous man falls into sin seven times a day? And, doubtless, they are all hypocrites or enthusiasts who pretend to be better than their neighbours.' If, at any time, a serious thought fix upon him, he stifles it as soon as possible, with, 'Why should I fear, since God is merciful, and Christ died for sinners?' Thus, he remains a willing servant of sin, content with the bondage of corruption; inwardly and out-wardly unholy, and satisfied therewith; not only not conquering sin, but not striving to conquer, particularly that sin which doth so easily beset him.

8. Such is the state of every *natural man*; whether he be a gross, scandalous transgressor, or a more reputable and decent sinner, having the form, though not the power, of godliness. But how can such an one be *convinced of sin?* How is he brought to *repent*, to be *under the law:* to receive the *spirit of bondage unto fear?* This is the point which is next to be considered.

II. 1. By some awful providence, or by His word applied with the demonstration of His Spirit, God touches the heart of him that lay asleep in darkness and in the shadow of death. He is terribly shaken out of his sleep, and awakes into a consciousness of his danger. Perhaps in a moment, perhaps by degrees, the eyes of his understanding are opened, and now first (the veil being in part removed) discern the real state he is in. Horrid light breaks in upon his soul; such light as may be conceived to gleam from the bottomless pit, from the lowest deep, from a lake of fire burning with brimstone. He at last sees the loving, the merciful God is also 'a consuming fire'; that He is a just God and a terrible, rendering to every man according to his works, entering into judgement with the ungodly for every idle word, yea, and for the imaginations of the heart. He now clearly perceives, that the great and holy God is 'of purer eyes than to behold iniquity'; that He is an avenger of every one who rebelleth against Him, and repayeth the wicked to his face; and that 'it is a fearful thing to fall into the hands of the living God.'

2. The inward, spiritual meaning of the law of God now begins to glare upon him. He perceives 'the commandment is exceeding broad,' and there is 'nothing hid from the light thereof.' He is convinced, that every part of it relates, not barely to outward sin or obedience, but to what passes in the secret recesses of the soul, which no eye but God's can penetrate. If he now hears, 'Thou shalt not kill,' God speaks in thunder, 'He that hateth his brother is a murderer;' 'He that saith unto his brother, Thou fool, is obnoxious to hell-fire.' If the law say, 'Thou shalt not commit adultery,' the voice of the Lord sounds in his ears, 'He that looketh on a woman to lust after her hath committed adultery with her already in this heart.' And thus, in every point, he feels the Word of God 'quick and powerful, sharper than a two-edged sword.' It 'pierces even to the dividing asunder of his soul and spirit, his joints and marrow.' And so much the more, because he is conscious to himself of having neglected so great salvation; of having 'trodden under foot the Son of God,' who would have saved him from his sins, and 'counted the blood of the covenant an unholy,' a common, unsanctifying 'thing.'

3. And as he knows, "all things are naked and open unto the eyes of Him with whom we have to do,' so he sees himself naked, stripped of all the fig-leaves which he had sewed together, of all his poor pretences to religion or virtue, and his wretched excuses for sinning against God. He now sees himself like the ancient sacrifices, τετραχηλισμένον, *cleft in sunder*, as it were, from the neck downward, so that all within him stands confessed. His heart is bare, and he sees it is all sin, 'deceitful above all things, desperately wicked'; that it is altogether corrupt and abominable, more than

8

it is possible for tongue to express; that there dwelleth therein no good thing, but unrighteousness and ungodliness only; every motion thereof, every temper and thought, being only evil continually.

4. And he not only sees, but feels in himself, by an emotion of soul which he cannot describe, that for the sins of his heart, were his life without blame (which yet it is not, and cannot be; seeing 'an evil tree cannot bring forth good fruit'), he deserves to be cast into the fire that never shall be quenched. He feels that 'the wages,' the just reward, 'of sin,' of his sin above all, 'is death'; even the second death, the death which dieth not, the destruction of body and soul in hell.

5. Here ends his pleasing dream, his delusive rest, his false peace, his vain security. His joy now vanishes as a cloud; pleasures, once loved, delight no more. They pall upon the taste: he loathes the nauseous sweet; he is weary to bear them The shadows of happiness flee away, and sink into oblivion: so that he is stripped of all, and wanders to and fro seeking rest, but finding none.

6. The fumes of those opiates being now dispelled, he feels the anguish of a wounded spirit. He finds that sin let loose upon the soul (whether it be pride, anger, or evil desire, whether self-will, malice, envy, revenge, or any other) is perfect misery: he feels sorrow of heart for the blessings he has lost, and the curse which is come upon him; remorse for having thus destroyed himself, and despised his own mercies; fear, from a lively sense of the wrath of God, and of the consequences of His wrath, of the punishment which he has justly deserved, and which he sees hanging over his head; fear of death, as being to him the gate of hell, the entrance of death eternal; fear of the devil, the executioner of the wrath and righteous vengeance of God; fear of men, who, if they were able to kill his body, would thereby plunge both body and soul into hell,—fear, sometimes arising to such a height, that the poor, sinful, guilty soul is terrified with everything, with nothing, with shades, with a leaf shaken of the wind. Yea, sometimes it may even border upon distraction, making a man 'drunken though not with wine,' suspending the exercise of the memory, of the understanding, of all the natural faculties.

Sometimes it may approach to the very brink of despair; so that he who trembles at the name of death, may yet be ready to plunge into it every moment, to 'choose strangling rather than life.' Well may such a man roar, like him of old, for the very disquietness of his heart. Well may he cry out, 'The spirit of a man may sustain his infirmities; but a wounded spirit who can bear?'

7. Now he truly desires to break loose from sin, and begins to struggle with it. But though he strive with all his might, he cannot conquer: sin is mightier than he. He would fain escape; but he is so fast in prison, that he cannot get forth. He resolves against sin, but yet sins on: he sees the snare, and abhors and runs into it. So much does his boasted reason avail—only to enhance his guilt, and increase his misery! Such is the freedom of his will; free only to evil; free to 'drink in iniquity like water'; to wander farther and farther from the living God, and do more 'despite to the Spirit of grace.'

8. The more he strives, wishes, labours to be free, the more does he feel his chains, the grievous chains of sin, wherewith Satan binds and 'leads him captive at his will'; his servant he is, though he repine ever so much; though he rebel, he cannot prevail. He is still in bondage and fear, by reason of sin: generally, of some outward sin, to which he is peculiarly disposed, either by nature, custom, or outward circumstances; but always, of some inward sin, some evil temper or unholy affection. And the more he frets against it the more it prevails; he may bite, but cannot break his chain. Thus he toils without end, repenting and sinning and repenting and sinning again, till at length the poor, sinful, helpless wretch is even at his wit's end, and can barely groan, 'O wretched man that I am! who shall deliver me from the body of this death?'

9. This whole struggle of one who is 'under the law,' under the 'spirit of fear and bondage,' is beautifully described by the Apostle in the foregoing chapter, speaking in the person of an awakened man. 'I,' saith he, 'was alive without the law once' (verse 9): I had much life, wisdom, strength, and virtue; so I thought: 'but when the commandment came, sin revived, and I died': when the commandment, in its spiritual meaning, came

to my heart, with the power of God, my inbred sin was stirred up, fretted, inflamed, and all my virtue died away. 'And the commandment, which was ordained to life, I found to be unto death. For sin, taking occasion by the commandment, deceived me, and by it slew me' (verses 10, 11): it came upon me unawares; slew all my hopes; and plainly showed, in the midst of life I was in death. Wherefore the law is holy, and the commandment holy, and just, and good' (verse 12): I no longer lay the blame on this, but on the corruption of my own heart. I acknowledge that 'the law is spiritual; but I am carnal, sold under sin' (verse 14): I now see both the spritiual nature of the law; and my own carnal, devilish heart 'sold under sin,' totally enslaved (like slaves bought with money, who were absolutely at their master's disposal): 'for that which I do, I allow not; for what I would, I do not: but what I hate, that I do'. (verse 15): such is the bondage under which I groan; such the tyranny of my hard master. 'To will is present with me; but how to perform that which is good I find not. For the good that I would, I do not; but the evil which I would not, that I do' (verses 18, 19): 'I find a law,' an inward constraining power, 'that, when I would do good, evil is present with me. For I delight in,' or consent to, 'the law of God, after the inward man' (verses 21, 22): in my 'mind' (so the Apostle explains himself in the words that immediately follow; and so ὁ ἔσω ἄνθρωπος, *the inward man* is understood in all other Greek writers): 'but I see another law in my members, another constraining power, 'warring against the law of my mind,' or inward man, 'and bringing me into captivity to the law' or power 'of sin' (verse 23): dragging me, as it were, at my conqueror's chariot-wheels, into the very thing which my soul abhors. 'O wretched man that I am! who shall deliver me from the body of this death?' (verse 24). Who shall deliver me from this helpless, dying life, from this bondage of sin and misery? Till this is done, 'I myself' (or rather, *that* I, αὐτὸς ἐγώ, that man I am now personating) 'with the mind,' or inward man, 'serve the law of God'; my mind, my conscience, is on God's side: 'but with my flesh,' with my body, 'the law of sin' (verse 25), being hurried away by a force I cannot resist.

10. How lively a portraiture is this of one 'under the law'!

one who feels the burden he cannot shake off; who pants after liberty, power, and love, but is in fear and bondage still! until the time that God answers the wretched man, crying out, 'Who shall deliver me' from this bondage of sin, from this body of death?—'The grace of God through Jesus Christ thy Lord.'

III. 1. Then it is that this miserable bondage ends, and he is no more 'under the law, but under grace.' This state we are, thirdly, to consider; the state of one who has found *grace* or favour in the sight of God, even the Father, and who has the *grace* or power of the Holy Ghost reigning in his heart; who has received, in the language of the Apostle, the 'Spirit of adoption, whereby' he now cries, 'Abba, Father!'

2. 'He cried unto the Lord in his trouble, and God delivers him out of his distress.' His eyes are opened in quite another manner than before even to see a loving, gracious God. While he is calling, 'I beseech Thee, show me Thy glory!'—he hears a voice in his inmost soul, 'I will make all My goodness pass before thee, and I will proclaim the name of the Lord: I will be gracious to whom I will be gracious, and I will show mercy to whom I will show mercy.' And it is not long before 'the Lord descends in the cloud, and proclaims the name of the Lord.' Then he sees but not with eyes of flesh and blood, 'The Lord, the Lord God, merciful and gracious, long-suffering, and abundant in goodness and truth; keeping mercy for thousands, and forgiving iniquities, and transgressions, and sin.'

3. Heavenly, healing light now breaks in upon his soul. He 'looks on Him whom he had pierced'; and 'God, who out of darkness commanded light to shine, shineth in his heart.' He sees the light of the glorious love of God, in the face of Jesus Christ. He hath a divine 'evidence of things not seen' by sense, even of 'the deep things of God'; more particularly of the love of God, of His pardoning love to him that believes in Jesus. Overpowered with the sight, his whole soul cries out, 'My Lord, and my God!' For he sees all his iniquities laid on Him who 'bare them in His own body on the tree': he beholds the Lamb of God taking away his sins. How clearly now does he discern, that 'God was in Christ, reconciling the world unto Himself;

making Him sin for us, who knew no sin, that we might be made the righteousness of God through Him'; and that he himself is reconciled to God, by that blood of the covenant!

4. Here end both the guilt and power of sin. He can now say, 'I am crucified with Christ; nevertheless I live; yet not I, but Christ liveth in me: and the life which I now live in the flesh' (even in this mortal body), 'I live by faith in the Son of God, who loved me, and gave Himself for me.' Here end remorse, and sorrow of heart, and the anguish of a wounded spirit. 'God turneth his heaviness into joy.' He made sore, and now His hands bind up. Here ends also that bondage unto fear; for 'his heart standeth fast, believing in the Lord.' He cannot fear any longer the wrath of God; for he knows it is now turned away from him, and looks upon Him no more as an angry Judge, but as a loving Father. He cannot fear the devil, knowing he has 'no power, except it be given him from above.' He fears not hell; being an heir of the kingdom of heaven: consequently, he has no fear of death; by reason whereof he was in time past, for so many years, 'subject to bondage.' Rather, knowing that 'if the earthly house of this tabernacle be dissolved, he hath a building of God, a house not made with hands, eternal in the heavens; he groaneth earnestly, desiring to be clothed upon with that house which is from heaven.' He groans to shake off this house of earth, that 'mortality' may be 'swallowed up of life'; knowing that God 'hath wrought him for the selfsame thing; who hath also given him the earnest of His Spirit.'

5. And 'where the Spirit of the Lord is, there is liberty'; liberty, not only from guilt and fear, but from sin, from that heaviest of all yokes, that basest of all bondage. His labour is not now in vain. The snare is broken, and he is delivered. He not only strives, but likewise prevails; he not only fights, but conquers also. 'Henceforth he does not serve sin' (chap. vi. 6, &c.). He is 'dead unto sin, and alive unto God'; 'sin doth not now reign,' even 'in his mortal body,' nor doth he 'obey it in the desires thereof..' He does not 'yield his members as instruments of unrighteousness unto sin, but as instruments of righteousness unto God.' For 'being now made free from sin, he is become the servant of righteousness.'

6. Thus 'having peace with God through our Lord Jesus Christ,' 'rejoicing in hope of the glory of God,' and having power over all sin, over every evil desire, and temper, and word, and work, he is a living witness of the 'glorious liberty of the sons of God'; all of whom, being partakers of like precious faith, bear record with one voice, 'We have received the Spirit of adoption, whereby we cry, Abba, Father!'

7. It is this Spirit which continually 'worketh in them, both to will and to do of His good pleasure.' It is He that sheds the love of God abroad in their hearts, and the love of all mankind; thereby purifying their hearts from the love of the world, from the lust of the flesh, the lust of the eye, and the pride of life. It is by Him they are delivered from anger and pride, from all vile and inordinate affections. In consequence, they are delivered from evil words and works, from all unholiness of conversation; doing no evil to any child of man, and being zealous of all good works.

8. To sum up all: the *natural* man neither fears nor loves God, one *under the law* fears, one *under grace* loves Him   The first has no light in the things of God, but walks in utter darkness; the second sees the painful light of hell; the third, the joyous light of heaven.   He that sleeps in death has a false peace; he that is awakened has no peace at all; he that believes has true peace,— the peace of God filling and ruling his heart.   The Heathen, baptized or unbaptized, hath a fancied liberty, which is indeed licentiousness; the Jew, or one under the Jewish dispensation, is in heavy, grievous bondage; the Christian enjoys the true glorious liberty of the sons of God.   An unawakened child of the devil sins willingly; one that is awakened sins unwillingly; a child of God 'sinneth not,' but 'keepeth himself, and the wicked one toucheth him not.'   To conclude: the natural man neither conquers nor fights; the man under the law fights with sin, but cannot conquer; the man under grace fights and conquers, yea, is 'more than conqueror through Him that loveth him.'

IV. 1. From this plain account of the threefold state of man, the *natural*, the *legal*, and the *evangelical*, it appears that it is not sufficient to divide mankind into sincere and insincere. A man may be sincere in any of these states; not only when he has the 'Spirit of adoption,' but while he has the 'spirit of bondage unto fear'; yea, while he has neither this fear, nor love. For undoubtedly there may be sincere Heathens, as well as sincere Jews or Christians. This circumstance, then, does by no means prove that a man is in a state of acceptance with God.

'Examine yourselves, therefore,' not only whether ye are sincere, but 'whether ye be in the faith.' Examine narrowly (for it imports you much), what is the ruling principle in your soul? Is it the love of God? Is it the fear of God? Or is it neither one nor the other? Is it not rather the love of the world? the love of pleasure, or gain? of ease, or reputation? If so, you are not come so far as a Jew. You are but a Heathen still. Have you heaven in your heart? Have you the Spirit of adoption, ever crying, Abba, Father? Or do you cry unto God, as 'out of the belly of hell,' overwhelmed with sorrow and fear? Or are you a stranger to this whole affair, and cannot imagine what I mean? Heathen, pull off the mask! Thou hast never put on Christ! Stand barefaced! Look up to heaven; and own before Him that liveth for ever and ever, thou hast no part either among the sons or servants of God!

Whosoever thou art, Dost thou commit sin, or dost thou not? If thou dost, is it willingly or unwillingly? In either case, God hath told thee whose thou art: 'He that committeth sin is of the devil.' If thou committest it willingly, thou art his faithful servant: he will not fail to reward thy labour. If unwillingly, still thou art his servant. God deliver thee out of his hands!

Art thou daily fighting against all sin? and daily more than conqueror? I acknowledge thee for a child of God. O stand fast in thy glorious liberty! Art thou fighting, but not conquering? striving for the mastery, but not able to attain? Then thou art not yet a believer in Christ; but follow on, and thou shalt know the Lord. Art thou not fighting at all, but leading an easy, indolent, fashionable life? O how hast thou dared to name the name of Christ, only to make it a reproach among the Heathen? Awake, thou sleeper! Call upon thy God, before the deep swallow thee up!

2. Perhaps one reason why so many think of themselves more

highly than they ought to think, why they do not discern what state they are in, is, because these several states of soul are often mingled together, and in some measure meet in one and the same person. Thus experience shows, that the legal state, or state of fear, is frequently mixed with the natural; for few men are so fast asleep in sin, but they are sometimes more or less awakened. As the Spirit of God does not 'wait for the call of man,' so, at some times He *will* be heard. He puts them in fear, so that, for a season at least, the Heathen 'know themselves to be but men.' They feel the burden of sin, and earnestly desire to flee from the wrath to come. But not long: they seldom suffer the arrows of conviction to go deep into their souls; but quickly stifle the grace of God, and return to their wallowing in the mire.

In like manner, the evangelical state, or state of love, is frequently mixed with the legal. For few of those who have the spirit of bondage and fear remain always without hope. The wise and gracious God rarely suffers this; 'for He remembereth that we are but dust'; and He willeth not that 'the flesh should fail before Him, or the spirit which He hath made.' Therefore at such times as He seeth good, He gives a dawning of light unto them that sit in darkness. He causes a part of His goodness to pass before them, and shows He is a 'God that heareth the prayer.' They see the promise, which is by faith in Christ Jesus, though it be yet afar off; and hereby they are encouraged to 'run with patience the race which is set before them.'

3. Another reason why many deceive themselves, is, because they do not consider how far a man may go, and yet be in a natural, or, at best, a legal state. A man may be of a compassionate and a benevolent temper; he may be affable, courteous, generous, friendly; he may have some degree of meekness, patience, temperance, and of many other moral virtues. He may feel many desires of shaking off all vice, and of attaining higher degrees of virtue. He may abstain from much evil; perhaps from all that is grossly contrary to justice, mercy, or truth. He may do much good, may feed the hungry, clothe the naked, relieve the widow and fatherless. He may attend public worship, use prayer in private, read many books of devotion; and yet, for all this, he

may be a mere natural man, knowing neither himself nor God, equally a stranger to the spirit of fear and to that of love; having neither repented, nor believed the gospel.

But suppose there were added to all this a deep conviction of sin, with much fear of the wrath of God; vehement desires to cast off every sin, and to fulfil all righteousness; frequent rejoicing in hope, and touches of love often glancing upon the soul; yet neither do these prove a man to be *under grace:* to have true, living, Christian faith, unless the Spirit of adoption abide in his heart, unless he can continually cry, 'Abba, Father!'

4. Beware, then, thou who art called by the name of Christ, that thou come not short of the mark of thy high calling. Beware thou rest not, either in a natural state, with too many that are accounted *good Christians*; or in a legal state, wherein those who are highly esteemed of men are generally content to live and die. Nay, but God hath prepared better things for thee, if thou follow on till thou attain. Thou art not called to fear and tremble, like devils; but to rejoice and love, like the angels of God. 'Thou shalt love the Lord thy God with all thy heart, and with all thy soul, and with all thy mind, and with all thy strength.' Thou shalt 'rejoice evermore'; thou shalt 'pray without ceasing'; thou shalt 'in everything give thanks.' Thou shalt do the will of God on earth as it is done in heaven. O prove thou 'what is that good, and acceptable, and 'perfect will of God'! Now present thyself 'a living sacrifice, holy, acceptable to God'! 'Whereunto thou hast already attained, hold fast,' by 'reaching forth unto those things which are before'; until 'the God of peace make thee perfect in every good work, working in thee that which is well-pleasing in His sight, through Jesus Christ; to whom be glory for ever and ever! Amen!'

SERMON X

THE WITNESS OF THE SPIRIT

DISCOURSE I

The Spirit itself beareth witness with our spirit, that we are the children of God
—ROM. viii. 16

How many vain men, not understanding what they spake, neither whereof they affirmed, have wrested this scripture to the great loss, if not the destruction, of their souls! How many have mistaken the voice of their own imagination for this witness of the Spirit of God, and thence idly presumed they were the children of God, while they were doing the works of the devil! These are truly and properly enthusiasts; and, indeed, in the worst sense of the word. But with what difficulty are they convinced thereof, especially if they have drank deep into that spirit of error. All endeavours to bring them to the knowledge of themselves, they will then account fighting against God; and that vehemence and impetuosity of spirit, which they call 'contending earnestly for the faith,' sets them so far above all the usual methods of conviction, that we may well say, 'With men it is impossible.'

2. Who then can be surprised, if many reasonable men, seeing the dreadful effects of this delusion, and labouring to keep at the utmost distance from it, should sometimes lean toward another extreme?—if they are not forward to believe any who speak of having this witness, concerning which others have so grievously erred?—if they are almost ready to set all down for enthusiasts who use the expressions which have been so terribly abused?—yea, if they should question whether the witness or testimony here spoken of be the privilege of *ordinary* Christians, and not, rather, one of those *extraordinary* gifts which they suppose belonged only to the apostolic age?

3. But is there any necessity laid upon us of running either into one extreme or the other? May we not steer a middle

course—keep a sufficient distance from that spirit of error and
enthusiasm, without denying the gift of God, and giving up the
great privilege of His children? Surely we may. In order thereto,
let us consider, in the presence and fear of God,—

I. WHAT IS THIS WITNESS OR TESTIMONY OF OUR SPIRIT; WHAT
IS THE TESTIMONY OF GOD'S SPIRIT; AND, HOW DOES HE
'BEAR WITNESS WITH OUR SPIRIT THAT WE ARE THE
CHILDREN OF GOD'?

II. HOW IS THIS JOINT TESTIMONY OF GOD'S SPIRIT AND OUR
OWN, CLEARLY AND SOLIDLY DISTINGUISHED FROM THE
PRESUMPTION OF A NATURAL MIND, AND FROM THE
DELUSION OF THE DEVIL?

I. 1. Let us first consider, what is the witness or testimony of
our spirit. But here I cannot but desire all those who are for
swallowing up the testimony of the Spirit of God in the rational
testimony of our own spirit, to observe, that in this text the
Apostle is so far from speaking of the testimony of our own
spirit *only*, that it may be questioned whether he speaks of it
at all—whether he does not speak *only* of the testimony of God's
Spirit. It does not appear but the original text may be fairly
understood thus. The Apostle had just said, in the preceding
verse, 'Ye have received the Spirit of adoption, whereby we cry,
Abba, Father'; and immediately subjoins, Αὐτὸ τὸ Πνεῦμα
(some copies read, τὸ αὐτὸ Πνεῦμα) συμμαρτυρεῖ τῷ πνεύματι
ἡμῶν ὅτι ἐσμὲν τεχνα Θεοῦ; which may be translated, 'The
same Spirit beareth witness to our spirit, that we are the children
of God' (The preposition σύν only denoting, that he witnesses
this *at the same time* that He enables us to cry, Abba, Father). But
I contend not; seeing so many other texts, with the experience
of all real Christians, sufficiently evince, that there is in every
believer, both the testimony of God's Spirit, and the testimony
of his own, that he is a child of God.

2. With regard to the latter, the foundation thereof is laid in
those numerous texts of Scripture which describe the marks of
the children of God; and that so plain, that he which runneth
may read them. These are also collected together, and placed in

the strongest light, by many both ancient and modern writers. If any need farther light, he may receive it by attending on the ministry of God's word; by meditating thereon before God in secret; and by conversing with those who have the knowledge of His ways. And by the reason or understanding that God has given him, which religion was designed not to extinguish, but to perfect—according to that of the Apostle, 'Brethren, be not children in understanding; in malice' or wickedness 'be ye children; but in understanding be ye men' (1 Cor. xiv. 20)— every man applying those scriptural marks to himself may know whether he is a child of God. Thus, if he know, first, 'as many as are led by the Spirit of God,' into all holy tempers and actions, 'they are the sons of God' (for which he has the infallible assurance of holy writ); secondly, I am thus 'led by the Spirit of God'; he will easily conclude, 'Therefore I am a son of God.'

3. Agreeable to this are all those plain declarations of St. John, in his First Epistle: 'Hereby we do know that we know Him, if we keep His commandments' (chap. ii. 3). 'Whoso keepeth His word, in him verily is the love of God perfected: hereby know we that we are in Him'; that we are indeed the children of God (verse 5). 'If ye know that He is righteous, ye know that every one that doeth righteousness is born of Him' (verse 29). 'We know that we have passed from death unto life, because we love the brethren' (chap. iii. 14). 'Hereby we know that we are of the truth, and shall assure our hearts before Him' (verse 19); namely, because we 'love one another, not in word, neither in tongue, but in deed and in truth.' 'Hereby know we that we dwell in Him, because He hath given us of His' loving 'Spirit' (chap. iv. 13). And, 'Hereby we know that He abideth in us, by the' obedient 'Spirit which He hath given us' (chap. iii. 24).

4. It is highly probable there never were any children of God, from the beginning of the world unto this day, who were farther advanced in the grace of God, and the knowledge of our Lord Jesus Christ, than the Apostle John, at the time when he wrote these words, and the fathers in Christ to whom he wrote. Notwithstanding which, it is evident, both the Apostle himself, and all those pillars in God's temple, were very far from despising these marks of their being the children of God; and that they

applied them to their own souls for the confirmation of their faith. Yet all this is no other than rational evidence, the witness of our spirit, our reason or understanding. It all resolves into this: Those who have these marks are children of God: but we have these marks: therefore we are children of God.

5. But how does it appear, that we have these marks? This is a question which still remains. How does it appear, that we do love God and our neighbour, and that we keep His commandments? Observe, that the meaning of the question is, How does it appear to *ourselves:* not to *others?* I would ask him, then, that proposes this question, How does it appear to you, that you are alive, and that you are now in ease, and not in pain? Are you not immediately conscious of it? By the same immediate consciousness, you will know if your soul is alive to God; if you are saved from the pain of proud wrath, and have the ease of a meek and quiet spirit. By the same means you cannot but perceive if you love, rejoice, and delight in God. By the same you must be directly assured if you love your neighbour as yourself; if you are kindly affectioned to all mankind, and full of gentleness and long-suffering. And with regard to the outward mark of the children of God, which is, according to St. John, the keeping His commandments, you undoubtedly know in your own breast, if, by the grace of God, it belongs to you. Your conscience informs you from day to day, if you do not take the name of God within your lips, unless with seriousness and devotion, with reverence and godly fear; if you remember the Sabbath-day to keep it holy; if you honour your father and mother; if you do to all as you would they should do unto you; if you possess your body in sanctification and honour; and if, whether you eat or drink, you are temperate therein, and do all to the glory of God.

6. Now this is properly the testimony of our own spirit; even the testimony of our own conscience, that God hath given us to be holy of heart, and holy in outward conversation. It is a consciousness of our having received, in and by the Spirit of adoption, the tempers mentioned in the Word of God, as belonging to His adopted children; even a loving heart toward God, and toward all mankind; hanging with child-like confidence on God our Father, desiring nothing but Him, casting all our care upon

Him, and embracing every child of man with earnest,
affection: a consciousness that we are inwardly conformed,
the Spirit of God, to the image of His Son, and that we walk
before Him in justice, mercy, and truth, doing the things which
are pleasing in His sight.

7. But what is that testimony of God's Spirit, which is super-
added to, and conjoined with, this? How does He 'bear witness
with our spirit that we are the children of God'? It is hard to
find words in the language of men to explain 'the deep things of
God.' Indeed, there are none that will adequately express what
the children of God experience. But perhaps one might say
(desiring any who are taught of God to correct, to soften, or
strengthen the expression), the testimony of the Spirit is an
inward impression on the soul, whereby the Spirit of God
directly witnesses to my spirit, that I am a child of God; that
Jesus Christ hath loved me, and given Himself for me; and that
all my sins are blotted out, and I, even I, am reconciled to
God.

8. That this testimony of the Spirit of God must needs, in the
very nature of things, be antecedent to the testimony of our own
spirit, may appear from this single consideration. We must be
holy of heart, and holy in life, before we can be conscious that
we are so; before we can have the testimony of our spirit, that
we are inwardly and outwardly holy. But we must love God,
before we can be holy at all; this being the root of all holiness
Now we cannot love God, till we know He loves us. 'We love
Him, because He first loved us.' And we cannot know His
pardoning love to us, till His Spirit witnesses it to our spirit.
Since, therefore, this testimony of His Spirit must precede the
love of God and all holiness, of consequence it must precede our
inward consciousness thereof, or the testimony of our spirit concerning them.

9. Then, and not till then—when the Spirit of God beareth
that witness to our spirit, 'God hath loved thee, and given His
own Son to be the propitiation for thy sins; the Son of God hath
loved thee, and hath washed thee from thy sins in His blood'
—'we love God, because He first loved us'; and, for His sake,
we love our brother also. And of this we cannot but be con-

scious to ourselves; we 'know the things that are freely given to us of God.' We know that we love God, and keep His commandments; and 'hereby also we know that we are of God.' This is that testimony of our own spirit, which, so long as we continue to love God and keep His commandments, continues joined with the testimony of God's Spirit, 'that we are the children of God.'

10. Not that I would by any means be understood, by anything which has been spoken concerning it, to exclude the operation of the Spirit of God, even from the testimony of our own spirit. In no wise. It is He that not only worketh in us every manner of thing that is good, but also shines upon His own work, and clearly shows what He has wrought. Accordingly, this is spoken of by St. Paul, as one great end of our receiving the Spirit, 'that we may know the things which are freely given to us of God': that He may strengthen the testimony of our conscience, touching our 'simplicity and godly sincerity'; and give us to discern, in a fuller and stronger light, that we now do the things which please him.

11. Should it still be inquired, 'How does the Spirit of God "bear witness with our spirit, that we are the children of God,'' so as to exclude all doubt, and evince the reality of our sonship?' —the answer is clear from what has been observed above. And first, as to the witness of our spirit: the soul as intimately and evidently perceives when it loves, delights, and rejoices in God, as when it loves and delights in anything on earth. And it can no more doubt, whether it loves, delights, and rejoices or no, than whether it exists or not. If, therefore, this be just reasoning, he that now loves God, that delights and rejoices in Him with an humble joy, an holy delight, and an obedient love, is a child of God:

But I thus love, delight, and rejoice in God;

Therefore, I am a child of God:—

Then a Christian can in no wise doubt of his being a child of God. Of the former proposition he has as full an assurance as he has that the Scriptures are of God; and of his thus loving God, he has an inward proof, which is nothing short of self-evidence. Thus, the testimony of our own spirit is with the most intimate conviction manifested to our hearts, in such a manner, as beyond all reasonable doubt to evince the reality of our sonship.

12. The manner how the *divine* testimony is manifested to the heart, I do not take upon me to explain. Such knowledge is too wonderful and excellent for me: I cannot attain unto it. The wind bloweth, and I hear the sound thereof; but I cannot tell how it cometh, or whither it goeth. As no one knoweth the things of a man, save the spirit of a man that is in him; so the *manner* of the things of God knoweth no one, save the Spirit of God. But the fact we know; namely, that the Spirit of God does give a believer such a testimony of his adoption, that while it is present to the soul, he can no more doubt the reality of his sonship, than he can doubt of the shining of the sun, while he stands in the full blaze of his beams.

II. 1. How this joint testimony of God's Spirit and our spirit may be clearly and solidly distinguished from the presumption of a natural mind, and from the delusion of the devil, is the next thing to be considered. And it highly imports all who desire the salvation of God, to consider it with the deepest attention, as they would not deceive their own souls. An error in this is generally observed to have the most fatal consequences: the rather, because he that errs, seldom discovers his mistake, till it is too late to remedy it.

2. And, first, how is this testimony to be distinguished from the presumption of a natural mind? It is certain, one who was never convinced of sin is always ready to flatter himself, and to think of himself, especially in spiritual things, more highly than he ought to think. And hence, it is in no wise strange, if one who is vainly puffed up by his fleshly mind, when he hears of this privilege of true Christians among whom he undoubtedly ranks himself, should soon work himself up into a persuasion that he is already possessed thereof. Such instances now abound in the world, and have abounded in all ages. How then may the real testimony of the Spirit with our spirit be distinguished from this damning presumption?

3. I answer, the holy Scriptures abound with marks, whereby the one may be distinguished from the other. They describe, in

9

the plainest manner, the circumstances which go before, which accompany, and which follow, the true, genuine testimony of the Spirit of God with the spirit of a believer. Whoever carefully weighs and attends to these will not need to put darkness for light. He will perceive so wide a difference, with respect to all these, between the real and the pretended witness of the Spirit, that there will be no danger, I might say, no possibility, of confounding the one with the other.

4. By these, one who vainly presumes on the gift of God might surely know, if he really desired it, that he hath been hitherto 'given up to a strong delusion,' and suffered to believe a lie. For the Scriptures lay down those clear, obvious marks, as preceding, accompanying, and following that gift, which a little reflection would convince him, beyond all doubt, were never found in his soul. For instance: the Scripture describes repentance, or conviction of sin, as constantly going before this witness of pardon. So, 'Repent; for the kingdom of heaven is at hand' (Matt. iii. 2). 'Repent ye, and believe the gospel' (Mark I. 15). 'Repent, and be baptized every one of you, for the remission of sins' (Acts ii. 38). 'Repent ye therefore, and be converted, that your sins may be blotted out' (Acts iii. 19). In conformity thereto, our Church also, continually places repentance before pardon, or the witness of it. "He pardoneth and absolveth all them that truly repent, and unfeignedly believe His holy gospel.' 'Almighty God . . . hath promised forgiveness of sins to all them who, with hearty repentance and true faith, turn unto Him.' But he is a stranger even to this repentance, he hath never known a broken and a contrite heart: 'the remembrance of his sins' was never 'grievous unto him,' nor 'the burden of them intolerable.' In repeating those words, he never meant what he said; he merely paid a compliment to God. And were it only from the want of this previous work of God, he hath too great reason to believe that he hath grasped a mere shadow, and never yet known the real privilege of the sons of God.

5. Again: the Scriptures describe the being born of God, which must precede the witness that we are His children, as a vast and mighty change; a change 'from darkness to light,' as

well as 'from the power of Satan unto God'; as a 'passing from death unto life,' a resurrection from the dead. Thus the Apostle to the Ephesians: 'You hath He quickened, who were dead in trespasses and sins' (ii. 1). And again, 'When we were dead in sins, He hath quickened us together with Christ; and hath raised us up together, and made us sit together in heavenly places in Christ Jesus' (verses 5, 6). But what knoweth he, concerning whom we now speak, of any such change as this? He is altogether unacquainted with this whole matter. This is a language which he does not understand. He tells you he always was a Christian. He knows no time when he had need of such a change. By this also, if he give himself leave to think, may he know, that he is not born of the Spirit; that he has never yet known God; but has mistaken the voice of nature for the voice of God.

6. But waiving the consideration of whatever he has or has not experienced in time past; by the present marks may we easily distinguish a child of God from a presumptuous self-deceiver. The Scriptures describe that joy in the Lord which accompanies the witness of His Spirit, as an humble joy; a joy that abases to the dust, that makes a pardoned sinner cry out, 'I am vile! What am I, or my father's house! Now mine eye seeth Thee, I abhor myself in dust and ashes!' And wherever lowliness is, there is meekness, patience, gentleness, long-suffering. There is a soft, yielding spirit; a mildness and sweetness, a tenderness of soul, which words cannot express. But do these fruits attend that *supposed* testimony of the Spirit in a presumptuous man? Just the reverse. The more confident he is of the favour of God, the more is he lifted up; the more does he exalt himself; the more haughty and assuming is his whole behaviour. The stronger witness he imagines himself to have, the more overbearing is he to all around him; the more incapable of receiving any reproof; the more impatient of contradiction. Instead of being more meek, and gentle, and teachable, more 'swift to hear, and slow to speak,' he is more slow to hear, and swift to speak; more unready to learn of any one; more fiery and vehement in his temper, and eager in his conversation. Yea, perhaps, there will sometimes appear a kind of fierceness in his air, his manner of speaking, his whole deportment, as if he were

just going to take the matter out of God's hands, and himself to 'devour the adversaries.'

7. Once more: the Scriptures teach, 'This is the love of God, the sure mark thereof, 'that we keep His commandments' (1 John v. 3). And our Lord Himself saith, 'He that keepeth My commandments, he it is that loveth Me' (John xiv. 21). Love rejoices to obey; to do, in every point, whatever is acceptable to the beloved. A true lover of God hastens to do His will on earth as it is done in heaven. But is this the character of the presumptuous pretender to the love of God? Nay, but His love gives him a liberty to disobey, to break, not keep, the commandments of God. Perhaps, when he was in fear of the wrath of God, he did labour to do His will. But now, looking on himself as 'not under the law,' he thinks he is no longer obliged to observe it. He is therefore less zealous of good works; less careful to abstain from evil; less watchful over his own heart; less jealous over his tongue. He is less earnest to deny himself, and to take up his cross daily. In a word, the whole form of his life is changed, since he has fancied himself to be *at liberty*. He is no longer 'exercising himself unto godliness'; 'wrestling not only with flesh and blood, but with principalities and powers,' enduring hardships, 'agonizing to enter in at the strait gate.' No; he has found an easier way to heaven; a broad, smooth, flowery path in which he can say to his soul, 'Soul, take thy ease; eat, drink, and be merry.' It follows, with undeniable evidence, that he has not the true testimony of his own spirit. He cannot be conscious of having those marks which he hath not; that lowliness, meekness, and obedience: nor yet can the Spirit of the God of truth bear witness to a lie; or testify that he is a child of God, when he is manifestly a child of the devil.

8. Discover thyself, thou poor self-deceiver!—thou who art confident of being a child of God; thou who sayest, 'I have the witness in myself,' and therefore defiest all thy enemies. Thou art weighed in the balance and found wanting; even in the balance of the sanctuary. The word of the Lord hath tried thy soul, and proved thee to be reprobate silver. Thou art not lowly of heart; therefore thou hast not received the Spirit of Jesus unto this day. Thou art not gentle and meek; therefore thy joy is

nothing worth: it is not joy in the Lord. Thou dost not keep His commandments: therefore thou lovest Him not, neither art thou partaker of the Holy Ghost. It is consequently as certain and as evident, as the oracles of God can make it. His Spirit doth not bear witness with thy spirit that thou art a child of God. O cry unto Him, that the scales may fall off thine eyes; that thou mayest know thyself as thou art known; that thou mayest receive the sentence of death in thyself, till thou hear the voice that raises the dead, saying, 'Be of good cheer: thy sins are forgiven; thy faith hath made thee whole.'

9. 'But how may one who has the real witness in himself distinguish it from presumption?' How, I pray, do you distinguish day from night? How do you distinguish light from darkness; or the light of a star, or a glimmering taper, from the light of the noonday sun? Is there not an inherent, obvious, essential difference between the one and the other? And do you not immediately and directly perceive that difference, provided your senses are rightly disposed? In like manner, there is an inherent, essential difference between spiritual light and spiritual darkness; and between the light wherewith the Sun of righteousness shines upon our heart, and that glimmering light which arises only from 'sparks of our own kindling': and this difference also is immediately and directly perceived, if our spiritual senses are rightly disposed.

10. To require a more minute and philosophical account of the manner whereby we distinguish these, and of the *criteria*, or intrinsic marks, whereby we know the voice of God, is to make a demand which can never be answered; no, not by one who has the deepest knowledge of God. Suppose, when Paul answered before Agrippa, the wise Roman had said, 'Thou talkest of hearing the voice of the Son of God. How dost thou know it was His voice? By what *criteria*, what intrinsic marks, dost thou know the voice of God? Explain to me the *manner* of distinguishing this from a human or angelic voice.' Can you belive, the Apostle himself would have once attempted to answer so idle a demand? And yet, doubtless, the moment he heard that voice, he knew it was the voice of God. But *how* he knew this, who is able to explain? Perhaps neither man nor angel.

11. To come yet closer: suppose God were now to speak to any soul, 'Thy sins are forgiven thee,' He must be willing that soul should know His voice; otherwise He would speak in vain. And he is able to effect this; for, whenever He wills, to do is present with Him. And He does effect it: that soul is absolutely assured, 'This voice is the voice of God.' But yet he who hath that witness in himself cannot explain it to one who hath it not: nor indeed is it to be expected that he should. Were there any natural medium to prove, or natural method to explain, the things of God to unexperienced men, then the natural man might discern and know the things of the Spirit of God. But this is utterly contrary to the assertion of the Apostle, that 'he cannot know them, because they are spiritually discerned'; even by spiritual senses, which the natural man hath not.

12. 'But how shall I know that my spiritual senses are rightly disposed?' This also is a question of vast importance; for if a man mistake in this, he may run on in endless error and delusion. 'And how am I assured that this is not my case; and that I do not mistake the voice of the Spirit?' Even by the testimony of your own spirit: by 'the answer of a good conscience toward God.' By the fruits which He hath wrought in your spirit, you shall know the testimony of the Spirit of God. Hereby you shall know that you are in no delusion, that you have not deceived your own soul. The immediate fruits of the Spirit, ruling in the heart, are 'love, joy, peace, bowels of mercies, humbleness of mind, meekness, gentleness, long-suffering.' And the outward fruits are, the doing good to all men; the doing no evil to any; and the walking in the light—a zealous, uniform obedience to all the commandments of God.

13. By the same fruits shall you distinguish this voice of God from any delusion of the devil. That proud spirit cannot humble thee before God. He neither can nor would soften thy heart, and melt it first into earnest mourning after God, and then into filial love. It is not the adversary of God and man that enables thee to love thy neighbour; or to put on meekness, gentleness, patience, temperance, and the whole armour of God. He is not divided against himself, or a destroyer of sin, his own work. No; it is none but the Son of God who cometh 'to destroy the works of

the devil.' As surely therefore as holiness is of God, and as sin is the work of the devil, so surely the witness thou hast in thyself is not of Satan, but of God.

14. Well then mayest thou say, 'Thanks be unto God for His unspeakable gift!' Thanks be unto God, who giveth me to 'know in whom I have believed'; who hath 'sent forth the Spirit of His Son into my heart, crying, Abba, Father, and even now, 'bearing witness with my spirit that I am a child of God'! And see, that not only thy lips, but thy life show forth His praise. He hath sealed thee for His own; glorify Him then in thy body and thy spirit, which are His. Beloved, if thou hast this hope in thyself, purify thyself, as He is pure. While thou beholdest what manner of love the Father hath given thee, that thou shouldest be called a child of God, cleanse thyself 'from all filthiness of flesh and spirit, perfecting holiness in the fear of God'; and let all thy thoughts, words, and works be a spiritual sacrifice, holy, acceptable to God through Christ Jesus!

SERMON XI

THE WITNESS OF OUR OWN SPIRIT

This is our rejoicing, the testimony of our conscience, that in simplicity and godly sincerity, not with fleshly wisdom, but by the grace of God, we have had our conversation in the world.—2 COR. i. 12.

SUCH is the voice of every true believer in Christ, so long as he abides in faith and love. 'He that followeth Me,' saith our Lord, 'walketh not in darkness': and while he hath the light, he rejoiceth therein. As he hath 'received the Lord Jesus Christ,' so he walketh in Him; and while he walketh in Him, the exhortation of the Apostle takes place in his soul, day by day, 'Rejoice in the Lord always; and again I say, Rejoice.'

2. But that we may not build our house upon the sand (lest when the rains descend, and the winds blow, and the floods

arise and beat upon it, it fall, and great be the fall thereof), I intend in the following discourse to show what is the nature and ground of a Christian's joy. We know, in general, it is that happy peace, that calm satisfaction of spirit which arises from such a testimony of his conscience, as is here described by the Apostle. But, in order to understand this the more thoroughly, it will be requisite to weigh all his words; whence will easily appear, both what we are to understand by *conscience*: and what by the *testimony* thereof; and also, how he that hath this testimony rejoiceth evermore.

3. And, first, what are we to understand by *conscience*? What is the meaning of this word that is in every one's mouth? One would imagine it was an exceeding difficult thing to discover this, when we consider how large and numerous volumes have been from time to time wrote on this subject; and how all the treasures of ancient and modern learning have been ransacked, in order to explain it. And yet it is to be feared, it has not received much light from all those elaborate inquiries. Rather, have not most of those writers puzzled the cause; 'darkening counsel by words without knowledge'; perplexing a subject, plain in itself and easy to be understood? For, set aside but hard words, and every man of an honest heart will soon understand the thing.

4. God has made us thinking beings, capable of perceiving what is present, and of reflecting or looking back on what is past. In particular, we are capable of perceiving whatsoever passes in our own hearts or lives; of knowing whatsoever we feel or do; and that either while it passes, or when it is past. This we mean when we say, man is a *conscious* being: he hath a *consciousness*, or inward perception, both of things present and past, relating to himself, of his own tempers and outward behaviour. But what we usually term *conscience* implies somewhat more than this. It is not barely the knowledge of our present or the remembrance of our preceding life. To remember, to bear witness either of past or present things, is only one, and the least office of conscience: its main business is to excuse or accuse, to approve or disapprove, to acquit or condemn.

5. Some late writers indeed have given a new name to this,

and have chose to style it a *moral sense*. But the old word seems preferable to the new, were it only on this account, that it is more common and familiar among men, and therefore easier to be understood. And to Christians it is undeniably preferable, on another account also; namely, because it is scriptural; because it is the word which the wisdom of God hath chose to use in the inspired writings.

And according to the meaning wherein it is generally used there, particularly in the Epistles of St. Paul, we may understand by conscience, a faculty or power, implanted by God in every soul that comes into the world, of perceiving what is right or wrong in his own heart or life, in his tempers, thoughts, words, and actions.

6. But what is the rule whereby men are to judge of right and wrong? whereby their conscience is to be directed? The rule of Heathens, as the Apostle teaches elsewhere, is 'the law written in their hearts.' 'These,' saith he, 'not having the' outward 'law, are a law unto themselves: who show the work of the law,' that which the outward law prescribes, 'written in their hearts,' by the finger of God; 'their conscience also bearing witness whether they walk by this rule or not, 'and their thoughts the meanwhile accusing, or even excusing,' acquitting, defending them; ἢ καὶ ἀπολογουμένων (Rom. ii. 14, 15). But the Christian rule of right and wrong is the Word of God, the writings of the Old and New Testament; all that the prophets and 'holy men of old' wrote 'as they were moved by the Holy Ghost'; all that Scripture which was 'given by inspiration of God,' and which is indeed 'profitable for doctrine,' or teaching the whole will of God; 'for reproof' of what is contrary thereto; for 'correction' of error; and 'for instruction,' or training us up, 'in righteousness' (2 Tim. iii. 16).

This is a lantern unto a Christian's feet, and a light in all his paths. This alone he receives as his rule of right or wrong, of whatever is really good or evil. He esteems nothing good, but what is here enjoined, either directly or by plain consequence; he accounts nothing evil but what is here forbidden, either in terms, or by undeniable inference. Whatever the Scripture neither forbids nor enjoins, either directly or by plain consequence, he believes to be of an indifferent nature; to be in itself neither good nor evil; this being the whole and sole outward rule whereby his conscience is to be directed in all things.

7. And if it be directed thereby in fact, then hath he 'the answer of a good conscience toward God.' 'A good conscience' is what is elsewhere termed by the Apostle, 'a conscience void of offence.' So, what he at one time expresses thus, 'I have lived in all good conscience before God until this day' (Acts xxiii. 1); he denotes at another by that expression, 'Herein do I exercise myself, to have always a conscience void of offence toward God, and toward men' (chap. xxiv. 16). Now, in order to this there is absolutely required, first, a right understanding of the Word of God, of His 'holy, and acceptable, and perfect will' concerning us, as it is revealed therein. For it is impossible we should walk by a rule, if we do not know what it means. There is, secondly, required (which how few have attained!) a true knowledge of ourselves; a knowledge both of our hearts and lives, of our inward tempers and outward conversation. seeing, if we know them not, it is not possible that we should compare them with our rule. There is required, thirdly, an agreement of our hearts and lives, of our tempers and conversation, of our thoughts, and words, and works, with that rule, with the written Word of God. For, without this, if we have any conscience at all, it can be only an evil conscience. There is, fourthly, required, an inward perception of this agreement with our rule; and this habitual perception, this inward consciousness itself, is properly a *good conscience*; or, in the other phrase of the Apostle, 'a conscience void of offence toward God, and toward men.'

8. But whoever desires to have a conscience thus void of offence, let him see that he lay the right foundation. Let him remember, 'other foundation' of this 'can no man lay, than that which is laid, even Jesus Christ.' And let him also be mindful, that no man buildeth on Him but by a living faith; that no man is a partaker of Christ, until he can clearly testify, 'The life which I now live, I live by faith in the Son of God'; in Him who is now *revealed* in my heart; who 'loved me, and gave Himself for me.' Faith alone is that evidence, that conviction, that

demonstration of things 'invisible, whereby, the eyes of our understanding being opened, and divine light poured in upon them, we 'see the wondrous things of God's law'; the excellency and purity of it; the height, and depth, and length, and breadth thereof, and of every commandment contained therein. It is by faith that, beholding 'the light of the glory of God in the face of Jesus Christ,' we perceive, as in a glass, all that is in ourselves, yea, the inmost motions of our souls. And by this alone can that blessed love of God be 'shed abroad in our hearts,' which enables us so to love one another as Christ loved us. By this is that gracious promise fulfilled unto all the Israel of God, 'I will put My laws into their mind, and write' (or engrave) 'them in their hearts' (Heb. viii. 10); hereby producing in their souls an entire agreement with His holy and perfect law, and 'bringing into captivity every thought to the obedience of Christ.'

And, as an evil tree cannot bring forth good fruit, so a good tree cannot bring forth evil fruit. As the heart therefore of a believer, so likewise his life, is thoroughly conformed to the rule of God's commandments; in a consciousness whereof, he can give glory to God, and say with the Apostle, 'This is our rejoicing, the testimony of our conscience, that in simplicity and godly sincerity, not with fleshly wisdom, but by the grace of God, we have had our conversation in the world.'

9. 'We have had our conversation.' The Apostle in the original expresses this by one single word, ἀνεστράφημεν; but the meaning thereof is exceeding broad, taking in our whole deportment, yea, every inward as well as outward circumstance, whether relating to our soul or body. It includes every motion of our heart, of our tongue, of our hands and bodily members. It extends to all our actions and words; to the employment of all our powers and faculties; to the manner of using every talent we have received, with respect either to God or man.

10. 'We have had our conversation in the world'; even in the world of the ungodly: not only among the children of God (that were comparatively a little thing); but among the children of the devil, among those that lie in wickedness, ἐν τῷ πονηρῷ, in the wicked one. What a world is this! How thoroughly impregnated with the spirit it continually breathes! As our God

is good, and doeth good, so the god of this world, and all his children, are evil, and do evil (so far as they are suffered) to all the children of God. Like their father, they are always lying in wait, or 'walking about, seeking whom they may devour'; using fraud or force, secret wiles or open violence, to destroy those who are not of the world; continually warring against our souls, and, by old or new weapons, and devices of every kind, labouring to bring them back into the snare of the devil, into the broad road that leadeth to destruction.

11. 'We have had our' whole 'conversation,' in such a world, 'in simplicity and godly sincerity.' First, in simplicity: this is what our Lord recommends under the name of a 'single eye.' 'The light of the body,' saith He, 'is the eye. If therefore thine eye be single, thy whole body shall be full of light.' The meaning whereof is this: What the eye is to the body, that the intention is to all the words and actions: if, therefore, this eye of thy soul be single, all thy actions and conversation shall be 'full of light,' of the light of heaven, of love, and peace, and joy in the Holy Ghost.

We are then simple of heart, when the eye of our mind is singly fixed on God; when in all things we aim at God alone, as our God, our portion, our strength, our happiness, our exceeding great reward, our all, in time and eternity. This is simplicity; when a steady view, a single intention of promoting His glory, of doing and suffering His blessed will, runs through our whole soul, fills all our heart, and is the constant spring of all our thoughts, desires, and purposes.

12. 'We have had our conversation in the world,' secondly, in 'godly sincerity.' The difference between simplicity and sincerity seems to be chiefly this: simplicity regards the intention itself, sincerity the execution of it; and this sincerity relates not barely to our words, but to our whole conversation, as described above. It is not here to be understood in that narrow sense, wherein St. Paul himself sometimes uses it, for speaking the truth, or abstaining from guile, from craft, and dissimulation; but in a more extensive meaning, as actually hitting the mark, which we aim at by simplicity, Accordingly, it implies in this place, that we do, in fact, speak and do all to the glory of God:

that all our words are not only pointed at this, but actually conducive thereto; that all our actions flow on in an even stream, uniformly subservient to this great end; and that in our whole lives, we are moving straight toward God, and that continually; walking steadily on in the highway of holiness, in the paths of justice, mercy, and truth.

13. This sincerity is termed by the Apostle, godly sincerity, or the sincerity of God; εἰλικρινεία Θεοῦ; to prevent our mistaking or confounding it with the sincerity of the Heathens (for they had also a kind of sincerity among them, for which they professed no small veneration); likewise to denote the object and end of this, as of every Christian virtue, seeing whatever does not ultimately tend to God, sinks among 'the beggarly elements of the world.' By styling it the sincerity of God, he also points out the Author of it, the 'Father of lights, from whom every good and perfect gift descendeth'; which is still more clearly declared in the following words, 'Not with fleshly wisdom, but by the grace of God.'

14. 'Not with fleshly wisdom': as if he had said, 'We cannot thus converse in the world, by any natural strength of understanding, neither by any naturally acquired knowledge or wisdom. We cannot gain this simplicity, or practise this sincerity, by the force either of good sense, good nature, or good breeding. It overshoots all our native courage and resolution, as well as all our precepts of philosophy. The power of custom is not able to train us up to this, nor the most exquisite rules of human education. Neither could I Paul ever attain hereto, notwithstanding all the advantages I enjoyed, so long as I was *in the flesh*, in my natural state, and pursued it only by *fleshly*, natural *wisdom*.'

And yet surely, if any man could, Paul himself might have attained thereto by that wisdom: for we can hardly conceive any who was more highly favoured with all the gifts both of nature and education. Besides his natural abilities, probably not inferior to those of any person then upon the earth, he had all the benefits of learning, studying at the University of Tarsus, afterwards brought up at the feet of Gamaliel, a person of the greatest account, both for knowledge and integrity, that was

then in the whole Jewish nation. And he had all the possible
advantages of religious education, being a Pharisee, the son of a
Pharisee, trained up in the very straitest sect or profession, distinguished from all others by a more eminent strictness. And
herein he had 'profited above many' others, 'who were his equals'
in years, 'being more abundantly zealous' of whatever he thought
would please God, and 'as touching the righteousness of the law,
blameless.' But it could not be, that he should hereby attain
this simplicity and godly sincerity. It was all but lost labour; in a
deep, piercing sense of which he was at length constrained to cry
out, 'the things which were gain to me, those I counted loss for
Christ. Yea doubtless, and I count all things but loss for the
excellency of the knowledge of Christ Jesus my Lord' (Phil. iii.
7, 8).

15. It could not be that ever he should attain to this, but by
the 'excellent knowledge of Jesus Christ' our Lord; or 'by the
grace of God'—another expression of nearly the same import.
By 'the grace of God' is sometimes to be understood that free
love, that unmerited mercy by which I a sinner, through the
merits of Christ, am now reconciled to God. But in this place
it rather means that power of God the Holy Ghost, which
'worketh in us both to will and to do of His good pleasure.'
As soon as ever the grace of God in the former sense, His pardoning love, is manifested to our souls, the grace of God in the
latter sense, the power of His Spirit, takes place therein. And
now we can perform, through God, what to man was impossible.
Now we can order our conversation aright. We can do all
things in the light and power of that love, through Christ
which strengtheneth us. We now have 'the testimony of our
conscience,' which we could never have by fleshly wisdom, 'that
in simplicity and godly sincerity we have our conversation in
the world.'

16. This is properly the ground of a Christian's joy. We may
now therefore readily conceive, how he that hath this testimony
in himself rejoiceth evermore. 'My soul,' may he say, 'doth
magnify the Lord, and my spirit rejoiceth in God my Saviour.'
I rejoice in Him, who, of His own unmerited love, of His own
free and tender mercy, 'hath called me into this state of salvation,'

wherein, through His power, I now stand. I rejoice, because His Spirit beareth witness to my spirit, that I am bought with the blood of the Lamb; and that, believing in Him, 'I am a member of Christ, a child of God, and an inheritor of the kingdom of heaven.' I rejoice, because the sense of God's love to me hath, by the same Spirit, wrought in me to love Him, and to love for His sake every child of man, every soul that He hath made. I rejoice, because He gives me to feel in myself 'the mind that was in Christ': simplicity, a single eye to Him in every motion of my heart; power always to fix the loving eye of my soul on Him who 'loved me, and gave Himself for me'; to aim at Him alone, at His glorious will, in all I think, or speak, or do: purity, desiring nothing more but God; 'crucifying the flesh with its affections and lusts'; 'setting my affections on things above, not on things of the earth'; holiness, a recovery of the image of God, a renewal of soul 'after His likeness': and godly sincerity, directing all my words and works, so as to conduce to His glory In this I likewise rejoice, yea, and will rejoice, because my conscience beareth me witness in the Holy Ghost, by the light He continually pours in upon it, that I 'walk worthy of the vocation wherewith I am called'; that I 'abstain from all appearance of evil,' fleeing from sin as from the face of a serpent; that as I have opportunity I do all possible good, in every kind, to all men; that I follow my Lord in all my steps, and do what is acceptable in His sight. I rejoice, because I both see and feel, through the inspiration of God's Holy Spirit, that all my works are wrought in Him, yea, and that it is He who worketh all my works in me. I rejoice in seeing through the light of God, which shines in my heart, that I have power to walk in His ways; and that, through His grace, I turn not therefrom, to the right hand or to the left.

17. Such is the ground and the nature of that joy whereby an adult Christian rejoiceth evermore. And from all this we may easily infer, first, that this is not a *natural* joy. It does not arise from any natural cause: not from any sudden flow of spirits. This may give a transient start of joy; but the Christian *rejoiceth always*. It cannot be owing to bodily health or ease; to strength and soundness of constitution: for it is equally strong in sickness and pain; yea, perhaps far stronger than before. Many Christians

have never experienced any joy, to be compared with that which then filled their soul, when the body was wellnigh worn out with pain, or consumed away with pining sickness. Least of all can it be ascribed to outward prosperity, to the favour of men, or plenty of worldly goods; for then, chiefly, when their faith has been tried as with fire, by all manner of outward afflictions, have the children of God rejoiced in Him, whom unseen they loved, even with joy unspeakable. And never surely did men rejoice like those who were used as 'the filth and offscouring of the world'; who wandered to and fro, being in want of all things; in hunger, in cold, in nakedness; who had trials, not only of 'cruel mockings,' but, 'moreover of bonds and imprisonments'; yea, who, at last, 'counted not their lives dear unto themselves, so they might finish their course with joy.'

18. From the preceding considerations, we may, secondly, infer, that the joy of a Christian does not arise from any blindness of conscience, from his not being able to discern good from evil. So far from it, that he was an utter stranger to this joy, till the eyes of his understanding were opened; that he knew it not, until he had spiritual senses, fitted to discern spiritual good and evil. And now the eye of his soul waxeth not dim: he was never so sharp-sighted before: he has so quick a perception of the smallest things, as is quite amazing to the natural man. As a mote is visible in the sunbeam, so to him who is walking in the light, in the beams of the uncreated Sun, every mote of sin is visible. Nor does he close the eyes of his conscience any more: that sleep is departed from him. His soul is always broad awake: no more slumber or folding of the hands to rest! He is always standing on the tower, and hearkening what his Lord will say concerning him; and always rejoicing in this very thing, in 'seeing Him that is invisible.'

19. Neither does the joy of a Christian arise, thirdly, from any dullness or callousness of conscience. A kind of joy, it is true, may arise from this, in those whose 'foolish hearts are darkened'; whose heart is callous, unfeeling, dull of sense, and consequently, without spiritual understanding. Because of their senseless, unfeeling hearts, they may rejoice even in committing sin; and this they may probably call *liberty*!—which is indeed mere

drunkenness of soul, a fatal numbness of spirit, the stupid insensibility of a seared conscience. On the contrary, a Christian has the most exquisite sensibility; such as he could not have conceived before. He never had such a tenderness of conscience as he has had since the love of God has reigned in his heart. And this also is his glory and joy, that God hath heard his daily prayer:

> O that my tender soul might fly
>   The first abhorr'd approach of ill;
> Quick as the apple of an eye,
>   The slightest touch of sin to feel.

20. To conclude. Christian joy is joy in obedience; joy in loving God, and keeping His commandments: and yet not in keeping them as if we were thereby to fulfil the terms of the covenant of works; as if by any works or righteousness of ours we were to procure pardon and acceptance with God. Not so: we are already pardoned and accepted through the mercy of God in Christ Jesus. Not as if we were by our own obedience to procure life, life from the death of sin: this also we have already through the grace of God. Us 'hath He quickened, who were dead in sins'; and now we are 'alive to God, through Jesus Christ our Lord.' But we rejoice in walking according to the covenant of grace, in holy love and happy obedience. We rejoice in knowing that, 'being justified through His grace,' we have 'not received that grace of God in vain'; that God having freely (not for the sake of our willing or running, but through the blood of the Lamb) reconciled us to Himself, we run, in the strength which He hath given us, the way of His commandments. He hath 'girded us with strength unto the war,' and we gladly 'fight the good fight of faith.' We rejoice, through Him who liveth in our hearts by faith, to 'lay hold of eternal life.' This is our rejoicing, that as our 'Father worketh hitherto,' so (not by our own might or wisdom, but through the power of His Spirit, freely given in Christ Jesus) we also work the works of God. And may He work in us whatsoever is well-pleasing in His sight! To whom be the praise for ever and ever!

SERMON XII

THE MEANS OF GRACE

Ye are gone away from Mine ordinances, and have not kept them.—MAL. iii. 7.

I. 1. But are there any *ordinances* now, since life and immortality were brought to light by the gospel? Are there, under the Christian dispensation, any *means ordained* of God, as the usual channels of His grace? This question could never have been proposed in the apostolical church, unless by one who openly avowed himself to be a Heathen; the whole body of Christians being agreed, that Christ had ordained certain outward means, for conveying His grace into the souls of men. Their constant practice set this beyond all dispute; for so long as 'all that believed were together, and had all things common' (Acts ii. 44), 'they continued steadfastly in the teaching of the Apostles, and in breaking of bread, and in prayers' (verse 42).

2. But in process of time, when 'the love of many waxed cold,' some began to mistake the *means* for the *end*, and to place religion, rather in doing those outward works, than in a heart renewed after the image of God. They forgot that 'the end of' every 'commandment is love, out of a pure heart,' with 'faith unfeigned'; the loving the Lord their God with all their heart, and their neighbour as themselves; and the being purified from pride, anger, and evil desire, by a 'faith of the operation of God.' Others seemed to imagine, that though religion did not principally consist in these outward means, yet there was something in them wherewith God was well pleased; something that would still make them acceptable in His sight, though they were not exact in the weightier matters of the law, in justice, mercy, and the love of God.

3. It is evident, in those who abused them thus, they did not conduce to the end for which they were ordained: rather, the things which should have been for their health, were to them an occasion of falling. They were so far from receiving any

blessing therein, that they only drew down a curse upon their head; so far from growing more heavenly in heart and life, that they were twofold more the children of hell than before. Others, clearly perceiving that these means did not convey the grace of God to those children of the devil, began, from this particular case, to draw a general conclusion,—that they were not means of conveying the grace of God.

4. Yet the number of those who *abused* the ordinances of God was far greater than of those who *despised* them, till certain men arose, not only of great understanding (sometimes joined with considerable learning), but who likewise appeared to be men of love, experimentally acquainted with true, inward religion. Some of these were burning and shining lights, persons famous in their generations, and such as had well deserved of the church of Christ, for standing in the gap against the overflowings of ungodliness.

It cannot be supposed, that these holy and venerable men intended any more, at first, than to show that outward religion is nothing worth, without the religion of the heart; that 'God is a Spirit, and they who worship Him must worship Him in spirit and in truth'; that, therefore, external worship is lost labour, without a heart devoted to God; that the outward ordinances of God then profit much, when they advance inward holiness; but, when they advance it not, are unprofitable and void, are lighter than vanity; yea, than when they are used, as it were, *in the place of* this, they are an utter abomination to the Lord.

5. Yet it is not strange, if some of these, being strongly convinced of that horrid profanation of the ordinances of God, which had spread itself over the whole church, and wellnigh driven true religion out of the world, in their fervent zeal for the glory of God, and the recovery of souls from that fatal delusion, spake as if outward religion were absolutely nothing, as if it had no place in the religion of Christ. It is not surprising at all, if they should not always have expressed themselves with sufficient caution; so that unwary hearers might believe they condemned all outward means, as altogether unprofitable, and as not designed of God to be the ordinary channels of conveying His grace into the souls of men.

Nay, it is not impossible, some of these holy men did, at length, themselves fall into this opinion: in particular those who not by choice, but by the providence of God, were cut off from all these ordinances; perhaps wandering up and down, having no certain abiding-place, or dwelling in dens and caves of the earth. These, experiencing the grace of God in themselves, though they were deprived of all outward means, might infer that the same grace would be given to them who of set purpose abstained from them.

6. And experience shows how easily this notion spreads, and insinuates itself into the minds of men; especially of those who are throughly awakened out of the sleep of death, and begin to feel the weight of their sins a burden too heavy to be borne. These are usually impatient of their present state; and, trying every way to escape from it, they are always ready to catch at any new thing, any new proposal of ease or happiness. They have probably tried most outward means, and found no ease in them: it may be, more and more of remorse, and fear, and sorrow, and condemnation. It is easy, therefore, to persuade these that it is better for them to abstain from all those means. They are already weary of striving (as it seems) in vain, of labouring in the fire; and are therefore glad of any pretence to cast aside that wherein their soul has no pleasure, to give over the painful strife, and sink down into an indolent inactivity.

II. 1. In the following discourse, I propose to examine at large whether there be any means of grace.

By 'means of grace,' I understand outward signs, words, or actions, ordained of God, and appointed for this end, to be the ordinary channels whereby He might convey to men, preventing, justifying, or sanctifying grace.

I use this expression, 'means of grace,' because I know none better; and because it has been generally used in the Christian church for many ages—in particular by our own Church, which directs us to bless God both for the means of grace, and hope of glory; and teaches us, that a sacrament is 'an outward sign of inward grace, and a means whereby we receive the same.'

The chief of these means are prayer, whether in secret or

with the great congregation; searching the Scriptures (which implies reading, hearing, and meditating thereon); and receiving the Lord's supper, eating bread and drinking wine in remembrance of Him; and these we believe to be ordained of God, as the ordinary channels of conveying His grace to the souls of men.

2. But we allow, that the whole value of the means depends on their actual subservience to the end of religion; that, consequently, all these means, when separate from the end, are less than nothing and vanity; that if they do not actually conduce to the knowledge and love of God, they are not acceptable in His sight, yea, rather, they are an abomination before Him, a stink in His nostrils; He is weary to bear them. Above all, if they are used as a kind of *commutation* for the religion they were designed to subserve, it is not easy to find words for the enormous folly and wickedness of thus turning God's arms against Himself; of keeping Christianity out of the heart by those very means which were ordained for the bringing it in.

3. We allow, likewise, that all outward means whatever, if separate from the Spirit of God, cannot profit at all, cannot conduce, in any degree, either to the knowledge or love of God. Without controversy, the help that is done upon earth, He doeth it Himself. It is He alone who, by His own almighty power, worketh in us what is pleasing in His sight; and all outward things, unless He work in them and by them, are mere weak and beggarly elements. Whosoever, therefore, imagines there is any intrinsic power in any means whatsoever, does greatly err, not knowing the Scriptures, neither the power of God. We know that there is no inherent power in the words that are spoken in prayer, in the letter of Scripture read, the sound thereof heard, or the bread and wine received in the Lord's supper; but that it is God alone who is the Giver of every good gift, the Author of all grace; that the whole power is of Him, whereby, through any of these, there is any blessing conveyed to our souls. We know, likewise, that He is able to give the same grace, though there were no means on the face of the earth. In this sense, we may affirm, that, with regard to God, there is no such thing as means; seeing He is equally able to work whatsoever pleaseth Him, by any, or by none at all.

4. We allow farther, that the use of all means whatever will never atone for one sin; that it is the blood of Christ alone whereby any sinner can be reconciled to God; there being no other propitiation for our sins, no other fountain for sin and uncleanness. Every believer in Christ is deeply convinced that there is no merit but in Him; that there is no merit in any of his own works; not in uttering the prayer, or searching the Scripture, or hearing the Word of God, or eating of that bread and drinking of that cup. So that if no more be intended by the expression some have used, 'Christ is the only means of grace,' than this,—that He is the only meritorious cause of it, it cannot be gainsaid by any who know the grace of God.

5. Yet once more: we allow, though it is a melancholy truth, that a large proportion of those who are called Christians, do to this day abuse the means of grace to the destruction of their souls. This is doubtless the case with all those who rest content in the form of godliness, without the power. Either they fondly presume they are Christians already, because they do thus and thus (although Christ was never yet revealed in their hearts, nor the love of God shed abroad therein); or else they suppose they shall infallibly be so, barely because they use these means; idly dreaming (though perhaps hardly conscious thereof), either that there is some kind of *power* therein, whereby, sooner or later (they know not when), they shall certainly be made holy; or that there is a sort of *merit* in using them, which will surely move God to give them holiness, or accept them without it.

6. So little do they understand that great foundation of the whole Christian building, 'By grace are ye saved'; ye are saved from your sins, from the guilt and power thereof, ye are restored to the favour and image of God, not for any works, merits, or deservings of yours, but by the free grace, the mere mercy of God, through the merits of His well-beloved Son: ye are thus saved, not by any power, wisdom, or strength, which is in you, or in any other creature; but merely through the grace or power of the Holy Ghost, which worketh all in all.

7. But the main question remains: 'We know this salvation is the gift and the work of God; but how (may one say who is convinced he hath it not) may I attain thereto?' If you say,

'Believe, and thou shalt be saved!' he answers, 'True; but how shall I believe?' You reply, 'Wait upon God.' 'Well; but how am I to wait? In the means of grace, or out of them? Am I to wait for the grace of God which bringeth salvation, by using these means, or by laying them aside?'

8. It cannot possibly be conceived, that the Word of God should give no direction in so important a point; or, that the Son of God, who came down from heaven for us men and for our salvation, should have left us undetermined with regard to a question wherein our salvation is so nearly concerned.

And, in fact, He hath not left us undetermined; He hath shown us the way wherein we should go. We have only to consult the oracles of God; to inquire what is written there; and, if we simply abide by their decision, there can be no possible doubt remain.

III. 1. According to this, according to the decision of holy writ, all who desire the grace of God are to wait for it in the means which He hath ordained; in using, not in laying them aside.

And, first, all who desire the grace of God are to wait for it in the way of prayer. This is the express direction of our Lord Himself. In His Sermon upon the Mount, after explaining at large wherein religion consists, and describing the main branches of it, He adds, 'Ask, and it shall be given you; seek, and ye shall find; knock, and it shall be opened unto you: for every one that asketh receiveth; and he that seeketh findeth; and to him that knocketh it shall be opened' (Matt. vii. 7, 8). Here we are in the plainest manner directed to ask, in order to, or as a means of, receiving; to seek, in order to find, the grace of God, the pearl of great price; and to knock, to continue asking and seeking, if we would enter into His kingdom.

2. That no doubt might remain, our Lord labours this point in a more peculiar manner. He appeals to every man's own heart: 'What man is there of you, who, if his son ask bread, will he give him a stone? or, if he ask a fish, will he give him a serpent? If ye then, being evil, know how to give good gifts unto your children, how much more shall your Father which is in heaven,'

the Father of angels and men, the Father of the spirits of all flesh 'give good things to them that ask Him'? (verses 9-11). Or, as He expresses Himself on another occasion, including all good things in one, 'How much more shall your heavenly Father give the Holy Spirit to them that ask Him?' (Luke xi. 13). It should be particularly observed here, that the persons directed to ask had not then received the Holy Spirit: nevertheless our Lord directs them to use this means, and promises that it should be effectual; that upon asking they should receive the Holy Spirit, from Him whose mercy is over all His works.

3. The absolute necessity of using this means, if we would receive any gift from God, yet farther appears from that remarkable passage which immediately precedes these words: 'And He said unto them,' whom He had just been teaching how to pray, 'Which of you shall have a friend, and shall go unto him at midnight, and shall say unto him, Friend, lend me three loaves: and he from within shall answer, Trouble me not; I cannot rise and give thee. I say unto you, Though he will not rise and give him, because he is his friend, yet because of his importunity he will rise and give him as many as he needeth. And I say unto you, Ask, and it shall be given you' (Luke xi. 5, 7-9). 'Though he will not give him, because he is his friend, yet because of his importunity he will rise and give him as many as he needeth.' How could our blessed Lord more plainly declare, that we may receive of God, by this means, by importunately asking, what otherwise we should not receive at all?

4. 'He spake also another parable, to this end, that men ought always to pray, and not to faint,' till through this means they should receive of God whatsoever petition they asked of Him: 'There was in a city a judge, which feared not God, neither regarded man: and there was a widow in that city; and she came unto him, saying, Avenge me of my adversary. And he would not for a while; but afterward he said within himself, Though I fear not God, nor regard man, yet because this widow troubleth me, I will avenge her, lest by her continual coming she weary me' (Luke xviii. 1-5). The application of this our Lord Himself hath made: 'Hear what the unjust judge saith!' Because she continues to ask, because she will take no denial, therefore I will

avenge her. 'And shall not God avenge His own elect, which cry day and night unto Him? I tell you He will avenge them speedily,' if they pray, and faint not.

5. A direction, equally full and express, to wait for the blessings of God in private prayer, together with a positive promise that, by this means, we shall obtain the request of our lips, He hath given us in those well-known words: 'Enter into thy closet, and when thou hast shut thy door, pray to thy Father which is in secret; and thy Father which seeth in secret shall reward thee openly' (Matt. vi. 6).

6. If it be possible for any direction to be more clear, it is that which God hath given us by the Apostle, with regard to prayer of every kind, public or private, and the blessing annexed thereto: 'If any of you lack wisdom, let him ask of God, that giveth to all men liberally' (if they ask; otherwise 'ye have not, because ye ask not,' Jas. iv. 2), 'and upbraideth not; and it shall be given him' (Jas. i. 5).

If it be objected, 'But this is no direction to unbelievers; to them who know not the pardoning grace of God: for the Apostle adds, "But let him ask in faith"; otherwise, "let him not think that he shall receive anything of the Lord" '; I answer, The meaning of the word *faith*, in this place, is fixed by the Apostle himself, as if it were on purpose to obviate this objection, in the words immediately following: 'Let him ask in faith, nothing wavering,' nothing *doubting: μηδὲν διακρινόμενος*: not doubting but God heareth his prayer, and will fulfil the desire of his heart.

The gross, blasphemous absurdity of supposing *faith*, in this place, to be taken in the full Christian meaning, appears hence: it is supposing the Holy Ghost to direct a man who knows he has not this faith (which is here termed *widsom*), to ask it of God, with a positive promise that 'it shall be given him'; and then immediately to subjoin, that it shall not be given him, unless he have it before he asks for it! But who can bear such a supposition? From this scripture, therefore, as well as those cited above, we must infer, that all who desire the grace of God are to wait for it in the way of prayer.

7. Secondly. All who desire the grace of God are to wait for it in searching the Scriptures.

Our Lord's direction, with regard to the use of this means, is likewise plain and clear. 'Search the Scriptures,' saith He to the unbelieving Jews, 'for they testify of Me' (John v. 39). And for this very end did He direct them to search the Scriptures, that they might believe in Him.

The objection, that 'this is not a command, but only an assertion, that they did search the Scriptures,' is shamelessly false. I desire those who urge it, to let us know how a command can be more clearly expressed, than in those terms, Ἐρευνᾶτε τὰς γραφάς. It is as peremptory as so many words can make it.

And what a blessing from God attends the use of this means, appears from what is recorded concerning the Bereans: who, after hearing St. Paul, 'searched the Scriptures daily, whether those things were so. Therefore many of them believed,'— found the grace of God, in the way which He had ordained (Acts xvii. 11, 12).

It is probable, indeed, that in some of those who had 'received the word with all readiness of mind,' 'faith came,' as the same Apostle speaks, 'by hearing,' and was only confirmed by reading the Scriptures: but it was observed above, that, under the general term of searching the Scriptures, both hearing, reading, and meditating are contained.

8. And that this is a means whereby God not only gives, but also confirms and increases, true wisdom, we learn from the words of St. Paul to Timothy; 'From a child thou hast known the holy Scriptures, which are able to make thee wise unto salvation through faith which is in Christ Jesus' (2 Tim. iii. 15). The same truth (namely, that this is the great means God has ordained for conveying His manifold grace to man) is delivered, in the fullest manner that can be conceived, in the words which immediately follow: 'All Scripture is given by inspiration of God'; consequently, all Scripture is infallibly true; 'and is profitable for doctrine, for reproof, for correction, for instruction in righteousness ; to the end 'that the man of God may be perfect, throughly furnished unto all good works' (verses 16, 17)

9. It should be observed, that this is spoken primarily and directly of the Scriptures which Timothy had known from a

child; which must have been those of the Old Testament, for the New was not then wrote. How far then was St. Paul (though he was 'not a whit behind the very chief of the Apostles,' nor, therefore, I presume, behind any man now upon earth) from making light of the Old Testament! Behold this, lest ye one day 'wonder and perish,' ye who make so small account of one half of the oracles of God! Yea, and that half of which the Holy Ghost expressly declares, that it is profitable,' as a means ordained of God for this very thing, 'for doctrine, for reproof, for correction, for instruction in righteousness'; to the end, 'the man of God may be perfect, throughly furnished unto all good works.'

10. Nor is this profitable only for the men of God, for those who walk already in the light of His countenance; but also for those who are yet in darkness, seeking Him whom they know not. Thus St. Peter: 'We have also a more sure word of prophecy': literally, 'And we have the prophetic word more sure': Καὶ ἔχομεν βεβαιότερον τὸν προφητικὸν λόγον confirmed by our being 'eye-witnesses of His majesty,' and 'hearing the voice which came from the excellent glory,' 'unto which' —prophetic word; so he styles the holy Scriptures—'ye do well that ye take heed, as unto a light that shineth in a dark place, until the day dawn, and the Day-star arise in your hearts' (2 Pet. i. 19). Let all therefore who desire that day to dawn upon their hearts, wait for it in searching the Scriptures.

11. Thirdly. All who desire an increase of the grace of God are to wait for it in partaking of the Lord's supper; for this also is a direction Himself hath given: 'The same night in which He was betrayed He took bread, and brake it, and said, 'Take, eat. this is My body'; that is, the sacred sign of My body. 'this do in remembrance of Me.' Likewise 'He took the cup, saying, This cup is the new testament,' or covenant, 'in My blood'; the sacred sign of that covenant. 'this do ye in remembrance of Me. For as often as ye eat this bread, and drink this cup, ye do show forth the Lord's death till He come' (1 Cor. xi. 23, &c.): ye openly exhibit the same, by these visible signs, before God, and angels and men; ye manifest your solemn remembrance of His death, till He cometh in the clouds of heaven.

Only 'let a man' first 'examine himself,' whether he understand the nature and design of this holy institution, and whether he really desire to be himself made conformable to the death of Christ; and so, nothing doubting, 'let him eat of that bread, and drink of that cup' (verse 28).

Here, then, the direction first given by our Lord is expressly repeated by the Apostle: 'Let him eat, let him drink' (ἐσθιέτω, πινέτω, both in the imperative mood); words not implying a bare permission only, but a clear, explicit command; a command to all those who either already are filled with peace and joy in believing, or can truly say, 'The remembrance of our sins is grievous unto us, the burden of them is intolerable.'

12. And that this is also an ordinary, stated means of receiving the grace of God, is evident from those words of the Apostle which occur in the preceding chapter: 'The cup of blessing which we bless, is it not the communion,' or *communication:* 'of the blood of Christ? The bread which we break, is it not the communion of the body of Christ?' (I Cor. x. 16). Is not the eating of that bread, and the drinking of that cup, the outward, visible means whereby God conveys into our souls all that spiritual grace, that righteousness, and peace, and joy in the Holy Ghost, which were purchased by the body of Christ once broken, and the blood of Christ once shed for us? Let all, therefore, who truly desire the grace of God, eat of that bread, and drink of that cup.

IV. 1. But as plainly as God hath pointed out the way wherein He will be inquired after, innumerable are the objections which men, wise in their own eyes, have from time to time raised against it. It may be needful to consider a few of these; not because they are of weight in themselves, but because they have so often been used, especially of late years, to turn the lame out of the way; yea, to trouble and subvert those who did run well, till Satan appeared as an angel of light.

The first and chief of these is, 'You cannot use these means (as you call them) without *trusting* in them.' I pray, where is this written? I expect you should show me plain Scripture for your assertion: otherwise I dare not receive it; because I am not convinced that you are wiser than God.

If it really had been as you assert, it is certain Christ must have known it. And if He had known it, He would surely have warned us; He would have revealed it long ago. Therefore, because He has not, because there is no tittle of this in the whole revelation of Jesus Christ, I am as fully assured your assertion is false, as that this revelation is of God.

'However, leave them off for a short time, to see whether you trusted in them or no.' So I am to disobey God, in order to know whether I trust in obeying Him! And do you avow this advice? Do you deliberately teach to 'do evil, that good may come'? O tremble at the sentence of God against such teachers! Their 'damnation is just.'

'Nay, if you are troubled when you leave them off, it is plain you trusted in them.' By no means. If I am troubled when I wilfully disobey God, it is plain His Spirit is still striving with me; but if I am not troubled at wilful sin, it is plain I am given up to a reprobate mind.

But what do you mean by *trusting* in them?'—looking for the blessing of God therein? believing, that if I wait in this way, I shall attain what otherwise I should not? So I do. And so I will, God being my helper, even to my life's end. By the grace of God, I will *thus* trust in them, till the day of my death; that is, I will believe, that whatever God hath promised, He is faithful also to perform. And seeing He hath promised to bless me in this way, I *trust* it shall be according to His word.

2. It has been, secondly, objected, 'This is seeking salvation by works.' Do you know the meaning of the expression you use? What is seeking salvation by works? In the writings of St. Paul, it means, either seeking to be saved by observing the ritual works of the Mosaic law; or expecting salvation for the sake of our own works, by the merit of our own righteousness. But how is either of these implied in my waiting in the way God has ordained, and expecting that He will meet me there, because He has promised so to do?

I do expect that He will fulfil His word, that He will meet and bless me in this way. Yet not for the sake of any works which I have done, nor for the merit of my righteousness; but merely through the merits, and sufferings, and love of His Son, in whom He is always well pleased.

3. It has been vehemently objected, thirdly, 'that Christ is the only means of grace.' I answer, This is mere playing upon words. Explain your term, and the objection vanishes away. When we say, 'Prayer is a means of grace,' we understand a channel through which the grace of God is conveyed. When you say, 'Christ is the means of grace,' you understand the sole price and purchaser of it; or, that 'no man cometh unto the Father, but through Him.' And who denies it? But this is utterly wide of the question.

4. 'But does not the Scripture' (it has been objected, fourthly) 'direct us to *wait* for salvation? Does not David say, "My soul waiteth upon God; for of Him cometh my salvation"? And does not Isaiah teach us the same thing saying, "O Lord, we have waited for Thee"?' All this cannot be denied. Seeing it is the gift of God, we are undoubtedly to *wait* on Him for salvation. But how shall we wait? If God Himself has appointed a way, can you find a better way of waiting for Him? But that He hath appointed a way, hath been shown at large, and also what that way is. The very words of the prophet which you cite, put this out of all question. For the whole sentence runs thus: 'In the way of Thy judgements,' or ordinances, 'O Lord, have we waited for Thee' (Isa. xxvi. 8). And in the very same way did David wait, as his own words abundantly testify: 'I have waited for thy saving health, O Lord, and have kept Thy law. Teach me, O Lord, the way of Thy statutes, and I shall keep it unto the end.'

5. 'Yea,' say some, 'but God has appointed another way: "Stand still, and see the salvation of God."'

Let us examine the Scriptures to which you refer. The first of them, with the context, runs thus,—

'And when Pharaoh drew nigh, the children of Israel lifted up their eyes; and they were sore afraid. And they said unto Moses, Because there were no graves in Egypt, hast thou taken us away to die in the wilderness? And Moses said unto the people, Fear ye not, stand still, and see the salvation of the Lord. And the Lord said unto Moses, Speak unto the children of Israel, that they go forward. But lift thou up thy rod, and stretch out thine hand over the sea, and divide it; and the children of Israel shall go on dry ground through the midst of the sea' (Exod. xiv. 10, &c.).

This was the *salvation of God*, which they *stood still* to see, by *marching forward* with all their might!

The other passage, wherein this expression occurs, stands thus: 'There came some that told Jehoshaphat, saying, There cometh a great multitude against thee from beyond the sea. And Jehoshaphat feared, and set himself to seek the Lord, and proclaimed a fast throughout all Judah. And Judah gathered themselves together to ask help of the Lord: even out of all the cities they came to seek the Lord. And Jehoshaphat stood in the congregation, in the house of the Lord. . . . Then upon Jahaziel came the Spirit of the Lord. And he said, Be not dismayed by reason of this great multitude. To-morrow go ye down against them: ye shall not need to fight in this battle. Set yourselves: stand ye still, and see the salvation of the Lord. And they rose early in the morning, and went forth. And when they began to sing and to praise, the Lord set ambushments against the children of Ammon, Moab, and mount Seir; . . . and every one helped to destroy another' (2 Chron. xx. 2, &c.).

Such was the salvation which the children of Judah saw. But how does all this prove, that we ought not to wait for the grace of God in the means which He hath ordained?

6. I shall mention but one objection more, which, indeed, does not properly belong to this head: nevertheless, because it has been so frequently urged, I may not wholly pass it by.

'Does not St. Paul say, "If ye be dead with Christ, why are ye subject to ordinances"? (Col. ii. 20). Therefore, a Christian, one that is dead with Christ, need not use the ordinances any more.'

So you say, 'If I am a Christian, I am not subject to the ordinances of Christ'! Surely, by the absurdity of this, you must see at the first glance, that the ordinances here mentioned cannot be the ordinances of Christ; that they must needs be the Jewish ordinances, to which it is certain a Christian is no longer subject.

And the same undeniably appears from the words immediately following, 'Touch not, taste not, handle not'; all evidently referring to the ancient ordinances of the Jewish law.

So that this objection is the weakest of all. And, in spite of all, that great truth must stand unshaken,—that all who desire the grace of God are to wait for it in the means which He hath ordained.

V. 1. But this being allowed, that all who desire the grace of God are to wait for it in the means He hath ordained; it may still be inquired, how those means should be used, both as to the order and the manner of using them.

With regard to the former, we may observe, there is a kind of order, wherein God Himself is generally pleased to use these means in bringing a sinner to salvation. A stupid, senseless wretch is going on in his own way, not having God in all his thoughts, when God comes upon him unawares, perhaps by an awakening sermon or conversation, perhaps by some awful providence, or, it may be, by an immediate stroke of His convincing Spirit, without any outward means at all. Having now a desire to flee from the wrath to come, he purposely goes to *hear* how it may be done. If he finds a preacher who speaks to the heart, he is amazed, and begins searching the Scriptures, whether these things are so. The more he *hears* and *reads*, the more convinced he is; and the more he meditates thereon day and night. Perhaps he finds some other book which explains and enforces what he has heard and read in Scripture. And by all these means, the arrows of conviction sink deeper into his soul. He begins also to *talk* of the things of God, which are ever uppermost in his thoughts; yea, and to talk with God; to *pray* to Him; although, through fear and shame, he scarce knows what to say. But whether he can speak or no, he cannot but pray, were it only in 'groans which cannot be uttered.' Yet, being in doubt, whether 'the high and lofty One that inhabiteth eternity' will regard such a sinner as him, he wants to pray with those who know God, with the faithful, in the great congregation. But here he observes others go up to the table of the Lord. He considers, 'Christ has said, "Do this!" How is it that I do not? I am too great a sinner. I am not fit. I am not worthy' After struggling with these scruples awhile, he breaks through. And thus he continues in God's way, in hearing, reading, meditating, praying, and partaking of the Lord's supper, till God, in the manner that pleases Him, speaks to his heart, 'Thy faith hath saved thee. Go in peace.'

2. By observing this order of God, we may learn what means to recommend to any particular soul. If any of these will reach a stupid, careless sinner, it is probably hearing, or conversation. To such, therefore, we might recommend these, if he has ever any thought about salvation. To one who begins to feel the weight of his sins, not only hearing the Word of God, but reading it too, and perhaps other serious books, may be a means of deeper conviction. May you not advise him also to meditate on what he reads, that it may have its full force upon his heart? Yea, and to speak thereof, and not be ashamed, particularly among those who walk in the same path. When trouble and heaviness take hold upon him, should you not then earnestly exhort him to pour out his soul before God; 'always to pray and not to faint'; and when he feels the worthlessness of his own prayers, are you not to work together with God, and remind him of going up into the house of the Lord, and praying with all that fear Him? But if he does this, the dying word of his Lord will soon be brought to his remembrance; a plain intimation, that this is the time when we should second the motions of the blessed Spirit. And thus may we lead him, step by step, through all the means which God has ordained; not according to our own will, but just as the providence and the Spirit of God go before and open the way.

3. Yet, as we find no command in holy writ for any particular order to be observed herein, so neither do the providence and the Spirit of God adhere to any without variation; but the means into which different men are led, and in which they find the blessing of God, are varied, transposed, and combined together, a thousand different ways. Yet still our wisdom is to follow the leadings of His providence and His Spirit; to be guided herein (more especially as to the means wherein we ourselves seek the grace of God), partly by His outward providence, giving us the opportunity of using sometimes one means, sometimes another, partly by our experience, which it is whereby His free Spirit is pleased most to work in our heart. And in the meantime, the sure and general rule for all who groan for the salvation of God

11

is this,—whenever opportunity serves, use all the means which God has ordained; for who knows in which God will meet thee with the grace that bringeth salvation?

4. As to the manner of using them—whereon indeed it wholly depends whether they shall convey any grace at all to the user—it behoves us, first, always to retain a lively sense, that God is above all means. Have a care, therefore, of limiting the Almighty. He doeth whatsoever and whensoever it pleaseth Him. He can convey His grace either in or out of any of the means which He hath appointed. Perhaps He will. 'Who hath known the mind of the Lord? or who hath been His counsellor?' Look, then, every moment for His appearing! Be it at the hour you are employed in His ordinances; or before, or after that hour; or when you are hindered therefrom. He is not hindered; He is always ready, always able, always willing to save. 'It is the Lord: let Him do what seemeth Him good!'

Secondly. Before you use any means, let it be deeply impressed on your soul,—there is no *power* in this. It is, in itself, a poor, dead, empty thing: separate from God, it is a dry leaf, a shadow. Neither is there any *merit* in my using this; nothing intrinsically pleasing to God; nothing whereby I deserve any favour at His hands, no, not a drop of water to cool my tongue. But, because God bids, therefore I do; because He directs me to wait in this way, therefore here I wait for His free mercy, whereof cometh my salvation.

Settle this in your heart, that the *opus operatum*, the mere *work done*, profiteth nothing; that there is no *power* to save but in the Spirit of God, no *merit* but in the blood of Christ; that, consequently, even what God ordains, conveys no grace to the soul, if you trust not in Him alone. On the other hand, he that does truly trust in Him cannot fall short of the grace of God, even though he were cut off from every outward ordinance, though he were shut up in the centre of the earth.

Thirdly. In using all means, seek God alone. In and through every outward thing, look singly to the *power* of His Spirit, and the *merits* of His Son. Beware you do not stick in the *work* itself; if you do, it is all lost labour. Nothing short of God can satisfy your soul. Therefore, eye Him in all, through all, and above all.

Remember also, to use all means *as means*; as ordained, not for their own sake, but in order to the renewal of your soul in righteousness and true holiness. If, therefore, they actually tend to this, well; but, if not, they are dung and dross.

Lastly. After you have used any of these, take care how you value yourself thereon; how you congratulate yourself as having done some great thing. This is turning all into poison. Think, 'If God was not there, what does this avail? Have I not been adding sin to sin? How long? O Lord, save, or I perish! O lay not this sin to my charge!' If God was there, if His love flowed into your heart, you have forgot, as it were, the outward work. You see, you know, you feel, God is all in all. Be abased. Sink down before Him. Give Him all the praise. 'Let God in all things be glorified through Christ Jesus.' Let all your bones cry out, 'My song shall be always of the lovingkindness of the Lord, with my mouth will I ever be telling of Thy truth from one generation to another!'

SERMON XIII

THE CIRCUMCISION OF THE HEART

PREACHED AT

ST. MARY'S, OXFORD, BEFORE THE UNIVERSITY,

ON JANUARY 1, 1733.

Circumcision is that of the heart, in the spirit, and not in the letter.
—ROM. ii. 29.

IT is the melancholy remark of an excellent man, that he who now preaches the most essential duties of Christianity runs the hazard of being esteemed, by a great part of his hearers, 'a setter forth of new doctrines.' Most men have so *lived away* the substance of that religion, the profession whereof they still retain, that no sooner are any of those truths proposed which difference the Spirit of Christ from the spirit of the world, than they cry out, 'Thou bringest strange things to our ears; we would know what these things mean': though he is only preaching to them 'Jesus and the resurrection,' with the necessary consequence of it,—If Christ be risen, ye ought then to die unto the world, and to live wholly unto God.

2. A hard saying this to the natural man, who is alive unto the world, and dead unto God; and one that he will not readily be persuaded to receive as the truth of God, unless it be so qualified in the interpretation, as to have neither use nor significancy left. He 'receiveth not the' words 'of the Spirit of God,' taken in their plain and obvious meaning; 'they are foolishness unto him: neither' indeed 'can he know them, because they are spiritually discerned': they are perceivable only by that spiritual sense, which in him was never yet awakened; for want of which he must reject, as idle fancies of men, what are both the wisdom and the power of God.

3. That 'circumcision is that of the heart, in the spirit, and not in the letter'—that the distinguishing mark of a true follower of Christ, of one who is in a state of acceptance with God, is not either outward circumcision, or baptism, or any other outward form, but a right state of soul, a mind and spirit renewed after the image of Him that created it—is one of those important truths that can only be spiritually discerned. And this the Apostle himself intimates in the next words: 'Whose praise is not of men, but of God.' As if he had said, 'Expect not, whoever thou art, who thus followest thy great Master, that the world, the men who follow Him not, will say, "Well done, good and faithful servant!" Know that the circumcision of the heart, the seal of thy calling, is foolishness with the world. Be content to wait for thy applause till the day of thy Lord's appearing. In that day shalt thou have praise of God, in the great assembly of men and angels.'

I design, first, particularly to inquire, wherein this circumcision of the heart consists; and, secondly, to mention some reflections that naturally arise from such an inquiry.

I. 1. I am, first, to inquire, wherein that circumcision of the heart consists, which will receive the praise of God. In general we may observe, it is that habitual disposition of soul which, in the sacred writings, is termed holiness; and which directly implies, the being cleansed from sin, 'from all filthiness both of flesh and spirit'; and, by consequence, the being endued with those virtues which were also in Christ Jesus; the being so 'renewed in the spirit of our mind,' as to be 'perfect as our Father in heaven is perfect.'

2.   To be more particular: circumcision of heart implies humility, faith, hope, and charity. Humility, a right judgement of ourselves, cleanses our minds from those high conceits of our own perfections, from that undue opinion of our own abilities and attainments, which are the genuine fruit of a corrupted nature. This entirely cuts off that vain thought, 'I am rich, and wise, and have need of nothing'; and convinces us that we are by nature 'wretched and poor, and miserable, and blind, and naked.' It convinces us, that in our best estate we are, of ourselves, all sin and vanity; that confusion, and ignorance, and error reign over our understanding; that unreasonable, earthly, sensual, devilish passions usurp authority over our will; in a word, that there is no whole part in our soul, that all the foundations of our nature are out of course.

3.   At the same time we are convinced, that we are not sufficient of ourselves to help ourselves; that, without the Spirit of God, we can do nothing but add sin to sin; that it is He alone who worketh in us by His almighty power, either to will or do that which is good; it being as impossible for us even to think a good thought, without the supernatural assistance of His Spirit, as to create ourselves, or to renew our whole souls in righteousness and true holiness.

4.   A sure effect of our having formed this right judgement of the sinfulness and helplessness of our nature, is a disregard of that 'honour which cometh of man,' which is usually paid to some supposed excellency in us. He who knows himself, neither desires nor values the applause which he knows he deserves not. It is therefore 'a very small thing with him, to be judged by man's judgement.' He has all reason to think, by comparing what it has said, either for or against him, with what he feels in his own breast, that the world, as well as the god of this world,

was 'a liar from the beginning.' And even as to those who are not of the world; though he would choose, if it were the will of God, that they should account of him as of one desirous to be found a faithful steward of his Lord's goods, if haply this might be a means of enabling him to be of more use to his fellow servants, yet as this is the one end of his wishing for their approbation, so he does not at all rest upon it: for he is assured, that whatever God wills, he can never want instruments to perform; since He is able, even of these stones, to raise up servants to do His pleasure.

5. This is that lowliness of mind, which they have learned of Christ, who follow His example and tread in His steps. And this knowledge of their disease, whereby they are more and more cleansed from one part of it, pride and vanity, disposes them to embrace, with a willing mind, the second thing implied in circumcision of the heart,—that faith which alone is able to make them whole, which is the one medicine given under heaven to heal their sickness.

6. The best guide of the blind, the surest light of them that are in darkness, the most perfect instructor of the foolish, is faith. But it must be such a faith as is 'mighty through God, to the pulling down of strongholds'—to the overturning all the prejudices of corrupt reason, all the false maxims revered among men, all evil customs and habits, all that 'wisdom of the world which is foolishness with God'; as 'casteth down imaginations,' reasonings, 'and every high thing that exalteth itself against the knowledge of God, and bringeth into captivity every thought to the obedience of Christ.'

7. 'All things are possible to him that' thus 'believeth.' 'The eyes of his understanding being enlightened,' he sees what is his calling; even to glorify God, who hath bought him with so high a price, in his body and in his spirit, which now are God's by redemption, as well as by creation. He feels what is 'the exceeding greatness of His power,' who, as He raised up Christ from the dead, so is able to quicken us, dead in sin, 'by His Spirit which dwelleth in us.' 'This is the victory which overcometh the world, even our faith'; that faith, which is not only an unshaken assent to all that God hath revealed in Scripture—

and in particular to those important truths, 'Jesus Christ came into the world to save sinners,' 'He bare our sins in His own body on the tree,' 'He is the propitiation for our sins, and not for ours only, but also for the sins of the whole world,'[1]—but likewise the revelation of Christ in our hearts; a divine evidence or conviction of His love, His free, unmerited love to me a sinner; a sure confidence in His pardoning mercy, wrought in us by the Holy Ghost; a confidence, whereby every true believer is enabled to bear witness, 'I know that my Redeemer liveth,' that I have an 'Advocate with the Father,' and that 'Jesus Christ the righteous' is my Lord, and 'the propitiation for my sins'— I know He hath 'loved me, and given Himself for me'—He hath reconciled me, even me, to God; and I 'have redemption through His blood, even the forgiveness of sins.'

8. Such a faith as this cannot fail to show evidently the power of Him that inspires it, by delivering His children from the yoke of sin, and 'purging their consciences from dead works'; by strengthening them so, that they are no longer constrained to obey sin in the desires thereof; but instead of 'yielding their members unto it, as instruments of unrighteousness,' they now 'yield themselves' entirely 'unto God, as those that are alive from the dead.'

9. Those who are thus by faith born of God have also strong consolation through hope. This is the next thing which the circumcision of the heart implies; even the testimony of their own spirit with the Spirit which witnesses in their hearts that they are the children of God. Indeed it is the same Spirit who works in them that clear and cheerful confidence that their heart is upright toward God; that good assurance, that they now do, through His grace, the things which are acceptable in His sight; that they are now in the path which leadeth to life, and shall, by the mercy of God, endure therein to the end. It is He who giveth them a lively expectation of receiving all good things at God's hand; a joyous prospect of that crown of glory which is reserved in heaven for them. By this anchor a Christian is kept

---

[1] N.B. The following part of this paragraph is now added to the Sermon formerly preached. [The foregoing footnote was added by Wesley to the first edition of the *Sermons*.]

steady in the midst of the waves of this troublesome world, and preserved from striking upon either of those fatal rocks,—presumption or despair. He is neither discouraged by the misconceived severity of his Lord, nor does he 'despise the riches of His goodness.' He neither apprehends the difficulties of the race set before him to be greater than he has strength to conquer, nor expects them to be so little as to yield in the conquest till he has put forth all his strength. The experience he already has in the Christian warfare, as it assures him his 'labour is not in vain' if 'whatever his hand findeth to do, he doeth it with his might'; so it forbids his entertaining so vain a thought, as that he can otherwise gain any advantage; as that any virtue can be shown, any praise attained, by faint hearts and feeble hands; or, indeed, by any but those who pursue the same course with the great Apostle of the Gentiles. 'I,' says he, 'so run, not as uncertainly; so fight I, not as one that beateth the air: but I keep under my body, and bring it into subjection; lest, by any means, when I have preached to others, I myself should be a castaway.'

10. By the same discipline is every good soldier of Christ to inure himself to endure hardship. Confirmed and strengthened by this, he will be able not only to renounce the works of darkness, but every appetite too, and every affection, which is not subject to the law of God. For 'every one,' saith St. John, 'who hath this hope, purifieth himself even as He is pure.' It is his daily care, by the grace of God in Christ, and through the blood of the covenant, to purge the inmost recesses of his soul from the lusts that before possessed and defiled it; from uncleanness, and envy, and malice, and wrath; from every passion and temper that is after the flesh, that either springs from or cherishes his native corruption: as well knowing, that he whose very body is the temple of God, ought to admit into it nothing common or unclean; and that holiness becometh that house for ever, where the Spirit of holiness vouchsafes to dwell.

11. Yet lackest thou one thing, whosoever thou art, that to a deep humility, and a steadfast faith, hast joined a lively hope, and thereby in a good measure cleansed thy heart from its inbred pollution. If thou wilt be perfect, add to all these, charity; add love, and thou hast the circumcision of the heart. 'Love is the

fulfilling of the law, the end of the commandment.' Very excellent things are spoken of love; it is the essence, the spirit, the life of all virtue. It is not only the first and great command, but it is all the commandments in one. 'Whatsoever things are just, whatsoever things are pure, whatsoever things are amiable,' or honourable; 'if there be any virtue, if there be any praise,' they are all comprised in this one word,—love. In this is perfection, and glory, and happiness. The royal law of heaven and earth is this, 'Thou shalt love the Lord thy God with all thy heart, and with all thy soul, and with all thy mind, and with all thy strength.'

12. Not that this forbids us to love anything besides God: it implies that we love our brother also. Nor yet does it forbid us (as some have strangely imagined) to take pleasure in anything but God. To suppose this, is to suppose the Fountain of holiness is directly the author of sin; since He has inseparably annexed pleasure to the use of those creatures which are necessary to sustain the life He has given us. This, therefore, can never be the meaning of His command. What the real sense of it is, both our blessed Lord and His Apostles tell us too frequently, and too plainly, to be misunderstood. They all with one mouth bear witness, that the true meaning of those several declarations, 'The Lord thy God is one Lord'; 'Thou shalt have no other gods but Me'; 'Thou shalt love the Lord thy God with all thy strength'; 'Thou shalt cleave unto Him'; 'The desire of thy soul shall be to His name,' is no other than this: The one perfect Good shall be your one ultimate end. One thing shall ye desire for its own sake,—the fruition of Him that is All in all. One happiness shall ye propose to your souls, even an union with Him that made them; the having 'fellowship with the Father and the Son'; the being joined to the Lord in one Spirit. One design you are to pursue to the end of time,—the enjoyment of God in time and in eternity. Desire other things, so far as they tend to this. Love the creature, as it leads to the Creator. But in every step you take, be this the glorious point that terminates your view. Let every affection, and thought, and word, and work, be subordinate to this. Whatever ye desire or fear, whatever ye seek or shun, whatever ye think, speak or do, be it in order to your

happiness in God, the sole End, as well as Source, of your being.

13. Have no end, no ultimate end, but God. Thus our Lord: 'One thing is needful'; and if thine eye be singly fixed on this one thing, 'thy whole body shall be full of light.' Thus St. Paul: 'This one thing I do; I press toward the mark, for the prize of the high calling in Christ Jesus.' Thus St. James: 'Cleanse your hands, ye sinners; and purify your hearts, ye double-minded.' Thus St. John: 'Love not the world, neither the things that are in the world. For all that is in the world, the lust of the flesh, the lust of the eye, and the pride of life, is not of the Father, but is of the world.' The seeking happiness in what gratifies either the desire of the flesh, by agreeably striking upon the outward senses; the desire of the eye, of the imagination, by its novelty, greatness, or beauty; or the pride of life, whether by pomp, grandeur, power, or, the usual consequence of them, applause and admiration,— 'is not of the Father,' cometh not from, neither is approved by, the Father of spirits: 'but of the world'; it is the distinguishing mark of those who will not have Him to reign over them.

II. 1. Thus have I particularly inquired, what that circumcision of heart is, which will obtain the praise of God. I am, in the second place, to mention some reflections that naturally arise from such an inquiry, as a plain rule whereby every man may judge of himself, whether he be of the world or of God.

And, first, it is clear from what has been said, that no man has a title to the praise of God, unless his heart is circumcised by humility; unless he is little, and base, and vile in his own eyes; unless he is deeply convinced of that inbred 'corruption of his nature,' 'whereby he is very far gone from original righteousness,' being prone to all evil, averse to all good, corrupt and abominable; having a 'carnal mind which is enmity against God, and is not subject to the law of God, nor indeed can be'; unless he continually feels in his inmost soul, that without the Spirit of God resting upon him, he can neither think, nor desire, nor speak, nor act anything good, or well-pleasing in His sight.

No man, I say, has a title to the praise of God, till he feels his want of God; nor indeed, till he seeketh that 'honour which cometh of God' only; and neither desires nor pursues that which cometh of man, unless so far only as it tends to this.

2. Another truth, which naturally follows from what has been said, is, that none shall obtain the honour that cometh of God, unless his heart be circumcised by faith; even a 'faith of the operation of God'; unless, refusing to be any longer led by his senses, appetites, or passions, or even by that blind leader of the blind, so idolized by the world, natural reason, he lives and walks by faith; directs every step, as 'seeing Him that is invisible'; 'looks not at the things that are seen, which are temporal, but at the things that are not seen, which are eternal'; and governs all his desires, designs, and thoughts, all his actions and conversations, as one who is entered in within the veil, where Jesus sits at the right hand of God.

3. It were to be wished, that they were better acquainted with this faith who employ much of their time and pains in laying another foundation; in grounding religion on the eternal *fitness* of things, on the intrinsic *excellence* of virtue, and the *beauty* of actions flowing from it; on the *reasons*, as they term them, of good and evil, and the *relations*, of beings to each other. Either these accounts of the grounds of Christian duty coincide with the scriptural, or not. If they do, why are well-meaning men perplexed, and drawn from the weightier matters of the law, by a cloud of terms, whereby the easiest truths are explained into obscurity? If they are not, then it behoves them to consider who is the author of this new doctrine; whether he is likely to be an angel from heaven, who preacheth another gospel than that of Christ Jesus; though, if he were, God, not we, hath pronounced his sentence: 'Let him be accursed.'

4. Our gospel, as it knows no other foundation of good works than faith, or of faith than Christ, so it clearly informs us, we are not His disciples while we either deny Him to be the Author, or His Spirit to be the Inspirer and Perfecter, both of our faith and works. 'If any man have not the Spirit of Christ, he is none of his.' He alone can quicken those who are dead unto God, can breathe into them the breath of Christian life, and so prevent, accompany, and follow them with His grace, as to bring their good desires to good effect. And, 'as many as are

thus led by the Spirit of God, they are the sons of God.' This is God's short and plain account of true religion and virtue; and 'other foundation can no man lay.'

5. From what has been said, we may, thirdly, learn, that none is truly 'led by the Spirit,' unless that 'Spirit bear witness with his spirit, that he is a child of God'; unless he see the prize and the crown before him, and 'rejoice in hope of the glory of God,' So greatly have they erred who have taught that, in serving God, we ought not to have a view to our own happiness! Nay, but we are often and expressly taught of God, to have 'respect unto the recompense of reward'; to balance the toil with the 'joy set before us,' these 'light afflictions' with that 'exceeding weight of glory.' Yea, we are 'aliens to the covenant of promise,' we are 'without God in the world,' until God, 'of His abundant mercy, hath begotten us again unto a living hope of the inheritance incorruptible, undefiled, and that fadeth not away.'

6. But if these things are so, it is high time for those persons to deal faithfully with their own souls, who are so far from finding in themselves this joyful assurance that they fulfil the terms, and shall obtain the promises, of that covenant, as to quarrel with the covenant itself, and blaspheme the terms of it; to complain, they are too severe; and that no man ever did or shall live up to them. What is this but to reproach God, as if He were a hard Master, requiring of His servants more than He enables them to perform?—as if He had mocked the helpless works of His hands, by binding them to impossibilities; by commanding them to overcome ,where neither their own strength nor His grace was sufficient for them?

7. These blasphemers might almost persuade those to imagine themselves guiltless, who, in the contrary extreme, hope to fulfil the commands of God without taking any pains at all. Vain hope! that a child of Adam should ever expect to see the kingdom of Christ and of God without striving, without *agonizing*, first 'to enter in at the strait gate'; that one who was 'conceived and born in sin,' and whose 'inward parts are very wickedness,' should once entertain a thought of being 'purified as his Lord is pure,' unless he tread in His steps ,and 'take up his cross daily,' unless he 'cut off his right hand,' and 'pluck out the right eye, and

cast it from him'; that he should ever dream of shaking off his old opinions, passions, tempers, of being 'sanctified throughout in spirit, soul, and body,' without a constant and continued course of general self-denial!

8. What less than this can we possibly infer from the above-cited words of St. Paul, who, living 'in infirmities, in reproaches, in necessities, in persecutions, in distresses' for Christ's sake; who, being full of 'signs and wonders, and mighty deeds,' who, having been 'caught up into the third heaven,'—yet reckoned, as a late author strongly expresses it, that all his virtues would be insecure, and even his salvation in danger, without this constant self-denial? 'So run I,' says he, 'not as uncertainly; so fight I, not as one that beateth the air': by which he plainly teaches us, that he who does not thus run, who does not thus deny himself daily, does run uncertainly, and fighteth to as little purpose as he that 'beateth the air.'

9. To as little purpose does he talk of 'fighting the fight of faith,' as vainly hope to attain the crown of incorruption (as we may, lastly, infer from the preceding observations), whose heart is not circumcised by love. Love, cutting off both the lust of the flesh, the lust of the eye, and the pride of life—engaging the whole man, body, soul, and spirit, in the ardent pursuit of that one object—is so essential to a child of God, that without it, whosoever liveth is counted dead before Him. 'Though I speak with the tongues of men and of angels, and have not love, I am as sounding brass, or a tinkling cymbal. Though I have the gift of prophecy, and understand all mysteries, and all knowledge; and though I have all faith, so as to remove mountains, and have not love, I am nothing.' Nay, 'though I give all my goods to feed the poor, and my body to be burned, and have not love, it profiteth me nothing.'

10. Here, then, is the sum of the perfect law; this is the true circumcision of the heart. Let the spirit return to God that gave it, with the whole train of its affections. 'Unto the place from whence all the rivers came,' thither let them flow again. Other sacrifices from us He would not; but the living sacrifice of the heart He hath chosen. Let it be continually offered up to God through Christ, in flames of holy love. And let no creature be

for want of observing, that the latter as well as the former part of these words were spoken by Moses himself to the people of Israel, and that concerning the covenant which then was (Deut. xxx. 11, 12, 14). But it is the covenant of grace, which God, through Christ, hath established with men in all ages (as well before and under the Jewish dispensation, as since God was manifest in the flesh), which St. Paul here opposes to the covenant of works, made with Adam while in paradise, but commonly supposed to be the only covenant which God had made with man, particularly by those Jews of whom the Apostle writes.

2. Of these it was that he so affectionately speaks in the beginning of this chapter: 'My heart's desire and prayer to God for Israel is, that they may be saved. For I bear them record, that they have a zeal for God, but not according to knowledge. For they being ignorant of God's righteousness' (of the justification that flows from His mere grace and mercy, freely forgiving our sins through the Son of His love, through the redemption which is in Jesus) 'and seeking to establish their own righteousness' (their own holiness, antecedent to faith in 'Him that justifieth the ungodly,' as the ground of their pardon and acceptance), 'have not submitted themselves unto the righteousness of God,' and consequently, seek death in the error of their life.

3. They were ignorant that 'Christ is the end of the law for righteousness to every one that believeth,'—that, by the oblation of Himself once offered, He had put an end to the first law or covenant (which, indeed, was not given by God to Moses, but to Adam in his state of innocence), the strict tenor whereof, without any abatement, was, 'Do this, and live'; and, at the same time, purchased for us that better covenant, 'Believe, and live'; believe, and thou shalt be saved; now saved, both from the guilt and power of sin, and, of consequence, from the wages of it.

4. And how many are equally ingorant now, even among those who are called by the name of Christ! How many who have now 'a zeal for God,' yet have it not 'according to knowledge'; but are still seeking 'to establish their own righteousness' as the ground of their pardon and acceptance; and therefore vehemently refuse to 'submit themselves unto the righteousness of God'! Surely my heart's desire, and prayer to God for you

2. Perhaps is it not needful to give a definition of this, seeing the Scripture gives none. But as the question is of the deepest concern to every child of man; since, 'except a man be born again' born of the Spirit, 'he cannot see the kingdom of God'; I propose to lay down the marks of it in the plainest manner, just as I find them laid down in Scripture.

I. 1. The first of these, and the foundation of all the rest, is faith. So St. Paul, 'Ye are all the children of God by faith in Christ Jesus' (Gal. iii. 26). So St. John, 'To them gave He power' (ἐξουσίαν, *right* or *privilege:* it might rather be translated) 'to become the sons of God, even to them that believe on His name; which were born,' when they believed, 'not of blood, nor of the will of the flesh,' not by natural generation, 'nor of the will of man,' like those children adopted by men, in whom no inward change is thereby wrought, 'but of God' (John i. 12, 13). And again, in his General Epistle, 'Whosoever believeth that Jesus is the Christ is born of God' (1 John v. 1).

2. But it is not a barely notional or speculative faith that is here spoken of by the Apostles. It is not a bare assent to this proposition, 'Jesus is the Christ'; nor indeed to all the propositions contained in our creed, or in the Old and New Testament. It is not merely an assent to any or all these credible things, as credible. To say this, were to say (which who could hear?) that the devils were born of God; for they have this faith. They, trembling believe, both that Jesus is the Christ, and that all Scripture, having been given by inspiration of God, is true as God is true. It is not only an assent to divine truth, upon the testimony of God, or upon the evidence of miracles; for *they* also heard the words of His mouth, and knew Him to be a faithful and true witness. They could not but receive the testimony He gave, both of Himself, and of the Father which sent Him. They saw likewise the mighty works which He did, and thence believed that He 'came forth from God.' Yet, notwithstanding this faith, they are still 'reserved in chains of darkness unto the judgement of the great day.'

3. For all this is no more than a dead faith. The true, living, Christian faith, which whosoever hath is born of God, is not

only assent, an act of the understanding; but a disposition, which God hath wrought in his heart; 'a sure trust and confidence in God, that, through the merits of Christ, his sins are forgiven, and he reconciled to the favour of God.' This implies, that a man first renounce himself; that, in order to be 'found in Christ,' to be accepted through Him, he totally rejects all 'confidence in the flesh'; that, 'having nothing to pay,' having no trust in his own works or righteousness of any kind, he comes to God as a lost, miserable, self-destroyed, self-condemned, undone, helpless sinner; as one whose mouth is utterly stopped, and who is altogether 'guilty before God.' Such a sense of sin (commonly called 'despair' by those who speak evil of the things they know not), together with a full conviction, such as no words can express, that of Christ only cometh our salvation, and an earnest desire of that salvation, must precede a living faith, a trust in Him, who 'for us paid our ransom by His death, and fulfilled the law in His life.' This faith then, whereby we are born of God, is 'not only a belief of all the articles of our faith, but also a true confidence of the mercy of God through our Lord Jesus Christ.'

4. An immediate and constant fruit of this faith whereby we are born of God, a fruit which can in no wise be separated from it, no, not for an hour, is power over sin,—power over outward sin of every kind; over every evil word and work; for wheresoever the blood of Christ is thus applied, it 'purgeth the conscience from dead works,'—and over inward sin; for it purifieth the heart from every unholy desire and temper. This fruit of faith St. Paul has largely described, in the sixth chapter of his Epistle to the Romans. 'How shall we,' saith he, 'who' by faith 'are dead to sin, live any longer therein.' 'Our old man is crucified with Christ, that the body of sin might be destroyed, that henceforth we should not serve sin.' 'Likewise, reckon ye yourselves to be dead unto sin, but alive unto God through Jesus Christ our Lord. Let not sin therefore reign' even 'in your mortal body,' 'but yield yourselves unto God, as those that are alive from the dead.' 'For sin shall not have dominion over you. . . . God be thanked, that ye were the servants of sin . . . but being made free,'—the plain meaning is, God be

thanked, that though ye were, in time past, the servants of sin, yet now, 'being free from sin, ye are become the servants of righteousness.'

5. The same invaluable privilege of the sons of God is as strongly asserted by St. John; particularly with regard to the former branch of it, namely, power over outward sin. After he had been crying out, as one astonished at the depth of the riches of the goodness of God, 'Behold, what manner of love the Father hath bestowed upon us, that we should be called the sons of God! Beloved, now are we the sons of God; and it doth not yet appear what we shall be: but we know that, when He shall appear, we shall be like Him; for we shall see Him as He is' (1 John iii. 1, &c.),—he soon adds, 'Whosoever is born of God doth not commit sin; for His seed remaineth in him: and he cannot sin, because he is born of God' (verse 9). But some men will say, 'True: whosoever is born of God doth not commit sin *habitually.*' *Habitually!* Whence is that? I read it not. It is not written in the Book. God plainly saith, 'He doth not commit sin'; and thou addest, *habitually!* Who art thou that *mendest* the oracles of God?—that 'addest to the words of this book'? Beware, I beseech thee, lest God 'add to thee all the plagues that are written therein'! especially when the comment thou addest is such as quite swallows up the text. so that by this μεθοδεία πλάνης, this artful method of deceiving, the precious promise is utterly lost; by this κυβεία ἀνθρώπων, this tricking and shuffling of men, the Word of God is made of none effect. O beware, thou that thus takest from the words of this book, that, taking away the whole meaning and spirit from them, leavest only what may indeed be termed a dead letter, lest God take away thy part out of the book of life!

6. Suffer we the Apostle to interpret his own words, by the whole tenor of his discourse. In the fifth verse of this chapter, he had said, 'Ye know that He,' Christ, 'was manifested to take away our sins; and in Him is no sin.' What is the inference he draws from this? Whosoever abideth in Him sinneth not: whosoever sinneth hath not seen Him, neither known Him' (1 John iii. 6). To his enforcement of this important doctrine, he premises an highly necessary caution: 'Little children, let no

12

man deceive you' (verse 7); for many will endeavour to so do; to persuade you that you may be unrighteous, that you may commit sin, and yet be children of God: 'He that doeth righteousness is righteous, even as He is righteous. He that committeth sin is of the devil; for the devil sinneth from the beginning.' Then follows, 'Whosoever is born of God doth not commit sin; for His seed remaineth in him: and he cannot sin, because he is born of God.' 'In this,' adds the Apostle, 'the children of God are manifest, and the children of the devil.' By this plain mark (the committing or not committing sin) are they distinguished from each other. To the same effect are those words in his fifth chapter: 'We know that whosoever is born of God sinneth not; but he that is begotten of God keepeth himself, and that wicked one toucheth him not' (verse 18).

7. Another fruit of this living faith is peace. For, 'being justified by faith,' having all our sins blotted out, 'we have peace with God through our Lord Jesus Christ' (Rom. v. 1). This indeed our Lord Himself, the night before His death, solemnly bequeathed to all His followers. 'Peace,' saith He, 'I leave with you' (you who 'believe in God,' and 'believe also in Me'); 'My peace I give unto you: not as the world giveth, give I unto you Let not your heart be troubled, neither let it be afraid' (John xiv. 27). And again: 'These things have I spoken unto you, that in Me ye might have peace' (John xvi. 33). This is that 'peace of God which passeth all understanding,' that serenity of soul which it hath not entered into the heart of a natural man to conceive, and which it is not possible for even the spiritual man to utter. And it is a peace which all the powers of earth and hell are unable to take from him. Waves and storms beat upon it, but they shake it not; for it is founded upon a rock. It keepeth the hearts and minds of the children of God, at all times and in all places. Whether they are in ease or in pain, in sickness or health, in abundance or want, they are happy in God. In every state they have learned to be content, yea, to give thanks unto God through Christ Jesus; being well assured, that 'whatsoever is, is best,' because it is His will concerning them: so that in all the vicissitudes of life their 'heart standeth fast, believing in the Lord.'

II. 1. A second scriptural mark of those who are born of God, is hope. Thus St. Peter, speaking to all the children of God who were then scattered abroad, saith, 'Blessed be the God and Father of our Lord Jesus Christ, which according to His abundant mercy, hath begotten us again unto a lively hope' (1 Pet. i. 3). Ἐλπίδα ζῶσαν, *a lively* or *living* hope, saith the Apostle; because there is also a *dead* hope, as well as a dead faith; a hope which is not from God, but from the enemy of God and man;—as evidently appears by its fruits; for, as it is the offspring of pride, so it is the parent of every evil word and work; whereas, every man that hath in him this living hope, is 'holy as He that calleth him is holy'; every man that can truly say to his brethren in Christ, 'Beloved, now are we the sons of God, and we shall see Him as He is,' 'purifieth himself, even as He is pure.'

2. This hope implies, first, the testimony of our own spirit, or conscience, that we walk 'in simplicity and godly sincerity'; secondly, the testimony of the Spirit of God, 'bearing witness with,' or to, 'our spirit, that we are the children of God,' 'and if children, then heirs, heirs of God, and joint-heirs with Christ.'

3. Let us well observe what is here taught us by God Himself, touching this glorious privilege of His children. Who is it that is here said to bear witness? Not our spirit only, but another; even the Spirit of God: He it is who 'beareth witness with our spirit.' What is it He beareth witness of? 'That we are the children of God; and if children, then heirs; heirs of God, and joint-heirs with Christ' (Rom. viii. 16, 17); 'if so be that we suffer with Him,' if we deny ourselves, if we take up our cross daily, if we cheerfully endure persecution or reproach for His sake, 'that we may also be glorified together.' And in whom doth the Spirit of God bear this witness? In all who are the children of God. By this very argument does the Apostle prove, in the preceding verses, that they are so: 'As many,' saith he, 'as are led by the Spirit of God, they are the sons of God.' 'For ye have not received the spirit of bondage again to fear; but ye have received the Spirit of adoption, whereby we cry, Abba, Father!' It follows, 'the Spirit itself beareth witness with our spirit, that we are the children of God' (Rom. viii. 14-16).

4. The variation of the phrase in the fifteenth verse is worthy our observation: 'Ye have received the Spirit of adoption, whereby we cry, Abba, Father!' *Ye*, as many as are the sons of God, have, in virtue of your sonship, received that self-same Spirit of adoption, whereby *we* cry, Abba, Father. *We*, the apostles, prophets, teachers (for so the word may not improperly be understood), *we*, through whom you have believed, the 'ministers of Christ, and stewards of the mysteries of God.' As *we* and *you* have one Lord, so we have one Spirit: as we have one faith, so we have one hope also. We and you are sealed with one 'Spirit of promise,' the earnest of *your* and of *our* inheritance: the same Spirit bearing witness with your and with our spirit, 'that we are the children of God.'

5. And thus is the Scripture fulfilled, 'Blessed are they that mourn; for they shall be comforted.' For it is easy to believe, that though sorrow may precede this witness of God's Spirit with our spirit (indeed *must*, in some degree, while we groan under fear, and a sense of the wrath of God abiding on us); yet, as soon as any man feeleth it in himself, his 'sorrow is turned into joy.' Whatsoever his pain may have been before; yet, as soon as that 'hour is come, he remembereth the anguish no more, for joy' that he is born of God. It may be, many of *you* have now sorrow, because you are 'aliens from the commonwealth of Israel'; because you are conscious to yourselves that you have not this Spirit; that you are 'without hope and without God in the world. But when the Comforter is come, 'then your heart shall rejoice': yea, 'your joy shall be full,' and 'that joy no man taketh from you' (John xvi. 22). 'We joy in God,' will ye say, 'through our Lord Jesus Christ, by whom we have now received the atonement'; 'by whom we have access into this grace, this state of grace, of favour, or reconciliation with God, 'wherein we stand, and rejoice in hope of the glory of God' (Rom. v. 2). 'Ye,' saith St. Peter, whom God hath 'begotten again unto a lively hope, are kept by the power of God unto, salvation: wherein ye greatly rejoice, though now for a season, if need be, ye are in heaviness through manifold temptations; that the trial of your faith may be found unto praise, and honour, and glory at the appearing of Jesus Christ; in whom, though

now ye see Him not, ye rejoice with joy unspeakable and full of glory' (1 Pet. i. 5, &c.). Unspeakable indeed! It is not for the tongue of man to describe this joy in the Holy Ghost. It is 'the hidden manna, which no man knoweth, save he that receiveth it.' But this we know, it not only remains, but overflows, in the depth of affliction. 'Are the consolations of God small' with His children, when all earthly comforts fail? Not so. But when sufferings most abound, the consolations of His Spirit do much more abound; insomuch that the sons of God 'laugh at destruction when it cometh'; at want, pain, hell, and the grave; as knowing Him who 'hath the keys of death and hell,' and will shortly 'cast them into the bottomless pit'; as hearing even now the great voice out of heaven, saying, 'Behold, the tabernacle of God is with men, and He will dwell with them, and they shall be His people, and God Himself shall be with them, and be their God. And God shall wipe away all tears from their eyes; and there shall be no more death, neither sorrow, nor crying, neither shall there be any more pain; for the former things are passed away' (Rev. xxi. 3, 4).

III. 1. A third scriptural mark of those who are born of God, and the greatest of all, is love; even 'the love of God shed abroad in their hearts by the Holy Ghost which is given unto them' (Rom. v. 5). 'Because they are sons, God hath sent forth the Spirit of His Son in their hearts, crying, Abba, Father!' (Gal. iv. 6). By this Spirit, continually looking up to God as their reconciled and loving Father, they cry to Him for their daily bread, for all things needful, whether for their souls or bodies. They continually pour out their hearts before Him, knowing 'they have the petitions which they ask of Him' (1 John v. 15). Their delight is in Him. He is the joy of their heart; their 'shield,' and their 'exceeding great reward.' The desire of their soul is toward Him; it is their 'meat and drink to do His will'; and they are 'satisfied as with marrow and fatness, while their mouth praiseth Him with joyful lips' (Ps. lxiii. 5).

2. And, in this sense also, 'every one who loveth Him that begat, loveth Him that is begotten of Him' (1 John v. 1). His spirit rejoiceth in God his Saviour. He 'loveth the Lord Jesus

Christ in sincerity.' He is so 'joined unto the Lord,' as to be one spirit. His soul hangeth upon Him, and chooseth Him as altogether lovely, 'the chiefest among ten thousand.' He knoweth, he feeleth what that means, 'My beloved is mine, and I am His' (Cant. ii. 16). 'Thou art fairer than the children of men; full of grace are Thy lips, because God hath anointed Thee forever!' (Ps. xlv. 2).

3. The necessary fruit of this love of God is the love of our neighbour; of every soul which God hath made; not excepting our enemies; not excepting those who are now 'despitefully using and persecuting us'—a love whereby we love every man as ourselves; as we love our own souls. Nay, our Lord has expressed it still more strongly, teaching us to 'love one another, even as He hath loved us.' Accordingly, the commandment written in the hearts of all those that love God is no other than this, 'As I have loved you, so love ye one another.' Now, 'herein perceive we the love of God, in that He laid down His life for us' (1 John iii. 16). 'We ought,' then, as the Apostle justly infers, 'to lay down our lives for the brethren.' If we feel ourselves ready to do this, then do we truly love our neighbour. Then 'we know that we have passed from death unto life, because we' thus 'love the brethren' (1 John iii. 14). 'Hereby know we' that we are born of God, that we 'dwell in Him, and He in us, because He hath given us of His' loving 'Spirit' (iv. 13). For 'love is of God; and every one that 'thus 'loveth is born of God, and knoweth God' (iv. 7).

4. But some may possibly ask, 'Does not the Apostle say, "This is the love of God, that we keep His commandments"?' (1 John v. 3). Yea, and this is the love of our neighbour also, in the same sense as it is the love of God. But what would you infer from hence? that the keeping the outward commandments is all that is implied in loving God with all your heart, with all your mind, and soul, and strength, and in loving your neighbour as yourself? that the love of God is not an affection of the soul? but merely an *outward service*? and that the love of our neighbour is not a disposition of heart, but barely a course of *outward works*? To mention so wild an interpretation of the Apostle's words, is sufficiently to confute it. The plain indisputable meaning of the

text is—this is the sign or proof of the love of God, of our keeping the first and great commandment, to keep all the rest of His commandments. For true love, if it be once shed abroad in our heart, will constrain us so to do; since, whosoever loves God with all his heart, cannot but serve Him with all his strength.

5. A second fruit, then, of the love of God (so far as it can be distinguished from it) is universal obedience to Him we love, and conformity to His will; obedience to all the commands of God, internal and external; obedience of the heart and of the life: in every temper, and in all manner of conversation. And one of the tempers most obviously implied herein is, the being 'zealous of good works'; the hungering and thirsting to do good, in every possible kind, unto all men; the rejoicing to 'spend and be spent for them,' for every child of man; not looking for any recompense in this world, but only in the resurrection of the just.

IV. 1. Thus have I plainly laid down those marks of the new birth which I find laid down in Scripture. Thus doth God Himself answer that weighty question, What is it to be born of God? Such, if the appeal be made to the oracles of God, is 'every one that is born of the Spirit.' This it is, in the judgement of the Spirit of God, to be a son or a child of God: it is, so to *believe* in God, through Christ, as 'not to commit sin,' and to enjoy at all times, and in all places, that 'peace of God which passeth all understanding.' It is, so to *hope* in God through the Son of His love, as to have not only the 'testimony of a good conscience,' but also the Spirit of God 'bearing witness with your spirits, that ye are the children of God'; whence cannot but spring the rejoicing in Him through whom ye 'have received the atonement.' It is, so to *love* God, who hath thus loved you, as you never did love any creature: so that ye are constrained to love all men as yourselves; with a love not only ever burning in your hearts, but flaming out in all your actions and conversations, and making your whole life one 'labour of love,' one continued obedience to those commands, 'Be ye merciful, as God is merciful'; 'Be ye holy, as I the Lord am holy'; 'Be ye perfect, as your Father which is in heaven is perfect.'

2. Who then are ye that are *thus* born of God? Ye 'know the things which are given to you of God.' Ye well know that ye are the children of God, and 'can assure your hearts before Him.' And every one of you who has observed these words cannot but feel, and know of a truth, whether at this hour (answer to God, and not to man!) you are thus a child of God or no. The question is not, what you was made in baptism (do not evade); but, what are you now? Is the Spirit of adoption now in your heart? To your own heart let the appeal be made. I ask not, whether you *were* born of water and of the Spirit; but are you *now* the temple of the Holy Ghost which dwelleth in you? I allow you were 'circumcised with the circumcision of Christ' (as St. Paul emphatically terms baptism); but does the Spirit of Christ and of glory *now* rest upon you? Else, 'your circumcision is become uncircumcision.'

3. Say not then in your heart, 'I *was once* baptized, therefore I *am now* a child of God.' Alas, that consequence will by no means hold. How many are the baptized gluttons and drunkards, the baptized liars and common swearers, the baptized railers and evil-speakers, the baptized whoremongers, thieves, extortioners? What think you? Are these now the children of God? Verily, I say unto you, whosoever you are, unto whom any one of the preceding characters belong, 'Ye are of your father the devil, and the works of your father ye do.' Unto you I call, in the name of Him whom you crucify afresh, and in His words to your circumcised predecessors, 'Ye serpents, ye generation of vipers, how can ye escape the damnation of hell?'

4. How, indeed, except ye be born again? For ye are now dead in trespasses and sins. To say, then, that ye cannot be born again, that there is no new birth but in baptism, is to seal you all under damnation, to consign you to hell, without help, without hope. And perhaps some may think this just and right. In their zeal for the Lord of Hosts, they may say, 'Yea, cut off the sinners, the Amalekites! Let these Gibeonites be utterly destroyed! They deserve no less.' No, nor I, nor you. Mine and your desert, as well as theirs, is hell! and it is mere mercy, free, undeserved mercy, that *we* are not now in unquenchable fire. You will say, 'But we are washed'; we were born again 'of water

and of the Spirit.' So *were* they: this, therefore, hinders not at all, but that ye may *now* be even as they. Know ye not, that 'what is highly esteemed of men is an abomination in the sight of God'? Come forth, ye 'saints of the world,' ye that are honoured of men, and see who will cast the first stone at them, at these wretches not fit to live upon the earth, these common harlots, adulterers, murderers. Only learn ye first what that meaneth, 'He that hateth his brother is a murderer' (1 John iii. 15). 'He that looketh on a woman to lust after her hath committed adultery with her already in his heart' (Matt. v. 28). 'Ye adulterers and adulteresses, know ye not that the friendship of the world is enmity with God?' (Jas. iv. 4).

5. 'Verily, verily, I say unto you, ye' also 'must be born again.' 'Except ye' also 'be born again, ye cannot see the kingdom of God.' Lean no more on the staff of that broken reed, that ye *were* born again in baptism. Who denies that ye were then made children of God, and heirs of the kingdom of heaven? But, notwithstanding this, ye are now children of the devil. Therefore, ye must be born again. And let not Satan put it into your heart to cavil at a word, when the thing is clear. Ye have heard what are the marks of the children of God: all ye who have them not on your souls, baptized or unbaptized, must needs receive them, or without doubt ye will perish everlastingly. And if ye have been baptized, your only hope is this,—that those who were made the children of God by baptism, but are now the children of the devil, may yet again receive 'power to become the sons of God'; that they may receive again what they have lost, even the 'Spirit of adoption, crying in their hearts, Abba, Father!'

Amen, Lord Jesus! May every one who prepareth his heart yet again to seek Thy face receive again that Spirit of adoption, and cry out, 'Abba, Father!' Let him now again have power so to believe in Thy name as to become a child of God; as to know and feel he hath 'redemption in Thy blood, even the forgiveness of sins'; and that he 'cannot commit sin, because he is born of God.' Let him be now 'begotten again unto a living hope,' so as to 'purify himself as Thou art pure'; and 'because he is a son,' let the Spirit of love and of glory rest upon him, cleansing him 'from all filthiness of flesh and spirit,' and teaching him to 'perfect holiness in the fear of God'!

SERMON XV

THE GREAT PRIVILEGE OF THOSE THAT ARE BORN OF GOD

Whosoever is born of God doth not commit sin.—1 JOHN iii. 9.

IT has been frequently supposed, that the being born of God was all one with the being justified; that the new birth and justification were only different expressions, denoting the same thing: it being certain, on the one hand, that whoever is justified is also born of God; and, on the other, that whoever is born of God is also justified; yea, that both these gifts of God are given to every believer in one and the same moment. In one point of time his sins are blotted out, and he is born again of God.

2. But though it be allowed, that justification and the new birth are, in point of time, inseparable from each other, yet are they easily distinguished, as being not the same, but things of a widely different nature. Justification implies only a relative, the new birth a real, change. God in justifying us does something *for* us; in begetting us again, He does the work *in* us. The former changes our outward relation to God, so that of enemies we become children; by the latter our inmost souls are changed, so that of sinners we become saints. The one restores us to the favour, the other to the image, of God. The one is the taking away the guilt, the other the taking away the power, of sin: so that, although they are joined together in point of time, yet are they of wholly distinct natures.

3. The not discerning this, the not observing the wide difference there is between being justified and being born again, has occasioned exceeding great confusion of thought in many who have treated on this subject; particularly when they have

attempted to explain this great privilege of the children of God; to show how 'whosoever is born of God doth not commit sin.'

4. In order to apprehend this clearly, it may be necessary, first, to consider what is the proper meaning of that expression, 'Whosoever is born of God'; and, secondly, to inquire in what sense he 'doth not commit sin.'

I. 1. First, we are to consider, what is the proper meaning of that expression, 'Whosoever is born of God.' And, in general, from all the passages of holy writ wherein this expression, 'the being born of God,' occurs, we may learn that it implies not barely the being baptized, or any outward change whatever; but a vast inward change, a change wrought in the soul, by the operation of the Holy Ghost; a change in the whole manner of our existence; for, from the moment we are born of God, we live in quite another manner than we did before; we are, as it were, in another world.

2. The ground and reason of the expression is easy to be understood. When we undergo this great change, we may, with much propriety, be said to be born again, because there is so near a resemblance between the circumstances of the natural and of the spiritual birth; so that to consider the circumstances of the natural birth is the most easy way to understand the spiritual.

3. The child which is not yet born subsists indeed by the air, as does everything which has life; but *feels* it not, nor anything else, unless in a very dull and imperfect manner. It *hears* little, if at all; the organs of hearing being as yet closed up. It *sees* nothing; having its eyes fast shut, and being surrounded with utter darkness. There are, it may be, some faint beginnings of life, when the time of its birth draws nigh, and some motion consequent thereon, whereby it is distinguished from a mere mass of matter; but it has no *senses*; all these avenues of the soul are hitherto quite shut up. Of consequence, it has scarce any intercourse with this visible world; nor any knowledge, conception, or idea, of the things that occur therein.

4. The reason why he that is not yet born is wholly a stranger to the visible world, is not because it is afar off (it is very nigh, it surrounds him on every side); but, partly, because he has not

those senses, they are not yet opened in his soul, whereby alone it is possible to hold commerce with the material world; and partly, because so thick a veil is cast between, through which he can discern nothing.

5. But no sooner is the child born into the world, than he exists in a quite different manner. He now *feels* the air with which he is surrounded, and which pours into him from every side, as fast as he alternately breathes it back, to sustain the flame of life: and hence springs a continual increase of strength, of motion, and of sensation; all the bodily senses being now awakened, and furnished with their proper objects.

His eyes are now opened to perceive the light, which, silently flowing in upon them, discovers not only itself, but an infinite variety of things, with which before he was wholly unacquainted His ears are unclosed, and sounds rush in with endless diversity Every sense is employed upon such objects as are peculiarly suitable to it; and by these inlets the soul, having an open intercourse with the visible world, acquires more and more knowledge of sensible things, of all the things which are under the sun.

6. So it is with him that is born of God. Before that great change is wrought, although he subsists by Him, in whom all that have life 'live, and move, and have their being,' yet he is not *sensible* of God; he does not *feel*, he has no inward consciousness of His presence. He does not perceive that divine breath of life, without which he cannot subsist a moment: nor is he sensible of any of the things of God; they make no impression upon his soul. God is continually calling to him from on high, but he heareth not; his ears are shut, so that the 'voice of the charmer' is lost to him, 'charm he never so wisely.' He seeth not the things of the Spirit of God; the eyes of his understanding being closed, and utter darkness covering his whole soul, surrounding him on every side. It is true he may have some faint dawnings of life, some small beginnings of spiritual motion; but as yet he has no spiritual senses capable of discerning spiritual objects; consequently, he 'discerneth not the things of the Spirit of God; he cannot know them, because they are spiritually discerned.'

7. Hence he has scarce any knowledge of the invisible world, as he has scarce any intercourse with it. Not that it is afar off: no: he is in the midst of it; it encompasses him round about. The *other world*, as we usually term it, is not far from every one of us: it is above, and beneath, and on every side. Only the natural man discerneth it not; partly, because he has no spiritual senses, whereby alone we can discern the things of God; partly, because so thick a veil is interposed as he knows not how to penetrate.

8. But when he is born of God, born of the Spirit, how is the manner of his existence changed! His whole soul is now sensible of God, and he can say, by sure experience, 'Thou art about my bed, and about my path'; I feel Thee in all my ways: 'Thou besettest me behind and before, and layest Thy hand upon me.' The spirit or breath of God is immediately inspired, breathed into the new-born soul; and the same breath which comes from, returns to, God: as it is continually received by faith, so it is continually rendered back by love, by prayer, and praise, and thanksgiving; love, and praise, and prayer being the breath of every soul which is truly born of God. And by this new kind of spiritual respiration, spiritual life is not only sustained, but increased day by day, together with spiritual strength, and motion, and sensation, all the senses of the soul being now awake, and capable of discerning spiritual good and evil.

9. 'The eyes of his understanding' are now 'open,' and he 'seeth Him that is invisible.' He sees what is 'the exceeding greatness of His power' and of His love towards them that believe. He sees that God is merciful to him a sinner; that he is reconciled through the Son of His love. He clearly perceives both the pardoning love of God, and all His 'exceeding great and precious promises.' 'God, who commanded the light to shine out of darkness, hath shined,' and doth shine, 'in his heart,' to enlighten him with 'the knowledge of the glory of God in the face of Jesus Christ.' All the darkness is now passed away, and he abides in the light of God's countenance.

10. His ears are now opened, and the voice of God no longer calls in vain. He hears and obeys the heavenly calling; he knows the voice of his Shepherd. All his spiritual senses being now

awakened, he has a clear intercourse with the invisible world; and hence he knows more and more of the things which before it could not 'enter in to his heart to conceive.' He now knows what the peace of God is; what is joy in the Holy Ghost; what the love of God which is shed abroad in the hearts of them that believe in Him through Christ Jesus. Thus the veil being removed which before intercepted the light and voice, the knowledge and love of God, he who is born of the Spirit dwelleth in love, 'dwelleth in God, and God in him.'

II. 1. Having considered the meaning of that expression, 'Whosoever is born of God,' it remains, in the second place, to inquire, in what sense he 'doth not commit sin.'

Now one who is so born of God, as hath been above described, who continually receives into his soul the breath of life from God, the gracious influence of His Spirit, and continually renders it back; one who thus believes and loves, who by faith perceives the continual actings of God upon his spirit, and, by a kind of spiritual reaction returns the grace he receives, in unceasing love, and praise, and prayer; not only doth not commit sin, while he thus keepeth himself, but so long as this 'seed remaineth in him, he cannot sin, because he is born of God.'

2. By sin, I here understand outward sin, according to the plain, common acceptation of the word; an actual, voluntary transgression of the law; of the revealed, written law of God; of any commandment of God, acknowledged to be such at the time that it is transgressed. But 'whosoever is born of God,' while he abideth in faith and love, and in the spirit of prayer and thanksgiving, not only doth not, but cannot, thus commit sin. So long as he thus believeth in God through Christ, and loves Him, and is pouring out his heart before Him, he cannot voluntarily transgress any command of God, either by speaking or acting what he knows God hath forbidden· so long that seed which remaineth in him, that loving, praying, thankful faith, compels him to refrain from whatsoever he knows to be an abomination in the sight of God.

3. But here a difficulty will immediately occur; and one that to many has appeared insuperable, and induced them to deny

the plain assertion of the Apostle, and give up the privilege of the children of God.

It is plain, in fact, that those whom we cannot deny to have been truly born of God (the Spirit of God having given us in His Word this infallible testimony concerning them), nevertheless, not only could, but did, commit sin, even gross, outward sin. They did transgress the plain, known laws of God, speaking or acting what they knew He had forbidden.

4. Thus David was unquestionably born of God or ever he was anointed king over Israel. He knew in whom he had believed; 'he was strong in faith, giving glory to God.' 'The Lord,' saith he, 'is my Shepherd; therefore can I lack nothing. He shall feed me in green pastures, and lead me forth beside the waters of comfort. Yea, though I walk through the valley of the shadow of death, I will fear no evil; for Thou art with me' (Ps. xxiii. 1, &c.). He was filled with love; such as often constrained him to cry out, 'I will love Thee, O Lord, my strength. The Lord is my stony rock, and my defence; . . . the horn also of my salvation, and my refuge' (Ps. xviii. 1, 2). He was a man of prayer; pouring out his soul before God in all circumstances of life; and abundant in praises and thanksgiving; 'Thy praise,' saith he, 'shall be ever in my mouth' (Ps. xxxiv. 1): 'Thou art my God, and I will thank Thee: Thou art my God, and I will praise Thee' (Ps. cxviii. 28). And yet such a child of God could and did commit sin; yea, the horrid sins of adultery and murder.

5. And even after the Holy Ghost was more largely given, after 'life and immortality were brought to light by the gospel,' we want not instances of the same melancholy kind, which were also doubtless written for our instruction. Thus he who (probably from his selling all that he had, and bringing the price for the relief of his poor brethren) was by the Apostles themselves 'surnamed Barnabas,' that is, 'the son of consolation' (Acts iv. 36, 37); who was so honoured at Antioch, as to be selected with Saul out of all the disciples, to carry their relief unto the brethren in Judea, (Acts xi. 29, 30); this Barnabas, who, at his return from Judea, was, by the peculiar direction of the Holy Ghost, solemnly 'separated from the other prophets and teachers, for the work whereunto God had called him' (xiii. 1-4), even to accompany

the great Apostle among the Gentiles, and to be his fellow labourer in every place;—nevertheless, was afterwards so sharp (xv. 35, 39), in his contention with St. Paul (because he 'thought it not good to take with them John,' in his visiting the brethren a second time, 'who had departed from them from Pamphylia, and went not with them to the work') that he himself also departed from the work; that he 'took John, and sailed unto Cyprus' (xv. 39); forsaking him to whom he had been in so immediate a manner joined by the Holy Ghost.

6. An instance more astonishing than both these is given by St. Paul in his Epistle to the Galatians. When Peter, the aged, the zealous, the first of the apostles, one of the three most highly favoured by his Lord, 'was come to Antioch, I withstood him to the face, because he was to be blamed. For before that certain came from James, he did eat with the Gentiles'—the Heathens converted to the Christian faith—as having been peculiarly taught of God, that he 'should not call any man common or unclean' (Acts x. 28). 'But when they were come, he separated himself, fearing them which were of the circumcision. And the other Jews dissembled likewise with him; insomuch that Barnabas also was carried away with their dissimulation. But when I saw that they walked not uprightly according to the truth of the gospel, I said unto Peter before them all, If thou, being a Jew, livest after the manner of the Gentiles'—not regarding the ceremonial law of Moses—'why compellest thou the Gentiles to live as do the Jews'? (Gal. ii. 11, &c.). Here is also plain, undeniable sin committed by óne who was undoubtedly born of God. But how can this be reconciled with the assertion of St. John, if taken in the obvious literal meaning, that 'whosoever is born of God, doth not commit sin'?

7. I answer, What has been long observed is this: so long as 'he that is born of God keepeth himself' (which he is able to do by the grace of God), 'the wicked one toucheth him not': but if he keepeth not himself, if he bideth not in the faith, he may commit sin even as another man.

It is easy therefore to understand, how any of these children of God might be moved from his own steadfastness, and yet the great truth of God, declared by the Apostle, remain steadfast and unshaken. He did not 'keep himself,' by that grace of God which was sufficient for him. He fell, step by step, first, into negative, inward sin, not 'stirring up the gift of God which was in him,' not 'watching unto prayer,' not 'pressing on to the mark of the prize of his high calling': then into positive inward sin, inclining to wickedness with his heart, giving way to some evil desire or temper: next, he lost his faith, his sight of a pardoning God, and consequently his love of God; and, being then weak and like another man, he was capable of committing even outward sin.

8. To explain this by a particular instance: David was born of God, and saw God by faith. He loved God in sincerity. He could truly say, 'Whom have I in heaven but Thee? and there is none upon earth, 'neither person nor thing, 'that I desire in comparison of Thee.' But still there remained in his heart that corruption of nature, which is the seed of all evil.

'He was walking upon the roof of his house' (2 Sam. xi. 2), probably praising the God whom his soul loved, when he looked down and saw Bathsheba. He felt a temptation; a thought which tended to evil. The Spirit of God did not fail to convince him of this. He doubtless heard and knew the warning voice; but he yielded in some measure to the thought, and the temptation began to prevail over him. Hereby his spirit was sullied; he saw God still; but it was more dimly than before. He loved God still; but not in the same degree; not with the same strength and ardour of affection. Yet God checked him again, though His Spirit was grieved; and His voice, though fainter and fainter, still whispered, 'Sin lieth at the door; look unto Me and be thou saved.' But he would not hear; he looked again, not unto God, but unto the forbidden object; till nature was superior to grace, and kindled lust in his soul.

The eye of his mind was now closed again, and God vanished out of his sight. Faith, the divine, supernatural intercourse with God, and the love of God, ceased together: he then rushed on as a horse into the battle, and knowingly committed the outward sin.

9. You see the unquestionable progress from grace to sin: thus it goes on, from step to step. (1) The divine seed of loving,

conquering faith, remains in him that is born of God. 'He keepeth himself,' by the grace of God, and 'cannot commit sin.' (2) A temptation arises; whether from the world, the flesh, or the devil, it matters not. (3) The Spirit of God gives him warning that sin is near, and bids him more abundantly watch unto prayer. (4) He gives way, in some degree, to the temptation, which now begins to grow pleasing to him. (5) The Holy Spirit is grieved; his faith is weakened; and his love of God grows cold. (6) The Spirit reproves him more sharply, and saith, 'This is the way; walk thou in it.' (7) He turns away from the painful voice of God, and listens to the pleasing voice of the tempter. (8) Evil desire begins and spreads in his soul, till faith and love vanish away: he is then capable of committing outward sin, the power of the Lord being departed from him.

10. To explain this by another instance: the Apostle Peter was full of faith and of the Holy Ghost; and hereby keeping himself, he had a conscience void of offence toward God and toward man

Walking thus in simplicity and godly sincerity, 'before that certain came from James, he did eat with the Gentiles,' knowing that what God had cleansed was not common or unclean.

But 'when they were come,' a temptation arose in his heart, 'to fear those of the circumcision' (the Jewish converts, who were zealous for circumcision and the other rites of the Mosaic law), and regard the favour and praise of these men, more than the praise of God.

He was warned by the Spirit that sin was near: nevertheless, he yielded to it in some degree, even to sinful fear of man, and his faith and love were proportionably weakened.

God reproved him again for giving place to the devil. Yet he would not hearken to the voice of his Shepherd; but gave himself up to that slavish fear, and thereby quenched the Spirit.

Then God disappeared, and faith and love being extinct, he committed the outward sin: *walking not uprightly:* not 'according to the truth of the gospel,' he 'separated himself' from his Christian brethren, and by his evil example, if not advice also, 'compelled even the Gentiles to live after the manner of the Jews'; to entangle themselves again with that 'yoke of bondage,' from which 'Christ had set them free.'

Thus it is unquestionably true, that he who is born of God, keeping himself, doth not, cannot commit sin; and yet, if he keepeth not himself, he may commit all manner of sin with greediness.

III. 1. From the preceding considerations we may learn, first, to give a clear and incontestable answer to a question which has frequently perplexed many who were sincere of heart: 'Does sin precede or follow the loss of faith? Does a child of God first commit sin, and thereby lose his faith? Or does he lose his faith first, before he can commit sin!'

I answer, Some sin of omission, at least, must necessarily precede the loss of faith; some inward sin: but the loss of faith must precede the committing outward sin.

The more any believer examines his own heart, the more will he be convinced of this: that faith, working by love, excludes both inward and outward sin from a soul watching unto prayer; that nevertheless we are even then liable to temptation, particularly to the sin that did easily beset us; that if the loving eye of the soul be steadily fixed on God, the temptation soon vanishes away: but if not, if we are ἐξελκόμενοι (as the Apostle James speaks, chap. i. 14), *drawn out* of God by our *own desire:* and δελεαζόμενοι, *caught by the bait* of present or promised pleasures; then that desire, conceived in us, brings forth sin; and having by that inward sin destroyed our faith, it casts us headlong into the snare of the devil, so that we may commit any outward sin whatever.

2. From what has been said, we may learn, secondly, what the life of God in the soul of a believer is; wherein it properly consists; and what is immediately and necessarily implied therein. It immediately and necessarily implies the continual inspiration of God's Holy Spirit; God's breathing into the soul, and the soul's breathing back what it first receives from God; a continual action of God upon the soul, and a reaction of the soul upon God; an unceasing presence of God, the loving, pardoning God, manifested to the heart, and perceived by faith; and an unceasing return of love, praise and prayer, offering up all the thoughts of our hearts, all the words of our tongues, all the works

of our hands, all our body, soul, and spirit, to be a holy sacrifice, acceptable unto God in Christ Jesus.

3. And hence we may, thirdly, infer the absolute necessity of this reaction of the soul (whatsoever it be called), in order to the continuance of the divine life therein. For it plainly appears, God does not continue to act upon the soul, unless the soul reacts upon God. He prevents us indeed with the blessings of His goodness. He first loves us, and manifests Himself unto us. While we are yet afar off, He calls us to Himself, and shines upon our hearts. But if we do not then love Him who first loved us; if we will not hearken to His voice; if we turn our eye away from Him, and will not attend to the light which He pours in upon us; His Spirit will not always strive: He will gradually withdraw, and leave us to the darkness of our own hearts. He will not continue to breathe into our soul, unless our soul breathes toward Him again; unless our love, and prayer, and thanksgiving return to Him, a sacrifice wherewith He is well pleased.

4. Let us learn, lastly, to follow that direction of the great Apostle, 'Be not high-minded, but fear.' Let us fear sin, more than death or hell. Let us have a jealous (though not painful) fear, lest we should lean to our own deceitful hearts. 'Let him that standeth take heed lest he fall.' Even he who now standeth fast in the grace of God, in the faith that overcometh the world, may nevertheless fall into inward sin, and thereby 'make shipwreck of his faith.' And how easily then will outward sin regain its dominion over him! Thou, therefore, O man of God! watch always, that thou mayest always hear the voice of God! Watch, that thou mayest pray without ceasing, at all times, and in all places, pouring out thy heart before Him! So shalt thou always believe, and always love, and never commit sin.

SERMON XVI

UPON OUR LORD'S SERMON ON THE MOUNT

DISCOURSE I

And seeing the multitudes, He went up into a mountain: and when He was set,
*   His disciples came unto Him:*
And He opened His mouth, and taught them, saying:
Blessed are the poor in spirit, for theirs is the kingdom of heaven.
Blessed are they that mourn, for they shall be comforted.

—MATT. v. 1-4

OUR Lord had now gone 'about all Galilee' (Matt. iv. 23), beginning at the time 'when John was cast into prison' (verse 12), not only 'teaching in their synagogues, and preaching the gospel of the kindgom,' but likewise 'healing all manner of sickness and all manner of disease among the people.' It was a natural consequence of this, that 'there followed Him great multitudes from Galilee, and from Decapolis, and from Jerusalem, and from Judea, and from the region beyond Jordan' (verse 25). 'And seeing the multitudes,' whom no synagogue could contain, even had there been any at hand, 'He went up into a mountain,' where there was room for all that came unto Him from every quarter. 'And when He was set,' as the manner of the Jews was, 'His disciples came unto Him. And He opened His mouth' (an expression denoting the beginning of a solemn discourse), 'and taught them, saying. . . '

2. Let us observe, who it is that is here speaking, that we may take heed how we hear. It is the Lord of heaven and earth, the Creator of all; who, as such, has a right to dispose of all His creatures; the Lord our Governor, whose kingdom is from everlasting, and ruleth over all; the great Lawgiver, who can well enforce all His laws, being 'able to save and to destroy,' yea, to punish with 'everlasting destruction from His presence and from the glory of His power' It is the eternal Wisdom of the Father,

I. 1. First, I am to show, who those are that 'are in Christ
Jesus.' And are they not those who believe in His name? those
who are 'found in Him, not having their own righteousness,
but the righteousness which is of God by faith'? These, 'who
have redemption through His blood,' are properly said to be
in Him; for they dwell in Christ, and Christ in them. They are
joined unto the Lord in one Spirit. They are ingrafted into Him
as branches into the vine. They are united, as members to their
head, in a manner which words cannot express, nor could it
before enter into their hearts to conceive.

2. Now 'whosoever abideth in Him, sinneth not'; 'walketh
not after the flesh.' The flesh, in the usual language of St. Paul,
signifies corrupt ntaure. In this sense he uses the word, writing
to the Galatians, 'The works of the flesh are manifest' (Gal. v. 19);
and a little before, 'Walk in the Spirit, and ye shall not fulfil the
lust' (or desire) 'of the flesh' (ver. 16). To prove which, namely,
that those who 'walk by the Spirit' do not 'fulfil the lusts of the
flesh,' he immediately adds, 'For the flesh lusteth against the
Spirit, and the Spirit lusteth against the flesh (for these are contrary to each other); that ye may not do the things which ye
would.' So the words are literally translated (ἵνα μὴ ἃ ἂν θέλητε,
ταῦτα ποιῆτε), not, 'So that ye cannot do the things that ye
would'; as if the flesh overcame the Spirit: a translation which
hath not only nothing to do with the original text of the Apostle,
but likewise makes his whole argument nothing worth; yea,
asserts just the reverse of what he is proving.

3. They who are of Christ, who abide in Him, 'have crucified
the flesh with its affections and lusts.' They abstain from all
those works of the flesh; from 'adultery and fornication'; from
'uncleanness and lasciviousness'; from 'idolatry, witchcraft,
hatred, variance'; from 'emulations, wrath, strife, sedition,
heresies, envyings, murders, drunkenness, revellings'; from every
design, and word, and work, to which the corruption of nature
leads. Although they feel the root of bitterness in themselves,
yet are they endued with power from on high to trample it
continually under foot, so that it cannot 'spring up to trouble
them'; insomuch that every fresh assault which they undergo
only gives them fresh occasion of praise, of crying out, 'Thanks

Word of God, and teach unwary souls to seek death in the error of their life.

4. And hence we are naturally led to observe, whom it is that He is here teaching. Not the Apostles alone: if so, He had no need to have gone up into the mountain. A room in the house of Matthew, or any of His disciples, would have contained the twelve. Nor does it in any wise appear that the disciples who came unto Him were the twelve only. Οἱ μαθηταὶ αὐτοῦ, without any force put upon the expression, may be understood of all who desired to learn of Him. But to put this out of all question, to make it undeniably plain that where it is said, 'He opened His mouth and taught them,' the word *them* includes all the multitudes who went up with Him into the mountain, we need only observe the concluding verses of the seventh chapter: 'And it came to pass, when Jesus had ended these sayings, the multitudes (οἱ ὄχλοι) were astonished at His doctrine,' or teaching; 'for He taught them,' the multitudes, 'as one having authority, and not as the Scribes.'

Nor was it only those multitudes who were with Him on the mount, to whom He now taught the way of salvation: but all the children of men; the whole race of mankind; the children that were yet unborn; all the generations to come, even to the end of the world, who should ever hear the words of this life.

5. And this all men allow, with regard to some parts of the ensuing discourse. No man, for instance, denies that what is said of poverty of spirit relates to all mankind. But many have supposed, that other parts concerned only the Apostles, or the first Christians, or the ministers of Christ; and were never designed for the generality of men, who, consequently, have nothing at all to do with them.

But may we not justly inquire, who told them this, that some parts of this discourse concerned only the Apostles, or the Christians of the apostolic age, or the ministers of Christ? Bare assertions are not a sufficient proof to establish a point of so great importance. Has then our Lord Himself taught us, that some parts of His discourse do not concern all mankind? Without doubt, had it been so, He would have told us; He could not have omitted so necessary an information. But has He told us so?

Where? In the discourse itself? No: here is not the least intimation of it. Has He said so elsewhere? in any other of His discourses? Not one word so much as glancing this way can we find in anything He ever spoke, either to the multitudes, or to His disciples. Has any one of the Apostles, or other inspired writers, left such an instruction upon record? No such thing. No assertion of this kind is to be found in all the oracles of God. Who then are the men who are so much wiser than God—wise so far above that is written?

6. Perhaps they will say, that the reason of the thing requires such a restriction to be made. If it does, it must be on one of these two accounts; because, without such a restriction, the discourse would either be apparently absurd, or would contradict some other scripture. But this is not the case. It will plainly appear, when we come to examine the several particulars, that there is no absurdity at all in applying all which our Lord hath here delivered to all mankind. Neither will it infer any contradiction to anything else He has delivered, nor to any other scripture whatever. Nay, it will farther appear, that either all the parts of this discourse are to be applied to men in general, or no part; seeing they are all connected together, all joined as the stones in an arch, of which you cannot take one away, without destroying the whole fabric.

7. We may, lastly, observe, how our Lord teaches here. And surely, as at all times, so particularly at this, He speaks 'as never man spake.' Not as the holy men of old; although they also spoke 'as they were moved by the Holy Ghost.' Not as Peter, or James, or John, or Paul: they were indeed wise master-builders in His church; but still in this, in the degrees of heavenly wisdom, the servant is not as his Lord. No, nor even as Himself at any other time, or on any other occasion. It does not appear, that it was ever His design, at any other time or place, to lay down at once the whole plan of His religion; to give us a full prospect of Christianity; to describe at large the nature of that holiness without which no man shall see the Lord. Particular branches of this He has indeed described, on a thousand different occasions; but never, besides here, did He give, of set purpose, a general view of the whole. Nay, we have nothing else of this kind

in all the Bible; unless one should except that short sketch of holiness delivered by God in those ten words or commandments to Moses, on Mount Sinai. But even here how wide a difference is there between one and the other! 'Even that which was made glorious had no glory in this respect, by reason of the glory that excelleth' (2 Cor. iii. 10).

8. Above all, with what amazing love does the Son of God here reveal His Father's will to man! He does not bring us again 'to the mount that burned with fire, nor unto blackness, and darkness, and tempest.' He does not speak as when He 'thundered out of heaven'; when the Highest 'gave His thunder, hailstones, and coals of fire.' He now addresses us with His still, small voice,—'Blessed,' or happy, 'are the poor in spirit.' Happy are the mourners; the meek; those that hunger after righteousness; the merciful; the pure in heart: happy in the end, and in the way; happy in this life, and in life everlasting! As if He had said, 'Who is he that lusteth to live, and would fain see good days? Behold, I show you the thing which your soul longeth for! See the way you have so long sought in vain; the way of pleasantness; the path to calm, joyous peace, to heaven below, and heaven above!'

9. At the same time, with what authority does He teach! Well might they say, 'Not as the Scribes.' Observe the manner (but it cannot be expressed in words), the air, with which He speaks! Not as Moses, the servant of God; not as Abraham, His friend; not as any of the prophets; nor as any of the sons of men It is something more than human; more than can agree to any created being. It speaks the Creator of all; A God, a God appears! Yea, 'Ο 'ΩN, the Being of beings, JEHOVAH, the Self-existent, the Supreme, the God who is over all blessed for ever.

10. This divine discourse, delivered in the most excellent method, every subsequent part illustrating those that precede, is commonly, and not improperly, divided into three principal branches: the first contained in the fifth, the second in the sixth, and the third in the seventh chapter. In the first, the sum of all true religion is laid down in eight particulars, which are explained, and guarded against the false glosses of man, in the following parts of the fifth chapter. In the second are rules for

that right intention which we are to preserve in all our outward actions, unmixed with worldly desires, or anxious cares for even the necessaries of life. In the third are cautions against the main hindrances of religion, closed with an application of the whole.

I. 1. Our Lord first lays down the sum of all true religion in eight particulars, which He explains and guards against the false glosses of men, to the end of the fifth chapter.

Some have supposed that He designed, in these, to point out the several stages of the Christian course—the steps which a Christian successively takes in his journey to the promised land; others, that all the particulars here set down belong at all times to every Christian. And why may we not allow both the one and the other? What inconsistency is there between them? It is undoubtedly true, that both poverty of spirit, and every other temper which is here mentioned, are at all times found, in a greater or less degree, in every real Christian. And it is equally true, that real Christianity always begins in poverty of spirit, and goes on in the order here set down, till the 'man of God is made perfect.' We begin at the lowest of these gifts of God; yet so as not to relinquish this, when we are called of God to come up higher; but 'whereunto we have already attained, we hold fast,' while we press on to what is yet before, to the highest blessings of God in Christ Jesus.

2. The foundation of all is poverty of spirit: here, therefore, our Lord begins: 'Blessed,' saith He, 'are the poor in spirit; for theirs is the kingdom of heaaven.'

It may not improbably be supposed, that our Lord looked on those who were round about Him, and, observing that not many rich were there, but rather the poor of the world, took occasion from thence to make a transition from temporal to spiritual things. 'Blessed,' saith He (or *happy*—so the word should be rendered, both in this and the following verses), 'are the poor in spirit.' He does not say, they that are poor as to outward circumstances, it being not impossible that some of these may be as far from happiness as a monarch upon his throne; but 'the poor in spirit'—they who, whatever their outward circumstances are, have that disposition of heart which is the first step to all real, substantial happiness, either in this world, or that which is to come.

3. Some have judged, that by the poor in spirit here, are meant those who love poverty; those who are free from covetousness, from the love of money; who fear, rather than desire, riches. Perhaps they have been induced so to judge, by wholly confining their thoughts to the very term; or by considering that weighty observation of St. Paul, that 'the love of money is the root of all evil.' And hence many have wholly divested themselves, not only of riches, but of all worldly goods. Hence also the vows of voluntary poverty seem to have arisen in the Romish Church; it being supposed that so eminent a degree of this fundamental grace must be a large step toward the 'kingdom of heaven.'

But these do not seem to have observed, first, that the expression of St. Paul must be understood with some restriction; otherwise it is not true; for the love of money is not the root, the sole root, of all evil. There are a thousand other roots of evil in the world, as sad experience daily shows. His meaning can only be, it is the root of very many evils; perhaps of more than any single vice besides. Secondly, that this sense of the expression, 'poor in spirit,' will by no means suit our Lord's present design, which is to lay a general foundation whereon the whole fabric of Christianity may be built; a design which would be in no wise answered by guarding against one particular vice: so that, if even this were supposed to be one part of His meaning, it could not possibly be the whole. Thirdly, that it cannot be supposed to be any part of His meaning, unless we charge Him with manifest tautology; seeing, if poverty of spirit were only freedom from covetousness, from the love of money, or the desire of riches, it would coincide with what He afterwards mentions, it would be only a branch of purity of heart.

4. Who then are 'the poor in spirit'? Without question, the humble; they who know themselves; who are convinced of sin; those to whom God hath given that first repentance, which is previous to faith in Christ.

One of these can no longer say, 'I am rich, and increased in goods, and have need of nothing'; as now knowing, that he is 'wretched, and poor, and miserable, and blind, and naked.' He is convinced that he is spiritually poor indeed; having no spiritual good abiding in him. 'In me,' saith he, 'dwelleth no good thing,' but whatsoever is evil and abominable. He has a deep sense of the loathsome leprosy of sin, which he brought with him from his mother's womb, which overspreads his whole soul, and totally corrupts every power and faculty thereof. He sees more and more of the evil tempers which spring from that evil root: the pride and haughtiness of spirit, the constant bias to think of himself more highly than he ought to think; the vanity, the thirst after the esteem or honour that cometh from men; the hatred or envy, the jealousy or revenge, the anger, malice, or bitterness; the inbred enmity both against God and man, which appears in ten thousand shapes; the love of the world, the self-will, the foolish and hurtful desires, which cleave to his inmost soul. He is conscious how deeply he has offended by his tongue; if not by profane, immodest, untrue, or unkind words, yet by discourse which was not 'good to the use of edifying,' not 'meet to minister grace to the hearers,' which, consequently, was all corrupt in God's account, and grievous to His Holy Spirit. His evil works are now likewise ever in his sight: if he tells them, they are more than he is able to express. He may as well think to number the drops of rain, the sands of the sea, or the days of eternity.

5. His guilt is now also before his face: he knows the punishment he has deserved, were it only on account of his carnal mind, the entire, universal corruption of his nature: how much more, on account of all his evil desires and thoughts, of all his sinful words and actions! He cannot doubt for a moment, but the least of these deserves the damnation of hell—'the worm that dieth not, and the fire that never shall be quenched.' Above all, the guilt of 'not believing on the name of the only-begotten Son of God' lies heavy upon him. How, saith he, shall I escape, who 'neglect so great salvation'! 'He that believeth not is condemned already,' and 'the wrath of God abideth on him.'

6. But what shall he give in exchange for his soul, which is forfeited to the just vengeance of God? 'Wherewithal shall he

come before the Lord?' How shall he pay Him that he oweth? Were he from this moment to perform the most perfect obedience to every command of God, this would make no amends for a single sin, for any one act of past disobedience; seeing he owes God all the service he is able to perform, from this moment to all eternity: could he pay this, it would make no manner of amends for what he ought to have done before. He sees himself therefore utterly helpless with regard to atoning for his past sins; utterly unable to make any amends to God, to pay any ransom for his own soul.

But if God would forgive him all that is past, on this one condition, that he should sin no more; that for the time to come he should entirely and constantly obey all His commands; he well knows that this would profit him nothing, being a condition he could never perform. He knows and feels that he is not able to obey even the outward commands of God; seeing these cannot be obeyed while his heart remains in its natural sinfulness and corruption; inasmuch as an evil tree cannot bring forth good fruit. But he cannot cleanse a sinful heart: with men this is impossible: so that he is utterly at a loss even how to begin walking in the path of God's commandments. He knows not how to get one step forward in the way. Encompassed with sin, and sorrow, and fear, and finding no way to escape, he can only cry out, 'Lord, save, or I perish!'

7. Poverty of spirit then, as it implies the first step we take in running the race which is set before us, is a just sense of our inward and outward sins, and of our guilt and helplessness. This some have monstrously styled 'the virtue of humility'; thus teaching us to be proud of knowing we deserve damnation! But our Lord's expression is quite of another kind; conveying no idea to the hearer, but that of mere want, of naked sin, of helpless guilt and misery.

8. The great apostle, where he endeavours to bring sinners to God, speaks in a manner just answerable to this. 'The wrath of God,' saith he, 'is revealed from heaven against all ungodliness and unrighteousness of men' (Rom. i. 18, &c.); a charge which he immediately fixes on the heathen world, and thereby proves they are under the wrath of God. He next shows that the Jews

were no better than they, and were therefore under the same condemnation; and all this, not in order to their attaining 'the noble virtue of humility,' but 'that every mouth might be stopped, and all the world become guilty before God.'

He proceeds to show, that they were helpless as well as guilty; which is the plain purport of all those expressions: 'Therefore by the deeds of the law there shall no flesh be justified'; 'But now the righteousness of God, which is by faith of Jesus Christ, without the law, is manifested'; 'We conclude, that a man is justified by faith, without the deeds of the law,'—expressions all tending to the same point, even to 'hide pride from man'; to humble him to the dust, without teaching him to reflect upon his humility as a virtue; to inspire him with that full, piercing conviction of his utter sinfulness, guilt, and helplessness, which casts the sinner, stripped of all, lost and undone, on his strong Helper, Jesus Christ the righteous.

9. One cannot but observe here, that Christianity begins just where heathen morality ends; poverty of spirit, conviction of sin, the renouncing ourselves, the not having our own right-eousness (the very first point in the religion of Jesus Christ), leaving all pagan religion behind. This was ever hid from the wise men of this world; insomuch that the whole Roman language, even with all the improvements of the Augustan age, does not afford so much as a name for *humility* (the word from whence we borrow this, as is well known, bearing in Latin a quite different meaning); no, nor was one found in all the copious language of Greece, till it was made by the great Apostle.

10. O that we may feel what they were not able to express! Sinner, awake! Know thyself! Know and feel, that thou were 'shapen in wickedness,' and that 'in sin did thy mother conceive thee'; and that thou thyself hast been heaping up sin upon sin, ever since thou couldest discern good from evil! Sink under the mighty hand of God, as guilty of death eternal; and cast off, renounce, abhor, all imagination of ever being able to help thy-self! Be it all thy hope to be washed in His blood, and renewed by His almighty Spirit, who Himself 'bare all our sins in His own body on the tree'! So shalt thou witness, 'Happy are the poor in spirit: for theirs is the kingdom of heaven.'

11. This is that kingdom of heaven, or of God, which is within us; even 'righteousness, and peace, and joy in the Holy Ghost.' And what is 'righteousness,' but the life of God in the soul; the mind which was in Christ Jesus; the image of God stamped upon the heart, now renewed after the likeness of Him that created it? What is it but the love of God, because He first loved us, and the love of all mankind for His sake?

And what is this 'peace,' the peace of God, but that calm serenity of soul, that sweet repose in the blood of Jesus, which leaves no doubt of our acceptance in Him; which excludes all fear, but the loving, filial fear of offending our Father which is in heaven?

This inward kingdom implies also 'joy in the Holy Ghost'; who seals upon our hearts 'the redemption which is in Jesus,' the righteousness of Christ imputed to us 'for the remission of the sins that are past'; who giveth us now 'the earnest of our inheritance,' of the crown which the Lord, the righteous Judge, will give at that day. And well may this be termed 'the kingdom of heaven'; seeing it is heaven already opened in the soul: the first springing up of those rivers of pleasure which flow at God's right hand for evermore.

12. 'Theirs is the kingdom of heaven.' Whosoever thou art, to whom God hath given to be 'poor in spirit,' to feel thyself lost, thou hast a right thereto, through the gracious promise of Him who cannot lie. It is purchased for thee by the blood of the Lamb. It is very nigh: thou art on the brink of heaven! Another step, and thou enterest into the kingdom of righteousness, and peace, and joy! Art thou all sin?—'Behold the Lamb of God, who taketh away the sin of the world!' All unholy?—see thy 'Advocate with the Father, Jesus Christ the righteous!' Art thou unable to atone for the least of thy sins?—'He is the propitiation for' all thy 'sins.' Now believe on the Lord Jesus Christ, and all thy sins are blotted out! Art thou totally unclean in soul and body?—here is the 'fountain for sin and uncleanness!' 'Arise, and wash away thy sins!' Stagger no more at the promise through unbelief! Give glory to God! Dare to believe! Now cry out, from the ground of thy heart,—

Yes, I yield, I yield at last,
  Listen to Thy speaking blood;
Me, with all my sins, I cast
  On my atoning God.

13. Then thou learnest of Him to be 'lowly of heart.' And this is the true, genuine, Christian humility, which flows from a sense of the love of God, reconciled to us in Christ Jesus. Poverty of spirit, in this meaning of the word, begins where a sense of guilt and of the wrath of God ends; and is a continual sense of our total dependence on Him, for every good thought, or word, or work; of our utter inability to all good, unless He 'water us every moment'; and an abhorrence of the praise of men, knowing that all praise is due unto God only. With this is joined a loving shame, a tender humiliation before God, even for the sins which we know He hath forgiven us, and for the sin which still remaineth in our hearts, although we know it is not imputed to our condemnation. Nevertheless, the conviction we feel of inbred sin is deeper and deeper every day. The more we grow in grace, the more do we see of the desperate wickedness of our heart. The more we advance in the knowledge and love of God, through our Lord Jesus Christ (as great a mystery as this may appear to those who know not the power of God unto salvation), the more do we discern of our alienation from God, of the enmity that is in our carnal mind, and the necessity of our being entirely renewed in righteousness and true holiness.

II. 1. It is true, he has scarce any conception of this who now begins to know the inward kingdom of heaven. 'In his prosperity he saith, I shall never be moved; Thou, Lord, hast made my hill so strong.' Sin is so utterly bruised beneath his feet, that he can scarce believe it remaineth in him. Even temptation is silenced, and speaks not again: it cannot approach, but stands afar off. He is borne aloft in the chariots of joy and love: he soars 'as upon the wings of an eagle.' But our Lord well knew that this triumphant state does not often continue long: He therefore presently subjoins, 'Blessed are they that mourn; for they shall be comforted.'

2. Not that we can imagine this promise belongs to those who mourn only on some worldly account; who are in sorrow and heaviness merely on account of some worldly trouble or disappointment, such as the loss of their reputation or friends, or the impairing of their fortune. As little title to it have they who are afflicting themselves, through fear of some temporal evil; or who pine away with anxious care, or that desire of earthly things which 'maketh the heart sick.' Let us not think these 'shall receive anything from the Lord': He is not in all their thoughts. Therefore it is that they thus 'walk in a vain shadow, and disquiet themselves in vain.' 'And this shall ye have at Mine hand,' saith the Lord, 'ye shall lie down in sorrow.'

3. The mourners of whom our Lord here speaks, are those that mourn on quite another account: they that mourn after God; after Him in whom they did 'rejoice with joy unspeakable, when He gave them to 'taste the good,' the pardoning 'word, and the powers of the world to come.' But He now 'hides His face and they are troubled'; they cannot see Him through the dark cloud. But they see temptation and sin, which they fondly supposed were gone never to return, arising again, following after them amain, and holding them in on every side. It is not strange if their soul is now disquieted within them, and trouble and heaviness take hold upon them. Nor will their great enemy fail to improve the occasion: to ask, 'Where is now thy God? Where is now the blessedness whereof thou spakest? the beginning of the kingdom of heaven? Yea, hath God said, "Thy sins are forgiven thee?" Surely God hath not said it. It was only a dream, a mere delusion, a creature of thy own imagination. If thy sins are forgiven, why art thou thus? Can a pardoned sinner be thus unholy?' And if then, instead of immediately crying to God, they reason with him that is wiser than they, they will be in heaviness indeed, in sorrow of heart, in anguish not to be expressed. Nay, even when God shines again upon the soul, and takes away all doubt of His past mercy, still he that is weak in faith may be tempted and troubled on account of what is to come; especially when inward sin revives, and thrusts sore at him that he may fall. Then may he again cry out,—

> I have a sin of fear, that when I've spun
> My last thread, I shall perish on the shore!—

lest I should make shipwreck of the faith, and my last state be worse than the first,—

> Lest all my bread of life should fail,
> And I sink down unchanged to hell!

4. Sure it is, that this 'affliction,' for the present, 'is not joyous, but grievous; nevertheless, afterward it bringeth forth peaceable fruit unto them that are exercised thereby.' Blessed, therefore, are they that thus mourn, if they 'tarry the Lord's leisure,' and suffer not themselves to be turned out of the way, by the miserable comforters of the world; if they resolutely reject all the comforts of sin, of folly, and vanity; all the idle diversions and amusements of the world; all the pleasures which 'perish in the using,' and which only tend to benumb and stupefy the soul, that it may neither be sensible of itself nor God. Blessed are they who 'follow on to know the Lord,' and steadily refuse all other comfort. They shall be comforted by the consolations of His Spirit; by a fresh manifestation of His love; by such a witness of His accepting them in the Beloved, as shall never more be taken away from them. This 'full assurance of faith' swallows up all doubt, as well as all tormenting fear; God now giving them a sure hope of an enduring substance, and 'strong consolation through grace.' Without disputing whether it be possible for any of those to 'fall away, who were once enlightened, and made partakers of the Holy Ghost,' it suffices them to say, by the power now resting upon them, 'Who shall separate us from the love of Christ? . . . I am persuaded, that neither death, nor life, nor things present, nor things to come, nor height, nor depth, shall be able to separate us from the love of God, which is in Christ Jesus our Lord' (Rom. viii. 35-39).

5. This whole process, both of mourning for an absent God, and recovering the joy of His countenance, seems to be shadowed out in what our Lord spoke to His Apostles, the night before His passion: 'Do ye inquire of that I said, A little while, and ye

shall not see Me: and again, a little while, and ye shall see Me?
Verily, verily, I say unto you, That ye shall weep and lament';
namely, when ye do not see Me; 'but the world shall rejoice';
shall triumph over you, as though your hope were now come to
an end. 'And ye shall be sorrowful,' through doubt, through
fear, through temptation, through vehement desire; 'but your
sorrow shall be turned into joy,' by the return of Him whom
your soul loveth. 'A woman when she is in travail hath sorrow,
because her hour is come: but as soon as she is delivered of the
child, she remembereth no more the anguish, for joy that a
man is born into the world. And ye now have sorrow': ye
mourn, and cannot be comforted: 'but I will see you again, and
your heart shall rejoice,' with calm inward joy, 'and your joy
no man taketh from you' (John xvi. 19-22).

6. But although this mourning is at an end, is lost in holy joy,
by the return of the Comforter, yet is there another, and a
blessed mourning it is, which abides in the children of God.
They still mourn for the sins and miseries of mankind: they
'weep with them that weep.' They weep for them that weep
not for themselves, for the sinners against their own souls. They
mourn for the weakness and unfaithfulness of those that are, in
some measure, saved from their sins. 'Who is weak, and they
are not weak? Who is offended, and they burn not?' They are
grieved for the dishonour continually done to the Majesty of
heaven and earth. At all times they have an awful sense of this,
which brings a deep seriousness upon their spirit; a seriousness
which is not a little increased, since the eyes of their understanding were opened, by their continually seeing the vast ocean
of eternity, without a bottom or a shore, which has already
swallowed up millions of millions of men, and is gaping to
devour them that yet remain. They see here the house of God
eternal in the heavens; there, hell and destruction without a
covering; and thence feel the importance of every moment,
which just appears, and is gone for ever!

7. But all this wisdom of God is foolishness with the world.
The whole affair of mourning and poverty of spirit is with them
stupidity and dullness. Nay, it is well if they pass so favourable a
judgement upon it; if they do not vote it to be mere moping and

melancholy, if not downright lunacy and distraction. And it is no wonder at all, that this judgement should be passed by those who know not God. Suppose, as two persons were walking together, one should suddenly stop, and with the strongest signs of fear and amazement, cry out, 'On what a precipice do we stand! See, we are on the point of being dashed in pieces! Another step, and we fall into that huge abyss! Stop! I will not go on for all the world!'—when the other, who seemed, to himself at least, equally sharp-sighted, looked forward and saw nothing of all this; what would he think of his companion, but that he was beside himself; that his head was out of order; that much religion (if he was not guilty of 'much learning') had certainly made him mad!

8. But let not the children of God, 'the mourners in Sion,' be moved by any of these things. Ye, whose eyes are enlightened, be not troubled by those who walk on still in darkness. Ye do not walk on in a vain shadow: God and eternity are real things. Heaven and hell are in very deed open before you; and ye are on the edge of the great gulf. It has already swallowed up more than words can express, nations, and kindreds, and peoples, and tongues; and still yawns to devour, whether they see it or no, the giddy, miserable children of men. O cry aloud! Spare not! Lift up your voice to Him who grasps both time and eternity, both for yourselves and your brethren, that ye may be counted worthy to escape the destruction that cometh as a whirlwind! that ye may be brought safe through all the waves and storms, into the haven where you would be! Weep for yourselves, till He wipes away the tears from your eyes. And even then, weep for the miseries that come upon the earth, till the Lord of all shall put a period to misery and sin, shall wipe away the tears from all faces, and 'the knowledge of the Lord shall cover the earth, as the waters cover the sea.'

SERMON XVII

UPON OUR LORD'S SERMON ON THE MOUNT

DISCOURSE II

Blessed are the meek, for they shall inherit the earth.
Blessed are they which do hunger and thirst after righteousness, for they shall
*   be filled.*
Blessed are the merciful, for they shall obtain mercy.

—MATT. v. 5-7

I. 1. WHEN 'the winter is past,' when 'the time of singing is come, and the voice of the turtle is heard in the land'; when He that comforts the mourners is now returned, 'that He may abide with them for ever'; when, at the brightness of His presence, the clouds disperse, the dark clouds of doubt and uncertainty, the storms of fear flee away, the waves of sorrow subside, and their spirit again rejoiceth in God their Saviour; then is it that this word is eminently fulfilled; then those whom He hath comforted can bear witness, 'Blessed,' or happy, 'are the meek; for they shall inherit the earth.'

2. But who are 'the meek'? Not those who grieve at nothing, because they know nothing; who are not discomposed at the evils that occur, because they discern not evil from good. Not those who are sheltered from the shocks of life by a stupid insensibility; who have, either by nature or art, the virtue of stocks and stones, and resent nothing, because they feel nothing. Brute philosophers are wholly unconcerned in this matter. Apathy is as far from meekness as from humanity. So that one would not easily conceive how any Christians of the purer ages, especially any of the Fathers of the Church, could confound these, and mistake one of the foulest errors of Heathenism for a branch of true Christianity.

3. Nor does Christian meekness imply, the being without zeal for God, any more than it does ignorance or insensibility.

No; it keeps clear of every extreme, whether in excess or defect. It does not destroy but balance the affections, which the God of nature never designed should be rooted out by grace, but only brought and kept under due regulations. It poises the mind aright. It holds an even scale, with regard to anger, and sorrow, and fear; preserving the mean in every circumstance of life, and not declining either to the right hand or the left.

4. Meekness, therefore, seems properly to relate to ourselves: but it may be referred either to God or our neighbour. When this due composure of mind has reference to God, it is usually termed 'resignation'; a calm acquiescence in whatsoever is His will concerning us, even though it may not be pleasing to nature; saying continually, 'It is the Lord; let Him do what seemeth Him good.' When we consider it more strictly with regard to ourselves, we style it 'patience' or 'contentedness.' When it is exerted toward other men, then it is 'mildness' to the good, and 'gentleness' to the evil.

5. They who are truly meek can clearly discern what is evil; and they can also suffer it. They are sensible of everything of this kind, but still, meekness holds the reins. They are exceeding 'zealous for the Lord of Hosts'; but their zeal is always guided by knowledge, and tempered, in every thought, and word, and work, with the love of man, as well as the love of God. They do not desire to extinguish any of the passions which God has for wise ends implanted in their nature; but they have the mastery of all: they hold them all in subjection, and employ them only in subservience to those ends. And thus even the harsher and more unpleasing passions are applicable to the noblest purposes; even hatred, and anger, and fear, when engaged against sin, and regulated by faith and love, are as walls and bulwarks to the soul, so that the wicked one cannot approach to hurt it.

6. It is evident, this divine temper is not only to abide but to increase in us day by day. Occasions of exercising, and thereby increasing it, will never be wanting while we remain upon earth. 'We have need of patience, that after we have done' and suffered 'the will of God, we may receive the promise.' We have need of resignation, that we may in all circumstances say, 'Not as I will, but as Thou wilt.' And we have need of 'gentleness

toward all men'; but especially toward the evil and unthankful: otherwise we shall be overcome of evil, instead of overcoming evil with good.

7. Nor does meekness restrain only the outward act, as the Scribes and Pharisees taught of old, and the miserable teachers who are not taught of God will not fail to do in all ages. Our Lord guards against this, and shows the true extent of it, in the following words: 'Ye have heard that it was said by them of old time, Thou shalt not kill; and whosoever shall kill shall be in danger of the judgement' (Matt. v. 21, &c.): 'But I say unto you, That whosoever is angry with his brother without a cause shall be in danger of the judgement: and whosoever shall say to his brother, Raca, shall be in danger of the council: but whosoever shall say, Thou fool, shall be in danger of hell-fire.'

8. Our Lord here ranks under the head of murder, even that anger which goes no farther than the heart; which does not show itself by any outward unkindness, no, not so much as a passionate word. 'Whosoever is angry with his brother,' with any man living, seeing we are all brethren; whosoever feels any unkindness in his heart, any temper contrary to love; whosoever is angry without a cause, without a sufficient cause, or farther than that cause requires, 'shall be in danger of the judgement'; ἔνοχος ἔσται; *shall*, in that moment, *be obnoxious to* the righteous judgement of God.

But would not one be inclined to prefer the reading of those copies which omit the word εἰκῆ, *without a cause*? Is it not entirely superfluous? For if *anger at persons* be a temper contrary to love, how can there be a cause, a sufficient cause for it,—any that will justify it in the sight of God?

Anger at sin we allow. In this sense we may be angry, and yet we sin not. In this sense our Lord Himself is once recorded to have been angry: 'He looked round about upon them with anger, being grieved for the hardness of their hearts.' He was grieved at the sinners, and angry at the sin. And this is undoubtedly right before God.

9. 'And whosoever shall say to his brother, Raca'—whosoever shall give way to anger, so as to utter any contemptuous word. It is observed by commentators, that Raca is a Syriac word,

which properly signifies, *empty*, *vain*, *foolish*; so that it is as inoffensive an expression as can well be used, toward one at whom we are displeased. And yet, whosoever shall use this, as our Lord assures us, 'shall be in danger of the council': rather, shall be obnoxious thereto: he shall be liable to a severer sentence from the Judge of all the earth.

'But whosoever shall say, Thou fool'—whosoever shall so give place to the devil, as to break out into reviling, into designedly reproachful and contumelious language—'shall be obnoxious to hell-fire'; shall, in that instant, be liable to the highest condemnation. It should be observed, that our Lord describes all these as obnoxious to capital punishment. The first, to strangling, usually inflicted on those who were condemned in one of the inferior courts; the second, to stoning, which was frequently inflicted on those who were condemned by the great Council at Jerusalem; the third, to burning alive, inflicted only on the highest offenders, in the 'valley of the sons of Hinnom'; Γαὶ 'Εννόμ, from which that word is evidently taken which we translate 'hell.'

10.   And whereas men naturally imagine, that God will excuse their defect in some duties, for their exactness in others; our Lord next takes care to cut off that vain, though common imagination. He shows, that it is impossible for any sinner to *commute* with God; who will not accept one duty for another, nor take a part of obedience for the whole. He warns us, that the performing our duty to God will not excuse us from our duty to our neighbour; that works of piety, as they are called, will be so far from commending us to God, if we are wanting in charity, that, on the contrary, that want of charity will make all those works an abomination to the Lord.

'Therefore, if thou bring thy gift to the altar, and there rememberest that thy brother hath aught against thee'—on account of thy unkind behaviour toward him, of thy calling him, 'Raca,' or, 'Thou fool'—think not that thy gift will atone for thy anger; or that it will find any acceptance with God, so long as thy conscience is defiled with the guilt of unrepented sin. 'Leave there thy gift before the altar, and go thy way; first be reconciled to thy brother' (at least do all that in thee lies toward being reconciled), 'and then come and offer thy gift' (Matt. v. 23,24).

11. And let there be no delay in what so nearly concerneth thy soul. 'Agree with thine adversary quickly'—now; upon the spot; 'whiles thou art in the way with him'—if it be possible, before he go out of thy sight; 'lest at any time the adversary deliver thee to the judge'—lest he appeal to God the Judge of all; 'and the judge deliver thee to the officer'—to Satan, the executioner of the wrath of God; 'and thou be cast into prison'—into hell, there to be reserved to the judgement of the great day. 'Verily I say unto thee, Thou shalt by no means come out thence, till thou hast paid the uttermost farthing.' But this it is impossible for thee ever to do: seeing thou hast nothing to pay. Therefore, if thou art once in that prison, the smoke of thy torment must 'ascend up for ever and ever.'

12. Meantime 'the meek shall inherit the earth.' Such is the foolishness of worldly wisdom! The wise of the world had warned them again and again, that if they did not resent such treatment, if they would tamely suffer themselves to be thus abused, there would be no living for them upon earth; that they would never be able to procure the common necessaries of life, nor to keep even what they had; that they could expect no peace, no quiet possession, no enjoyment of anything. Most true, suppose there were no God in the world; or suppose He did not concern Himself with the children of men: but 'when God ariseth to judgement, and to help all the meek upon earth,' how doth He laugh all this heathen wisdom to scorn, and turn the 'fierceness of man to His praise! He takes a peculiar care to provide them with all things needful for life and godliness; He secures to them the provision He hath made, in spite of the force, fraud, or malice of men; and what He secures He gives them richly to enjoy. It is sweet to them, be it little or much. As in patience they possess their souls, so they truly possess whatever God hath given them. They are always content, always pleased with what they have: it pleases them, because it pleases God: so that while their heart, their desire, their joy is in heaven, they may truly be said to 'inherit the earth.'

13. But there seems to be a yet farther meaning in these words,

even that they shall have a more eminent part in 'the new earth,
wherein dwelleth righteousness'; in that inheritance, a general
description of which (and the particulars we shall know hereafter) St. John hath given in the twentieth chapter of the Revelation: 'And I saw an angel come down from heaven, . . . and
he laid hold on the dragon, that old serpent, . . . and bound him
a thousand years. . . . And I saw the souls of them that were
beheaded for the witness of Jesus, and for the Word of God, and
of them which had not worshipped the beast, neither his image,
neither had received his mark upon their foreheads, or in their
hands; and they lived and reigned with Christ a thousand years.
But the rest of the dead lived not again until the thousand years
were finished. This is the first resurrection. Blessed and holy is
he that hath part in the first resurrection: on such the second
death hath no power, but they shall be priests of God and of
Christ, and shall reign with Him a thousand years.'

II. 1. Our Lord has hitherto been more immediately employed in removing the hindrances of true religion: such is pride,
the first grand hindrance of all religion, which is taken away by
poverty of spirit; levity and thoughtlessness, which prevent any
religion from taking root in the soul, till they are removed by
holy mourning: such are anger, impatience, discontent, which
are all healed by Christian meekness. And when once these
hindrances are removed, these evil diseases of the soul, which
were continually raising false cravings therein, and filling it
with sickly appetites, the native appetite of a heaven-born spirit
returns; it hungers and thirsts after righteousness: and 'blessed
are they which do hunger and thirst after righteousness: for they
shall be filled.'

2. Righteousness, as was observed before, is the image of God,
the mind which was in Christ Jesus. It is every holy and heavenly
temper in one; springing from, as well as terminating in, the love
of God, as our Father and Redeemer, and the love of all men for
His sake.

3. 'Blessed are they which do hunger and thirst after' this:
in order fully to understand which expression, we should observe,
first, that hunger and thirst are the strongest of all our bodily

appetites. In like manner this hunger in the soul, this thirst after the image of God, is the strongest of all our spiritual appetites, when it is once awakened in the heart; yea, it swallows up all the rest in that one great desire,—to be renewed after the likeness of Him that created us. We should, secondly, observe, that from the time we begin to hunger and thirst, those appetites do not cease, but are more and more craving and importunate, till we either eat and drink, or die. And even so, from the time that we begin to hunger and thirst after the whole mind which was in Christ, these spiritual appetites do not cease, but cry after their food with more and more importunity; nor can they possibly cease, before they are satisfied, while there is any spiritual life remaining. We may, thirdly, observe, that hunger and thirst are satisfied with nothing but meat and drink. If you would give to him that is hungry all the world beside, all the elegance of apparel, all the trappings of state, all the treasure upon earth, yea, thousands of gold and silver; if you would pay him ever so much honour,—he regards it not: all these things are then of no account with him. He would still say, 'These are not the things I want: give me food, or else I die.' The very same is the case with every soul that truly hungers and thirsts after righteousness. He can find no comfort in anything but this: he can be satisfied with nothing else. Whatever you offer besides, it is lightly esteemed: whether it be riches, or honour, or pleasure, he still says 'This is not the thing which I want! Give me love, or else I die!'

4. And it is as impossible to satisfy such a soul, a soul that is athirst for God, the living God, with what the world accounts religion, as with what they account happiness. The religion of the world implies three things: (1) The doing no harm, the abstaining from outward sin; at least from such as is scandalous, as robbery, theft, common swearing, drunkenness: (2) The doing good, the relieving the poor; the being charitable, as it is called: (3) The using the means of grace: at least the going to church and to the Lord's supper. He in whom these three marks are found is termed by the world 'a religious man.' But will this satisfy him who hungers after God? No: it is not food for his soul. He wants a religion of a nobler kind, a religion higher and

deeper than this. He can no more feed on this poor, shallow, formal thing, than he can 'fill his belly with the east wind.' True, he is careful to abstain from the very appearance of evil; he is zealous of good works; he attends all the ordinances of God: but all this is not what he longs for. This is only the outside of that religion which he insatiably hungers after. The knowledge of God in Christ Jesus; 'the life which is hid with Christ in God'; the being 'joined unto the Lord in one spirit'; the having 'fellowship with the Father and the Son'; the 'walking in the light as God is in the light'; the being 'purified even as He is pure,'—this is the religion, the righteousness he thirsts after; nor can he rest, till he thus rests in God.

5. 'Blessed are they who' thus 'hunger and thirst after righteousness; for they shall be filled.' They shall be filled with the things which they long for; even with righteousness and true holiness. God shall satisfy them with the blessings of His goodness, with the felicity of His chosen. He shall feed them with the bread of heaven, with the manna of His love. He shall give them to drink of His pleasures as out of the river, which he that drinketh of shall never thirst, only for more and more of the water of life. This thirst shall endure forever.

> The painful thirst, the fond desire,
>   Thy joyous presence shall remove:
> But my full soul shall still require
>   A whole eternity of love.

6. Whosoever then thou art, to whom God hath given to 'hunger and thirst after righteousness,' cry unto Him that thou mayest never lose that inestimable gift—that this divine appetite may never cease. If many rebuke thee, and bid thee hold thy peace, regard them not; yea, cry so much the more, 'Jesus, Master, have mercy on me!' 'Let me not live, but to be holy as Thou art holy!' No more 'spend thy money for that which is not bread, nor thy labour for that which satisfieth not.' Canst thou hope to dig happiness out of the earth—to find it in the things of the world? O trample under foot all its pleasures, despise its honours, count its riches as dung and dross—yea, and

all the things which are beneath the sun—'for the excellency of the knowledge of Christ Jesus,' for the entire renewal of thy soul in that image of God wherein it was originally created. Beware of quenching that blessed hunger and thrist, by what the world calls 'religion'; a religion of form, of outside show, which leaves the heart as earthly and sensual as ever. Let nothing satisfy thee but the power of godliness, but a religion that is spirit and life; thy dwelling in God, and God in thee—the being an inhabitant of eternity; the entering in by the blood of sprinkling 'within the veil,' and sitting 'in heavenly places with Christ Jesus.'

III. 1. And the more they are filled with the life of God, the more tenderly will they be concerned for those who are still without God in the world, still dead in trespasses and sins. Nor shall this concern for others lose its reward. 'Blessed are the merciful: for they shall obtain mercy.'

The word used by our Lord more immediately implies the compassionate, the tender-hearted; those who, far from despising, earnestly grieve for, those that do not hunger after God.

This eminent part of brotherly love is here, by a common figure, put for the whole; so that 'the merciful,' in the full sense of the term, are they who love their neighbours as themselves.

2. Because of the vast importance of this love—without which, 'though we spake with the tongues of men and angels, though we had the gift of prophecy, and understood all mysteries, and all knowledge; though we had all faith, so as to remove mountains; yea, though we gave all our goods to feed the poor, and our very bodies to be burned, it would profit us nothing' —the wisdom of God has given us, by the Apostle Paul, a full and particular account of it; by considering which we shall most clearly discern who are the merciful that shall obtain mercy.

3. 'Charity,' or love (as it were to be wished it had been rendered throughout, being a far plainer and less ambiguous word), the love of our neighbour as Christ hath loved us, 'suffereth long'; is patient towards all men: it suffers all the weakness, ignorance, errors, infirmities, all the frowardness and little-ness of faith, of the children of God; all the malice and wicked-ness of the children of the world. And it suffers all this, not only

for a time, for a short season, but to the end; still feeding our enemy when he hungers; if he thirst, still giving him drink; thus continually 'heaping coals of fire,' of melting love, 'upon his head.'

4. And in every step toward this desirable end, the 'over-coming evil with good,' 'love is kind' (χρηστεύεται, a word not easily translated): it is *soft, mild, benign*. It stands at the utmost distance from moroseness, from all harshness or sourness of spirit; and inspires the sufferer at once with the most amiable sweetness, and the most fervent and tender affection.

5. Consequently, 'love envieth not': it is impossible it should; it is directly opposite to that baneful temper. It cannot be, that he who has this tender affection to all, who earnestly wishes all temporal and spiritual blessings, all good things in this world and the world to come, to every soul that God hath made, should be pained at His bestowing any good gift on any child of man. If he has himself received the same, he does not grieve, but rejoice, that another partakes of the common benefit. If he has not, he blesses God that his brother at least has, and is herein happier than himself. And the greater his love, the more does he rejoice in the blessings of all mankind; the farther is he removed from every kind and degree of envy toward any creature.

6. Love οὐ περπερεύεται,—not 'vaunteth not itself'; which coincides with the very next words; but rather (as the word likewise properly imports), *is not rash* or *hasty* in judging; it will not hastily condemn any one. It does not pass a severe sentence, on a slight or sudden view of things: it first weighs all the evidence, particularly that which is brought in favour of the accused. A true lover of his neighbour is not like the generality of men, who, even in cases of the nicest nature, 'see a little, presume a great deal, and so jump to the conclusion.' No: he proceeds with wariness and circumspection, taking heed to every step; willingly subscribing to that rule of the ancient Heathen (O where will the modern Christian appear!) 'I am so far from lightly believing what one man says against another, that I will not easily believe what a man says against himself. I will always allow him second thoughts, and many times counsel too.'

7. It follows, love 'is not puffed up': it does not incline or

suffer any man 'to think more highly of himself than he ought to think'; but rather to think soberly: yea, it humbles the soul unto the dust. It destroys all high conceits engendering pride; and makes us rejoice to be as nothing, to be little and vile, the lowest of all, the servant of all. They who are 'kindly affectioned one to another with brotherly love,' cannot but 'in honour prefer one another.' Those who, having the same love, are of one accord, do in lowliness of mind 'each esteem other better than themselves.'

8. 'It doth not behave itself unseemly'; it is not rude, or willingly offensive to any. It 'renders to all their due; fear to whom fear, honour to whom honour'; courtesy, civility, humanity to all the world; in their several degrees 'honouring all men.' A late writer defines good breeding, nay, the highest degree of it, politeness, 'A continual desire to please, appearing in all the behaviour.' But if so, there is none so well-bred as a Christian, a lover of all mankind. For he cannot but desire to 'please all men for their good to edification': and this desire cannot be hid; it will necessarily appear in all his intercourse with men. For his 'love is without dissimulation': it will appear in all his actions and conversation: yea, and will constrain him, though without guile, 'to become all things to all men, if by any means he may save some.'

9. And in becoming all things to all men, 'love seeketh not her own.' In striving to please all men, the lover of mankind has no eye at all to his own temporal advantage. He covets no man's silver, or gold, or apparel: he desires nothing but the salvation of their souls: yea, in some sense, he may be said, *not to seek his own* spiritual, any more than temporal, advantage; for while he is on the full stretch to save their souls from death, he, as it were, forgets himself. He does not think of himself, so long as that zeal for the glory of God swallows him up. Nay, at some times he may almost seem, through an excess of love, to give up himself, both his soul and his body; while he cries out, with Moses, 'O, this people have sinned a great sin; yet now, if Thou wilt forgive their sin—; and if not, blot me out of the book which Thou hast written' (Exod. xxxii. 31, 32); or, with St. Paul, 'I could wish that myself were accursed from Christ for

my brethren, my kinsmen according to the flesh' (Rom. ix. 3).

10. No marvel that such 'love is not provoked'; οὐ παροξύνεται. Let it be observed, the word *easily*, strangely inserted in the translation, is not in the original. St. Paul's words are absolute. 'Love is not provoked'; it is not provoked to unkindness toward any one. Occasions indeed will frequently occur; outward provocations of various kinds; but love does not yield to provocation; it triumphs over all. In all trials it looketh unto Jesus, and is more than conqueror in His love.

It is not improbable that our translators inserted that word, as it were, to *excuse* the Apostle; who, as they supposed, might otherwise appear to be wanting in the very love which he so beautifully describes. They seem to have supposed this from a phrase in the Acts of the Apostles, which is likewise very inaccurately translated. When Paul and Barnabas disagreed concerning John, the translation runs thus, 'And the contention was so sharp between them, that they departed asunder' (Acts xv. 39). This naturally induces the reader to suppose, that they were equally sharp therein; that St. Paul, who was undoubtedly right, with regard to the point in question (it being quite improper to take John with them again, who had deserted them before), was as much provoked as Barnabas, who gave such a proof of his anger, as to leave the work for which he had been set apart by the Holy Ghost. But the original imports no such thing; nor does it affirm that St. Paul was provoked at all. It simply says, Ἐγένετο οὖν παροξυσμός, —'And there was a sharpness,' a *paroxysm* of anger; in consequence of which Barnabas left St. Paul, took John, and went his own way. Paul then 'chose Silas and departed, being recommended by the brethren to the grace of God' (which is not said concerning Barnabas); 'and he went through Syria and Cilicia,' as he had proposed, 'confirming the churches.' But to return.

11. Love prevents a thousand provocations which would otherwise arise, because it 'thinketh no evil.' Indeed, the merciful man cannot avoid knowing many things that are evil; he cannot but see them with his own eyes, and hear them with his own ears. For love does not put out his eyes, so that is impossible for him not to see that such things are done; neither does it take

away his understanding, any more than his senses, so that he cannot but know that they are evil. For instance; when he sees a man strike his neighbour, or hears him blaspheme God, he cannot either question the thing done, or the words spoken, or doubt of their being evil: yet, οὐ λογίζεται τὸ κακόν. The word λογίζεται, 'thinketh,' does not refer either to our seeing and hearing, or to the first and involuntary acts of our understanding; but to our *willingly thinking* what we need not; our *inferring* evil, where it does not appear; to our *reasoning* concerning things which we do not see; our *supposing* what we have neither seen nor heard. This is what true love absolutely destroys. It tears up root and branch, all *imagining* what we have not known. It casts out all jealousies, all evil surmisings, all readiness to believe evil. It is frank, open, unsuspicious; and, as it cannot design, so neither does it fear, evil.

12. It rejoiceth not in iniquity'; common as this is, even among those who bear the name of Christ, who scruple not to rejoice over their enemy, when he falleth either into affliction, or error, or sin. Indeed, how hardly can they avoid this, who are zealously attached to any party! How difficult is it for them not to be pleased with any fault which they discover in those of the opposite party,—with any real or supposed blemish, either in their principles or practice! What warm defender of any cause is clear of these? Yea, who is so calm as to be altogether free? Who does not rejoice when his adversary makes a false step, which he thinks will advantage his own cause? Only a man of love. He alone weeps over either the sin or folly of his enemy, takes no pleasure in hearing or in repeating it, but rather desires that it may be forgotten for ever.

13. But he 'rejoiceth in the truth,' wheresoever it is found; in 'the truth which is after godliness'; bringing forth its proper fruit,—holiness of heart, and holiness of conversation. He rejoices to find that even those who oppose him, whether with regard to opinions, or some points of practice, are nevertheless lovers of God, and in other respects unreprovable. He is glad to hear good of them, and to speak all he can consistently with truth and justice. Indeed, good in general is his glory and joy, wherever diffused throughout the race of mankind. As a citizen

15

of the world he claims a share in the happiness of all the inhabitants of it. Because he is a man, he is not unconcerned in the welfare of any man; but enjoys whatsoever brings glory to God, and promotes peace and good-will among men.

14. This 'love covereth all things' (so, without all doubt, πάντα στέγει should be translated; for otherwise it would be the very same with πάντα ὑπομένει, 'endureth all things'): because the merciful man rejoiceth not in iniquity, neither does he willingly make mention of it. Whatever evil he sees, hears, or knows, he nevertheless conceals, so far as he can without making himself 'partaker of other men's sins.' Wheresoever or with whomsoever he is, if he sees anything which he approves not, it goes not out of his lips, unless to the person concerned, if haply he may gain his brother. So far is he from making the faults or failings of others the matter of his conversation, that of the absent he never does speak at all, unless he can speak well. A talebearer, a backbiter, a whisperer, an evil-speaker, is to him all one as a murderer. He would just as soon cut his neighbour's throat, as thus murder his reputation. Just as soon would he think of diverting himself by setting fire to his neighbour's house, as of thus 'scattering abroad arrows, fire-brands, and death,' and saying, 'Am I not in sport?'

He makes one only exception. Sometimes he is convinced that it is for the glory of God, or (which comes to the same) the good of his neighbour, that an evil should not be covered. In this case, for the benefit of the innocent, he is constrained to declare the guilty. But even here, (1) He will not speak at all, till love, superior love, constrains him. (2) He cannot do it from a general confused view of doing good, or promoting the glory of God, but from a clear sight of some particular end, some determinate good, which he pursues. (3) Still he cannot speak, unless he be fully convinced that this very means is necessary to that end; that the end cannot be answered, at least not so effectually, by any other way. (4) He then doeth it with the utmost sorrow and reluctance; using it as the last and worst medicine, a desperate remedy in a desperate case, a kind of poison never to be used but to expel poison. Consequently, (5) He uses it as sparingly as possible. And this he does with fear and trembling, lest he should transgress the law of love by speaking too much, more than he would have done by not speaking at all.

15. Love 'believeth all things.' It is always willing to think the best; to put the most favourable construction on everything. It is ever ready to believe whatever may tend to the advantage of any one's character. It is easily convinced of (what it earnestly desires) the innocence and integrity of any man; or, at least, of the sincerity of his repentance, if he had once erred from the way. It is glad to excuse whatever is amiss; to condemn the offender as little as possible; and to make all the allowance for human weakness which can be done without betraying the truth of God.

16. And when it can no longer believe, then love 'hopeth all things.' Is any evil related of any man? Love hopes that the relation is not true, that the thing related was never done. Is it certain it was?—'But perhaps it was not done with such circumstances as are related; so that, allowing the fact, there is room to hope it was not so ill as it is represented.' Was the action apparently undeniably evil? Love hopes the intention was not so. Is it clear, the design was evil too?—'Yet might it not spring from the settled temper of the heart, but from a start of passion, or from some vehement temptation, which hurried the man beyond himself.' And even when it cannot be doubted, but all the actions, designs, and tempers are equally evil; still love hopes that God will at last make bare His arm, and get Himself the victory; and that there shall be 'joy in heaven over' this 'one sinner that repenteth, more than over ninety and nine just persons that need no repentance.'

17. Lastly. It 'endureth all things.' This completes the character of him that is truly merciful. He endureth not some, not many, things only; not most, but absolutely *all things*. Whatever the injustice, the malice, the cruelty of men can inflict, he is able to suffer. He calls nothing intolerable; he never says of anything, 'This is not to be borne.' No; he can not only do, but suffer, all things through Christ which strengtheneth him. And all he suffers does not destroy his love, nor impair it in the least. It is proof against all. It is a flame that burns even in the midst of the great deep. 'Many waters cannot quench' his

'love, neither can the floods drown it.' It triumphs over all. It 'never faileth,' either in time or in eternity.

> In obedience to what heaven decrees,
> Knowledge shall fail, and prophecy shall cease;
> But lasting charity's more ample sway,
> Nor bound by time, nor subject to decay,
> In happy triumph shall for ever live,
> And endless good diffuse, and endless praise receive.

So shall the 'merciful obtain mercy'; not only by the blessing of God upon all their ways, by His now repaying the love they bear to their brethren a thousand-fold into their own bosom; but likewise by 'an exceeding and eternal weight of glory,' in the 'kingdom prepared for them from the beginning of the world.'

18. For a little while you may say, 'Woe is me, that I' am constrained to 'dwell with Mesech, and to have my habitation among the tents of Kedar!' You may pour out your soul, and bemoan the loss of true, genuine love in the earth: lost indeed! You may well say (but not in the ancient sense), 'See how *these Christians* love one another!' these Christian kindgoms, that are tearing out each other's bowels, desolating one another with fire and sword! these Christian armies, that are sending each other by thousands, by ten thousands, quick into hell! these Christian nations, that are all on fire with intestine broils, party against party, faction against faction! these Christian cities, where deceit and fraud, oppression and wrong, yea robbery and murder, go not out of their streets! these Christian families, torn asunder with envy, jealousy, anger, domestic jars, without number, without end! yea, what is most dreadful, most to be lamented of all, these Christian churches!—churches ('tell it not in Gath,'—but, alas! how can we hide it, either from Jews, Turks, or Pagans?) that bear the name of Christ, the Prince of Peace, and wage continual war with each other! that convert sinners by burning them alive! that are 'drunk with the blood of the saints'! Does this praise belong only to 'Babylon the Great, the mother of harlots and abominations of the earth'? Nay, verily; but Reformed churches (so called) have fairly

learned to tread in her steps. Protestant churches too know how to persecute, when they have power in their hands, even unto blood. And meanwhile, how do they also anathematize each other! devote each other to the nethermost hell! What wrath, what contention, what malice, what bitterness, is everywhere found among them, even where they agree in essentials, and only differ in opinions, or in the circumstantials of religion! Who follows after *only* the 'things that make for peace, and things wherewith one may edify another'? O God! how long? Shall Thy promise fail? Fear it not, ye little flock! Against hope, believe in hope! It is your Father's good pleasure yet to renew the face of the earth. Surely all these things shall come to an end, and the inhabitatns of the earth shall learn righteousness. 'Nation shall not lift up sword against nation, neither shall they know war any more.' 'The mountain of the Lord's house shall be established on the top of the mountains'; and 'all the kingdoms of the earth shall become the kingdoms of our God.' 'They shall not' then 'hurt or destroy in all His holy mountain'; but they shall call their 'walls salvation, and their gates praise.' They shall all be without spot or blemish, loving one another, even as Christ hath loved us.—Be thou part of the first-fruits, if the harvest is not yet. Do thou love thy neighbour as thyself. The Lord God fill thy heart with such a love to every soul, that thou mayest be ready to lay down thy life for his sake! May thy soul continually overflow with love, swallowing up every unkind and unholy temper, till He calleth thee up into the region of love, there to reign with Him for ever and ever!

SERMON XVIII

UPON OUR LORD'S SERMON ON THE MOUNT

DISCOURSE III

Blessed are the pure in heart, for they shall see God.

Blessed are the peace-makers, for they shall be called the children of God

Blessed are they which are persecuted for righteousness' sake, for theirs is the kingdom of heaven.

Blessed are ye, when men shall revile you, and persecute you, and shall say all manner of evil against you falsely, for My sake.

Rejoice, and be exceeding glad, for great is your reward in heaven, for so persecuted they the prophets which were before you.—MATT. v. 8-12.

I. 1. How excellent things are spoken of the love of our neighbour! It is 'the fulfilling of the law,' 'the end of the commandment.' Without this, all we have, all we do, all we suffer, is of no value in the sight of God. But it is that love of our neighbour which springs from the love of God: otherwise itself is nothing worth. It behoves us, therefore, to examine well upon what foundation our love of our neighbour stands; whether it is really built upon the love of God; whether we do 'love Him because He first loved us'; whether we are pure in heart: for this is the foundation which shall never be moved. 'Blessed are the pure in heart: for they shall see God.'

2. 'The pure in heart' are they whose hearts God hath 'purified even as He is pure'; who are purified, through faith in the blood of Jesus, from every unholy affection; who, being 'cleansed from all filthiness of flesh and spirit, perfect holiness in the' loving 'fear of God.' They are, through the power of His grace, purified from pride, by the deepest poverty of spirit; from anger, from every unkind or turbulent passion, by meekness and gentleness; from every desire but to please and enjoy God, to know and love Him more and more, by that hunger and thirst after righteousness which now engrosses their whole soul: so that now they love the Lord their God with all their heart, and with all their soul, and mind, and strength.

3. But how little has this purity of heart been regarded by the false teachers of all ages! They have taught men barely to abstain from such outward impurities as God hath forbidden by name; but they did not strike at the heart; and by not guarding against, they in effect countenanced, inward corruptions.

A remarkable instance of this our Lord has given us in the following words: 'Ye have heard that it was said by them of old time, Thou shalt not commit adultery' (verse 27); and, in explaining this, those blind leaders of the blind only insisted on men's abstaining from the outward act. 'But I say unto you, That whosoever looketh on a woman to lust after her hath committed adultery with her already in his heart' (verse 28); for God requireth truth in the inward parts: He searcheth the heart, and trieth the reins; and if thou incline unto iniquity with thy heart, the Lord will not hear thee.

4. And God admits no excuse for retaining anything which is an occasion of impurity. Therefore, 'if thy right eye offend thee, pluck it out, and cast it from thee: for it is profitable for thee that one of thy members should perish, and not that thy whole body should be cast into hell' (verse 29). If persons as dear to thee as thy right eye be an occasion of thy thus offending God, a means of exciting unholy desire in thy soul, delay not, forcibly separate from them. 'And if thy right hand offend thee, cut it off, and cast it from thee: for it is profitable for thee that one of thy members should perish, and not that thy whole body should be cast into hell' (verse 30). If any who seem as necessary to thee as thy right hand be an occasion of sin, of impure desire; even though it were never to go beyond the heart, never to break out in word or action; constrain thyself to an entire and final parting: cut them off at a stroke: give them up to God. Any loss, whether of pleasure, or substance, or friends, is preferable to the loss of thy soul.

Two steps only it may not be improper to take before such an absolute and final separation. First, try whether the unclean spirit may not be driven out by fasting and prayer, and by carefully abstaining from every action, and word, and look, which thou hast found to be an occasion of evil. Secondly, if thou art not by this means delivered, ask counsel of him that watcheth over thy soul, or, at least, of some who have experience in the ways of God, touching the time and manner of that separation; but confer not with flesh and blood, lest thou be 'given up to a strong delusion to believe a lie.'

5. Nor may marriage itself, holy and honourable as it is, be used as a pretence for giving a loose to our desires. Indeed, 'it hath been said, Whosoever will put away his wife, let him give her a writing of divorcement': and then all was well; though he alleged no cause, but that he did not like her, or liked another better. 'But I say unto you, That whosoever shall put away his wife, saving for the cause of fornication' (that is, adultery; the word πορνεία signifying unchastity in general, either in the married or unmarried state), 'causeth her to commit adultery,' if she marry again: 'and whosoever shall marry her that is put away committeth adultery' (verses 31, 32).

All polygamy is clearly forbidden in these words, wherein our Lord expressly declares, that for any woman who has a husband alive, to marry again is adultery. By parity of reason, it is adultery for any man to marry again, so long as he has a wife alive, yea, although they were divorced; unless that divorce had been for the cause of adultery: in that only case there is no scripture which forbids to marry again.

6. Such is the purity of heart which God requires, and works in those who believe on the Son of His love. And 'blessed are' they who are thus 'pure in heart: for they shall see God.' He will 'manifest Himself unto them,' not only 'as He doth not unto the world,' but as He doth not always to His own children. He will bless them with the clearest communications of His Spirit, the most intimate 'fellowship with the Father and with the Son.' He will cause His presence to go continually before them, and the light of His countenance to shine upon them. It is the ceaseless prayer of their heart, 'I beseech Thee, show me Thy glory'; and they have the petition they ask of Him. They now see Him by faith (the veil of flesh being made, as it were, transparent), even in these His lowest works, in all that surrounds them, in all that God has created and made. They see Him in the height above, and in the depth beneath; they see Him filling all in all. The pure in heart see all things full of God. They see

Him in the firmament of heaven; in the moon, walking in brightness; in the sun, when he rejoiceth as a giant to run his course. They see Him 'making the clouds His chariots, and walking upon the wings of the wind.' They see Him 'preparing rain for the earth, and blessing the increase of it; giving grass for the cattle, and green herb for the use of man.' They see the Creator of all, wisely governing all, and 'upholding all things by the word of His power.' 'O Lord our Governor, how excellent is Thy name in all the world!'

7. In all His providences relating to themselves, to their souls or bodies, the pure in heart do more particularly see God. They see His hand ever over them for good; giving them all things in weight and measure, numbering the hairs of their head, making a hedge round about them and all that they have, and disposing all the circumstances of their life according to the depth both of His wisdom and mercy.

8. But in a more especial manner they see God in His ordinances. Whether they appear in the great congregation, to 'pay Him the honour due unto His name,' 'and worship Him in the beauty of holiness'; or 'enter into their closets,' and there pour out their souls before their 'Father which is in secret'; whether they search the oracles of God, or hear the ambassadors of Christ proclaiming glad tidings of salvation: or, by eating of that bread, and drinking of that cup, 'show forth His death till He come' in the clouds of heaven,—in all these His appointed ways, they find such a near approach as cannot be expressed. They see Him, as it were, face to face, and 'talk with Him, as a man talketh with his friend'—a fit preparation for those mansions above, wherein they shall see Him as He is.

9. But how far were they from seeing God, who, having heard 'that it had been said by them of old time, Thou shalt not forswear thyself, but shalt perform unto the Lord thine oaths' (verse 33), interpreted it thus, Thou shalt not forswear thyself, when thou swearest by the Lord Jehovah: thou 'shalt perform unto the Lord' these 'thine oaths'; but as to other oaths, He regardeth them not.

So the Pharisees taught. They not only allowed all manner of swearing in common conversation; but accounted even for-

swearing a little thing, so they had not sworn by the peculiar
name of God.

But our Lord here absolutely forbids all common swearing
as well as all false swearing; and shows the heinousness of both.
by the same awful consideration, that every creature is God's.
and He is everywhere present, in all, and over all. 'I say unto
you, Swear not at all; neither by heaven, for it is God's throne'
(verse 34); and, therefore, this is the same as to swear by Him
who sitteth upon the circle of the heavens: 'Nor by the earth,
for it is His footstool' (verse 35); and He is as intimately present
in earth as heaven: 'Neither by Jerusalem; for it is the city of
the great King'; and God is well known in her palaces. 'Neither
shalt thou swear by thy head; because thou canst not make one
hair white or black' (verse 36); because even this, it is plain, is
not thine, but God's, the sole disposer of all in heaven and earth
'But let your communication' (verse 37), your conversation
your discourse with each other, 'be, Yea, yea; Nay, nay'; a bare,
serious affirming or denying; 'for whatsoever is more than these
cometh of evil': ἐκ τοῦ πονηροῦ ἐστιν, *is of the evil one*; proceedeth from the devil, and is a mark of his children.

10. That our Lord does not here forbid the 'swearing in
judgement and truth,' when we are required so to do by a
magistrate, may appear (1), From the occasion of this part of
His discourse—the abuse He was here reproving—which was
false swearing, and common swearing; the swearing before a
magistrate being quite out of the question. (2) From the very
words wherein He forms the general conclusion: 'Let your
communication,' or discourse, 'be, Yea, yea; Nay, nay.' (3)
From His own example: for He answered Himself upon oath,
when required by a magistrate. When the high-priest said unto
him, 'I adjure thee by the living God, that thou tell us whether
thou be the Christ, the Son of God,' Jesus immediately answered
in the affirmative, 'Thou hast said' (that is, the truth); 'nevertheless' (or, rather, *moreover*), 'I say unto you, Hereafter shall ye
see the Son of Man sitting on the right hand of power, and
coming in the clouds of heaven' (Matt. xxvi. 63, 64). (4) From
the example of God, even the Father, who, 'willing more
abundantly to show unto the heirs of promise the immutability

of His counsel, confirmed it by an oath' (Heb. vi. 17). (5) From
the example of St. Paul, who we think had the Spirit of God,
and well understood the mind of his Master. 'God is my witness,'
saith he, to the Romans, 'that without ceasing I make mention
of you always in my prayers' (Rom. i. 9): to the Corinthians,
'I call God for a record upon my soul, that to spare you I came
not as yet unto Corinth' (2 Cor. i. 23): and to the Philippians,
'God is my record, how greatly I long after you in the bowels
of Jesus Christ' (Phil. i. 8). Hence it undeniably appears, that if
the Apostle knew the meaning of his Lord's words, they do not
forbid swearing on weighty occasions even to one another: how
much less before a magistrate! And, lastly, from that assertion
of the great Apostle, concerning solemn swearing in general
(which it is impossible he could have mentioned without
any touch of blame, if his Lord had totally forbidden it): 'Men
verily swear by the greater'; by one greater than themselves;
'and an oath for confirmation is to them an end of all strife'
(Heb. vi. 16).

11. But the great lesson which our blessed Lord inculcates
here, and which He illustrates by this example, is, that God is
in all things, and that we are to see the Creator in the glass of
every creature; that we should use and look upon nothing as
separate from God, which indeed is a kind of practical Atheism;
but, with a true magnificence of thought, survey heaven and
earth, and all that is therein, as contained by God in the hollow
of His hand, who by His intimate presence holds them all in
being, who pervades and actuates the whole created frame, and
is, in a true sense, the soul of the universe.

II. 1. Thus far our Lord has been more directly employed
in teaching the religion of the heart. He has shown what
Christians are to be. He proceeds to show what they are to
do also,—how inward holiness is to exert itself in our outward
conversation. 'Blessed,' saith He, 'are the peace-makers; for
they shall be called the children of God.'

2. 'The peace-makers': the word in the original is οἱ
εἰρηνοποιοί. It is well known that εἰρήνη, in the sacred
writings, implies all manner of good; every blessing that relates

either to the soul or the body, to time or eternity. Accordingly, when St. Paul, in the titles of his epistles, wishes grace and peace to the Romans or the Corinthians, it is as if he had said, 'As a fruit of the free, undeserved love and favour of God, may you enjoy all blessings, spiritual and temporal; all the good things which God hath prepared for them that love Him.'

3. Hence we may easily learn, in how wide a sense the term 'peace-makers' is to be understood. In its literal meaning it implies those lovers of God and man who utterly detest and abhor all strife and debate, all variance and contention; and accordingly labour with all their might, either to prevent this fire of hell from being kindled, or, when it is kindled, from breaking out, or, when it is broke out, from spreading any farther. They endeavour to calm the stormy spirits of men, to quiet their turbulent passions, to soften the minds of contending parties, and, if possible, reconcile them to each other. They use all innocent arts, and employ all their strength, all the talents which God has given them, as well to preserve peace where it is, as to restore it where it is not. It is the joy of their heart to promote, to confirm, to increase, mutual good-will among men, but more especially among the children of God, however distinguished by things of smaller importance; that as they have all 'one Lord, one faith,' as they are all 'called in one hope of their calling,' so they may all 'walk worthy of the vocation wherewith they are called; with all lowliness and meekness, with long-suffering, forbearing one another in love; endeavouring to keep the unity of the Spirit in the bond of peace.'

4. But, in the full extent of the word, a peace-maker, is one that, as he hath opportunity, 'doeth good unto all men'; one that, being filled with the love of God and of all mankind, cannot confine the expressions of it to his own family, or friends, or acquaintance, or party, or to those of his own opinions,— no, nor those who are partakers of like precious faith; but steps over all these narrow bounds, that he may do good to every man, that he may, some way or other, manifest his love to neighbours and strangers, friends and enemies. He doeth good to them all, as he hath opportunity, that is, on every possible occasion; 'redeeming the time,' in order thereto; buying up

every opportunity, improving every hour, losing no moment wherein he may profit another. He does good, not of one particular kind, but good in general, in every possible way; employing herein all his talents of every kind, all his powers and faculties of body and soul, all his fortune, his interest, his reputation; desiring only, that when his Lord cometh He may say, 'Well done, good and faithful servant.'

5. He doeth good to the uttermost of his power, even to the bodies of all men. He rejoices to 'deal his bread to the hungry,' and to 'cover the naked with a garment.' Is any a stranger? He takes him in, and relieves him according to his necessities. Are any sick or in prison? He visits them, and administers such help as they stand most in need of. And all this he does, not as unto man; but remembering Him that hath said, 'Inasmuch as ye have done it unto one of the least of these My brethren, ye have done it unto Me.'

6. How much more does he rejoice, if he can do any good to the soul of any man! This power, indeed, belongeth unto God. It is He only that changes the heart, without which every other change is lighter than vanity. Nevertheless, it pleases Him who worketh all in all, to help man chiefly by man; to convey His own power, and blessing, and love, through one man to another. Therefore, although it be certain that, 'the help which is done upon earth, God doeth it Himself'; yet has no man need, on this account, to stand idle in his vineyard. The peace-maker cannot: he is ever labouring therein, and, as an instrument in God's hand, preparing the ground for his Master's use, or sowing the seed of the kingdom, or watering what is already sown, if haply God may give the increase. According to the measure of grace which he has received, he uses all diligence, either to reprove the gross sinner, to reclaim those who run on headlong in the broad way of destruction; or' to give light to them that sit in darkness,' and are ready to 'perish for lack of knowledge'; or to 'support the weak, to lift up the hands that hang down, and the feeble knees'; or to bring back and heal that which was lame and turned out of the way. Nor is he less zealous to confirm those who are already striving to enter in at the strait gate; to strengthen those that stand, that they may 'run with patience

the race which is set before them'; to build up in their most holy faith those that know in whom they have believed; to exhort them to stir up the gift of God which is in them, that daily growing in grace, 'an entrance may be ministered unto them abundantly into the everlasting kingdom of our Lord and Saviour Jesus Christ.'

7. 'Blessed' are they who are thus continually employed in the work of faith and the labour of love; 'for they shall be called,' that is, *shall be* (a common Hebraism), 'the children of God.' God shall continue unto them the Spirit of adoption, yea, shall pour it more abundantly into their hearts. He shall bless them with all the blessings of His children. He shall acknowledge them as sons before angels and men; 'and if sons, then heirs; heirs of God, and joint-heirs with Christ.'

III. 1. One would imagine such a person as has been above described, so full of genuine humility, so unaffectedly serious, so mild and gentle, so free from all selfish design, so devoted to God, and such an active lover of men, should be the darling of mankind. But our Lord was better acquainted with human nature in its present state. He therefore closes the character of this man of God with showing him the treatment he is to expect in the world. 'Blessed,' saith He, 'are they which are persecuted for righteousness' sake; for theirs is the kingdom of heaven.'

2. In order to understand this throughly, let us, first, inquire, Who are they that are persecuted? And this we may easily learn from St. Paul: 'As of old, he that was born after the flesh persecuted him that was born after the Spirit, even so it is now' (Gal. iv. 29). 'Yea,' saith the Apostle, 'and all that will live godly in Christ Jesus shall suffer persecution' (2 Tim. iii. 12). The same we are taught by St. John: 'Marvel not, my brethren, if the world hate you. We know that we have passed from death unto life, because we love the brethren' (1 John iii. 13, 14). As if he had said, The brethren, the Christians, cannot be loved, but by them who have passed from death unto life. And most expressly by our Lord: 'If the world hate you, ye know that it hated Me before it hated you. If ye were of the world, the world would love his own; but because ye are not of the world, there-

fore the world hateth you. Remember the word that I said unto you, The servant is not greater than his lord. If they have persecuted Me, they will also persecute you' (John xv. 18, &c.).

By all these scriptures it manifestly appears who they are that are persecuted; namely, the righteous: he 'that is born of the Spirit'; 'all that will live godly in Christ Jesus'; they that are 'passed from death unto life'; those who are 'not of the world'; all those who are meek and lowly in heart, that mourn for God, that hunger after His likeness; all that love God and their neighbour, and therefore, as they have opportunity, do good unto all men.

3. If it be, secondly, inquired, why they are persecuted, the answer is equally plain and obvious. It is 'for righteousness' sake'; because they are righteous; because they are born after the Spirit; because they 'will live godly in Christ Jesus'; because they 'are not of the world.' Whatever may be pretended, this is the real cause: be their infirmities more or less, still, if it were not for this, they would be borne with, and the world would love its own. They are persecuted because they are *poor in spirit*; that is, say the world, 'poor-spirited, mean, dastardly souls, good for nothing, not fit to live in the world';—because they *mourn*: 'They are such dull, heavy, lumpish creatures, enough to sink any one's spirits that sees them! They are mere deathheads; they kill innocent mirth, and spoil company wherever they come';—because they are *meek*: 'Tame, passive fools, just fit to be trampled upon';—because they *hunger and thirst after righteousness*: 'A parcel of hot-brained enthusiasts, gaping after they know not what, not content with rational religion, but running mad after raptures and inward feelings';—because they are *merciful*, lovers of all, lovers of the evil and unthankful; 'Encouraging all manner of wickedness; nay, tempting people to do mischief by impunity: and men who, it is to be feared, have their own religion still to seek; very loose in their principles', —because they are *pure in heart*: 'Uncharitable creatures, that damn all the world, but those that are of their own sort! Blasphemous wretches, that pretend to make God a liar, to live without sin!'—Above all, because they are *peace-makers*; because they take all opportunities of doing good to all men This is the

grand reason why they have been persecuted in all ages, and will be till the restitution of all things: 'If they would but keep their religion to themselves, it would be tolerable: but it is this spreading their errors, this infecting so many others, which is not to be endured. They do so much mischief in the world, that they ought to be tolerated no longer. It is true, the men do some things well enough; they relieve some of the poor: but this, too, is only done to gain the more to their party; and so, in effect, to do the more mischief!' Thus the men of the world sincerely think and speak. And the more the kingdom of God prevails, the more the peace-makers are enabled to propagate lowliness, meekness, and all other divine tempers, the more mischief is done, in their account: consequently, the more are they enraged against the authors of this, and the more vehemently will they presecute them.

4. Let us, thirdly, inquire, Who are they that persecute them? St. Paul answers, 'He that is born after the flesh': every one who is not 'born of the Spirit,' or, at least, desirous so to be; all that do not at least labour to 'live godly in Christ Jesus'; all that are not 'passed from death unto life,' and, consequently, cannot 'love the brethren'; 'the world,' that is, according to our Saviour's account, they who 'know not Him that sent Me'; they who know not God, even the loving, pardoning God, by the teaching of His own Spirit.

The reason is plain: the spirit which is in the world is directly opposite to the Spirit which is of God. It must therefore needs be that those who are of the world will be opposite to those who are of God. There is the utmost contrariety between them, in all their opinions, their desires, designs, and tempers. And hitherto the leopard and the kid cannot lie down in peace together. The proud, because he is proud, cannot but persecute the lowly: the light and airy, those that mourn: and so in every other kind; the unlikeness of disposition (were there no other) being a perpetual ground of enmity. Therefore, were it only on this account, all the servants of the devil will persecute the children of God.

5. Should it be inquired, fourthly, how they will persecute them, it may be answered in general, Just in that manner and

measure which the wise Disposer of all sees will be most for His glory,—will tend most to His children's growth in grace, and the enlargement of His own kingdom. There is no one branch of God's government of the world which is more to be admired than this. His ear is never heavy to the threatenings of the persecutor, or the cry of the persecuted. His eye is ever open, and His hand stretched out to direct every, the minutest circumstance. When the storm shall begin, how high it shall rise, which way it shall point its course, when and how it shall end, are all determined by His unerring wisdom. The ungodly are only a sword of His; an instrument which He uses as it pleaseth Him, and which itself, when the gracious ends of His providence are answered, is cast into the fire.

At some rare times, as when Christianity was planted first, and while it was taking root in the earth; as also when the pure doctrine of Christ began to be planted again in our nation; God permitted the storm to rise high, and His children were called to resist unto blood. There was a peculiar reason why He suffered this with regard to the Apostles, that their evidence might be the more unexceptionable. But from the annals of the church we learn another, and a far different reason, why He suffered the heavy presecutions which arose in the second and third centuries; namely, because 'the mystery of iniquity' did so strongly 'work'; because of the monstrous corruptions which even then reigned in the church: these God chastised, and at the same time strove to heal, by those severe but necessary visitations.

Perhaps the same observation may be made, with regard to the grand persecution in our own land. God had dealt very graciously with our nation: He had poured out various blessings upon us: He had given us peace abroad and at home; and a king, wise and good beyond his years: and, above all, He had caused the pure light of His gospel to arise and shine amongst us. But what return did He find? 'He looked for righteousness; but behold a cry'—a cry of oppression and wrong, of ambition and injustice, of malice, and fraud, and covetousness. Yea, the cry of those who even then expired in the flames entered into the ears of the Lord of Sabaoth. It was then God arose to maintain His own cause against those that held the truth in unright-

eousness. Then He sold them into the hands of their persecutors,
by a judgement mixed with mercy; an affliction to punish, and
yet a medicine to heal, the grievous backslidings of His people.

6. But it is seldom God suffers the storm to rise so high as
torture or death, or bonds, or imprisonment.   Whereas His
children are frequently called to endure the lighter kinds of
persecution; they frequently suffer the estrangement of kins-
folks the loss of the friends that were as their own soul. They
find the truth of their Lord's word (concerning the *event*, though
not the *design*, of His coming), 'Suppose ye that I am come to
give peace upon earth? I tell you, Nay; but rather division'
(Luke xii. 51). And hence will naturally follow loss of business
or employment, and consequently of substance. But all these
circumstances likewise are under the wise direction of God,
who allots to every one what is most expedient for him.

7. But the persecution which attends *all* the children of God
is that our Lord describes in the following words: 'Blessed are
ye when men shall revile you and persecute you'—shall persecute by reviling you—'and say all manner of evil against you
falsely, for My sake.' This cannot fail; it is the very badge of our
discipleship; it is one of the seals of our calling; it is a sure portion
entailed on all the children of God: if we have it not, we are
bastards, and not sons: straight through evil report, as well as
good report, lies the only way to the kingdom.   The meek,
serious, humble, zealous lovers of God and man are of good
report among their brethren; but of evil report with the world,
who count and treat them 'as the filth and offscouring of all things.'

8. Indeed, some have supposed that before the fullness of
the Gentiles shall come in, the scandal of the cross will cease; that
God will cause Christians to be esteemed and loved even by
those who are as yet in their sins. Yea, and sure it is, that even
now He at some times suspends the contempt as well as the
fierceness of men; 'He makes a man's enemies to be at peace
with him' for a season, and gives him favour with his bitterest
persecutors. But setting aside this exempt case, the scandal of the
cross is not yet ceased; but a man may say still, 'If I please men,
I am not the servant of Christ.' Let no man therefore regard
that pleasing suggestion (pleasing doubtless to flesh and blood),

'that bad men only *pretend* to hate and despise them that are good, but do indeed love and esteem them in their hearts.' Not so: they may employ them sometimes; but it is for their own profit. They may put confidence in them; for they know their ways are not like other men's. But still they love them not; unless so far as the Spirit of God may be striving with them. Our Saviour's words are express: 'If ye were of the world, the world would love its own; but because ye are not of the world, therefore the world hateth you.' Yea (setting aside what exceptions may be made by the preventing grace, or the peculiar providence, of God), it hateth them as cordially and sincerely as ever it did their Master.

9. It remains only to inquire, How are the children of God to behave with regard to persecution? And, first, they ought not knowingly or designedly to bring it upon themselves. This is contrary both to the example and advice of our Lord and all His Apostles; who teach us not only not to seek, but to avoid it, as far as we can, without injuring our conscience; without giving up any part of that righteousness which we are to prefer before life itself. So our Lord expressly: 'When they persecute you in this city, flee ye into another'; which is indeed, when it can be taken, the most unexceptionable way of avoiding persecution.

10. Yet think not that you can always avoid it, either by this or any other means. If ever that idle imagination steals into your heart, put it to flight by that earnest caution, 'Remember the word that I said unto you, The servant is not greater than his lord. If they have persecuted Me, they will also persecute you.' 'Be ye wise as serpents, and harmless as doves.' But will this screen you from persecution? Not unless you have more wisdom than your Master, or more innocence than the Lamb of God.

Neither desire to avoid it, to escape it wholly; for if you do, you are none of His. If you escape the persecution, you escape the blessing; the blessing of those who are persecuted for righteousness' sake. If you are not persecuted for righteousness' sake, you cannot enter into the kingdom of heaven. 'If we suffer with Him, we shall also reign with Him. But if we deny Him, He will also deny us.'

11. Nay, rather, 'rejoice and be exceeding glad,' when men

persecute you for His sake; when they persecute you by reviling you, and by 'saying all manner of evil against you falsely'; which they will not fail to mix with every kind of persecution: they must blacken you to excuse themselves: 'For so persecuted they the prophets which were before you,'—those who were most eminently holy in heart and life; yea, and all the righteous which ever have been from the beginning of the world. Rejoice, because by this mark also ye know unto whom ye belong; and 'because great is your reward in heaven'—the reward purchased by the blood of the covenant, and freely bestowed in proportion to your sufferings, as well as to your holiness of heart and life. 'Be exceeding glad'; knowing that these 'light afflictions, which are but for a moment, work out for you a far more exceeding and eternal weight of glory.'

12. Meantime, let no persecution turn you out of the way of lowliness and meekness, of love and beneficence. 'Ye have heard' indeed 'that it hath been said, An eye for an eye, and a tooth for a tooth' (Matt. v. 38): and your miserable teachers have hence allowed you to avenge yourselves, to return evil for evil: 'but I say unto you, That ye resist not evil,'—not thus; not by returning it in kind. 'But,' rather than do this, 'whosoever smiteth thee on thy right cheek, turn to him the other also. And if any man will sue thee at the law, and take away thy coat, let him have thy cloak also. And whosoever shall compel thee to go a mile, go with him twain.'

So invincible let thy meekness be. And be thy love suitable thereto. 'Give to him that asketh thee, and from him that would borrow of thee turn not thou away.' Only, give not away that which is another man's, that which is not thine own. Therefore, (1) Take care to owe no man anything: for what thou owest is not thine own, but another man's. (2) Provide for those of thine own household. This also God hath required of thee; and what is necessary to sustain them in life and godliness is also not thine own. Then, (3) Give or lend all that remains, from day to day, or from year to year: only, first, seeing thou canst not give or lend to all, remember the household of faith.

13. The meekness and love we are to feel, the kindness we are to show to them which persecute us for righteousness' sake, our

blessed Lord describes farther in the following verses: O that
they were engraven upon our hearts! 'Ye have heard that it
hath been said, Thou shalt love thy neighbour, and hate thy
enemy' (Matt. v. 43, &c.): God indeed had said only the former
part, 'Thou shalt love thy neighbour'; the children of the devil
had added the latter, 'and hate thy enemy': 'But I say unto you,'
(1) 'Love your enemies': see that you bear a tender good-will to
those who are most bitter of spirit against you; who wish you
all manner of evil. (2) 'Bless them that curse you.' Are there
any whose bitterness of spirit breaks forth in bitter words? who
are continually cursing and reproaching you when you are
present, and 'saying all evil against you' when absent? So much
the rather do you bless: in conversing with them, use all mildness
and softness of language. Reprove them, by repeating a better
lesson before them; by showing them how they ought to have
spoken. And, in speaking of them, say all the good you can,
without violating the rules of truth and justice. (3) 'Do good to
them that hate you': let your actions show that you are as real
in love, as they in hatred. Return good for evil. 'Be not overcome of evil, but overcome evil with good.' (4) If you can do
nothing more, at least 'pray for them that despitefully use you
and persecute you.' You can never be disabled from doing this;
nor can all their malice or violence hinder you. Pour out your
souls to God, not only for those who did this once, but now
repent; this is a little thing: 'If thy brother, seven times a day,
turn and say unto thee, I repent' (Luke xvii. 4); that is, if, after
ever so many relapses, he give thee reason to believe that he is
really and throughly changed; then thou shalt forgive him, so as
to trust him, to put him in thy bosom, as if he had never sinned
against thee at all; but pray for, wrestle with God for, those
that do not repent, that now despitefully use thee and persecute
thee. Thus far forgive them, 'not until seven times only, but
until, seventy times seven' (Matt. xviii. 22). Whether they
repent or no, yea, though they appear farther and farther from
it, yet show them this instance of kindness; 'that ye may be the
children,' that ye may approve yourselves the genuine children,
'of your Father which is in heaven'; who shows His goodness by
giving such blessings as they are capable of, even to His stub-

bornest enemies; 'who maketh His sun to rise on the evil and on
the good, and sendeth rain on the just and on the unjust.' 'For
if ye love them which love you, what reward have ye? do not
even the publicans the same?' (Matt. v. 46)—who pretend to no
religion; whom ye yourselves acknowledge to be without God
in the world. 'And if ye salute,' show kindness in word or
deed to, 'your brethren,' your friends or kinsfolk, 'only; what
do ye more than others?'—than those who have no religion at
all? 'do not even the publicans so?' (Matt. v. 47). Nay, but
follow ye a better pattern than them. In patience, in long-
suffering, in mercy, in beneficence of every kind, to all, even to
your bitterest persecutors; 'be ye,' Christians, 'perfect,' in kind,
though not in degree, 'even as your Father which is in heaven is
perfect' (Matt. v. 48).

IV. Behold Christianity in its native form, as delivered by its
great Author! This is the genuine religion of Jesus Christ! Such
He presents it to him whose eyes are opened. See a picture of
God so far as He is imitable by man! a picture drawn by God's
own hand. 'Behold, ye despisers, and wonder, and perish!
Or, rather, wonder and adore! Rather cry out, 'Is this the
religion of Jesus of Nazareth? the religion which I persecuted?
Let me no more be found even to fight against God. Lord,
what wouldest Thou have me to do?' What beauty appears in
the whole! How just a symmetry! What exact proportion in
every part! How desirable is the happiness here described! How
venerable, how lovely the holiness! This is the spirit of religion;
the quintessence of it. These are indeed the fundamentals of
Christianity. O that we may not be hearers of it only!—'like a
man beholding his own face in a glass, who goeth his way, and
straightway forgetteth what manner of man he was. Nay, but
let us steadily 'look into this perfect law of liberty, and continue
therein.' Let us not rest, until every line thereof is transcribed
into our own hearts. Let us watch, and pray, and believe, and
love, and 'strive for the mastery,' till every part of it shall appear
in our soul, graven there by the finger of God; till we are 'holy
as He which hath called us is holy, perfect as our Father which
is in heaven is perfect.'

SERMON XIX

UPON OUR LORD'S SERMON ON THE MOUNT

DISCOURSE IV

*Ye are the salt of the earth, but if the salt have lost his savour, wherewith shall
    it be salted? it is thenceforth good for nothing, but to be cast out, and to be
    trodden under foot of men.*
Ye are the light of the world. A city that is set on an hill cannot be hid.
*Neither do men light a candle, and put it under a bushel, but on a candlestick;
    and it giveth light unto all that are in the house.*
*Let your light so shine before men, that they may see your good works, and
    glorify your Father which is in heaven.*

—MATT. v. 13-16.

THE beauty of holiness, of that inward man of the heart which
is renewed after the image of God, cannot but strike every eye
which God hath opened—every enlightened understanding.
The ornament of a meek, humble, loving spirit, will at least
excite the approbation of all those who are capable, in any
degree, of discerning spiritual good and evil. From the hour
men begin to emerge out of the darkness which covers the giddy,
unthinking world, they cannot but perceive how desirable a
thing it is to be thus transformed into the likeness of Him that
created us. This inward religion bears the shape of God so
visibly impressed upon it, that a soul must be wholly immersed
in flesh and blood when he can doubt of its divine original. We
may say of this, in a secondary sense, even as of the Son of God
Himself, that it is 'the brightness of His glory, the express image
of His person'—ἀπαύγασμα τῆς δόξης αὐτοῦ—'the beaming
forth of His' eternal 'glory'; and yet so tempered and softened,
that even the children of men may herein see God and live;
χαρακτὴρ τῆς ὑποστάσεως αὐτοῦ—'the character, the stamp, the
living impression of His person,' who is the fountain of beauty
and love, the original source of all excellency and perfection.

2. If religion, therefore, were carried no farther than this,

they could have no doubt concerning it; they should have no objection against pursuing it with the whole ardour of their souls. 'But why,' say they, 'is it clogged with other things? What need of loading it with *doing* and *suffering*? These are what damps the vigour of the soul, and sinks it down to earth again. Is it not enough to "follow after charity"; to soar upon the wings of love? Will it not suffice to worship God, who is a Spirit, with the spirit of our minds, without encumbering ourselves with outward things, or even thinking of them at all? Is it not better, that the whole extent of our thought should be taken up with high and heavenly contemplation; and that instead of busying ourselves at all about externals, we should only commune with God in our hearts?'

3. Many eminent men have spoken thus; have advised us 'to cease from all outward action'; wholly to withdraw from the world; to leave the body behind us; to abstract ourselves from all sensible things; to have no concern at all about outward religion, but *to work all virtues in the will*; as the far more excellent way, more perfective of the soul as well as more acceptable to God.

4. It needed not that any should tell our Lord of this masterpiece of the wisdom from beneath, this fairest of all the devices wherewith Satan hath ever perverted the right ways of the Lord! And O! what instruments hath he found, from time to time, to employ in this his service, to wield this grand engine of hell against some of the most important truths of God!— men that would 'deceive, if it were possible, the very elect,' the men of faith and love; yea, that have for a season deceived and led away no inconsiderable number of them, who have fallen in all ages into the gilded snare, and hardly escaped with the skin of their teeth.

5. But has our Lord been wanting on His part? Has He not sufficiently guarded us against this pleasing delusion? Has He not armed us here with armour of proof against Satan 'transformed into an angel of light'? Yea, verily: He here defends, in the clearest and strongest manner, the active, patient religion He had just described. What can be fuller and plainer than the words He immediately subjoins to what He had said of doing

and suffering? 'Ye are the salt of the earth: but if the salt have lost his savour, wherewith shall it be salted? It is thenceforth good for nothing but to be cast out, and trodden under foot of men. Ye are the light of the world. A city that is set on an hill cannot be hid. Neither do men light a candle and put it under a bushel, but on a candlestick; and it giveth light to all that are in the house. Let your light so shine before men, that they may see your good works, and glorify your Father which is in heaven.'

In order fully to explain and enforce these important words, I shall endeavour to show, first, that Christianity is essentially a social religion; and that to turn it into a solitary one is to destroy it. Secondly, that to conceal this religion is impossible, as well as utterly contrary to the design of its Author. I shall, thirdly, answer some objections; and conclude the whole with a practical application.

I. 1. First. I shall endeavour to show, that Christianity is essentially a social religion; and that to turn it into a solitary religion, is indeed to destroy it.

By Christianity, I mean that method of worshipping God which is here revealed to man by Jesus Christ. When I say, This is essentially a social religion, I mean not only that it cannot subsist so well, but that it cannot subsist at all, without society, —without living and conversing with other men. And in showing this, I shall confine myself to those considerations which will arise from the very discourse before us. But if this be shown, then, doubtless, to turn this religion into a solitary one is to destroy it.

Not that we can in any wise condemn the intermixing solitude or retirement with society. This is not only allowable, but expedient; nay, it is necessary, as daily experience shows, for every one that either already is, or desires to be a real Christian. It can hardly be, that we should spend one entire day in a continued intercourse with men, without suffering loss in our soul, and in some measure grieving the Holy Spirit of God. We have need daily to retire from the world, at least morning and evening, to converse with God, to commune more freely with our Father which is in secret. Nor indeed can a man of experience condemn even longer seasons of religious retirement, so they do not imply any neglect of the worldly employ wherein the providence of God has placed us.

2. Yet such retirement must not swallow up all our time: this would be to destroy, not advance, true religion. For, that the religion described by our Lord in the foregoing words cannot subsist without society, without our living and conversing with other men, is manifest from hence, that several of the most essential branches thereof can have no place if we have no intercourse with the world.

3. There is no disposition, for instance, which is more essential to Christianity than meekness. Now although this, as it implies resignation to God, or patience in pain and sickness, may subsist in a desert, in a hermit's cell, in total solitude; yet as it implies (which it no less necessarily does) mildness, gentleness, and long-suffering, it cannot possibly have a being, it has no place under heaven, without an intercourse with other men: so that to attempt turning this into a solitary virtue is to destroy it from the face of the earth.

4. Another necessary branch of true Christianity is peace-making, or doing of good. That this is equally essential with any of the other parts of the religion of Jesus Christ, there can be no stronger argument to evince (and therefore it would be absurd to allege any other), than that it is here inserted in the original plan He has laid down of the fundamentals of His religion. Therefore, to set aside this is the same daring insult on the authority of our Great Master as to set aside mercifulness, purity of heart, or any other branch of His institution. But this is apparently set aside by all who call us to the wilderness; who recommend entire solitude either to the babes, or the young men, or the fathers in Christ. For will any man affirm that a solitary Christian (so-called, though it is little less than a contradiction in terms) can be a merciful man,—that is, one that takes every opportunity of doing all good to all men? What can be more plain than that this fundamental branch of the religion of Jesus Christ cannot possibly subsist without society, without our living and conversing with other men?

5. 'But is it not expedient, however' one might naturally ask,

'to converse only with good men,—only with those whom we know to be meek and merciful, holy of heart, and holy of life? Is it not expedient to refrain from any conversation or intercourse with men of the opposite character,—men who do not obey, perhaps do not believe, the gospel of our Lord Jesus Christ?' The advice of St. Paul to the Christians at Corinth may seem to favour this: 'I wrote unto you in an epistle not to company with fornicators' (1 Cor. v. 9). And it is certainly not advisable so to company with them or with any of the workers of iniquity, as to have any particular familiarity or any strictness of friendship with them. To contract or continue an intimacy with any such is no way expedient for a Christian. It must necessarily expose him to abundance of dangers and snares, out of which he can have no reasonable hope of deliverance.

But the Apostle does not forbid us to have any intercourse at all even with the men that know not God: 'For then,' says he, 'ye must needs go out of the world'; which he could never advise them to do. But he subjoins, 'If any man that is called a brother,' that professes himself a Christian, 'be a fornicator, or covetous, or an idolater, or a railer, or a drunkard, or an extortioner' (1 Cor. v. 11); 'now I have written unto you not to keep company with' him; 'with such an one no not to eat.' This must necessarily imply, that we break off all familiarity, all intimacy of acquaintance, with him. 'Yet count him not,' saith the Apostle elsewhere, 'as an enemy, but admonish him as a brother' (2 Thess. iii. 15); plainly showing that even in such a case as this, we are not to renounce all fellowship with him. So that here is no advice to separate wholly even from wicked men. Yea, these very words teach us quite the contrary.

6. Much more the words of our Lord; who is so far from directing us to break off all commerce with the world, that without it, according to His account of Christianity, we cannot be Christians at all. It would be easy to show, that some intercourse even with ungodly and unholy men is absolutely needful, in order to the full exertion of every temper which He has described as the way to the kingdom; that it is indispensably necessary, in order to the complete exercise of poverty of spirit, of mourning, and of every other disposition which has a place

here, in the genuine religion of Jesus Christ. Yea, it is necessary to the very being of several of them: of that meekness, for example, which, instead of demanding 'an eye for an eye, or a tooth for a tooth,' doth 'not resist evil,' but causes us rather, when smitten 'on the right cheek, to turn the other also'; of that mercifulness, whereby we 'love our enemies, bless them that curse us, do good to them that hate us, and pray for them which despitefuly use us and persecute us'; and of that complication of love and all holy tempers which is exercised in suffering for righteousness' sake. Now all these, it is clear, could have no being, were we to have no commerce with any but real Christ- ians.

7. Indeed, were we wholly to separate ourselves from sinners, how could we possibly answer that character which our Lord gives us in these very words? 'Ye' (Christians, ye that are lowly, serious, and meek; ye that hunger after righteousness, that love God and man, that do good to all, and therefore suffer evil; ye) 'are the salt of the earth': it is your very nature to season whatever is round about you. It is the nature of the divine savour which is in you, to spread to whatsoever you touch; to diffuse itself, on every side, to all those among whom you are. This is the great reason why the providence of God has so mingled you together with other men, that whatever grace you have received of God may through you be communicated to others; that every holy temper and word and work of yours may have an influence on them also. By this means a check will, in some measure, be given to the corruption which is in the world; and a small part, at least, saved from the general infection, and rendered holy and pure before God.

8. That we may the more diligently labour to season all we can with every holy and heavenly temper, our Lord proceeds to show the desperate state of those who do not impart the religion they have received; which indeed they cannot possibly fail to do, so long as it remains in their own hearts. 'If the salt have lost his savour, wherewith shall it be salted? It is thenceforth good for nothing but to be cast out, and trodden under foot of men': if ye who were holy and heavenly-minded, and con- sequently zealous of good works, have no longer that savour in

yourselves, and do therefore no longer season others: if you are grown flat, insipid, dead, both careless of your own souls, and useless to the souls of other men; wherewith shall ye be salted? How shall ye be recovered? What help? What hope? Can tasteless salt be restored to its savour? No; 'it is thenceforth good for nothing but to be cast out,' even as the mire in the streets, 'and to be trodden under foot of men,' to be overwhelmed with everlasting contempt. If ye had never known the Lord, there might have been hope,—if ye had never been 'found in Him': but what can you now say to that, His solemn declaration just parallel to what He hath here spoken? 'Every branch in Me that beareth not fruit, He,' the Father, 'taketh away. He that abideth in Me, and I in him, bringeth forth much fruit.' 'If a man abide not in Me,' or do not bring forth fruit, 'he is cast out as a branch, and withered; and men gather them,' not to plant them again, but 'to cast them into the fire' (John xv. 2, 5, 6).

9. Toward those who have never tasted of the good word, God is indeed pitiful and of tender mercy. But justice takes place with regard to those who have tasted that the Lord is gracious, and have afterwards turned back 'from the holy commandment' then 'delivered to them.' 'For it is impossible for those who were once enlightened' (Heb. vi. 4, &c.); in whose hearts God had once shined, to enlighten them with the knowledge of the glory of God in the face of Jesus Christ; 'who have tasted of the heavenly gift,' of redemption in His blood, the forgiveness of sins; 'and were made partakers of the Holy Ghost,' of lowliness, of meekness, and of the love of God and man shed abroad in their hearts by the Holy Ghost which was given unto them; and 'have fallen away'—καὶ παραπεσόντας (here is not a supposition, but a flat declaration of matter of fact), 'to renew them again unto repentance; seeing they crucify to themselves the Son of God afresh, and put Him to an open shame.

But that none may misunderstand these awful words, it should be carefully observed, (1) Who they are that are here spoken of; namely, they, and they only, who were once thus 'enlightened'; they only, 'who did taste of' that 'heavenly gift, and were' thus 'made partakers of the Holy Ghost.' So that

all who have not experienced these things are wholly unconcerned in this scripture. (2) What that falling away is, which
is here spoken of: it is an absolute, total apostasy. A believer
may fall, and not fall away. He may fall and rise again. And
if he should fall, even into sin, yet this case, dreadful as it is,
is not desperate. For 'we have an Advocate with the Father,
Jesus Christ the righteous; and He is the propitiation for our
sins.' But let him above all things beware, lest his 'heart be
hardened by the deceitfulness of sin'; lest he should sink lower
and lower, till he wholly fall away, till he become as salt that
hath lost its savour: for if we thus sin wilfully, after we have
received the experimental 'knowledge of the truth, there remaineth no more sacrifice for sins; but a certain fearful looking
for of judgement and fiery indignation, which shall devour the
adversaries.'

II. 1. 'But although we may not wholly separate ourselves
from mankind, although it be granted we ought to season
them with the religion which God has wrought in our hearts,
yet may not this be done insensibly? May we not convey this
into others in a secret and almost imperceptible manner, so
that scarce any one shall be able to observe how or when it is
done?—even as salt conveys its own savour into that which is
seasoned thereby, without any noise, and without being liable
to any outward observation. And if so, although we do not go
out of the world, yet we may lie hid in it. We may thus far
keep our religion to ourselves; and not offend those whom we
cannot help.'

2. Of this plausible reasoning of flesh and blood our Lord was
well aware also: and He has given a full answer to it in those
words which come now to be considered; in explaining which,
I shall endeavour to show, as I proposed to do in the second
place, that so long as true religion abides in our hearts, it is
impossible to conceal it, as well as absolutely contrary to the
design of its great Author.

And, first, it is impossible for any that have it, to conceal
the religion of Jesus Christ. This our Lord makes plain beyond
all contradiction, by a two-fold comparison: 'Ye are the light of

the world: a city set upon an hill cannot be hid.' Ye Christians
are 'the light of the world,' with regard both to your tempers
and actions. Your holiness makes you as conspicuous as the sun
in the midst of heaven. As ye cannot go out of the world, so
neither can ye stay in it without appearing to all mankind. Ye
may not flee from men; and while ye are among them, it is
impossible to hide your lowliness and meekness, and those other
dispositions whereby ye aspire to be perfect as your Father
which is in heaven is perfect. Love cannot be hid any more
than light; and least of all, when it shines forth in action, when
ye exercise yourselves in the labour of love, in beneficence of
every kind. As well may men think to hide a city, as to hide a
Christian; yea, as well may they conceal a city set upon a hill, as
a holy, zealous, active lover of God and man.

3. It is true, men who love darkness rather than light, because
their deeds are evil, will take all possible pains to prove, that the
light which is in you is darkness. They will say evil, all manner
of evil, falsely, of the good which is in you; they will lay to your
charge that which is farthest from your thoughts, which is the
very reverse of all you are, and all you do. And your patient
continuance in well-doing, your meek suffering all things for
the Lord's sake, your calm, humble joy in the midst of persecution, your unwearied labour to overcome evil with good, will
make you still more visible and conspicuous than ye were before.

4. So impossible it is, to keep our religion from being seen,
unless we cast it away; so vain is the thought of hiding the light,
unless by putting it out! Sure it is, that a secret, unobserved
religion cannot be the religion of Jesus Christ. Whatever religion
can be concealed, is not Christianity. If a Christian could be
hid, he could not be compared to a city set upon a hill; to the
light of the world, the sun shining from heaven, and seen by all
the world below. Never, therefore, let it enter into the heart
of him whom God hath renewed in the spirit of his mind, to
hide that light, to keep his religion to himself; especially considering it is not only impossible to conceal true Christianity,
but likewise absolutely contrary to the design of the great
Author of it.

5. This plainly appears from the following words: 'Neither

do men light a candle to put it under a bushel.' As if he had
said, As men do not light a candle, only to cover and conceal it,
so neither does God enlighten any soul with His glorious knowledge and love, to have it covered or concealed, either by
prudence, falsely so called, or shame, or voluntary humility; to
have it hid either in a desert, or in the world; either by avoiding
men, or in conversing with them. 'But they put it on a candlestick, and it giveth light to all that are in the house': in like manner, it is the design of God that every Christian should be in an
open point of view; that he may give light to all around, that he
may visibly express the religion of Jesus Christ.

6. Thus hath God in all ages spoken to the world, not only
by precept, but by example also. He hath 'not left Himself
without witness,' in any nation where the sound of the gospel
hath gone forth, without a few who have testified His truth by
their lives as well as their words. These have been 'as light
shining in a dark place.' And from time to time they have been
the means of enlightening some, of preserving a remnant, a
little seed which was 'counted unto the Lord for a generation.'
They have led a few poor sheep out of the darkness of the world,
and guided their feet into the way of peace.

7. One may imagine that, where both Scripture and the
reason of things speak so clearly and expressly, there could not
be much advanced on the other side, at least not with any appearance of truth. But they who imagine thus know little of the
depths of Satan. After all that Scripture and reason have said, so
exceeding plausible are the pretences for solitary religion, for a
Christian's going out of the world, or at least hiding himself in it,
that we need all the wisdom of God to see through the snare, and
all the power of God to escape it; so many and strong are the
objections which have been brought against being social, open,
active Christians.

III. 1. To answer these, was the third thing which I proposed.
And, first, it has been often objected, that religion does not lie in
outward things, but in the heart, the inmost soul; that it is the
union of the soul with God, the life of God in the soul of man;
that outside religion is nothing worth; seeing God 'delighteth not

in burnt-offerings,' in outward services, but a pure and holy heart is the 'sacrifice He will not despise.'

I answer, It is most true, that the root of religion lies in the heart, in the inmost soul; that this is the union of the soul with God, the life of God in the soul of man. But if this root be really in the heart, it cannot but put forth branches. And these are the several instances of outward obedience, which partake of the same nature with the root; and, consequently, are not only marks or signs, but substantial parts, of religion.

It is also true, that bare outside religion, which has no root in the heart, is nothing worth; that God delighteth not in *such* outward services, no more than in Jewish burnt-offerings; and that a pure and holy heart is a sacrifice with which He is always well pleased. But He is also well pleased with all that outward service which arises from the heart; with the sacrifice of our prayers (whether public or private), of our praises and thanksgivings; with the sacrifice of our goods, humbly devoted to Him, and employed wholly to His glory; and with that of our bodies, which He peculiarly claims, which the Apostle beseeches us, 'by the mercies of God, to present unto Him, a living sacrifice, holy and acceptable unto God.'

2. A second objection, nearly related to this, is, that love is all in all; that it is 'the fulfilling of the law,' 'the end of the commandment,' of every commandment of God; that all we do, and all we suffer, if we have not charity or love, profiteth us nothing; and therefore the Apostle directs us to 'follow after charity,' and terms this 'the more excellent way,'

I answer, It is granted, that the love of God and man, arising from faith unfeigned, is all in all, the fulfilling of the law, the end of every commandment of God. It is true, that without this, whatever we do, whatever we suffer, profits us nothing. But it does not follow, that love is all in such a sense as to supersede either faith or good works. It is 'the fulfilling of the law,' not by releasing us from but by constraining us to obey it. It is 'the end of the commandment,' as every commandment leads to and centres in it. It is allowed, that whatever we do or suffer without love profits us nothing: but withal, whatever we do or suffer in love, though it were only the suffering reproach for Christ, or

17

the giving a cup of cold water in His name, it shall in no wise lose its reward.

3. 'But does not the Apostle direct us to "follow after charity"? And does he not term it "a more excellent way"?'—He does direct us to 'follow after charity'; but not after that alone. His, words are, 'Follow after charity, and desire spiritual gifts' (1 Cor. xiv. 1). Yea, 'follow after charity'; and desire to spend and be spent for your brethren. 'Follow after charity'; and, as you have opportunity, do good to all men.

In the same verse wherein he terms this, the way of love, 'a more excellent way,' he directs the Corinthians to desire other gifts besides it; yea, to desire them earnestly. 'Covet earnestly,' saith he, 'the best gifts; and yet I show unto you a more excellent way' (1 Cor. xii. 31). More excellent than what? Than the gifts of healing, of speaking with tongues, and of interpreting mentioned in the preceding verse; but not more excellent than the way of obedience. Of this the Apostle is not speaking; neither is he speaking of outward religion at all: so that this text is quite wide of the present question.

But suppose the Apostle had been speaking of outward as well as inward religion, and comparing them together; suppose, in the comparison, he had given the preference ever so much to the latter; suppose he had preferred (as he justly might) a loving heart, before all outward works whatever; yet it would not follow that we were to reject either one or the other. No; God hath joined them together from the beginning of the world; and let not man put them asunder.

4. 'But "God is a Spirit; and they that worship Him, must worship Him in spirit and in truth." And is not this enough? Nay, ought we not to employ the whole strength of our mind herein? Does not attending to outward things clog the soul, that it cannot soar aloft in holy contemplation? Does it not damp the vigour of our thought? Has it not a natural tendency to encumber and distract the mind? Whereas St. Paul would have us to be "without carefulness," and to "wait upon the Lord without distraction." '

I answer, 'God is a Spirit; and they that worship Him, must worship Him in spirit and in truth.' Yea, and this is enough:

we ought to employ the whole strength of our mind therein. But then I would ask, What is it to worship God, a Spirit, in spirit and in truth? Why, it is to worship Him with our spirit; to worship Him in that manner which none but spirits are capable of. It is to believe in Him, as a wise, just, holy Being, of purer eyes than to behold iniquity; and yet merciful, gracious, and longsuffering; forgiving iniquity, and transgression, and sin; casting all our sins behind His back, and accepting us in the Beloved. It is, to love Him, to delight in Him, to desire Him, with all our heart, and mind, and soul, and strength; to imitate Him we love, by purifying ourselves even as He is pure; and to obey Him whom we love, and in whom we believe, both in thought, and word, and work. Consequently, one branch of the worshipping God in spirit and in truth is, the keeping His outward conmandments. To glorify Him, therefore, with our bodies as well as with our spirits; to go through outward work with hearts lifted up to Him; to make our daily employment a sacrifice to God; to buy and sell, to eat and drink, to His glory, —this is worshipping God in spirit and in truth, as much as the praying to Him in a wilderness.

5. But if so, then contemplation is only one way of worshipping God in spirit and in truth. Therefore to give ourselves up entirely to this, would be to destroy many branches of spiritual worship, all equally acceptable to God, and equally profitable, not hurtful to the soul. For it is a great mistake, to suppose that an attention to those outward things, whereto the providence of God hath called us, is any clog to a Christian, or any hindrance at all to his always seeing Him that is invisible. It does not at all damp the ardour of his thought; it does not encumber or distract his mind; it gives him no uneasy or hurtful care, who does it all as unto the Lord; who hath learned, whatsoever he doeth in word or deed, to do all in the name of the Lord Jesus; having only one eye of the soul, which moves round on outward things, and one immovably fixed on God. Learn what this meaneth, ye poor recluses, that you may clearly discern your own littleness of faith: yea, that you may no longer judge others by yourselves, go and learn what that meaneth,—

Thou, O Lord, in tender love,
  Dost all my burdens bear;
Lift my heart to things above,
  And fix it ever there.
Calm on tumult's wheel I sit;
  'Midst busy multitudes alone;
Sweetly waiting at Thy feet,
  Till all Thy will be done.

6. But the grand objection is still behind. 'We appeal,' say they, 'to experience. Our light did shine; we used outward things many years; and yet they profited nothing. We attended on all the ordinances; but we were no better for it; nor indeed any one else: nay, we were the worse; for we fancied ourselves Christians for so doing, when we knew not what Christianity meant.

I allow the fact: I allow that you and ten thousand more have thus abused the ordinances of God; mistaking the means for the end; supposing that the doing these, or some other outward works, either was the religion of Jesus Christ, or would be accepted in the place of it. But let the abuse be taken away, and the use remain. Now use all outward things, but use them with a constant eye to the renewal of your soul in righteousness and true holiness.

7. But this is not all: they affirm, 'Experience likewise shows, that the trying to do good is but lost labour. What does it avail to feed or clothe men's bodies, if they are just dropping into everlasting fire? And what good can any man do to their souls? If these are changed, God doeth it Himself. Besides, all men are either good, at least desirous so to be, or obstinately · evil. Now the former have no need of us; let them ask help of God, and it shall be given them: and the latter will receive no help from us. Nay, and our Lord forbids to "cast our pearls before swine."'

I answer, (1) Whether they will finally be lost or saved, you are expressly commanded to feed the hungry, and clothe the naked. If you can, and do not, whatever becomes of them, you shall go away into everlasting fire. (2) Though it is God only changes hearts, yet He generally doeth it by man. It is our part to do all that in us lies, as diligently as if we could change them ourselves, and then to leave the event to Him. (3) God, in answer to their prayers, builds up His children by each other in every good gift; nourishing and strengthening the whole 'body by that which every joint supplieth.' So that 'the eye cannot say to the hand, I have no need of thee'; no, nor even 'the head to the feet, I have no need of you.' Lastly. How are you assured, that the persons before you are dogs or swine? Judge them not, until you have tried. 'How knowest thou, O man, but thou mayest gain thy brother'—but thou mayest, under God, save his soul from death? When he spurns thy love, and blasphemes the good word, then it is time to give him up to God.

8. 'We have tried; we have laboured to reform sinners; and what did it avail? On many we could make no impression at all: and if some were changed for a while, yet their goodness was but as the morning dew, and they were soon as bad, nay, worse than ever: so that we only hurt them, and ourselves too; for our minds were hurried and discomposed,—perhaps filled with anger instead of love: therefore, we had better have kept our religion to ourselves.'

It is very possible this fact also may be true; that you have tried to do good, and have not succeeded; yea, that those who seemed reformed, relapsed into sin, and their last state was worse than the first. And what marvel? Is the servant above his Master? But how often did He strive to save sinners, and they would not hear; or, when they had followed Him awhile, they turned back as a dog to his vomit! But He did not therefore desist from striving to do good: no more should you, whatever your success be. It is your part to do as you are commanded: the event is in the hand of God. You are not accountable for this: leave it to Him, who orders all things well. 'In the morning sow thy seed, and in the evening withhold not thy hand: for thou knowest not whether shall prosper' (Eccles. xi. 6).

But the trial hurries and frets your own soul. Perhaps it did so for this very reason, because you thought you was accountable for the event, which no man is, nor indeed can be; or perhaps, because you was off your guard—you was not watchful over your own spirit. But this is no reason for disobeying God. Try

again: but try more warily than before. Do good (as you forgive) 'not seven times only, but until seventy times seven.'
Only be wiser by experience: attempt it every time more cau-
tiously than before. Be more humbled before God, more deeply
convinced that of yourself you can do nothing. Be more
jealous over your own spirit; more gentle, and watchful unto
prayer. Thus 'cast your bread upon the waters, and you shall
find it again after many days.'

IV. 1. Notwithstanding all these plausible pretences for
hiding it, 'let your light so shine before men, that they may see
your good works, and glorify your Father which is in heaven.'
This is the practical application which our Lord Himself makes
of the foregoing considerations.

'Let your light so shine,'—your lowliness of heart; your
gentleness, and meekness of wisdom; your serious, weighty
concern for the things of eternity, and sorrow for the sins and
miseries of men; your earnest desire of universal holiness, and
full happiness in God; your tender goodwill to all mankind,
and fervent love to your supreme Benefactor. Endeavour not
to conceal this light, wherewith God hath enlightened your soul;
but let it shine before men, before all with whom you are, in
the whole tenor of your conversation. Let it shine still more
eminently in your actions, in your doing all possible good to
all men; and in your suffering for righteousness' sake, while
you 'rejoice and are exceeding glad,' knowing that 'great is
your reward in heaven.'

2. 'Let your light so shine before men, that they may see
your good works,'—so far let a Christian be from ever designing
or desiring to conceal his religion! On the contrary, let it be
your desire, not to conceal it; not to put the light under a bushel.
Let it be your care to place it 'on a candlestick, that it may give
light to all that are in the house.' Only take heed, not to seek
your own praise herein, not to desire any honour to yourselves.
But let it be your sole aim, that all who see your good works
may 'glorify your Father which is in heaven.'

3. Be this your one ultimate end in all things. With this
view, be plain, open, undisguised. Let your love be without

dissimulation: why should you hide fair, disinterested love? Let there be no guile found in your mouth: let your words be the genuine picture of your heart. Let there be no darkness or reservedness in your conversation, no disguise in your behaviour. Leave this to those who have other designs in view; designs which will not bear the light. Be ye artless and simple to all mankind; that all may see the grace of God which is in you. And although some will harden their hearts, yet others will take knowledge that ye have been with Jesus, and, by returning themselves to the great Bishop of their souls, 'glorify your Father which is in heaven.'

4. With this one design, that men may glorify God in you, go on in His name, and in the power of His might. Be not ashamed even to stand alone, so it be in the ways of God. Let the light which is in your heart shine in all good works, both works of piety and works of mercy. And in order to enlarge your ability of doing good, renounce all superfluities. Cut off all unnecessary expense in food, in furniture, in apparel. Be a good steward of every gift of God, even of these His lowest gifts. Cut off all unnecessary expense of time, all needless or useless employments; and 'whatsoever thy hand findeth to do, do it with thy might.' In a word, be thou full of faith and love; do good; suffer evil. And herein be thou 'steadfast, unmovable'; yea, 'always abounding in the work of the Lord; forasmuch as thou knowest that thy labour is not in vain in the Lord.'

SERMON XX

UPON OUR LORD'S SERMON ON THE MOUNT

DISCOURSE V

Think not that I am come to destroy the Law, or the Prophets: I am not come to destroy, but to fulfil.

For verily I say unto you: Till heaven and earth pass, one jot or one tittle shall in no wise pass from the law, till all be fulfilled.

Whosoever therefore shall break one of these least commandments, and shall teach men so, he shall be called the least in the kingdom of heaven: but whosoever shall do and teach them, the same shall be called great in the kingdom of heaven.

For I say unto you: That except your righteousness shall exceed the righteousness of the Scribes and Pharisees, ye shall in no case enter into the kingdom of heaven.—MATT. v. 17-20.

AMONG the multitude of reproaches which fell upon Him who 'was despised and rejected of men,' it could not fail to be one, that He was a teacher of novelties, an introducer of *a new religion.* This might be affirmed with the more colour, because many of the expressions He had used were not common among the Jews: either they did not use them at all, or not in the same sense, not in so full and strong a meaning. Add to this, that the worshipping God 'in spirit and in truth' must always appear a new religion to those who have hitherto known nothing but outside worship, nothing but the 'form of godliness.'

2. And it is not improbable, some might hope it was so; that He was abolishing the old religion, and bringing in another —one which, they might flatter themselves, would be an easier way to heaven. But our Lord refutes, in these words, both the vain hopes of the one, and the groundless calumnies of the other.

I shall consider them in the same order as they lie, taking each verse for a distinct head of discourse.

I. 1. And first, 'Think not that I am come to destroy the Law, or the Prophets: I am not come to destroy, but to fulfil.'

The ritual or ceremonial law, delivered by Moses to the children of Israel, containing all the injunctions and ordinances which related to the old sacrifices and service of the temple, our Lord indeed did come to destroy, to dissolve, and utterly abolish. To this bear all the Apostles witness; not only Barnabas and Paul, who vehemently withstood those who taught that Christians ought 'to keep the law of Moses' (Acts xv. 5); not only St. Peter, who termed the insisting on this, on the observance of the ritual law, a 'tempting God,' and 'putting a yoke upon the neck of the disciples, which neither our fathers,' saith he, 'nor we, were able to bear'; but all the Apostles, elders, and brethren, being assembled with one accord (verse 22), declared, that to command them to keep this law, was to 'subvert their souls'; and that 'it seemed good to the Holy Ghost' and to them, to lay no such burden upon them (verse 28). This 'hand-writing of ordinances our Lord did blot out, take away, and nail to His cross.

2. But the moral law, contained in the Ten Commandments, and enforced by the prophets, He did not take away. It was not the design of His coming to revoke any part of this. This is a law which never can be broken, which 'stands fast as the faithful witness in heaven.' The moral stands on an entirely different foundation from the ceremonial or ritual law, which was only designed for a temporary restraint upon a disobedient and stiff-necked people; whereas this was from the beginning of the world, being 'written not on tables of stone,' but on the hearts of all the children of men, when they came out of the hands of the Creator. And, however the letters once wrote by the finger of God are now in a great measure defaced by sin, yet can they not wholly be blotted out, while we have any consciousness of good and evil. Every part of this law must remain in force upon all mankind, and in all ages; as not depending either on time or place, or any other circumstances liable to change, but on the nature of God, and the nature of man, and their unchangeable relation to each other.

3. 'I am not come to destroy, but to fulfil.' Some have conceived our Lord to mean, I am come to fulfil this, by My entire and perfect obedience to it. And it cannot be doubted but He did, in this sense, fulfil every part of it. But this does not appear to be what He intends here, being foreign to the scope of His present discourse. Without question, His meaning in this place is (consistently with all that goes before and follows after), I am come to establish it in its fullness, in spite of all the glosses of men: I am come to place in a full and clear view whatsoever was dark or obscure therein: I am come to declare the true and full import of every part of it; to show the length and breadth, the entire extent, of every commandment contained therein, and the height and depth, the inconceivable purity and spirituality of it in all its branches

4. And this our Lord has abundantly performed in the preceding and subsequent parts of the discourse before us; in which He has not introduced a new religion into the world, but the same which was from the beginning,—a religion, the substance of which is, without question, as old as the creation, being coeval with man, and having proceeded from God at the very time when 'man became a living soul' (the *substance*, I say; for some circumstances of it now relate to man as a fallen creature); a religion witnessed to both by the law and by the prophets, in all succeeding generations. Yet was it never so fully explained, nor so thoroughly understood, till the great Author of it Himself condescended to give mankind this authentic comment on all the essential branches of it; at the same time declaring it should never be changed, but remain in force to the end of the world

II. 1. 'For verily I say unto you' (a solemn preface, which denotes both the importance and certainty of what is spoken), 'Till heaven and earth pass, one jot or one tittle shall in no wise pass from the law, till all be fulfilled.'

'One jot': it is literally, *not one iota*, not the most inconsiderable vowel. 'Or one tittle,' μία κεραία,—one *corner* or *point* of a consonant. It is a proverbial expression, which signifies that no one commandment contained in the moral law, nor the least part of any one, however inconsiderable it might seem, should ever be disannulled.

'Shall in no wise pass from the law'; οὐ μὴ παρέλθῃ ἀπὸ τοῦ νόμου. The double negative, here used, strengthens the sense, so as to admit of no contradiction: and the word παρέλθῃ, it may be observed, is not barely *future*, declaring what *will* be; but has likewise the force of an *imperative*, ordering what *shall* be. It is a word of authority, expressing the sovereign will and power of Him that spake; of Him whose word is the law of heaven and earth, and stands fast for ever and ever.

'One jot or one tittle shall in no wise pass, till heaven and earth pass'; or, as it is expressed immediately after, ἕως ἂν πάντα γένηται,—*till all* (or rather *all things*) *be fulfilled*, till the consummation of all things. Here is therefore no room for that poor evasion (with which some have delighted themselves greatly), that 'no part of the law was to pass away, till *all the law* was fulfilled: but it has been fulfilled by Christ; and therefore now must pass, for the gospel to be established.' Not so: the word *all* does not mean all the law, but all things in the universe; as neither has the term *fulfilled* any reference to the law, but to all things in heaven and earth.

2. From all this we may learn, that there is no contrariety at all between the law and the gospel; that there is no need for the law to pass away, in order to the establishing the gospel. Indeed neither of them supersedes the other, but they agree perfectly well together. Yea, the very same words, considered in different respects, are parts both of the law and of the gospel: if they are considered as commandments, they are parts of the law; if as promises, of the gospel. Thus, 'Thou shalt love the Lord thy God with all thy heart,' when considered as a commandment, is a branch of the law; when regarded as a promise, is an essential part of the gospel—the gospel being no other than the commands of the law, proposed by way of promise. Accordingly, poverty of spirit, purity of heart, and whatever else is enjoined in the holy law of God, are no other, when viewed in a gospel light, than so many great and precious promises.

3. There is, therefore, the closest connexion that can be conceived between the law and the gospel. On the one hand, the law continually makes way for, and points us to, the gospel; on the other, the gospel continually leads us to a more exact fulfilling of the law. The law, for instance, requires us to love God, to love our neighbour, to be meek, humble, or holy: we feel that we are not sufficient for these things; yea, that 'with man this is impossible.' But we see a promise of God, to give us that love, and to make us humble, meek, and holy: we lay hold of this gospel, of these glad tidings: it is done unto us according to our faith; and 'the righteousness of the law is fulfilled in us,' through faith which is in Christ Jesus.

We may yet farther observe, that every command in holy writ is only a covered promise. For by that solemn declaration, 'This is the covenant I will make after those days, saith the Lord. I will put My laws in your minds, and write them in your hearts,' God hath engaged to give whatsoever He commands.

Does He command us then to 'pray without ceasing,' to 'rejoice evermore,' to be 'holy as He is holy'? It is enough: He will work in us this very thing: it shall be unto us according to His word.

4. But if these things are so, we cannot be at a loss what to think of those who, in all ages of the church, have undertaken to change or supersede some commands of God, as they professed, by the peculiar direction of His Spirit. Christ has here given us an infallible rule, whereby to judge of all such pretensions. Christianity, as it includes the whole moral law of God, both by way of injunction and of promise, if we will hear Him, is designed of God to be the last of all His dispensations. There is no other to come after this. This is to endure till the consummation of all things. Of consequence, all such new revelations are of Satan, and not of God; and all pretences to another more perfect dispensation fall to the ground of course. 'Heaven and earth shall pass away'; but *this* word 'shall not pass away.'

III. 1. 'Whosoever, therefore, shall break one of these least commandments, and shall teach men so, he shall be called the least in the kingdom of heaven: but whosoever shall do and teach them, the same shall be called great in the kingdom of heaven.'

Who, what are they, that make the preaching of the law a character of reproach? Do they not see on whom the reproach must fall—on whose head it must light at last? Whosoever on this ground despiseth us despiseth Him that sent us. For did ever any man preach the law like Him, even when He came not to condemn but to save the world; when He came purposely to 'bring life and immortality to light through the gospel'? Can any preach the law more expressly, more rigorously, than Christ does in these words? And who is he that shall amend them? Who is he that shall instruct the Son of God how to preach? Who will teach Him a better way of delivering the message which He hath received of the Father?

2. 'Whosoever shall break one of these least commandments,' or one of the least of these commandments. 'These commandments,' we may observe, is a term used by our Lord as an equivalent with the law, or the law and the prophets,—which

is the same thing, seeing the prophets added nothing to the law, but only declared, explained, or enforced it, as they were moved by the Holy Ghost.

'Whosoever shall break one of these least commandments,' especially if it be done wilfully or presumptuously;—*one*—for 'he that keepeth the whole law, and' thus 'offends in one point, is guilty of all'; the wrath of God abideth on him, as surely as if he had broken every one. So that no allowance is made for one darling lust; no reserve for one idol; no excuse for refraining from all besides, and only giving way to one bosom sin. What God demands is, an entire obedience; we are to have an eye to all His commandments; otherwise we lose all the labour we take in keeping some, and our poor souls for ever and ever.

'One of these least,' or one of the least of these commandments: here is another excuse cut off, whereby many, who cannot deceive God, miserably deceive their own souls. 'This sin,' saith the sinner, 'is it not a little one? Will not the Lord spare me in this thing? Surely He will not be extreme to mark this, since I do not offend in the greater matters of the law.' Vain hope! Speaking after the manner of men, we may term these great, and those little, commandments; but, in reality they are not so. If we use propriety of speech, there is no such thing as a little sin; every sin being a transgression of the holy and perfect law, and an affront on the great Majesty of heaven.

3. 'And shall teach men so.' In some sense it may be said, that whosoever openly breaks any commandment teaches others to do the same; for example speaks, and many times louder than precept. In this sense, it is apparent, every open drunkard is a teacher of drunkenness; every Sabbath-breaker is constantly teaching his neighbour to profane the day of the Lord. But this is not all: an habitual breaker of the law is seldom content to stop here; he generally teaches other men to do so too, by word as well as example; especially when he hardens his neck, and hateth to be reproved. Such a sinner soon commences an advocate for sin; he defends what he is resolved not to forsake; he excuses the sin which he will not leave, and thus directly teaches every sin which he commits.

'He shall be called least in the kingdom of heaven'—that is, shall have no part therein. He is a stranger to the kingdom of heaven which is on earth: he hath no portion in that inheritance; no share of that 'righteousness, and peace, and joy in the Holy Ghost.' Nor, by consequence, can he have any part in the glory which shall be revealed.

4. But if those who even thus break, and teach others to break, 'one of the least of these commandments, shall be called least in the kingdom of heaven,' shall have no part in the kingdom of Christ and of God; if even these shall be cast into 'outer darkness, where is wailing and gnashing of teeth'; then where will they appear, whom our Lord chiefly and primarily intends in these words—they who, bearing the character of teachers sent from God, do nevertheless themselves break His commandments; yea, and openly teach others so to do; being corrupt both in life and doctrine?

5. These are of several sorts. Of the first sort are they who live in some wilful, habitual sin. Now, if an ordinary sinner teaches by his example, how much more a sinful minister—even if he does not attempt to defend, excuse, or extenuate his sin! If he does, he is a murderer indeed; yea, the murderer-general of his congregation He peoples the regions of death. He is the choicest instrument of the prince of darkness. When he goes hence, 'hell from beneath is moved to meet him at his coming.' Nor can he sink into the bottomless pit, without dragging a multitude after him.

6. Next to these are the good-natured, good sort of men; who live an easy, harmless life, neither troubling themselves with outward sin, nor with inward holiness; men who are remarkable neither one way nor the other, neither for religion nor irreligion; who are very regular both in public and private, but do not pretend to be any stricter than their neighbours. A minister of this kind breaks, not one, or a few only, of the least commandments of God; but all the great and weighty branches of His law which relate to the power of godliness, and all that require us to 'pass the time of our sojourning in fear,' to 'work out our salvation with fear and trembling,' to have our 'loins always girt, and our lights burning,' to 'strive' or agonize 'to enter in at the strait gate.' And he *teaches men so*, by the whole

form of his life, and the general tenor of his preaching, which uniformly tends to soothe those in their pleasing dream who imagine themselves Christians and are not; to persuade all who attend upon his ministry to sleep on and take their rest. No marvel, therefore, if both he, and they that follow him, wake together in everlasting burnings!

7. But above all these, in the highest rank of the enemies of the gospel of Christ are they who openly and explicitly 'judge the law' itself, and 'speak evil of the law'; who teach men to break (λῦσαι, to *dissolve*, to *loose*, to *untie*, the obligation of) not one only, whether of the least or of the greatest, but all the commandments at a stroke; who teach, without any cover, in so many words, 'What did our Lord do with the law? He abolished it. There is but one duty, which is that of believing. All commands are unfit for our times. From any demand of the law, no man is obliged now to go one step, or give away one farthing, to eat or omit one morsel. This, is, indeed, carrying matters with a high hand; this is withstanding our Lord to the face, and telling Him that He understood not how to deliver the message on which He was sent. O Lord, lay not this sin to their charge! Father, forgive them; for they know not what they do!

8. The most surprising of all the circumstances that attend this strong delusion is, that they who are given up to it really believe that they honour Christ by overthrowing His law, and that they are magnifying His office, while they are destroying His doctrine. Yea, they honour Him just as Judas did, when he said, 'Hail, Master!' and kissed Him. And He may as justly say to every one of them, 'Betrayest thou the Son of Man with a kiss?' It is no other than betraying Him with a kiss, to talk of His blood, and take away His crown; to set light by any part of His law, under pretence of advancing His gospel. Nor, indeed, can any one escape this charge, who preaches faith in any such manner as either directly or indirectly tends to set aside any branch of obedience; who preaches Christ so as to disannul, or weaken in any wise, the least of the commandments of God.

9. It is impossible, indeed, to have too high an esteem for 'the faith of God's elect.' And we must all declare. 'By grace ye are saved through faith; not of works, lest any man should boast.'

We must cry aloud to every penitent sinner, 'Believe in the
Lord Jesus Christ, and thou shalt be saved.' But, at the same time,
we must take care to let all men know, we esteem no faith but
that which worketh by love; and that we are not saved by faith,
unless so far as we are delivered from the power as well as the
guilt of sin. And when we say, 'Believe, and thou shalt be saved,'
we do not mean, 'Believe, and thou shalt step from sin to heaven,
without any holiness coming between; faith supplying the place
of holiness'; but, 'Believe, and thou shalt be holy; believe in the
Lord Jesus, and thou shalt have peace and power together: thou
shalt have power from Him in whom thou believest, to trample
sin under thy feet: power to love the Lord thy God with all thy
heart, and to serve Him with all thy strength; thou shalt have
power, "by patient continuance in well-doing, to seek for glory,
and honour, and immortality"; thou shalt both do and teach all
the commandments of God, from the least even to the greatest:
thou shalt teach them by thy life as well as thy words, and so
"be called great in the kingdom of heaven." '

IV. 1. Whatever other way we teach to the kingdom of
heaven, to glory, honour, and immortality, be it called 'the
way of faith,' or by any other name, it is, in truth, the way to
destruction. It will not bring a man peace at the last. For thus
saith the Lord, 'I say unto you, That except your righteousness
shall exceed the righteousness of the Scribes and Pharisees, ye
shall in no case enter into the kingdom of heaven.'

The Scribes, mentioned so often in the New Testament, as
some of the most constant and vehement opposers of our Lord,
were not secretaries, or men employed in writing only, as that
term might incline us to believe. Neither were they lawyers,
in our common sense of the word: although the word νομικοί,
is so rendered in our translation. Their employment had no
affinity at all to that of a lawyer among us. They were conversant with the laws of God, and not with the laws of man.
These were their study: it was their proper and peculiar business
to read and expound the law and the prophets; particularly in
the synagogues. They were the ordinary, stated preachers among
the Jews. So that if the sense of the original word was attended

to, we might render it, 'the divines.' For these were the men
who made divinity their profession; and they were generally
(as their name literally imports) men of letters; men of the
greatest account for learning that were then in the Jewish nation.

2. The Pharisees were a very ancient sect, or body of men,
among the Jews; originally so called from the Hebrew word
פָּרַשׁ, which signifies to *separate* or *divide*. Not that they made
any formal separation from, or division in, the national Church:
they were only distinguished from others by greater strictness
of life, by more exactness of conversation. For they were
zealous of the law in the minutest points; paying tithes of mint,
anise, and cummin: and hence they were had in honour of all
the people, and generally esteemed the holiest of men.

Many of the Scribes were of the sect of the Pharisees. Thus
St. Paul himself, who was educated for a Scribe, first at the
university of Tarsus, and after that in Jerusalem, at the feet of
Gamaliel (one of the most learned Scribes or Doctors of the Law
that were then in the nation), declares of himself before the
council, 'I am a Pharisee, the son of a Pharisee' (Acts xxiii. 6);
and before King Agrippa, 'After the straitest sect of our religion
I lived a Pharisee' (xxvi. 5). And the whole body of the Scribes
generally esteemed and acted in concert with the Pharisees.
Hence we find our Saviour so frequently coupling them together,
as coming in many respects under the same consideration. In
this place they seemed to be mentioned together as the most
eminent professors of religion; the former of whom were
accounted the wisest, the latter the holiest of men.

3. What 'the righteousness of the Scribes and Pharisees'
really was, it is not difficult to determine. Our Lord has preserved an authentic account which one of them gave of himself:
and he is clear and full in describing his own righteousness;
and cannot be supposed to have omitted any part of it. He went
up indeed 'into the temple to pray'; but was so intent upon his
own virtues, that he forgot the design upon which he came.
For it is remarkable, he does not properly pray at all: he only
tells God how wise and good he was. 'God, I thank Thee, that
I am not as other men are, extortioners, unjust, adulterers; or
even as this publican. I fast twice in the week; I give tithes of

18

all that I possess.' His righteousness therefore consisted of three parts: first, saith he, 'I am not as other men are'; I am not an extortioner, not unjust, not an adulterer; not 'even as this publican': secondly, 'I fast twice in the week': and, thirdly, 'I give tithes of all that I possess.'

'I am not as other men are.' This is not a small point. It is not every man that can say this. It is as if he had said, 'I do not suffer myself to be carried away by that great torrent, custom. I live not by custom, but by reason; not by the examples of men, but by the Word of God. I am not an extortioner, not unjust, not an adulterer; however common these sins are, even among those who are called the people of God (extortion, in particular —a kind of legal injustice, not punishable by any human law, the making gain of another's ignorance or necessity having filled every corner of the land); nor even as this publican; not guilty of any open or presumptuous sin; not an outward sinner; but a fair, honest man, of blameless life and conversation.'

4. 'I fast twice in the week.' There is more implied in this than we may at first be sensible of. All the stricter Pharisees observed the weekly fasts; namely, every Monday and Thursday On the former day, they fasted in memory of Moses receiving on that day (as their tradition taught) the two tables of stone written by the finger of God; on the latter, in memory of his casting them out of his hand, when he saw the people dancing round the golden calf. On these days, they took no sustenance at all, till three in the afternoon; the hour at which they began to offer up the evening sacrifice in the temple. Till that hour, it was their custom to remain in the temple, in some of the corners, apartments, or courts thereof; that they might be ready to assist at all the sacrifices, and to join in all the public prayers. The time between they were accustomed to employ, partly in private addresses to God, partly in searching the Scriptures, in reading the law and the prophets, and in meditating thereon. Thus much is implied in 'I fast twice in the week'; the second branch of the righteousness of a Pharisee.

5. 'I give tithes of all that I possess.' This the Pharisees did with the utmost exactness. They would not except the most inconsiderable thing; no, not mint, anise, and cummin. They

would not keep back the least part of what they believed properly to belong to God; but gave a full tenth of their whole substance yearly, and of all their increase, whatsoever it was.

Yes, the stricter Pharisees (as has been often observed by those who are versed in the ancient Jewish writings), not content with giving one tenth of their substance to God in His priests and Levites, gave another tenth to God in the poor, and that continually. They gave the same proportion of all they had in alms, as they were accustomed to give in tithes. And this likewise they adjusted with the utmost exactness; that they might not keep back any part, but might fully render unto God the things which were God's, as they accounted this to be. So that, upon the whole, they gave away, from year to year, an entire fifth of all that they possessed.

6. This was 'the righteousness of the Scribes and Pharisees'; a righteousness which, in many respects, went far beyond the conception which many have been accustomed to entertain concerning it. But perhaps it will be said, 'It was all false and feigned; for they were all a company of hypocrites.' Some of them doubtless were; men who had really no religion at all, no fear of God, or desire to please Him; who had no concern for the honour that cometh of God, but only for the praise of men. And these are they whom our Lord so severely condemns, so sharply reproves, on many occasions. But we must not suppose, because many Pharisees were hypocrites, therefore all were so. Nor indeed is hypocrisy by any means essential to the character of a Pharisee. This is not the distinguishing mark of their sect. It is rather this, according to our Lord's account, 'They trusted in themselves that they were righteous, and despised others.' This is their genuine badge. But the Pharisee of this kind cannot be a hypocrite. He must be, in the common sense, sincere; otherwise he could not 'trust in himself that he is righteous.' The man who was here commending himself to God, unquestionably thought himself righteous. Consequently he was no hypocrite; he was not conscious to himself of any insincerity. He now spoke to God just what he thought, namely, that he was abundantly better than other men.

But the example of St. Paul were there no other, is sufficient to put this out of all question. He could not only say when he was a Christian, 'Herein do I exercise myself, to have always a conscience void of offence toward God, and toward men' (Acts xxiv. 16); but even concerning the time when he was a Pharisee, 'Men and brethren, I have lived in all good conscience before God until this day' (xxiii. 1). He was therefore sincere when he was a Pharisee, as well as when he was a Christian. He was no more a hypocrite when he persecuted the church, than when he preached the faith which once he persecuted. Let this then be added to 'the righteousness of the Scribes and Pharisees' —a sincere belief that they are righteous, and in all things 'doing God service.'

7. And yet, 'except your righteousness,' saith our Lord, 'shall exceed the righteousness of the Scribes and Pharisees, ye shall in no case enter into the kingdom of heaven.' A solemn and weighty declaration, and which it behoves all who are called by the name of Christ seriously and deeply to consider. But before we inquire how our righteousness may exceed theirs, let us examine whether at present we come up to it.

First. A Pharisee was 'not as other men are.' In externals he was singularly good. Are we so? Do we dare to be singular at all? Do we not rather swim with the stream? Do we not many times dispense with religion and reason together, because we would not *look particular*? Are we not often more afraid of being out of the fashion, than being out of the way of salvation? Have we courage to stem the tide, to run counter to the world, 'to obey God rather than man'? Otherwise, the Pharisee leaves us behind at the very first step. It is well if we overtake him any more.

But to come closer. Can we use his first plea with God?— which is, in substance, 'I do no harm: I live in no outward sin: I do nothing for which my own heart condemns me.' Do you not? Are you sure of that? Do you live in no practice for which your own heart condemns you? If you are not an adulterer, if you are not unchaste, either in word or deed, are you not unjust? The grand measure of justice, as well as of mercy, is, 'Do unto others as thou wouldest they should do unto thee.' Do you walk by this rule? Do you never do unto any what you would

not they should do unto you? Nay, are you not grossly unjust
Are not you an extortioner? Do you not make a gain of any
one's ignorance or necessity; neither in buying nor selling?
Suppose you were engaged in trade: do you demand, do you
receive, no more than the real value of what you sell? Do you
demand, do you receive, no more of the ignorant than of the
knowing—of a little child, than of an experienced trader? If you
do, why does not your heart condemn you? You are a barefaced extortioner. Do you demand no more than the usual price
of goods of any who is in pressing want—who must have, and
that without delay, the things which you only can furnish him
with? If you do, this also is flat extortion. Indeed you do not
come up to the righteousness of a Pharisee.

8. A Pharisee, secondly (to express his sense in our common
way), used all the means of grace. As he fasted often and much,
twice in every week, so he attended all the sacrifices. He was
constant in public and private prayer, and in reading and hearing
the Scriptures. Do you go as far as this? Do you fast much and
often?—twice in the week? I fear not. Once at least—'on all
Fridays in the year'? (So our Church clearly and peremptorily
enjoins all her members to do; to observe all these, as well as the
vigils and the forty days of Lent, as days of fasting or abstinence.)
Do you fast twice in the year? I am afraid some among us cannot
plead even this! Do you neglect no opportunity of attending
and partaking of the Christian sacrifice? How many are they who
call themselves Christians, and yet are utterly regardless of it
—yet do not eat of that bread, or drink of that cup, for months,
perhaps years together! Do you, every day, either hear the
Scriptures or read them, and meditate thereon? Do you join in
prayer with the great congregation, daily, if you have opportunity; if not, whenever you can; particularly on that day which
you 'remember to keep it holy'? Do you strive to *make* opportunities? Are you glad when they say unto you, 'We will go
into the house of the Lord'? Are you zealous of, and diligent in,
private prayer? Do you suffer no day to pass without it? Rather,
are not some of you so far from spending therein (with the
Pharisee) several hours in one day, that you think one hour full
enough, if not too much? Do you spend an hour in a day, or in

a week, in praying to your Father which is in secret? yea, an hour
in a month? Have you spent one hour together in private
prayer ever since you was born? Ah, poor Christian! Shall not
the Pharisee rise up in the judgement against thee and condemn
thee? His righteousness is as far above thine as the heaven is
above the earth!

9. The Pharisee, thirdly, paid tithes and gave alms of all that
he possessed. And in how ample a manner! So that he was (as
we phrase it) 'a man that did much good.' Do we come up to
him here? Which of us is so abundant as he was in good works?
Which of us gives a fifth of all his substance to God, both of
the principal and of the increase? Who of us, out of (suppose)
an hundred pounds a year, gives twenty to God and the poor;
out of fifty, ten; and so in a larger or a smaller proportion?
When shall our righteousness, in using all the means of grace, in
attending all the ordinances of God, in avoiding evil and doing
good, equal at least the righteousness of the Scribes and Pharisees?

10. Although if it only equalled theirs, what would that
profit? 'For verily I say unto you, Except your righteousness
shall exceed the righteousness of the Scribes and Pharisees, ye
shall in no case enter into the kingdom of heaven.' But how can
it exceed theirs? Wherein does the righteousness of a Christian
exceed that of a Scribe or Pharisee? Christian righteousness
exceeds theirs, first, in the extent of it. Most of the Pharisees,
though they were rigorously exact in many things, yet were
emboldened, by the traditions of the elders, to dispense with
others of equal importance. Thus, they were extremely punctual
in keeping the fourth commandment—they would not even
rub an ear of corn on the Sabbath day; but not at all in keeping
the third—making little account of light, or even false, swearing.
So that their righteousness was partial; whereas the righteousness
of a real Christian is universal. He does not observe one, or
some parts of the law of God, and neglect the rest; but keeps all
His commandments, loves them all, values them above gold or
precious stones.

11. It may be, indeed, that some of the Scribes and Pharisees
endeavoured to keep all the commandments, and consequently
were, as touching the righteousness of the law, that is, according

to the letter of it, blameless. But still the righteousness of a
Christian exceeds all this righteousness of a Scribe or Pharisee, by
fulfilling the spirit as well as the letter of the law; by inward as
well as outward obedience. In this, in the spirituality of it, it
admits of no comparison. This is the point which our Lord has
so largely proved, in the whole tenor of this discourse. Their
righteousness was external only; Christian righteousness is in the
inner man. The Pharisee 'cleansed the outside of the cup and the
platter'; the Christian is clean within. The Pharisee laboured to
present God with a good life; the Christian with a holy heart.
The one shook off the leaves, perhaps the fruits, of sin; the other
'lays the axe to the root'; as not being content with the outward
form of godliness, how exact soever it be, unless the life, the
Spirit, the power of God unto salvation be felt in the inmost soul.

Thus, to do no harm, to do good, to attend the ordinances of
God (the righteousness of a Pharisee), are all external; whereas,
on the contrary, poverty of spirit, mourning, meekness, hunger
and thirst after righteousness, the love of our neighbour, and
purity of heart (the righteousness of a Christian), are all internal.
And even peace-making (or doing good), and suffering for
righteousness' sake, stand entitled to the blessings annexed to
them, only as they imply these inward dispositions, as they
spring from, exercise, and confirm them. So that whereas the
righteousness of the Scribes and Pharisees was external only, it
may be said, in some sense, that the righteousness of a Christian
is internal only: all his actions and sufferings being as nothing in
themselves, being estimated before God only by the tempers
from which they spring.

12. Whosoever therefore thou art, who bearest the holy and
venerable name of a Christian, see, first, that thy righteousness
fall not short of the righteousness of the Scribes and Pharisees.
Be not thou 'as other man are'! 'Dare to stand alone'; to be,
'against example, singularly good.' If thou 'follow a multitude'
at all, it must be 'to do evil.' Let not custom or fashion be thy
guide, but reason and religion. The practice of others is nothing
to thee: 'Every man must give an account of himself to God.'
Indeed, if thou canst save the soul of another, do; but at least
save one,—thy own. Walk not in the path of death because it is

broad, and many walk therein. Nay, by this very token thou mayest know it. Is the way wherein thou now walkest, a broad, well-frequented, fashionable way? Then it infallibly leads to destruction. O be not thou 'damned for company'! Cease from evil: fly from sin as from the face of a serpent! At least, do no harm. 'He that committeth sin is of the devil.' Be not thou found in that number. Touching outward sins, surely the grace of God is even now sufficient for thee. 'Herein,' at least, 'exercise thyself to have a conscience void of offence toward God, and toward men.'

Secondly. Let not thy righteousness fall short of theirs with regard to the ordinances of God. If thy labour or bodily strength will not allow of thy fasting twice in the week, however, deal faithfully with thy own soul, and fast as often as thy strength will permit. Omit no public, no private opportunity of pouring out thy soul in prayer. Neglect no occasion of eating that bread and drinking that cup which is the communion of the body and blood of Christ. Be diligent in searching the Scriptures; read as thou mayest, and meditate therein day and night. Rejoice to embrace every opportunity of hearing, the word of reconciliation' declared by the 'ambassadors of Christ,' the 'stewards of the mysteries of God.' In using all the means of grace, in a constant and careful attendance on every ordinance of God, live up to (at least till thou canst go beyond) 'the righteousness of the Scribes and Pharisees.'

Thirdly, Fall not short of a Pharisee in doing good. Give alms of all thou dost possess. Is any hungry? Feed him. Is he athirst? Give him drink. Naked? Cover him with a garment If thou hast this world's goods, do not limit thy beneficence to a scanty proportion. Be merciful to the uttermost of thy power. Why not even as this Pharisee? Now 'make thyself friends,' while the time is, 'of the mammon of unrighteousness, that when thou failest,' when this earthly tabernacle is dissolved, they 'may receive thee into everlasting habitations.'

13. But rest not here. Let thy righteousness 'exceed the righteousness of the Scribes and Pharisees.' Be not thou content to keep the whole law, and offend in one point.' Hold thou fast all His commandments, and all 'false ways do thou utterly

abhor.' Do all the things whatsoever He hath commanded, and that with all thy might. Thou canst do all things through Christ strengthening thee; though without Him thou canst do nothing.

Above all, let thy righteousness exceed theirs in the purity and spirituality of it. What is the exactest form of religion to thee? the most perfect outside righteousness? Go thou higher and deeper than all this! Let thy religion be the religion of the heart. Be thou poor in spirit; little, and base, and mean, and vile in thy own eyes; amazed and humbled to the dust at the love of God which is in Christ Jesus thy Lord! Be serious: let the whole stream of thy thoughts, words, and works be such as flows from the deepest conviction that thou standest on the edge of the great gulf, thou and all the children of men, just ready to drop in, either into everlasting glory or everlasting burnings! Be meek: let thy soul be filled with mildness, gentleness, patience, long-suffering toward all men; at the same time that all which is in thee is athirst for God, the living God, longing to awake up after His likeness, and to be satisfied with it. Be thou a lover of God, and of all mankind. In this spirit, do and suffer all things. Thus 'exceed the righteousness of the Scribes and Pharisees,' and thou shalt be 'called great in the kingdom of heaven.'

SERMON XXI

UPON OUR LORD'S SERMON ON THE MOUNT

DISCOURSE VI

Take heed that ye do not your alms before men, to be seen of them, otherwise ye have no reward of your Father which is in heaven.

Therefore when thou doest thine alms, do not sound a trumpet before thee, as the hypocrites do in the synagogues and in the streets, that they may have glory of men. Verily I say unto you, They have their reward.

But when thou doest alms, let not thy left hand know what thy right hand doeth.

That thine alms may be in secret, and thy Father which seeth in secret Himself shall reward thee openly.

And when thou prayest, thou shalt not be as the hypocrites are, for they love to pray standing in the synagogues and in the corners of the streets: that they may be seen of men. Verily I say unto you, They have their reward.

But thou, when thou prayest, enter into thy closet, and when thou hast shut thy door, pray to thy Father which is in secret, and thy Father which seeth in secret shall reward thee openly.

But when ye pray, use not vain repetitions, as the Heathen do, for they think that they shall be heard for their much speaking.

Be not ye therefore like unto them, for your Father knoweth what things ye have need of, before ye ask Him.

After this manner therefore pray ye: Our Father which art in heaven, Hallowed be Thy name Thy kingdom come. Thy will be done in earth, as it is in heaven. Give us this day our daily bread And forgive us our debts, as we forgive our debtors. And lead us not into temptation, but deliver us from evil: For thine is the kingdom, and the power, and the glory, for ever. Amen.

For if ye forgive men their trespasses, your heavenly Father will also forgive you: But if ye forgive not men their trespasses, neither will your Father forgive your trespasses.—MATT. vi. 1-15.

IN the preceding chapter our Lord has described inward religion in its various branches. He has laid before us those dispositions of soul which constitute real Christianity; the inward tempers contained in that 'holiness, without which no man shall see the Lord'; the affections which, when flowing from their proper fountain, from a living faith in God through Christ Jesus, are intrinsically and essentially good, and acceptable to God. He proceeds to show, in this chapter, how all our actions likewise, even those that are indifferent in their own nature, may be made holy, and good, and acceptable to God, by a pure and holy intention. Whatever is done without this, He largely declares, is of no value before God. Whereas, whatever outward works are thus consecrated to God, they are, in His sight, of great price.

2. The necessity of this purity of intention, He shows, first, with regard to those which are usually accounted religious actions, and indeed are such when performed with a right intention. Some of these are commonly termed 'works of piety'; the rest, 'works of charity' or mercy. Of the latter sort, He particularly names almsgiving; of the former, prayer and fasting.

But the directions given for these are equally to be applied to every work, whether of charity or mercy.

I. 1. And, first, with regard to works of mercy. 'Take heed,' saith He, 'that ye do not your alms before men, to be seen of them: otherwise ye have no reward of your Father which is in heaven.' 'That ye do not your alms': although this only is named, yet is every work of charity included, everything which we give, or speak, or do, whereby our neighbour may be profited; whereby another man may receive any advantage, either in his body or soul. The feeding the hungry, the clothing the naked, the entertaining or assisting the stranger, the visiting those that are sick or in prison, the comforting the afflicted, the instructing the ignorant, the reproving the wicked, the exhorting and encouraging the well-doer; and if there be any other work of mercy, it is equally included in this direction.

2. 'Take heed that ye do not your alms before men, to be seen of them.' The thing which is here forbidden is not barely the doing good in the sight of men; this circumstance alone, that others see what we do, makes the action neither worse nor better; but the doing it before men, 'to be seen of them,' with this view, from this intention only. I say, from this intention only; for this may, in some cases, be a part of our intention; we may design that some of our actions should be seen, and yet they may be acceptable to God. We may intend that our light should shine before men, when our conscience bears us witness in the Holy Ghost, that our ultimate end in designing they should see our good works is, 'that they may glorify our Father which is in heaven.' But take heed that ye do not the least thing with a view to your own glory: take heed that a regard to the praise of men have no place at all in your works of mercy. If ye seek your own glory, if you have any design to gain the honour that cometh of men, whatever is done with this view is nothing worth; it is not done unto the Lord; He accepteth it not; 'ye have no reward' for this 'of our Father which is in heaven.'

3. 'Therefore when thou doest thine alms, do not sound a trumpet before thee, as the hypocrites do in the synagogues and in the streets, that they may have praise of men.' The word

synagogue does not here mean a place of worship, but any place
of public resort, such as the market-place, or exchange. It was a
common thing among the Jews who were men of large fortunes,
particularly among the Pharisees, to cause a trumpet to be
sounded before them in the most public parts of the city, when
they were about to give any considerable alms. The pretended
reason for this was to call the poor together to receive it; but the
real design, that they might have praise of men. But be not thou
like unto them. Do not thou cause a trumpet to be sounded
before thee. Use no ostentation in doing good. Aim at the
honour which cometh of God only. They who seek the praise
of men have their reward: they shall have no praise of God.

4. 'But when thou doest alms, let not thy left hand know
what thy right hand doeth.' This is a proverbial expression,
the meaning of which is, Do it in as secret a manner as is possible;
as secret as is consistent with the doing it at all (for it must not
be left undone; omit no opportunity of doing good, whether
secretly or openly), and with the doing it in the most effectual
manner. For here is also an exception to be made: when you
are fully persuaded in your own mind, that by your not con-
cealing the good which is done, either you will yourself be
enabled, or others excited, to do the more good, then you may
not conceal it; then let your light appear, and, 'shine to all that
are in the house.' But, unless where the glory of God and the
good of mankind oblige you to the contrary, act in as private
and unobserved a manner as the nature of the thing will admit;
'that thy alms may be in secret; and thy Father which seeth in
secret, He shall reward thee openly'; perhaps in the present
world—many instances of this stand recorded in all ages; but
infallibly in the world to come, before the general assembly of
men and angels.

II. 1. From works of charity or mercy our Lord proceeds to
those which are termed 'works of piety.' 'And when thou
prayest,' saith He, 'thou shalt not be as the hypocrites are; for
they love to pray standing in the synagogues, and in the corners
of the streets, that they may be seen of men.' 'Thou shalt not be
as the hypocrites are.' Hypocrisy, then, or insincerity, is the

first thing we are to guard against in prayer. Beware not to speak what thou dost not mean. Prayer is the lifting up of the heart to God: all words of prayer, without this, are mere hypocrisy. Whenever therefore thou attemptest to pray, see that it be thy one design to commune with God, to lift up thy heart to Him, to pour out thy soul before Him; not as the hypocrites, who love, or are wont, 'to pray standing in the synagogues,' the exchange, or market-places, 'and in the corners of the streets,' wherever the most people are, 'that they may be seen of men': this was the sole design, the motive, and end, of the prayers which they there repeated. 'Verily I say unto you, They have their reward.' They are to expect none from your Father which is in heaven.

2. But it is not only the having an eye to the praise of men, which cuts us off from any reward in heaven; which leaves us no room to expect the blessing of God upon our works, whether of piety or mercy. Purity of intention is equally destroyed by a view to any temporal reward whatever. If we repeat our prayers, if we attend the public worship of God, if we relieve the poor, with a view to gain or interest, it is not a whit more acceptable to God, than if it were done with a view to praise. Any temporal view, any motive whatever on this side eternity, any design but that of promoting the glory of God, and the happiness of men for God's sake, makes every action, however fair it may appear to men, an abomination unto the Lord.

3. 'But when thou prayest, enter into thy closet, and when thou hast shut thy door, pray to thy Father which is in secret.' There is a time when thou art openly to glorify God, to pray, and praise Him in the great congregation. But when thou desirest more largely and more particularly to make thy requests known unto God, whether it be in the evening, or in the morning, or at noonday, 'enter into thy closet, and shut thy door.' Use all the privacy thou canst. (Only leave it not undone, whether thou hast any closet, any privacy, or no. Pray to God, if it be possible, when none seeth but He; but if otherwise, pray to God.) Thus 'pray to thy Father which is in secret'; pour out all thy heart before Him; 'and thy Father which seeth in secret, He shall reward thee openly.'

4. 'But when ye pray,' even in secret, 'use not vain repetitions, as the Heathen do'; μὴ βαττολογήσητε. Do not use abundance of words without any meaning. Say not the same thing over and over again; think not the fruit of your prayers depends on the length of them, like the Heathens; for 'they think they shall be heard for their much speaking.'

The thing here reproved is not simply the length, any more than the shortness, of our prayers;—but, first, length without meaning; speaking much, and meaning little or nothing; the using (not all repetitions; for our Lord Himself prayed thrice, repeating the same words; but) vain repetitions, as the Heathens did, reciting the names of their gods over and over; as they do among Christians (vulgarly so called), and not among the Papists only, who say over and over the same string of prayers, without ever feeling what they speak: secondly, the thinking to be heard for our much speaking, the fancying God measures prayers by their length, and is best pleased with those which contain the most words, which sound the longest in His ears. These are such instances of superstition and folly as all who are named by the name of Christ should leave to the Heathens, to them on whom the glorious light of the gospel hath never shined.

5. 'Be not ye therefore like unto them.' Ye who have tasted of the grace of God in Christ Jesus are throughly convinced, 'your Father knoweth what things ye have need of, before ye ask Him.' So that the end of your praying is not to inform God, as though He knew not your wants already; but rather to inform yourselves; to fix the sense of those wants more deeply in your hearts, and the sense of your continual dependence on Him who only is able to supply all your wants. It is not so much to move God, who is always more ready to give than you to ask, as to move yourselves, that you may be willing and ready to receive the good things He has prepared for you.

III. 1. After having taught the true nature and ends of prayer, our Lord subjoins an example of it; even that divine form of prayer which seems in this place to be proposed by way of pattern chiefly, as the model and standard of all our prayers: 'After this manner therefore pray ye.' Whereas, elsewhere He enjoins the use of these very words: 'He said unto them, When ye pray, say . . .' (Luke xi. 2).

2. We may observe, in general, concerning this divine prayer, first, that it contains all we can reasonably or innocently pray for. There is nothing which we have need to ask of God, nothing which we can ask without offending Him, which is not included, either directly or indirectly, in this comprehensive form. Secondly, that it contains all we can reasonably or innocently desire: whatever is for the glory of God, whatever is needful or profitable, not only for ourselves, but for every creature in heaven and earth. And, indeed, our prayers are the proper test of our desires; nothing being fit to have a place in our desires which is not fit to have a place in our prayers: what we may not pray for, neither should we desire. Thirdly, that it contains all our duty to God and man; whatsoever things are pure and holy, whatsoever God requires of the children of men, whatsoever is acceptable in His sight, whatsoever it is whereby we may profit our neighbour, being expressed or implied therein.

3. It consists of three parts,—the preface, the petitions, and the doxology, or conclusion. The preface, 'Our Father which art in heaven,' lays a general foundation for prayer; comprising what we must first know of God, before we can pray in confidence of being heard. It likewise points out to us all those tempers with which we are to approach to God, which are most essentially requisite, if we desire either our prayers or our lives should find acceptance with Him.

4. 'Our Father': if He is a Father, then He is good, then He is loving, to His children. And here is the first and great reason for prayer. God is willing to bless; let us ask for a blessing. 'Our Father,'—our Creator; the Author of our being; He who raised us from the dust of the earth; who breathed into us the breath of life, and we became living souls. But if He made us, let us ask, and He will not withhold any good thing from the work of His own hands. 'Our Father,'—our Preserver; who, day by day, sustains the life He has given; of whose continuing love we now and every moment receive life, and breath, and all things. So much the more boldly let us come to Him, and we shall 'obtain mercy, and find grace to help in time of need.'

Above all, the Father of our Lord Jesus Christ, and of all that believe in Him; who justifies us 'freely by His grace, through the redemption that is in Jesus'; who hath 'blotted out all our sins, and healed all our infirmities'; who hath received us for His own children, by adoption and grace; and, 'because' we 'are sons, hath sent forth the Spirit of His Son into' our 'hearts, crying, Abba, Father'; who 'hath begotten us again of incorruptible seed,' and 'created us anew in Christ Jesus.' Therefore we know that He heareth us always; therefore we pray to Him without ceasing. We pray, because we love; and 'we love Him, because He first loved us.'

5. 'Our Father': not *mine* only who now cry unto Him, but *ours* in the most extensive sense. The God and 'Father of the spirits of all flesh'; the Father of angels and men: so the very Heathens acknowledge Him to be, Πατὴρ ἀνδρῶν τε θεῶν τε. The Father of the universe, of all the families both in heaven and earth. Therefore with Him there is no respect of persons. He loveth all that He hath made. 'He is loving unto every man, and His mercy is over all His works.' And the Lord's delight is in them that fear Him, and put their trust in His mercy; in them that trust in Him through the Son of His love, knowing they are 'accepted in the Beloved.' But 'if God so loved us, we ought also to love one another'; yea, all mankind; seeing 'God so loved the world, that He gave His only-begotten Son,' even to die the death, that they 'might not perish, but have everlasting life.'

6. 'Which art in heaven': high and lifted up, God over all, blessed for ever; who, sitting on the circle of the heavens, beholdeth all things both in heaven and earth; whose eye pervades the whole sphere of created being, yea, and of uncreated night; unto whom 'are known all His works,' and all the works of every creature, not only 'from the beginning of the world' (a poor, low, weak translation), but ἀπ' αἰῶνος, from all *eternity*, from everlasting to everlasting; who constrains the host of heaven, as well as the children of men, to cry out with wonder and amazement, O the depth! 'the depth of the riches, both of the wisdom and of the knowledge of God'! 'Which art in heaven': the Lord and Ruler of all, superintending and disposing

all things; who art the King of kings, and Lord of lords, the blessed and only Potentate; who art strong and girded about with power, doing whatsoever pleaseth Thee; the Almighty; for whensoever Thou willest, to do is present with Thee. 'In heaven': eminently there. Heaven is Thy throne, 'the place where Thine honour' particularly 'dwelleth.' But not there alone; for Thou fillest heaven and earth, the whole expanse of space. 'Heaven and earth are full of Thy Glory. Glory be to Thee, O Lord most high!'

Therefore should we 'serve the Lord with fear, and rejoice unto Him with reverence.' Therefore should we think, speak, and act, as continually under the eye, in the immediate presence, of the Lord, the King.

7. 'Hallowed be Thy name.' This is the first of the six petitions whereof the prayer itself is composed. The name of God is God Himself; the nature of God, so far as it can be discovered to man. It means therefore, together with His existence, all His attributes or perfections:—His Eternity, particularly signified by His great and incommunicable name, JEHOVAH, as the Apostle John translates it, Τὸ Α καὶ τὸ Ω, ἀρχὴ καὶ τέλος, ὁ ὤν καὶ ὁ ἦν καὶ ὁ ἐρχόμενος—'The Alpha and Omega, the beginning and the end; He which is, and which was, and which is to come';—His fullness of Being, denoted by His other great name, I AM THAT I AM!—His omnipresence;—His omnipotence; who is indeed the only Agent in the material world; all matter being essentially dull and inactive, and moving only as it is moved by the finger of God; and He is the spring of action in every creature, visible and invisible, which could neither act not exist, without the continual influx and agency of His almighty power;—His wisdom, clearly deduced from the things that are seen, from the goodly order of the universe; —His Trinity in Unity, and Unity in Trinity, discovered to us in the very first line of His written Word; בָּרָא אֱלֹהִים,— literally, the Gods created, a plural noun joined with a verb of the singular number; as well as in every part of His subsequent revelations, given by the mouth of all His holy Prophets and Apostles;—His essential purity and holiness;—and, above all, His love, which is the very brightness of His glory.

19

In praying that God, or His name, may be hallowed or glorified, we pray that He may be known, such as He is, by all that are capable thereof, by all intelligent beings, and with affections suitable to that knowledge; that He may be duly honoured, and feared, and loved, by all in heaven above and in the earth beneath; by all angels and men, whom for that end He has made capable of knowing and loving Him to eternity.

8. 'Thy kingdom come.' This has a close connexion with the preceding petition. In order that the name of God might be hallowed, we pray that His kingdom, the kingdom of Christ, may come. This kingdom then comes to a particular person, when he 'repents and believes the gospel'; when he is taught of God, not only to know himself, but to know Jesus Christ and Him crucified. As 'this is life eternal, to know the only true God, and Jesus Christ whom He hath sent'; so it is the kingdom of God begun below, set up in the believer's heart; 'the Lord God Omnipotent' then 'reigneth,' when He is known through Christ Jesus. He taketh unto Himself His mighty power, that He may subdue all things unto Himself. He goeth on in the soul conquering and to conquer, till He hath put all things under His feet, till 'every thought is brought into captivity to the obedience of Christ.'

When therefore God shall 'give His Son the heathen for His inheritance, and the uttermost parts of the earth for His possession'; when 'all kingdoms shall bow before Him, and all nations shall do Him service'; when 'the mountain of the Lord's house,' the church of Christ, 'shall be established in the top of the mountains'; when 'the fullness of the Gentiles shall come in, and all Israel shall be saved'; then shall it be seen, that 'the Lord is King, and hath put on glorious apparel,' appearing to every soul of man as King of kings and Lord of lords. And it is meet for all those who love His appearing, to pray that He would hasten the time; that this His kingdom, the kingdom of grace, may come quickly, and swallow up all the kingdoms of the earth; that all mankind, receiving Him for their King, truly believing in His name, may be filled with righteousness, and peace, and joy, with holiness and happiness; till they are removed hence into His heavenly kingdom, there to reign with Him for ever and ever.

For this also we pray in those words, 'Thy kingdom come': we pray for the coming of His everlsting kingdom, the kingdom of glory in heaven, which is the continuation and perfection of the kingdom of grace on earth. Consequently this, as well as the preceding petition, is offered up for the whole intelligent creation, who are all interested in this grand event, the final renovation of all things, by God's putting an end to misery and sin, to infirmity and death, taking all things into His own hands, and setting up the kingdom which endureth throughout all ages.

Exactly answerable to all this are those awful words in the prayer at the burial of the dead: 'Beseeching Thee, that it may please Thee of Thy gracious goodness, shortly to accomplish the number of Thine elect, and to hasten Thy kindgom: that we, with all those that are departed in the true faith of Thy holy name, may have our perfect consummation and bliss, both in body and soul, in Thy everlasting glory.'

9. 'Thy will be done in earth, as it is in heaven.' This is the necessary and immediate consequence wherever the kingdom of God is come; wherever God dwells in the soul by faith, and Christ reigns in the heart by love.

It is probable, many, perhaps the generality of men, at the first view of these words, are apt to imagine they are only an expression of, or petition for, resignation; for a readiness to suffer the will of God, whatsoever it be, concerning us: And this is unquestionably a divine and excellent temper, a most precious gift of God. But this is not what we pray for in this petition; at least, not in the chief and primary sense of it. We pray, not so much for a passive, as for an active conformity to the will of God, in saying, 'Thy will be done in earth, as it is in heaven.'

How is it done by the angels of God in heaven—those who now circle His throne rejoicing? They do it willingly; they love His commandments, and gladly hearken to His words. It is their meat and drink to do His will; it is their highest glory and joy. They do it *continually*; there is no interruption in their willing service. They rest not day nor night, but employ every hour (speaking after the manner of men; otherwise our measures of duration, days, and nights, and hours, have no place in eternity) in fulfilling His commands, in executing His designs, in performing the counsel of His will. And they do it *perfectly*. No sin, no defect belongs to angelic minds. It is true, 'the stars are not pure in His sight,' even the morning-stars that sing together before Him. 'In His sight,' that is, in comparison of Him, the very angels are not pure. But this does not imply, that they are not pure *in themselves*. Doubtless they are; they are without spot and blameless. They are altogether devoted to His will, and perfectly obedient in all things.

If we view this in another light, we may observe, the angels of God in heaven do *all* the will of God. And they do nothing else, nothing but what they are absolutely assured is His will. Again: they do all the will of God *as* He willeth; in the manner which pleases Him, and no other. Yea, and they do this, only *because* it is His will; for this end, and no other reason.

10. When therefore we pray, that the will of God may 'be done in earth as it is in heaven,' the meaning is, that all the inhabitants of the earth, even the whole race of mankind, may do the will of their Father which is in heaven, as *willingly* as the holy angels; that these may do it *continually*, even as they, without any interruption of their willing service; yea, and that they may do it *perfectly*—that 'the God of peace, through the blood of the everlasting covenant, may make them perfect in every good work to do His will, and work in them' all 'which is well-pleasing in His sight.'

In other words, we pray that we and all mankind may do the whole will of God in all things; and nothing else, not the least thing but what is the holy and acceptable will of God: we pray that we may do the whole will of God *as* He willeth, in the manner that pleases Him: and, lastly, that we may do it *because* it is His will; that this may be the sole reason and ground, the whole and only motive, of whatsoever we think, or whatsoever we speak or do.

11 'Give us this day our daily bread.' In the three former petitions we have been praying for all mankind. We come now more particularly to desire a supply for our own wants. Not

that we are directed, even here, to confine our prayer altogether to ourselves; but this, and each of the following petitions, may be used for the whole church of Christ upon earth.

By 'bread' we may understand all things needful, whether for our souls or bodies; τὰ πρὸς ζωὴν καὶ εὐσέβειαν—*the things pertaining to life and godliness*: we understand not barely the outward bread, what our Lord terms 'the meat which perisheth'; but much more the spiritual bread, the grace of God, the food 'which endureth unto everlasting life' It was the judgement of many of the ancient Fathers, that we are here to understand the sacramental bread also; daily received in the beginning by the whole church of Christ, and highly esteemed, till the love of many waxed cold, as the grand channel whereby the grace of His Spirit was conveyed to the souls of all the children of God.

'Our daily bread.' The word we render *daily* has been differently explained by different commentators But the most plain and natural sense of it seems to be this, which is retained in almost all translations, as well ancient as modern,—what is sufficient for this day; and so for each day as it succeeds.

12. 'Give us': for we claim nothing of right, but only of free mercy. We deserve not the air we breathe, the earth that bears, or the sun that shines upon us. All our desert, we own, is hell: but God loves us freely; therefore, we ask Him to give, what we can no more procure for ourselves, than we can merit it at His hands.

Not that either the goodness or the power of God is a reason for us to stand idle. It is His will that we should use all diligence in all things, that we should employ our utmost endeavours, as much as if our success were the natural effect of our own wisdom and strength; and then, as though we had done nothing, we are to depend on Him, the Giver of every good and perfect gift.

'This day': for we are to take no thought for the morrow. For this very end has our wise Creator divided life into these little portions of time, so clearly separated from each other, that we might look on every day as a fresh gift of God, another life, which we may devote to His glory; and that every evening may be as the close of life, beyond which we are to see nothing but eternity.

13. 'And forgive us our trespasses, as we forgive them that trespass against us.' As nothing but sin can hinder the bounty of God from flowing forth upon every creature, so this petition naturally follows the former; that, all hindrances being removed, we may the more clearly trust in the God of love for every manner of thing which is good.

'Our trespasses': the word properly signifies *our debts*. Thus our sins are frequently represented in Scripture; every sin laying us under a fresh debt to God, to whom we already owe, as it were, ten thousand talents. What, then, can we answer when He shall say, 'Pay me that thou owest'? We are utterly insolvent; we have nothing to pay; we have wasted all our substance. Therefore, if He deal with us according to the rigour of His law, if He exact what He justly may, He must command us to be 'bound hand and foot, and delivered over to the tormentors.'

Indeed we are already bound hand and foot by the chains of our own sins. These, considered with regard to ourselves, are chains of iron and fetters of brass. They are wounds wherewith the world, the flesh, and the devil have gashed and mangled us all over. They are diseases that drink up our blood and spirits, that bring us down to the chambers of the grave. But, considered as they are here, with regard to God, they are debts immense and numberless. Well, therefore, seeing we have nothing to pay, may we cry unto Him, that He would frankly forgive us all!

The word translated *forgive*, implies either to forgive a debt, or to unloose a chain. And if we attain the former, the latter follows of course: if our debts are forgiven, the chains fall off our hands. As soon as ever, through the free grace of God in Christ, we 'receive forgiveness of sins,' we receive likewise 'a lot among those which are sanctified, by faith which is in Him.' Sin has lost its power: it has no dominion over those who are under grace, that is, in favour with God. As 'there is now no condemnation to them that are in Christ Jesus,' so they are freed from sin as well as from guilt. 'The righteousness of the law is fulfilled in them, and they 'walk not after the flesh, but after the Spirit.'

14. 'As we forgive them that trespass against us.' In these words our Lord clearly declares both on what condition, and

in what degree or manner, we may look to be forgiven of God. All our trespasses and sins are forgiven us *if* we forgive, and *as* we forgive others. This is a point of the utmost importance. And our blessed Lord is so jealous lest at any time we should let it slip out of our thoughts, that He not only inserts it ir the body of His prayer, but presently after repeats it twice over. 'If,' saith He, 'ye forgive men their trespasses, your heavenly Father will also forgive you: but if ye forgive not men their trespasses, neither will your Father forgive your trespasses' (verses 14, 15). Secondly, God forgives us *as* we forgive others. So that if any malice or bitterness, if any taint of unkindness or anger remains, if we do not clearly, fully, and from the heart, forgive all men their trespasses, we so far cut short the forgiveness of our own: God cannot clearly and fully forgive us: He may show us some degree of mercy; but we will not suffer Him to blot out all our sins, and forgive all our iniquities.

In the meantime, while we do not from our hearts forgive our neighbour his trespasses, what manner of prayer are we offering to God whenever we utter these words? We are indeed setting God at open defiance; we are daring Him to do His worst. 'Forgive us our trespasses, as we forgive them that trespass against us!' That is, in plain terms, 'Do not Thou forgive us at all; we desire no favour at Thy hands. We pray that Thou wilt keep our sins in remembrance, and that Thy wrath may abide upon us.' But can you seriously offer such a prayer to God? And hath He not yet cast you quick into hell? O tempt Him no longer! Now, even now, by His grace, forgive as you would be forgiven! Now have compassion on thy fellow servant, as God hath had, and will have, pity on thee!

15. 'And lead us not into temptation, but deliver us from evil.'—'And lead us not into temptation.' The word translated *temptation* means trial of any kind. And so the English word temptation, was formerly taken in an indifferent sense; although now it is usually understood of solicitation to sin. St. James uses the word in both these senses; first, in its general, then in its restrained, acceptation. He takes it in the former sense when he saith, 'Blessed is the man that endureth temptation: for when he is tried,' or approved of God, 'He shall receive the

crown of life' (Jas. i. 12). He immediately adds, taking the word
in the latter sense, 'Let no man say when he is tempted, I am
tempted of God: for God cannot be tempted with evil, neither
tempteth He any man: but every man is tempted, when he is
drawn away of his own lust,' or *desire*, ἐξελκόμενος—drawn out
of God, in whom alone he is safe—'*and enticed*'; caught as a fish
with a bait. Then it is, when he is thus *drawn away and enticed*,
that he properly enters into temptation. Then temptation covers
him as a cloud; it overspreads his whole soul. Then how hardly
shall he escape out of the snare! Therefore we beseech God 'not
to lead us into temptation,' that is (seeing God tempteth no
man), not to suffer us to be led into it. 'But deliver us from
evil.' Rather, '*from the evil one*,' ἀπὸ τοῦ πονηροῦ. Ὁ πονηρός
is unquestionably *the wicked one*, emphatically so called, the
prince and god of this world, who works with mighty power
in the children of disobedience. But all those who are the
children of God by faith are delivered out of his hands. He
may fight against them; and so he will. But he cannot conquer,
unless they betray their own souls. He may torment for a time,
but he cannot destroy; for God is on their side, who will not
fail, in the end, to 'avenge His own elect, that cry unto Him
day and night,' Lord, when we are tempted, suffer us not to
enter into temptation! Do thou make a way for us to escape,
that the wicked one touch us not!

16. The conclusion of this divine prayer, commonly called
'the doxology,' is a solemn thanksgiving, a compendious
acknowledgement of the attributes and works of God. 'For
Thine is the kingdom,'—the sovereign right of all things that
are, or ever were created; yea, Thy kindgom is an everlasting
kingdom, and Thy dominion endureth throughout all ages.
'The power,'—the executive power whereby Thou governest
all things in Thy everlasting kingdom, whereby Thou doest
whatsoever pleaseth Thee, in all places of Thy dominion. 'And
the glory,'—the praise due from every creature, for Thy power,
and the mightiness of Thy kingdom, and for all Thy wondrous
works which Thou workest from everlasting, and shalt do,
world without end, 'for ever and ever. Amen!' So be it!

I believe it will not be unacceptable to the serious reader to subjoin

A PARAPHRASE ON THE LORD'S PRAYER

1 FATHER of all! whose powerful voice
    Called forth this universal frame;
  Whose mercies over all rejoice,
    Through endless ages still the same.
  Thou, by Thy word, upholdest all
    Thy bounteous love to all is showed:
  Thou hear'st Thy every creature's call,
    And fillest every mouth with good.

2 In heaven Thou reign'st, enthroned in light,
    Nature's expanse beneath Thee spread;
  Earth, air, and sea, before Thy sight,
    And hell's deep gloom, are open laid.
  Wisdom, and might, and love, are Thine;
    Prostrate before Thy face we fall,
  Confess Thine attributes divine,
    And hail Thee Sovereign Lord of all!

3 Thee, Sovereign Lord, let all confess,
    That moves in earth, or air, or sky,
  Revere Thy power, Thy goodness bless,
    Tremble before Thy piercing eye.
  All ye who owe to Him your birth,
    In praise your every hour employ:
  Jehovah reigns! Be glad, O earth!
    And shout, ye morning stars, for joy!

4 Son of Thy Sire's eternal love,
    Take to Thyself Thy mighty power;
  Let all earth's sons Thy mercy prove,
    Let all Thy bleeding grace adore.
  The triumphs of Thy love display:
    In every heart reign Thou alone;
  Till all Thy foes confess Thy sway,
    And glory ends what grace begun.

5 Spirit of grace, and health, and power,
    Fountain of light and love below;

Abroad Thine healing influence shower,
   O'er all the nations let it flow.
Inflame our hearts with perfect love;
   In us the work of faith fulfil;
So not heaven's host shall swifter move,
   Than we on earth to do Thy will.

6 Father, 'tis Thine each day to yield
   Thy children's wants a fresh supply:
Thou cloth'st the lilies of the field,
   And hearest the young ravens cry.
On Thee we cast our care; we live
   Through Thee, who know'st our every need:
O feed us with Thy grace, and give
   Our souls this day the living bread!

7 Eternal, spotless Lamb of God,
   Before the world's foundation slain,
Sprinkle us ever with Thy blood;
   O cleanse, and keep us ever clean
To every soul (all praise to Thee!)
   Our bowels of compassion move;
And all mankind by this may see
   God is in us; for God is love.

8 Giver and Lord of life, whose power
   And guardian care for all are free,
To Thee, in fierce temptation's hour,
   From sin and Satan let us flee.
Thine, Lord, we are, and ours Thou art;
   In us be all Thy goodness showed;
Renew, enlarge, and fill our heart
   With peace, and joy, and heaven, and God.

9 Blessing and honour, praise and love,
   Co-equal, co-eternal Three,
In earth below, in heaven above,
   By all Thy works be paid to Thee.
Thrice Holy! Thine the kingdom is,
   The power omnipotent is Thine;
And when created nature dies,
   Thy never-ceasing glories shine.

SERMON XXII

UPON OUR LORD'S SERMON ON THE MOUNT

DISCOURSE VII

Moreover when ye fast, be not, as the hypocrites of a sad countenance, for they disfigure their faces, that they may appear unto men to fast. Verily I say unto you, They have their reward.
But thou, when thou fastest, anoint thine head, and wash thy face;
That thou appear not unto men to fast, but unto thy Father which is in secret: and thy Father, which seeth in secret, shall reward thee openly.—MATT. vi. 16-18.

IT has been the endeavour of Satan, from the beginning of the world, to put asunder what God hath joined together; to separate inward from outward religion; to set one of these at variance with the other. And herein he has met with no small success among those who were 'ignorant of his devices.'

Many, in all ages, having a zeal for God, but not according to knowledge, have been strictly attached to the 'righteousness of the law,' the performance of outward duties, but in the meantime wholly regardless of inward righteousness, 'the righteousness which is of God by faith.' And many have run into the opposite extreme, disregarding all outward duties, perhaps even 'speaking evil of the law, and judging the law,' so far as it enjoins the performance of them.

2. It is by this very device of Satan, that faith and works have been so often set at variance with each other. And many who had a real zeal for God have, for a time, fallen into the snare on either hand. Some have magnified faith to the utter exclusion of good works, not only from being the cause of our justification (for we know that a man is justified freely by the redemption which is in Jesus), but from being the necessary fruit of it, yea, from having any place in the religion of Jesus Christ. Others, eager to avoid this dangerous mistake, have run as much too far the contrary way; and either maintained that good works

were the cause, at least the previous condition, of justification —or spoken of them as if they were all in all, the whole religion of Jesus Christ.

3. In the same manner have the end and the means of religion been set at variance with each other. Some well-meaning men have seemed to place all religion in attending the prayers of the Church, in receiving the Lord's supper, in hearing sermons, and reading books of piety; neglecting, meantime, the end of all these, the love of God and their neighbour. And this very thing has confirmed others in the neglect, if not contempt, of the ordinances of God—so wretchedly abused, to undermine and overthrow the very end they were designed to establish.

4. But of all the means of grace there is scarce any concerning which men have run into greater extremes, than that of which our Lord speaks in the above-mentioned words; I mean religious fasting. How have some exalted this beyond all Scripture and reason; and others utterly disregarded it—as it were, revenging themselves by undervaluing as much as the former had over-valued it! Those have spoken of it as if it were all in all; if not the end itself, yet infallibly connected with it: these, as if it were just nothing; as if it were a fruitless labour, which had no relation at all thereto. Whereas it is certain the truth lies between them both. It is not all, nor yet is it nothing. It is not the end, but it is a precious means thereto; a means which God Himself has ordained, and in which therefore, when it is duly used, He will surely give us His blessing.

In order to set this in the clearest light, I shall endeavour to show, first, what is the nature of fasting, and what the several sorts and degrees thereof: secondly, what are the reasons, grounds and ends of it: thirdly, how we may answer the most plausible objections against it: and, fourthly, in what manner it should be performed.

I. 1. I shall endeavour to show, first, what is the nature of fasting, and what the several sorts and degrees thereof. As to the nature of it, all the inspired writers, both in the Old Testament and the New, take the word, to *fast*, in one single sense, for not to eat, to abstain from food. This is so clear, that it would be

labour lost to quote the words of David, Nehemiah, Isaiah, and
the prophets which followed, or of our Lord and His apostles;
all agreeing in this, that to fast is, not to eat for a time prescribed.

2. To this, other circumstances were usually joined by them
of old, which had no necessary connexion with it. Such were,
the neglect of their apparel; the laying aside those ornaments
which they were accustomed to wear; the putting on mourning;
the strewing ashes upon their head; or wearing sackcloth next
their skin. But we find little mention made in the New Testament of any of these indifferent circumstances. Nor does it
appear that any stress was laid upon them by the Christians of
the purer ages; however some penitents might voluntarily use
them, as outward sings of inward humiliation. Much less did the
Apostles, or the Christians contemporary with them, beat or tear
their own flesh: such discipline as this was not unbecoming the
priests or worshippers of Baal. The gods of the Heathens were
but devils; and it was doubtless acceptable to their devil-god,
when his priests (1 Kings xviii. 28) 'cried aloud, and cut themselves after their manner, till the blood gushed out upon them':
but it cannot be pleasing to Him, nor become His followers,
who 'came not to destroy men's lives, but to save them.'

3. As to the degrees or measures of fasting, we have instances
of some who have fasted several days together. So Moses,
Elijah, and our blessed Lord, being endued with supernatural
strength for that purpose, are recorded to have fasted, without
intermission, 'forty days and forty nights.' But the time of
fasting, more frequently mentioned in Scripture, is one day,
from morning till evening. And this was the fast commonly
observed among the ancient Christians. But besides these, they
had also their half-fasts (*semijejunia*, as Tertullian styles them) on
the fourth and sixth days of the week (Wednesday and Friday),
throughout the year; on which they took no sustenance till
three in the afternoon, the time when they returned from the
public service.

4. Nearly related to this, is what our Church seems peculiarly
to mean by the term *abstinence*; which may be used when we
cannot fast entirely, by reason of sickness or bodily weakness.
This is the eating little; the abstaining in part: the taking a

smaller quantity of food than usual. I do not remember any
scriptural instance of this. But neither can I condemn it; for the
Scripture does not. It may have its use, and receive a blessing
from God.

5. The lowest kind of fasting, if it can be called by that name,
is the abstaining from pleasant food. Of this, we have several
instances in Scripture, besides that of Daniel and his brethren,
who, from a peculiar consideration, namely, that they might
'not defile themselves with the portion of the king's meat, nor
with the wine which he drank' (a daily provision of which the
king had appointed for them), requested and obtained, of the
prince of the eunuchs, pulse to eat, and water to drink (Dan. i.
8, &c.). Perhaps from a mistaken imitation of this might spring
the very ancient custom of abstaining from flesh and wine
during such times as were set apart for fasting and abstinence,—
if it did not rather arise from a supposition that these were the
most pleasant food, and a belief that it was proper to use what
was least pleasing at those times of solemn approach to God.

6. In the Jewish Church there were some stated fasts. Such
was the fast of the seventh month, appointed by God Himself
to be observed by all Israel under the severest penalty. 'The
Lord spake unto Moses, saying, On the tenth day of this seventh
month there shall be a day of atonement: and ye shall afflict
your souls, . . . to make an atonement for you before the Lord
your God. For whatsoever soul it be that shall not be afflicted
in that same day, he shall be cut off from among his people'
(Lev. xxiii. 26, &c.). In after-ages, several other stated fasts
were added to these. So mention is made, by the Prophet
Zechariah, of the fast, not only 'of the seventh, but also of the
fourth, of the fifth, and of the tenth month' (viii. 19).

In the ancient Christian church there were likewise stated
fasts, and those both annual and weekly. Of the former sort
was that before Easter; observed by some for eight-and-forty
hours; by others, for an entire week; by many, for two weeks;
taking no sustenance till the evening of each day: of the latter,
those of the fourth and sixth days of the week, observed (as
Epiphanius writes, remarking it as an undeniable fact) ἐν ὅλῃ
τῇ οἰκουμένῃ—in the whole habitable earth; at least in every

place where any Christians made their abode. The annual fasts in our Church are, 'the forty days of Lent, the Ember days at the four seasons, the Rogation days, and the Vigils or Eves of several solemn festivals; the weekly, all Fridays in the year, except Christmas-day.'

But beside those which were fixed, in every nation fearing God there have always been occasional fasts, appointed from time to time, as the particular circumstances and occasions of each required. So when 'the children of Moab, and the children of Ammon, came against Jehoshaphat to battle, Jehoshaphat set himself to seek the Lord, and proclaimed a fast throughout all Judah' (2 Chron. xx. 1, 3). And so, 'in the fifth year of Jehoiakim the son of Josiah, in the ninth month,' when they were afraid of the king of Babylon, the princes of 'Judah proclaimed a fast before the Lord, to all the people in Jerusalem' (Jer. xxxvi. 9).

And, in like manner, particular persons, who take heed unto their ways, and desire to walk humbly and closely with God, will find frequent occasion for private seasons of thus afflicting their souls before their Father which is in secret. And it is to this kind of fasting that the directions here given do chiefly and primarily refer.

II. 1. I proceed to show, in the second place, what are the grounds, the reasons, and ends of fasting.

And, first, men who are under strong emotions of mind, who are affected with any vehement passion, such as sorrow or fear, are often swallowed up therein, and even forget to eat their bread. At such seasons they have little regard for food, not even what is needful to sustain nature, much less for any delicacy or variety; being taken up with quite different thoughts. Thus when Saul said, 'I am sore distressed; for the Philistines make war against me, and God is departed from me'; it is recorded, 'He had eaten no bread all the day, nor all the night' (1 Sam. xxviii. 15, 20). Thus those who were in the ship with St. Paul, 'when no small tempest lay upon them, and all hope that they should be saved was taken away,' 'continued fasting, having taken nothing,' no regular meal, for fourteen days together' (Acts xxvii. 33). And thus David, and all the men that were with him, when they heard that the people were fled from the battle, and that many of the people were fallen and dead, and Saul and Jonathan his son were dead also, 'mourned, and wept, and fasted until even, for Saul and Jonathan, and for the house of Israel' (2 Sam. i. 12).

Nay, many times they whose minds are deeply engaged are impatient of any interruption, and even loathe their needful food, as diverting their thoughts from what they desire should engross their whole attention: even as Saul, when, on the occasion mentioned before, he had 'fallen all along upon the earth, and there was no strength in him,' yet said, 'I will not eat,' till 'his servants together with the woman, compelled him.'

2. Here, then is, the natural ground of fasting. One who is under deep affliction, overwhelmed with sorrow for sin, and a strong apprehension of the wrath of God, would, without any rule, without knowing or considering whether it were a command of God or not, 'forget to eat his bread,' abstain not only from pleasant but even from needful food; like St. Paul, who, after he was led into Damascus, 'was three days without sight, and did neither eat nor drink' (Acts ix. 9).

Yea, when the storm rose high, 'when an horrible dread overwhelmed' one who had been without God in the world, his soul would 'loathe all manner of meat'; it would be unpleasing and irksome to him; he would be impatient of anything that should interrupt his ceaseless cry, 'Lord, save! or I perish.'

How strongly is this expressed by our Church in the first part of the Homily on Fasting!—'When men feel in themselves the heavy burden of sin, see damnation to be the reward of it, and behold, with the eye of their mind, the horror of hell, they tremble, they quake, and are inwardly touched with sorrowfulness of heart, and cannot but accuse themselves, and open their grief unto Almighty God, and call unto Him for mercy. This being done seriously, their mind is so occupied [taken up], partly with sorrow and heaviness, partly with an earnest desire to be delivered from this danger of hell and damnation, that all desire of meat and drink is laid apart, and loathsomeness [or loathing] of all worldly things and pleasure cometh in place. So that nothing then liketh them more than to weep, to lament, to mourn, and both with words and behaviour of body to show themselves weary of life.'

3. Another reason or ground of fasting is this: many of those who now fear God are deeply sensible how often they have sinned against Him, by the abuse of these lawful things. They know how much they have sinned by excess of food; how long they have transgressed the holy law of God, with regard to temperance, if not sobriety too; how they have indulged their sensual appetites, perhaps to the impairing even their bodily health, certainly to the no small hurt of their soul. For hereby they continually fed and increased that sprightly folly, that airiness of mind, that levity of temper, that gay inattention to things of the deepest concern, that giddiness and carelessness of spirit, which were no other than drunkenness of soul, which stupefied all their noblest faculties, no less than excess of wine or strong drink. To remove, therefore, the effect, they remove the cause: they keep at a distance from all excess. They abstain, as far as is possible, from what had well nigh plunged them in everlasting perdition. They often wholly refrain: always take care to be sparing and temperate in all things.

4. They likewise well remember how fullness of bread increased not only carelessness and levity of spirit, but also foolish and unholy desires, yea, unclean and vile affections. And this experience puts beyond all doubt. Even a genteel, regular sensuality is continually sensualizing the soul, and sinking it into a level with the beasts that perish. It cannot be expressed what an effect a variety and delicacy of food have on the mind as well as the body; making it just ripe for every pleasure of sense, as soon as opportunity shall invite. Therefore, on this ground also, every wise man will refrain his soul, and keep it low; will wean it more and more from all those indulgences of the inferior appetites, which naturally tend to chain it down to earth, and to pollute as well as debase it. Here is another perpetual reason for fasting; to remove the food of lust and sensuality, to withdraw the incentives of foolish and hurtful desires, of vile and vain affections.

5. Perhaps we need not altogether omit (although I know

not if we should do well to lay any great stress upon it) another
reason for fasting, which some good men have largely insisted
on; namely, the punishing themselves for having abused the
good gifts of God, by sometimes wholly refraining from them;
thus exercising a kind of holy revenge upon themselves, for
their past folly and ingratitude, in turning the things which
should have been for their health into an occasion of falling.
They suppose David to have had an eye to this, when he said,
'I wept and chastened,' or punished, 'my soul with fasting'; and
St. Paul, when he mentions 'what revenge' godly sorrow occasioned in the Corinthians.

6. A fifth and more weighty reason for fasting is, that it is an
help to prayer; particularly when we set apart larger portions
of time for private prayer. Then especially it is that God is
often pleased to lift up the souls of His servants above all the
things of earth, and sometimes to rap them up, as it were, into
the third heavens. And it is chiefly, as it is an help to prayer, that
it has so frequently been found a means, in the hand of God, of
confirming and increasing, not one virtue, not chastity only (as
some have idly imagined, without any ground either from
Scripture, reason, or experience), but also seriousness of spirit,
earnestness, sensibility and tenderness of conscience, deadness to
the world, and consequently the love of God, and every holy
and heavenly affection.

7. Not that there is any natural or necessary connexion
between fasting, and the blessings God conveys thereby. But
He will have mercy *as* He will have mercy; He will convey
whatsoever seemeth Him good by whatsoever means He is
pleased to appoint. And He hath, in all ages, appointed this to be
a means of averting His wrath, and obtaining whatever blessings
we, from time to time, stand in need of.

How powerful a means this is to avert the wrath of God,
we may learn from the remarkable instance of Ahab. 'There
was none like him who did sell himself'—wholly give himself
up, like a slave bought with money—'to work wickedness.'
Yet, when he 'rent his clothes, and put sackcloth upon his flesh,
and fasted, and went softly, the word of the Lord came to Elijah,
saying, Seest thou how Ahab humbleth himself before Me?

Because he humbleth himself before Me, I will not bring the evil in his days.'

It was for this end, to avert the wrath of God, that Daniel sought God 'with fasting, and sackcloth, and ashes.' This appears from the whole tenor of his prayer, particularly from the solemn conclusion of it: 'O Lord, according to all Thy righteousness,' or mercies, 'let Thy anger be turned away from Thy holy mountain. . . . Hear the prayer of Thy servant, and cause Thy face to shine upon Thy sanctuary that is desolate. . . . O Lord, hear; O Lord, forgive; O Lord, hearken and do, for Thine own sake' (Dan. ix. 3, 16, &c.).

8. But it is not only from the people of God that we learn, when His anger is moved, to seek Him by fasting and prayer; but even from the Heathens. When Jonah had declared, 'Yet forty days, and Nineveh shall be overthrown,' the people of Nineveh 'proclaimed a fast, and put on sackcloth, from the greatest of them unto the least. For the king of Nineveh arose from his throne, and laid his robe from him, and covered him with sackcloth, and sat in ashes. And he caused it to be proclaimed and published through Nineveh. Let neither man nor beast, herd nor flock, taste anything: let them not feed, nor drink water' (not that the beasts had sinned, or could repent; but that, by their example, man might be admonished, considering that, for his sin, the anger of God was hanging over all creatures): 'who can tell if God will turn and repent, and turn away from His fierce anger, that we perish not?' And their labour was not in vain. The fierce anger of God was turned away from them. 'God saw their works' (the fruits of that repentance and faith which He had wrought in them by His prophet); 'and God repented of the evil, that He had said He would do unto them; and He did it not' (Jonah iii. 4, &c.).

9. And it is a means not only of turning away the wrath of God, but also of obtaining whatever blessings we stand in need of. So, when the other tribes were smitten before the Benjamites, 'all the children of Israel went up unto the house of God, and wept, and fasted that day until even'; and then the Lord said, 'Go up' again; 'for to-morrow I will deliver them into thine hand' (Judges xx. 26, &c.). So Samuel gathered all Israel

together, when they were in bondage to the Philistines, 'and they fasted on that day' before the Lord: and when 'the Philistines drew near to battle against Israel, the Lord thundered' upon them 'with a great thunder, and discomfited them; and they were smitten before Israel' (1 Sam. vii. 6). So Ezra: 'I proclaimed a fast at the river Ahava, that we might afflict ourselves before our God, to seek of Him a right way for us, and for our little ones; and He was entreated of us' (viii. 21). So Nehemiah: 'I fasted and prayed before the God of heaven, and said, Prosper, I pray Thee, Thy servant this day, and grant him mercy in the sight of this man': and God granted him mercy in the sight of the king (i. 4-11).

10. In like manner, the Apostles always joined fasting with prayer when they desired the blessing of God on any important undertaking. Thus we read (Acts xiii.), 'There were in the church that was at Antioch certain prophets and teachers: as they ministered to the Lord, and fasted,' doubtless for direction in this very affair, 'the Holy Ghost said, Separate Me Barnabas and Saul for the work whereunto I have called them. And when they had' a second time 'fasted and prayed, and laid their hands on them, they sent them away' (verses 1-3).

Thus also Paul and Barnabas themselves, as we read in the following chapter, when they 'returned again to Lystra, Iconium, and Antioch, confirming the souls of the disciples, and when they had ordained them elders in every church, and had prayed with fasting, commended them to the Lord' (Acts xiv. 23).

Yea, that blessings are to be obtained in the use of this means, which are no otherwise attainable, our Lord expressly declares in His answer to His disciples, asking, 'Why could not we cast him out? Jesus said unto them, Because of your unbelief: for verily I say unto you, If ye have faith as a grain of mustard-seed, ye shall say unto this mountain, Remove hence to yonder place; and it shall remove; and nothing shall be impossible unto you. Howbeit this kind' of devils 'goeth not out but by prayer and fasting' (Matt xvii. 19, &c.) —these being the appointed means of attaining that faith whereby the very devils are subject unto you.

11. These were the appointed means: for it was not merely

by the light of reason, or of natural conscience, as it is called, that the people of God have been, in all ages, directed to use fasting as a means to these ends; but they have been, from time to time, taught it of God Himself, by clear and open revelations of His will. Such is that remarkable one by the Prophet Joel: 'Therefore saith the Lord, Turn ye to Me with all your heart, and with fasting, and with weeping, and with mourning; . . . who knoweth if He will return and repent, and leave a blessing behind Him? Blow the trumpet in Zion, sanctify a fast, call a solemn assembly: . . . then will the Lord be jealous for His land, and pity His people. Yea, I will send you corn, and wine, and oil; . . . I will no more make you a reproach among the Heathen' (Joel ii. 12, &c.).

Nor are they only temporal blessings which God directs His people to expect in the use of these means. For, at the same time that He promised to those who should seek Him with fasting, and weeping, and mourning, 'I will restore to you the years which the locust hath eaten, the canker-worm, and the caterpillar, and the palmer-worm, My great army': He subjoins, 'So shall ye eat and be satisfied, and praise the name of the Lord your God. . . . Ye shall also know that I am in the midst of Israel, and that I am the Lord your God.' And then immediately follows the great gospel promise: 'I will pour out My Spirit upon all flesh; and your sons and your daughters shall prophesy, your old men shall dream dreams, and your young men shall see visions: and also upon the servants and upon the handmaids in those days will I pour out My Spirit.'

12. Now whatsoever reasons there were to quicken those of old, in the zealous and constant discharge of this duty, they are of equal force still to quicken us. But above all these, we have a peculiar reason for being 'in fastings often'; namely, the command of Him by whose name we are called. He does not, indeed, in this place expressly enjoin either fasting, giving of alms, or prayer; but His directions *how* to fast, to give alms, and to pray, are of the same force with such injunctions. For the commanding us to do anything *thus*, is an unquestionable command to do that thing; seeing it is impossible to perform it *thus*, if it be not performed at all. Consequently, the saying, 'Give alms, pray, fast,

in such a manner, is a clear command to perform all those duties; as well as to perform them in that *manner* which shall in no wise lose its reward.

And this is a still farther motive and encouragement to the performance of this duty; even the promise which our Lord has graciously annexed to the due discharge of it: 'Thy Father, which seeth in secret, shall reward thee openly.' Such are the plain grounds, reasons, and ends of fasting; such our encouragement to persevere therein, notwithstanding abundance of objections which men, wiser than their Lord, have been continually raising against it.

III. 1. The most plausible of these I come now to consider. And, first, it has been frequently said, 'Let a Christian fast from sin, and not from food: this is what God requires at his hands.' So He does; but He requires the other also. Therefore this ought to be done, and that not left undone.

View your argument in its full dimensions; and you will easily judge of the strength of it:—

If a Christian ought to abstain from sin, then he ought not to abstain from food:

But a Christian ought to abstain from sin:

Therefore he ought not to abstain from food.

That a Christian ought to abstain from sin, is most true; but how does it follow from hence that he ought not to abstain from food? Yea, let him do both the one and the other. Let him, by the grace of God, always abstain from sin; and let him often abstain from food, for such reasons and ends as experience and Scripture plainly show to be answered thereby.

2. 'But is it not better' (as it has, secondly, been objected) 'to abstain from pride and vanity, from foolish and hurtful desires, from peevishness, and anger, and discontent, than from food?' Without question, it is. But here again we have need to remind you of our Lord's words: These things ought ye to have done, and not to leave the other undone.' And, indeed, the latter is only in order to the former; it is a means to that great end. We abstain from food with this view,—that, by the grace of God conveyed into our souls through this outward means, in

conjunction with all the other channels of His grace which He hath appointed, we may be enabled to abstain from every passion and temper which is not pleasing in His sight. We refrain from the one, that, being endued with power from on high, we may be able to refrain from the other. So that your argument proves just the contrary to what you designed. It proves that we ought to fast. For if we ought to abstain from evil tempers and desires, then we ought thus to abstain from food; since these little instances of self-denial are the ways God hath chose, wherein to bestow that great salvation.

3. 'But we do not find it so in fact' (this is a third objection): we have fasted much and often; but what did it avail? We were not a whit better; we found no blessing therein. Nay, we have found it an hindrance rather than an help. Instead of preventing anger, for instance, or fretfulness, it has been a means of increasing them to such a height, that we could neither bear others nor ourselves.' This may very possibly be the case. It is possible either to fast or pray in such a manner as to make you much worse than before; more unhappy, and more unholy. Yet the fault does not lie in the means itself, but in the manner of using it. Use it still, but use it in a different manner. Do what God commands *as* He commands it; and then, doubtless, His promise shall not fail: His blessing shall be withheld no longer; but, when thou fastest in secret, He that seeth in secret shall reward thee openly.'

4. But is it not mere superstition' (so it has been, fourthly, objected), to imagine that God regards such little things as these?' If you say it is, you condemn all the generations of God's children. But will you say, These were all weak, superstitious men? Can you be so hardy as to affirm this, both of Moses and Joshua, of Samuel and David, of Jehoshaphat, Ezra, Nehemiah, and all the prophets? yea, of a greater than all,—the Son of God Himself? It is certain, both our Master, and all these His servants, did imagine that fasting is not a little thing, and that He who is higher than the highest doth regard it. Of the same judgement, it is plain, were all His Apostles, after they were filled with the Holy Ghost, and with wisdom.' · When they had the 'unction of the Holy One, teaching them all things,' they still approved themselves the ministers of God, 'by fastings,' as well as 'by the

armour of righteousness on the right hand and on the left.' After 'the bridegroom was taken from them, then did they fast in those days.' Nor would they attempt anything (as we have seen above) wherein the glory of God was nearly concerned, such as the sending forth labourers into the harvest. without solemn fasting as well as prayer.

5. 'But if fasting be indeed of so great importance, and attended with such a blessing, is it not best,' say some, fifthly, 'to fast always? not to do it now and then, but to keep a continual fast? to use as much abstinence, at all times, as our bodily strength will bear?' Let none be discouraged from doing this. By all means use as little and plain food, exercise as much self-denial herein, at all times, as your bodily strength will bear. And this may conduce, by the blessing of God, to several of the great ends above mentioned. It may be a considerable help, not only to chastity, but also to heavenly-mindedness; to the weaning your affections from things below, and setting them on things above. But this is not fasting, scriptural fasting; it is never termed so in all the Bible. It, in some measure, answers some of the ends thereof; but still it is another thing. Practise it by all means; but not so as thereby to set aside a command of God, and an instituted means of averting His judgements, and obtaining the blessings of His children.

6. Use continually then as much abstinence as you please; which, taken thus, is no other than Christian temperance; but this need not at all interfere with your observing solemn times of fasting and prayer. For instance: your habitual abstinence or temperance would not prevent your fasting in secret, if you were suddenly overwhelmed with huge sorrow and remorse, and with horrible fear and dismay. Such a situation of mind would almost constrain you to fast; you would loathe your daily food; you would scarce endure even to take such supplies as were needful for the body, till God 'lifted you up out of the horrible pit, and set your feet upon a rock, and ordered your goings.' The same would be the case, if you were in agony of desire, vehemently wrestling with God for His blessing. You would need none to instruct you not to eat bread till you had obtained the request of your lips.

7. Again: had you been at Nineveh when it was proclaimed throughout the city, 'Let neither man nor beast, herd nor flock, taste anything; let them not feed or drink water, but let them cry mightily unto God'; would your continual fast have been any reason for not bearing part in that general humiliation? Doubtlesss it would not. You would have been as much concerned as any other not to taste food on that day.

No more would abstinence, or the observing a continual fast, have excused any of the children of Israel from fasting on the tenth day of the seventh month, the great annual day of atonement. There was no exception for these in that solemn decree, 'Whatsoever soul it be, that shall not be afflicted,' shall not fast, 'in that day, he shall be cut off from among his people.'

Lastly, had you been with the brethren in Antioch, at the time when they fasted and prayed, before the sending forth of Barnabas and Saul, can you possibly imagine that your temperance or abstinence would have been a sufficient cause for not joining therein? Without doubt, if you had not, you would soon have been cut off from the Christian community. You would have deservedly been cast out from among them, as bringing confusion into the church of God.

IV. 1. I am, in the last place, to show, in what manner we are to fast, that it may be an acceptable service unto the Lord. And, first, let it be done unto the Lord, with our eye singly fixed on Him. Let our intention herein be this, and this alone, to glorify our Father which is in heaven; to express our sorrow and shame for our manifold transgressions of His holy law; to wait for an increase of purifying grace, drawing our affections to things above; to add seriousness and earnestness to our prayers; to avert the wrath of God; and to obtain all the great and precious promises which He hath made to us in Jesus Christ.

Let us beware of mocking God, of turning our fast, as well as our prayers, into an abomination unto the Lord, by the mixture of any temporal view, particularly by seeking the praise of men. Against this our blessed Lord more peculiarly guards us in the words of the text. 'Moreover, when ye fast, be ye not as the hypocrites'—such were too many who were called the people of God; 'of a sad countenance'; sour, affectedly sad, putting their looks into a peculiar form. 'For they disfigure their faces,' not only by unnatural distortions, but also by covering them with dust and ashes, 'that they may appear unto men to fast'; this is their chief, if not only, design. 'Verily I say unto you, they have their reward'; even the admiration and praise of men. 'But thou when thou fastest, anoint thy head and wash thy face': do as thou art accustomed to do at other times; 'that thou appear not unto men to fast': let this be no part of thy intention; if they know it without any desire of thine, it matters not, thou art neither the better nor the worse; 'but unto thy Father which is in secret: and thy Father, which seeth in secret, shall reward thee openly.'

2. But, if we desire this reward, let us beware, secondly, of fancying we *merit* anything of God by our fasting. We cannot be too often warned of this; inasmuch as a desire to 'establish our own righteousness,' to procure salvation of debt and not of grace, is so deeply rooted in all our hearts. Fasting is only a way which God hath ordained, wherein we wait for His unmerited mercy: and wherein, without any desert of ours, He hath promised freely to give us His blessing.

3. Not that we are to imagine, the performing the bare outward act will receive any blessing from God. 'Is it such a fast that I have chosen, saith the Lord; a day for a man to afflict his soul? is it to bow down his head as a bulrush, and to spread sackcloth and ashes under him?' Are these outward acts, however strictly performed, all that is meant by a man's 'afflicting his soul'? 'Wilt thou call this a fast, and an acceptable day to the Lord?' No, surely: if it be a mere external service, it is all but lost labour. Such a performance may possibly afflict the body; but, as to the soul, it profiteth nothing.

4. Yea, the body may sometimes be afflicted too much, so as to be unfit for the works of our calling. This also we are diligently to guard against; for we ought to preserve our health, as a good gift of God. Therefore care is to be taken, whenever we fast, to proportion the fast to our strength. For we may not offer God murder for sacrifice, or destroy our bodies to help our souls.

But at these solemn seasons, we may, even in great weakness of body, avoid that other extreme, for which God condemns those who of old expostulated with Him for not accepting their fasts 'Wherefore have we fasted, say they, and Thou seest not? . . Behold, in the day of your fast you find pleasure, saith the Lord.' If we cannot wholly abstain from food, we may, at least, abstain from pleasant food; and then we shall not seek His face in vain.

5. But let us take care to afflict our souls as well as our bodies. Let every season, either of public or private fasting, be a season of exercising all those holy affections which are implied in a broken and contrite heart Let it be a season of devout mourning of godly sorrow for sin; such a sorrow as that of the Corinthians, concerning which the Apostle saith, 'I rejoice, not that ye were made sorry, but that ye sorrowed to repentance. For ye were made sorry after a godly manner, that ye might receive damage by us in nothing. For godly sorrow,' ἡ κατὰ Θεὸν λύπη— the sorrow which is according to God, which is a precious gift of His Spirit, lifting the soul to God from whom it flows— 'worketh repentance to salvation, not to be repented of.' Yea, and let our sorrowing after a godly sort work in us the same inward and outward *repentance*; the same entire change of heart, renewed after the image of God, in righteousness and true holiness; and the same change of life, till we are holy as He is holy, in all manner of conversation. Let it work in us the same *carefulness* to be found in Him, without spot and blameless; the same *clearing of ourselves*, by our lives rather than words, by our abstaining from all appearance of evil; the same *indignation*, vehement abhorrence of every sin; the same *fear* of our own deceitful hearts; the same *desire* to be in all things conformed to the holy and acceptable will of God; the same zeal for whatever may be a means of His glory, and of our growth in the knowledge of our Lord Jesus Christ; and the same *revenge* against Satan and all his works, against all filthiness both of flesh and spirit (2 Cor. vii. 9, &c.).

6. And with fasting let us always join fervent prayer, pouring out our whole souls before God, confessing our sins with all their aggravations, humbling ourselves under His mighty hand, laying open before Him all our wants, all our guiltiness and

helplessness. This is a season for enlarging our prayers, both in behalf of ourselves and of our brethren. Let us now bewail the sins of our people; and cry aloud for the city of our God, that the Lord may build up Zion, and cause His face to shine on her desolations. Thus, we may observe, the men of God, in ancient times, always joined prayer and fasting together; thus the Apostles, in all the instances cited above; and thus our Lord joins them in the discourse before us.

7. It remains only, in order to our observing such a fast as is acceptable to the Lord, that we add alms thereto; works of mercy, after our power, both to the bodies and souls of men: 'With such sacrifices' also 'God is well pleased.' Thus the angel declares to Cornelius, fasting and praying in his house, 'Thy prayers and thine alms are come up for a memorial before God' (Acts x. 4, &c.). And thus God Himself expressly and largely declares: 'Is not this the fast that I have chosen? to loose the bands of wickedness, to undo the heavy burdens, and to let the oppressed go free, and that ye break every yoke? Is it not to deal thy bread to the hungry, and that thou bring the poor that are cast out to thy house? when thou seest the naked, that thou cover him; and that thou hide not thyself from thine own flesh? Then shall thy light break forth as the morning, and thine health shall spring forth speedily: and thy righteousness shall go before thee; the glory of the Lord shall be thy reward. Then shalt thou call, and the Lord shall answer: thou shalt cry, and He shall say, Here I am. . . . If,' when thou fastest, 'thou draw out thy soul to the hungry, and satisfy the afflicted soul; then shall thy light rise in obscurity, and thy darkness be as the noon-day. And the Lord shall guide thee continually, and satisfy thy soul in drought, and make fat thy bones: and thou shalt be like a watered garden, and like a spring of water, whose waters fail not.' (Isa. lviii. 6, &c.).

SERMON XXIII

UPON OUR LORD'S SERMON ON THE MOUNT

DISCOURSE VIII

Lay not up for yourselves treasures upon earth, where moth and rust doth corrupt: and where thieves break through and steal:

But lay up for yourselves treasures in heaven, where neither moth nor rust doth corrupt, and where thieves do not break through nor steal:

For where your treasure is, there will your heart be also.

The light of the body is the eye: if therefore thine eye be single thy whole body shall be full of light.

But if thine eye be evil, thy whole body shall be full of darkness. If therefore the light that is in thee be darkness: how great is that darkness!—MATT. vi. 19-23.

FROM those which are commonly termed religious actions, and which are real branches of true religion, where they spring from a pure and holy intention, and are performed in a manner suitable thereto, our Lord proceeds to the actions of common life; and shows that the same purity of intention is as indispensably required in our ordinary business, as in giving alms, or fasting, or prayer.

And without question, the same purity of intention, 'which makes our alms and devotions acceptable, must also make our labour or employment a proper offering to God. If a man pursues his business, that he may raise himself to a state of figure and riches in the world, he is no longer serving God in his employment, and has no more title to a reward from God, than he who gives alms that he may be seen, or prays that he may be heard, of men. For vain and earthly designs are no more allowable in our employments, than in our alms and devotions. They are not only evil when they mix with our good works,' with our religious actions, 'but they have the same evil nature when they enter into the common business of our employments. If it were allowable to pursue them in our worldly employments, it would be allowable to pursue them in our devotions. But as our alms and devotions are not an acceptable service but when they proceed from a pure intention, so our common employment cannot be reckoned a service to Him but when it is performed with the same piety of heart.'

2. This our blessed Lord declares in the liveliest manner, in those strong and comprehensive words, which He explains, enforces, and enlarges upon, throughout this whole chapter: 'The light of the body is the eye: if therefore thine eye be single, thy whole body shall be full of light. But if thine eye be evil, thy whole body shall be full of darkness.' The eye is the intention: what the eye is to the body, the intention is to the soul. As the one guides all the motions of the body, so does the other those of the soul. This eye of the soul is then said to be single, when it looks at one thing only; when we have no other design, but to 'know God, and Jesus Christ whom He hath sent'—to know Him with suitable affections, loving Him as He hath loved us; to please God in all things; to serve God (as we love Him) with all our heart, and mind, and soul, and strength; and to enjoy God in all, and above all things, in time and in eternity.

3. 'If thine eye be' thus 'single,' thus fixed on God, 'thy whole body shall be full of light.' 'Thy whole body':—all that is guided by the intention, as the body is by the eye: all thou art; all thou doest; thy desires, tempers, affections; thy thoughts, and words, and actions. The whole of these 'shall be full of light'; full of true, divine knowledge. This is the first thing we may here understand by light. 'In His light thou shalt see light.' 'He which of old commanded light to shine out of darkness, shall shine in thy heart': He shall enlighten the eyes of thy understanding with the knowledge of the glory of God. His Spirit shall reveal unto thee the deep things of God. The inspiration of the Holy One shall give thee understanding, and cause thee to know wisdom secretly. Yea, the anointing which thou receivest of Him 'shall abide in thee, and teach thee of all things.'

How does experience confirm this! Even after God hath opened the eyes of our understanding, if we seek or desire anything else than God, how soon is our foolish heart darkened! Then clouds again rest upon our souls. Doubts and fears again overwhelm us. We are tossed to and fro, and know not what to do, or which is the path wherein we should go. But when we desire and seek nothing but God, clouds and doubts vanish away. We who 'were sometimes darkness are now light in the Lord.' The night now shineth as the day; and we find 'the path of the upright is light.' God showeth us the path wherein we should go, and maketh plain the way before our face.

4. The second thing which we may here understand by light, is holiness. While thou seekest God in all things, thou shalt find Him in all—the fountain of all holiness continually filling thee with His own likeness, with justice, mercy, and truth. While thou lookest unto Jesus, and Him alone, thou shalt be filled with the mind that was in Him. Thy soul shall be renewed day by day, after the image of Him that created it. If the eye of thy mind be not removed from Him, if thou endurest 'seeing Him that is invisible,' and seeking nothing else in heaven or earth, then as thou beholdest the glory of the Lord, thou shalt be transformed 'into the same image, from glory to glory, by the Spirit of the Lord.'

And it is also matter of daily experience, that 'by grace we are' thus 'saved through faith.' It is by faith that the eye of the mind is opened, to see the light of the glorious love of God: and as long as it is steadily fixed thereon, on God in Christ, reconciling the world unto Himself, we are more and more filled with the love of God and man; with meekness, gentleness, long-suffering; with all the fruits of holiness which are through Christ Jesus, to the glory of God the Father.

5. This light which fills him who has a single eye implies, thirdly, happiness, as well as holiness. Surely 'light is sweet, and a pleasant thing it is to see the sun.' But how much more, to see the Sun of righteousness continually shining upon the soul! And if there be any consolation in Christ, if any comfort of love, if any peace that passeth all understanding, if any rejoicing in hope of the glory of God, they all belong to him whose eye is single. Thus is his 'whole body full of light.' He walketh in the light as God is in the light, rejoicing evermore, praying without ceasing, and in everything giving thanks; enjoying whatever is the will of God concerning him in Christ Jesus.

6. 'But if thine eye be evil, thy whole body shall be full of darkness.' 'If thine eye be evil': we see there is no medium between a single and an evil eye. If the eye be not single, then it

is evil. If the intention, in whatever we do, be not singly to God, if we seek anything else, then our mind and conscience are defiled.

Our eye therefore is evil, if, in anything we do, we aim at any other end than God; if we have any view, but to know and to love God, to please and serve Him in all things; if we have any other design than to enjoy God, to be happy in Him both now and for ever.

7. If thine eye be not singly fixed on God, 'thy whole body shall be full of darkness.' The veil shall still remain on thy heart. Thy mind shall be more and more blinded by 'the god of this world,' 'lest the light of the glorious gospel of Christ should shine upon thee.' Thou wilt be full of ignorance and error touching the things of God, not being able to receive or discern them. And even when thou hast some desire to serve God, thou wilt be full of uncertainty as to the manner of serving Him; finding doubts and difficulties on every side, and not seeing any way to escape.

Yea, if thine eye be not single, if thou seek any of the things of earth, thou shalt be full of ungodliness and unrighteousness; thy desires, tempers, affections, being all out of course; being all dark, and vile, and vain. And thy conversation will be evil, as well as thy heart; not 'seasoned with salt,' or 'meet to minister grace unto the hearers'; but idle, unprofitable, corrupt, grievous to the Holy Spirit of God.

8. Both destruction and unhappiness are in thy ways; 'for the way of peace hast thou not known.' There is no peace, no settled, solid peace, for them that know not God. There is no true nor lasting content for any who do not seek Him with their whole heart. While thou aimest at any of the things that perish, 'all that cometh is vanity'; yea not only vanity, but 'vexation of spirit'; and that both in the pursuit and the enjoyment also. Thou walkest indeed in a vain shadow, and disquietest thyself in vain. Thou walkest in darkness that may be felt. Sleep on; but thou canst not take thy rest. The dreams of life can give pain; and that thou knowest: but ease they cannot give. There is no rest in this world or the world to come, but only in God, the centre of spirits.

'If the light which is in thee be darkness, how great is that darkness!' If the intention, which ought to enlighten the whole soul, to fill it with knowledge, and love, and peace, and which in fact does, so long as it is single, as long as it aims at God alone,— if this be darkness; if it aim at anything beside God, and consequently cover the soul with darkness instead of light, with ignorance and error, with sin and misery; O how great is that darkness! It is the very smoke which ascends out of the bottomless pit! It is the essential night which reigns in the lowest deep, in the land of the shadow of death!

9. Therefore, 'lay not up for yourselves treasures upon earth, where moth and rust doth corrupt, and where thieves break through and steal.' If you do, it is plain your eye is evil; it is not singly fixed on God.

With regard to most of the commandments of God, whether relating to the heart or life, the Heathens of Africa or America stand much on a level with those that are called Christians. The Christians observe them (a few only being excepted) very near as much as the Heathens. For instance: the generality of the natives of England, commonly called Christians, are as sober and as temperate as the generality of the Heathens near the Cape of Good Hope. And so the Dutch or French Christians are as humble and as chaste as the Choctaw or Cherokee Indians. It is not easy to say, when we compare the bulk of the nations in Europe with those in America, whether the superiority lies on the one side or the other. At least, the American has not much the advantage. But we cannot affirm this with regard to the command now before us. Here the Heathen has far the pre-eminence. He desires and seeks nothing more than plain food to eat, and plain raiment to put on; and he seeks this only from day to day: he reserves, he lays up nothing; unless it be as much corn at one season of the year as he will need before that season returns. This command, therefore, the Heathens though they know it not, do constantly and punctually observe. They 'lay up for themselves no treasures upon earth'; no stores of purple or fine linen, of gold or silver, which either 'moth or rust may corrupt, or thieves break through and steal.' But how do the Christians observe what they profess to receive as a command of the most high God? Not at all; not in any degree; no more than if no such command had ever been given to man. Even the good Christians, as they are accounted by others as well as themselves, pay no manner of regard thereto. It might as well be still hid in its original Greek, for any notice they take of it. In what Christian city do you find one man of five hundred, who makes the least scruple of laying up just as much treasure as he can—of increasing his goods just as far as he is able? There are, indeed, those who would not do this unjustly: there are many who will neither rob nor steal; and some who will not defraud their neighbour; nay, who will not gain either by his ignorance or necessity. But this is quite another point. Even these do not scruple the thing, but the manner of it. They do not scruple the 'laying up treasures upon earth'; but the laying them up by dishonesty. They do not start at disobeying Christ, but at a breach of heathen morality. So that even these honest men do no more obey this command than a highwayman or a house-breaker. Nay, they never designed to obey it. From their youth up, it never entered into their thoughts. They were bred up by their Christian parents, masters, and friends, without any instruction at all concerning it; unless it were this,—to break it as soon and as much as they could, and to continue breaking it to their lives' end.

10. There is no one instance of spiritual infatuation in the world which is more amazing than this. Most of these very men read, or hear the Bible read—many of them every Lord's day. They have read or heard these words an hundred times, and yet never suspect that they are themselves condemned thereby, any more than by those which forbid parents to offer up their sons or daughters unto Moloch. O that God would speak to these miserable self-deceivers with His own voice, His mighty voice; that they may at last awake out of the snare of the devil, and the scales may fall from their eyes!

11. Do you ask what it is to 'lay up treasures on earth'? It will be needful to examine this thoroughly. And let us, first, observe what is not forbidden in this command, that we may then clearly discern what it is.

We are not forbidden in this command, first, to 'provide things honest in the sight of all men,' to provide wherewith we may render unto all their due, whatsoever they can justly demand of us. So far from it, that we are taught of God to 'owe no man anything.' We ought, therefore, to use all diligence in our calling, in order to owe no man anything; this being no other than a plain law of common justice, which our Lord came 'not to destroy, but to fulfil.'

Neither, secondly, does He here forbid the providing for ourselves such things as are needful for the body; a sufficiency of plain, wholesome food to eat, and clean raiment to put on. Yea, it is our duty, so far as God puts it into our power, to provide these things also; to the end we may eat our own bread, and be burdensome to no man.

Nor yet are we forbidden, thirdly, to provide for our children, and for those of our own household. This also it is our duty to do, even upon principles of heathen morality. Every man ought to provide the plain necessaries of life, both for his own wife and children; and to put them into a capacity of providing these for themselves, when he is gone hence and is no more seen. I say, of providing *these*; the plain necessaries of life; not delicacies; not superfluities:—and that by their diligent labour; for it is no man's duty to furnish them, any more than himself, with the means either of luxury or idleness. But if any man provide not thus far for his own children (as well as for the widows of his own house, of whom primarily St. Paul is speaking in those well-known words to Timothy), he hath practically 'denied the faith, and is worse than an infidel,' or Heathen.

Lastly. We are not forbidden, in these words, to lay up, from time to time, what is needful for the carrying on our worldly business, in such a measure and degree as is sufficient to answer the foregoing purposes,—in such a measure as, first, to owe no man anything; secondly, to procure for ourselves the necessaries of life; and, thirdly, to furnish those of our own house with them while we live, and with the means of procuring them when we are gone to God.

12. We may now clearly discern (unless we are unwilling to discern it) what that is which is forbidden here. It is, the designedly procuring more of this world's goods than will answer the foregoing purposes. The labouring after a larger measure of worldly substance, a larger increase of gold and silver—the

laying up any more than these ends require—is what is here expressly and absolutely forbidden. If the words have any meaning at all, it must be this; for they are capable of no other. Consequently, whoever he is that, owing no man anything, and having food and raiment for himself and his household, together with a sufficiency to carry on his worldly business, so far as answers these reasonable purposes; whosoever, I say, being already in these circumstances, seeks a still larger portion on earth; he lives in an open, habitual denial of the Lord that bought him. 'He hath' practically 'denied the faith, and is worse than' an African or American 'infidel.'

13. Hear ye this, all ye that dwell in the world, and love the world wherein ye dwell! Ye may be 'highly esteemed of men'; but ye are 'an abomination in the sight of God'! How long shall your souls cleave to the dust? How long will ye load yourselves with thick clay? When will ye awake and see, that the open, speculative Heathens are nearer the kingdom of heaven than you? When will ye be persuaded to choose the better part; that which cannot be taken away from you? When will ye seek only to 'lay up treasures in heaven'; renouncing, dreading, abhorring all other? If you aim at 'laying up treasures on earth,' you are not barely losing your time, and spending your strength for that which is not bread; for what is the fruit if you succeed? You have murdered your own soul! You have extinguished the last spark of spiritual life therein! Now indeed, in the midst of life, you are in death! You are a living man, but a dead Christian! For where your treasure is, there will your heart be also.' Your heart is sunk into the dust; your soul cleaveth to the ground. Your affections are set, not on things above, but on things of the earth; on poor husks, that may poison, but cannot satisfy, an everlasting spirit, made for God. Your love, your joy, your desire, are all placed on the things which perish in the using. You have thrown away the treasure in heaven. God and Christ are lost! You have gained riches and hell-fire!

14. O how hardly shall they that have riches enter into the kingdom of God!' When our Lord's disciples were astonished at His speaking thus, He was so far from retracting it, that He repeated the same important truth in stronger terms than before.

It is easier for a camel to go through the eye of a needle, than for a rich man to enter into the kingdom of God.' How hard is it for them, whose every word is applauded, not to be wise in their own eyes! How hard for them not to think themselves better than the poor, base, uneducated herd of men! How hard not to seek happiness in their riches, or in things dependent upon them; in gratifying the desire of the flesh, the desire of the eye, or the pride of life! O ye rich, how can ye escape the damnation of hell? Only with God all things are possible!

15. And even if you do not succeed, what is the fruit of your endeavouring to lay up treasures on earth? They that will be rich' οἱ βουλόμενοι πλουτεῖν, they that *desire*, that *endeavour* after it, (whether they succeed or no), 'fall into temptation and a snare'—a gin, a trap of the devil; and into many foolish and hurtful lusts'—ἐπιθυμίας ἀνοήτους, *desires*, with which *reason hath nothing to do*; such as properly belong not to rational and immortal beings, but only to the brute beasts, which have no understanding; which drown men in destruction and perdition,' in present and eternal misery. Let us but open our eyes, and we may daily see the melancholy proofs of this—men who, desiring, resolving to be rich, coveting after money, the root of all evil, have already pierced themselves through with many sorrows, and anticipted the hell to which they are going.!

The cautiousness with which the Apostle here speaks is highly observable. He does not affirm this absolutely of the rich: for a man may possibly be rich, without any fault of his, by an over-ruling Providence, preventing his own choice; but he affirms it of οἱ βουλόμενοι πλουτεῖν, *those who desire* or seek *to be rich.* Riches, dangerous as they are, do not always 'drown men in destruction and perdition'; but the *desire of riches* does. Those who calmly desire, and deliberately seek to attain them, whether they do, in fact, gain the world or no, do infallibly lose their own souls. These are they that sell Him who bought them with His blood, for a few pieces of gold or silver. These enter into a covenant with death and hell; and their covenant shall stand: for they are daily making themselves meet to partake of their inheritance with the devil and his angels.

16. O who shall warn this generation of vipers to flee from the

wrath to come! Not those who lie at their gate, or cringe at their feet, desiring to be fed with the crumbs that fall from their tables. Not those who court their favour, or fear their frown; none of those who mind earthly things. But if there be a Christian upon earth, if there be a man who hath overcome the world, who desires nothing but God, and fears none but Him that is able to destroy both body and soul in hell; thou, O man of God, speak, and spare not; lift up thy voice like a trumpet! Cry aloud, and show these honourable sinners the desperate condition wherein they stand! It may be, one in a thousand may have ears to hear; may arise and shake himself from the dust; may break loose from these chains that bind him to the earth, and at length lay up treasures in heaven.

17. And if it should be, that one of these by the mighty power of God awoke and asked, 'What must I do to be saved?' the answer, according to the oracles of God, is clear, full, and express. God doth not say to thee, 'Sell all that thou hast.' Indeed, He who seeth the hearts of men saw it needful to enjoin this in one peculiar case, that of the young rich ruler. But He never laid it down for a general rule to all rich men, in all succeeding generations. His general direction is, first, 'Be not high minded.' God seeth not as man seeth. He esteems thee not for thy riches, for thy grandeur or equipage, for any qualification or accomplishment which is directly or indirectly owing to thy wealth, which can be bought or procured thereby. All these are with Him as dung and dross: let them be so with thee also. Beware thou think not thyself to be one jot wiser or better for all these things. Weigh thyself in another balance: estimate thyself only by the measure of faith and love which God hath given thee. If thou hast more of the knowledge and love of God than he, thou art on this account, and no other, wiser and better, more valuable and honourable, than him who is with the dogs of thy flock. But if thou hast not this treasure, thou art more foolish, more vile, more truly contemptible, I will not say than the lowest servant under thy roof, but than the beggar laid at thy gate full of sores.

18. Secondly. 'Trust not in uncertain riches.' Trust not in them for help: and trust not in them for happiness.

First. Trust not in them for help. Thou art miserably mistaken, if thou lookest for this in gold or silver. These are no
more able to set thee *above the world*, than to set thee above the
devil. Know that both the world, and the prince of this world,
laugh at all such preparations against them. These will little
avail in the day of trouble; even if they remain in the trying
hour. But it is not certain that they will; for how oft do they
'make themselves wings and fly away'! But if not, what support
will they afford, even in the ordinary troubles of life? The desire
of thy eyes, the wife of thy youth, thy son, thine only son, or the
friend which was as thy own soul, is taken away at one stroke.
Will thy riches reanimate the breathless clay, or call back its late
inhabitant? Will they secure thee from sickness, diseases, pain?
Do these visit the poor only? Nay, he that feeds thy flocks, or
tills thy ground, has less sickness and pain than thou. He is more
rarely visited by these unwelcome guests; and if they come there
at all, they are more easily driven away from the little cot, than
from the 'the cloud-topt palaces.' And during the time that thy
body is chastened with pain, or consumes away with pining
sickness, how do thy treasures help thee? Let the poor Heathen
answer,—

> *Ut lippum pictae tabulae: fomenta podagrum,*
> *Auriculas citharae collectâ sorde dolentes.*[1]

19. But there is at hand a greater trouble than all these. Thou
art to die! Thou art to sink into dust; to return to the ground
from which thou wast taken; to mix with common clay. Thy
body is to go to the earth as it was, while thy spirit returns to
God that gave it. And the time draws on: the years slide away
with a swift, though silent, pace. Perhaps your day is far spent:
the noon of life is past, and the evening shadows begin to rest
upon you. You feel in yourself sure approaching decay. The
springs of life wear away apace. Now what help is there in your
riches? Do they sweeten death? Do they endear that solemn
hour? Quite the reverse. 'O death, how bitter art thou to a man
that liveth at rest in his possessions!' How unacceptable to him

[1] Such help as pictures to sore eyes afford,
As heap'd-up tables to their gouty lord.

is that awful sentence, 'This night shall thy soul be required of thee'! Or will they prevent the unwelcome stroke, or protract the dreadful hour? Can they deliver your soul, that it should not see death? Can they restore the years that are past? Can they add to your appointed time a month, a day, an hour, a moment? Or will the good things you have chosen for your portion here follow you over the great gulf? Not so: naked came you into this world; naked must you return.

> Linquenda tellus, et domus: et placens
> Uxor; neque harum: quas colis: arborum,
>   Te, praeter invisam cupressum,
>   Ulla brevem dominum sequetur![1]

Surely, were not these truths too plain to be observed, because they are too plain to be denied, no man that is to die could possibly trust for help in uncertain riches.

20. And trust not in them for happiness: for here also they will be found 'deceitful upon the weights.' Indeed this every reasonable man may infer from what has been observed already. For if neither thousands of gold and silver, nor any of the advantages or pleasures purchased thereby, can prevent our being miserable, it evidently follows, they cannot make us happy. What happiness can they afford to him who in the midst of all, is constrained to cry out,

> To my new courts sad thought does still repair,
> And round my gilded roofs hangs hovering care?

Indeed experience is here so full, strong, and undeniable, that it makes all other arguments needless. Appeal we therefore to fact. Are the rich and great the only happy men? And is each of them more or less happy in proportion to his measure of riches? Are they happy at all? I had well nigh said, they are of all men most miserable! Rich man, for once speak the truth from thy heart! Speak, both for thyself and for thy brethren!

---

[1] The following is Boscawen's translation of these verses from Horace:—
> Thy lands, thy dome, thy pleasing wife,
>   These must thou quit; 'tis nature's doom:
> No tree, whose culture charms thy life,
>   Save the sad cypress, waits thy tomb.—ED.

> Amidst our plenty something still,—
> To me, to thee, to him is wanting!
> That cruel something, unpossess'd,
> Corrodes and leavens all the rest.

Yea, and so it will, till thy wearisome day of vanity are shut up in the night of death.

Surely, then, to trust in riches for happiness is the greatest folly of all that are under the sun! Are you not convinced of this? Is it possible you should still expect to find happiness in money, or all it can procure? What! can silver and gold, and eating and drinking, and horses and servants, and glittering apparel, and diversions and pleasures (as they are called) make thee happy? They can as soon make thee immortal!

21. These are all dead show. Regard them not. Trust thou in the living God; so shalt thou be safe under the shadow of the Almighty; His faithfulness and truth shall be thy shield and buckler. He is a very present help in time of trouble; such an help as can never fail. Then shalt thou say, if all thy other friends die, 'The Lord liveth, and blessed be my strong Helper!' He shall remember thee when thou liest sick upon thy bed; when vain is the help of man. When all the things of the earth can give no support, He will 'make all thy bed in thy sickness,' He will sweeten thy pain: the consolations of God shall cause thee to clap thy hands in the flames. And even when this house of earth is wellnigh shaken down, when it is just ready to drop into the dust, He will teach thee to say, 'O death! where is thy sting? O grave where is thy victory? Thanks be unto God which giveth' me 'the victory, through' my 'Lord Jesus Christ.'

O trust in Him for happiness as well as for help. All the springs of happiness are in Him. Trust 'in Him who giveth us all things richly to enjoy,' παρέχοντι ἡμῖν πλουσίως πάντα εἰς ἀπόλαυσιν—who, of His own rich and free mercy, holds them out to us, as in His own hand, that, receiving them as His gifts, and as pledges of His love, we may enjoy all that we possess. It is His love gives a relish to all we taste—puts life and sweetness into all; while every creature leads us up to the great Creator, and all earth is a scale to heaven. He transfuses the joys that are

at His own right hand into all He bestows on His thankful
children; who, having fellowship with the Father and His Son
Jesus Christ, enjoy Him in all, and above all.

22. Thirdly. Seek not to increase in goods. 'Lay not up for'
thyself 'treasures upon earth.' This is a flat, positive command;
full as clear as, 'Thou shalt not commit adultery.' How then is it
possible for a rich man to grow richer, without denying the
Lord that bought him? Yea, how can any man who has already
the necessaries of life, gain or aim at more, and be guiltless?
'Lay not up,' saith our Lord, 'treasures upon earth.' If, in spite
of this, you do and will lay up money or goods which 'moth or
rust may corrupt, or thieves break through and steal'; if you will
add house to house, or field to field,—why do you call yourself
a Christian? You do not obey Jesus Christ. You do not design
it. Why do you name yourself by His name? 'Why call ye Me,
Lord, Lord,' saith He Himself, 'and do not the things which I say?'

23. If you ask, 'But what must we do with our goods, seeing
we have more than we have occasion to use, if we must not lay
them up? Must we throw them away?' I answer, If you threw
them into the sea, if you were to cast them into the fire and
consume them, they would be better bestowed than they are
now. You cannot find so mischievous a manner of throwing
them away, as either the laying them up for your posterity, or
the laying them out upon yourselves in folly and superfluity. Of
all possible methods of throwing them away, these two are the
very worst; the most opposite to the gospel of Christ, and the
most pernicious to your own soul.

How pernicious to your own soul the latter of these is, has
been excellently shown by a late writer:—

'If we waste our money, we are not only guilty of wasting a
talent which God has given us, but we do ourselves this farther
harm, we turn this useful talent into a powerful means of corrupting ourselves; because so far as it is spent wrong, so far it is
spent in the support of some wrong temper, in gratifying some
vain and unreasonable desires, which, as Christians, we are
obliged to renounce.

'As wit and fine parts cannot be only trifled away, but will
expose those that have them to greater follies; so money cannot

be only trifled away, but, if it is not used according to reason and religion, will make people live a more silly and extravagant life, than they would have done without it: if, therefore, you do not spend your money in doing good to others, you must spend it to the hurt of yourself. You act like one that refuses the cordial to his sick friend, which he cannot drink himself without inflaming his blood. For this is the case of superfluous money: if you give it to those that want it, it is a cordial; if you spend it upon yourself, in something that you do not want, it only inflames and disorders your mind.

'In using riches where they have no real use, nor we any real want, we only use them to our great hurt, in creating unreasonable desires, in nourishing ill tempers, in indulging foolish passions, and supporting a vain turn of mind. For high eating and drinking, fine clothes and fine houses, state and equipage, gay pleasures and diversions, do all of them naturally hurt and disorder our heart. They are the food and nourishment of all the folly and weakness of our nature. They are all of them the support of something that ought not to be supported. They are contrary to that sobriety and piety of heart which relishes divine things. They are so many weights upon our mind, that make us less able and less inclined to raise our thoughts and affections to things above.

'So that money thus spent is not merely wasted or lost, but it is spent to bad purposes and miserable effects; to the corruption and disorder of our hearts; to the making us unable to follow the sublime doctrines of the gospel. It is but like keeping money from the poor, to buy poison for ourselves.'

24. Equally inexcusable are those who lay up what they do not need for any reasonable purposes:—

'If a man had hands, and eyes, and feet, that he could give to those that wanted them; if he should lock them up in a chest, instead of giving them to his brethren that were blind and lame, should we not justly reckon him an inhuman wretch? If he should rather choose to amuse himself with hoarding them up, than entitle himself to an eternal reward, by giving them to those that wanted eyes and hands, might we not justly reckon him mad?

'Now, money has very much the nature of eyes and feet. If therefore we lock it up in chests, while the poor and distressed want it for their necessary uses, we are not far from the cruelty of him that chooses rather to hoard up the hands and eyes, than to give them to those that want them. If we choose to lay it up, rather than to entitle oursleves to an eternal reward by disposing of our money well, we are guilty of his madness that rather chooses to lock up eyes and hands, than to make himself for ever blessed by giving them to those that want them.'

25. May not this be another reason why rich men shall so hardly enter into the kingdom of heaven? A vast majority of them are under a curse, under the peculiar curse of God; inasmuch as, in the general tenor of their lives, they are not only robbing God, continually embezzling and wasting their Lord's goods, and, by that very means, corrupting their own souls, but also robbing the poor, the hungry, the naked; wronging the widow and the fatherless; and making themselves accountable for all the want, affliction, and distress which they may but do not remove. Yea, doth not the blood of all those who perish for want of what they either lay up, or lay out needlessly, cry against them from the earth? O what account will they give to Him who is ready to judge both the quick and the dead!

26. The true way of employing what you do not want yourselves, you may, fourthly, learn from those words of our Lord, which are the counterpart of what went before: 'Lay up for yourselves treasures in heaven; where neither moth nor rust doth corrupt, and where thieves do not break through and steal.' Put out whatever thou canst spare, upon better security than this world can afford. Lay up thy treasures in the bank of heaven; and God shall restore them in that day. 'He that hath pity upon the poor lendeth unto the Lord: and look, what he layeth out, it shall be paid him again.' 'Place that,' saith He, 'unto My account. Howbeit, thou owest Me thine own self besides!'

Give to the poor with a single eye, with an upright heart, and write, 'So much given to God.' For 'inasmuch as ye did it unto one of the least of these My brethren, ye have done it unto Me.'

This is the part of a 'faithful and wise steward': not to sell either his houses or lands, or principal stock, be it more or less, unless some peculiar circumstance should require it; and not to desire or endeavour to increase it, any more than to squander it away in vanity; but to employ it wholly to those wise and reasonable purposes for which his Lord has lodged it in his hands. The wise steward, after having provided his own household with what is needful for life and godliness, makes himself friends with all that remains, from time to time, of the 'mammon of unrighteousness; that when he fails, they may receive him into everlasting habitations'—that whensoever his earthly tabernacle is dissolved, they who were before carried into Abraham's bosom, after having eaten his bread, and worn the fleece of his flock, and praised God for the consolation, may welcome him into paradise, and into 'the house of God, eternal in the heavens.'

27. We 'charge' you, therefore, 'who are rich in this world,' as having authority from our great Lord and Master, ἰγαθοεργεῖν —to be *habitually doing good*, to live in a course of good works. 'Be ye merciful, as your Father which is in heaven is merciful'; who doeth good, and ceaseth not. 'Be ye merciful'—how far? After your power; with all the ability which God giveth. Make this your only measure of doing good; not any beggarly maxims or customs of the world. We 'charge you to be rich in good works'; as you have much, to give plenteously. 'Freely ye have received, freely give'; so as to lay up no treasure but in heaven. Be ye 'ready to distribute' to every one, according to his necessity. Disperse abroad; give to the poor; deal your bread to the hungry. Cover the naked with a garment; entertain the stranger; carry or send relief to them that are in prison. Heal the sick; not by miracle, but through the blessing of God upon your seasonable support. Let the blessing of him that was ready to perish, through pining want, come upon thee. Defend the oppressed, plead the cause of the fatherless, and make the widow's heart sing for joy.

28. We exhort you, in the name of the Lord Jesus Christ, to be willing 'to communicate'; κοινωνικοὺς εἶναι; to be of the same spirit (though not in the same outward state) with those believers of ancient times, who remained steadfast, ἐν τῇ ποινωνίᾳ, in that blessed and holy *fellowship*, wherein 'none said that anything was his own, but they had all things common.'

Be a steward, a faithful and wise steward, of God and of the poor; differing from them in these two circumsatnces only,—that your wants are first supplied, out of the portion of your Lord's goods which remains in your hands; and, that you have the blessedness of giving. Thus 'lay up for yourselves a good foundation,' not in the world which now is, but rather 'for the time to come, that ye may lay hold on eternal life.' The great foundation indeed of all the blessings of God, whether temporal or eternal, is the Lord Jesus Christ. His righteousness and blood, what He hath done, and what He hath suffered for us. And 'other foundation,' in this sense, 'can no man lay': no, not an apostle; no, not an angel from heaven. But through His merits, whatever we do in His name is a foundation for a good reward, in the day when 'every man shall receive his own reward, according to his own labour.' Therefore 'labour thou,' 'not for the meat that perisheth, but for that which endureth unto everlasting life.' Therefore 'whatsoever thy hand' now 'findeth to do, do it with thy might.' Therefore let

> No fair occasion pass unheeded by;
> Snatching the golden moments as they fly,
> Thou by few fleeting years ensure eternity!

'By patient continuance in well-doing, seek' thou 'for glory, and honour, and immortality.' In a constant, zealous performance of all good works, wait thou for that happy hour when the King shall say, 'I was an hungered, and ye gave Me meat: I was thirsty and ye gave Me drink: I was a stranger, and ye took Me in; naked, and ye clothed Me: I was sick, and ye visited Me: I was in prison, and ye came unto Me ... Come, ye blessed of My Father, receive the kingdom prepared for you from the foundation of the world!'

SERMON XXIV

UPON OUR LORD'S SERMON ON THE MOUNT

DISCOURSE IX

No man can serve two masters: for either he will hate the one, and love the other; or else he will hold to the one, and despise the other. Ye cannot serve God and mammon.

Therefore I say unto you, Take no thought for your life, what ye shall eat, or what ye shall drink; nor yet for your body, what ye shall put on. Is not the life more than meat, and the body than raiment?

Behold the fowls of the air: for they sow not, neither do they reap, nor gather into barns; yet your heavenly Father feedeth them. Are ye not much better than they?

Which of you by taking thought can add one cubit unto his stature?

And why take ye thought for raiment? Consider the lilies of the field, how they grow; they toil not, neither do they spin:

And yet I say unto you, That even Solomon in all his glory was not arrayed like one of these.

Wherefore, if God so clothe the grass of the field, which to-day is, and to-morrow is cast into the oven, shall He not much more clothe you, O ye of little faith?

Therefore take no thought, saying: What shall we eat? or, What shall we drink? or, Wherewithal shall we be clothed?

(For after all these things do the Gentiles seek:) for your heavenly Father knoweth that ye have need of all these things.

But seek ye first the kingdom of God, and His righteousness; and all these things shall be added unto you.

Take therefore no thought for the morrow: for the morrow shall take thought for the things of itself. Sufficient unto the day is the evil thereof.

—MATT. vi. 24-34

IT is recorded of the nations whom the king of Assyria, after he had carried Israel away into captivity, placed in the cities of Samaria, that 'they feared the Lord, and served their own gods.' These nations,' saith the inspired writer, 'feared the Lord', performed an outward service to Him (a plain proof that they had a fear of God, though not according to knowledge); 'and served their graven images, both their children, and their chil-

dren's children: as did their fathers, so do they unto this day'
(2 Kings xvii. 33, &c.).

How nearly does the practice of most modern Christians
resemble this of the ancient Heathens! 'They fear the Lord';
they also perform an outward service to Him, and hereby show
they have some fear of God; but they likewise 'serve their own
gods.' There are those who 'teach them,' as there were who
taught the Assyrians, 'the manner of the God of the land'; the
God whose name the country bears to this day, and who was
once worshipped there with an holy worship: 'Howbeit,' they
do not serve Him alone; they do not fear Him enough for this:
but 'every nation maketh gods of their own: every nation in the
cities wherein they dwell' 'These nations fear the Lord'; they
have not laid aside the outward form of worshipping Him; but
'they serve their graven images,' silver and gold, the work of
men's hands: money, pleasure, and praise, the gods of this world,
more than divide their service with the God of Israel. This is the
manner both of 'their children and their children's children: as
did their fathers, so do they unto this day.'

2. But although, speaking in a loose way, after the common
manner of men, those poor Heathens were said to 'fear the Lord,'
yet we may observe the Holy Ghost immediately adds, speaking
according to the truth and real nature of things, 'They fear not
the Lord, neither do after the law and the commandment which
the Lord commanded the children of Jacob; with whom the
Lord made a covenant, and charged them, saying, Ye shall not
fear other gods, nor serve them, but the Lord your God ye shall
fear; and He shall deliver you out of the hand of your enemies.'

The same judgement is passed by the unerring Spirit of God,
and indeed by all, the eyes of whose understanding He hath
opened to discern the things of God, upon these poor Christians,
commonly so called. If we speak according to the truth and real
nature of things, 'they fear not the Lord, neither do they serve
Him.' For they do not 'after the covenant the Lord hath made
with them, neither after the law and commandment which He
hath commanded them, saying, Thou shalt worship the Lord thy
God, and Him only shalt thou serve.' 'They serve other gods unto
this day.' And 'no man can serve two masters.'

3. How vain is it for any man to aim at this,—to attempt the serving of two masters! Is it not easy to foresee what must be the unavoidable consequence of such an attempt? 'Either he will hate the one and love the other; or else he will hold to the one, and despise the other.' The two parts of this sentence, although separately proposed, are to be understood in connexion with each other; for the latter part is a consequence of the former. He will naturally hold to him whom he loves. He will so cleave to him, as to perform to him a willing, faithful, and diligent service. And, in the meantime, he will so far at least despise the master he hates as to have little regard to his commands, and to obey them, if at all, in a slight and careless manner. Therefore, whatsoever the wise men of the world may suppose, 'ye cannot serve God and mammon.'

4. Mammon was the name of one of the heathen gods, who was supposed to preside over riches. It is here understood of riches themselves; gold and silver; or in general, money; and, by a common figure of speech, of all that may be purchased thereby: such as ease, honour, and sensual pleasure.

But what are we here to understand by serving God, and what by serving mammon?

We cannot serve God, unless we *believe* in Him. This is the only true foundation of serving Him. Therefore, the believing in God, as 'reconciling the world to Himself through Christ Jesus,' the believing in Him, as a loving, pardoning God, is the first great branch of His service.

And thus to believe in God implies, to trust in Him as our strength, without whom we can do nothing, who every moment endues us with power from on high, without which it is impossible to please Him; as our help, our only help in time of trouble, who compasseth us about with songs of deliverance; as our shield, our defender, and the lifter up of our head above all our enemies that are round about us.

It implies, to trust in God as our happiness; as the centre of spirits; the only rest of our souls; the only good who is adequate to all our capacities, and sufficient to satisfy all the desires He hath given us.

It implies (what is nearly allied to the other), to trust in God

22

as our end; to have an eye to Him in all things; to use all things only as means of enjoying Him: wheresoever we are, or whatsoever we do, to see Him that is invisible, looking on us well pleased, and to refer all things to Him in Christ Jesus.

5. Thus to believe, is the first thing we are to understand by serving God. The second is, to *love* Him.

Now to love God, in the manner the Scripture describes, in the manner God Himself requires of us, and by requiring engages to work in us, is to love Him as the ONE GOD; that is, 'with all our heart, and with all our soul, and with all our mind, and with all our strength,'—it is to desire God alone for His own sake; and nothing else, but with reference to Him,—to rejoice in God,—to delight in the Lord; not only to seek, but find, happiness in Him, to enjoy God as the chiefest among ten thousand; to rest in Him, as our God and our all: in a word, to have such a possession of God as makes us always happy.

6. A third thing we are to understand by serving God is, to *resemble* or *imititate* Him.

So the ancient Father: *Optimus Dei cultus! imitare quem colis*: 'It is the best worship or service of God, to imitate Him you worship.'

We here speak of imitating or resembling Him in the spirit of our minds: for here the true Christian imitation of God begins. 'God is a Spirit'; and they that imitate or resemble Him must do it 'in spirit and in truth.'

Now God is love: therefore, they who resemble Him in the spirit of their minds are transformed into the same image. They are merciful even as He is merciful. Their soul is all love. They are kind, benevolent, compassionate, tender-hearted; and that not only to the good and gentle, but also to the froward. Yea, they are, like Him, loving unto every man, and their mercy extends to all His works.

7. One thing more we are to understand by serving God, and that is, the *obeying* Him; the glorifying Him with our bodies, as well as with our spirits; the keeping His outward commandments; the zealously doing whatever He hath enjoined; the carefully avoiding whatever He hath forbidden; the performing all the ordinary actions of life with a single eye and a pure heart,

offering them all in holy, fervent love, as sacrifices to God through Jesus Christ.

8. Let us consider now, what we are to understand, on the other hand, by serving mammon. And, first, it implies, the *trusting* in riches, in money, or the things purchasable thereby, as our strength, the means whereby we shall perform whatever cause we have in hand; the trusting in them as our help, by which we look to be comforted in, or delivered out of trouble.

It implies, the trusting in the world for happiness; the supposing that 'a man's life,' the comfort of his life, 'consisteth in the abundance of the things which he possesseth'; the looking for rest in the things that are seen; for content in outward plenty; the expecting that satisfaction in the things of the world, which can never be found out of God.

And if we do this, we cannot but make the world our end; the ultimate end, if not of all, at least of many, of our undertakings, many of our actions and designs; in which we shall aim only at an increase of wealth, at the obtaining pleasure or praise, at the gaining a larger measure of temporal things, without any reference to things eternal.

9. The serving mammon implies, secondly, *loving* the world; desiring it for its own sake; the placing our joy in the things thereof, and setting our hearts upon them; the seeking (what indeed it is impossible we should find) our happiness therein; the resting, with the whole weight of our souls, upon the staff of this broken reed; although daily experience shows it cannot support, but will only 'enter into our hand and pierce it.'

10. To *resemble*, to be *conformed* to, the world, is a third thing we are to understand by serving mammon; to have not only designs, but desires, tempers, affections, suitable to those of the world; to be of an earthly, sensual mind, chained down to the things of earth; to be self-willed, inordinate lovers of ourselves, to think highly of our own attainments; to desire and delight in the praise of men; to fear, shun, and abhor reproach; to be impatient of reproof, easy to be provoked, and swift to return evil for evil.

11. To serve mammon is lastly, to *obey* the world, by outwardly conforming to its maxims and customs; to walk as other

men walk, in the common road, in the broad, smooth, beaten path: to be in the fashion; to follow a multitude; to do like the rest of our neighbours: that is, to do the will of the flesh and the mind, to gratify our appetites and inclinations; to sacrifice to ourselves; aim at our own ease and pleasure, in the general course both of our words and actions.

Now what can be more undeniably clear than that we cannot thus serve God and mammon?

12. Does not every man see, that he cannot *comfortably* serve both? that to trim between God and the world is the sure way to be disappointed in both, and to have no rest either in one or the other? How uncomfortable a condition must he be in, who, having the fear but not the love of God—who, serving Him, but not with all his heart—has only the toils and not the joys of religion! He has religion enough to make him miserable, but not enough to make him happy: his religion will not let him enjoy the world; and the world will not let him enjoy God. So that, by halting between both, he loses both, and has no peace either in God or the world.

13. Does not every man see, that he cannot serve both *consistently* with himself? What more glaring inconsistency can be conceived, than must continually appear in his whole behaviour, who is endeavouring to obey both these masters,—striving to 'serve God and mammon'? He is indeed 'a sinner that goeth two ways'; one step forward and another backward. He is continually building up with one hand, and pulling down with the other. He loves sin, and he hates it: he is always seeking, and yet always fleeing from, God. He would, and he would not. He is not the same man for one day; no, not for an hour together. He is a motley mixture of all sorts of contrarieties; a heap of contradictions jumbled in one. O be consistent with thyself one way or the other! Turn to the right hand or to the left. If mammon be God, serve thou him; if the Lord, then serve Him. But never think of serving either at all, unless it be with thy whole heart.

14. Does not every reasonable, every thinking man see, that he cannot *possibly* serve God and mammon? because there is the most absolute contrariety, the most irreconcilable enmity'

between them.   The contrariety between the most opposite
things on earth, between fire and water, darkness and light,
vanishes into nothing, when compared to the contrariety between God and mammon.   So that, in whatsoever respect you
serve the one, you necessarily renounce the other.   Do you
believe in God through Christ?   Do you trust in Him as your
strength, your help, your shield, and your exceeding great
reward?—as your happiness, your end in all, above all things?
Then you cannot trust in riches.   It is absolutely impossible you
should, so long as you have this faith in God.   Do you thus trust
in riches?   Then you have denied the faith.   You do not trust in
the living God.   Do you love God?   Do you seek and find
happiness in Him?   Then you cannot love the world, neither the
things of the world.   You are crucified to the world, and the
world crucified to you.   Do you love the world?   Are your
affections set on things beneath?   Do you seek happiness in
earthly things?   Then it is impossible you should love God.
Then the love of the Father is not in you.   Do you resemble
God?   Are you merciful, as your Father is merciful?   Are you
transformed, by the renewal of your mind, into the image of
Him that created you?   Then you cannot be conformed to the
present world.   You have renounced all its affections and lusts
Are you conformed to the world?   Does your soul still bear
the image of the earthly?   Then you are not renewed in the
spirit of your mind.   You do not bear the image of the heavenly.   Do you obey God?   Are you zealous to do His will on
earth as the angels do in heaven?   Then it is impossible you
should obey mammon.   Then you set the world at open defiance.
You trample its customs and maxims under foot, and will
neither follow nor be led by them.   Do you follow the world?
Do you live like other men?   Do you please men?   Do you
please yourself?   Then you cannot be a servant of God.   You are
of your master and father, the devil.

15.   Therefore, 'thou shalt worship the Lord thy God, and
Him only shalt thou serve.'   Thou shalt lay aside all thoughts of
obeying two masters, of serving God and mammon.   Thou shalt
propose to thy self no end, no help, no happiness, but God.
Thou shalt seek nothing in earth or heaven but Him: thou

shalt aim at nothing, but to know, to love, and enjoy Him. And because this is all your business below, the only view you can reasonably have, the one design you are to pursue in all things,—'Therefore I say unto you' (as our Lord continues His discourse), 'Take no thought for your life, what ye shall eat, or what ye shall drink; nor yet for your body, what ye shall put on': a deep and weighty direction, which it imports us well to consider, and thoroughly to understand.

16. Our Lord does not here require, that we should be utterly without thought, even touching the concerns of this life. A giddy, careless temper is at the farthest remove from the whole religion of Jesus Christ. Neither does He require us to be 'slothful in business,' to be slack and dilatory therein. This, likewise, is contrary to the whole spirit and genius of His religion. A Christian abhors sloth as much as drunkenness; and flees from idleness as he does from adultery. He well knows, that there is one kind of thought and care with which God is well pleased; which is absolutely needful for the due performance of those outward works unto which the providence of God has called him.

It is the will of God, that every man should labour to eat his own bread; yea, and that every man should provide for his own, for them of his own household. It is likewise His will, that we should 'owe no man anything, but provide things honest in the sight of all men.' But this cannot be done without taking some thought, without having some care upon our minds; yea, often, not without long and serious thought, not without much and earnest care. Consequently this care, to provide for ourselves and our household, this thought how to render to all their dues, our blessed Lord does not condemn. Yea, it is good and acceptable in the sight of God our Saviour.

It is good and acceptable to God, that we should so take thought concerning whatever we have in hand, as to have a clear comprehension of what we are about to do, and to plan our business before we enter upon it. And it is right that we should carefully consider, from time to time, what steps we are to take therein; as well as that we should prepare all things beforehand, for the carrying it on in the most effectual manner. This care, termed by some, 'the care of the head,' it was by no means our Lord's design to condemn.

17. What He here condemns is, the care of the heart; the anxious, uneasy care; the care that hath torment: all such care as does hurt, either to the soul or body. What He forbids is, that care which, sad experience shows, wastes the blood and drinks up the spirits; which anticipates all the misery it fears, and comes to torment us before the time. He forbids only that care which poisons the blessings of to-day, by fear of what may be to-morrow; which cannot enjoy the present plenty, through apprehensions of future want. This care is not only a sore disease, a grievous sickness of soul, but also a heinous offence against God, a sin of the deepest dye. It is a high affront to the gracious Governor and wise Disposer of all things; necessarily implying, that the great Judge does not do right; that He does not order all things well. It plainly implies, that He is wanting, either in wisdom, if He does not know what things we stand in need of; or in goodness, if He does not provide those things for all who put their trust in Him. Beware, therefore, that you take not thought in this sense: be ye anxiously careful for nothing. Take no uneasy thought: this is a plain, sure rule, Uneasy care is unlawful care. With a single eye to God, do all that in you lies to provide things honest in the sight of all men: and then give up all into better hands; leave the whole event to God.

18. 'Take no thought' of this kind, no uneasy thought, even 'for your life, what ye shall eat, or what ye shall drink; nor yet for your body, what ye shall put on. Is not the life more than meat, and the body than raiment?' If then God gave you life, the greater gift, will He not give you food to sustain it? If He hath given you the body, how can ye doubt but He will give you raiment to cover it? more especially, if you give yourselves up to Him, and serve Him with your whole heart. 'Behold,' see before your eyes, 'the fowls of the air: for they sow not, neither do they reap, nor gather into barns'; and yet they lack nothing; 'yet your heavenly Father feedeth them. Are ye not much better than they?' Ye that are creatures capable of God, are ye not of more account in the eyes of God? of a higher rank in the scale of beings? 'And which of you, by taking thought, can add one

cubit to his stature?' What profit have you then from this anxious thought? It is every way fruitless and unavailing.

'And why take ye thought for raiment?' Have ye not a daily reproof wherever you turn your eyes? 'Consider the lilies of the field, how they grow; they toil not, neither do hey spin; and yet I say unto you, that even Solomon in all his glory was not arrayed like one of these. Wherefore, if God so clothe the grass of the field, which to-day is, and to-morrow is cast into the oven' (is cut down, burned up, and seen no more), 'shall He not much more clothe you, O ye of little faith?' you, whom He made to endure for ever and ever, to be pictures of His own eternity! Ye are indeed of little faith: otherwise ye could not doubt of His love and care; no, not for a moment.

19. 'Therefore take no thought, saying, What shall we eat,' if we lay up no treasure upon earth? 'What shall we drink,' if we serve God with all our strength, if our eye be singly fixed on Him? 'Wherewithal shall we be clothed,' if we are not conformed to the world, if we disoblige those by whom we might be profited? 'For after all these things do the Gentiles seek'— the Heathens who know not God. But ye are sensible 'your heavenly Father knoweth that ye have need of all these things.' And He hath pointed out to you an infallible way of being constantly supplied therewith: 'Seek ye first the kingdom of God, and His righteousness; and all these things shall be added unto you.'

20. 'Seek ye first the kingdom of God': before ye give place to any other thought or care, let it be your concern that the God and Father of our Lord Jesus Christ (who 'gave His only-begotten Son,' to the end that, believing in Him, 'ye might not perish, but have everlasting life') may reign in your heart, may manifest Himself in your soul, and dwell and rule there; that He may 'cast down every high thing which exalteth itself against the knowledge of God, and bring into captivity every thought to the obedience of Christ.' Let God have the sole dominion over you: let Him reign without a rival: let Him possess all your heart, and rule alone. Let Him be your one desire, your joy, your love; so that all that is within you may continually cry out, 'The Lord God omnipotent reigneth.'

'Seek the kingdom of God, and His righteousness.' Righteousness is the fruit of God's reigning in the heart. And what is righteousness, but love?—the love of God and of all mankind, flowing from faith in Jesus Christ, and producing humbleness of mind, meekness, gentleness, long-suffering, patience, deadness to the world; and every right disposition of heart, toward God and toward man. And by these it produces all holy actions, whatsoever are lovely or of good report; whatsoever works of faith and labour of love are acceptable to God, and profitable to man.

'His righteousness': this is all His righteousness still: it is His own free gift to us, for the sake of Jesus Christ the righteous, through whom alone it is purchased for us: and it is His work. it is He alone that worketh it in us, by the inspiration of the Holy Spirit.

21. Perhaps the well observing this may give light to some other scriptures, which we have not always so clearly understood. St. Paul, speaking in his Epistle to the Romans concerning the unbelieving Jews, saith, 'They, being ignorant of God's righteousness, and going about to establish their own righteousness, have not submitted themselves unto the righteousness of God.' I believe this may be one sense of the words: they were 'ignorant of God's righteousness,' not only of the righteousness of Christ, imputed to every believer, whereby all his sins are blotted out, and he is reconciled to the favour of God; but (which seems here to be more immediately understood) they were ignorant of that inward righteousness, of that holiness of heart, which is with the utmost propriety termed 'God's righteousness,' as being both His own free gift through Christ, and His own work by His almighty Spirit. And because they were 'ignorant' of this, they 'went about to establish their own righteousness.' They laboured to establish that outside righteousness which might very properly be termed their own. For neither was it wrought by the Spirit of God, nor was it owned or accepted of Him. They might work this themselves, by their own natural strength; and when they had done, it was a stink in His nostrils. And yet, trusting in this, they would 'not submit themselves unto the righteousness of God.' Yea, they hardened themselves against that faith whereby alone it was possible to attain it. 'For Christ is the end of the law

for righteousness to every one that believeth.' Christ, when He said, 'It is finished!' put an end to the law,—to the law of external rites and ceremonies, that He might bring a better righteousness through His blood, by that one oblation of Himself once offered, even the image of God, into the inmost soul of every one that believeth.

22. Nearly related to these are those words of the Apostle, in his Epistle to the Philippians. 'I count all things but dung, that I may win Christ'; an entrance into His everlasting kingdom; 'and be found in Him,' believing in Him, 'not having mine own righteousness, which is of the law, but that which is through the faith of Christ, the righteousness which is of God by faith.' 'Not having my own righteousness, which is of the law'; a barely external righteousness, the outside religion I formerly had, when I hoped to be accepted of God because I was, 'touching the righteousness which is of the law, blameless'; 'but that which is through the faith of Christ, the righteousness which is of God by faith'; that holiness of heart, that renewal of the soul in all its desires, tempers, and affections, 'which is of God' (it is the work of God, and not of man), 'by faith'; through the faith of Christ, through the revelation of Jesus Christ in us, and by faith in His blood; whereby alone we obtain the remission of our sins, and an inheritance among those that are sanctified.

23. 'Seek ye first' this 'kingdom of God' in your hearts; this righteousness, which is the gift and work of God, the image of God renewed in your souls; 'and all these things shall be added unto you'; all things needful for the body; such a measure of all as God sees most for the advancement of His kingdom. These shall be added—they shall be thrown in, over and above. In seeking the peace and the love of God, you shall not only find what you more immediately seek, even the kingdom that cannot be moved; but also what you seek not—not at all for its own sake, but only in reference to the other. You shall find, in your way to the kingdom, all outward things, so far as they are expedient for you. This care God hath taken upon Himself: cast you all your care upon Him. He knoweth your wants; and whatsoever is lacking He will not fail to supply.

24. 'Therefore take no thought for the morrow.' Not only,

take ye no thought how to lay up treasures on earth, how to increase in worldly substance; take no thought how to procure more food than you can eat, or more raiment than you can put on, or more money than is required from day to day, for the plain, reasonable purposes of life;—but take no uneasy thought, even concerning those things which are absolutely needful for the body. Do not trouble yourself now, with thinking what you shall do at a season which is yet afar off. Perhaps that season will never come; or it will be no concern of yours; before then you will have passed through all the waves, and be landed in eternity. All those distant views do not belong to you, who are but a creature of a day. Nay, what have you to do with the morrow, more strictly speaking? Why should you perplex yourself without need? God provides for you to-day what is needful to sustain the life which He hath given you. It is enough; give yourself up into His hands. If you live another day, He will provide for that also.

25. Above all, do not make the care of future things a pretence for neglecting present duty. This is the most fatal way of 'taking thought for the morrow.' And how common is it among men! Many, if we exhort them to keep a conscience void of offence, to abstain from what they are convinced is evil, do not scruple to reply, 'How then must we live? Must we not take care of ourselves and of our families?' And this they imagine to be a sufficient reason for continuing in known, wilful sin. They say, and perhaps think, they would serve God now, were it not that they should, by-and-by, lose their bread. They would prepare for eternity; but they are afraid of wanting the necessaries of life. So they serve the devil for a morsel of bread; they rush into hell for fear of want; they throw away their poor souls, lest they should, some time or other, fall short of what is needful for their bodies!

It is not strange that they who thus take the matter out of God's hands should be so often disappointed of the very things they seek; that, while they throw away heaven to secure the things of earth, they lose the one, but do not gain the other. The jealous God, in the wise course of His providence, frequently suffers this. So that they who will not cast their care on God, who, taking thought for temporal things, have little concern for things eternal, lose the very portion which they have chosen. There is a visible blast on all their undertakings; whatsoever they do, it doth not prosper; insomuch, that after they have forsaken God for the world, they lose what they sought, as well as what they sought not: they fall short of the kingdom of God, and His righteousness; nor yet are other things added unto them.

26. There is another way of 'taking thought for the morrow,' which is equally forbidden in these words. It is possible to take thought in a wrong manner, even with regard to spiritual things; to be so careful about what may be by-and-by, as to neglect what is now required at our hands. How insensibly do we slide into this, if we are not continually watching unto prayer! How easily we are carried away, in a kind of waking dream, projecting distant schemes, and drawing fine scenes in our own imagination! We think, what good we will do when we are in such a place, or when such a time is come! How useful we will be, how plenteous in good works, when we are easier in our circumstances! How earnestly we will serve God, when once such an hindrance is out of the way!

Or perhaps you are now in heaviness of soul: God, as it were, hides His face from you. You see little of the light of His countenance: you cannot taste His redeeming love. In such a temper of mind, how natural is it to say, 'O how I will praise God, when the light of His countenance shall be again lifted up upon my soul! How will I exhort others to praise Him, when His love is again shed abroad in my heart! Then I will do thus and thus: I will speak for God in all places: I will not be ashamed of the gospel of Christ. Then I will redeem the time: I will use to the uttermost every talent I have received.' Do not believe thyself. Thou wilt not do it then, unless thou doest it now. 'He that is faithful in that which is little,' of whatsoever kind it be, whether it be worldly substance or the fear or love of God, 'will be faithful in that which is much.' But if thou now hidest one talent in the earth, thou wilt then hide five: that is, if ever they are given; but there is small reason to expect they ever will. Indeed, 'unto him that hath,' that is, uses what he hath, 'shall be given, and he shall have more abundantly. But from him that hath not,' that is, uses not the grace which he hath already received, whether in a larger or smaller degree, 'shall be taken away even that which he hath.'

27. And take no thought for the temptations of to-morrow. This also is a dangerous snare. Think not, 'When such a temptation comes, what shall I do? how shall I stand? I feel I have not power to resist: I am not able to conquer that enemy.' Most true: you have not now the power which you do not now stand in need of. You are not able at this time to conquer that enemy; and at this time he does not assault you. With the grace you have now, you could not withstand the temptations which you have not. But when the temptation comes, the grace will come. In greater trials you will have greater strength. When sufferings abound, the consolations of God will, in the same proportion, abound also. So that, in every situation, the grace of God will be sufficient for you. He doth not suffer you 'to be tempted' to-day above that ye are able to bear'; and 'in every temptation He will make a way to escape." 'As thy days, so thy strength shall be.'

28. 'Let the morrow,' therefore, 'take thought for the things of itself'; that is, when the morrow comes, then think of it. Live thou to-day. Be it thy earnest care to improve the present hour. This is your own; and it is your all. The past is as nothing, as though it had never been. The future is nothing to you: it is not yours; perhaps it never will be. There is no depending on what is yet to come; for you 'know not what a day may bring forth.' Therefore live to-day: lose not an hour: use this moment: for it is your portion. Who knoweth the things which have been before him, or which shall be after him under the sun?' The generations that were from the beginning of the world, where are they now? Fled away: forgotten. They were; they lived their day; they were shook off the earth, as leaves off their trees: they mouldered away into common dust! Another and another race succeeded; then they 'followed the generation of their fathers, and shall never more see the light.' Now is thy turn upon the earth. 'Rejoice, O young man, in the days of thy youth!' Enjoy the very, very now, by enjoying Him 'whose years fail not.' Now let thine eye be singly fixed on Him in 'whom is no variableness neither shadow of turning'! Now give Him thy heart; now stay

thyself on Him; now be thou holy, as He is holy! Now lay hold
on the blessed opportunity of doing His acceptable and perfect
will! Now rejoice to 'suffer the loss of all things,' so thou mayest
'win Christ.'

29. Gladly suffer to-day, for His name's sake, whatsoever He
permits this day to come upon thee. But look not at the sufferings of to-morrow. 'Sufficient unto the day is the evil thereof.'
Evil it is, speaking after the manner of men; whether it be reproach or want, pain or sickness; but in the language of God, all
is blessing: it is a precious balm prepared by the wisdom of God,
and variously dispensed among His children, according to the
various sicknesses of their souls. And He gives in one day sufficient for that day; proportioned to the want and strength of the
patient. If, therefore, thou snatchest to-day what belongs to the
morrow; if thou addest this to what is given thee already, it will
be more than thou canst bear: this is the way, not to heal, but to
destroy thy own soul. Take, therefore, just as much as He gives
thee to-day: to-day, do and suffer His will! To-day, give up
thyself, thy body, soul and spirit to God, through Christ Jesus;
desiring nothing, but that God may be glorified in all thou art,
all thou doest, all thou sufferest; seeking nothing, but to know
God, and His Son Jesus Christ, through the eternal Spirit;
pursuing nothing, but to love Him, to serve Him, and to enjoy
Him at this hour, and to all eternity!

Now unto 'God the Father, who hath made me and all the
world'; unto 'God the Son, who hath redeemed me and all mankind'; unto 'God the Holy Ghost who sanctifieth me and all the
elect people of God'; be honour and praise, majesty and dominion, for ever and ever! Amen.

SERMON XXV

UPON OUR LORD'S SERMON ON THE MOUNT

DISCOURSE X

Judge not, that ye be not judged.

*For with what judgement ye judge, ye shall be judged: and with what measure
ye mete, it shall be measured to you again.*

*And why beholdest thou the mote that is in thy brother's eye, but considerest not
the beam that is in thine own eye?*

*Or how wilt thou say to thy brother, Let me pull out the mote out of thine eye;
and, behold, a beam is in thine own eye?*

*Thou hypocrite, first cast out the beam out of thine own eye; and then shalt thou
see clearly to cast out the mote out of thy brother's eye.*

*Give not that which is holy unto the dogs, neither cast ye your pearls before
swine, lest they trample them under their feet and turn again and rend you.*

*Ask: and it shall be given you; seek, and ye shall find; knock and it shall be
opened unto you:*

*For every one that asketh receiveth; and he that seeketh findeth; and to him that
knocketh it shall be opened.*

*Or what man is there of you, whom if his son ask bread, will he give him a
stone?*

Or if he ask a fish, will he give him a serpent?

*If ye then, being evil, know how to give good gifts unto your children, how
much more shall your Father which is in heaven give good things to them
that ask Him.?*

*Therefore all things whatsoever ye would that men should do to you, do ye even
so to them, for this is the law and the prophets.*—MATT. vii. 1-12.

OUR blessed Lord, having now finished His main design, having
first delivered the sum of true religion, carefully guarded against
those glosses of men whereby they would make the Word of
God of none effect; and having next laid down rules touching
that right intention which we are to preserve in all outward
actions; now proceeds to point out the main hindrances of this
religion, and concludes all with a suitable application.

2. In the fifth chapter, our great Teacher has fully described

inward religion in its various branches. He has there laid before
us those dispositions of soul which constitute real Christianity;
the tempers contained in that 'holiness, without which no man
shall see the Lord'; the affections which, when flowing from their
proper fountain, from a living faith in God through Christ Jesus,
are intrinsically and essentially good and acceptable to God. In
the sixth He hath shown how all our actions, likewise, even those
that are indifferent in their own nature, may be made holy, and
good, and acceptable to God, by a pure and holy intention.
Whatever is done without this, He declares, is of no value with
God: whereas, whatever outward works are thus consecrated to
God are, in His sight, of great price.

3. In the former part of this chapter, He points out the most
common and most fatal hindrances of this holiness: in the latter,
he exhorts us, by various motives, to break through all, and
secure that prize of our high calling.

4. The first hindrance He cautions us against is judging.
'Judge not, that ye be not judged.' Judge not others, that ye be
not judged of the Lord; that ye bring not vengeance on your
own heads. 'For with what judgement ye judge, ye shall be
judged; and with what measure ye mete, it shall be measured
to you again': a plain and equitable rule, whereby God permits
you to determine for yourselves, in what manner He shall deal
with you in the judgement of the great day.

5. There is no station of life, nor any period of time, from the
hour of our first repenting and believing the gospel, till we are
made perfect in love, wherein this caution is not needful for
every child of God. For occasions of judging can never be
wanting: and the temptations to it are innumerable; many
whereof are so artfully disguised, that we fall into the sin before
we suspect any danger. And unspeakable are the mischiefs
produced hereby,—always to him that judges another, thus
wounding his own soul, and exposing himself to the righteous
judgement of God; and frequently to those who are judged,
whose hands hang down, who are weakened and hindered in
their course, if not wholly turned out of the way, and caused to
turn back even to perdition. Yea, how often, when this 'root of
bitterness springs up, are many defiled thereby': by reason

whereof the way of truth itself is evil spoken of, and that worthy name blasphemed whereby we are called!

6. Yet it does not appear that our Lord designed this caution only, or chiefly, for the children of God; but rather for the children of the world, for the men who know not God. These cannot but hear of those who are not of the world: who follow after the religion above described; who endeavour to be humble, serious, gentle, merciful, and pure in heart; who earnestly desire such measures of these holy tempers, as they have not yet attained, and wait for them in doing all good to all men, and patiently suffering evil. Whoever go but thus far, cannot be hid, no more than 'a city set upon a hill.' And why do not those who 'see their good works, glorify their Father which is in heaven?' What excuse have they for not treading in their steps—for not imitating their example, and being followers of them, as they are also of Christ? Why, in order to provide an excuse for themselves, they condemn those whom they ought to imitate. They spend their time in finding out their neighbours' faults, instead of amending their own. They are so busied about others going out of the way, that themselves never come into it at all; at least, never get forward; never go beyond a poor dead form of godliness, without the power.

7. It is to these more especially that our Lord says, 'Why beholdest thou the mote that is in thy brother's eye'—the infirmities, the mistakes, the imprudence, the weakness of the children of God—'but considerest not the beam that is in thine own eye?' Thou considerest not the damnable impenitence, the satanic pride, the accursed self-will, the idolatrous love of the world, which are in thyself, and which make thy whole life an abomination to the Lord. Above all, with what supine carelessness and indifference art thou dancing over the mouth of hell! And, how then,' with what grace, with what decency or modesty 'wilt thou say to thy brother, Let me pull out the mote out of thine eye': the excess of zeal for God, the extreme of self-denial, the too great disengagement from worldly cares and employments, the desire to be day and night in prayer, or hearing the words of eternal life? 'And, behold, a beam is in thine own eye!' Not a mote, like one of these.—'Thou hypocrite!' who pre-

23

tendest to care for others, and hast no care for thy own soul; who makest a show of zeal for the cause of God, when in truth thou neither lovest nor fearest Him! 'First cast out the beam out of thine own eye': cast out the beam of impenitence! Know thyself! See and feel thyself a sinner! Feel that thy inward parts are very wickedness, that thou art altogether corrupt and abominable, and that the wrath of God abideth on thee! Cast out the beam of pride; abhor thyself; sink down as in dust and ashes; be more and more little, and mean, and base, and vile in thine own eyes! Cast out the beam of self-will! Learn what that meaneth, 'If any man will come after Me, let him renounce himself.' Deny thyself, and take up thy cross daily. Let thy whole soul cry out, 'I came down from heaven'—for so thou didst, thou never-dying spirit, whether thou knowest it or no—'not to do my own will, but the will of Him that sent me.' Cast out the beam of love of the world. Love not the world, neither the things of the world. Be thou crucified unto the world, and the world crucified unto thee. Only *use* the world, but *enjoy* God. Seek all thy happiness in Him! Above all, cast out the grand beam, that supine carelessness and indifference! Deeply consider that 'one thing is needful'; the one thing which thou hast scarce ever thought of. Know and feel, that thou art a poor, vile, guilty worm, quivering over the great gulf! What art thou? A sinner born to die: a leaf driven before the wind; a vapour ready to vanish away: just appearing, and then scattered into air, to be no more seen! See this! 'And then shalt thou see clearly to cast out the mote out of thy brother's eye.' Then, if thou hast leisure from the concerns of thy own soul, thou shalt know how to correct thy brother also.

8. But what is properly the meaning of this word, 'Judge not?' What is the judging which is here forbidden? It is not the same as evil-speaking, although it is frequently joined therewith. Evil-speaking is the relating anything that is evil concerning an absent person; whereas judging may indifferently refer either to the absent or the present. Neither does it necessarily imply the speaking at all, but only the thinking evil of another. Not that all kind of thinking evil of others is that judging which our Lord condemns. If I see one commit robbery or murder, or hear him

blaspheme the name of God, I cannot refrain from thinking ill of the robber or murderer. Yet this is not evil judging: there is no sin in this, nor anything contrary to tender affection.

9. The thinking of another in a manner that is contrary to love, is that judging which is here condemned; and this may be of various kinds. For, first we may think another to blame when he is not. We may lay to his charge (at least in our own mind) the things of which he is not guilty; the words which he has never spoke, or the actions which he has never done. Or we may think his manner of acting was wrong, although in reality it was not. And even where nothing can justly be blamed, either in the thing itself, or in the manner of doing it, we may suppose his intention was not good, and so condemn him on that ground; at the same time that He who searches the heart sees his simplicity and godly sincerity.

10. But we may not only fall into the sin of judging, by condemning the innocent; but also, secondly, by condemning the guilty to a higher degree than he deserves. This species of judging is likewise an offence against justice, as well as mercy; and yet such an offence as nothing can secure us from but the strongest and tenderest affection. Without this, we readily suppose one who is acknowledged to be in fault, to be more in fault than he really is. We undervalue whatever good is found in him. Nay, we are not easily induced to believe that anything good can remain in him in whom we have found anything that is evil.

11. All this shows a manifest want of that love which οὐ λογίζεται κακόν—*thinketh no evil*; which never draws an unjust or unkind conclusion from any premisses whatsoever. Love will not infer from a person's falling once into an act of open sin, that he is accustomed so to do; that he is habitually guilty of it: and if he was habitually guilty once, love does not conclude he is so still; much less, that if he is now guilty of this, therefore he is guilty of other sins also. These evil reasonings all pertain to that sinful judging which our Lord here guards us against; and which we are in the highest degree concerned to avoid, if we love either God or our own souls.

12. But supposing we do not condemn the innocent, neither

the guilty any farther than they deserve; still we may not be altogether clear of the snare: for there is a third sort of sinful judging, which is the condemning any person at all where there is not a sufficient evidence. And be the facts we suppose ever so true, yet that does not acquit us. For they ought not to have been supposed, but proved; and till they were, we ought to have formed no judgement. I say, 'till they were'; for neither are we excused, although the facts admit of ever so strong a proof, unless that proof be produced before we pass sentence, and compared with the evidence on the other side. Nor can we be excused, if ever we pass a full sentence before the accused has spoken for himself. Even a Jew might teach us this, as a mere lesson of justice, abstracted from mercy and brotherly love: 'Doth our law,' says Nicodemus, 'judge any man, before it hear him, and know what he doeth?' (John vii. 51). Yea, a Heathen could reply, when the chief of the Jewish nation desired to have judgement against his prisoner, 'It is not the manner of the Romans' to judge 'any man, before he that is accused have the accusers face to face, and have license to answer for himself concerning the crime laid against him.'

13. Indeed we could not easily fall into sinful judging, were we only to observe that rule which another[1] of those heathen Romans affirms to have been the measure of his own practice. 'I am so far,' says he, 'from lightly believing every man's or any man's evidence against another, that I do not easily or immediately believe a man's evidence against himself. I always allow him second thoughts, and many times counsel too.' Go, thou who art called a Christian, and do likewise: lest the Heathen rise and condemn thee in that day!

14. But how rarely should we condemn or judge one another, at least how soon would that evil be remedied, were we to walk by that clear and express rule which our Lord Himself has taught us!—'If thy brother shall trespass against thee,' or if thou hear or believe that he hath, 'go and tell him of his fault between thee and him alone.' This is the first step thou art to take. 'But if he will not hear, take with thee one or two more, that in the

[1] Seneca.

mouth of two or three witnesses every word may be established.' This is the second step. 'If he neglect to hear them, tell it unto the church'; either to the overseers thereof, or to the whole congregation, Thou hast then done thy part. Then think of it no more, but commend the whole to God.

15. But supposing thou hast by the grace of God 'cast the beam out of thine own eye,' and dost now clearly see 'the mote' or the beam 'which is in thy brother's eye,' yet beware thou dost not receive hurt thyself by endeavouring to help him. Still 'give not that which is holy unto dogs.' Do not lightly account any to be of this number; but if it evidently appear that they deserve the title, then 'cast ye not your pearls before swine.' Beware of that zeal which is not according to knowledge. For this is another great hindrance in their way who would be 'perfect as their heavenly Father is perfect.' They who desire this cannot but desire that all mankind should partake of the common blessing. And when we ourselves first partake of the heavenly gift, the divine 'evidence of things not seen,' we wonder that all mankind do not see the things which we see so plainly; and make no doubt at all but we shall open the eyes of all we have any intercourse with. Hence we are for attacking all we meet without delay, and constraining them to see, whether they will or no; and by the ill success of this intemperate zeal we often suffer in our own souls. To prevent this spending our strength in vain, our Lord adds this needful caution (needful to all, but more especially to those who are now warm in their first love), 'Give not that which is holy unto the dogs, neither cast ye your pearls before swine, lest they trample them under their feet, and turn again and rend you.'

16. 'Give not that which is holy unto the dogs.' Beware of thinking that any deserve this appellation, till there is full and incontestable proof, such as you can no longer resist. But when it is clearly and indisputably proved, that they are unholy and wicked men, not only strangers to but enemies to God, to all righteousness and true holiness; 'give not that which is holy,' τὸ ἅγιον—'the holy thing,' emphatically so called, unto these. The holy, the peculiar doctrines of the gospel—such as were hid from the ages and generations of old, and are now made known

to us, only by the revelation of Jesus Christ, and the inspiration of His Holy Spirit—are not to be prostituted unto these men, who know not if there be any Holy Ghost. Not indeed that the ambassadors of Christ can refrain from declaring them in the great congregation, wherein some of these may probably be: we must speak, whether men will hear or whether they will forbear; but this is not the case with private Christians. They do not bear that awful character; nor are they under any manner of obligation to force these great and glorious truths on them who contradict and blaspheme, who have a rooted enmity against them. Nay, they ought not so to do, but rather to lead them as they are able to bear. Do not begin a discourse with these upon remission of sins, and the gift of the Holy Ghost; but talk with them in their own manner, and upon their own principles. With the rational, honourable, and unjust Epicure, reason of 'righteousness, temperance, and judgement to come.' This is the most probable way to make Felix tremble. Reserve higher subjects for men of higher attainments.

17. Neither 'cast your pearls before swine.' Be very unwilling to pass this judgement on any man; but if the fact be plain and undeniable, if it is clear beyond all dispute, if the swine do not endeavour to disguise themselves, but rather glory in their shame, making no pretence to purity, either of heart or life, but working all uncleanness with greediness; then cast not ye your pearls before them. Talk not to them of the mysteries of the kingdom; of the things which eye hath not seen, nor ear heard; which, of consequence, as they have no other inlets of knowledge, no spiritual senses, it cannot enter into their hearts to conceive. Tell not them of the exceeding great and precious promises which God hath given us in the Son of His love. What conception can they have of being made partakers of the divine nature, who do not even desire to escape the corruption that is in the world through lust? Just as much knowledge as swine have of pearls, and as much relish as they have for them, so much relish have they for the deep things of God, so much knowledge of the mysteries of the gospel, who are immersed in the mire of this world, in worldly pleasures, desires, and cares. O cast not those pearls before these, 'lest they trample them under their feet!'

—lest they utterly despise what they cannot understand, and speak evil of the things which they know not. Nay, it is probable, this would not be the only inconvenience which would follow: it would not be strange, if they were, according to their nature, to 'turn again and rend you'; if they were to return you evil for good, cursing for blessing, and hatred for your good will. Such is the enmity of the carnal mind against God, and all the things of God. Such is the treatment you are to expect from these, if you offer them the unpardonable affront of endeavouring to save their souls from death, to pluck them as brands out of the burning.

18. And yet you need not utterly despair even of these, who, for the present, 'turn again and rend you.' For if all your arguments and persuasives fail, there is yet another remedy left, and one that is frequently found effectual, when no other method avails; this is prayer. Therefore, whatever you desire or want, either for others or for your own soul, 'ask, and it shall be given you; seek, and ye shall find; knock, and it shall be opened unto you.' The neglect of this is a third grand hindrance of holiness. Still we 'have not, because we ask not.' O how meek and gentle, how lowly in heart, how full of love both to God and men, might ye have been at this day, if you had only asked; if you had continued instant in prayer! Therefore, now, at least, 'ask, and it shall be given unto you.' 'Ask,' that ye may throughly experience, and perfectly practise, the whole of that religion which our Lord has here so beautifully described. It shall then be given you to be holy as He is holy, both in heart and in all manner of conversation. 'Seek,' in the way He hath ordained, in searching the Scriptures, in hearing His word, in meditating thereon, in fasting, in partaking of the Supper of the Lord; and surely ye shall find: ye shall find that pearl of great price, that faith which overcometh the world, that peace which the world cannot give, that love which is the earnest of your inheritance. 'Knock,'; continue in prayer, and in every other way of the Lord: be not weary or faint in your mind: press on to the mark: take no denial; let Him not go until He bless you. 'And the door' of mercy, of holiness, of heaven, 'shall be opened unto you.'

19. It is in compassion to the hardness of our heart, so unready

to believe the goodness of God, that our Lord is pleased to enlarge upon this head, and to repeat and confirm what He hath spoken. 'For every one,' saith He, 'that asketh, receiveth'; so that none need come short of the blessing; 'and he that seeketh,' even every one that seeketh, 'findeth' the love and the image of God; 'and to him that knocketh,' to every one that knocketh, the gate of righteousness shall be opened. So that here is no room for any to be discouraged, as though they might ask, or seek or knock in vain. Only remember always to pray, to seek, to knock, and not to faint. And then the promise standeth sure. It is firm as the pillars of heaven,—yea, more firm; for heaven and earth shall pass away; but His word shall not pass away.

20. To cut off every pretence for unbelief, our blessed Lord, in the following verses, illustrates yet farther what He had said, by an appeal to what passes in our own breasts: 'What man,' saith He, 'is there of you, whom if his son ask bread, will give him a stone?' Will even natural affection permit you to refuse the reasonable request of one you love? 'Or if he ask a fish, will he give him a serpent?' Will he give him hurtful instead of profitable things? So that even from what you feel and do yourselves, you may receive the fullest assurance, as, on the one hand, that no ill effect can possibly attend your asking, so, on the other, that it will be attended with that good effect, a full supply of all your wants. For 'if ye, being evil, know how to give good gifts unto your children, how much more shall your Father which is in heaven,' who is pure, unmixed, essential goodness, 'give good things to them that ask Him?' or (as He expresses it on another occasion), 'give the Holy Ghost to them that ask Him?' In Him are included all good things: all wisdom, peace, joy, love; the whole treasures of holiness and happiness; all that God hath prepared for them that love Him.

21. But that your prayer may have its full weight with God, see that ye be in charity with all men. For, otherwise, it is more likely to bring a curse than a blessing on your own head; nor can you expect to receive any blessing from God while you have not charity towards your neighbour. Therefore, let this hindrance be removed without delay. Confirm your love towards one another, and towards all men. And love them not in word only,

but in deed and in truth. 'Therefore, all things whatsoever ye would that men should do to you, do ye even so to them; for this is the law and the prophets.'

22. This is that royal law, that golden rule of mercy, as well as justice, which even the heathen Emperor caused to be written over the gate of his palace; a rule which many believe to be naturally engraved on the mind of every one that comes into the world. And thus much is certain, that it commends itself, as soon as heard, to every man's conscience and understanding; insomuch that no man can knowingly offend against it, without carrying his condemnation in his own breast.

23. 'This is the law and the prophets.' Whatsoever is written in that law which God of old revealed to mankind, and whatsoever precepts God has given by His holy prophets which have been since the world began, they are all summed up in these few words, they are all contained in this short direction. And this, rightly understood, comprises the whole of that religion which our Lord came to establish upon earth.

24. It may be understood either in a positive or negative sense. If understood in a negative sense, the meaning is, 'Whatever ye would not that men should do to you, do not ye unto them.' Here is a plain rule, always ready at hand, always easy to be applied. In all cases relating to your neighbour, make his case your own. Suppose the circumstances to be changed, and yourself to be just as he is now; and then beware that you indulge no temper or thought, that no word pass out of your lips, that you take no step, which you should have condemned in him, upon such a change of circumstances. If understood in a direct and positive sense, the plain meaning of it is, 'Whatsoever you could reasonably desire of him, supposing yourself to be in his circumstances, that do, to the uttermost of your power, to every child of man.'

25. To apply this in one or two obvious instances: it is clear to every man's own conscience, we would not that others should judge us, should causelessly or lightly think evil of us; much less would we that any should speak evil of us—should publish our real faults or infirmities. Apply this to yourself. Do not unto another what you would not he should do unto you; and you

will never more judge your neighbour, never causelessly or lightly think evil of any one; much less will you speak evil; you will never mention even the real fault of an absent person, unless so far as you are convinced it is absolutely needful for the good of other souls.

26. Again: we would that all men should love and esteem us, and behave towards us according to justice, mercy, and truth. And we may reasonably desire, that they should do us all the good they can do, without injuring themselves; yea, that in outward things (according to the known rule), their superfluities should give way to our conveniences; their conveniences, to our necessities; and their necessities, to our extremities. Now, then, let us walk by the same rule: let us do unto all as we would they should do to us. Let us love and honour all men. Let justice, mercy, and truth govern all our minds and action. Let our superfluities give way to our neighbour's conveniences (and who then will have any superfluities left?); our conveniences, to our neighbour's necessities; our necessities, to his extremities.

27. This is pure and genuine morality. This do, and thou shalt live. 'As many as walk by this rule, peace be to them and mercy'; for they are 'the Israel of God.' But then, be it observed, none can walk by this rule (nor ever did from the beginning of the world), none can love his neighbour as himself, unless he first love God. And none can love God, unless he believe in Christ; unless he have redemption through His blood, and the Spirit of God bearing witness with his spirit that he is a child of God. Faith, therefore, is still the root of all, of present as well as future salvation. Still we must say to every sinner, 'Believe in the Lord Jesus Christ, and thou shalt be saved': thou shalt be saved now, that thou mayest be saved for ever; saved on earth, that thou mayest be saved in heaven. Believe in Him, and thy faith will work by love. Thou wilt love the Lord thy God, because He hath loved thee: thou wilt love thy neighbour as thyself: and then it will be thy glory and joy, to exert and increase this love; not barely by abstaining from what is contrary thereto, from every unkind thought, word, and action, but by showing all that kindness to every man which thou wouldest he should show unto thee.

SERMON XXVI

UPON OUR LORD'S SERMON ON THE MOUNT

DISCOURSE XI

Enter ye in at the strait gate, for wide is the gate, and broad is the way, that leadeth to destruction, and many there be which go in thereat:
Because strait is the gate, and narrow is the way, which leadeth unto life, and few there be that find it.—MATT. vii. 13, 14.

OUR Lord, having warned us of the dangers which easily beset us at our first entrance upon real religion, the hindrances which naturally arise from within, from the wickedness of our own hearts; now proceeds to apprise us of the hindrances from without, particularly ill example and ill advice. By one or the other of these, thousands, who once ran well, have drawn back unto perdition—yea, many of those who were not novices in religion, who had made some progress in righteousness. His caution, therefore, against these He presses upon us with all possible earnestness, and repeats again and again, in variety of expressions, lest by any means we should let it slip. Thus, effectually to guard us against the former, 'Enter ye in,' saith He, 'at the strait gate: for wide is the gate, and broad is the way, that leadeth to destruction, and many there be which go in thereat: because strait is the gate, and narrow is the way, which leadeth unto life, and few there be that find it': to secure us from the latter, 'Beware,' saith He, 'of false prophets.' We shall, at present, consider the former only.

2. 'Enter ye in,' saith our Blessed Lord, 'at the strait gate: for wide is the gate, and broad is the way, that leadeth to destruction, and many there be which go in thereat: because strait is the gate, and narrow is the way, which leadeth unto life, and few there be that find it.'

3. In these words we may observe, first, the inseparable properties of the way to hell: 'Wide is the gate, broad the way,

that leadeth to destruction, and many there be that go in thereat':
secondly, the inseparable properties of the way to heaven:
'Strait is that gate, and few there be that find it': thirdly, a serious
exhortation grounded thereon, 'Enter ye in at the strait gate.'

I. 1. We may observe, first, the inseparable properties of the
way to hell: 'wide is the gate, and broad is the way, that leadeth
to destruction, and many there be which go in thereat.'

2. Wide indeed is the gate, and broad the way, that leadeth
to destruction! For sin is the gate of hell, and wickedness the
way to destruction. And how wide a gate is that of sin! How
broad is the way of wickedness! The 'commandment' of God
'is exceeding broad'; as extending not only to all our actions, but
to every word which goeth out of our lips, yea, every thought
that rises in our heart. And sin is equally broad with the
commandment, seeing any breach of the commandment is sin.
Yea, rather, it is a thousand times broader; since there is only one
way of keeping the commandment; for we do not properly keep
it, unless both the thing done, the manner of doing it, and all the
other circumstances, are right: but there are a thousand ways of
breaking every commandment; so that this gate is wide indeed

3. To consider this a little more particularly: how wide do
those parent-sins extend, from which all the rest derive their
being; that carnal mind which is enmity against God, pride of
heart, self-will, and love of the world! Can we fix any bounds
to them? Do they not diffuse themselves through all our thoughts
and mingle with all our tempers? Are they not the leaven which
leavens, more or less, the whole mass of our affections? May we
not, on a close and faithful examination of ourselves, perceive
these roots of bitterness continually springing up, infecting all
our words, and tainting all our actions? And how innumerable
an offspring do they bring forth, in every age and nation! Even
enough to cover the whole earth with darkness and cruel habitations.

4. O who is able to reckon up their accursed fruits; to count
all the sins, whether against God or our neighbour, not which
imagination might paint, but which may be matter of daily
melancholy experience! Nor need we range over all the earth to

find them. Survey any one kingdom, any single country, or city, or town; and how plenteous is this harvest! And let it not be one of those which are still overspread with Mahometan or Pagan darkness; but of those which name the name of Christ, which profess to see the light of His glorious gospel. Go no farther than the kingdom to which we belong, the city wherein we are now. We call ourselves Christians; yea, and that of the purest sort: we are Protestants; Reformed Christians! But, alas! who shall carry on the reformation of our opinions into our hearts and lives? Is there not a cause? For how innumerable are our sins; and those of the deepest dye! Do not the grossest abominations, of every kind, abound among us from day to day? Do not sins of every sort cover the land, as the waters cover the sea? Who can count them? Rather go and count the drops of rain, or the sands on the sea-shore. So 'wide is the gate,' so 'broad is the way, that leadeth to destruction'!

5. 'And many there are who go in at' that gate; many who walk in that way; almost as many as go in at the gate of death, as sink into the chambers of the grave. For it cannot be denied (though neither can we acknowledge it but with shame and sorrow of heart), that even in this, which is called a Christian country, the generality of every age and sex, of every profession and employment, of every rank and degree, high and low, rich and poor, are walking in the way of destruction. The far greater part of the inhabitants of this city, to this day, live in sin; in some palpable, habitual, known transgression of the law they profess to observe; yea, in some outward transgression, some gross, visible kind of ungodliness or unrighteousness, some open violation of their duty, either to God or man. These then, none can deny, are all in the way that leadeth to destruction. Add to these, those who have a name indeed that they live, but were never yet alive to God; those that outwardly appear fair to men, but are inwardly full of all uncleanness; full of pride or vanity, of anger or revenge, of ambition or covetousness; lovers of themselves, lovers of the world, lovers of pleasure, more than lovers of God. These, indeed, may be highly esteemed of men; but they are an abomination to the Lord. And how greatly will these saints of the world swell the number of the children of hell! Yea, add all,

whatever they be in other respects, whether they have more or less of the form of godliness, who, 'being ignorant of God's righteousness, and seeking to establish their own righteousness' as the ground of their reconciliation to God and acceptance with Him, of consequence have not 'submitted themselves unto the righteousness which is of God' by faith. Now, all these things joined together in one, how terribly true is our Lord's assertion, 'Wide is the gate, and broad is the way, that leadeth to destruction, and many there be which go in thereat!'

6. Nor does this only concern the vulgar herd—the poor, base, stupid part of mankind. Men of eminence in the world, men who have many fields and yoke of oxen, do not desire to be excused from this. On the contrary, 'many wise men after the flesh,' according to the human methods of judging, 'many mighty,' in power, in courage, in riches, many 'noble, are called'; called into the broad way, by the world, the flesh, and the devil; and they are not disobedient to that calling. Yea, the higher they are raised in fortune and power, the deeper do they sink into wickedness. The more blessings they have received from God, the more sins do they commit; using their honour or riches, their learning or wisdom, not as means of working out their salvation, but rather of excelling in vice, and so ensuring their own destruction.

II. 1. And the very reason why many of these go on so securely in the broad way, is, because it is broad; not considering that this is the inseparable property of the way to destruction. 'Many there be,' saith our Lord, 'which go in thereat'; for the very reason why they should flee from it; even 'because strait is the gate, and narrow the way, that leadeth unto life, and few there be that find it.'

2. This is an inseparable property of the way to heaven. So narrow is the way that leadeth unto life—unto life everlasting— so strait the gate, that nothing unclean, nothing unholy, can enter. No sinner can pass through that gate, until he is saved from all his sins. Not only from his outward sins, from his evil 'conversation received by tradition from his fathers.' It will not suffice, that he hath 'ceased to do evil,' and 'learned to do well';

he must not only be saved from all sinful actions, and from all evil and useless discourse; but inwardly changed, throughly renewed in the spirit of his mind: otherwise he cannot pass through the gate of life, he cannot enter into glory.

3. For, 'narrow is the way that leadeth unto life'; the way of universal holiness. Narrow indeed is the way of poverty of spirit; the way of holy mourning; the way of meekness; and that of hungering and thirsting after righteousness. Narrow is the way of mercifulness; of love unfeigned; the way of purity of heart; of doing good unto all men; and of gladly suffering evil, all manner of evil, for righteousness' sake.

4. 'And few there be that find it.' Alas! how few find even the way of heathen honesty! How few are there that do nothing to another which they would not another should do unto them! How few that are clear before God, from acts either of injustice or unkindness! How few that do not 'offend with their tongue'! that speak nothing unkind, nothing untrue! What a small proportion of mankind are innocent even of outward transgressions! And how much smaller a proportion have their hearts right before God,—clean and holy in His sight! Where are they, whom His all-searching eye discerns to be truly humble; to abhor themselves in dust and ashes in the presence of God their Saviour; to be deeply and steadily serious, feeling their wants, and 'passing the time of their sojourning with fear'; truly meek and gentle, never 'overcome of evil, but overcoming evil with good'; throughly athirst for God, and continually panting after a renewal in His likeness? How thinly are they scattered over the earth whose souls are enlarged in love to all mankind; and who love God with all their strength, who have given Him their hearts, and desire nothing else in earth or heaven! How few are those lovers of God and man, that spend their whole strength in doing good unto all men; and are ready to suffer all things, yea, death itself, to save one soul from eternal death!

5. But while so few are found in the way of life, and so many in the way of destruction, there is great danger lest the torrent of example should bear us away with them. Even a single example, if it be always in our sight, is apt to make much impression upon us; especially when it has nature on its side, when

it falls in with our own inclinations. How great then must be the force of so numerous examples, continually before our eyes; and all conspiring, together with our own hearts, to carry us down the stream of nature! How difficult must it be to stem the tide, and to keep 'ourselves unspotted in the world'!

6. What heightens the difficulty still more is, that they are not the rude and senseless part of mankind, at least not these alone, who set us the example, who throng the downward way; but the polite, the well-bred, the genteel, the wise, the men who understand the world, the men of knowledge, of deep and various learning, the rational, the eloquent! These are all, or nearly all, against us. And how shall we stand against these? Do not their tongues drop manna, and have they not learned all the arts of soft persuasion?—and of reasoning too? for these are versed in all controversies, and strife of words. It is therefore a small thing with them to prove, that the way is *right*, because it is *broad*; that he who follows a multitude cannot do evil, but only he who will not follow them; that your way must be *wrong*, because it is *narrow*, and because there are so few that find it. These will make it clear to a demonstration, that evil is good, and good is evil; that the way of holiness is the way of destruction, and the way of the world the only way to heaven.

7. O how can unlearned and ignorant men maintain their cause against such opponents! And yet these are not all with whom they must contend, however unequal to the task: for there are many mighty, and noble, and powerful men, as well as wise, in the road that leadeth to destruction; and these have a shorter way of confuting, than that of reason and argument. They usually apply, not to the understanding, but to the fears, of any that oppose them,—a method that seldom fails of success, even where argument profits nothing, as lying level to the capacities of all men; for all can fear, whether they can reason or no. And all who have not a firm trust in God, a sure reliance both on His power and love, cannot but fear to give any disgust to those who have the power of the world in their hands. What wonder, therefore, if the example of these is a law to all who know not God?

8. Many rich are likewise in the broad way. And these apply

to the hopes of men, and to all their foolish desires, as strongly and effectually as the mighty and noble to their fears. So that hardly can you hold on in the way of the kingdom, unless you are dead to all below, unless you are crucified to the world, and the world crucified to you, unless you desire nothing more but God.

9. For how dark, how uncomfortable, how forbidding, is the prospect on the opposite side! A strait gate; a narrow way! and few finding that gate; few walking in the way! Besides, even those few are not wise men, not men of learning or eloquence. They are not able to reason either strongly or clearly; they cannot propose an argument to any advantage. They know not how to prove what they profess to believe; or to explain even what they say they experience. Surely such advocates as these will never recommend, but rather discredit, the cause they have espoused:

10. Add to this, that they are not noble, not honourable men. if they were, you might bear with their folly. They are men of no interest, no authority, of no account in the world. They are mean and base; low in life; and such as have no power, if they had the will, to hurt you. Therefore there is nothing at all to be feared from them; and there is nothing at all to hope: for the greater part of them may say, 'Silver and gold have I none'; at least a very moderate share. Nay, some of them have scarce food to eat, or raiment to put on. For this reason, as well as because their ways are not like those of other men, they are everywhere spoken against, are despised, have their names cast out as evil, are variously persecuted, and treated as the filth and offscouring of the world. So that both your fears, your hopes, and all your desires (except those which you have immediately from God), yea, all your natural passions, continually incline you to return into the broad way.

III. 1. Therefore it is, that our Lord so earnestly exhorts, 'Enter ye in at the strait gate.' Or (as the same exhortation is elsewhere expressed), 'Strive to enter in': 'Ἀγωνίζεσθε εἰσελθεῖν —'strive as in an agony': 'For many,' saith our Lord, 'shall seek to enter in,' indolently strive, 'and shall not be able.'

2. It is true, He intimates what may seem another reason for

this, for their not being able to enter in, in the words which immediately follow these. For after He had said, 'Many, I say unto you, will seek to enter in, and shall not be able,' He subjoins, 'When once the master of the house is risen up, and hath shut to the door, and ye begin to stand without,' ἄρξησθε ἔξω ἐστάναι—rather, *ye stand without*; for ἄρξησθε seems to be only an elegant expletive—'and to knock at the door, saying, Lord, Lord, open unto us; He shall answer and say unto you, I know you not: depart from Me, all ye workers of iniquity' (Luke xiii. 24, &c.).

3. It may appear, upon a transient view of these words, that their delaying to seek at all, rather than their manner of seeking, was the reason why they were not able to enter in. But it comes, in effect, to the same thing. They were, therefore, commanded to depart, because they had been 'workers of iniquity'; because they had walked in the broad road; in other words, because they had not agonized to 'enter in at the strait gate.' Probably they did *seek*, before the door was shut; but that did not suffice: and they did *strive*, after the door was shut; but then it was too late.

4. Therefore strive ye now, in this your day, to 'enter in at the strait gate.' And in order thereto, settle it in your heart, and let it be ever uppermost in your thoughts, that if you are in a broad way, you are in the way that leadeth to destruction. If many go with you, as sure as God is true, both they and you are going to hell! If you are walking as the generality of men walk, you are walking to the bottomless pit! Are many wise, many rich, many mighty, or noble, travelling with you in the same way? By this token, without going any farther, you know it does not lead to life. Here is a short, a plain, an infallible rule, before you enter into particulars. In whatever profession you are engaged, you must be singular, or be damned! The way to hell has nothing singular in it; but the way to heaven is singularity all over. If you move but one step towards God, you are not as other men are. But regard not this. It is far better to stand alone, than to fall into the pit. Run, then, with patience the race which is set before thee, though thy companions therein are but few. They will not always be so. Yet a little while, and thou wilt 'come to an innumerable company of angels, to the general assembly and

church of the first-born, and to the spirits of just men made perfect.'

5. Now, then, 'strive to enter in at the strait gate,' being penetrated with the deepest sense of the inexpressible danger your soul is in, so long as you are in a broad way,—so long as you are void of poverty of spirit, and all that inward religion, which the many, the rich, the wise, account madness. 'Strive to enter in'; being pierced with sorrow and shame for having so long run on with the unthinking crowd, utterly neglecting, if not despising, that 'holiness without which no man can see the Lord.' Strive, as in an agony of holy fear, lest 'a promise being made you of entering into His rest,' even that 'rest which remaineth for the people of God,' you should nevertheless 'come short of it.' Strive, in all the fervour of desire, with 'groanings which cannot be uttered.' Strive by prayer without ceasing; at all times, in all places, lifting up your heart to God, and giving Him no rest, till you 'awake up after His likeness,' and are 'satisfied' with it.

6. To conclude. 'Strive to enter in at the strait gate, not only by this agony of soul, of conviction, of sorrow, of shame, of desire, of fear, of unceasing prayer; but likewise by ordering thy conversation aright, by walking with all thy strength in all the ways of God, the way of innocence, of piety, and of mercy. Abstain from all appearance of evil; do all possible good to all men; deny thyself, thy own will, in all things, and take up thy cross daily. Be ready to cut off thy right hand, to pluck out thy right eye, and cast it from thee, to suffer the loss of goods, friends, health, all things on earth, so thou mayest enter into the kingdom of heaven.

SERMON XXVII

UPON OUR LORD'S SERMON ON THE MOUNT

DISCOURSE XII

Beware of false prophets, which come to you in sheep's clothing, but inwardly they are ravening wolves.

Ye shall know them by their fruits. Do men gather grapes of thorns, or figs of thistles?

Even so every good tree bringeth forth good fruit; but a corrupt tree bringeth forth evil fruit.

A good tree cannot bring forth evil fruit, neither can a corrupt tree bring forth good fruit.

Every tree that bringeth not forth good fruit is hewn down, and cast into the fire. Wherefore by their fruits ye shall know them.

MATT. vii. 15-20.

It is scarce possible to express or conceive what multitudes of souls run on to destruction, because they would not be persuaded to walk in a *narrow* way, even though it were the way to ever-lasting salvation. And the same thing we may still observe daily. Such is the folly and madness of mankind, that thousands of men still rush on in the way to hell, only because it is a *broad* way. They walk in it themselves, because others do: because so many perish, they will add to the number. Such is the amazing influence of example over the weak, miserable children of men! It continually peoples the regions of death, and drowns number-less souls in everlasting perdition.

2. To warn mankind of this, to guard as many as possible against this spreading contagion, God has commanded His watchmen to cry aloud, and show the people the danger they are in. For this end He has sent His servants, the prophets, in their succeeding generations, to point out the narrow path, and exhort all men not to be conformed to this world. But what, if the watchmen themselves fall into the snare against which they should warn others? What if 'the prophets prophesy deceits'? if they 'cause the people to err from the way'? What shall be

done, if they point out, as the way to eternal life, what is in truth the way to eternal death; and exhort others to walk, as they do themselves, in the broad, not the narrow way?

3. Is this an unheard-of, is it an uncommon thing? Nay, God knoweth it is not. The instances of it are almost innumerable. We may find them in every age and nation. But how terrible is this—when the ambassadors of God turn agents for the devil! —when they who are commissioned to teach men the way to heaven do in fact teach them the way to hell! These are like the locusts of Egypt, 'which eat up the residue that had escaped, that had remained after the hail.' They devour even the residue of men that had escaped, that were not destroyed by ill example. It is not, therefore, without cause, that our wise and gracious Master so solemnly cautions us against them: 'Beware,' saith He, of false prophets, which come to you in sheep's clothing, but inwardly they are ravening wolves.'

4. A caution this of the utmost importance. That it may the more effectually sink into our hearts, let us inquire, first, who these false prophets are: secondly, what appearance they put on: and, thirdly, how we may know what they really are, notwithstanding their fair appearance.

I. 1. We are, first, to inquire who these false prophets are. And this it is needful to do the more diligently, because these very men have so laboured to 'wrest this scripture to their own,' though not only their own, 'destruction.' In order, therefore, to cut off all dispute, I shall raise no dust (as the manner of some is), neither use any loose, rhetorical exclamations, to deceive the hearts of the simple; but speak rough, plain truths, such as none can deny who has understanding or modesty left, and such truths as have the closest connexion with the whole tenor of the preceding discourse: whereas too many have interpreted these words without any regard to all that went before; as if they bore no manner of relation to the sermon in the close of which they stand.

2. By *prophets* here (as in many other passages of Scripture, particularly in the new Testament) are meant, not those who foretell things to come, but those who speak in the name of God;

those men who profess to be sent of God, to teach others the way to heaven.

Those are *false* prophets, who teach a false way to heaven, a way which does not lead thither; or (which comes in the end to the same point), who do not teach the true.

3. Every broad way is infallibly a false one. Therefore this is one plain, sure rule: 'They who teach men to walk in a broad way, a way that many walk in, are false prophets.'

Again: the true way to heaven is a narrow way. Therefore this is another plain, sure rule: 'They who do not teach men to walk in a narrow way, to be singular, are false prophets.

4. To be more particular: the only true way to heaven is that pointed out in the preceding sermon. Therefore they are false prophets who do not teach men to walk in this way.

Now the way to heaven pointed out in the preceding sermon is the way of lowliness, mourning, meekness, and holy desire, love of God and of our neighbour, doing good, and suffering evil for Christ's sake. They are, therefore, false prophets, who teach, as the way to heaven, any other way than this.

5. It matters not what they call that other way. They may call it faith; or good works; or faith and works; or repentance; or repentance, faith, and new obedience. All these are good words: but if, under these, or any other terms whatever, they teach men any way distinct from this, they are properly false prophets.

6. How much more do they fall under that condemnation, who speak evil of this good way; but above all, they who teach the directly opposite way, the way of pride, of levity, of passion, of worldly desires, of loving pleasure more than God, of unkindness to our neighbour, of unconcern for good works, and suffering no evil, no persecution, for righteousness' sake!

7. If it be asked, 'Why, who ever did teach this, or who does teach it, as the way to heaven?' I answer, Ten thousand wise and honourable men; even all those, of whatever denomination, who encourage the proud, the trifler, the passionate, the lover of the world, the man of pleasure, the unjust or unkind, the easy, careless, harmless, useless creature, the man who suffers no reproach for righteousness' sake, to imagine he is in the way to

heaven. These are false prophets in the highest sense of the word. These are traitors both to God and man. These are no other than the first-born of Satan; the eldest sons of Apollyon, the destroyer. These are far above the rank of ordinary cut-throats; for they murder the souls of men. They are continually peopling the realms of night; and whenever they follow the poor souls whom they have destroyed, 'hell shall be moved from beneath to meet them at their coming.'

II. 1. But do they come now in their own shape? By no means. If it were so, they could not destroy. You would take the alarm, and flee for your life. Therefore they put on a quite contrary appearance (which was the second thing to be considered): 'they come to you in sheep's clothing, although inwardly they are ravening wolves.'

2. 'They come to you in sheep's clothing'; that is, with an appearance of harmlessness. They come in the most mild, inoffensive manner, without any mark or token of enmity. Who can imagine that these quiet creatures would do any hurt to any one? Perhaps they may not be so zealous and active in doing good as one would wish they were. However, you see no reason to suspect that they have even the desire to do any harm. But this is not all.

3. They come, secondly, with an appearance of usefulness. Indeed to this, to do good, they are particularly called. They are set apart for this very thing. They are particularly commissioned to watch over your soul, and to train you up to eternal life. It is their whole business, to 'go about doing good, and healing those that are oppressed of the devil.' And you have been always accustomed to look upon them in this light, as messengers of God, sent to bring you a blessing.

4. They come, thirdly, with an appearance of religion. All they do is for conscience' sake! They assure you, it is out of mere zeal for God, that they are making God a liar. It is out of pure concern for religion, that they would destroy it, root and branch. All they speak is only from a love of truth, and a fear lest it should suffer; and, it may be, from a regard for the Church, and a desire to defend her from all her enemies.

5. Above all, they come with an appearance of love. They take all these pains only for *your* good. They should not trouble themselves about you, but that they have a kindness for you. They will make large professions of their goodwill, of their concern for the danger you are in, and of their earnest desire to preserve you from error, from being entangled in new and mischievous doctrines. They should be very sorry to see one who *means* so well, hurried into any extreme, perplexed with strange and unintelligible notions, or deluded into enthusiasm. Therefore it is that they advise you to keep still in the plain middle way; and to beware of 'being righteous over-much,' lest you should 'destroy yourself.'

III. 1. But how may we know what they really are, notwithstanding their fair appearance? This was the third thing into which it was proposed to inquire. Our blessed Lord saw how needful it was for all men to know false prophets, however disguised. He saw, likewise, how unable most men were to deduce a truth through a long train of consequences. He therefore gives us a short and plain rule, easy to be understood by men of the meanest capacities, and easy to be applied upon all occasions: 'Ye shall know them by their fruits.'

2. Upon all occasions you may easily apply this rule. In order to know whether any who speak in the name of God are false or true prophets, it is easy to observe, first, What are the fruits of their doctrine as to themselves? What effect has it had upon their lives? Are they holy and unblamable in all things? What effect has it had upon their hearts? Does it appear by the general tenor of their conversation, that their tempers are holy, heavenly, divine? that the mind is in them which was in Christ Jesus? that they are meek, lowly, patient, lovers of God and man, and zealous of good works?

3. You may easily observe, secondly, what are the fruits of their doctrine as to those that hear them—in many, at least, though not in all; for the Apostles themselves did not convert all that heard them. Have these the mind that was in Christ? And do they walk as He also walked? And was it by hearing these men that they began so to do? Were they inwardly and

outwardly wicked till they heard them? If so, it is a manifest proof that those are true prophets, teachers sent of God. But if it is not so, if they do not effectually teach either themselves or others to love and serve God, it is a manifest proof that they are false prophets: that God hath not sent them.

4. A hard saying this! How few can bear it? This our Lord was sensible of, and therefore condescends to prove it at large, by several clear and convincing arguments. 'Do men,' says he, 'gather grapes of thorns, or figs of thistles?' (verse 16). Do you expect that these evil men should bring forth good fruit? As well might you expect that thorns should bring forth grapes, or that figs should grow upon thistles! 'Every good tree bringeth forth good fruit; but a corrupt tree bringeth forth evil fruit' (verse 17). Every true prophet, every teacher whom I have sent, bringeth forth the good fruit of holiness. But a false prophet, a teacher whom I have not sent, brings forth only sin and wickedness. 'A good tree cannot bring forth evil fruit, neither can a corrupt tree bring forth good fruit.' A true prophet, a teacher sent from God, does not bring forth good fruit sometimes only, but always; not accidentally, but by a kind of necessity In like manner, a false prophet, one whom God hath not sent, does not bring forth evil fruit accidentally, or sometimes only, but always, and of necessity. 'Every tree that bringeth not forth good fruit is hewn down, and cast into the fire' (verse 19). Such infallibly will be the lot of those prophets who bring not forth good fruit, who do not save souls from sin, who do not bring sinners to repentance. 'Wherefore,' let this stand as an eternal rule, 'By their fruits ye shall know them' (verse 20). They who, in fact, bring the proud, passionate, unmerciful, lovers of the world, to be lowly, gentle, lovers of God and man,—they are true prophets; they are sent from God, who therefore confirms their word. On the other hand, they whose hearers, if unrighteous before, remain unrighteous still, or, at least, void of any righteousness which 'exceeds the righteousness of the Scribes and Pharisees,'—they are false prophets; they are not sent of God; therefore their word falls to the ground: and, without a miracle of grace, they and their hearers together will fall into the bottomless pit!

5. O 'beware of these false prophets'! For though they 'come in sheep's clothing, yet inwardly they are ravening wolves.' They only destroy and devour the flock: they tear them in pieces, if there is none to help them. They will not, cannot, lead you in the way to heaven. How should they, when they know it not themselves? O beware they do not turn you out of the way, and cause you to 'lose what you have wrought'!

6. But perhaps you will ask, 'If there is such danger in hearing them, ought I to hear them at all?' It is a weighty question, such as deserves the deepest consideration, and ought not to be answered but upon the calmest thought, the most deliberate reflection. For many years I have been almost afraid to speak at all concerning it; being unable to determine one way or the other, or to give any judgement upon it. Many reasons there are which readily occur and incline me to say, 'Hear them not.' And yet what our Lord speaks concerning the false prophets of His own times seems to imply the contrary: 'Then spake Jesus unto the multitude, and to His disciples, saying, The Scribes and the Pharisees sit in Moses' seat'—are the ordinary, stated teachers in your Church: 'all, therefore, whatsoever they bid you observe, that observe and do. But do not ye after their works; for they say, and do not.' Now, that these were false prophets in the highest sense, our Lord hath shown during the whole course of His ministry; as indeed He does in those very words, 'They say, and do not.' Therefore, by their fruits His disciples could not but know them, seeing they were open to the view of all men. Accordingly, He warns them again and again, to beware of these false prophets. And yet He does not forbid them to hear even these: nay, He, in effect, commands them so to do, in those words, 'All, therefore, whatsoever they bid you observe, that observe and do': for unless they heard them, they could not know, much less observe, whatsoever they bade them do. Here, then, our Lord Himself gives a plain direction, both to His Apostles and the whole multitude, in some circumstances, to hear even false prophets, known and acknowledged so to be.

7. But perhaps it will be said, 'He only directed to hear them when they read the Scripture to the congregation.' I answer, At the same time that they thus read the Scripture, they generally

expounded it too. And here is no kind of intimation that they were to hear the one, and not the other also. Nay, the very terms, 'All things whatsoever they bid you observe,' exclude any such limitation.

8. Again: unto them, unto false prophets, undeniably such, is frequently committed (O grief to speak! for surely these things ought not so to be) the administration of the sacrament also. To direct men, therefore, not to hear them, would be, in effect, to cut them off from the ordinance of God. But this we dare not do; considering the validity of the ordinance doth not depend on the goodness of him that administers, but on the faithfulness of Him that ordained it, who will and doth meet us in His appointed ways. Therefore, on this account, likewise, I scruple to say, 'Hear not even the false prophets.' Even by these who are under a curse themselves, God can and doth give us His blessing. For the bread which they break, we have experiment-ally known to be 'the communion of the body of Christ', and the cup which God blessed, even by their unhallowed lips, was to us the communion of the blood of Christ.

9. All, therefore, which I can say is this: In any particular case, wait upon God by humble and earnest prayer, and then act according to the best light you have: act according to what you are persuaded, upon the whole, will be most for your spiritual advantage. Take great care that you do not judge rashly; that you do not lightly think any to be false prophets: and when you have full proof, see that no anger or contempt have any place in your heart. After this, in the presence and in the fear of God, determine for yourself. I can only say, if by experience you find that the hearing them hurts your soul, then hear them not; then quietly refrain, and hear those that profit you. If, on the other hand, you find it does not hurt your soul, you then may hear them still. Only, 'take heed how you hear': beware of them and of their doctrine. Hear with fear and trembling, lest you should be deceived, and given up, like them, to a strong delusion. As they continually mingle truth and lies, how easily may you take in both together! Hear with fervent and continual prayer to Him who alone teacheth man wisdom. And see that you bring whatever you hear 'to the law and to the

testimony.' Receive nothing untried, nothing till it is weighed in the balance of the sanctuary: believe nothing they say, unless it is clearly confirmed by passages of holy writ. Wholly reject whatsoever differs therefrom, whatever is not confirmed thereby. And, in particular, reject, with the utmost abhorrence, whatsoever is described as the way of salvation, that is either different from, or short of, the way our Lord has marked out in the foregoing discourse.

10. I cannot conclude without addressing a few plain words to those of whom we have now been speaking. O ye false prophets! O ye dry bones! hear ye, for once, the word of the Lord! How long will ye lie in the name of God, saying, 'God hath spoken!' and God hath not spoken by you? How long will ye pervert the right ways of the Lord, putting darkness for light, and light for darkness? How long will ye teach the way of death, and call it the way of life? How long will ye deliver to Satan the souls whom ye profess to bring unto God?

11. 'Woe unto you, ye blind leaders of the blind; for ye shut the kingdom of heaven against men. Ye neither go in yourselves, neither suffer ye them that are entering to go in.' Them that would 'strive to enter in at the strait gate,' ye call back into the broad way. Them that have scarce gone one step in the ways of God, you devilishly caution against going too far. Them that just begin to 'hunger and thirst after righteousness,' you warn not to 'be righteous overmuch.' Thus you cause them to stumble at the very threshold; yea, to fall and rise no more. O wherefore do ye this? What profit is there in their blood, when they go down to the pit? Miserable profit to you! 'They shall perish in their iniquity; but their blood will God require at your hands!'

12. Where are your eyes? Where is your understanding? Have ye deceived others, till you have deceived yourselves also? Who hath required this at your hands, to teach a way which ye never knew? Are you 'given up to' so 'strong a delusion,' that ye not only teach but 'believe a lie'? And can you possibly believe that God hath sent you? that ye are His messengers? Nay, if the Lord had sent you, the work of the Lord would prosper in your hand. As the Lord liveth, if ye were messengers

of God, He would 'confirm the word of His messengers.' But the work of the Lord doth not prosper in your hand: you bring no sinners to repentance. The Lord doth not confirm your word; for you save no souls from death.

13. How can you possibly evade the force of our Lord's words—so full, so strong, so express? How can ye evade knowing yourselves by your fruits—evil fruits of evil trees? And how should it be otherwise? 'Do men gather grapes of thorns, or figs of thistles?' Take this to yourselves, ye to whom it belongs! O ye barren trees, why cumber ye the ground? 'Every good tree bringeth forth good fruit.' See ye not, that here is no exception? Take knowledge, then, ye are not good trees; for ye do not bring forth good fruit. 'But a corrupt tree bringeth forth evil fruit'; and so have ye done from the beginning. Your speaking, as from God, has only confirmed them that heard you in the tempers, if not works, of the devil. O take warning of Him in whose name ye speak, before the sentence He hath pronounced take place: 'Every tree which bringeth not forth good fruit is hewn down and cast into the fire.'

14. My dear brethren, harden not your hearts! You have too long shut your eyes against the light. Open them now before it is too late; before you are cast into outer darkness! Let not any temporal consideration weigh with you; for eternity is at stake. Ye have run before ye were sent. O go no farther! Do not persist to damn yourselves and them that hear you! You have no fruit of your labours. And why is this? Even because the Lord is not with you. But can you go this warfare at your own cost? It cannot be. Then humble yourselves before Him. Cry unto Him out of the dust, that He may first quicken *thy* soul; give *thee* the faith that worketh by love; that is lowly and meek, pure and merciful, zealous of good works, rejoicing in tribulation, in reproach, in distress, in persecution for righteousness' sake! So shall 'the Spirit of glory and of Christ rest upon thee,' and it shall appear that God hath sent thee. So shalt thou indeed 'do the work of an Evangelist, and make full proof of thy ministry.' So shall the word of God in thy mouth be 'an hammer that breaketh the rocks in pieces'! It shall then be known by thy fruits that thou art a prophet of the Lord, even by the children whom God

hath given thee. And having 'turned many to righteousness,'
thou shalt 'shine as the stars for ever and ever!'

SERMON XXVIII

UPON OUR LORD'S SERMON ON THE MOUNT

DISCOURSE XIII

*Not every one that saith unto Me, Lord, Lord, shall enter into the kingdom of
heaven; but he that doeth the will of My Father which is in heaven.*

*Many will say to Me in that day, Lord, Lord, have we not prophesied in Thy
name? and in Thy name have cast out devils? and in Thy name done
many wonderful works?*

*And then will I profess unto them, I never knew you: depart from Me, ye that
work iniquity.*

*Therefore whosoever heareth these sayings of Mine, and doeth them, I will
liken him unto a wise man, which built his house upon a rock:*

*And the rain descended, and the floods came, and the winds blew, and beat upon
that house; and it fell not: for it was founded upon a rock.*

*And every one that heareth these sayings of Mine, and doeth them not, shall be
likened unto a foolish man, which built his house upon the sand:*

*And the rain descended, and the floods came, and the winds blew, and beat upon
that house; and it fell, and great was the fall of it.*

—MATT. vii. 21-27.

OUR Divine Teacher, having declared the whole counsel of God
with regard to the way of salvation, and observed the chief
hindrances of those who desire to walk therein, now closes the
whole with these weighty words; thereby, as it were, setting His
seal to His prophecy, and impressing His whole authority on
what He had delivered, that it might stand firm to all generations.

2. For thus saith the Lord, that none may ever conceive there
is any other way than this, 'Not every one that saith unto Me,
Lord, Lord, shall enter into the kingdom of heaven; but he that
doeth the will of My Father which is in heaven. Many will say

to Me in that day, Lord, Lord, have we not prophesied in Thy name? and in Thy name have cast out devils? and in Thy name done many wonderful works? And then will I profess unto them, I never knew you: depart from Me, ye that work iniquity. Therefore, everyone that heareth these sayings of Mine and doeth them not, shall be likened unto a foolish man, which built his house upon the sand: and the rain descended, and the floods came, and the winds blew, and beat upon that house; and it fell: and great was the fall of it.'

3. I design, in the following discourse, first, to consider the case of him who thus builds his house upon the sand: secondly, to show the wisdom of him who builds upon a rock: and, thirdly, to conclude with a practical application.

I. 1. And, first, I am to consider the case of him who builds his house upon the sand. It is concerning him our Lord saith, 'Not every one that saith unto Me, Lord, Lord, shall enter into the kingdom of heaven.' And this is a decree which cannot pass; which standeth fast for ever and ever. It therefore imports us in the highest degree, throughly to understand the force of these words. Now, what are we to understand by that expression, 'That saith unto Me, Lord, Lord'? It undoubtedly means, *that thinks of going to heaven by any other way than that which I have now described.* It therefore implies (to begin at the lowest point) all good words, all verbal religion. It includes whatever creeds we may rehearse, whatever professions of faith we make, whatever number of prayers we may repeat, whatever thanksgivings we read or say to God. We may speak good of His name, and declare His lovingkindness to the children of men. We may be talking of all His mighty acts, and telling of His salvation from day to day. By comparing spiritual things with spiritual, we may show the meaning of the oracles of God. We may explain the mysteries of His kingdom, which have been hid from the beginning of the world. We may speak with the tongue of angels, rather than men, concerning the deep things of God. We may proclaim to sinners, 'Behold the Lamb of God, who taketh away the sin of the world!' Yea, we may do this with such a measure of the power of God, and such demonstration of His

Spirit, as to save many souls from death, and hide a multitude of sins. And yet it is very possible, all this may be no more than saying, 'Lord, Lord.' After I have thus successfully preached to others, still I myself may be a castaway. I may, in the hand of God, snatch many souls from hell, and yet drop into it when I have done. I may bring many others to the kingdom of heaven and yet myself never enter there. Reader, if God hath ever blessed my word to *thy* soul, pray that He may be merciful to *me* a sinner!

2. The saying, 'Lord, Lord,' may, secondly, imply the doing no harm. We may abstain from every presumptuous sin, from every kind of outward wickedness. We may refrain from all those ways of acting or speaking which are forbidden in holy writ. We may be able to say to all those among whom we live, 'Which of you convinceth me of sin?' We may have a conscience void of any external offence, towards God and towards man. We may be clear of all uncleanness, ungodliness, and unrighteousness, as to the outward act; or (as the Apostle testifies concerning himself), 'touching the righteousness of the law,' that is, outward righteousness, 'blameless.' But yet we are not hereby justified Still this is no more than saying, 'Lord, Lord'; and if we go no farther than this, we shall never 'enter into the kingdom of heaven.'

3. The saying, 'Lord, Lord,' may imply, thirdly, many of what are usually styled good works. A man may attend the supper of the Lord, may hear abundance of excellent sermons, and omit no opportunity of partaking all the other ordinances of God. I may do good to my neighbour, deal my bread to the hungry, and cover the naked with a garment. I may be so zealous of good works as even to 'give all my goods to feed the poor.' Yea, and I may do all this with a desire to please God, and a real belief that I do please Him thereby (which is undeniably the case of those our Lord introduces, saying unto Him, 'Lord, Lord'); and still I may have no part in the glory which shall be revealed.

4. If any man marvels at this, let him acknowledge he is a stranger to the whole religion of Jesus Christ; and, in particular, to that perfect portraiture thereof which He has set before us in this discourse. For how far short is all this of that righteousness

and true holiness which He has described therein! How widely distant from that inward kingdom of heaven which is now opened in the believing soul!—which is first sown in the heart as a grain of mustard-seed, but afterwards putteth forth great branches, on which grow all the fruits of righteousness, every good temper, and word, and work.

5. Yet as clearly as He had declared this, as frequently as He had repeated, that none who have not this kingdom of God within them shall enter into the kingdom of heaven; our Lord well knew, that many would not receive this saying, and therefore confirms it yet again: 'Many' (saith He: not one; not a few only; it is not a rare or an uncommon case) 'shall say unto Me in that day,' not only, We have said many prayers; We have spoken Thy praise; We have refrained from evil; We have exercised ourselves in doing good —but, what is abundantly more than this, 'We have prophesied in Thy name; in Thy name have we cast out devils; in Thy name done many wonderful works.' 'We have prophesied,'—we have declared Thy will to mankind; we have showed sinners the way to peace and glory. And we have done this 'in Thy name,' according to the truth of Thy gospel; yea, and by Thy authority, who didst confirm the word with the Holy Ghost sent down from heaven. For in or by Thy name, by the power of Thy Word and of Thy Spirit, 'have we cast out devils'; out of the souls which they had long claimed as their own, and whereof they had full and quiet possession. 'And in Thy name,' by Thy power, not our own, 'have we done many wonderful works'; insomuch that 'even the dead heard the voice of the Son of God' speaking by us, and lived. 'And then will I profess' even 'unto them, I never knew you'; no, not then, when you were 'casting out devils in My name', even then I did not know you as My own; for your heart was not right toward God. Ye were not yourselves meek and lowly; ye were not lovers of God, and of all mankind; ye were not renewed in the image of God; ye were not holy as I am holy. 'Depart from Me, ye' who, notwithstanding all this, are 'workers of iniquity';—ἀνομία: ye are transgressors of My law, My law of holy and perfect love.

6. It is to put this beyond all possibility of contradiction, that our Lord confirms it by that apposite comparison: 'Every one,'

25

saith He, 'who heareth these sayings of Mine, and doeth them not, shall be likened unto a foolish man, which built his house upon the sand. And the rain descended, and the floods came, and the winds blew, and beat upon that house'—as they will surely do, sooner or later, upon every soul of man; even the floods of outward affliction, or inward temptation; the storms of pride, anger, fear, or desire—'and it fell: and great was the fall of it'; so that it perished for ever and ever. Such must be the portion of all who rest in anything short of that religion which is above described. And the greater will their fall be, because they 'heard those sayings,' and 'yet did them not.'

II. 1. I am, secondly, to show the wisdom of him that doeth them, that buildeth his house upon a rock. He indeed is wise, 'who doeth the will of My Father which is in heaven.' He is truly wise, whose 'righteousness exceeds the righteousness of the Scribes and Pharisees.' He is poor in spirit; knowing himself even as also he is known. He sees and feels all his sin, and all his guilt, till it is washed away by the atoning blood. He is conscious of his lost estate, of the wrath of God abiding on him, and of his utter inability to help himself, till he is filled with peace and joy in the Holy Ghost. He is meek and gentle, patient toward all men, never 'returning evil for evil, or railing for railing, but contrariwise blessing,' till he overcomes evil with good. His soul is athirst for nothing on earth, but only for God, the living God. He has bowels of love for all mankind, and is ready to lay down his life for his enemies. He loves the Lord his God with all his heart, and with all his mind, and soul, and strength. He alone shall enter into the kingdom of heaven, who, in this spirit, doeth good unto all men; and who, being for this cause despised and rejected of men, being hated, reproached, and persecuted, rejoices and is 'exceeding glad,' knowing in whom he hath believed, and being assured these light, momentary afflictions will 'work out for him an eternal weight of glory.'

2. How truly wise is this man! He knows himself: an ever-lasting spirit, which came forth from God, and was sent down into an house of clay, not to do his own will, but the will of Him that sent him. He knows the world: the place in which he is to

pass a few days or years, not as an inhabitant, but as a stranger and sojourner, in his way to the everlasting habitations; and accordingly he uses the world as not abusing it, and as knowing the fashion of it passes away. He knows God: his Father and his Friend, the parent of all good, the centre of the spirits of all flesh, the sole happiness of all intelligent beings. He sees, clearer than the light of the noon-day sun, that this is the end of man, to glorify Him who made him for Himself, and to love and enjoy Him for ever. And with equal clearness he sees the means to that end, to the enjoyment of God in glory; even now to know, to love, to imitate God, and to believe in Jesus Christ whom He hath sent.

3. He is a wise man, even in God's account; for 'he buildeth his house upon a rock'; upon the Rock of Ages, the everlasting Rock, the Lord Jesus Christ. Fitly is He so called: for He changeth not: He is 'the same yesterday, and to-day, and for ever.' To Him both the men of God of old, and the Apostle citing His words, bear witness: 'Thou, Lord, in the beginning hast laid the foundation of the earth; and the heavens are the works of Thine hands. They shall perish; but Thou remainest: and they all shall wax old as doth a garment; and as a vesture shalt Thou fold them up, and they shall be changed: but Thou art the same, and Thy years shall not fail' (Heb. i. 10-12). Wise, therefore, is the man who buildeth on Him; who layeth Him for his only foundation; who builds only upon His blood and right-eousness, upon what He hath done and suffered for us. On this corner-stone he fixes his faith, and rests the whole weight of his soul upon it. He is taught of God to say, 'Lord, I have sinned! I deserve the nethermost hell; but I am justified freely by Thy grace, through the redemption that is in Jesus Christ; and the life I now live, I live by faith in Him, who loved me, and gave Himself for me. The life I now live; namely, a divine, heavenly life; a life which is hid with Christ in God. I now live, even in the flesh, a life of love; of pure love both to God and man; a life of holiness and happiness; praising God, and doing all things to His glory.'

4. Yet, let not such an one think that he shall not see war any more; that he is now out of the reach of temptation. It still

remains for God to prove the grace He hath given: he shall be tried as gold in the fire. He shall be tempted not less than they who know not God: perhaps abundantly more; for Satan will not fail to try to the uttermost those whom he is not able to destroy. Accordingly, 'the rain' will impetuously descend; only at such times and in such a manner as seems good, not to the prince of the power of the air, but to Him 'whose kindgom ruleth over all.' 'The floods,' or torrents, will come; they will lift up their waves and rage horribly. But to them also, the Lord that sitteth above the water-floods, that remaineth a King for ever, will say, 'Hitherto shall ye come, and no farther: here shall your proud waves be stayed.' 'The winds will blow, and beat upon that house,' as though they would tear it up from the foundation: but they cannot prevail: it falleth not; for it is founded upon a rock. He buildeth on Christ by faith and love; therefore, he shall not be cast down. He 'shall not fear though the earth be moved, and though the hills be carried into the midst of the sea.' 'Though the waters thereof rage and swell, and the mountains shake at the tempest of the same'; still he 'dwelleth under the defence of the Most High, and is safe under the shadow of the Almighty.'

III. 1. How nearly then does it concern every child of man, practically to apply these things to himself; diligently to examine on what foundation he builds, whether on a rock or on the sand! How deeply are *you* concerned to inquire, 'What is the foundation of *my* hope? Whereon do I build my expectation of entering into the kingdom of heaven? Is it not built on the sand? upon my *orthodoxy*, or right opinions, which, by a gross abuse of words, I have called *faith*? upon my having a set of notions, suppose more rational or scriptural than others have?' Alas! what madness is this! Surely this is building on the sand, or, rather, on the froth of the sea! Say, I am convinced of this: 'Am I not, again, building my hope on what is equally unable to support it? Perhaps on my belonging to "so excellent a Church; reformed after the true Scripture model; blessed with the purest doctrine, the most primitive Liturgy, the most apostolical form of government!"' These are, doubtless, so many reasons for praising God, as they may be so many helps to holiness; but they are not holiness itself: and if they are separate from it, they will profit me nothing; nay, they will leave me the more without excuse, and exposed to the greater damnation. Therefore, if I build my hope upon this foundation, I am still building upon the sand.

2. You cannot, you dare not, rest here. Upon what next will you build your hope of salvation?—upon your innocence? upon your doing no harm? your not wronging or hurting any one? Well; allow this plea to be true. You are just in all your dealings: you are a downright honest man; you pay every man his own; you neither cheat nor extort; you act fairly with all mankind; and you have a conscience towards God; you do not live in any known sin. Thus far is well: but still it is not the thing. You may go thus far, and yet never come to heaven. When all this harmlessness flows from a right principle, it is the *least part* of the religion of Christ. But in you it does not flow from a right principle, and therefore is no part at all of religion. So that in grounding your hope of salvation on this, you are still building upon the sand.

3. Do you go farther yet? Do you add to the doing no harm, the attending all the ordinances of God? Do you, at all opportunities, partake of the Lord's supper? use public and private prayer? fast often? hear and search the Scriptures, and meditate thereon? These things, likewise, ought you to have done, from the time you first set your face towards heaven. Yet these things also are nothing, being alone. They are nothing without 'the weightier matters of the law.' And those you have forgotten; at least, you experience them not: faith, mercy, and the love of God; holiness of heart; heaven opened in the soul. Still, therefore, you build upon the sand.

4. Over and above all this, are you zealous of good works? Do you, as you have time, do good to all men? Do you feed the hungry, and clothe the naked, and visit the fatherless and widow in their affliction? Do you visit those that are sick? relieve them that are in prison? Is any a stranger, and you take him in? Friend, come up higher! Do you 'prophesy' in the 'name 'of Christ? Do you preach the truth as it is in Jesus? And does the influence of His Spirit attend your word, and make it the power of God

unto Salvation? Does He enable you to bring sinners from darkness to light, from the power of Satan unto God? Then go and learn what thou hast so often taught, 'By grace are ye saved through faith'; 'Not by works of righteousness which we have done, but of His own mercy He saveth us.' Learn to hang naked upon the cross of Christ, counting all thou hast done but dung and dross! Apply to Him just in the spirit of the dying thief, of the harlot with her seven devils! else thou art still on the sand; and, after saving others, thou wilt lose thy own soul.

5. Lord, increase my faith, if I now believe! else, give me faith, though but as a grain of mustard-seed!—But 'what doth it profit, if a man say he hath faith, and have not works? Can' that 'faith save him'? O no! That faith which hath not works, which doth not produce both inward and outward holiness, which does not stamp the whole image of God on the heart, and purify us as He is pure; that faith which does not produce the whole of the religion described in the foregoing chapters, is not the faith of the gospel, not the Christian faith, not the faith which leads to glory. O beware of this, above all other snares of the devil,—of resting on unholy, unsaving faith! If thou layest stress on this, thou art lost for ever: thou still buildest thy house upon the sand. When 'the rain descends, and the floods come,' it will surely fall, 'and great will be the fall of it.'

6. Now, therefore, build thou upon a rock. By the grace of God, know thyself. Know and feel that thou wast shapen in wickedness, and in sin did thy mother conceive thee; and that thou thyself hast been heaping sin upon sin, ever since thou couldest discern good from evil. Own thyself guilty of eternal death; and renounce all hope of ever being able to save thyself. Be it all thy hope, to be washed in His blood, and purified by His Spirit, 'who Himself bore' all 'thy sins in His own body upon the tree.' And if thou knowest He hath taken away thy sins, so much the more abase thyself before Him, in a continual sense of thy total dependence on Him for every good thought, and word, and work, and of thy utter inability to all good unless He 'water thee every moment.'

7. Now weep for your sins, and mourn after God, till He turns your heaviness into joy. And even then weep with them

that weep; and for them that weep not for themselves. Mourn for the sins and miseries of mankind; and see, but just before your eyes, the immense ocean of eternity, without a bottom or a shore, which has already swallowed up millions of millions of men, and is gaping to devour them that yet remain! See here, the house of God eternal in the heavens! there, hell and destruction without a covering!—and thence learn the importance of every moment, which just appears, and is gone for ever!

8. Now add to your seriousness, meekness of wisdom. Hold an even scale as to all your passions, but in particular, as to anger, sorrow, and fear. Calmly acquiesce in whatsoever is the will of God Learn in every state wherein you are, therewith to be content. Be mild to the good: be gentle toward all men; but especially toward the evil and the unthankful. Beware, not only of outward expressions of anger, such as calling thy brother, *Raca*, or *Thou fool*; but of every inward emotion contrary to love, though it go no farther than the heart. Be angry at sin, as an affront offered to the Majesty of heaven; but love the sinner still: like our Lord, who 'looked round about upon the Pharisees with anger, being grieved for the hardness of their hearts.' He was grieved at the sinners, angry at sin. Thus be thou 'angry, and sin not'!

9. Now do thou hunger and thirst, not for 'the meat that perisheth, but for that which endureth unto everlasting life'. Trample under foot the world, and the things of the world; all these riches, honours, pleasures. What is the world to thee? Let the dead bury their dead; but follow thou after the image of God. And beware of quenching that blessed thirst, if it is already excited in thy soul, by what is vulgarly called religion; a poor, dull farce, a religion of form, of outside show, which leaves the heart still cleaving to the dust, as earthly and sensual as ever. Let nothing satisfy thee but the power of godliness, but a religion that is spirit and life; the dwelling in God and God in thee; the being an inhabitant of eternity; the entering in by the blood of sprinkling 'within the veil,' and 'sitting in heavenly places with Christ Jesus'!

10. Now, seeing thou canst do all things through Christ strengthening thee, be merciful as thy Father in heaven is merci-

ful! Love thy neighbour as thyself! Love friends and enemies as thy own soul: and let thy love be long-suffering and patient towards all men. Let it be kind, soft, benign; inspiring thee with the most amiable sweetness, and the most fervent and tender affection. Let it rejoice in the truth wheresoever it is found; the truth that is after godliness. Enjoy whatsoever brings glory to God, and promotes peace and good-will among men. In love, cover all things: of the dead and the absent speaking nothing but good; believe all things which may any way tend to clear your neighbour's character; hope all things in his favour; and endure all things, triumphing over all opposition: for true love never faileth, in time or in eternity.

11. Now be thou pure in heart; purified through faith from every unholy affection; 'cleansing thyself from all filthiness of flesh and spirit, and perfecting holiness in the fear of God.' Being, through the power of His grace, purified from pride, by deep poverty of spirit; from anger, from every unkind or turbulent passion, by meekness and mercifulness; from every desire but to please and enjoy God, by hunger and thirst after righteousness; now love the Lord thy God with all thy heart, and with all thy strength!

12. In a word: let thy religion be the religion of the heart. Let it lie deep in thy inmost soul. Be thou little, and base, and mean, and vile (beyond what words can express) in thy own eyes; amazed and humbled to the dust by the love of God which is in Christ Jesus. Be serious. Let the whole stream of thy thoughts, words, and actions flow from the deepest conviction that thou standest on the edge of the great gulf, thou and all the children of men, just ready to drop in, either into everlasting glory or everlasting burnings! Let thy soul be filled with mildness, gentleness, patience, long-suffering towards all men; at the same time that all which is in thee is athirst for God, the living God, longing to awake up after His likeness and to be satisfied with it! Be thou a lover of God and of all mankind! In this spirit do and suffer all things! Thus show thy faith by thy works; thus 'do the will of thy Father which is in heaven'! And, as sure as thou now walkest with God on earth, thou shalt also reign with Him in glory!

SERMON XXIX

THE ORIGINAL, NATURE, PROPERTY, AND USE OF THE LAW

Wherefore the law is holy, and the commandment holy, and just, and good.
—ROM. vii. 12.

PERHAPS there are few subjects within the whole compass of religion so little understood as this. The reader of this Epistle is usually told, by 'the law' St. Paul means the Jewish law; and so, apprehending himself to have no concern therewith, passes on without farther thought about it. Indeed some are not satisfied with this account; but observing the Epistle is directed to the Romans, thence infer that the Apostle in the beginning of this chapter alludes to the old Roman law. But as they have no more concern with this, than with the ceremonial law of Moses, so they spend not much thought on what they suppose is occasionally mentioned barely to illustrate another thing.

2. But a careful observer of the Apostle's discourse will not be content with these light explications of it. And the more he weighs the words, the more convinced he will be, that St. Paul, by 'the law' mentioned in this chapter, does not mean either the ancient law of Rome, or the ceremonial law of Moses. This will clearly appear to all who attentively consider the tenor of his discourse. He begins the chapter, 'Know ye not, brethren (for I speak to them that know the law),' to them who have been instructed therein from their youth, 'that the law hath dominion over a man as long as he liveth?' (What! the law of Rome only, or the ceremonial law? No, surely; but the moral law.) 'For,' to give a plain instance, 'the woman which hath a husband is bound by the ' moral 'law to her husband so long as he liveth; but if the husband be dead, she is loosed from the law of her husband. So then if, while her husband liveth, she be married to another man, she shall be called an adulteress: but if her husband be dead, she is free from that law; so that she is no adulteress, though she

be married to another man.' From this particular instance the Apostle proceeds to draw that general conclusion: 'Wherefore, my brethren,' by a plain parity of reason, 'ye also are become dead to the law,' the whole Mosaic institution, by the body of Christ,' offered for you, and bringing you under a new dispensation: 'That ye should' without any blame 'be married to another, even to Him who is raised from the dead'; and hath thereby given proof of His authority to make the change; 'that we should bring forth fruit unto God.' And this we can do now, whereas before we could not: 'for when we were in the flesh' —under the power of the flesh, that is, of corrupt nature, which was necessarily the case till we knew the power of Christ's resurrection, 'the motions of sins, which were by the law'— which were shown and inflamed by the Mosaic law, not conquered, 'did work in our members'—broke out various ways, 'to bring forth fruit unto death.' 'But now we are delivered from the law'; from that whole moral, as well as ceremonial economy; 'that being dead whereby we were held'—that entire institution being now as it were dead, and having no more authority over us than the husband, when dead, hath over his wife: 'That we should serve Him'—who died for us and rose again, 'in newness of spirit'—in a new spiritual dispensation; 'and not in the oldness of the letter'—with a bare outward service, according to the letter of the Mosaic institution (verses 1-6).

3. The Apostle, having gone thus far in proving that the Christian had set aside the Jewish dispensation, and that the moral law itself, though it could never pass away, yet stood on a different foundation from what it did before,—now stops to propose and answer an objection: 'What shall we say then? Is the law sin?' So some might infer from a misapprehension of those words, 'the motions of sins, which were by the law.' 'God forbid!' saith the Apostle, that we should say so. Nay, the law is an irreconcilable enemy to sin; searching it out, wherever it is. 'I had not known sin, but by the law: for I had not known lust,' evil desire, to be sin, 'except the law had said, Thou shalt not covet' (verse 7). After opening this farther, in the four following verses, he subjoins this general conclusion, with regard more especially to the moral law, from which the preceding instance

was taken: 'Wherefore the law is holy, and the commandment holy, and just, and good.'

4. In order to explain and enforce these deep words, so little regarded, because so little understood, I shall endeavour to show, first, the original of this law; secondly, the nature thereof; thirdly, the properties—that it is holy, and just, and good; and, fourthly, the uses of it.

I. 1. I shall, first, endeavour to show the original of the moral law, often called 'the law,' by way of eminence. Now this is not, as some may have possibly imagined, of so late an institution as the time of Moses. Noah declared it to men long before that time, and Enoch before him. But we may trace its original higher still, even beyond the foundation of the world; to that period, unknown indeed to men, but doubtless enrolled in the annals of eternity, when 'the morning stars' first 'sang together,' being newly called into existence. It pleased the great Creator to make these, His first-born sons, intelligent beings, that they might know Him that created them. For this end He endued them with understanding, to discern truth from falsehood, good from evil; and, as a necessary result of this, with liberty, a capacity of choosing the one and refusing the other. By this they were, likewise, enabled to offer Him a free and willing service; a service rewardable in itself, as well as most acceptable to their gracious Master.

2. To employ all the faculties which He had given them, particularly their understanding and liberty, He gave them a law, a complete model of all truth, so far as is intelligible to a finite being; and of all good, so far as angelic minds were capable of embracing it. It was also the design of their beneficent Governor herein to make way for a continual increase of their happiness; seeing every instance of obedience to that law would both add to the perfection of their nature, and entitle them to an higher reward, which the righteous Judge would give in its season.

3. In like manner, when God, in His appointed time, had created a new order of intelligent beings, when He had raised man from the dust of the earth, breathed into him the breath of life, and caused him to become a living soul endued with power

to choose good or evil; he gave to this free, intelligent creature the same law as to His first-born children,—not wrote, indeed, upon tables of stone, or any corruptible substance, but engraven on his heart by the finger of God; wrote in the inmost spirit both of men and of angels; to the intent it might never be far off, never hard to be understood, but always at hand, and always shining with clear light, even as the sun in the midst of heaven.

4. Such was the original of the law of God. With regard to man, it was coeval with his nature; but with regard to the elder sons of God, it shone in its full splendour 'or ever the mountains were brought forth, or the earth and the round world were made.' But it was not long before man rebelled against God, and by breaking this glorious law, wellnigh effaced it out of his heart; the eyes of his understanding being darkened in the same measure as his soul was 'alienated from the life of God.' And yet God did not despise the work of His own hands; but, being reconciled to man through the Son of His love, He, in some measure, re-inscribed the law on the heart of His dark, sinful creature, 'He' again 'showed thee, O man, what is good,' although not as in the beginning, 'even to do justly, and to love mercy, and to walk humbly with thy God.'

5. And this He showed, not only to our first parents, but like-wise to all their posterity, by 'that true light which enlightens every man that cometh into the world.' But, notwithstanding this light, all flesh had, in process of time, 'corrupted their way before Him'; till He chose out of mankind a peculiar people, to whom He gave a more perfect knowledge of His law: and the heads of this, because they were slow of understanding, He wrote on two tables of stone, which He commanded the fathers to teach their children, through all succeeding generations.

6. And thus it is, that the law of God is now made known to them that know not God. They hear, with the hearing of the ear, the things that were written aforetime for our instruction. But this does not suffice; they cannot, by this means, comprehend the height, and depth, and length, and breadth thereof. God alone can reveal this by His Spirit. And so He does to all that truly believe, in consequence of that gracious promise made to all the Israel of God: 'Behold, the days come, saith the Lord, that I will

make a new covenant with the house of Israel. And this shall be the covenant that I will make; I will put My law in their inward parts, and write it in their hearts; and I will be their God, and they shall be My people' (Jer. xxxi. 31, &c.).

II. 1. The nature of that law which was originally given to angels in heaven and man in paradise, and which God has so mercifully promised to write afresh in the hearts of all true believers, was the second thing I proposed to show. In order to which, I would first observe, that although the 'law' and the 'commandment' are sometimes differently taken (the commandment meaning but a part of the law), yet in the text they are used as equivalent terms, implying one and the same thing. But we cannot understand here, either by one or the other, the ceremonial law. It is not the ceremonial law, whereof the Apostle says, in the words above recited 'I had not known sin, but by the law': this is too plain to need a proof. Neither is it the ceremonial law which saith, in the words immediately subjoined, 'Thou shalt not covet.' Therefore the ceremonial law has no place in the present question.

2. Neither can we understand by 'the law' mentioned in the text the Mosaic dispensation. It is true, the word is sometimes so understood; as when the Apostle says, speaking to the Galatians (iii. 17), 'The covenant that was confirmed before'; namely, with Abraham, the father of the faithful, 'the law,' that is, the Mosaic dispensation, 'which was four hundred and thirty years after, cannot disannul.' But it cannot be understood so in the text; for the Apostle never bestows so high commendations as these upon that imperfect and shadowy dispensation. He nowhere affirms the Mosaic to be a spiritual law; or, that it is holy, and just, and good. Neither is it true, that God will write that law in the hearts of those whose iniquities He remembers no more. It remains, that 'the law,' eminently so termed, is no other than the moral law.

3. Now, this law is an incorruptible picture of the High and Holy ONE that inhabiteth eternity. It is He whom, in His essence, no man hath seen, or can see, made visible to men and angels. It is the face of God unveiled; God manifested to His

creatures as they are able to bear it; manifested to give, and not to destroy, life—that they may see God and live. It is the heart of God disclosed to man. Yea, in some sense, we may apply to this law what the Apostle says of His Son: it is ἀπαύγασμα τῆς δόξης, καὶ χαρακτὴρ τῆς ὑποστάσεως αὐτοῦ—*the streaming forth* or *outbeaming of His glory, the express image of His person.*

4. 'If virtue,' said the ancient Heathen, 'could assume such a shape as that we could behold her with our eyes, what wonderful love would she excite in us!' If virtue could do this! It is done already. The law of God is all virtues in one, in such a shape as to be beheld with open face by all those whose eyes God hath enlightened. What is the law but divine virtue and wisdom assuming a visible form? What is it but the original ideas of truth and good, which were lodged in the uncreated mind from eternity, now drawn forth and clothed with such a vehicle as to appear even to human understanding.

5. If we survey the law of God in another point of view, it is supreme, unchangeable reason; it is unalterable rectitude; it is the everlasting fitness of all things that are or ever were created. I am sensible, what a shortness, and even impropriety, there is, in these and all other human expressions, when we endeavour by these faint pictures to shadow out the deep things of God. Nevertheless, we have no better, indeed no other way, during this our infant state of existence. As we now 'know' but 'in part,' so we are constrained to 'prophesy,' that is, speak of the things of God, 'in part' also. 'We cannot order our speech by reason of darkness,' while we are in this house of clay. While I am 'a child,' I must 'speak as a child': but I shall soon 'put away childish things'; for 'when that which is perfect is come, that which is in part shall be done away.'

6. But to return. The law of God (speaking after the manner of men) is a copy of the eternal mind, a transcript of the divine nature; yea, it is the fairest offspring of the everlasting Father, the brightest efflux of His essential wisdom, the visible beauty of the Most High. It is the delight and wonder of cherubim and seraphim, and all the company of heaven, and the glory and joy of every wise believer, every well-instructed child of God upon earth.

III. 1. Such is the nature of the ever-blessed law of God. I am, in the third place, to show the properties of it:—not all; for that would exceed the wisdom of an angel; but those only which are mentioned in the text. These are three: it is holy, just, and good. And, first, the law is holy.

2. In this expression the Apostle does not appear to speak of its effects, but rather of its nature: as St. James, speaking of the same thing under another name, says, 'The wisdom from above' (which is no other than this law, written in our heart) 'is first pure' (iii. 17); ἀγνή,—*chaste, spotless*; eternally and essentially holy. And, consequently, when it is transcribed into the life, as well as the soul, it is (as the same Apostle terms it, i 27) θρησκεία καθαρὰ καὶ ἀμίαντος,—*pure religion and undefiled*; or the pure, clean, unpolluted worship of God.

3. It is, indeed, in the highest degree, pure, chaste, clean, holy. Otherwise it could not be the immediate offspring, and much less the express resemblance, of God, who is essential holiness. It is pure from all sin, clean and unspotted from any touch of evil. It is a chaste virgin, incapable of any defilement, of any mixture with that which is unclean or unholy. It has no fellowship with sin of any kind: for 'what communion hath light with darkness?' As sin is, in its very nature, enmity to God, so His law is enmity to sin.

4. Therefore it is that the Apostle rejects with such abhorrence that blasphemous supposition, that the law of God is either sin itself, or the cause of sin. God forbid that we should suppose it is the cause of sin, because it is the discoverer of it; because it detects the hidden things of darkness, and drags them out into open day. It is true, by this means (as the Apostle observes, Rom. vii. 13), 'sin appears to be sin.' All its disguises are torn away, and it appears in its native deformity. It is true likewise, that 'sin, by the commandment, becomes exceeding sinful': being now committed against light and knowledge, being stripped even of the poor plea of ignorance, it loses its excuse, as well as disguise, and becomes far more odious both to God and man. Yea, and it is true, that 'sin worketh death by that which is good'; which in itself is pure and holy. When it is dragged out to light, it rages the more: when it is restrained, it bursts out

with great violence. Thus the Apostle (speaking in the person
of one who was convinced of sin, but not yet delivered from it),
'Sin, taking occasion by the commandment' detecting and
endeavouring to restrain it, disdained the restraint, and so much
the more 'wrought in me all manner of concupiscence' (verse 8);
all manner of foolish and hurtful desire, which that commandment sought to restrain. Thus, 'when the commandment came,
sin revived' (verse 9): it fretted and raged the more. But this is
no stain on the commandment. Though it is abused, it cannot be
defiled. This only proves that 'the heart of man is desperately
wicked.' But 'the law' of God 'is holy' still.

5. And it is, secondly, just. It renders to all their due. It
prescribes exactly what is right, precisely what ought to be done,
said, or thought, both with regard to the Author of our being,
with regard to ourselves, and with regard to every creature which
He has made. It is adapted, in all respects to the nature of things,
of the whole universe, and every individual. It is suited to all the
circumstances of each, and to all their mutual relations, whether
such as have existed from the beginning, or such as commenced
in any following period. It is exactly agreeable to the fitnesses of
things, whether essential or accidental. It clashes with none of
these in any degree; nor is ever unconnected with them. If the
word be taken in that sense, there is nothing arbitrary in the law
of God. Although still the whole and every part thereof is
totally dependent upon His will; so that, 'Thy will be done,' is
the supreme, universal law both in earth and heaven.

6. 'But is the will of God the cause of His law? Is His will the
original of right and wrong? Is a thing *therefore* right, because
God wills it? or does He will it because it is right?'

I fear this celebrated question is more curious than useful.
And perhaps in the manner it is usually treated of, it does not so
well consist with the regard that is due from a creature to the
Creator and Governor of all things. It is hardly decent for man
to call the supreme God to give an account to him. Nevertheless,
with awe and reverence we may speak a little. The Lord pardon
us if we speak amiss!

7. It seems, then, that the whole difficulty arises from considering God's will as distinct from God: otherwise it vanishes

away. For none can doubt but God is the cause of the law of God. But the will of God is God Himself. It is God considered as willing thus or thus. Consequently, to say that the will of God, or that God Himself, is the cause of the law, is one and the same thing.

8. Again: If the law, the immutable rule of right and wrong, depends upon the nature and fitnesses of things, and on their essential relations to each other (I do not say, their eternal relations; because the eternal relation of things existing in time, is little less than a contradiction); if, I say, this depends on the nature and relations of things, then it must depend on God, or the will of God; because those things themselves, with all their relations, are the works of His hands. By His will, 'for His pleasure' alone, they all 'are and were created.'

9. And yet it may be granted (which is probably all that a considerate person would contend for), that in every particular case, God wills this or this (suppose, that men should honour their parents) because it is right, agreeable to the fitness of things, to the relation wherein they stand.

10. The law, then, is right and just concerning all things. And it is good as well as just. This we may easily infer from the fountain whence it flowed. For what was this, but the goodness of God? What but goodness alone inclined Him to impart that divine copy of Himself to the holy angels? To what else can we impute His bestowing upon man the same transcript of His own nature? And what but tender love constrained Him afresh to manifest His will to fallen man—either to Adam, or any of his seed, who like him were 'come short of the glory of God'? Was it not mere love that moved Him to publish His law after the understandings of men were darkened? and to send His prophets to declare that law to the blind, thoughtless children of men? Doubtless His goodness it was which raised up Enoch and Noah to be preachers of righteousness; which caused Abraham, His friend, and Isaac, and Jacob, to bear witness to His truth. It was His goodness alone, which, when 'darkness had covered the earth, and thick darkness the people,' gave a written law to Moses, and, through Him, to the nation whom He had chosen. It was love which explained these living oracles by David and

26

all the prophets that followed; until, when the fullness of time was come, He sent His only-begotten Son, 'not to destroy the law, but to fulfil,' confirm every jot and tittle thereof; till, having wrote it in the hearts of all His children, and put all His enemies under His feet, 'He shall deliver up' His mediatorial 'kingdom to the Father, that God may be all in all.'

11. And this law, which the goodness of God gave at first, and has preserved through all ages, is, like the fountain from whence it springs, full of goodness and benignity: it is mild and kind; it is, as the Psalmist expresses it, 'sweeter than honey and the honey-comb.' It is winning and amiable. It includes 'whatsoever things are lovely or of good report. If there be any virtue, if there be any praise' before God and His holy angels, they are all comprised in this; wherein are hid all the treasures of the divine wisdom, and knowledge, and love.

12. And it is good in its effects, as well as in its nature. As the tree is, so are its fruits. The fruits of the law of God written in the heart are 'righteousness, and peace, and assurance for ever.' Or rather, the law itself is righteousness, filling the soul with a peace which passeth all understanding, and causing us to rejoice evermore, in the testimony of a good conscience toward God. It is not so properly a pledge, as 'an earnest, of our inheritance,' being a part of the purchased possession. It is God made manifest in our flesh, and bringing with Him eternal life; assuring us by that pure and perfect love, that we are 'sealed unto the day of redemption'; that He will 'spare us as a man spareth his own son that serveth him,' 'in the day when He maketh up His jewels'; and that there remaineth for us 'a crown of glory which fadeth not away.'

IV. 1. It remains only to show, in the fourth and last place, the uses of the law. And the first use of it, without question, is, to convince the world of sin. This is, indeed, the peculiar work of the Holy Ghost; who can work it without any means at all, or by whatever means it pleaseth Him, however insufficient in themselves, or even improper, to produce such an effect. And, accordingly, some there are whose hearts have been broken in pieces in a moment, either in sickness or in health, without any visible cause, or any outward means whatever; and others (one in an age) have been awakened to a sense of the 'wrath of God abiding on them,' by hearing that 'God was in Christ, reconciling the world unto Himself.' But it is the ordinary method of the Spirit of God to convict sinners by the law. It is this which, being set home on the conscience, generally breaketh the rocks in pieces. It is more especially this part of the word of God which is ζῶν καὶ ἐνεργής, —*quick and powerful*, full of life and energy, 'and sharper than any two-edged sword.' This, in the hand of God, and of those whom He hath sent, pierces through all the folds of a deceitful heart, and 'divides asunder even the soul and the spirit'; yea, as it were, the very 'joints and marrow.' By this is the sinner discovered to himself. All his fig-leaves are torn away, and he sees that he is 'wretched, and poor, and miserable, and blind, and naked.' The law flashes conviction on every side. He feels himself a mere sinner. He has nothing to pay. His 'mouth is stopped,' and he stands 'guilty before God.'

2. To slay the sinner is, then, the first use of the law; to destroy the life and strength wherein he trusts, and convince him that he is dead while he liveth; not only under the sentence of death, but actually dead unto God, void of all spiritual life, 'dead in trespasses and sins.' The second use of it is, to bring him unto life, unto Christ, that he may live. It is true, in performing both these offices, it acts the part of a severe schoolmaster. It drives us by force, rather than draws us by love. And yet love is the spring of all. It is the spirit of love which, by this painful means, tears away our confidence in the flesh, which leaves us no broken reed whereon to trust, and so constrains the sinner, stripped of all, to cry out in the bitterness of his soul, or groan in the depth of his heart,

> I give up every plea beside,—
> Lord, I am damn'd, but Thou hast died.

3. The third use of the law is, to keep us alive. It is the grand means whereby the blessed Spirit prepares the believer for larger communications of the life of God.

I am afraid this great and important truth is little understood, not only by the world, but even by many whom God hath taken out of the world, who are real children of God by faith. Many of these lay it down as an unquestioned truth, that when we come to Christ, we have done with the law; and that, in this sense, 'Christ is the end of the law to every one that believeth.' 'The end of the law': so He is, 'for righteousness,' for justification, 'to every one that believeth.' Herein the law is at an end. It justifies none, but only brings them to Christ; who is also, in another respect, the end or scope of the law—the point at which it continually aims. But when it has brought us to Him, it has yet a farther office, namely, to keep us with Him. For it is continually exciting all believers, the more they see of its height, and depth, and length, and breadth, to exhort one another so much the more,—

> Closer and closer let us cleave
> To His beloved embrace;
> Expect His fullness to receive,
> And grace to answer grace.

4. Allowing then, that every believer has done with the law, as it means the Jewish ceremonial law, or the entire Mosaic dispensation (for these Christ hath taken out of the way); yea, allowing we have done with the moral law, as a means of procuring our justification; for we are 'justified freely by His grace, (through the redemption that is in Jesus'); yet, in another sense, we have not done with this law: for it is still of unspeakable use, first, in convincing us of the sin that yet remains both in our hearts and lives, and thereby keeping us close to Christ, that His blood may cleanse us every moment; secondly, in deriving strength from our Head into His living members, whereby He empowers them to do what His law commands; and, thirdly, in confirming our hope of whatsoever it commands and we have not yet attained,—of receiving grace upon grace, till we are in actual possession of the fullness of His promises.

5. How clearly does this agree with the experience of every true believer! While he cries out, 'O what love have I unto Thy law! all the day long is my study in it'; he sees daily, in that divine mirror, more and more of his own sinfulness. He sees more and more clearly, that he is still a sinner in all things—that

neither his heart nor his ways are right before God; and that every moment sends him to Christ. This shows him the meaning of what is written, 'Thou shalt make a plate of pure gold, and grave upon it, 'HOLINESS TO THE LORD. And it shall be upon Aaron's forehead' (the type of our great High-Priest), 'that Aaron may bear the iniquity of the holy things, which the children of Israel shall hallow in all their holy gifts' (so far are our prayers or holy things from atoning for the rest of our sin); 'and it shall be always upon his forehead, that they may be accepted before the Lord' (Exod. xxviii. 36, 38).

6. To explain this by a single instance: the law says, 'Thou shalt not kill'; and hereby (as our Lord teaches), forbids not only outward acts, but every unkind word or thought. Now, the more I look into this perfect law, the more I feel how far I come short of it; and the more I feel this, the more I feel my need of His blood to atone for all my sin, and of His Spirit to purify my heart, and make me 'perfect and entire, lacking nothing.'

7. Therefore I cannot spare the law one moment, no more than I can spare Christ; seeing I now want it as much to keep me to Christ, as I ever wanted it to bring me to Him. Otherwise, this 'evil heart of unbelief' would immediately 'depart from the living God.' Indeed each is continually sending me to the other —the law to Christ, and Christ to the law. On the one hand, the height and depth of the law constrain me to fly to the love of God in Christ; on the other, the love of God in Christ endears the law to me 'above gold or precious stones'; seeing I know every part of it is a gracious promise which my Lord will fulfil in its season.

8. Who art thou then, O man, that 'judgest the law, and speakest evil of the law?'—that rankest it with sin, Satan, and death, and sendest them all to hell together? The Apostle James esteemed judging or 'speaking evil of the law' so enormous a piece of wickedness, that he knew not how to aggravate the guilt of judging our brethren more, than by showing it included this. 'So now,' says he, 'thou art not a doer of the law, but a judge!' A judge of that which God hath ordained to judge thee! So thou hast set up thyself in the judgement-seat of Christ, and cast down the rule whereby He will judge the world! O take

knowledge what advantage Satan hath gained over thee; and, for the time to come, never think or speak lightly of, much less dress up as a scarecrow, this blessed instrument of the grace of God. Yea, love and value it for the sake of Him from whom it came, and of Him to whom it leads. Let it be thy glory and joy, next to the cross of Christ. Declare its praise, and make it honourable before all men.

9. And if thou art throughly convinced that it is the offspring of God, that it is the copy of all His imitable perfections, and that it is 'holy, and just, and good,' but especially to them that believe; then, instead of casting it away as a polluted thing, see that thou cleave to it more and more. Never let the law of mercy and truth, of love to God and man, of lowliness, meekness, and purity, forsake thee. 'Bind it about thy neck; write it on the table of thy heart.' Keep close to the law, if thou wilt keep close to Christ; hold it fast; let it not go. Let this continually lead thee to the atoning blood, continually confirm thy hope, till all the 'righteousness of the law is fulfilled in thee,' and thou art 'filled with all the fullness of God.''

10. And if thy Lord hath already fulfilled His word, if He hath already 'written His law in thy heart,' then 'stand fast in the liberty wherewith Christ hath made thee free.' Thou art not only made free from Jewish ceremonies, from the guilt of sin, and the fear of hell (these are so far from being the whole, that they are the least and lowest part of Christian liberty); but, what is infinitely more, from the power of sin, from serving the devil, from offending God. O stand fast in this liberty; in comparison of which, all the rest is not even worthy to be named! Stand fast in loving God with all thy heart, and serving Him with all thy strength! This is perfect freedom; thus to keep His law, and to walk in all His commandments blameless. 'Be not entangled again with the yoke of bondage.' I do not mean of Jewish bondage; nor yet of bondage to the fear of hell: these, I trust, are far from thee. But beware of being entangled again with the yoke of sin, of any inward or outward transgression of the law. Abhor sin far more than death or hell; abhor sin itself, far more than the punishment of it. Beware of the bondage of pride, of desire, of anger; of every evil temper, or word, or work. 'Look

unto Jesus'; and in order thereto, look more and more into the perfect law, 'the law of liberty'; and 'continue therein'; so shalt thou daily 'grow in grace, and in the knowledge of our Lord Jesus Christ.'

SERMON XXX

THE LAW ESTABLISHED THROUGH FAITH

DISCOURSE I

Do we then make void the law through faith? God forbid, yea, we establish the law.—ROM. iii. 31.

St. PAUL, having in the beginning of this Epistle laid down his general proposition, namely, that 'the gospel of Christ is the power of God unto salvation to every one that believeth'— the powerful means whereby God makes every believer a partaker of present and eternal salvation—goes on to show that there is no other way under heaven whereby men can be saved. He speaks particularly of salvation from the guilt of sin, which he commonly terms justification. And that all men stood in need of this, that none could plead their own innocence, he proves at large by various arguments, addressed to the Jews as well as the Heathens. Hence he infers (in the 19th verse of this chapter), 'that every mouth,' whether of Jew or Heathen, must be 'stopped' from excusing or justifying himself, 'and all the world become guilty before God.' 'Therefore,' saith he, by his own obedience, 'by the works of the law, shall no flesh be justified in His sight.' But now the righteousness of God without the law'—without our previous obedience thereto—'is manifested'; even 'the righteousness of God which is by faith of Jesus Christ unto all and upon all that believe.' 'For there is no difference'—as to their need of justification, or the manner wherein they attain it—'for all have sinned, and come short of the glory of God'; the glorious image of God wherein they were created: and all (who attain) 'are justified freely by His grace through the redemption that is in Jesus Christ; whom God hath set forth to be a propitiation through faith in His blood: that He might be just, and yet the justifier of him which believeth in Jesus'—that without any impeachment to His justice, He might show him mercy for the sake of that propitiation. 'Therefore we conclude' (which was the grand position he had undertaken to establish), 'that a man is justified by faith, without the works of the law' (verses 20-28).

2. It was easy to foresee an objection which might be made, and which has in fact been made in all ages; namely, that to say we are justified without the works of the law, is to abolish the law. The Apostle, without entering into a formal dispute, simply denies the charge. 'Do we then,' says he, 'make void the law through faith? God forbid! yea, we establish the law.'

3. The strange imagination of some, that St. Paul, when he says, 'A man is justified without the works of the law,' means only the ceremonial law, is abundantly confuted by these very words. For did St. Paul establish the ceremonial law? It is evident he did not. He did make void that law through faith, and openly avowed his doing so. It was the moral law only, of which he might truly say, We do not make void, but establish this through faith.

4. But all men are not herein of his mind. Many there are who will not agree to this. Many in all ages of the church, even among those who bore the name of Christians, have contended, that 'the faith once delivered to the saints' was designed to make void the whole law. They would no more spare the moral than the ceremonial law, but were for 'hewing,' as it were, both 'in pieces before the Lord'; vehemently maintaining, 'If you establish any law, Christ shall profit you nothing; Christ is become of no effect to you; ye are fallen from grace.'

5. But is the zeal of these men according to knowledge? Have they observed the connexion between the law and faith? and that, considering the close connexion between them, to destroy one is indeed to destroy both—that, to abolish the moral law, is, in truth, to abolish faith and the law together? as leaving no proper means, either of bringing us to faith, or of stirring up that gift of God in our soul.

6. It therefore behoves all who desire either to come to Christ, or to walk in Him whom they have received, to take heed how they 'make void the law through faith'; to secure us effectually against which, let us inquire, first, Which are the most usual ways of making 'void the law through faith'? And, secondly, how we may follow the Apostle, and by faith 'establish the law.'

I. 1. Let us, first, inquire, Which are the most usual ways of making void the law through faith? Now the way for a preacher to make it all void at a stroke, is, not to preach it at all. This is just the same thing as to blot it out of the oracles of God. More especially, when it is done with design; when it is made a rule, not to preach the law: and the very phrase, 'a preacher of the law,' is used as a term of reproach, as though it meant little less than an enemy to the gospel.

2. All this proceeds from the deepest ignorance of the nature, properties, and use of the law; and proves, that those who act thus, either know not Christ—are utter strangers to living faith —or, at least, that they are but babes in Christ, and, as such, 'unskilled in the word of righteousness.'

3. Their grand plea is this: that preaching the gospel, that is, according to their judgement, the speaking of nothing but the sufferings and merits of Christ, answers all the ends of the law. But this we utterly deny. It does not answer the very first end of the law, namely, the convincing men of sin; the awakening those who are still asleep on the brink of hell. There may have been here and there an exempt case. One in a thousand may have been awakened by the gospel: but this is no general rule: the ordinary method of God, is to convict sinners by the law, and that only. The gospel is not the means which God hath ordained, or which our Lord Himself used, for this end. We have no authority in Scripture for applying it thus, nor any ground to think it will prove effectual. Nor have we any more ground to expect this, from the nature of the thing. 'They that be whole,' as our Lord Himself observes, 'need not a physician, but they that are sick.' It is absurd, therefore to offer a physician to them that are whole or that at least imagine themselves so to be. You are first to convince them that they are sick; otherwise they will

not thank you for your labour. It is equally absurd to offer
Christ to them whose heart is whole, having never yet been broken.
It is, in the proper sense 'casting pearls before swine.' Doubtless
'they will trample them under foot'; and it is no more than you
have reason to expect, if they also 'turn again and rend you.'

4. 'But although there is no command in Scripture, to offer
Christ to the careless sinner, yet are there not scriptural prece-
dents for it?' I think not; I know not any. I believe you cannot
produce one, either from the four Evangelists, or the Acts of the
Apostles. Neither can you prove this to have been the practice of
any of the Apostles, from any passage in all their writings.

5. 'Nay, does not the Apostle Paul say, in his former Epistle to
the Corinthians, "We preach Christ crucified"? (i. 23); and in his
latter, "We preach not ourselves, but Christ Jesus the Lord"?'
(iv. 5.)

We consent to rest the cause on this issue; to tread in his steps,
to follow his example. Only preach you just as Paul preached,
and the dispute is at an end.

For although we are certain he preached Christ in as perfect a
manner as the very chief of the Apostles, yet who preached the
law more than St. Paul? Therefore he did not think the gospel
answered the same end.

6. The very first sermon of St. Paul's which is recorded, concludes in these words: 'By Him all that believe are justified from
all things, from which ye could not be justified by the law of
Moses. Beware therefore, lest that come upon you, which is
spoken of in the prophets; Behold, ye despisers, and wonder,
and perish: for I work a work in your days, a work which you
will in no wise believe, though a man declare it unto you' (Acts
xiii. 39, &c.). Now, it is manifest all this is preaching the law, in
the sense wherein you understand the term; even although
great part of, if not all, his hearers were either Jews or religious
proselytes (verse 43), and, therefore, probably many of them,
in some degree at least, convinced of sin already. He first reminds them, that they could not be justified by the law of Moses,
but only by faith in Christ; and then severely threatens them with
the judgements of God, which is, in the strongest sense, preaching
the law.

7. In his next discourse, that to the Heathens at Lystra (xiv. 15, &c.), we do not find so much as the name of Christ: the whole purport of it is, that they should 'turn from those vain idols unto the living God.' Now confess the truth. Do not you think, if you had been there, you could have preached much better than he? I should not wonder if you thought too that his *preaching so ill* occasioned his being *so ill treated*; and that his being *stoned* was a just judgement upon him for not *preaching Christ*!

8. To the jailor indeed, when 'he sprang in, and came trembling, and fell down before Paul and Silas, and said, Sirs, what must I do to be saved?' he immediately said, 'Believe on the Lord Jesus Christ' (Acts xvi. 29, &c.); and in the case of one so deeply convinced of sin, who would not have said the same? But to the men of Athens you find him speaking in a quite different manner; reproving their superstition, ignorance, and idolatry; and strongly moving them to repent, from the consideration of a future judgement, and of the resurrection from the dead (xvii. 24-31). Likewise when Felix sent for Paul, on purpose that he might 'hear him concerning the faith in Christ'; instead of preaching Christ in *your* sense (which would probably have caused the Governor either to mock or to contradict and blaspheme), 'he reasoned of righteousness, temperance and judgement to come,' till Felix (hardened as he was) 'trembled' (xxiv. 24, 25). Go thou, and tread in his steps. Preach Christ to the careless sinner, by reasoning 'of righteousness, temperance, and judgement to come'!

9. If you say, 'But he preached Christ in a different manner in his Epistles': I answer, (1) He did not there preach at all; not in that sense wherein we speak: for preaching, in our present question, means speaking before a congregation. But waiving this, I answer, (2) His Epistles are directed, not to unbelievers, such as those we are now speaking of, but 'to the saints of God,' in Rome, Corinth, Philippi, and other places. Now, unquestionably, he would speak more of Christ to these, than to those who were without God in the world. And yet, (3) Every one of these is full of the law, even the Epistles to the Romans and the Galatians; in both of which he does what you term 'preaching the law,' and that to believers, as well as unbelievers.

10. From hence it is plain, you know not what it is to preach Christ, in the sense of the Apostle. For doubtless St. Paul judged himself to be preaching Christ, both to Felix, and at Antioch, Lystra, and Athens: from whose example every thinking man must infer, that not only the declaring the love of Christ to sinners, but also the declaring that He will come from heaven in flaming fire, is, in the Apostle's sense, preaching Christ; yea, in the full scriptural meaning of the word. To preach Christ, is to preach what He hath revealed, either in the Old or New Testament; so that you are then as really preaching Christ, when you are saying, 'The wicked shall be turned into hell, and all the people that forget God,' as when you are saying, 'Behold the Lamb of God, which taketh away the sin of the world!'

11. Consider this well: that to preach Christ, is to preach all things that Christ hath spoken—all His promises; all His threatenings and commands; all that is written in His book; and then you will know how to preach Christ without making void the law.

12. 'But does not the greatest blessing attend those discourses wherein we peculiarly preach the merits and sufferings of Christ?'

Probably when we preach to a congregation of mourners, or of believers, these will be attended with the greatest blessing; because such discourses are peculiarly suited to their state. At least, these will usually convey the most comfort. But this is not always the greatest blessing. I may sometimes receive a far greater by a discourse that cuts me to the heart, and humbles me to the dust. Neither should I receive that comfort, if I were to preach or to hear no discourses but on the sufferings of Christ. These, by constant repetition, would lose their force, and grow more and more flat and dead, till at length they would become a dull round of words, without any spirit, or life, or virtue. So that thus to preach Christ must, in process of time, make void the gospel, as well as the law.

II. 1. A second way of making void the law through faith is, the teaching that faith supersedes the necessity of holiness. This divides itself into a thousand smaller paths, and many there are that walk therein. Indeed there are few that wholly escape it;

few who are convinced, we are saved by faith, but are sooner or later, more or less, drawn aside into this by-way.

2. All those are drawn into this by-way who, if it be not their settled judgement that faith in Christ entirely sets aside the necessity of keeping His law; yet suppose, either, (1) That holiness is less necessary now than it was before Christ came; or, (2) That a less degree of it is necessary; or, (3) That it is less necessary to believers than to others. Yea, and so are all those who, although their judgement be right in the general, yet think they may take more liberty in particular cases than they could have done before they believed. Indeed, the using the term *liberty*, in such a manner, for liberty from obedience or holiness, shows at once that their judgement is perverted, and that they are guilty of what they imagined to be far from them; namely, of making void the law through faith, by supposing faith to supersede holiness.

3. The first plea of those who teach this expressly is, that we are now under the covenant of grace, not works; and therefore we are no longer under the necessity of performing the works of the law.

And who ever was under the covenant of works? None but Adam before the fall. He was fully and properly under that covenant, which required perfect, universal obedience, as the one condition of acceptance; and left no place for pardon, upon the very least transgression. But no man else was ever under this, neither Jew nor Gentile; neither before Christ nor since. All his sons were and are under the covenant of grace. The manner of their acceptance is this: the free grace of God, through the merits of Christ, gives pardon to them that believe; that believe with such a faith as, working by love, produces all obedience and holiness.

4. The case is not, therefore, as you suppose, that men were *once* more obliged to obey God, or to work the works of His law, than they are *now*. This is a supposition you cannot make good. But we should have been obliged, if we had been under the covenant of works, to have done those works antecedent to our acceptance. Whereas now all good works, though as necessary as ever, are not antecedent to our acceptance, but consequent upon it. Therefore the nature of the covenant of grace gives you

no ground, no encouragement at all, to set aside any instance or degree of obedience; any part or measure of holiness.

5. 'But are we not justified by faith, without the works of the law?' Undoubtedly we are; without the works either of the ceremonial or the moral law. And would to God all men were convinced of this! It would prevent innumerable evils; Antinomianism in particular: for, generally speaking, they are the Pharisees who make the Antinomians. Running into an extreme so palpably contrary to Scripture, they occasion others to run into the opposite one. These, seeking to be justified by works, affright those from allowing any place for them.

6. But the truth lies between both. We are, doubtless, justified by faith. This is the corner-stone of the whole Christian building. We are justified without the works of the law, as any previous condition of justification; but they are an immediate fruit of that faith whereby we are justified. So that if good works do not follow our faith, even all inward and outward holiness, it is plain our faith is nothing worth; we are yet in our sins. Therefore, that we are justified by faith, even by faith without works, is no ground for making void the law through faith; or for imagining that faith is a dispensation from any kind or degree of holiness.

7. 'Nay, but does not St. Paul expressly say, "Unto him that worketh not, but believeth on Him that justifieth the ungodly, his faith is counted for righteousness"? And does it not follow from hence, that faith is to a believer in the room, in the place, of righteousness? But if faith is in the room of righteousness or holiness, what need is there of this too?'

This, it must be acknowledged, comes home to the point, and is, indeed, the main pillar of Antinomianism. And yet it needs not a long or laboured answer. We allow, (1) That God justifies the ungodly; him that, till that hour, is totally ungodly —full of all evil, void of all good: (2) That He justifies the ungodly that worketh not; that, till that moment, worketh no good work—neither can he; for an evil tree cannot bring forth good fruit: (3) That He justifies him by faith alone, without any goodness or righteousness preceding: and, (4) That faith is then counted to him for righteousness; namely, for preceding righteousness; that is God, through the merits of Christ, accepts him that believes, as if he had already fulfilled all righteousness. But what is all this to your point? The Apostle does not say, either here or elsewhere, that this faith is counted to him for *subsequent righteousness*. He does teach that there is no righteousness *before* faith; but where does he teach that there is none *after it*? He does assert, holiness cannot *precede* justification; but not, that it need not *follow* it. St. Paul, therefore, gives you no colour for making void the law, by teaching that faith supersedes the necessity of holiness.

III. 1. There is yet another way of making void the law through faith, which is more common than either of the former: and that is, the doing it practically; the making it void in *fact*, though not in *principle*; the *living* as if faith was designed to excuse us from holiness.

How earnestly does the Apostle guard us against this, in those well-known words: 'What then? shall we sin, because we are not under the law, but under grace? God forbid' (Rom. vi. 15): a caution which it is needful thoroughly to consider, because it is of the last importance.

2. The being 'under the law,' may here mean, (1) The being obliged to observe the ceremonial law: (2) The being obliged to conform to the whole Mosaic institution: (3) The being obliged to keep the whole moral law, as the condition of our acceptance with God: and, (4) The being under the wrath and curse of God; under sentence of eternal death; under a sense of guilt and condemnation, full of horror and slavish fear.

3. Now although a believer is 'not without law to God, but under the law to Christ,' yet from the moment he believes, he is not 'under the law,' in any of the preceding senses. On the contrary, he is 'under grace,' under a more benign, gracious dispensation. As he is no longer under the ceremonial law, nor under the Mosaic institution; as he is not obliged to keep even the moral law, as the condition of his acceptance; so he is delivered from the wrath and the curse of God, from all sense of guilt and condemnation, and from all that horror and fear of death and hell whereby he was all his life before subject to

bondage. And he now performs (which while 'under the law' he could not do) a willing and universal obedience. He obeys not from the motive of slavish fear, but on a nobler principle; namely, the grace of God ruling in his heart, and causing all his works to be wrought in love.

4. What then? Shall this evangelical principle of action be less powerful than the legal? Shall we be less obedient to God from filial love than we were from servile fear?

It is well if this is not a common case; if this practical Antinomianism, this unobserved way of making void the law through faith, has not infected thousands of believers.

Has it not infected you? Examine yourself honestly and closely. Do you not do now what you durst not have done when you was 'under the law,' or (as we commonly call it) under conviction? For instance: you durst not then indulge yourself in food: you took just what was needful, and that of the cheapest kind. Do you not allow yourself more latitude now? Do you not indulge yourself a *little* more than you did? O beware lest you 'sin because you are not under the law, but under grace.'

5. When you was under conviction, you durst not indulge the lust of the eye in any degree. You would not do anything, great or small, merely to gratify your curiosity. You regarded only cleanliness and necessity, or at most very moderate convenience, either in furniture or apparel; superfluity and finery of whatever kind, as well as fashionable elegance, were both a terror and an abomination to you.

Are they so still? Is your conscience as tender now in these things as it was then? Do you still follow the same rule both in furniture and apparel, trampling all finery, all superfluity, everything useless, everything merely ornamental, however fashionable, under foot? Rather, have you not resumed what you had once laid aside, and what you could not then use without wounding your conscience? And have you not learned to say, 'O, I am not so scrupulous now'? I would to God you were! Then you would not *sin* thus; 'because you are not under the law, but under grace!'

6. You was once scrupulous too of commending any to their face; and still more, of suffering any to commend you. It was

a stab to your heart; you could not bear it; you sought the honour that cometh of God only. You could not endure such conversation; nor any conversation which was not good to the use of edifying. All idle talk, all trifling discourse, you abhorred; you hated as well as feared it; being deeply sensible of the value of time, of every precious, fleeting moment. In like manner, you dreaded and abhorred idle expense; valuing your money only less than your time, and trembling lest you should be found an unfaithful steward, even of the mammon of unrighteousness.

Do you now look upon praise as deadly poison, which you can neither give nor receive but at the peril of your soul? Do you still dread and abhor all conversation which does not tend to the use of edifying; and labour to improve every moment, that it may not pass without leaving you better than it found you? Are not you less careful as to the expense both of money and time? Cannot you now lay out either, as you could not have done once? Alas! how has that 'which should have been for your health, proved to you an occasion of falling'! How have you 'sinned because you was not under the law, but under grace'!

7. God forbid you should any longer continue thus to 'turn the grace of God into lasciviousness'! O remember how clear and strong a conviction you once had concerning all these things! And, at the same time, you was fully satisfied from whom that conviction came. The world told you, you was in a delusion; but you knew it was the voice of God. In these things you was not too scrupulous then; but you are not now scrupulous enough. God kept you longer in that painful school, that you might learn those great lessons the more perfectly. And have you forgot them already? O recollect them before it is too late! Have you suffered so many things in vain? I trust it is not yet in vain. Now use the conviction without the pain! Practise the lesson without the rod! Let not the mercy of God weigh less with you now, than His fiery indignation did before. Is love a less powerful motive than fear? If not, let it be an invariable rule, 'I will do nothing now I am "under grace," which I durst not have done when "under the law." '

8. I cannot conclude this head without exhorting you to examine yourself, likewise, touching sins of omission. Are you as

clear of these, now you 'are under grace,' as you was when
'under the law'? How diligent was you then in hearing the
Word of God! Did you neglect any opportunity? Did you not
attend thereon day and night? Would a small hindrance have
kept you away? a little business? a visitant? a slight indisposition?
a soft bed? a dark or cold morning? Did not you then fast often;
or use abstinence to the uttermost of your power? Was not you
much in prayer (cold and heavy as you was), while you was
hanging over the mouth of hell? Did you not speak and not
spare even for an unknown God? Did you not boldly plead His
cause, reprove sinners, and avow the truth before an adulterous
generation? And are you now a believer in Christ? Have you
the faith that overcometh the world? What! and are less zealous
for your Master now, than you was when you knew Him not?
less diligent in fasting, in prayer, in hearing His word, in calling
sinners to God? O repent! See and feel your grievous loss!
Remember from whence you are fallen! Bewail your unfaithfulness! Now be zealous and do the first works; lest, if you continue to 'make void the law through faith,' God cut you off, and
appoint you your portion with the unbelievers.

SERMON XXXI

THE LAW ESTABLISHED THROUGH FAITH

DISCOURSE II

*Do we then make void the law through faith? God forbid: yea, we establish the
law.*—ROM. iii. 31.

IT has been shown in the preceding discourse, which are the
most usual ways of making void the law through faith; namely,
first, the not preaching it at all; which effectually makes it all
void at a stroke; and this under colour of preaching Christ and
magnifying the gospel, though it be, in truth, destroying both
the one and the other;—secondly, the teaching (whether directly

or indirectly), that faith supersedes the necessity of holiness; that this is less necessary now, or a less degree of it necessary, than before Christ came; that it is less necessary to us, because we believe, than otherwise it would have been; or, that Christian liberty is a liberty from any kind or degree of holiness (so perverting those great truths, that we are now under the covenant of grace, and not of works; that a man is justified by faith, without the works of the law; and that 'to him that worketh not, but believeth, his faith is counted for righteousness');—or, thirdly, the doing this practically; the making void the law in practice, though not in principle; the living or acting as if faith was designed to excuse us from holiness; the allowing ourselves in sin, 'because we are not under the law, but under grace.' It remains to inquire how we may follow a better pattern, how we may be able to say, with the Apostle, 'Do we then make void the law through faith? God forbid: yea, we establish the law.'

2. We do not, indeed, establish the old ceremonial law: we know that is abolished for ever. Much less do we establish the whole Mosaic dispensation: this we know our Lord has nailed to His cross. Nor yet do we so establish the moral law (which it is to be feared too many do), as if the fulfilling it, the keeping all the commandments, were the condition of our justification: if it were so, surely 'in His sight should no man living be justified.' But all this being allowed, we still, in the Apostle's sense, 'establish the law,' the moral law.

I. 1. We establish the law, first by our doctrine; by endeavouring to preach it in its whole extent, to explain and enforce every part of it, in the same manner as our great Teacher did while upon earth. We establish it by following St. Peter's advice: 'If any man speak, let him speak as the oracles of God'; as the holy men of old, moved by the Holy Ghost, spoke and wrote for our instruction: and as the Apostles of our blessed Lord, by the direction of the same Spirit. We establish it whenever we speak in His name, by keeping back nothing from them that hear; by declaring to them, without any limitation or reserve, the whole counsel of God. And in order the more effectually to establish it, we use herein great plainness of speech. 'We are not

as many that *corrupt* the word of God': καπηλεύοντες (as artful
men their bad wine); we do not *cauponize, mix, adulterate,* or
soften it, to make it suit the taste of the hearers: 'but as of sincerity,
but as of God, in the sight of God, speak we in Christ'; as having
no other aim, than 'by manifestation of the truth to commend
ourselves to every man's conscience in the sight of God.'

2. We then, by our doctrine, establish the law, when we thus
openly declare it to all men; and that in the fullness wherein it
is delivered by our blessed Lord and His Apostles; when we
publish it in the height, and depth, and length, and breadth
thereof. We then establish the law, when we declare every part
of it, every commandment contained therein, not only in its full,
literal sense, but likewise in its spiritual meaning: not only with
regard to the outward actions, which it either forbids or enjoins,
but also with respect to the inward principle, to the thoughts,
desires, and intents of the heart.

3. And indeed this we do the more diligently, not only because it is of the deepest importance,—inasmuch as all the fruit,
every word and work, must be only evil continually, if the tree
be evil, if the dispositions and tempers of the heart be not right
before God,—but likewise, because as important as these things
are, they are little considered or understood—so little, that we
may truly say of the law too, when taken in its full spiritual
meaning, it is 'a mystery which was hid from ages and generations since the world began.' It was utterly hid from the heathen
world. They, with all their boasted wisdom, neither found out
God, nor the law of God; not in the letter, much less in the spirit
of it. 'Their foolish hearts were' more and more 'darkened';
while professing themselves wise, they became fools.' And it
was almost equally hid, as to its spiritual meaning, from the
bulk of the Jewish nation. Even these, who were so ready to
declare concerning others. 'This people that knoweth not the
law are cursed,' pronounced their own sentence therein, as
being under the same curse, the same dreadful ignorance.
Witness our Lord's continual reproof of the wisest among them,
for their gross misinterpretations of it. Witness the supposition
almost universally received among them, that they needed only
to make clean the outside of the cup; that the paying tithe of

mint, anise, and cummin—outward exactness—would atone for inward unholiness, for the total neglect both of justice and mercy, of faith and the love of God. Yea, so absolutely was the spiritual meaning of the law hidden from the wisest of them, that one of their most eminent Rabbis comments thus on those words of the Psalmist, 'If I incline unto iniquity with my heart, the Lord will not hear me': 'That is,' saith he, 'if it be only in my heart, if I do not commit outward wickedness, the Lord will not regard it; He will not punish me, unless I proceed to the outward act'!

4. But, alas! the law of God, as to its inward, spiritual meaning, is not hid from the Jews or Heathens only, but even from what is called the Christian world; at least, from a vast majority of them. The spiritual sense of the commandments of God is still a mystery to these also. Nor is this observable only in those lands which are overspread with Romish darkness and ignorance: but this is too sure, that the far greater part even of those who are called *Reformed Christians* are utter strangers at this day to the law of Christ, in the purity and spirituality of it.

5. Hence it is that to this day 'the Scribes and Pharisees,' the men who have the form but not the power of religion, and who are generally wise in their own eyes, and righteous in their own conceits,—'hearing these things, are offended'; are deeply offended, when we speak of the religion of the heart; and particularly when we show, that, without this, were we to 'give all our goods to feed the poor,' it would profit us nothing. But offended they must be; for we cannot but speak the truth as it is in Jesus. It is our part, whether they will hear, or whether they will forbear, to deliver our own soul. All that is written in the book of God we are to declare, not as pleasing men, but the Lord. We are to declare, not only all the promises, but all the threatenings too, which we find therein. At the same time that we proclaim all the blessings and privileges which God hath prepared for His children, we are likewise to 'teach all the things whatsoever He hath commanded.' And we know that all these have their use; either for the awakening those that sleep, the instructing the ignorant, the comforting the feeble-minded, or the building up and perfecting of the saints. We know that 'all Scripture, given by inspiration of God, is profitable,' either 'for

doctrine,' or 'for reproof'; either 'for correction, or for instruction in righteousness'; and that 'the man of God,' in the process of the work of God in his soul, has need of every part thereof, that he may at length 'be perfect, throughly furnished unto all good works.'

6. It is our part thus to preach Christ, by preaching all things whatsoever He hath revealed. We may indeed, without blame, yea, and with a peculiar blessing from God, declare the love of our Lord Jesus Christ; we may speak, in a more especial manner, of the 'Lord our Righteousness'; we may expatiate upon the grace of God in Christ, 'reconciling the world unto Himself'; we may, at proper opportunities, dwell upon His praise, as 'bearing the iniquities of us all, as wounded for our transgressions, and bruised for our iniquities, that by His stripes we might be healed': but still we should not preach Christ according to His word, if we were wholly to confine ourselves to this; we are not ourselves clear before God, unless we proclaim Him in all His offices. To preach Christ, as a workman that needeth not to be ashamed, is to preach Him, not only as our great High-Priest, 'taken from among men, and ordained for men, in things pertaining to God'—as such 'reconciling us to God by His blood, and 'ever living to make intercession for us';—but likewise as the Prophet of the Lord, 'who of God is made unto us wisdom'; who, by His Word and His Spirit, is with us always, 'guiding us into all truth';—yea, and as remaining a King for ever; as giving laws to all whom He has bought with His blood; as restoring those to the image of God, whom He had first reinstated in His favour; as reigning in all believing hearts until He has 'subdued all things to Himself,'—until He hath utterly cast out all sin, and brought in everlasting righteousness.

II. 1. We establish the law, secondly, when we so preach faith in Christ as not to supersede, but produce, holiness; to produce all manner of holiness, negative and positive, of the heart and of the life.

In order to this, we continually declare (what should be frequently and deeply considered by all who would not 'make void the law through faith'), that faith itself, even Christian faith, the faith of God's elect, the faith of the operation of God, still is only the handmaid of love. As glorious and honourable as it is, it is not the end of the commandment. God hath given this honour to love alone: love is the end of all the commandments of God. Love is the end, the sole end, of every dispensation of God, from the beginning of the world to the comsummation of all things. And it will endure when heaven and earth flee away; for 'love' alone 'never faileth.' Faith will totally fail; it will be swallowed up in sight, in the everlasting vision of God. But even then, love,—

> Its nature and its office still the same,
> Lasting its lamp, and unconsumed its flame,
> In deathless triumph shall for ever live,
> And endless good diffuse, and endless praise receive.

2. Very excellent things are spoken of faith; and whosoever is a partaker thereof may well say with the Apostle, 'Thanks be to God for His unspeakable gift.' Yet still it loses all its excellence when brought into a comparison with love. What St. Paul observes concerning the superior glory of the gospel, above that of the law, may, with great propriety, be spoken of the superior glory of love, above that of faith: 'Even that which was made glorious hath no glory, in this respect, by reason of the glory that excelleth. For if that which is done away is glorious, much more doth that which remaineth exceed in glory.' Yea, all the glory of faith, before it is done away, arises hence, that it ministers to love: it is the great temporary means which God has ordained to promote that eternal end.

3. Let those who magnify faith beyond all proportion, so as to swallow up all things else, and who so totally misapprehend the nature of it as to imagine it stands in the place of love, consider farther, that as love will exist after faith, so it did exist long before it. The angels who, from the moment of their creation, beheld the face of their Father that is in heaven, had no occasion for faith, in its general notion, as it is the evidence of things not seen. Neither had they need of faith, in its more particular acceptation, faith in the blood of Jesus: for He took not upon Him the nature of angels; but only the seed of Abraham There

was, therefore, no place before the foundation of the world for faith, either in the general or particular sense. But there was for love. Love existed from eternity, in God, the great ocean of love. Love had a place in all the children of God, from the moment of their creation: they received at once, from their gracious Creator, to exist and to love.

4. Nor is it certain (as ingeniously and plausibly as many have descanted upon this), that faith, even in the general sense of the word, had any place in paradise. It is highly probable, from that short and uncircumstantial account which we have in holy writ, that Adam, before he rebelled against God, walked with Him by sight, and not by faith.

> For then his reason's eye was strong and clear,
>   And (as an eagle can behold the sun)
> Might have beheld his Maker's face as near
>   As th' intellectual angels could have done.

He was then able to talk with Him face to face, whose face we cannot now see and live; and consequently had no need of that faith, whose office it is to supply the want of sight.

5. On the other hand, it is absolutely certain, faith, in its particular sense, had then no place. For in that sense, it necessarily pre-supposes sin, and the wrath of God declared against the sinner; without which there is no need of an atonement for sin, in order to the sinner's reconciliation with God. Consequently, as there was no need of an atonement before the fall, so there was no place for faith in that atonement; man being then pure from every stain of sin; holy as God is holy. But love even then filled his heart; it reigned in him without a rival, and it was only when love was lost by sin, that faith was added, not for its own sake, nor with any design that it should exist any longer than until it had answered the end for which it was ordained,—namely, to restore man to the love from which he was fallen. At the fall, therefore, was added this evidence of things unseen, which before was utterly needless; this confidence in redeeming love, which could not possibly have any place till the promise was made, that 'the Seed of the woman should bruise the serpent's head.'

6. Faith, then was originally designed of God to re-establish

the law of love. Therefore, in speaking thus, we are not under-valuing it, or robbing it of its due praise; but, on the contrary, showing its real worth, exalting it in its just proportion, and giving it that very place which the wisdom of God assigned it from the beginning. It is the grand means of restoring that holy love wherein man was originally created. It follows, that although faith is of no value in itself (as neither is any other means whatsoever), yet as it leads to that end, the establishing anew the law of love in our hearts; and as, in the present state of things, it is the only means under heaven for effecting it; it is on that account an unspeakable blessing to man, and of unspeakable value before God.

III. 1. And this naturally brings us to observe, thirdly, the most important way of establishing the law; namely, the estab-lishing it in our own hearts and lives. Indeed, without this, what would all the rest avail? We might establish it by our doctrine; we might preach it in its whole extent; might explain and enforce every part of it; we might open it in its most spiritual meaning, and declare the mysteries of the kingdom; we might preach Christ in all His offices, and faith in Christ as opening all the treasures of His love; and yet all this time, if the law we preached were not established in our hearts, we should be of no more account before God, than 'sounding brass, or tinkling cymbals': all our preaching would be so far from profiting ourselves, that it would only increase our damnation.

2. This is, therefore, the main point to be considered,—How may we establish the law in our own hearts, so that it may have its full influence on our lives? And this can only be done by faith.

Faith alone it is which effectually answers this end, as we learn from daily experience. For so long as we walk by faith, not by sight, we go swiftly on in the way of holiness. While we steadily look, not at the things which are seen, but at those which are not seen, we are more and more crucified to the world, and the world crucified to us. Let but the eye of the soul be constantly fixed, not on the things which are temporal, but on those which are eternal, and our affections are more and more loosened from earth, and fixed on things above. So that faith, in general, is the most direct and effectual means of promoting all righteousness and true holiness; of establishing the holy and spiritual law in the hearts of them that believe.

3. And by faith, taken in its more particular meaning, for a confidence in a pardoning God, we establish His law in our own hearts, in a still more effectual manner. For there is no motive which so powerfully inclines us to love God, as the sense of the love of God in Christ. Nothing enables us like a piercing conviction of this to give our hearts to Him who was given for us. And from this principle of grateful love to God arises love to our brother also. Neither can we avoid loving our neighbour, if we truly believe the love wherewith God hath loved us. Now this love to man, grounded on faith, and love to God, 'worketh no ill to' our 'neighbour': consequently, it is, as the Apostle observes 'the fulfilling of the' whole negative 'law.' 'For this, Thou shalt not commit adultery: Thou shalt not kill: Thou shalt not steal: Thou shalt not bear false witness: Thou shalt not covet: and if there be any other commandment, it is briefly comprehended in this saying, Thou shalt love thy neighbour as thyself.' Neither is love content with barely working no evil to our neighbour It continually incites us to do good, as we have time and opportunity; to do good, in every possible kind, and in every possible degree, to all men. It is, therefore, the fulfilling of the positive, likewise, as well as of the negative, law of God.

4. Nor does faith fulfil either the negative or positive law as to the external part only; but it works inwardly by love, to the purifying of the heart, the cleansing it from all vile affections. Every one that hath this faith in himself 'purifieth himself even as He is pure,'—purifieth himself from every earthly, sensual desire; from all vile and inordinate affections; yea, from the whole of that carnal mind which is enmity against God. At the same time, if it have its perfect work, it fills him with all goodness, righteousness, and truth. It brings all heaven into his soul; and causes him to walk in the light, even as God is in the light.

5. Let us thus endeavour to establish the law in ourselves; not sinning 'because we are under grace,' but rather using all the power we receive thereby, 'to fulfil all righteousness.' Calling to

mind what light we received from God while His Spirit was convincing us of sin, let us beware we do not put out that light; what we had then attained let us hold fast. Let nothing induce us to build again what we have destroyed; to resume anything, small or great, which we then clearly saw was not for the glory of God, or the profit of our own soul; or to neglect anything, small or great, which we could not then neglect, without a check from our own conscience. To increase and perfect the light which we had before, let us now add the light of faith. Confirm we the former gift of God, by a deeper sense of whatever He had then shown us; by a greater tenderness of conscience, and a more exquisite sensibility of sin. Walking now with joy, and not with fear, in a clear, steady sight of things eternal, we shall look on pleasure, wealth, praise, all the things of earth, as on bubbles upon the water; counting nothing important, nothing desirable, nothing worth a deliberate thought, but only what is 'within the veil,' where Jesus 'sitteth at the right hand of God.'

6. Can *you* say, 'Thou art merciful to my unrighteousness; my sins Thou rememberest no more'? Then, for the time to come, see that you fly from sin, as from the face of a serpent! For how exceeding sinful does it appear to you now! How heinous above all expression! On the other hand, in how amiable a light do you now see the holy and perfect will of God! Now, therefore, labour that it may be fulfilled, both in you, by you, and upon you! Now watch and pray, that you may sin no more, that you may see and shun the least transgression of His law! You see the motes which you could not see before, when the sun shines into a dark place. In like manner, you see the sins which you could not see before, now the Sun of Righteousness shines in your heart. Now then do all diligence to walk, in every respect, according to the light you have received! Now be zealous to receive more light daily, more of the knowledge and love of God, more of the Spirit of Christ, more of His life, and of the power of His resurrection! Now use all the knowledge, and love, and life, and power you have already attained; so shall you continually go on from faith to faith; so shall you daily increase in holy love, till faith is swallowed up in sight, and the law of love is established to all eternity!

SERMON XXXII

THE NATURE OF ENTHUSIASM

And Festus said with a loud voice, Paul, thou art beside thyself
—Acts xxvi. 24.

AND so say all the world, the men who know not God, of all that
are of Paul's religion: of every one who is so a follower of him,
as he was of Christ. It is true, there is a sort of religion, nay, and
it is called Christianity too, which may be practised without any
such imputation, which is generally allowed to be consistent
with common sense,—that is, a religion of form, a round of outward duties, performed in a decent, regular manner. You may
add orthodoxy thereto, a system of right opinions, yea, and some
quantity of heathen morality; and yet not many will pronounce,
that 'much religion hath made you mad.' But if you aim at the
religion of the heart, if you talk of 'righteousness, and peace, and
joy in the Holy Ghost,' then it will not be long before your
sentence is passed, 'Thou art beside thyself.'

2. And it is no compliment which the men of the world pay
you herein. They, for once, mean what they say They not only
affirm, but cordially believe, that every man is beside himself
who says, 'the love of God is shed abroad in' his 'heart by the
Holy Ghost given unto him'; and that God has enabled him to
rejoice in Christ 'with joy unspeakable and full of glory.' If a
man is indeed alive to God, and dead to all things here below; if
he continually sees Him that is invisible, and accordingly walks
by faith, and not by sight; then they account it a clear case:
beyond all dispute, 'much religion hath made him mad.'

3. It is easy to observe, that the determinate thing which the
world account madness is, that utter contempt of all temporal
things, and steady pursuit of things eternal; that divine conviction of things not seen; that rejoicing in the favour of God;
that happy, holy love of God; and that testimony of His Spirit
with our spirit, that we are the children of God,—that is, in

truth, the whole spirit, and life, and power of the religion of Jesus Christ.

4. They will, however, allow, in other respects, the man acts and talks like one in his senses. In other things, he is a reasonable man; it is in these instances only his head is touched. It is therefore acknowledged, that the madness under which he labours is of a particular kind; and accordingly they are accustomed to, distinguish it by a particular name, 'enthusiasm.'

5. A term this, which is exceeding frequently used, which is scarce ever out of some men's mouths; and yet it is exceeding rarely understood, even by those who use it most. It may be, therefore, not unacceptable to serious men, to all who desire to understand what they speak or hear, if I endeavour to explain the meaning of this term—to show what enthusiasm is. It may be an encouragement to those who are unjustly charged therewith; and may possibly be of use to some who are justly charged with it; at least to others who might be so, were they not cautioned against it.

6. As to the word itself, it is generally allowed to be of Greek extraction. But whence the Greek word, ἐνθουσιασμός, is derived, none has yet been able to show. Some have endeavoured to derive it from ἐν Θεῷ—in God; because all enthusiasm has reference to Him. But this is quite forced; there being small resemblance between the word derived, and those they strive to derive it from. Others would derive it from ἐν θυσίᾳ—in sacrifice; because many of the enthusiasts of old were affected in the most violent manner during the time of sacrifice. Perhaps it is a fictitious word, invented from the noise which some of those made who were so affected.

7. It is not improbable, that one reason why this uncouth word has been retained in so many languages was, because men were not better agreed concerning the meaning than concerning the derivation of it. They therefore adopted the Greek word, because they did not understand it: they did not translate it into their own tongues, because they knew not how to translate it; it having been always a word of a loose, uncertain sense, to which no determinate meaning was affixed.

8. It is not, therefore, at all surprising, that it is so variously

taken at this day; different persons understanding it in different senses, quite inconsistent with each other. Some take it in a good sense, for a divine impulse or impression, superior to all the natural faculties, and suspending, for the time, either in whole or in part, both the reason and the outward senses. In this meaning of the word, both the Prophets of old, and the Apostles, were proper enthusiasts; being, at divers times, so filled with the Spirit, and so influenced by Him who dwelt in their hearts, that the exercise of their own reason, their senses, and all their natural faculties, being suspended, they were wholly actuated by the power of God, and 'spake' only 'as they were moved by the Holy Ghost.'

9. Others take the word in an indifferent sense, such as is neither morally good nor evil: thus they speak of the enthusiasm of the poets; of Homer and Virgil in particular. And this a late eminent writer extends so far as to assert, there is no man excellent in his profession, whatsoever it be, who has not in his temper a strong tincture of enthusiasm. By 'enthusiasm' these appear to understand, an uncommon vigour of thought, a peculiar fervour of spirit, a vivacity and strength not to be found in common men: elevating the soul to greater and higher things than cool reason could have attained.

10. But neither of these is the sense wherein the word 'enthusiasm' is most usually understood. The generality of men, if no farther agreed, at least agree thus far concerning it, that it is something evil: and this is plainly the sentiment of all those who call the religion of the heart 'enthusiasm.' Accordingly, I shall take it in the following pages, as an evil; a misfortune, if not a fault.

11. As to the nature of enthusiasm, it is undoubtedly a disorder of the mind; and such a disorder as greatly hinders the exercise of reason. Nay, sometimes it wholly sets it aside: it not only dims but shuts the eyes of the understanding. It may, therefore, well be accounted a species of madness; of madness rather than of folly: seeing a fool is properly one who draws wrong conclusions from right premisses; whereas a madman draws right conclusions, but from wrong premisses. And so does an enthusiast. Suppose his premisses true, and his conclusions would

necessarily follow. But here lies his mistake: his premisses are false. He imagines himself to be what he is not: and therefore, setting out wrong, the farther he goes, the more he wanders out of the way.

12. Every enthusiast, then, is properly a madman. Yet his is not an ordinary, but a religious, madness. By 'religious,' I do not mean, that it is any part of religion: quite the reverse. Religion is the spirit of a sound mind; and, consequently, stands in direct opposition to madness of every kind. But I mean, it has religion for its object; it is conversant about religion. And so the enthusiast is generally talking of religion, of God, or of the things of God; but talking in such a manner that every reasonable Christian may discern the disorder of his mind. Enthusiasm in general may then be described in some such manner as this: a religious madness arising from some falsely imagined influence or inspiration of God; at least, from imputing something to God which ought not to be imputed to Him, or expecting something from God which ought not to be expected from Him.

13. There are innumerable sorts of enthusiasm. Those which are most common, and for that reason most dangerous, I shall endeavour to reduce under a few general heads, that they may be more easily understood and avoided.

The first sort of enthusiasm which I shall mention, is that of those who imagine they have the grace which they have not. Thus some imagine, when it is not so, that they have redemption through Christ, 'even the forgiveness of sins.' These are usually such as 'have no root in themselves'; no deep repentance, or thorough conviction. 'Therefore they receive the word with joy.' And 'because they have no deepness of earth,' no deep work in their heart, therefore the seed 'immediately springs up.' There is immediately a superficial change, which, together with that light joy, striking in with the pride of their unbroken heart, and with their inordinate self-love, easily presuades them they have already 'tasted the good word of God, and the powers of the world to come.'

14. This is properly an instance of the first sort of enthusiasm: it is a kind of madness, arising from the imagination that they have that grace which, in truth, they have not: so that they only

deceive their own souls. Madness it may be justly termed: for the reasonings of these poor men are right, were their premises good; but as those are a mere creature of their own imagination, so all that is built on them falls to the ground. The foundation of all their reveries is this: they imagine themselves to have faith in Christ. If they had this, they would be 'kings and priests to God'; possessed of a' kingdom which cannot be moved': but they have it not; consequently, all their following behaviour is as wide of truth and soberness as that of the ordinary madman, who, fancying himself an earthly king, speaks and acts in that character.

15. There are many other enthusiasts of this sort. Such, for instance, is the fiery zealot for religion; or, more properly, for the opinions and modes of worship which he dignifies with that name. This man, also, strongly imagines himself to be a believer in Jesus; yea, that he is a champion for the faith which was once delivered to the saints. Accordingly, all his conduct is formed upon that vain imagination. And allowing his supposition to be just, he would have some tolerable plea for his behaviour; whereas now it is evidently the effect of a distempered brain, as well as of a distempered heart.

16. But the most common of all the enthusiasts of this kind are those who imagine themselves Christians, and are not. These abound, not only in all parts of our land, but in most parts of the habitable earth. That they are not Christians, is clear and undeniable, if we believe the oracles of God. For Christians are holy; these are unholy: Christians love God; these love the world: Christians are humble; these are proud: Christians are gentle; these are passionate; Christians have the mind which was in Christ; these are at the utmost distance from it. Consequently, they are no more Christians, than they are archangels. Yet they imagine themselves so to be; and they can give several reasons for it: for they have been *called so* ever since they can remember; they were *christened* many years ago; they embrace the *Christian opinions*, vulgarly termed the Christian or catholic faith; they use the *Christian modes of worship*, as their fathers did before them; they live what is called a good *Christian life*, as the rest of their neighbours do. And who shall presume to think or say

that these men are not Christians?—though without one grain of true faith in Christ, or of real, inward holiness; without ever having tasted the love of God, or been 'made partakers of the Holy Ghost'!

17. Ah poor self-deceivers! Christians ye are not. But you are enthusiasts in a high degree. Physicians, heal yourselves! But first know your disease: your whole life is enthusiasm; as being all suitable to the imagination, that you have received that grace of God which you have not. In consequence of this grand mistake, you blunder on, day by day, speaking and acting under a character which does in no wise belong to you. Hence arises that palpable, glaring inconsistency that runs through your whole behaviour; which is an awkward mixture of real Heathenism and imaginary Christianity. Yet still, as you have so vast a majority on your side, you will always carry it by mere dint of numbers, 'that you are the only men in your senses, and all are lunatics who are not as you are.' But this alters not the nature of things. In the sight of God, and His holy angels, yea, and all the children of God upon earth, you are mere madmen, mere enthusiasts all! Are you not? Are you not 'walking in a vain shadow, a shadow of religion, a shadow of happiness? Are you not still 'disquieting yourselves in vain' with misfortunes as imaginary as your happiness or religion? Do you not fancy yourselves great or good—very knowing and very wise? How long? Perhaps till death brings you back to your senses, to bewail your folly for ever and ever!

18. A second sort of enthusiasm is that of those who imagine they have such gifts from God as they have not. Thus some have imagined themselves to be endued with a power of working miracles, of healing the sick by a word or a touch, of restoring sight to the blind: yea, even of raising the dead—a notorious instance of which is still fresh in our own history. Others have undertaken to prophesy, to foretell things to come, and that with the utmost certainty and exactness. But a little time usually convinces these enthusiasts. When plain facts run counter to their predictions, experience performs what reason could not, and sinks them down into their senses.

19. To the same class belong those who, in preaching or

prayer, imagine themselves to be so influenced by the Spirit of
God, as, in fact, they are not. I am sensible, indeed, that without
Him we can do nothing, more especially in our public ministry;
that all our preaching is utterly vain, unless it be attended with
His power; and all our prayer, unless His Spirit therein help our
infirmities. I know, if we do not both preach and pray by the
Spirit, it is all but lost labour; seeing the help that is done upon
earth He doeth it Himself, who worketh all in all. But this does
not affect the case before us. Though there is a real influence of
the Spirit of God, there is also an imaginary one: and many there
are who mistake the one for the other. Many suppose themselves
to be under that influence, when they are not, when it is far from
them.   And many others suppose they are more under that
influence than they really are. Of this number, I fear, are all they
who imagine that God dictates the very words they speak; and
that, consequently, it is impossible they should speak anything
amiss, either as to the matter or manner of it. It is well known
how many enthusiasts of this sort also have appeared during
the present century; some of whom speak in a far more authorit-
ative manner than either St. Paul or any of the Apostles.

20. The same sort of enthusiasm, though in a lower degree,
is frequently found in men of a private character. They may
likewise imagine themselves to be influenced or directed by the
Spirit when they are not. I allow, 'if any man have not the
Spirit of Christ, he is none of His'; and that if ever we either
think, speak, or act aright, it is through the assistance of that
blessed Spirit. But how many impute things to Him, or expect
things from Him, without any rational or scriptural ground!
Such are they who imagine, they either do or shall receive
particular directions from God, not only in points of importance,
but in things of no moment; in the most trifling circumstances of
life. Whereas in these cases God has given us our own reason for
a guide; though never excluding the secret assistance of His
Spirit.

21. To this kind of enthusiasm they are peculiarly exposed,
who expect to be directed of God, either in spiritual things or in
common life, in what is justly called an *extraordinary* manner: I
mean, by visions or dreams, by strong impressions or sudden

impulses on the mind. I do not deny, that God has, of old times, manifested His will in this manner; or, that He can do so now: nay, I believe He does, in some very rare instances. But how frequently do men mistake herein! How are they misled by pride, and a warm imagination, to ascribe such impulses or impressions, dreams or visions, to God, as are utterly unworthy of Him! Now this is all pure enthusiasm; all as wide of religion, as it is of truth and soberness.

22. Perhaps some may ask, 'Ought we not then to inquire what is the will of God in all things? And ought not His will to be the rule of our practice?' Unquestionably it ought. But how is a sober Christian to make this inquiry? to know what is the will of God? Not by waiting for supernatural dreams; not by expecting God to reveal it in visions; not by looking for any *particular impressions* or sudden impulses on his mind: no; but by consulting the oracles of God. 'To the law and to the testimony!' This is the general method of knowing what is 'the holy and acceptable will of God.'

23. 'But how shall I know what is the will of God, in such and such a particular case? The thing proposed is, in itself, of an indifferent nature, and so left undetermined in Scripture.' I answer, the Scripture itself gives you a general rule, applicable to all particular cases: 'The will of God is our sanctification.' It is His will that we should be inwardly and outwardly holy; that we should be good, and do good, in every kind and in the highest degree whereof we are capable. Thus far we tread upon firm ground. This is as clear as the shining of the sun. In order, therefore, to know what is the will of God in a particular case, we have only to apply this general rule.

24. Suppose, for instance, it were proposed to a reasonable man to marry, or to enter into a new business: in order to know whether this is the will of God, being assured, 'It is the will of God concerning me, that I should be as holy and do as much good as I can,' he has only to inquire, 'In which of these states can I be most holy, and do the most good?' And this is to be determined, partly by reason, and partly by experience. Experience tells him what advantages he has in his present state, either for being or doing good; and reason is to show, what he certainly or probably

will have in the state proposed. By comparing these, he is to judge which of the two may most conduce to his being and doing good; and as far as he knows this, so far he is certain what is the will of God.

25. Meantime, the assistance of His Spirit is supposed, during the whole process of the inquiry. Indeed it is not easy to say, in how many ways that assistance is conveyed. He may bring many circumstances to our remembrance; may place others in a stronger and clearer light; may insensibly open our mind to receive conviction, and fix that conviction upon our heart. And to a concurrence of many circumstances of this kind, in favour of what is acceptable in His sight, He may superadd such an unutterable peace of mind, and so uncommon a measure of His love, as will leave us no possibility of doubting, that this, even this, is His will concerning us.

26. This is the plain, scriptural, rational way to know what is the will of God in a particular case. But considering how seldom this way is taken, and what a flood of enthusiasm must needs break in on those who endeavour to know the will of God by unscriptural, irrational ways; it were to be wished that the expression itself were far more sparingly used. The using it, as some do, on the most trivial occasions, is a plain breach of the third commandment. It is a gross way of taking the name of God in vain, and betrays great irreverence toward Him. Would it not be far better, then, to use other expressions, which are not liable to such objections? For example: instead of saying, on any particular occasion, 'I want to know what is the will of God'; would it not be better to say, 'I want to know what will be most for my improvement; and what will make me most useful?' This way of speaking is clear and unexceptionable: it is putting the matter on a plain, scriptural issue, and that without any danger of enthusiasm.

27. A third very common sort of enthusiasm (if it does not coincide with the former) is that of those who think to attain the end without using the means, by the immediate power of God. If, indeed, those means were providentially withheld, they would not fall under this charge. God can, and sometimes does, in cases of this nature, exert His own immediate power. But they

who expect this when they have those means, and will not use them, are proper enthusiasts. Such are they who expect to understand the holy Scriptures, without reading them, and meditating thereon; yea, without using all such helps as are in their power, and may probably conduce to that end. Such are they who designedly speak in the public assembly without any premeditation. I say 'designedly'; because there may be such circumstances as, at some times, make it unavoidable. But whoever despises that great means of speaking profitably is so far an enthusiast.

28. It may be expected that I should mention what some have accounted a fourth sort of enthusiasm, namely, the imagining those things to be owing to the providence of God which are not owing thereto. But I doubt: I know not what things they are which are not owing to the providence of God; in ordering, or at least in governing, of which, this is not either directly or remotely concerned. I except nothing but sin; and even in the sins of others, I see the providence of God to me. I do not say His *general* providence; for this I take to be a sounding word which means just nothing. And if there be a *particular* providence, it must extend to all persons and all things. So our Lord understood it, or He could never have said, 'Even the hairs of your head are all numbered'; and, 'Not a sparrow falleth to the ground without' the will of 'your Father' which is in heaven. But if it be so, if God preside *universis tanquam singulis, et singulis tanquam universis*; 'over the whole universe as over every single person, and over every single person as over the whole universe'; what is it (except only our own sins) which we are not to ascribe to the providence of God? So that I cannot apprehend there is any room here for the charge of enthusiasm.

29. If it be said, the charge lies here: 'When you impute *this* to Providence, you imagine yourself the peculiar favourite of heaven': I answer, you have forgot some of the last words I spoke: *Praesidet universis tanquam singulis*; 'His providence is over all men in the universe, as much as over any single person.' Do you not see that he who, believing this, imputes anything which befalls him to Providence, does not therein make himself any more the favourite of heaven, than he supposes every man under

heaven to be? Therefore you have no pretence, upon this ground, to charge him with enthusiasm.

30. Against every sort of this it behoves us to guard with the utmost diligence; considering the dreadful effects it has so often produced, and which, indeed, naturally result from it. Its immediate offspring is pride; it continually increases this source from whence it flows; and hereby it alienates us more and more from the favour and from the life of God. It dries up the very springs of faith and love, of righteousness and true holiness; seeing all these flow from grace: but 'God resisteth the proud, and giveth grace' only 'to the humble.'

31. Together with pride there will naturally arise an unadvisable and unconvincible spirit. So that into whatever error or fault the enthusiast falls, there is small hope of his recovery. For reason will have little weight with him (as has been frequently and justly observed) who imagines he is led by a higher guide,—by the immediate wisdom of God. And as he grows in pride, so he must grow in unadvisableness and in stubbornness also. He must be less and less capable of being convinced, less susceptible of persuasion; more and more attached to his own judgement and his own will, till he is altogether fixed and immovable.

32. Being thus fortified both against the grace of God, and against all advice and help from man, he is wholly left to the guidance of his own heart, and of the king of the children of pride. No marvel, then, that he is daily more rooted and grounded in contempt of all mankind, in furious anger, in every unkind disposition, in every earthly and devilish temper. Neither can we wonder at the terrible outward effects which have flowed from such dispositions in all ages; even all manner of wickedness, all the works of darkness, committed by those who call themselves Christians, while they wrought with greediness such things as were hardly named even among the Heathens.

Such is the nature, such the dreadful effects, of that many-headed monster, Enthusiasm! From the consideration of which we may now draw some plain inferences, with regard to our own practice.

33. And, first, if enthusiasm be a term, though so frequently used, yet so rarely understood, take you care not to talk of you

know not what; not to use the word till you understand it. As in all other points, so likewise in this, learn to think before you speak. First know the meaning of this hard word; and then use it, if need require.

34. But if so few, even among men of education and learning, much more among the common sort of men, understand this dark, ambiguous word, or have any fixed notion of what it means; then, secondly, beware of judging or calling any man an enthusiast, upon common report. This is by no means a sufficient ground for giving any name of reproach to any man; least of all is it a sufficient ground for so black a term of reproach as this. The more evil it contains, the more cautious you should be how you apply it to any one; to bring so heavy an accusation, without full proof, being neither consistent with justice nor mercy.

35. But if enthusiasm be so great an evil, beware you are not entangled therewith yourself. Watch and pray, that you fall not into the temptation. It easily besets those who fear or love God. O beware you do not think of yourself more highly than you ought to think. Do not imagine you have attained that grace of God which you have not attained. You may have much joy; you may have a measure of love; and yet not have living faith. Cry unto God, that He would not suffer you, blind as you are, to go out of the way; that you may never fancy yourself a believer in Christ, till Christ is revealed in you, and till His Spirit witnesses with your spirit that you are a child of God.

36. Beware you are not a fiery, persecuting enthusiast. Do not imagine that God has called you (just contrary to the spirit of Him you style your Master) to destroy men's lives, and not to save them. Never dream of forcing men into the ways of God. Think yourself, and let think. Use no constraint in matters of religion. Even those who are farthest out of the way never compel to come in by any other means than reason, truth, and love.

37. Beware you do not run with the common herd of enthusiasts, fancying you are a Christian when you are not. Presume not to assume that venerable name, unless you have a clear, scriptural title thereto; unless you have the mind which was in Christ, and walk as He also walked.

38. Beware you do not fall into the second sort of enthusiasm, —fancying you have those gifts from God which you have not. Trust not in visions or dreams; in sudden impressions, or strong impulses of any kind. Remember, it is not by these you are to know what is the will of God on any particular occasion; but by applying the plain Scripture rule, with the help of experience and reason, and the ordinary assistance of the Spirit of God. Do not lightly take the name of God in your mouth; do not talk of the will of God on every trifling occasion: but let your words, as well as your actions, be all tempered with reverence and godly fear.

39. Beware, lastly, of imagining you shall obtain the end without using the means conducive to it. God can give the end without any means at all; but you have no reason to think He will. Therefore constantly and carefully use all those means which He has appointed to be the ordinary channels of His grace. Use every means which either reason or Scripture recommends, as conducive (through the free love of God in Christ) either to the obtaining or increasing any of the gifts of God. Thus expect a daily growth in that pure and holy religion which the world always did, and always will, call 'enthusiasm'; but which, to all who are saved from real enthusiasm, from merely nominal Christianity, is 'the wisdom of God, and the power of God'; the glorious image of the Most High; 'righteousness and peace'; a 'fountain of living water, springing up into everlasting life'!

SERMON XXXIII

A CAUTION AGAINST BIGOTRY

And John answered Him, saying, Master, we saw one casting out devils in Thy name: and he followeth not us: and we forbad him, because he followeth not us. But Jesus said, Forbid him not.—MARK ix. 38, 39.

IN the preceding verses we read, that after the twelve had been disputing 'which of them should be the greatest,' Jesus took a little child, and set him in the midst of them, and taking him in His arms, said unto them, 'Whosoever shall receive one of these little children in My name, receiveth Me; and whosoever receiveth Me, receiveth not Me' only, 'but Him that sent Me'. Then 'John answered,' that is, said, with reference to what our Lord had spoken just before, 'Master, we saw one casting out devils in Thy name, and we forbad him, because he followeth not us.' As if he had said, 'Ought we to have received him? In receiving him, should we have received Thee? Ought we not rather to have forbidden him? Did not we do well therein?' 'But Jesus said, Forbid him not.'

2. The same passage is recited by St. Luke, and almost in the same words. But it may be asked, 'What is this to us, seeing no man now *casts out devils*? Has not the power of doing this been withdrawn from the church, for twelve or fourteen hundred years? How then are *we* concerned in the case here proposed, or in our Lord's decision of it?'

3. Perhaps more nearly than is commonly imagined; the case proposed being no uncommon case. That we may reap our full advantage from it, I design to show, first, in what sense men may, and do, now cast out devils: secondly, what we may understand by, 'He followeth not us.' I shall, thirdly, explain our Lord's direction, 'Forbid him not'; and conclude with an inference from the whole.

I. 1. I am, in the first place, to show, in what sense men may, and do, now cast out devils.

In order to have the clearest view of this, we should remember, that (according to the scriptural account) as God dwells and works in the children of light, so the devil dwells and works in the children of darkness. As the Holy Spirit possesses the souls of good men, so the evil spirit possesses the souls of the wicked. Hence it is that the Apostle terms him 'the god of this world'; from the uncontrolled power he has over worldly men   Hence our blessed Lord styles him 'the prince of this world'; so absolute is his dominion over it. And hence St. John: 'We know that we are of God, and' all who are not of God, 'the whole world,' ἐν τῷ πονηρῷ κεῖται,—not *lieth in wickedness:* but '*lieth in the wicked one*'; lives and moves in him, as they who are not of the world do in God.

2. For the devil is not to be considered only as 'a roaring lion, going about seeking whom he may devour'; nor barely as a subtle enemy, who cometh unawares upon poor souls, and 'leads them captive at his will'; but as he who dwelleth in them, and walketh in them; who ruleth the darkness or wickedness of this world (of worldly men and all their dark designs and actions), by keeping possession of their hearts, setting up his throne there, and bringing every thought into obedience to himself. Thus the 'strong one armed keepeth his house'; and if this 'unclean spirit' sometimes 'go out of a man,' yet he often returns with 'seven spirits worse than himself, and they enter in and dwell there.' Nor can he be idle in his dwelling. He is continually 'working in' these 'children of disobedience.' He works in them with power, with mighty energy, transforming them into his own likeness, effacing all the remains of the image of God, and preparing them for every evil word and work.

3. It is, therefore, an unquestionable truth, that the god and prince of this world still possesses all who know not God. Only the manner wherein he possesses them now differs from that wherein he did it of old time. *Then* he frequently tormented their bodies as well as souls, and that openly, without any disguise: *now* he torments their souls only (unless in some rare cases), and that as covertly as possible. The reason of this difference is plain: it was then his aim to drive mankind into superstition; therefore, he wrought as openly as he could. But it is his aim to drive us into infidelity; therefore, he works as privately as he can: for the more secret he is, the more he prevails.

4. Yet, if we may credit historians, there are countries, even now, where he works as openly as aforetime. 'But why in savage and barbarous countries only? Why not in Italy, France, or England?' For a very plain reason: he knows his men; and he knows what he hath to do with each. To Laplanders he appears barefaced; because he is to fix them in superstition and gross idolatry. But with you he is pursuing a different point. He is to make you idolize yourselves; to make you wiser in your own eyes than God Himself, than all the oracles of God. Now, in

order to do this, he must not appear in his own shape: that would frustrate his design. No: he uses all his art to make you deny his being, till he has you safe in his own place.

5. He reigns, therefore, although in a different way, yet as absolute in one land as in the other. He has the gay Italian infidel in his teeth, as sure as the wild Tartar. But he is fast asleep in the mouth of the lion, who is too wise to wake him out of sleep. So he only plays with him for the present, and when he pleases, swallows him up!

The god of this world holds his English worshippers full as fast as those in Lapland. But it is not his business to affright them, lest they should fly to the God of heaven. The prince of darkness, therefore, does not appear, while he rules over these his willing subjects. The conqueror holds his captives so much the safer, because they imagine themselves at liberty. Thus 'the strong one armed keepeth his house, and his goods are in peace'; neither the Deist nor nominal Christian suspects he is there: so he and they are perfectly at peace with each other.

6. All this while he works with energy in them. He blinds the eyes of their understanding, so that the light of the glorious gospel of Christ cannot shine upon them. He chains their souls down to earth and hell, with the chains of their own vile affections. He binds them down to the earth, by love of the world, love of money, of pleasure, of praise. And by pride, envy, anger, hate, revenge, he causes their souls to draw nigh unto hell; acting the more secure and uncontrolled, because they know not that he acts at all.

7. But how easily may we know the cause from its effects! These are sometimes gross and palpable. So they were in the most refined of the heathen nations. Go no farther than the admired, the virtuous Romans; and you will find these, when at the height of their learning and glory, 'filled with all unrighteousness, fornication, wickedness, covetousness, maliciousness; full of envy, murder, debate, deceit, malignity; whisperers, backbiters, despiteful, proud, boasters, disobedient to parents, covenant-breakers, without natural affection, implacable, unmerciful.'

8. The strongest parts of this description are confirmed by one whom some may think a more unexceptionable witness. I mean,

their brother Heathen, Dion Cassius; who observes, that, before Caesar's return from Gaul, not only gluttony and lewdness of every kind were open and barefaced; not only falsehood, injustice, and unmercifulness abounded, in public courts, as well as private families; but the most outrageous robberies, rapine, and murders were so frequent in all parts of Rome, that few men went out of doors without making their wills, as not knowing if they should return alive!

9. As gross and palpable are the works of the devil among many (if not all) the modern Heathens. The natural religion of the Creeks, Cherokees, Chickasaws, and all other Indians bordering on our southern settlements (not of a few single men, but of entire nations), is to torture all their prisoners from morning till night, till at length they roast them to death; and upon the slightest undesigned provocation, to come behind and shoot any of their own countrymen! Yea, it is a common thing among them, for the son, if he thinks his father lives too long, to knock out his brains; and for mother, if she is tired of her children, to fasten stones about their necks, and throw three or four of them into the river, one after another!

10. It were to be wished, that none but Heathens had practised such gross, palpable works of the devil. But we dare not say so. Even in cruelty and bloodshed, how little have the Christians come behind them! And not the Spaniards or Portuguese alone, butchering thousands in South America: not the Dutch only in the East Indies, or the French in North America, following the Spaniards step by step: our own countrymen, too, have wantoned in blood, and exterminated whole nations; plainly proving thereby what spirit it is that dwells and works in the children of disobedience.

11. These monsters might almost make us overlook the works of the devil that are wrought in our own country. But, alas! we cannot open our eyes even here, without seeing them on every side. Is it a small proof of his power, that common swearers, drunkards, whoremongers, adulterers, thieves, robbers, sodomites, murderers, are still found in every part of our land? How triumphant does the prince of this world reign in all these children of disobedience!

12. He less openly, but no less effectually, works in dissemblers, tale-bearers, liars, slanderers; in oppressors and extortioners; in the perjured, the seller of his friend, his honour, his conscience, his country. And yet these may talk of religion or conscience still; of honour, virtue, and public spirit! But they can no more deceive Satan than they can God. He likewise knows those that are his: and a great multitude they are, out of every nation and people, of whom he has full possession at this day.

13. If you consider this, you cannot but see in what sense men may now also cast out devils: yea, and every minister of Christ does cast them out, if his Lord's work prosper in his hand.

By the power of God attending his word, he brings these sinners to repentance; an entire inward as well as outward change, from all evil to all good. And this is, in a sound sense, to cast out devils, out of the souls wherein they had hitherto dwelt. The strong one can no longer keep his house. A stronger than he is come upon him, and hath cast him out, and taken possession for himself, and made it an habitation of God through His Spirit. Here, then, the energy of Satan ends, and the Son of God 'destroys the works of the devil.' The understanding of the sinner is now enlightened, and his heart sweetly drawn to God. His desires are refined, his affections purified; and, being filled with the Holy Ghost, he grows in grace till he is not only holy in heart, but in all manner of conversation.

14. All this is indeed the work of God. It is God alone who can cast out Satan. But He is generally pleased to do this by man, as an instrument in His hand: who is then said to cast out devils in His name, by His power and authority. And He sends whom He will send upon this great work; but usually such as man would never have thought of: for 'His ways are not as our ways, neither His thoughts as our thoughts.' Accordingly, He chooses the weak to confound the mighty; the foolish to confound the wise; for this plain reason, that He may secure the glory to Himself; that 'no flesh may glory in His sight.'

II. 1. But shall we not forbid one who thus 'casteth out devils,' if 'he followeth not us'? This, it seems, was both the judgement and practice of the Apostle, till he referred the case to his Master. 'We forbad him,' saith he, 'because he followeth not us!' which he supposed to be a very sufficient reason. What we may understand by this expression, 'He followeth not us,' is the next point to be considered.

The lowest circumstance we can understand thereby, is, He has no outward connexion with us. We do not labour in conjunction with each other. He is not our fellow-helper in the gospel. And indeed whensoever our Lord is pleased to send many labourers into His harvest, they cannot all act in subordination to, or connexion with, each other. Nay, they cannot all have personal acquaintance with, nor be so much as known to, one another. Many there will necessarily be, in different parts of the harvest, so far from having any mutual intercourse, that they will be as absolute strangers to each other, as if they had lived in different ages. And concerning any of these whom we know not, we may doubtless say, 'He followeth not us.'

2. A second meaning of this expression may be, He is not of our party. It has long been matter of melancholy consideration to all who pray for the peace of Jerusalem, that so many several parties are still subsisting among those who are all styled Christians. This has been particularly observable in our own countrymen, who have been continually dividing from each other, upon points of no moment, and many times such as religion had no concern in. The most trifling circumstances have given rise to different parties, which have continued for many generations; and each of these would be ready to object to one who was on the other side, 'He followeth not us.'

3. That expression may mean, thirdly, He differs from us in our religious opinions. There was a time when all Christians were of one mind, as well as of one heart; so great grace was upon them all, when they were first filled with the Holy Ghost! But how short a space did this blessing continue! How soon was that unanimity lost! and difference of opinion sprang up again, even in the church of Christ,—and that not in nominal but in real Christians; nay, in the very chief of them, the Apostles themselves! Nor does it appear that the difference which then began was ever entirely removed. We do not find that even those

pillars in the temple of God, so long as they remained upon the earth, were ever brought to think alike, to be of one mind, particularly with regard to the ceremonial law. It is therefore no way surprising, that infinite varieties of opinion should now be found in the Christian church. A very probable consequence of this is, that whenever we see any 'casting out devils,' he will be one that, in this sense, 'followeth not us'—that is not of our opinion. It is scarce to be imagined he will be of our mind in all points, even of religion. He may very probably think in a different manner from us, even on several subjects of importance; such as the nature and use of the moral law, the eternal decrees of God, the sufficiency and efficacy of His grace, and the perseverance of His children.

4. He may differ from us, fourthly, not only in opinion, but likewise in some point of practice. He may not approve of that manner of worshipping God which is practised in our congregation; and may judge that to be more profitable for his soul which took its rise from Calvin or Martin Luther. He may have many objections to that Liturgy which we approve of beyond all others; many doubts concerning that form of church government which we esteem both apostolical and scriptural. Perhaps he may go farther from us yet: he may, from a principle of conscience, refrain from several of those which we believe to be the ordinances of Christ. Or, if we both agree that they are ordained of God, there may still remain a difference between us, either as to the manner of administering those ordinances, or the persons to whom they should be administered. Now the unavoidable consequence of any of these differences will be, that he who thus differs from us must separate himself, with regard to those points, from our society. In this respect, therefore, 'he followeth not us': he is not (as we phrase it) 'of our Church.'

5. But in a far stronger sense 'he followeth not us,' who is not only of a different Church, but of such a Church as we account to be in many respects anti-scriptural and anti-Christian,—a Church which we believe to be utterly false and erroneous in her doctrines, as well as very dangerously wrong in her practice; guilty of gross superstition as well as idolatry,—a Church that has added many articles to the faith which was once delivered to

the saints; that has dropped one whole commandment of God, and made void several of the rest by her traditions; and that, pretending the highest veneration for, and strictest conformity to, the ancient Church, has nevertheless brought in numberless innovations, without any warrant either from antiquity or Scripture. Now, most certainly, 'he followeth not us,' who stands at so great a distance from us.

6. And yet there may be a still wider difference than this. He who differs from us in judgement or practice, may possibly stand at a greater distance from us in affection than in judgement. And this indeed is a very natural and a very common effect of the other. The differences which begin in points of opinion seldom terminate there. They generally spread into the affections, and then separate chief friends. Nor are any animosities so deep and irreconcilable as those that spring from disagreement in religion. For this cause the bitterest enemies of a man are those of his own household. For this the father rises against his own children, and the children against the father; and perhaps persecute each other even to the death, thinking all the time they are doing God service. It is therefore nothing more than we may expect, if those who differ from us, either in religious opinions or practice, soon contract a sharpness, yea, bitterness towards us; if they are more and more prejudiced against us, till they conceive as ill an opinion of our persons as of our principles. An almost necessary consequence of this will be, they will speak in the same manner as they think of us. They will set themselves in opposition to us, and, as far as they are able, hinder our work; seeing it does not appear to them to be the work of God, but either of man or of the devil. He that thinks, speaks, and acts in such a manner as this, in the highest sense, 'followeth not us.'

7. I do not indeed conceive, that the person of whom the Apostle speaks in the text (although we have no particular account of him, either in the context, or in any other part of holy writ) went so far as this. We have no ground to suppose that there was any material difference between him and the Apostles; much less that he had any prejudice either against them or their Master. It seems we may gather thus much from our Lord's own words, which immediately follow the text: 'There is no

man which shall do a miracle in My name, that can lightly speak evil of Me.' But I purposely put the case in the strongest light, adding all the circumstances which can well be conceived; that, being forewarned of the temptation in its full strength, we may in no case yield to it, and fight against God.

III. 1. Suppose, then, a man have no intercourse with us, suppose he be not of our party, suppose he separate from our Church, yea, and widely differ from us, both in judgement, practice, and affection; yet if we see even this man 'casting out devils,' Jesus saith, 'Forbid him not.' This important direction of our Lord I am, in the third place, to explain.

2. If we see this man casting out devils: But it is well if, in such a case, we would believe even what we saw with our eyes, if we did not give the lie to our own senses. He must be little acquainted with human nature who does not immediately perceive how extremely unready we should be to believe that any man does cast out devils who 'followeth not us' in all or most of the senses above recited: I had almost said, in any of them; seeing we may easily learn even from what passes in our own breasts, how unwilling men are to allow anything good in those who do not in all things agree with themselves.

3. 'But what is a sufficient, reasonable proof, that a man does (in the sense above) cast out devils?' The answer is easy. Is there full proof, (1) That a person before us was a gross, open sinner? (2) That he is not so now? that he has broke off his sins, and lives a Christian life? And (3) That this change was wrought by his hearing this man preach? If these three points be plain and undeniable, then you have sufficient, reasonable proof, such as you cannot resist without wilful sin, that this man casts out devils.

4. Then 'forbid him not.' Beware how you attempt to hinder him, either by your authority, or arguments, or persuasions. Do not in any wise strive to prevent his using all the power which God has given him. If you have *authority* with him, do not use that authority to stop the work of God. Do not furnish him with *reasons* why he ought not any more to speak in the name of Jesus. Satan will not fail to supply him with these, if you do not second him therein. *Persuade* him not to depart from the

29

work. If he should give place to the devil and you, many souls
might perish in their iniquity, but their blood would God require
at *your* hands.

5. 'But what, if he be only a layman, who casts out devils!
Ought I not to forbid him then?'

Is the fact allowed? Is there reasonable proof that this man has
or does cast out devils? If there is, forbid him not; no, not at the
peril of your soul. Shall not God work by whom He will work?
No man can do these works unless God is with him; unless God
hath sent him for this very thing. But if God hath sent him, will
you call him back? Will you forbid him to go?

6. 'But I do not know that he is sent of God.' 'Now herein is a
marvellous thing' (may any of the seals of his mission say, any
whom he hath brought from Satan to God), 'that ye know not
whence this man is, and, behold, he hath opened mine eyes! If
this man were not of God, he could do nothing.' If you doubt
the fact, send for the parents of the man: send for his brethren,
friends, acquaintance. But if you cannot doubt this, if you must
needs acknowledge 'that a notable miracle hath been wrought';
then with what conscience, with what face, can you charge him
whom God hath sent, 'not to speak any more in His name'?

7. I allow, that it is highly expedient, whoever preaches in
His name should have an outward as well as an inward call; but
that it is *absolutely necessary*, I deny.

'Nay, is not the Scripture express? "No man taketh this
honour unto himself, but he that is called of God, as was Aaron"'
(Heb. v. 4).

Numberless times has this text been quoted on the occasion,
as containing the very strength of the cause; but surely never was
so unhappy a quotation. For, first, Aaron was not called to
preach at all: he was called 'to offer gifts and sacrifice for sin.'
That was his peculiar employment. Secondly, these men do not
offer sacrifice at all, but only preach; which Aaron did not
Therefore it is not possible to find one text in all the Bible which
is more wide of the point than this.

8. 'But what was the practice of the apostolic age?' You may
easily see in the Acts of the Apostles. In the eighth chapter we
read, 'There was a great persecution against the church which

was at Jerusalem; and they were all scattered abroad throughout the regions of Judea and Samaria, except the Apostles' (verse 1). 'Therefore they that were scattered abroad went everywhere preaching the word' (verse 4). Now, were all these outwardly called to preach? No man in his senses can think so. Here, then, is an undeniable proof, what was the practice of the apostolic age. Here you see not one, but a multitude of lay preachers, men that were only sent of God.

9. Indeed, so far is the practice of the apostolic age from inclining us to think it was *unlawful* for a man to preach before he was ordained, that we have reason to think it was then accounted *necessary*. Certainly the practice and the direction of the Apostle Paul was, to *prove* a man before he was ordained at all. 'Let these' (the deacons), says he, 'first be proved; then let them use the office of a deacon' (1 Tim. iii. 10). *Proved*, how? By setting them to construe a sentence of Greek and asking them a few commonplace questions? O amazing proof of a minister of Christ! Nay; but by making a clear, open trial (as is still done by most of the Protestant Churches of Europe) not only whether their lives be holy and unblamable, but whether they have such gifts as are absolutely and indispensably necessary in order to edify the church of Christ.

10. But what if a man has these, and has brought sinners to repentance, and yet the Bishop will not ordain him? Then the Bishop does forbid him to cast out devils. But I dare not forbid him: I have published my reasons to all the world. Yet it is still insisted I ought to do it. You who insist upon it answer those reasons. I know not that any have done this yet, or even made an attempt of doing it. Only some have spoken of them as very weak and trifling: and this was prudent enough; for it is far easier to despise, at least seem to despise, an argument, than to answer it. Yet till this is done I must say, when I have reasonable proof that any man does cast out devils, whatever others do, I dare not forbid him, lest I be found even to fight against God.

11. And whosoever thou art that fearest God, 'forbid him not,' either directly or indirectly. There are many ways of doing this. You indirectly forbid him, if you either wholly deny, or despise and make little account of, the work which God has wrought by

his hands. You indirectly forbid him, when you discourage him in his work, by drawing him into disputes concerning it by raising objections against it, or frightening him with consequences which very possibly will never be. You forbid him when you show any unkindness toward him either in language or behaviour; and much more when you speak of him to others either in an unkind or a contemptuous manner; when you endeavour to represent him to any, either in an odious or a despicable light. You are forbidding him all the time you are speaking evil of him, or making no account of his labours. O forbid him not in any of these ways; nor by forbidding others to hear him,—by discouraging sinners from hearing that word which is able to save their souls!

12. Yea, if you would observe our Lord's direction in its full meaning and extent, then remember His word: 'He that is not for us is against us; and he that gathereth not with Me scattereth': he that gathereth not men into the kingdom of God, assuredly scatters them from it. For there can be no neuter in this war. Every one is either on God's side, or on Satan's. Are you on God's side? Then you will not only not forbid any man that casts out devils, but you will labour, to the uttermost of your power, to forward him in the work. You will readily acknowledge the work of God, and confess the greatness of it. You will remove all difficulties and objections, as far as may be, out of his way. You will strengthen his hands by speaking honourably of him before all men, and avowing the things which you have seen and heard. You will encourage others to attend upon his word, to hear him whom God hath sent. And you will omit no actual proof of tender love, which God gives you an opportunity of showing him.

IV. 1. If we willingly fail in any of these points, if we either directly or indirectly forbid him, 'because he followeth not us,' then we are bigots. This is the inference I draw from what has been said. But the term 'bigotry,' I fear, as frequently as it is used, is almost as little understood as 'enthusiasm.' It is too strong an attachment to, or fondness for, our own party, opinion, church, and religion. Therefore he is a bigot who is so fond of any of these, so strongly attached to them, as to forbid any who casts out devils because he differs from himself in any or all these particulars.

2. Do *you* beware of this. Take care (1) That you do not convict yourself of bigotry, by your unreadiness to believe that any man does cast out devils, who differs from you. And if you are clear thus far, if you acknowledge the fact, then examine yourself, (2) Am I not convicted of bigotry in this, in forbidding him directly or indirectly? Do I not directly forbid him on this ground, because he is not of my party, because he does not fall in with my opinions, or because he does not worship God according to that scheme of religion which I have received from my fathers?

3. Examine yourself, Do I not indirectly at least forbid him, on any of these grounds? Am I not sorry that God should thus own and bless a man that holds such erroneous opinions? Do I not discourage him, because he is not of my Church, by disputing with him concerning it, by raising objections, and by perplexing his mind with distant consequences? Do I show no anger, contempt, or unkindness of any sort, either in my words or actions? Do I not mention behind his back, his (real or supposed) faults—his defects or infirmities? Do not I hinder sinners from hearing his word? If you do any of these things, you are a bigot to this day.

4. 'Search me, O Lord, and prove me. Try out my reins and my heart! Look well if there be any way of' bigotry 'in me, and lead me in the way everlasting.' In order to examine ourselves thoroughly, let the case be proposed in the strongest manner. What, if I were to see a Papist, an Arian, a Socinian, casting out devils? If I did, I could not forbid even him, without convicting myself of bigotry. Yea, if it could be supposed that I should see a Jew, a Deist, or a Turk, doing the same, were I to forbid him either directly or indirectly, I should be no better than a bigot still.

5. O stand clear of this! But be not content with not forbidding any that casts out devils. It is well to go tnus far; but do not stop here. If you will avoid all bigotry, go on. In every instance of this kind, whatever the instrument be, acknowledge the finger of God. And not only acknowledge,

but rejoice in His work, and praise His name with thanksgiving. Encourage whomsoever God is pleased to employ, to give himself wholly up thereto. Speak well of him wheresoever you are; defend his character and his mission. Enlarge, as far as you can, his sphere of action; show him all kindness in word and deed; and cease not to cry to God in his behalf, that he may save both himself and them that hear him.

6. I need add but one caution: Think not the bigotry of another is any excuse for your own. It is not impossible, that one who casts out devils himself, may yet forbid you so to do. You may observe, this is the very case mentioned in the text. The Apostles forbade another to do what they did themselves. But beware of retorting. It is not your part to return evil for evil. Another's not observing the direction of our Lord, is no reason why you should neglect it. Nay, but let him have all the bigotry to himself. If he forbid *you*, do not you forbid *him*. Rather labour, and watch, and pray the more, to confirm your love toward him. If he speak all manner of evil of *you*, speak all manner of good (that is true) of *him*. Imitate herein that gloroius saying of a great man (O that he had always breathed the same spirit!), 'Let Luther call me a hundred devils; I will still reverence him as a messenger of God.'

SERMON XXXIV

CATHOLIC SPIRIT

And when he was departed thence, he lighted on Jehonadab the son of Rechab coming to meet him, and he saluted him, and said to him, Is thine heart right, as my heart is with thy heart? And Jehonadab answered: It is. If it be, give me thine hand.—2 KINGS x. 15.

IT is allowed even by those who do not pay this great debt, that love is due to all mankind; the royal law, 'Thou shalt love thy neighbour as thyself,' carrying its own evidence to all that hear it: and that, not according to the miserable construction put upon it by the zealots of old times, 'Thou shalt love thy neighbour,' thy relation, acquaintance, friend, 'and hate thine enemy'; not so; 'I say unto you,' saith our Lord, 'Love your enemies, bless them that curse you, do good to them that hate you, and pray for them that despitefully use you, and persecute you; that ye may be the children,' may appear so to all mankind, 'of your Father which is in heaven; who maketh His sun to rise on the evil and on the good, and sendeth rain on the just and on the unjust.'

2. But it is sure, there is a peculiar love which we owe to those that love God. So David: 'All my delight is upon the saints that are in the earth, and upon such as excel in virtue.' And so a greater than he: 'A new commandment I give unto you, That ye love one another: as I have loved you, that ye also love one another By this shall all men know that ye are My disciples, if ye have love one to another' (John xiii. 34, 35). This is that love on which the Apostle John so frequently and strongly insists: 'This,' saith he, 'is the message that ye heard from the beginning, that we should love one another' (1 John iii. 11). 'Hereby perceive we the love of God, because He laid down His life for us: and we ought,' if love should call us thereto, 'to lay down our lives for the brethren' (verse 16). And again: 'Beloved, let us love one another: for love is of God. He that loveth not, knoweth not God; for God is love' (iv. 7, 8). 'Not that we loved God, but that He loved us, and sent His Son to be the propitiation for our sins. Beloved, if God so loved us, we ought also to love one another' (verses 10, 11).

3. All men approve of this; but do all men practise it? Daily experience shows the contrary. Where are even the Christians who 'love one another as He hath given us commandment'? How many hindrances lie in the way! The two grand, general hindrances are, first, that they cannot all think alike and, in consequence of this, secondly, they cannot all walk alike; but in several smaller points their practice must differ in proportion to the difference of their sentiments.

4. But although a difference in opinions or modes of worship may prevent an entire external union, yet need it prevent our union in affection? Though we cannot think alike, may we not

love alike? May we not be of one heart, though we are not of one opinion? Without all doubt, we may. Herein all the children of God may unite, notwithstanding these smaller differences. These remaining as they are, they may forward one another in love and in good works.

5. Surely in this respect the example of Jehu himself, as mixed a character as he was of, is well worthy both the attention and imitation of every serious Christian. 'And when he was departed thence, he lighted on Jehonadab the son of Rechab coming to meet him; and he saluted him, and said to him, Is thine heart right, as my heart is with thy heart? And Jehonadab answered, It is. If it be, give me thine hand.'

The text naturally divides itself into two parts:—First, a question proposed by Jehu to Jehonadab: 'Is thine heart right, as my heart is with thy heart?' Secondly, an offer made on Jehonadab's answering, 'It is': 'If it be, give me thine hand.'

I. 1. And, first, let us consider the question proposed by Jehu to Jehonadab, 'Is thine heart right, as my heart is with thy heart?'

The very first thing we may observe in these words, is, that here is no inquiry concerning Jehonadab's opinions. And yet it is certain, he held some which were very uncommon, indeed quite peculiar to himself; and some which had a close influence upon his practice; on which, likewise, he laid so great a stress, as to entail them upon his children's children, to their latest posterity. This is evident from the account given by Jeremiah, many years after his death: 'I took Jaazaniah and his brethren, and all his sons, and the whole house of the Rechabites, . . . and set before them pots full of wine, and cups, and said unto them, Drink ye wine. But they said, We will drink no wine: for Jonadab,' or Jehonadab, 'the son of Rechab, our father' (it would be less ambiguous, if the words were placed thus: 'Jehonadab *our father, the son of* Rechab'; out of love and reverence to whom, he probably desired his descendants might be called by his name), 'commanded us, saying, Ye shall drink no wine, neither ye, nor your sons for ever. Neither shall ye build house, nor sow seed, nor plant vineyard, nor have any: but all your days ye shall dwell in tents. . . . And we have obeyed, and done according to all that Jonadab our father commanded us' (Jer. xxxv. 3-10).

2. And yet Jehu (although it seems to have been his manner, both in things secular and religious, to *drive furiously*) does not concern himself at all with any of these things, but lets Jehonadab abound in his own sense. And neither of them appears to have given the other the least disturbance touching the opinions which he maintained.

3. It is very possible, that many good men now also may entertain peculiar opinions; and some of them may be as singular herein as even Jehonadab was. And it is certain, so long as we know but *in part*, that all men will not see all things alike. It is an unavoidable consequence of the present weakness and shortness of human understanding, that several men will be of several minds in religion as well as in common life. So it has been from the beginning of the world, and so it will be 'till the restitution of all things.'

4. Nay, farther: although every man necessarily believes that every particular opinion which he holds is true (for to believe any opinion is not true, is the same thing as not to hold it); yet can no man be assured that all his own opinions, taken together, are true. Nay, every thinking man is assured they are not, seeing *humanum est errare et nescire!* 'to be ignorant of many things, and to mistake in some, is the necessary condition of humanity.' This, therefore, he is sensible, is his own case. He knows, in the general, that he himself is mistaken; although in what particulars he mistakes, he does not, perhaps he cannot, know.

5. I say, 'perhaps he cannot know'; for who can tell how far invincible ignorance may extend? or (that comes to the same thing) invincible prejudice?—which is often so fixed in tender minds, that it is afterwards impossible to tear up what has taken so deep a root. And who can say, unless he knew every circumstance attending it, how far any mistake is culpable? seeing all guilt must suppose some concurrence of the will; of which He only can judge who searcheth the heart.

6. Every wise man, therefore, will allow others the same

liberty of thinking which he desires they should allow him;
and will no more insist on their embracing his opinions, than
he would have them to insist on his embracing theirs. He bears
with those who differ from him, and only asks him with whom
he desires to unite in love that single question, 'Is thy heart right,
as my heart is with thy heart?'

7. We may, secondly, observe, that here is no inquiry made
concerning Jehonadab's mode of worship; although it is highly
probable there was, in this respect also, a very wide difference
between them. For we may well believe Jehonadab, as well as
all his posterity, worshipped God at Jerusalem! whereas Jehu
did not: he had more regard to state-policy than religion. And,
therefore, although he slew the worshippers of Baal, and 'destroyed Baal out of Israel'; yet from the convenient sin of Jero-
boam, the worship of the 'golden calves,' he 'departed not'
(2 Kings x. 29).

8. But even among men of an upright heart, men who
desire to 'have a conscience void of offence,' it must needs be,
that, as long as there are various opinions, there will be various
ways of worshipping God; seeng a variety of opinion necessarily
implies a variety of practice. And as, in all ages, men have
differed in nothing more than in their opinions concerning the
Supreme Being, so in nothing have they more differed from
each other, than in the manner of worshipping Him. Had this
been only in the heathen world, it would not have been at all
surprising: for we know, these 'by' their 'wisdom knew not
God'; nor, therefore, could they know how to worship Him.
But is it not strange, that even in the Christian world, although
they all agree in the general, 'God is a Spirit; and they that worship
Him must worship Him in spirit and in truth'; yet the particular
modes of worshipping God are almost as various as among the
Heathens?

9. And how shall we choose among so much variety? No
man can choose for, or prescribe to, another. But every one
must follow the dictates of his own conscience, in simplicity and
godly sincerity. He must be fully persuaded in his own mind;
and then act according to the best light he has. Nor has any
creature power to constrain another to walk by his own rule.

God has given no right to any of the children of men thus to lord it over the conscience of his brethren; but every man must judge for himself, as every man must give an account of himself to God.

10. Although, therefore, every follower of Christ is obliged, by the very nature of the Christian institution, to be a member of some particular congregation or other, some Church, as it is usually termed (which implies a particular manner of worshipping God; for 'two cannot walk together unless they be agreed'); yet none can be obliged by any power on earth but that of his own conscience, to prefer this or that congregation to another, this or that particular manner of worship. I know it is commonly supposed, that the place of our birth fixes the Church to which we ought to belong; that one, for instance, who is born in England, ought to be a member of that which is styled the Church of England; and consequently, to worship God in the particular manner which is prescribed by that Church. I was once a zealous maintainer of this; but I find many reasons to abate of this zeal. I fear it is attended with such difficulties as no reasonable man can get over. Not the least of which is, that if this rule had took place, there could have been no Reformation from Popery; seeing it entirely destroys the right of private judgement, on which that whole Reformation stands.

11. I dare not, therefore, presume to impose my mode of worship on any other. I believe it is truly primitive and apostolical: but my belief is no rule for another. I ask not, therefore, of him with whom I would unite in love, Are you of my church, of my congregation? Do you receive the same form of church government, and allow the same church officers, with me? Do you join in the same form of prayer wherein I worship God? I inquire not, Do you receive the supper of the Lord in the same posture and manner that I do? nor whether, in the administration of baptism, you agree with me in admitting sureties for the baptized; in the manner of administering it; or the age of those to whom it should be administered. Nay, I ask not of you (as clear as I am in my own mind), whether you allow baptism and the Lord's supper at all. Let all these things stand by: we will

talk of them, if need be, at a more convenient season; my only question at present is this, 'Is thine heart right, as my heart is with thy heart?'

12. But what is properly implied in the question? I do not mean, What did Jehu imply therein? But, What should a follower of Christ understand thereby, when he proposes it to any of his brethren?

The first thing implied is this: Is thy heart right with God? Dost thou believe His being and His perfections? His eternity, immensity, wisdom, power? His justice, mercy, and truth? Dost thou believe that He now 'upholdeth all things by the word of His power'? and that He governs even the most minute, even the most noxious, to His own glory, and the good of them that love Him? Hast thou a divine evidence, a supernatural conviction, of the things of God? Dost thou 'walk by faith, not by sight'? looking not at temporal things, but things eternal?

13. Dost thou believe in the Lord Jesus Christ, 'God over all, blessed for ever'? Is He revealed in thy soul? Dost thou know Jesus Christ and Him crucified? Does He dwell in thee, and thou in Him? Is He formed in thy heart by faith? Having absolutely disclaimed all thy own works, thy own righteousness hast thou 'submitted thyself unto the righteousness of God, which is by faith in Christ Jesus? Art thou 'found in Him, not having thy own righteousness, but the righteousness which is by faith'? And art thou, through Him, 'fighting the good fight of faith, and laying hold of eternal life'?

14. Is thy faith ἐνεργουμένη δι ἀγάπης—filled with the energy, of love? Dost thou love God (I do not say 'above all things,' for it is both an unscriptural and an ambiguous expression, but) 'with all thy heart, and with all thy mind, and with all thy soul, and with all thy strength'? Dost thou seek all thy happiness in Him alone? And dost thou find what thou seekest? Does thy soul continually 'magnify the Lord, and thy spirit rejoice in God thy Saviour'? Having learned 'in everything to give thanks, dost thou find 'it is a joyful and a pleasant thing to be thankful'? Is God the centre of thy soul, the sum of all thy desires? Art thou accordingly laying up thy treasure in heaven, and counting all things else dung and dross? Hath the love of God cast the

love of the world out of thy soul? Then thou art 'crucified to the world'; thou art dead to all below; and thy 'life is hid with Christ in God.'

15. Art thou employed in doing, 'not thy own will, but the will of Him that sent thee'—of Him that sent thee down to sojourn here awhile, to spend a few days in a strange land, till, having finished the work He hath given thee to do, thou return to thy Father's house? Is it thy meat and drink 'to do the will of thy Father which is in heaven'? Is thine eye single in all things? always fixed on Him? always looking unto Jesus? Dost thou point at Him in whatsoever thou doest? in all thy labour, thy business, thy conversation? aiming only at the glory of God in all; 'whatsoever thou doest, either in word or deed, doing it all in the name of the Lord Jesus; giving thanks unto God, even the Father, through Him'?

16. Does the love of God constrain thee to serve Him with fear, to 'rejoice unto Him with reverence'? Art thou more afraid of displeasing God, than either of death or hell? Is nothing so terrible to thee as the thought of offending the eyes of His glory? Upon this ground, dost thou 'hate all evil ways,' every transgression of His holy and perfect law; and herein 'exercise thyself, to have a conscience void of offence toward God, and toward man'?

17. Is thy heart right toward thy neighbour? Dost thou love as thyself, all mankind, without exception? 'If you love those only that love you, what thank have ye?' Do you 'love your enemies'? Is your soul full of good-will, of tender affection, toward them? Do you love even the enemies of God, the unthankful and unholy? Do your bowels yearn over them? Could you 'wish yourself' temporally 'accursed' for their sake? And do you show this by 'blessing them that curse you, and praying for those that despitefully use you, and persecute you'?

18. Do you show your love by your works? While you have time as you have opportunity, do you in fact 'do good to all men,' neighbours or strangers, friends or enemies, good or bad? Do you do them all the good you can; endeavouring to supply all their wants; assisting them both in body and soul, to the uttermost of your power?—If thou art thus minded may

every Christian say, yea, if thou art but sincerely desirous of it, and following on till thou attain, then 'thy heart is right, as my heart is with thy heart.'

II. 1. 'If it be, give me thy hand.' I do not mean, 'Be of my opinion.' You need not: I do not expect or desire it. Neither do I mean, 'I will be of your opinion.' I cannot; it does not depend on my choice: I can no more think, than I can see or hear, as I will. Keep you your opinion; I mine; and that as steadily as ever. You need not even endeavour to come over to me, or bring me over to you. I do not desire you to dispute those points, or to hear or speak one word concerning them. Let all opinions alone on one side and the other: only 'give me thine hand.'

2. I do not mean, 'Embrace my modes of worship'; or, 'I will embrace yours.' This also is a thing which does not depend either on your choice or mine. We must both act as each is fully persuaded in his own mind. Hold you fast that which you believe is most acceptable to God, and I will do the same. I believe the Episcopal form of church government to be scriptural and apostolical. If you think the Presbyterian or Independent is better, think so still, and act accordingly. I believe infants ought to be baptized; and that this may be done either by dipping or sprinkling. If you are otherwise persuaded, be so still, and follow your own persuasion. It appears to me, that forms of prayer are of excellent use, particularly in the great congregation. If you judge extemporary prayer to be of more use, act suitable to your own judgement. My sentiment is, that I ought not to forbid water, wherein persons may be baptized; and that I ought to eat bread and drink wine, as a memorial of my dying Master: however, if you are not convinced of this, act according to the light you have. I have no desire to dispute with you one moment upon any of the preceding heads. Let all these smaller points stand aside. Let them never come into sight. 'If thine heart is as my heart,' if thou lovest God and all mankind, I ask no more: 'give me thine hand.'

3. I mean, first, love me: and that not only as thou lovest all mankind; not only as thou lovest thine enemies, or the enemies of God, those that hate thee, that 'despitefully use thee, and

persecute thee'; not only as a stranger, as one of whom thou knowest neither good nor evil,—I am not satisfied with this,—no; 'if thine heart be right, as mine with thy heart,' then love me with a very tender affection, as a friend that is closer than a brother; as a brother in Christ, a fellow citizen of the New Jerusalem, a fellow soldier engaged in the same warfare, under the same Captain of our salvation. Love me as a companion in the kingdom and patience of Jesus, and a joint heir of His glory.

4. Love me (but in a higher degree than thou dost the bulk of mankind) with the love that is *long-suffering and kind*; that is patient,—if I am ignorant or out of the way, bearing and not increasing my burden; and is tender, soft, and compassionate still; that *envieth not*, if at any time it please God to prosper me in His work even more than thee. Love me with the love that *is not provoked*, either at my follies or infirmities; or even at my acting (if it should sometimes so appear to thee) not according to the will of God. Love me so as to *think no evil* of me; to put away all jealousy and evil-surmising. Love me with the love that *covereth all things*; that never reveals either my faults or infirmities,—that *believeth all things*; is always willing to think the best, to put the fairest construction on all my words and actions,—that *hopeth all things*; either that the thing related was never done; or not done with such circumstances as are related; or, at least, that it was done with a good intention, or in a sudden stress of temptation. And hope to the end, that whatever is amiss will, by the grace of God, be corrected; and whatever is wanting, supplied, through the riches of His mercy in Christ Jesus.

5. I mean, secondly, commend me to God in all thy prayers; wrestle with Him in my behalf, that He would speedily correct what He sees amiss, and supply what is wanting in me. In thy nearest access to the throne of grace, beg of Him who is then very present with thee, that my heart may be more as thy heart, more right both toward God and toward man; that I may have a fuller conviction of things not seen, and a stronger view of the love of God in Christ Jesus; may more steadily walk by faith, not by sight; and more earnestly grasp eternal life. Pray that the love of God and of all mankind may be more

largely poured into my heart; that I may be more fervent and
active in doing the will of my Father which is in heaven; more
zealous of good works, and more careful to abstain from all
appearance of evil.

6. I mean, thirdly, provoke me to love and to good works.
Second thy prayer, as thou hast opportunity, by speaking to me,
in love, whatsoever thou believest to be for my soul's health.
Quicken me in the work which God has given me to do, and
instruct me how to do it more perfectly. Yea, 'smite me friendly,
and reprove me,' whereinsoever I appear to thee to be doing
rather my own will, than the will of Him that sent me. O speak
and spare not, whatever thou believest may conduce, either to
the amending my faults, the strengthening my weakness, the
building me up in love, or the making me more fit, in any kind,
for the Master's use.

7. I mean, lastly, love me not in word only, but in deed and
in truth. So far as in conscience thou canst (retaining still thy
own opinions, and thy own manner of worshipping God), join
with me in the work of God; and let us go on hand in hand.
And thus far, it is certain, thou mayest go. Speak honourably,
wherever thou art, of the work of God, by whomsoever He
works, and kindly of His messengers. And, if it be in thy power,
not only sympathize with them when they are in any difficulty
or distress, but give them a cheerful and effectual assistance, that
they may glorify God on thy behalf.

8. Two things should be observed with regard to what has
been spoken under this last head: the one, that whatsoever love,
whatsoever offices of love, whatsoever spiritual or temporal
assistance, I claim from him whose heart is right, as my heart is
with his, the same I am ready, by the grace of God, according
to my measure, to give him: the other, that I have not made
this claim in behalf of myself only, but of all whose heart is
right toward God and man, that we may all love one another
as Christ hath loved us.

III. 1. One inference we may make from what has been said.
We may learn from hence, what is a catholic spirit.

There is scarce any expression which has been more grossly

misunderstood, and more dangerously misapplied, than this: but it will be easy for any who calmly consider the preceding observations, to correct any such misapprehensions of it, and to prevent any such misapplication.

For, from hence we may learn, first, that a catholic spirit is not *speculative* latitudinarianism. It is not an indifference to all opinions: this is the spawn of hell, not the offspring of heaven. This unsettledness of thought, this being 'driven to and fro, and tossed about with every wind of doctrine,' is a great curse, not a blessing; an irreconcilable enemy, not a friend, to true catholicism. A man of a truly catholic spirit has not now his religion to seek. He is fixed as the sun in his judgement concerning the main branches of Christian doctrine. It is true, he is always ready to hear and weigh whatsoever can be offered against his principles; but as this does not show any wavering in his own mind, so neither does it occasion any. He does not halt between two opinions, nor vainly endeavour to blend them into one. Observe this, you who know not what spirit ye are of: who call yourselves men of a catholic spirit, only because you are of a muddy understanding; because your mind is all in a mist; because you have no settled, consistent principles, but are for jumbling all opinions together. Be convinced, that you have quite missed your way; you know not where you are. You think you are got into the very spirit of Christ; when, in truth, you are nearer the spirit of Antichrist. Go, first, and learn the first elements of the gospel of Christ, and then shall you learn to be of a truly catholic spirit.

2. From what has been said, we may learn, secondly, that a catholic spirit is not any kind of *practical* latitudinarianism. It is not indifference as to public worship, or as to the outward manner of performing it. This, likewise, would not be a blessing but a curse. Far from being an help thereto, it would, so long as it remained, be an unspeakable hindrance to the worshipping of God in spirit and in truth. But the man of a truly catholic spirit, having weighed all things in the balance of the sanctuary, has no doubt, no scruple at all, concerning that particular mode of worship wherein he joins. He is clearly convinced, that *this* manner of worshipping God is both scriptural and rational. He

30

knows none in the world which is more scriptural, none which is more rational. Therefore, without rambling hither and thither, he cleaves close thereto, and praises God for the opportunity of so doing.

3. Hence we may, thirdly, learn, that a catholic spirit is not indifference to all congregations. This is another sort of latitudinarianism, no less absurd and unscriptural than the former. But it is far from a man of a truly catholic spirit. He is fixed in his congregation as well as his principles. He is united to one, not only in spirit, but by all the outward ties of Christian fellowship. There he partakes of all the ordinances of God. There he receives the supper of the Lord. There he pours out his soul in public prayer, and joins in public praise and thanksgiving. There he rejoices to hear the word of reconciliation, the gospel of the grace of God. With these his nearest, his best-beloved brethren, on solemn occasions, he seeks God by fasting. These particularly he watches over in love, as they do over his soul; admonishing, exhorting, comforting, reproving, and every way building up each other in the faith. These he regards as his own household; and therefore, according to the ability God has given him, naturally cares for them, and provides that they may have all the things that are needful for life and godliness.

4. But while he is steadily fixed in his religious principles, in what he believes to be the truth as it is in Jesus; while he firmly adheres to that worship of God which he judges to be most acceptable in His sight; and while he is united by the tenderest and closest ties to one particular congregation,—his heart is enlarged toward all mankind, those he knows and those he does not; he embraces with strong and cordial affection neighbours and strangers, friends and enemies. This is catholic or universal love. And he that has this is of a catholic spirit. For love alone gives the title to this character: catholic love is a catholic spirit.

5. If, then, we take this word in the strictest sense, a man of a catholic spirit is one who, in the manner above-mentioned, gives his hand to all whose hearts are right with his heart: one who knows how to value, and praise God for, all the advantages he enjoys, with regard to the knowledge of the things of God,

the true scriptural manner of worshipping Him, and, above all, his union with a congregation fearing God and working righteousness: one who, retaining these blessings with the strictest care, keeping them as the apple of his eye, at the same time loves —as friends, as brethren in the Lord, as members of Christ and children of God, as joint partakers now of the present kingdom of God, and fellow heirs of His eternal kingdom—all, of whatever opinion or worship, or congregation, who believe in the Lord Jesus Christ; who love God and man; who, rejoicing to please, and fearing to offend God, are careful to abstain from evil, and zealous of good works. He is the man of a truly catholic spirit, who bears all these continually upon his heart; who having an unspeakable tenderness for their persons, and longing for their welfare, does not cease to commend them to God in prayer, as well as to plead their cause before men; who speaks comfortably to them, and labours, by all his words, to strengthen their hands in God. He assists them to the uttermost of his power in all things, spiritual and temporal. He is ready 'to spend and be spent for them'; yea, to lay down his life for their sake.

6. Thou, O man of God, think on these things! If thou art already in this way, go on. If thou hast heretofore mistook the path, bless God who hath brought thee back! And now run the race which is set before thee, in the royal way of universal love. Take heed, lest thou be either wavering in thy judgement, or straitened in thy bowels: but keep an even pace, rooted in the faith once delivered to the saints, and grounded in love, in true catholic love, till thou art swallowed up in love for ever and ever!

CATHOLIC LOVE

1 Weary of all this wordy strife,
    These notions, forms, and modes, and names,
To Thee, the Way, the Truth, the Life,
    Whose love my simple heart inflames,
Divinely taught, at last I fly,
With Thee and Thine to live and die.

2 Forth from the midst of *Babel* brought,
　　Parties and sects I cast behind;
　Enlarged my heart, and free my thought,
　　Where'er the latent truth I find,
　The latent truth with joy to own,
　And bow to Jesu's name alone.

3 Redeem'd by Thine almighty grace,
　　I taste my glorious liberty,
　With open arms the world embrace,
　　But *cleave* to those who cleave to Thee;
　But only in Thy saints delight,
　Who walk with God in purest white.

4 One with the little flock I rest,
　　The-members sound who hold the Head,
　The chosen few, with pardon blest,
　　And by th' anointing Spirit led
　Into the mind that was in Thee,
　Into the depths of Deity.

5 My brethren, friends, and kinsmen these,
　　Who do my heavenly Father's will;
　Who *aim* at perfect holiness,
　　And all Thy counsels to fulfil,
　Athirst to be whate'er Thou art,
　And love their God with all their heart.

6 For these, howe'er in flesh disjoin'd,
　　Where'er dispersed o'er earth abroad,
　Unfeign'd, unbounded love I find,
　　And constant as the life of God;
　Fountain of life, from thence it sprung,
　As pure, as even, and as strong.

7 Join'd to the hidden church unknown
　　In this sure bond of perfectness,
　Obscurely safe, I dwell alone,
　　And glory in th' uniting grace,
　To me, to each believer given,
　To all Thy saints in earth and heaven.

C. W.

SERMON XXXV

CHRISTIAN PERFECTION

Not as though I had already attained, either were already perfect.
—PHIL. iii. 12.

THERE is scarce any expression in holy writ, which has given more offence than this. The word *perfect* is what many cannot bear. The very sound of it is an abomination to them; and whosoever *preaches perfection* (as the phrase is), that is, asserts that it is attainable in this life, runs great hazard of being accounted by them worse than a heathen man or a publican.

2. And hence, some have advised, wholly to lay aside the use of those expressions, 'because they have given so great offence.' But are they not found in the oracles of God? If so, by what authority can any messenger of God lay them aside, even though all men should be offended? We have not so learned Christ; neither may we thus give place to the devil. Whatsoever God hath spoken, that will we speak, whether men will hear, or whether they will forbear; knowing, that then alone can any minister of Christ be 'pure from the blood of all men,' when he hath 'not shunned to declare unto them all the counsel of God.'

3. We may not, therefore, lay these expressions aside, seeing they are the words of God and not of man. But we may and ought to explain the meaning of them; that those who are sincere of heart may not err to the right hand or left, from the mark of the prize of their high calling. And this is the more needful to be done, because, in the verse already repeated, the Apostle speaks of himself as not perfect: 'Not,' saith he, 'as though I were already perfect.' And yet immediately after, in the fifteenth verse, he speaks of himself, yea, and many others, as perfect. 'Let us,' saith he, 'as many as be perfect, be thus minded.'

4. In order, therefore, to remove the difficulty arising from

this seeming contradiction, as well as to give light to them who are pressing forward to the mark, and that those who are lame be not turned out of the way, I shall endeavour to show,—

I. In what sense Christians are not; and,
II. In what sense they are, perfect.

I. 1. In the first place, I shall endeavour to show, in what sense Christians are *not perfect*. And both from experience and Scripture it appears, first, that they are not perfect in knowledge: they are not *so* perfect in this life as to be free from ignorance. They know, it may be, in common with other men, many things relating to the present world; and they know, with regard to the world to come, the general truths which God hath revealed. They know likewise (what the natural man receiveth not; for these things are spiritually discerned) 'what manner of love' it is, wherewith 'the Father' hath loved them, 'that they should be called the sons of God.' They know the mighty working of His Spirit in their hearts; and the wisdom of His providence, directing all their paths, and causing all things to work together for their good. Yea, they know in every circumstance of life what the Lord requireth of them, and how to keep a conscience void of offence both toward God and toward man.

2. But innumerable are the things which they know not. Touching the Almighty Himself, they cannot search Him out to perfection. 'Lo, these are but a part of His ways; but the thunder of His power, who can understand?' They cannot understand, I will not say, how 'there are Three that bear record in heaven, the Father, the Son, and the Holy Spirit, and these Three are One'; or how the eternal Son of God 'took upon Himself the form of a servant';—but not any one attribute, not any one circumstance, of the divine nature. Neither is it for them to know the times and seasons when God will work His great works upon the earth; no, not even those which He hath in part revealed by His servants and prophets since the world began. Much less do they know when God, having 'accomplished the number of His elect, will hasten His kingdom'; when 'the

heavens shall pass away with a great noise, and the elements shall melt with fervent heat.'

3. They know not the reasons even of many of His present dispensations with the sons of men; but are constrained to rest here: Though 'clouds and darkness are round about Him, righteousness and judgement are the habitation of His seat.' Yea, often with regard to His dealings with themselves, doth their Lord say unto them, 'What I do, thou knowest not now; but thou shalt know hereafter.' And how little do they know of what is ever before them, of even the visible works of His hands! —how 'He spreadeth the north over the empty place, and hangeth the earth upon nothing'; how He unites all the parts of this vast machine by a secret chain, which cannot be broken. So great is the ignorance, so very little the knowledge, of even the best of men!

4. No one, then, is so perfect in this life, as to be free from ignorance. Nor, secondly, from mistake; which indeed is almost an unavoidable consequence of it; seeing those who 'know but in part' are ever liable to err touching the things which they know not. It is true, the children of God do not mistake as to the things essential to salvation: they do not 'put darkness for light, or light for darkness'; neither 'seek death in the error of their life.' For they are 'taught of God'; and the way which He teaches them, the way of holiness, is so plain, that 'the wayfaring man, though a fool, need not err therein.' But in things unessential to salvation they do err, and that frequently. The best and wisest of men are frequently mistaken even with regard to facts; believing those things not to have been which really were, or those to have been done which were not. Or, suppose they are not mistaken as to the fact itself, they may be with regard to its circumstances; believing them, or many of them, to have been quite different from what, in truth, they were. And hence cannot but arise many farther mistakes. Hence they may believe either past or present actions which were or are evil, to be good; and such as were or are good, to be evil. Hence also they may judge not according to truth with regard to the characters of men; and that, not only by supposing good men to be better, or wicked men to be worse, than they

are; but by believing them to have been or to be good men, who were or are very wicked; or perhaps those to have been or to be wicked men, who were or are holy and unreprovable.

5. Nay, with regard to the holy Scriptures themselves, as careful as they are to avoid it, the best of men are liable to mistake, and do mistake day by day; especially with respect to those parts thereof which less immediately relate to practice. Hence, even the children of God are not agreed as to the interpretation of many places in holy writ; nor is their difference of opinion any proof that they are not the children of God, on either side; but it is a proof that we are no more to expect any living man to be infallible, than to be omniscient.

6. If it be objected to what has been observed under this and the preceding head, that St. John, speaking to his brethren in the faith, says, 'Ye have an unction from the Holy One, and ye know all things' (1 John ii. 20); the answer is plain: 'Ye know all things that are needful for your soul's health.' That the Apostle never designed to extend this farther, that he could not speak it in an absolute sense, is clear, first, from hence: that otherwise he would describe the disciple as 'above his Master'; seeing Christ Himself, as man, knew not all things. 'Of that hour,' saith He, 'knoweth no man: no, not the Son, but the Father only.' It is clear, secondly, from the Apostle's own words that follow, 'These things have I written unto you concerning them that deceive you'; as well as from his frequently repeated caution, 'Let no man deceive you'; which had been altogether needless, had not those very persons who had that unction from the Holy One been liable, not to ignorance only, but to mistake also.

7. Even Christians, therefore, are not *so* perfect as to be free either from ignorance or error: we may, thirdly, add, nor from infirmities. Only let us take care to understand this word aright: only let us not give that soft title to known sins, as the manner of some is. So, one man tells us, 'Every man has his infirmity, and mine is drunkenness'; another has the infirmity of uncleanness; another, that of taking God's holy name in vain; and yet another has the infirmity of calling his brother, 'Thou fool,' or returning 'railing for railing.' It is plain that all you who thus speak, if

ye repent not, shall, with your infirmities, go quick into hell! But I mean hereby, not only those which are properly termed *bodily infirmities*, but all those inward or outward imperfections which are not of a moral nature. Such are the weakness or slowness of understanding, dullness or confusedness of apprehension, incoherency of thought, irregular quickness or heaviness of imagination. Such (to mention no more of this kind) is the want of a ready or retentive memory. Such, in another kind, are those which are commonly, in some measure, consequent upon these; namely, slowness of speech, impropriety of language, ungracefulness of pronunciation; to which one might add a thousand nameless defects, either in conversation or behaviour. These are the infirmities which are found in the best of men, in a larger or smaller proportion. And from these none can hope to be perfectly freed, till the spirit returns to God that gave it.

8. Nor can we expect, till then, to be wholly free from temptation. Such perfection belongeth not to this life. It is true, there are those who, being given up to work all uncleanness with greediness, scarce perceive the temptations which they resist not; and so seem to be without temptation. There are also many whom the wise enemy of souls seeing to be fast asleep in the dead form of godliness, will not tempt to gross sin, lest they should awake before they drop into everlasting burnings. I know there are also children of God who, being now justified freely, having found redemption in the blood of Christ, for the present feel no temptation. God hath said to their enemies, 'Touch not Mine anointed, and do My children no harm.' And for this season, it may be for weeks or months, He causeth them to ride on high places, He beareth them as on eagles' wings, above all the fiery darts of the wicked one. But this state will not last always; as we may learn from that single consideration, that the Son of God Himself, in the days of His flesh, was tempted even to the end of His life. Therefore, so let his servant expect to be; for 'it is enough that he be as his Master.'

9. Christian perfection, therefore, does not imply (as some men seem to have imagined) an exemption either from ignorance, or mistake, or infirmities, or temptations. Indeed, it is only another term for holiness. They are two names for the same

thing. Thus, every one that is holy is, in the Scripture sense, perfect. Yet we may, lastly, observe, that neither in this respect is there any absolute perfection on earth. There is no *perfection of degrees*, as it is termed; none which does not admit of a continual increase. So that how much soever any man has attained, or in how high a degree soever he is perfect, he hath still need to 'grow in grace,' and daily to advance in the knowledge and love of God his Saviour.

II. 1. In what sense, then are Christians perfect? This is what I shall endeavour, in the second place, to show. But it should be premised, that there are several stages in Christian life, as in natural; some of the children of God being but new-born babes, others having attained to more maturity. And accordingly St. John, in his First Epistle (ii. 12, &c.), applies himself severally to those he terms 'little children,' those he styles 'young men,' and those whom he entitles 'fathers.' 'I write unto you, little children,' saith the Apostle, 'because your sins are forgiven you': because thus far you have attained; being 'justified freely,' you 'have peace with God through Jesus Christ.' 'I write unto you, young men, because ye have overcome the wicked one': or (as he afterwards addeth), 'because ye are strong, and the word of God abideth in you.' Ye have quenched the fiery darts of the wicked one, the doubts and fears wherewith he disturbed your first peace; and the witness of God, that your sins are forgiven, now abideth in your heart. 'I write unto you, fathers, because ye have known Him that is from the beginning.' Ye have known both the Father, and the Son, and the Spirit of Christ, in your inmost soul. Ye are 'perfect men,' being grown up to 'the measure of the stature of the fullness of Christ.'

2. It is of these chiefly I speak in the latter part of this discourse; for these only are perfect Christians. But even babes in Christ are in such a sense perfect, or born of God (an expression taken also in divers senses), as, first, not to commit sin. If any doubt of this privilege of the sons of God, the question is not to be decided by abstract reasonings, which may be drawn out into an endless length, and leave the pooint just as it was before. Neither is it to be determined by the experience of this

or that particular person. Many may suppose they do not commit sin, when they do; but this proves nothing either way. To the law and to the testimony we appeal. 'Let God be true, and every man a liar.' By His Word will we abide, and that alone. Hereby we ought to be judged.

3. Now, the Word of God plainly declares, that even those who are justified, who are born again in the lowest sense, 'do not continue in sin'; that they cannot 'live any longer therein' (Rom. vi. 1, 2); that they are 'planted together in the likeness of the death' of Christ (verse 5); that their 'old man is crucified with Him,' the body of sin being destroyed, so that henceforth they do not serve sin; that, being dead with Christ, they are free from sin (verses 6, 7); that they are 'dead unto sin, and alive unto God' (verse 11); that 'sin hath no more dominion over them,' who are 'not under the law, but under grace'; but that these, 'being free from sin are become the servants of righteousness' (verses 14, 18). *and become perfect*

4. The very least which can be implied in these words, is, that the persons spoken of therein, namely, all real Christians, or believers in Christ, are made free from outward sin. And the same freedom, which St. Paul here expresses in such variety of phrases, St. Peter expresses in that one (1 Pet. iv. 1, 2): 'He that hath suffered in the flesh hath ceased from sin; that he no longer should live to the desires of men, but to the will of God.' For this *ceasing from sin*, if it be interpreted in the lowest sense, as regarding only the outward behaviour, must denote the ceasing from the outward act, from any outward transgression of the law.

5. But most express are the well-known words of St. John, in the third chapter of his First Epistle, verse 8, &c.: 'He that committeth sin is of the devil; for the devil sinneth from the beginning. For this purpose the Son of God was manifested, that He might destroy the works of the devil. Whosoever is born of God doth not commit sin; for His seed remaineth in him: and he cannot sin, because he is born of God.' And those in the fifth (verse 18): 'We know that whosoever is born of God sinneth not; but he that is begotten of God keepeth himself, and that wicked one toucheth him not.'

6. Indeed it is said, this means only, He sinneth not *wilfully*; or he doth not commit sin *habitually*; or, *not as other men do*; or, *not as he did before.* But by whom is this said? by St. John? No: there is no such word in the text; nor in the whole chapter; nor in all his Epistle; nor in any part of his writings whatsoever. Why, then, the best way to answer a bold assertion is, simply to deny it. And if any man can prove it from the Word of God, let him bring forth his strong reasons.

7. And a sort of reason there is, which has been frequently brought to support these strange assertions, drawn from the examples recorded in the Word of God: 'What!' say they, 'did not Abraham himself commit sin—prevaricating, and denying his wife? Did not Moses commit sin, when he provoked God at the waters of strife? Nay, to produce one for all, did not even David, "the man after God's own heart," commit sin, in the matter of Uriah the Hittite; even murder and adultery?' It is most sure he did. All this is true. But what is it you would infer from hence? It may be granted, first, that David, in the general course of his life, was one of the holiest men among the Jews; and, secondly, that the holiest men among the Jews did sometimes commit sin. But if you would hence infer, that all Christians do and must commit sin as long as they live, this consequence we utterly deny: it will never follow from those premises.

8. Those who argue thus seem never to have considered that declaration of our Lord (Matt. xi. 11): 'Verily I say unto you, Among them that are born of women there hath not risen a greater than John the Baptist: notwithstanding he that is least in the kingdom of heaven is greater than he.' I fear, indeed, there are some who have imagined 'the kingdom of heaven,' here, to mean the kingdom of glory; as if the Son of God had just discovered to us, that the least glorified saint in heaven is greater than any man upon earth! To mention this is sufficiently to refute it. There can, therefore, no doubt be made, but 'the kingdom of heaven,' here (as in the following verse, where it is said to be taken by force), or, 'the kingdom of God,' as St. Luke expresses it, is that kingdom of God on earth whereunto all true believers in Christ, all real Christians, belong. In these

words, then, our Lord declares two things: First, that before His coming in the flesh, among all the children of men there had not been one greater than John the Baptist; whence it evidently follows, that neither Abraham, David, nor any Jew, was greater than John. Our Lord, secondly, declares, that he which is least in the kingdom of God (in that kingdom which He came to set upon earth, and which the violent now began to take by force) is greater than he,—not a greater prophet, as some have interpreted the word; for this is palpably false in fact; but greater in the grace of God, and the knowledge of our Lord Jesus Christ. Therefore we cannot measure the privileges of real Christians by those formerly given to the Jews. Their 'ministration' (or dispensation) we allow, 'was glorious'; but ours 'exceeds in glory.' So that whosoever would bring down the Christian dispensation to the Jewish standard, whosoever gleans up the examples of weakness, recorded in the law and the prophets, and thence infers that they who have 'put on Christ' are endued with no greater strength, doth greatly err, neither 'knowing the Scriptures, nor the power of God.'

9. 'But are there not assertions in Scripture which prove the same thing, if it cannot be inferred from those examples? Does not the Scripture say expressly, "Even a just man sinneth seven times a day"?' I answer, No; the Scripture says no such thing. There is no such text in all the Bible. That which seems to be intended is the sixteenth verse of the twenty-fourth chapter of the Proverbs; the words of which are these: 'A just man falleth seven times, and riseth up again.' But this is quite another thing. For, first, the words 'a day' are not in the text. So that if a just man fall seven times in his life, it is as much as is affirmed here. Secondly, here is no mention of *falling into sin* at all: what is here mentioned is, *falling into temporal affliction*. This plainly appears from the verse before, the words of which are these: 'Lay not wait, O wicked man, against the dwelling of the righteous; spoil not his resting-place.' It follows, 'For a just man falleth seven times, and riseth up again: but the wicked shall fall into mischief.' As if he had said, 'God will deliver him out of his trouble; but when thou fallest, there shall be none to deliver thee.'

10. 'But, however, in other places,' continue the objectors

'Solomon does assert plainly, "There is no man that sinneth not" (1 Kings viii. 46; 2 Chron. vi. 36); yea, "There is not a just man upon earth, that doeth good, and sinneth not"' (Eccles. vii. 20). I answer, Without doubt, thus it was in the days of Solomon. Yea, thus it was from Adam to Moses, from Moses to Solomon, and from Solomon to Christ. There was then no man that sinned not. Even from the day that sin entered into the world, there was not a just man upon earth that did good and sinned not, until the Son of God was manifested to take away our sins. It is unquestionably true, that 'the heir, as long as he is a child, differeth nothing from a servant.' And that even so they (all the holy men of old, who were under the Jewish dispensation) were, during that infant state of the church, 'in bondage under the elements of the world.' 'But when the fullness of the time was come, God sent forth His Son, made under the law, to redeem them that were under the law, that they might receive the adoption of sons,'—that they might receive that 'grace which is now made manifest by the appearing of our Saviour Jesus Christ; who hath abolished death, and brought life and immortality to light through the gospel' (2 Tim. i. 10). Now, therefore, they 'are no more servants, but sons.' So that, whatsoever was the case of those under the law, we may safely affirm with St. John, that, since the gospel was given, 'he that is born of God sinneth not.'

11. It is of great importance to observe, and that more carefully than is commonly done, the wide difference there is between the Jewish and the Christian dispensation; and that ground of it which the same Apostle assigns in the seventh chapter of his Gospel (verses 38, &c.). After he had there related those words of our blessed Lord, 'He that believeth on Me, as the Scripture hath said, out of his belly shall flow rivers of living water,' he immediately subjoins, 'This spake He of the Spirit—οὗ ἔμελλον λαμβάνειν οἱ πιστεύοντες εἰς αὐτόν —*which they who should believe on Him were afterwards to receive.* For the Holy Ghost was not yet given; because that Jesus was not yet glorified.' Now, the Apostle cannot mean here (as some have taught), that the miracle-working power of the Holy Ghost was not yet given. For this was

given: our Lord had given it to all the Apostles, when He first sent them forth to preach the gospel. He then gave them power over unclean spirits to cast them out; power to heal the sick; yea, to raise the dead. But the Holy Ghost was not yet given in His sanctifying graces, as He was after Jesus was glorified It was then when 'He ascended up on high, and led captivity captive, that He 'received' those 'gifts for men, yea, even for the rebellious, that the Lord God might dwell among them.' And when the day of Pentecost was fully come, then first it was, that they who 'waited for the promise of the Father' were made more than conquerors over sin by the Holy Ghost given unto them.

12. That this great salvation from sin was not given till Jesus was glorified, St. Peter also plainly testifies; where, speaking of his brethren in the flesh, as now 'receiving the end of their faith, the salvation of their souls,' he adds (1 Pet. i. 9, 10, &c.), 'Of which salvation the prophets have inquired and searched diligently, who prophesied of the grace,' that is, the gracious dispensation, 'that should come unto you: searching what, or what manner of time the Spirit of Christ which was in them did signify, when it testified beforehand the sufferings of Christ, and the glory,' the glorious salvation, 'that should follow. Unto whom it was revealed, that not unto themselves, but unto us they did minister the things, which are now reported unto you by them that have preached the gospel unto you with the Holy Ghost sent down from heaven'; namely, at the day of Pentecost, and so unto all generations, into the hearts of all true believers. On this ground, even 'the grace which was brought unto them by the revelation of Jesus Christ,' the Apostle might well build that strong exhortation, 'Wherefore girding up the loins of your mind, . . . as He which hath called you is holy, so be ye holy in all manner of conversation.'

13. Those who have duly considered these things must allow, that the privileges of Christians are in no wise to be measured by what the Old Testament records concerning those who were under the Jewish dispensation; seeing the fullness of time is now come, the Holy Ghost is now given, the great salvation of God is brought unto men by the revelation of

Jesus Christ. The kingdom of heaven is now set up on earth;
concerning which the Spirit of God declared of old (so far is
David from being the pattern or standard of Christian perfection), 'He that is feeble among them at that day shall be as
David; and the house of David shall be as God, as the angel of
the Lord before them' (Zech. xii. 8).

14. If, therefore, you would prove that the Apostle's words,
'He that is born of God sinneth not, are not to be understood
according to their plain, natural, obvious meaning, it is from
the New Testament you are to bring your proofs, else you will
fight as one that beateth the air. And the first of these which is
usually brought is taken from the examples recorded in the
New Testament. 'The Apostles themselves, it is said, 'committed sin; nay, the greatest of them, Peter and Paul: St. Paul,
by his sharp contention with Barnabas; and St. Peter, by his
dissimulation at Antioch. Well, suppose both Peter and Paul
did then commit sin; what is it you would infer from hence?
that all the other Apostles committed sin sometimes? There is
no shadow of proof in this. Or would you thence infer, that all
the other Christians of the apostolic age committed sin? Worse
and worse: this is such an inference as, one would imagine, a
man in his senses could never have thought of. Or will you
argue thus: 'If two of the Apostles did once commit sin, then all
other Christians, in all ages, do and will commit sin as long as
they live? Alas, my brother! a child of common understanding
would be ashamed of such reasoning as this. Least of all can you
with any colour of argument infer, that any man *must* commit
sin at all. No; God forbid we should thus speak! No necessity
of sinning was laid upon them. The grace of God was surely
sufficient for them. And it is sufficient for us at this day. With
the temptation which fell on them, there was a way to escape;
as there is to every soul of man in every temptation. So that
whosoever is tempted to any sin, need not yield; for no man is
tempted above that he is able to bear.

15. 'But St. Paul besought the Lord thrice, and yet he could
not escape from his temptation. Let us consider his own words
literally translated: 'There was given to me a thorn to the flesh,
an angel' or messenger 'of Satan, to buffet me. Touching this

I besought the Lord thrice, that it,' or he, 'might depart from me. And He said unto me, My grace is sufficient for thee: for My strength is made perfect in weakness. Most gladly therefore will I rather glory in' these 'my weaknessses, that the strength of Christ may rest upon me. Therefore I take pleasure in weaknesses; . . . for when I am weak, then am I strong.'

16. As this scripture is one of the strongholds of the patrons of sin, it may be proper to weigh it throughly. Let it be observed, then, first, it does by no means appear that this thorn, whatsoever it was, occasioned St. Paul to commit sin; much less laid him under any necessity of doing so. Therefore, from hence it can never be proved that any Christian must commit sin. Secondly, the ancient Fathers inform us, it was bodily pain,—a violent headache, saith Tertullian (*De Pudic.*); to which both Chrysostom and St. Jerome agree. St. Cyprian[1] expresses it, a little more generally, in those terms, 'Many and grievous torments of the flesh and of the body.'[2] Thirdly, to this exactly agree the Apostle's own words: 'A thorn to the flesh, to smite, beat, or buffet me.' 'My strength is made perfect in weakness': which same word occurs no less than four times in these two verses only. But, fourthly, whatsoever it was, it could not be either inward or outward sin. It could no more be inward stirrings, than outward expressions, of pride, anger, or lust. This is manifest, beyond all possible exception, from the words that immediately follow: 'Most gladly will I glory in' these 'my weaknesses, that the strength of Christ may rest upon me.' What! did he glory in pride, in anger, in lust? Was it through these *weaknesses* that the strength of Christ rested upon him? He goes on: 'Therefore, I take pleasure in weaknesses; for when I am weak, then am I strong'; that is, when I am weak *in body*, then am I strong *in spirit*. But will any man dare to say, 'When I am weak by pride or lust, then am I strong in spirit'? I call you all to record this day, who find the strength of Christ resting upon you, can you glory in anger, or pride, or lust? Can you take pleasure in these infirmities? Do these weaknesses make you strong? Would you not leap into hell, were it possible, to escape them? Even by yourselves, then, judge, whether the

---

[1] *De Mortalitate.*   [2] *Carnis et corporis multa ac gravia tormenta.*

Apostle could glory and take pleasure in them. Let it be, lastly, observed, that this thorn was given to St. Paul above fourteen years before he wrote this Epistle; which itself was wrote several years before he finished his course. So that he had, after this, a long course to run, many battles to fight, many victories to gain, and great increase to receive in all the gifts of God, and the knowledge of Jesus Christ. Therefore, from any spiritual weakness (if such had been) which he at that time felt, we could by no means infer that he was never made strong; that Paul the aged, the father in Christ, still laboured under the same weaknesses: that he was in no higher state till the day of his death. From all which it appears, that this instance of St. Paul is quite foreign to the question, and does in no wise clash with the assertion of St. John, 'He that is born of God sinneth not.'

17. 'But does not St. James directly contradict this? His words are, "In many things we offend all" (iii. 2): and is not offending the same as committing sin?' In this place, I allow it is: I allow the persons here spoken of did commit sin; yea, that they all committed many sins. But who are the persons here spoken of? Why, those many masters or teachers, whom God had not sent (probably the same vain men who taught that faith without works, which is so sharply reproved in the preceding chapter); not the Apostle himself, nor any real Christian. That in the word *we* (used by a figure of speech common in all other, as well as the inspired writings) the Apostle could not possibly include himself or any other true believer, appears evidently, first, from the same word in the ninth verse: 'Therewith,' saith he, 'bless we God, and therewith curse we men. Out of the same mouth proceedeth blessing and cursing.' True, but not out of the mouth of the Apostle, nor of any one who is in Christ a new creature. Secondly, from the verse immediately preceding the text, and manifestly connected with it: 'My brethren, be not many masters' (or teachers), 'knowing that we shall receive the greater condemnation.' 'For in many things *we* offend all.' *We!* Who? Not the Apostles, nor true believers; but they who knew they should *receive the greater condemnation*, because of those many offences. But this could not be spoke of the Apostle himself, or of any who trod in his steps; seeing 'there is no con-

demnation to them who walk not after the flesh, but after the Spirit.' Nay, thirdly, the very verse itself proves, that, 'We offend all,' cannot be spoken either of all men, or of all Christians: for in it there immediately follows the mention of a man who *offends not*, as the *we* first mentioned did; from whom, therefore, he is professedly contradistinguished, and pronounced *a perfect man.*

18. So clearly does St. James explain himself, and fix the meaning of his own words. Yet, lest any one should still remain in doubt, St. John, writing many years after St. James, puts the matter entirely out of dispute by the express declarations above recited. But here a fresh difficulty may arise: how shall we reconcile St. John with himself? In one place he declares, 'Whosoever is born of God doth not commit sin ; and again, 'We know that he which is born of God sinneth not': and yet in another, he saith, 'If we say that we have no sin, we deceive ourselves, and the truth is not in us'; and again, 'If we say that we have not sinned, we make Him a liar, and His word is not in us.'

19. As great a difficulty as this may at first appear, it vanishes away, if we observe, first, that the tenth verse fixes the sense of the eighth: 'If we say we have no sin,' in the former, being explained by, 'If we say we have not sinned,' in the latter verse. Secondly, that the point under present consideration is not whether we *have or have not sinned heretofore*; and neither of these verses asserts that we *do sin, or commit sin now.* Thirdly, that the ninth verse explains both the eighth and tenth: 'If we confess our sins, He is faithful and just to forgive us our sins, and to cleanse us from all unrighteousness': as if he had said, 'I have before affirmed, "The blood of Jesus Christ cleanseth us from all sin"; but let no man say, I need it not; I have no sin to be cleansed from. If we say that we have no sin, that we have not sinned, we deceive ourselves, and make God a liar: but "if we confess our sins, He is faithful and just," not only "to forgive our sins," but also "to cleanse us from all unrighteousness"; that we may "go and sin no more." '

20. St. John, therefore, is well consistent with himself, as well as with the other holy writers; as will yet more evidently appear, if we place all his assertions touching this matter in one view;

he declares, first, the blood of Jesus Christ cleanseth us from all sin. Secondly, no man can say, I have not sinned, I have no sin to be cleansed from. Thirdly, but God is ready both to forgive our past sins, and to save us from them for the time to come. Fourthly, 'These things write I unto you,' saith the Apostle, 'That you may not sin. But if any man' should 'sin,' or *have sinned* (as the word might be rendered), he need not continue in sin; seeing 'we have an Advocate with the Father, Jesus Christ the righteous.' Thus far all is clear. But lest any doubt should remain in a point of so vast importance, the Apostle resumes this subject in the third chapter, and largely explains his own meaning: 'Little children,' saith he, 'let no man deceive you': (as though I had given any encouragement to those that continue in sin): 'he that doeth righteousness is righteous, even as He is righteous. He that committeth sin is of the devil; for the devil sinneth from the beginning. For this purpose the Son of God was manifested, that He might destroy the works of the devil. Whosoever is born of God doth not commit sin; for His seed remaineth in him: and he cannot sin, because he is born of God. In this the children of God are manifest, and the children of the devil' (verses 7-10). Here the point, which till then might possibly have admitted of some doubt in weak minds, is purposely settled by the last of the inspired writers, and decided in the clearest manner. In conformity, therefore, both to the doctrine of St. John, and to the whole tenor of the New Testament, we fix this conclusion,—*a Christian is so far perfect, as not to commit sin.*

21. This is the glorious privilege of every Christian; yea, though he be but a *babe in Christ.* But it is only of those who *are strong* in the Lord, 'and have overcome the wicked one,' or rather of those who 'have known Him that is from the beginning,' that it can be affirmed they are in such a sense perfect, as, secondly, to be freed from evil thoughts and evil tempers. First, from evil or sinful thoughts. But here let it be observed, that thoughts concerning evil are not always evil thoughts; that a thought concerning sin, and a sinful thought, are widely different. A man, for instance, may think of a murder which another has committed; and yet this is no evil or sinful thought.

So our blessed Lord Himself doubtless thought of, or understood, the thing spoken by the devil, when he said, 'All these things will I give Thee, if Thou wilt fall down and worship me.' Yet had He no evil or sinful thought; nor indeed was capable of having any. And even hence it follows, that neither have real Christians: for 'every one that is perfect is as his Master' (Luke vi. 40). Therefore, if He was free from evil or sinful thoughts, so are they likewise.

22. And, indeed, whence should evil thoughts proceed, in the servant who is *as his Master*? 'Out of the heart of man' (if at all) 'proceed evil thoughts' (Mark vii. 21). If, therefore, his heart be no longer evil, then evil thoughts can no longer proceed out of it. If the tree were corrupt, so would be the fruit: but the tree is good; the fruit, therefore, is good also (Matt. xii. 33); our Lord Himself bearing witness, 'Every good tree bringeth forth good fruit. A good tree cannot bring forth evil fruit,' as 'a corrupt tree cannot bring forth good fruit' (Matt. vii. 17, 18).

23. The same happy privilege of real Christians, St. Paul asserts from his own experience. 'The weapons of our warfare,' saith he, 'are not carnal, but mighty through God to the pulling down of strongholds; casting down imaginations' (or *reasonings* rather, for so the word λογισμούς signifies; all the reasonings of pride and unbelief against the declarations, promises, or gifts of God), 'and every high thing that exalteth itself against the knowledge of God, and bringing into captivity every thought to the obedience of Christ' (2 Cor. x. 4, &c.).

24. And as Christians indeed are freed from evil thoughts, so are they, secondly, from evil tempers. This is evident from the above-mentioned declaration of our Lord Himself: 'The disciple is not above his Master: but every one that is perfect shall be as his Master.' He had been delivering, just before, some of the sublimest doctrines of Christianity, and some of the most grievous to flesh and blood. 'I say unto you, Love your enemies, do good to them which hate you; . . . and unto him that smiteth thee on the one cheek, offer also the other.' Now these He well knew the world would not receive; and therefore immediately adds, 'Can the blind lead the blind? will they not both fall into

the ditch?' As if He had said, 'Do not confer with flesh and blood, touching these things—with men void of spiritual discernment, the eyes of whose understanding God hath not opened—lest they and you perish together.' In the next verse He removes the two grand objections with which these wise fools meet us at every turn: 'These things are too grievous to be borne'; or, 'They are too high to be attained,'—saying, ' "The disciple is not above his Master"; therefore, if I have suffered, be content to tread in My steps. And doubt ye not then, but I will fulfil My word: "For every one that is perfect shall be as his Master." ' But his Master was free from all sinful tempers. So, therefore, is His disciple, even every real Christian.

25. Every one of these can say with St. Paul, 'I am crucified with Christ: nevertheless I live; yet not I, but Christ liveth in me.'—words that manifestly describe a deliverance from inward as well as from outward sin. This is expressed both negatively, *I live not* (my evil nature, the body of sin, is destroyed); and positively, *Christ liveth in me*; and, therefore, all that is holy, and just, and good. Indeed, both these, *Christ liveth in me*, and *I live not*, are inseparably connected; for 'what communion hath light with darkness, or Christ with Belial?'

26. He, therefore, who liveth in true believers hath 'purified their hearts by faith'; insomuch that every one that hath Christ in him, the hope of glory, 'purifieth himself, even as He is pure' (1 John iii. 3). He is purified from pride; for Christ was lowly of heart. He is pure from self-will or desire; for Christ desired only to do the will of His Father, and to finish His work. And he is pure from anger, in the common sense of the word; for Christ was meek and gentle, patient and long-suffering. I say, in the common sense of the word; for all anger is not evil. We read of our Lord Himself (Mark iii. 5), that He once 'looked round with anger.' But with what kind of anger? The next word shows, συλλυπούμενος, 'being,' at the same time, 'grieved for the hardness of their hearts.' So then He was angry at the sin, and in the same moment grieved for the sinners; angry or displeased at the offence, but sorry for the offenders. With anger, yea, hatred, He looked upon the thing; with grief and love upon the persons. Go, thou that art perfect, and do likewise.

Be thus angry, and thou sinnest not; feeling a displacency at every offence against God, but only love and tender compassion to the offender.

27. Thus doth Jesus 'save His people from their sins': and not only from outward sins, but also from the sins of their hearts; from evil thoughts, and from evil tempers. 'True,' say some, we shall thus be saved from our sins; but not till death; not in this world.' But how are we to reconcile this with the express words of St. John?—'Herein is our love made perfect, that we may have boldness in the day of judgement: because as He is, so are we in this world.' The Apostle here, beyond all contradiction, speaks of himself and other living Christians, of whom (as though he had foreseen this very evasion, and set himself to overturn it from the foundation) he flatly affirms, that not only at or after death, but *in this world*, they are as their Master (1 John iv. 17).

28. Exactly agreeable to this are his words in the first chapter of this Epistle (verse 5, &c.), 'God is light, and in Him is no darkness at all If we walk in the light, . . we have fellowship one with another, and the blood of Jesus Christ His Son cleanseth us from all sin.' And again: 'If we confess our sins, He is faithful and just to forgive us our sins, and to cleanse us from all unrighteousness.' Now, it is evident, the Apostle here also speaks of a deliverance wrought *in this world*. For he saith not, The blood of Christ will cleanse at the hour of death, or in the day of judgement; but, it 'cleanseth,' at the time present, 'us,' living Christians, 'from all sin.' And it is equally evident, that if *any sin* remain, we are not cleansed from *all sin*; if *any* unrighteousness remain in the soul, it is not cleansed from *all* unrighteousness. Neither let any sinner against his own soul say, that this relates to justification only, or the cleansing us from the guilt of sin; first, because this is confounding together what the Apostle clearly distinguishes, who mentions first, *to forgive us our sins*, and then *to cleanse us from all unrighteousness*. Secondly, because this is asserting justification by works, in the strongest sense possible; it is making all inward as well as outward holiness necessarily previous to justification. For if the cleansing here spoken of is no other than the cleansing us from the guilt of

sin, then we are not cleansed from guilt, that is, are not justified, unless on condition of 'walking in the light, as He is in the light.' It remains, then, that Christians are saved in this world from all sin, from all unrighteousness; that they are now in such a sense perfect, as not to commit sin, and to be freed from evil thoughts and evil tempers.

29.   Thus hath the Lord fulfilled the things He spake by His holy prophets, which have been since the world began,—by Moses in particular, saying (Deut. xxx. 6), I 'will circumcise thine heart, and the heart of thy seed, to love the Lord thy God with all thy heart, and with all thy soul'; by David, crying out, 'Create in me a clean heart, and renew a right spirit within me'; and most remarkably by Ezekiel, in those words, 'Then will I sprinkle clean water upon you, and ye shall be clean: from all your filthiness, and from all your idols, will I cleanse you.   A new heart also will I give you, and a new spirit will I put within you; . . . and cause you to walk in My statutes, and ye shall keep My judgements, and do them. . . . Ye shall be My people, and I will be your God. I will also save you from all your uncleannesses. . . . Thus saith the Lord God: In the day that I shall have cleansed you from all your iniquities, . . . the Heathen shall know that I the Lord build the ruined places; . . . I the Lord have spoken it, and I will do it' (Ezek. xxxvi. 25, &c.).

30.   'Having therefore these promises, dearly beloved,' both in the law and in the prophets, and having the prophetic word confirmed unto us in the gospel, by our blessed Lord and His Apostles; 'let us cleanse ourselves from all filthiness of flesh and spirit, perfecting holiness in the fear of God.' 'Let us fear, lest' so many 'promises being made us of entering into His rest,' which he that hath entered into has ceased from his own works, 'any of us should come short of it.' 'This one thing let us do, forgetting those things which are behind, and reaching forth unto those things which are before, let us press toward the mark for the prize of the high calling of God in Christ Jesus'; crying unto Him day and night, till we also are 'delivered from the bondage of corruption, into the glorious liberty of the sons of God'!

THE PROMISE OF SANCTIFICATION

(Ezek. xxxvi. 25, &c.)

BY THE REV. CHARLES WESLEY

1 GOD of all power, and truth, and grace,
   Which shall from age to age endure;
 Whose word, when heaven and earth shall pass,
   Remains, and stands for ever sure.

2 Calmly to Thee my soul looks up,
   And waits Thy promises to prove;
 The object of my steadfast hope,
   The seal of Thine eternal love.

3 That I Thy mercy may proclaim,
   That all mankind Thy truth may see,
 Hallow Thy great and glorious name,
   And perfect holiness in me.

4 Chose from the world if now I stand,
   Adorn'd in righteousness divine;
 If, brought unto the promised land,
   I justly call the Saviour mine;

5 Perform the work Thou hast begun,
   My inmost soul to Thee convert:
 Love me, for ever love Thine own,
   And sprinkle with Thy blood my heart.

6 Thy sanctifying Spirit pour,
   To quench my thirst and wash me clean:
 Now, Father, let the gracious shower
   Descend, and make me pure from sin.

7 Purge me from every sinful blot;
   My idols all be cast aside;
 Cleanse me from every evil thought,
   From all the filth of self and pride.

8 Give me a new, a perfect heart,
   From doubt, and fear, and sorrow free;
 The mind which was in Christ impart,
   And let my spirit cleave to Thee.

9 O take this heart of stone away!
  (Thy rule it doth not, cannot own;)
  In me no longer let it stay:
  O take away this heart of stone!

10 The hatred of my carnal mind
   Out of my flesh at once remove;
   Give me a tender heart, resigned,
   And pure, and fill'd with faith and love.

11 Within me Thy good Spirit place,
   Spirit of health, and love, and power;
   Plant in me Thy victorious grace,
   And sin shall never enter more.

12 Cause me to walk in Christ my way,
   And I Thy statutes shall fulfil;
   In every point Thy law obey,
   And perfectly perform Thy will.

13 Hast Thou not said, who canst not lie,
   That I Thy law shall keep and do?
   Lord, I believe, though men deny:
   They all are false; but Thou art true.

14 O that I now, from sin released,
   Thy word might to the utmost prove!
   Enter into the promised rest,
   The Canaan of Thy perfect love!

15 There let me ever, ever dwell;
   Be Thou my God, and I will be
   Thy servant! O set to Thy seal!
   Give me eternal life in Thee.

16 From all remaining filth within
   Let me in Thee salvation have:
   From actual and from inbred sin,
   My ransom'd soul persist to save.

17 Wash out my old original stain;
   Tell me no more it cannot be,
   Demons or men! The Lamb was slain,
   His blood was all pour'd out for me.

18 Sprinkle it, Jesu, on my heart:
    One drop of Thy all-cleansing blood
Shall make my sinfulness depart,
    And fill me with the life of God.

19 Father, supply my every need;
    Sustain the life Thyself hast given;
Call for the corn, the living bread,
    The manna that comes down from heaven.

20 The gracious fruits of righteousness,
    Thy blessings' unexhausted store,
In me abundantly increase;
    Nor let me ever hunger more.

21 Let me no more, in deep complaint,
    'My leanness, O my leanness!' cry;
Alone consumed with pining want,
    Of all my Father's children I!

22 The painful thirst, the fond desire,
    Thy joyous presence shall remove;
While my full soul doth still require
    The whole eternity of love.

23 Holy, and true, and righteous Lord,
    I wait to prove Thy perfect will!
Be mindful of Thy gracious word,
    And stamp me with Thy Spirit's seal.

24 Thy faithful mercies let me find,
    In which Thou causest me to trust;
Give me Thy meek and lowly mind,
    And lay my spirit in the dust.

25 Show me how foul my heart hath been,
    When all renew'd by grace I am;
When Thou hast emptied me of sin,
    Show me the fullness of my shame.

26 Open my faith's interior eye,
    Display Thy glory from above;
And all I am shall sink and die,
    Lost in astonishment and love.

27 Confound, o'erpower me, with Thy grace;
    I would be by myself abhorr'd;
  (All might, all majesty, all praise,
    All glory be to Christ my Lord!)

28 Now let me gain perfection's height!
    Now let me into nothing fall!
  Be less than nothing in my sight,
    And feel that Christ is all in all!

SERMON XXXVI

WANDERING THOUGHTS

Bringing into captivity every thought to the obedience of Christ.—
2 COR. X. 5.

BUT will God so 'bring every thought into captivity to the obedience of Christ,' that no wandering thought will find a place in the mind, even while we remain in the body? So some have vehemently maintained; yea, have affirmed that none are perfected in love unless they are so far perfected in understanding, that all wandering thoughts are done away; unless not only every affection and temper be holy and just and good, but every individual thought which arises in the mind be wise and regular.

2. This is a question of no small importance. For how many of those who fear God, yea, and love Him, perhaps with all their heart, have been greatly distressed on this account! How many, by not understanding it right, have not only been distressed, but greatly hurt in their souls; cast into unprofitable, yea, mischievous reasonings, such as slackened their motion towards God, and weakened them in running the race set before them! Nay, many, through misapprehensions of this very thing, have cast away the precious gift of God. They have been induced, first to doubt of, and then to deny, the work God

had wrought in their souls; and hereby have grieved the Spirit of God, till He withdrew and left them in utter darkness!

3. How is it then, that amidst the abundance of books which have been lately published almost on all subjects, we should have none upon wandering thoughts? at least none that will at all satisfy a calm and serious mind? In order to do this in some degree, I purpose to inquire,—

I. WHAT ARE THE SEVERAL SORTS OF WANDERING THOUGHTS?
II. WHAT ARE THE GENERAL OCCASIONS OF THEM?
III. WHICH OF THEM ARE SINFUL, AND WHICH NOT?
IV. WHICH OF THEM WE MAY EXPECT AND PRAY TO BE DELIVERED FROM?

I. 1. I purpose to inquire, first, What are the several sorts of wandering thoughts? The particular sorts are innumerable; but, in general, they are of two sorts: thoughts that wander from God; and thoughts that wander from the particular point we have in hand.

2. With regard to the former, all our thoughts are naturally of this kind: for they are continually wandering from God: we think nothing about Him: God is not in all our thoughts: we are, one and all, as the Apostle observes, 'without God in the world.' We think of what we love; but we do not love God; therefore, we think not of Him. Or, if we are now and then constrained to think of Him for a time, yet, as we have no pleasure therein, nay, rather, as these thoughts are not only insipid, but distasteful and irksome to us, we drive them out as soon as we can, and return to what we love to think of. So that the world, and the things of the world—what we shall eat, what we shall drink, what we shall put on; what we shall see, what we shall hear, what we shall gain; how we shall please our senses or our imagination—takes up all our time, and engrosses all our thought. So long, therefore, as we love the world; that is, so long as we are in our natural state; all our thoughts, from morning to evening, and from evening to morning, are no other than wandering thoughts.

3. But many times we are not only 'without God in the world,' but also fighting against Him; as there is in every man by nature a 'carnal mind which is enmity against God': no wonder, therefore, that men abound with unbelieving thoughts; either saying in their hearts, 'There is no God,' or questioning, if not denying, His power or wisdom, His mercy, or justice, or holiness. No wonder that they so often doubt of His providence, at least, of its extending to all events; or that, even though they allow it, they still entertain murmuring or repining thoughts. Nearly related to these, and frequently connected with them, are proud and vain imaginations. Again: sometimes they are taken up with angry, malicious, or revengeful thoughts; at other times, with airy scenes of pleasure, whether of sense or imagination; whereby the earthy, sensual mind becomes more earthy and sensual still. Now by all these they make flat war with God: these are wandering thoughts of the highest kind.

4. Widely different from these are the other sort of wandering thoughts; in which the heart does not wander from God, but the understanding wanders from the particular point it had then in view. For instance: I sit down to consider those words in the verse preceding the text: 'The weapons of our warfare are not carnal, but mighty through God.' I think, 'This ought to be the case with all that are called Christians. But how far is it otherwise! Look round into almost every part of what is termed "the Christian world." What manner of weapons are these using? In what kind of warfare are they engaged,—

> While men, like fiends, each other tear,
> In all the hellish rage of war?

See how *these* Christians love one another! Wherein are they preferable to Turks and Pagans? What abomination can be found among Mahometans or Heathens which is not found among Christians also?' And thus my mind runs off, before I am aware, from one circumstance to another. Now, all these are, in some sense, wandering thoughts: for although they do not wander from God, much less fight against Him, yet they do wander from the particular point I had in view.

II. Such is the nature, such are the sorts (to speak rather usefully, than philosophically) of wandering thoughts. But what are the general occasions of them? This we are, in the second place, to consider.

1. And it is easy to observe, that the occasions of the former sort of thoughts, which oppose or wander from God, are, in general, sinful tempers. For instance: why is not God in all the thoughts, in any of the thoughts, of a natural man? For a plain reason: be he rich or poor, learned or unlearned, he is an Atheist (though not vulgarly so called); he neither knows nor loves God. Why are his thoughts continually wandering after the world? Because he is an idolater. He does not indeed worship an image, or bow down to the stock of a tree; yet is he sunk into equally damnable idolatry: he loves, that is, worships, the world. He seeks happiness in the things that are seen, in the pleasures that perish in the using. Why is it that his thoughts are perpetually wandering from the very end of his being, the knowledge of God in Christ? Because he is an unbeliever; because he has no faith; or, at least, no more than a devil. So all these wandering thoughts easily and naturally spring from that evil root of unbelief.

2. The case is the same in other instances: pride, anger, revenge, vanity, lust, covetousness—every one of them occasions thoughts suitable to its own nature. And so does every sinful temper of which the human mind is capable. The particulars it is hardly possible, nor is it needful, to enumerate: it suffices to observe, that as many evil tempers as find a place in any soul, so many ways that soul will depart from God, by the worst kind of wandering thoughts.

3. The occasions of the latter kind of wandering thoughts are exceeding various. Multitudes of them are occasioned by the natural union between the soul and body. How immediately and how deeply is the understanding affected by a diseased body! Let but the blood move irregularly in the brain, and all regular thinking is at an end. Raging madness ensues; and then farewell to all evenness of thought. Yea, let only the spirits be hurried or agitated to a certain degree, and a temporary madness, a delirium, prevents all settled thought. And is not the same irregularity of

thought, in a measure, occasioned by every nervous disorder?
So does 'the corruptible body press down the soul, and cause it
to muse about many things.'

4. But does it only cause this in the time of sickness or preternatural disorder? Nay, but more or less, at all times, even in a
state of perfect health. Let a man be ever so healthy, he will be
more or less delirious every four-and-twenty hours. For does he
not sleep? And while he sleeps, is he not liable to dream? And
who then is master of his own thoughts, or able to preserve
the order and consistency of them? Who can then keep them
fixed to any one point, or prevent their wandering from pole to
pole?

5. But suppose we are awake, are we always so awake that
we can steadily govern our thoughts? Are we not unavoidably
exposed to contrary extremes, by the very nature of this machine,
the body? Sometimes we are too heavy, too dull and languid,
to pursue any chain of thought. Sometimes, on the other hand,
we are too lively. The imagination, without leave, starts to and
fro, and carries us away hither and thither, whether we will or
no; and all this from the merely natural motion of the spirits, or
vibration of the nerves.

6. Farther: How many wanderings of thought may arise from
those various associations of our ideas which are made entirely
without our knowledge, and independently on our choice!
How these connexions are formed, we cannot tell; but they
are formed in a thousand different manners. Nor is it in the
power of the wisest or holiest of men to break those associations,
or prevent what is the necessary consequence of them, and matter
of daily observation. Let the fire but touch one end of the train,
and it immediately runs on to the other.

7. Once more: Let us fix our attention as studiously as we are
able on any subject, yet let either pleasure or pain arise, especially
if it be intense, and it will demand our immediate attention, and
attach our thought to itself. It will interrupt the steadiest contemplation, and divert the mind from its favourite subject.

8. These occasions of wandering thoughts lie within, are
wrought into our very nature. But they will likewise naturally
and necessarily arise from the various impulse of outward

objects. Whatever strikes upon the organ of sense, the eye or ear, will raise a perception in the mind. And, accordingly, whatever we see or hear will break in upon our former train of thought. Every man, therefore, that does anything in our sight, or speaks anything in our hearing, occasions our mind to wander, more or less, from the point it was thinking of before.

9. And there is no question but those evil spirits who are continually seeking whom they may devour make use of all the foregoing occasions to hurry and distract our minds. Sometimes by one, sometimes by another of these means, they will harass and perplex us, and, so far as God permits, interrupt our thoughts, particularly when they are engaged on the best subjects. Nor is this at all strange: they well understand the very springs of thought; and know on which of the bodily organs the imagination, the understanding, and every other faculty of the mind more immediately depends. And hereby they know how, by affecting those organs, to affect the operations dependent on them. Add to this, that they can inject a thousand thoughts, without any of the preceding means; it being as natural for spirit to act upon spirit, as for matter to act upon matter. These things being considered, we cannot admire that our thought so often wanders from any point which we have in view.

III. 1. What kind of wandering thoughts are sinful, and what not, is the third thing to be inquired into. And, first, all those thoughts which wander from God, which leave Him no room in our minds, are undoubtedly sinful. For all these imply practical Atheism; and by these we are without God in the world. And so much more are all those which are contrary to God, which imply opposition or enmity to Him. Such are all murmuring, discontented thoughts, which say, in effect, 'We will not have Thee to rule over us'; all unbelieving thoughts, whether with regard to His being, His attributes, or His providence. I mean, His particular providence over all things, as well as all persons, in the universe; that without which 'not a sparrow falls to the ground,' by which 'the hairs of our head are all numbered'; for as to a general providence (vulgarly so called), contradistinguished from a particular, it is only a decent, well-sounding word, which means just nothing.

2. Again: All thoughts which spring from sinful tempers are undoubtedly sinful. Such, for instance, are those that spring from a revengeful temper, from pride, or lust, or vanity. 'An evil tree cannot bring forth good fruit': therefore, if the tree be evil, so must the fruit be also.

3. And so must those be which either produce or feed any sinful temper; those which either give rise to pride or vanity, to anger or love of the world, or confirm and increase these or any other unholy temper, passion, or affection. For not only whatever flows from evil is evil; but also whatever leads to it; whatever tends to alienate the soul from God, and to make or keep it earthly, sensual, and devilish.

4. Hence, even those thoughts which are occasioned by weakness or disease, by the natural mechanism of the body, or by the laws of vital union, however innocent they may be in themselves, do nevertheless become sinful, when they either produce or cherish and increase in us any sinful temper; suppose the desire of the flesh, the desire of the eye, or the pride of life. In like manner, the wandering thoughts, which are occasioned by the words or actions of other men, if they cause or feed any wrong disposition, then commence sinful. And the same we may observe of those which are suggested or injected by the devil. When they minister to any earthly or devilish temper (which they do, whenever we give place to them, and thereby make them our own), then they are equally sinful with the tempers to which they minister.

5. But, abstracting from these cases, wandering thoughts, in the latter sense of the word, that is, thoughts wherein our understanding wanders from the point it has in view, are no more sinful than the motion of the blood in our veins, or of the spirits in our brain. If they arise from an infirm constitution, or from some accidental weakness or distemper, they are as innocent as it is to have a weak constitution or a distempered body. And surely no one doubts but a bad state of nerves, a fever of any kind, and either a transient or a lasting delirium, may consist with perfect innocence. And if they should arise

in a soul which is united to a healthful body, either from the natural union between the body and soul, or from any of ten thousand changes which may occur in those organs of the body that minister to thought,—in any of these cases they are as perfectly innocent as the causes from which they spring. And so they are when they spring from the casual, involuntary associations of our ideas.

6. If our thoughts wander from the point we had in view, by means of other men variously affecting our senses, they are equally innocent still: for it is no more a sin to understand what I see and hear, and in many cases cannot help seeing, hearing, and understanding, than it is to have eyes and ears. 'But if the devil injects wandering thoughts, are not those thoughts evil?' They are troublesome, and in that sense evil; but they are not sinful. I do not know that he spoke to our Lord with an audible voice; perhaps he spoke to His heart only, when he said, 'All these things will I give Thee, if Thou wilt fall down and worship me.' But whether he spoke inwardly or outwardly, our Lord doubtless understood what he said. He had therefore a thought correspondent to those words. But was it a sinful thought? We know it was not. In Him was no sin, either in action, or word, or thought. Nor is there any sin in a thousand thoughts of the same kind, which Satan may inject into any of our Lord's followers.

7. It follows, that none of these wandering thoughts (whatever unwary persons have affirmed, thereby grieving whom the Lord had not grieved) are inconsistent with perfect love. Indeed, if they were, then not only sharp pain, but sleep itself, would be inconsistent with it. Sharp pain; for whenever this supervenes, whatever we were before thinking of, it will interrupt our thinking, and of course draw our thoughts into another channel. Yea, and sleep itself; as it is a state of insensibility and stupidity; and such as is generally mixed with thoughts wandering over the earth, loose, wild, and incoherent. Yet certainly these are consistent with perfect love: so then are all wandering thoughts of this kind

IV. 1. From what has been observed, it is easy to **give** a clear answer to the last question, What kind of wandering thoughts we may expect and pray to be delivered from.

From the former sort of wandering thoughts—those wherein the heart wanders from God; from all that are contrary to His will, or that leave us without God in the world—every one that is perfected in love is unquestionably delivered. This deliverance, therefore, we may expect; this we may, we ought to pray for. Wandering thoughts of this kind imply unbelief, if not enmity against God; but both of these He will destroy, will bring utterly to an end. And indeed, from all sinful wandering thoughts we shall be absolutely delivered. All that are perfected in love are delivered from these; else they were not saved from sin. Men and devils will tempt them all manner of ways; but they cannot prevail over them.

2. With regard to the latter sort of wandering thoughts, the case is widely different. Till the cause is removed, we cannot in reason expect the effect should cease. But the causes or occasions of these will remain as long as we remain in the body. So long, therefore, we have all reason to believe the effects will remain also.

3. To be more particular: Suppose a soul, however holy, to dwell in a distempered body; suppose the brain be so thoroughly disordered, as that raging madness follows; will not all the thoughts be wild and unconnected as long as that disorder continues? Suppose a fever occasions that temporary madness which we term 'a delirium'; can there be any just connexion of thought till that delirium is removed? Yea, suppose what is called 'a nervous disorder' to rise to so high a degree as to occasion at least a partial madness; will there not be a thousand wandering thoughts? And must not these irregular thoughts continue as long as the disorder which occasions them?

4. Will not the case be the same with regard to those thoughts that necessarily arise from violent pain? They will more or less continue, while that pain continues, by the inviolable order of nature. This order, likewise, will obtain, where the thoughts are disturbed, broken, or interrupted by any defect of the apprehension, judgement, or imagination, flowing from the natural constitution of the body. And how many interruptions may spring from the unaccountable and involuntary association

of our ideas! Now, all these are directly or indirectly caused by the corruptible body pressing down the mind. Nor, therefore, can we expect them to be removed till 'this corruptible shall put on incorruption.'

5. And then only, when we lie down in the dust, shall we be delivered from those wandering thoughts which are occasioned by what we see and hear, among those by whom we are now surrounded. To avoid these, we must go out of the world: for as long as we remain therein, as long as there are men and women round about us, and we have eyes to see, and ears to hear, the things which we daily see and hear will certainly affect our mind, and will more or less break in upon and interrupt our preceeding thoughts.

6. And as long as evil spirits roam to and fro in a miserable, disordered world, so long they will assault (whether they can prevail or no) every inhabitant of flesh and blood. They will trouble even those whom they cannot destroy: they will attack, if they cannot conquer. And from these attacks of our restless, unwearied enemies, we must not look for an entire deliverance, till we are lodged 'where the wicked cease from troubling, and where the weary are at rest.'

7. To sum up the whole: To expect deliverance from those wandering thoughts which are occasioned by evil spirits is to expect that the devil should die or fall asleep, or, at least, should no more go about as a roaring lion. To expect deliverance from those which are occasioned by other men is to expect either that men should cease from the earth, or that we should be absolutely secluded from them, and have no intercourse with them; or that having eyes we should not see, neither hear with our ears, but be as senseless as stocks or stones. And to pray for deliverance from those which are occasioned by the body is, in effect, to pray that we may leave the body: otherwise it is praying for impossibilities and absurdities; praying that God would reconcile contradictions, by continuing our union with a corruptible body without the natural, necessary consequences of that union. It is as if we should pray to be angels and men, mortal and immortal, at the same time. Nay!—but when that which is immortal is come, mortality is done away.

8. Rather let us pray, both with the spirit and with the understanding, that all these things may work together for our good; that we may suffer all the infirmities of our nature, all the interruptions of men, all the assaults and suggestions of evil spirits, and in all be 'more than conquerors.' Let us pray, that we may be delivered from all sin; that both root and branch may be destroyed; that we may be 'cleansed from all pollution of flesh and spirit,' from every evil temper, and word, and work; that we may 'love the Lord our God with all our heart, with all our mind, with all our soul, and with all our strength'; that all the fruit of the Spirit may be found in us—not only love, joy, peace, but also 'long-suffering, gentleness, goodness, fidelity, meekness, temperance.' Pray that all these things may flourish and abound, may increase in you more and more, till an abundant entrance be ministered unto you, into the everlasting kingdom of our Lord Jesus Christ!

SERMON XXXVII

SATAN'S DEVICES

We are not ignorant of his devices.—2 COR. ii. 11.

THE devices whereby the subtle god of this world labours to destroy the children of God—or at least to torment whom he cannot destroy, to perplex and hinder them in running the race which is set before them—are numberless as the stars of heaven, or the sand upon the sea-shore. But it is of one of them only that I now propose to speak (although exerted in various ways), whereby he endeavours to divide the gospel against itself, and by one part of it to overthrow the other.

2. The inward kingdom of heaven, which is set up in the hearts of all that repent and believe the gospel, is no other than 'righteousness, and peace, and joy in the Holy Ghost.' Every babe in Christ knows we are made partakers of these, the very hour that we believe in Jesus. But these are only the first-fruits

of His Spirit; the harvest is not yet. Although these blessings are inconceivably great, yet we trust to see greater than these. We trust to love the Lord our God, not only as we do now, with a weak, though sincere affection, but 'with all our heart, with all our mind, with all our soul, and with all our strength.' We look for power to 'rejoice evermore, to pray without ceasing, and in everything to give thanks'; knowing, 'this is the will of God in Christ Jesus concerning us.'

3. We expect to be 'made perfect in love'; in that which casts out all painful fear, and all desire but that of glorifying Him we love, and of loving and serving Him more and more. We look for such an increase in the experimental knowledge and love of God our Saviour, as will enable us always 'to walk in the light as He is in the light.' We believe the whole mind will be in us 'which was also in Christ Jesus'; that we shall love every man so as to be ready to lay down our life for his sake; so as, by this love, to be freed from anger, and pride, and from every unkind affection. We expect to be 'cleansed from all our idols,' 'from all filthiness,' whether 'of flesh or spirit'; to be 'saved from all our uncleannesses,' inward or outward; to be purified 'as He is pure.'

4. We trust in His promise who cannot lie, that the time will surely come, when, in every word and work, we shall do His blessed will on earth, as it is done in heaven; when all our conversation shall be seasoned with salt, all meet to minister grace to the hearers; when, whether we eat or drink, or whatever we do, it shall be done to the glory of God; when all our words and deeds shall be 'in the name of the Lord Jesus, giving thanks unto God, even the Father, through Him.'

5. Now this is the grand device of Satan, to destroy the first work of God in the soul, or at least to hinder its increase, by our expectation of that greater work. It is therefore my present design, first, to point out the several ways whereby he endeavours this: and, secondly, to observe how we may retort these fiery darts of the wicked one; how we may rise the higher, by what he intends for an occasion of our falling.

I. I am, first, to point out the several ways whereby Satan

endeavours to destroy the first work of God in the soul, or at least to hinder its increase, by our expectation of that greater work. And, 1. He endeavours to damp our joy in the Lord, by the consideration of our own vileness, sinfulness, unworthiness; added to this, that there must be a far greater change than is yet, or we cannot see the Lord. If we knew we must remain as we are, even to the day of our death, we might possibly draw a kind of comfort, poor as it was, from that necessity. But as we know we need not remain in this state, as we are assured there is a greater change to come, and that unless sin be all done away in this life, we cannot see God in glory, that subtle adversary often damps the joy we should otherwise feel in what we have already attained, by a perverse representation of what we have not attained, and the absolute necessity of attaining it. So that we cannot rejoice in what we have, because there is more which we have not. We cannot rightly taste the goodness of God, who hath done so great things for us, because there are so much greater things which, as yet, He hath not done. Likewise, the deeper conviction God works in us of our present unholiness, and the more vehement desire we feel in our heart of the entire holiness He hath promised, the more are we tempted to think lightly of the present gifts of God, and to undervalue what we have already received, because of what we have not received.

2. If he can prevail thus far, if he can damp our joy, he will soon attack our peace also. He will suggest, 'Are you fit to see God? He is of purer eyes than to behold iniquity. How, then, can you flatter yourself, so as to imagine He beholds you with approbation? God is holy: you are unholy. What communion hath light with darkness? How is it possible that you, unclean as you are, should be in a state of acceptance with God? You see indeed the mark, the prize of your high calling; but do you not see it is afar off? How can you presume, then, to think that all your sins are already blotted out? How can this be until your are brought nearer to God, until you bear more resemblance to Him?' Thus will he endeavour not only to shake your peace, but even to overturn the very foundation of it; to bring you back, by insensible degrees, to the point from whence

you set out first, even to seek for justification by works, or by your own righteousness,—to make something in you the ground of your acceptance, or, at least, necessarily previous to it.

3. Or, if we hold fast, 'Other foundation can no man lay than that which is laid, even Jesus Christ'; and, 'I am justified freely by God's grace, through the redemption which is in Jesus'; yet he will not cease to urge, 'But the tree is known by its fruits: and have you the fruits of justification? Is that mind in you which was in Christ Jesus? Are you dead unto sin, and alive unto righteousness? Are you made conformable to the death of Christ, and do you know the power of His resurrection?' And then, comparing the small fruits we feel in our souls with the fullness of the promises, we shall be ready to conclude, 'Surely God hath not said that my sins are forgiven me! Surely I have not received the remission of my sins; for what lot have I among them that are sanctified?'

4. More especially in the time of sickness and pain, he will press this with all his might: 'Is it not the word of Him that cannot lie, "Without holiness no man shall see the Lord"? But you are not holy; you know it well; you know holiness is the full image of God; and how far is this above, out of your sight? You cannot attain unto it. Therefore, all your labour has been in vain. All these things you have suffered in vain. You have spent your strength for nought. You are yet in your sins, and must therefore perish at the last.' And thus, if your eye be not steadily fixed on Him who hath borne all your sins, he will bring you again under that 'fear of death,' whereby you was so long 'subject unto bondage,' and, by this means, impair, if not wholly destroy, your peace, as well as joy in the Lord.

5. But his masterpiece of subtlety is still behind. Not content to strike at your peace and joy, he will carry his attempts farther yet: he will level his assault against your righteousness also. He will endeavour to shake, yea, if it be possible, to destroy, the holiness you have already received, by your very expectation of receiving more, of attaining all the image of God.

6. The manner wherein he attempts this, may partly appear from what has been already observed. For, first, by striking at our joy in the Lord, he strikes likewise at our holiness: seeing

joy in the Holy Ghost is a precious means of promoting every holy temper, a choice instrument of God, whereby He carries on much of His work in a believing soul. And it is a considerable help, not only to inward, but also to outward, holiness. It strengthens our hands to go on in the work of faith, and in the labour of love; manfully to 'fight the good fight of faith, and to lay hold on eternal life.' It is peculiarly designed of God to be a balance both against inward and outward sufferings: to 'lift up the hands that hang down, and confirm the feeble knees.' Consequently, whatever damps our joy in the Lord, proportionably obstructs our holiness. And therefore, so far as Satan shakes our joy, he hinders our holiness also.

7. The same effect will ensue, if he can, by any means, either destroy or shake our peace. For the peace of God is another precious means of advancing the image of God in us. There is scarce a greater help to holiness than this, a continual tranquillity of spirit, the evenness of a mind stayed upon God, a calm repose in the blood of Jesus. And without this, it is scarce possible to 'grow in grace,' and in the vital 'knowledge of our Lord Jesus Christ.' For all fear (unless the tender, filial fear) freezes and benumbs the soul. It binds up all the springs of spiritual life, and stops all motion of the heart toward God. And doubt, as it were, bemires the soul, so that it sticks fast in the deep clay. Therefore, in the same proportion as either of these prevail, our growth in holiness is hindered.

8. At the same time that our wise adversary endeavours to make our conviction of the necessity of perfect love an occasion of shaking our peace by doubts and fears, he endeavours to weaken, if not destroy, our faith. Indeed these are inseparably connected, so that they must stand or fall together. So long as faith subsists, we remain in peace; our heart stands fast, while it believes in the Lord. But if we let go our faith, our filial confidence in a loving, pardoning God, our peace is at an end, the very foundation on which it stood being overthrown. And this is the only foundation of holiness, as well as of peace; consequently, whatever strikes at this, strikes at the very root of all holiness: for without this faith, without an abiding sense that Christ loved me, and gave Himself for me, without a continuing

conviction that God for Christ's sake is merciful to me a sinner, it is impossible that I should love God: 'We love Him, because He first loved us'; and in proportion to the strength and clearness of our conviction that He hath loved us, and accepted us in His Son. And unless we love God, it is not possible that we should love our neighbour as ourselves: nor, consequently, that we should have any right affections, either toward God, or toward man. It evidently follows, that whatever weakens our faith, must in the same degree, obstruct our holiness: and this is not only the most effectual, but also the most compendious way of destroying all holiness; seeing it does not affect any one Christian temper, any single grace or fruit of the Spirit, but, so far as it succeeds, tears up the very root of the whole work of God.

9. No marvel, therefore, that the ruler of the darkness of this world should here put forth all his strength. And so we find by experience. For it is far easier to conceive, than it is to express, the unspeakable violence wherewith this temptation is frequently urged on them who hunger and thirst after righteousness. When they see, in a strong and clear light, on the one hand the desperate wickedness of their own hearts, on the other hand the unspotted holiness to which they are called in Christ Jesus; on the one hand the depth of their own corruption, of their total alienation from God, on the other the height of the Glory of God, that image of the Holy One, wherein they are to be renewed; there is, many times, no spirit left in them; they could almost cry out, 'With God this is impossible!' They are ready to give up both faith and hope; to cast away that very confidence, whereby they are to overcome all things, through Christ strengthening them; whereby, 'after they have done the will of God,' they are to 'receive the promise.'

10. And if they 'hold fast the beginning of their confidence steadfast unto the end,' they shall undoubtedly receive the promise of God, reaching through both time and eternity. But here is another snare laid for our feet: while we earnestly pant for that part of the promise which is to be accomplished here, 'for the glorious liberty of the children of God,' we may be led unawares from the consideration of the glory which shall hereafter be revealed. Our eye may be insensibly turned aside

from that crown which the righteous Judge hath promised to give at that day 'to all that love His appearing'; and we may be drawn away from the view of that incorruptible inheritance which is reserved in heaven for us. But this also would be a loss to our souls, and an obstruction to our holiness. For to walk in the continual sight of our goal, is a needful help in our running the race that is set before us. This it was, the having 'respect unto the recompense of the reward,' which, of old time, encouraged Moses, rather 'to suffer affliction with the people of God, than to enjoy the pleasures of sin for a season; esteeming the reproach of Christ greater riches than the treasures of Egypt.' Nay, it is expressly said of a greater than he, that, 'for the joy that was set before Him, He endured the cross, and despised the shame,' till He 'sat down at the right hand of the throne of God.' Whence we may easily infer, how much more needful for us is the view of that joy set before us, that we may endure whatever cross the wisdom of God lays upon us and press on through holiness to glory.

11. But while we are reaching to this, as well as to that glorious liberty which is preparatory to it, we may be in danger of falling into another snare of the devil, wherein he labours to entangle the children of God. We may take too much thought for to-morrow, so as to neglect the improvement of to-day. We may so expect perfect love, as not to use that which is already shed abroad in our hearts. There have not been wanting instances of those who have greatly suffered hereby. They were so taken up with what they were to receive hereafter, as utterly to neglect what they had already received. In expectation of having five talents more, they buried their one talent in the earth. At least, they did not improve it as they might have done, to the glory of God, and the good of their own souls.

12. Thus does the subtle adversary of God and man endeavour to make void the counsel of God, by dividing the gospel against itself, and making one part of it overthrow the other; while the first work of God in the soul is destroyed by the expectation of His perfect work. We have seen several of the ways wherein he attempts this, by cutting off, as it were, the springs of holiness. But this he likewise does more directly, by making that blessed hope an occasion of unholy tempers.

13. Thus, whenever our heart is eagerly athirst for all the great and precious promises; when we pant after the fullness of God, as the hart after the water-brook; when our soul breaketh out in fervent desire, 'Why are His chariot-wheels so long a-coming?'—he will not neglect the opportunity of tempting us to murmur against God. He will use all his wisdom, and all his strength, if haply, in an unguarded hour, we may be influenced to repine at our Lord for thus delaying His coming. At least, he will labour to excite some degree of fretfulness or impatience; and, perhaps, of envy at those whom we believe to have already attained the prize of our high calling. He well knows, that, by giving way to any of these tempers, we are pulling down the very thing we would build up. By *thus* following after perfect holiness, we become more unholy than before. Yea, there is great danger that our last state should be worse than the first; like them of whom the Apostle speaks in those dreadful words, 'It had been better for them not to have known the way of righteousness, than, after they have known it, to turn from the holy commandment delivered to them.'

14. And from hence he hopes to reap another advantage, even to bring up an evil report of the good way. He is sensible, how few are able to distinguish (and too many are not willing so to do) between the accidental abuse, and the natural tendency, of a doctrine. These, therefore, will he continually blend together, with regard to the doctrine of Christian perfection; in order to prejudice the minds of unwary men against the glorious promises of God. And how frequently, how generally, I had almost said how universally, has he prevailed herein! For who is there that observes any of these accidental ill effects of this doctrine, and does not immediately conclude, this is its natural tendency; and does not readily cry out, 'See, these are the fruits (meaning the natural, necessary fruits) of such doctrine?' Not so: they are fruits which may accidentally spring from the abuse of a great and precious truth: but the abuse of this, or any other scriptural doctrine, does by no means destroy its use. Neither can the unfaithfulness of man, perverting his right way, make the promise of God of no effect. No: let God be true, and every man a liar. The word of the Lord, it shall stand. 'Faithful is He

that hath promised: He also will do it.' Let not us then be 'removed from the hope of the gospel.' Rather let us observe, which was the second thing proposed, how we may retort these fiery darts of the wicked one; how we may rise the higher by what he intends for an occasion of our falling.

II. 1. And, first, does Satan endeavour to damp your joy in the Lord, by the consideration of your sinfulness; added to this, that without entire, universal holiness, no man can see the Lord? You may cast back this dart upon his own head, while, through the grace of God, the more you feel of your own vileness the more you rejoice in confident hope, that all this shall be done away While you hold fast this hope, every evil temper you feel, though you hate it with a perfect hatred, may be a means, not of lessening your humble joy, but rather of increasing it. 'This and this,' may you say, 'shall likewise perish from the presence of the Lord. Like as the wax melteth at the fire, so shall this melt away before His face.' By this means, the greater that change is which remains to be wrought in your soul, the more you may triumph in the Lord, and rejoice in the God of your salvation, who hath done so great things for you already, and will do so much greater things than these.

2. Secondly: the more vehemently he assaults your peace with that suggestion. 'God is holy, you are unholy; you are immensely distant from that holiness without which you cannot see God: how then can you be in the favour of God? How can you fancy you are justified?'—take the more earnest heed to hold fast that, 'Not by works of righteousness which I have done, I am found in Him; I am accepted in the Beloved, not having my own righteousness (as the cause, either in whole or in part, of our justification before God), but that which is by faith in Christ, the righteousness which is of God by faith.' O bind this about your neck: write it upon the table of thy heart. Wear it as a bracelet upon thy arm, as frontlets between thine eyes: 'I am justified freely by His grace, through the redemption that is in Jesus Christ.' Value and esteem, more and more, that precious truth, 'By grace we are saved through faith.' Admire, more and more, the free grace of God, in so loving the world as to give

'His only-begotten Son, that whosoever believeth on Him might not perish, but have everlasting life.' So shall the sense of the sinfulness you feel, on the one hand, and of the holiness you expect, on the other, both contribute to establish your peace, and to make it flow as a river. So shall that peace flow on with an even stream, in spite of all those mountains of ungodliness, which shall become a plain in the day when the Lord cometh to take full possession of your heart. Neither will sickness, or pain, or the approach of death occasion any doubt or fear. You know a day, an hour, a moment, with God, is as a thousand years. He cannot be straitened for time wherein to work whatever remains to be done in your soul. And God's time is always the best time. Therefore be thou careful for nothing: only make thy requests known unto Him, and that, not with doubt or fear, but thanksgiving; as being previously assured, He cannot withhold from thee any manner of thing that is good.

3. Thirdly: the more you are tempted to give up your shield, to cast away your faith, your confidence in His love, so much the more take heed that you hold fast that whereunto you have attained; so much the more labour to stir up the gift of God which is in you. Never let that slip, 'I have "an Advocate with the Father, Jesus Christ the righteous"; and, "The life I now live, I live by faith in the Son of God, who loved me, and gave Himself for me." ' Be this thy glory, and crown of rejoicing; and see that no one take thy crown. Hold that fast: 'I know that my Redeemer liveth, and shall stand at the latter day upon the earth': and, 'I now "have redemption in His blood, even the forgiveness of sins." ' Thus, being filled with all peace and joy in believing, press on, in the peace and joy of faith, to the renewal of thy whole soul in the image of Him that created thee! Meanwhile, cry continually to God, that thou mayest see that prize of thy high calling, not as Satan represents it, in a horrid, dreadful shape, but in its genuine, native beauty; not as something that must be, or thou wilt go to hell, but as what may be, to lead thee to heaven. Look upon it as the most desirable gift which is in all the stores of the rich mercies of God. Beholding in it this true point of light, thou wilt hunger after it more and more;

thy whole soul will be athirst for God, and for this glorious conformity to His likeness; and, having received a good hope of this, and strong consolation through grace, thou wilt no more be weary or faint in thy mind, but wilt follow on till thou attainest.

4. In the same power of faith, press on to glory. Indeed, this is the same prospect still. God hath joined from the beginning, pardon, holiness, heaven. And why should man put them asunder? O beware of this! Let not one link of the golden chain be broken. 'God for Christ's sake hath forgiven me. He is now renewing me in His own image. Shortly He will make me meet for Himself, and take me to stand before His face. I, whom He hath justified through the blood of His Son, being throughly sanctified by His Spirit, shall quickly ascend to the "New Jerusalem, the city of the living God." Yet a little while and I shall "come to the general assembly and church of the first-born, and to God the Judge of all, and to Jesus the Mediator of the new covenant." How soon will these shadows flee away, and the day of eternity dawn upon me! How soon shall I drink of "the river of the water of life, going out of the throne of God and of the Lamb! There all His servants shall praise Him, and shall see His face, and His name shall be upon their foreheads. And no night shall be there; and they have no need of a candle, or the light of the sun. For the Lord God enlighteneth them, and they shall reign for ever and ever." '

5. And if you thus 'taste of the good word, and of the powers of the world to come,' you will not murmur against God, because you are not yet 'meet for the inheritance of the saints in light.' Instead of repining at your not being wholly delivered, you will praise God for thus far delivering you. You will magnify God for what He hath done, and take it as an earnest of what He will do. You will not fret against Him, because you are not yet renewed, but bless Him because you shall be; and because 'now is your salvation' from all sin 'nearer than when you' first 'believed.' Instead of uselessly tormenting yourself because the time is not fully come, you will calmly and quietly wait for it, knowing that it 'will come, and will not tarry.' You may therefore the more cheerfully endure, as yet, the

burden of sin that still remains in you, because it will not always remain. Yet a little while, and it shall be clean gone. Only 'tarry thou the Lord's leisure': be strong, and 'He shall comfort thy heart'; and put thou thy trust in the Lord!

6. And if you see any who appear (so far as man can judge, but God alone searcheth the hearts) to be already partakers of their hope, already 'made perfect in love'; far from envying the grace of God in them, let it rejoice and comfort your heart. Glorify God for their sake! 'If one member is honoured,' shall not 'all the members rejoice with it'? Instead of jealousy or evil surmising concerning them, praise God for the consolation! Rejoice in having a fresh proof of the faithfulness of God, in fulfilling all His promises; and stir yourself up the more to 'apprehend that for which you are also apprehended of Christ Jesus'!

7. In order to this, redeem the time. Improve the present moment. Buy up every opportunity of growing in grace, or of doing good. Let not the thought of receiving more grace tomorrow, make you negligent of to-day. You have one talent now: if you expect five more, so much the rather improve that you have. And the more you expect to receive hereafter, the more labour for God now. Sufficient for the day is the grace thereof. God is now pouring His benefits upon you: now approve yourself a faithful steward of the present grace of God. Whatever may be to-morrow, give all diligence to-day to 'add to your faith courage, temperance, patience, brotherly kindness,' and the fear of God, till you attain that pure and perfect love! Let these things be now 'in you, and abound'! Be not now slothful or unfruitful: 'so shall an entrance be ministered unto you into the everlasting kingdom of our Lord Jesus Christ'!

8. Lastly: if in time past you have abused this blessed hope of being holy as He is holy, yet do not therefore cast it away. Let the abuse cease, the use remain. Use it now to the more abundant glory of God, and profit of your own soul. In steadfast faith, in calm tranquillity of spirit, in full assurance of hope, rejoicing evermore for what God hath done, press ye on unto perfection! Daily growing in the knowledge of our Lord Jesus Christ, and going on from strength to strength, in resignation,

33

in patience, in humble thankfulness for what ye have attained, and for what ye shall, run the race set before you, 'looking unto Jesus,' till through perfect love, ye enter into His glory!

SERMON XXXVIII

ORIGINAL SIN

And God saw that the wickedness of man was great in the earth, and that every imagination of the thoughts of his heart was only evil continually.— GEN. vi. 5.

How widely different is this from the fair pictures of human nature which men have drawn in all ages! The writings of many of the ancients abound with gay descriptions of the dignity of man; whom some of them paint as having all virtue and happiness in his composition; or, at least, entirely in his power, without being beholden to any other being; yea, as self-sufficient, able to live on his own stock, and little inferior to God Himself.

2. Nor have Heathens alone, men who are guided in their researches by little more than the dim light of reason, but many likewise of them that bear the name of Christ, and to whom are entrusted the oracles of God, spoken as magnificently concerning the nature of man, as if it were all innocence and perfection. Accounts of this kind have particularly abounded in the present century: and perhaps in no part of the world more than in our own country. Here not a few persons of strong understanding, as well as extensive learning, have employed their utmost abilities to show, what they termed, 'the fair side of human nature.' And it must be acknowledged, that, if their accounts of him be just, man is still but 'a little lower than the angels'; or, as the words may be more literally rendered, 'a little less than God.'

3. Is it any wonder, that these accounts are very readily received by the generality of men? For who is not easily per-

suaded to think favourably of himself? Accordingly, writers of this kind are most universally read, admired, applauded. And innumerable are the converts they have made, not only in the gay but the learned world. So that it is now quite unfashionable to talk otherwise, to say anything to the disparagement of human nature; which is generally allowed, notwithstanding a few infirmities, to be very innocent, and wise, and virtuous!

4. But, in the meantime, what must we do with our Bibles? —for they will never agree with this. These accounts, however pleasing to flesh and blood, are utterly irreconcilable with the scriptural. The Scripture avers, that 'by one man's disobedience all men were constituted sinners'; that 'in Adam all died,' spiritually died, lost the life and the image of God; that fallen, sinful Adam then 'begat a son in his own likeness'—nor was it possible he should beget him in any other; for 'who can bring a clean thing out of an unclean?'—that consequently we, as well as other men, were by nature 'dead in trespasses and sins,' 'without hope, without God in the world,' and, therefore, 'children of wrath'; that every man may say, 'I was shapen in wickedness, and in sin did my mother conceive me'; that 'there is no difference,' in that 'all have sinned and come short of the glory of God,' of that glorious image of God wherein man was originally created. And hence, when 'the Lord looked down from heaven upon the children of men, He saw they were all gone out of the way; they were altogether become abominable, there was none righteous, no, not one,' none that truly sought after God: just agreeable this to what is declared by the Holy Ghost in the words above recited, 'God saw,' when He looked down from heaven before, 'that the wickedness of man was great in the earth'; so great, that 'every imagination of the thoughts of his heart was only evil continually.'

This is God's account of man: from which I shall take occasion, first, to show what men were before the flood: secondly, to inquire, whether they are not the same now: and, thirdly, to add some inferences.

I. 1. I am, first, by opening the words of the text, to show what men were before the flood. And we may fully depend on the account here given: for God saw it, and He cannot be deceived. He 'saw that the wickedness of man was great': —not of this or that man; not of a few men only; not barely of the greater part, but of man in general; of men universally. The word includes the whole human race, every partaker of human nature. And it is not easy for us to compute their numbers, to tell how many thousands and millions they were. The earth then retained much of its primaeval beauty and original fruitfulness. The face of the globe was not rent and torn as it is now; and spring and summer went hand in hand. It is therefore probable, it afforded sustenance for far more inhabitants than it is now capable of sustaining; and these must be immensely multiplied, while men begat sons and daughters for seven or eight hundred years together. Yet, among all this inconceivable number, only 'Noah found favour with God.' He alone (perhaps including part of his household) was an exception from the universal wickedness, which, by the just judgement of God, in a short time after brought on universal destruction. All the rest were partakers in the same guilt, as they were in the same punishment.

2. 'God saw all the imaginations of the thoughts of his heart'—of his soul, his inward man, the spirit within him, the principle of all his inward and outward motions. He 'saw all the imaginations'—it is not possible to find a word of a more extensive signification. It includes whatever is formed, made, fabricated within; all that is or passes in the soul; every inclination, affection, passion, appetite; every temper, design, thought. It must of consequence include every word and action, as naturally flowing from these fountains, and being either good or evil according to the fountain from which they severally flow.

3. Now God saw that all this, the whole thereof, was evil—contrary to moral rectitude; contrary to the nature of God, which necessarily includes all good; contrary to the divine will, the eternal standard of good and evil; contrary to the pure, holy image of God, wherein man was originally created, and wherein he stood when God, surveying the works of His hands, saw them all to be very good; contrary to justice, mercy, and

truth, and to the essential relations which each man bore to his Creator and his fellow creatures.

4. But was there not good mingled with the evil? Was there not light intermixed with the darkness? No, none at all: 'God saw that the whole imagination of the heart of man was only evil.' It cannot indeed be denied, but many of them, perhaps all, had good motions put into their hearts; for the Spirit of God did then also 'strive with man,' if haply he might repent, more especially during that gracious reprieve, the hundred and twenty years, while the ark was preparing. But still 'in his flesh dwelt no good thing'; all his nature was purely evil: it was wholly consistent with itself, and unmixed with anything of an opposite nature.

5. However, it may still be matter of inquiry, 'Was there no intermission of this evil? Were there no lucid intervals, wherein something good might be found in the heart of man?' We are not here to consider, what the grace of God might occasionally work in his soul; and, abstracted from this, we have no reason to believe there was any intermission of that evil. For God, who 'saw the whole imagination of the thoughts of his heart to be *only* evil,' saw likewise, that it was always the same, that it 'was only evil *continually*'; every year, every day, every hour, every moment. He never deviated into good.

II. Such is the authentic account of the whole race of mankind which He who knoweth what is in man, who searcheth the heart and trieth the reins, hath left upon record for our instruction Such were all men before God brought the flood upon the earth. We are, secondly, to inquire, whether they are the same now.

1. And this is certain, the Scripture gives us no reason to think any otherwise of them. On the contrary, all the above-cited passages of Scripture refer to those who lived after the flood. It was above a thousand years after, that God declared by David concerning the children of men, 'They are all gone out of the way' of truth and holiness; 'there is none righteous, no, not one.' And to this bear all the prophets witness, in their several generations. So Isaiah, concerning God's peculiar people (and certainly the Heathens were in no better condition),

'The whole head is sick, and the whole heart faint. From the sole of the foot even unto the head there is no soundness; but wounds, and bruises, and putrefying sores.' The same account is given by all the Apostles, yea, by the whole tenor of the oracles of God. From all these we learn, concerning man in his natural state, unassisted by the grace of God, that 'every imagination of the thoughts of his heart is' still 'evil, only evil,' and that 'continually.'

2. And this account of the present state of man is confirmed by daily experience. It is true, the natural man discerns it not: and this is not to be wondered at. So long as a man born blind continues so, he is scarce sensible of his want: much less, could we suppose a place where all were born without sight, would they be sensible of the want of it. In like manner, so long as men remain in their natural blindness of understanding, they are not sensible of their spiritual wants, and of this in particular. But as soon as God opens the eyes of their understanding, they see the state they were in before; they are then deeply convinced, that 'every man living,' themselves especially, are, by nature, 'altogether vanity'; that is, folly and ignorance, sin and wickedness.

3. We see, when God opens our eyes, that we were before ἄθεοι ἐν τῷ κόσμῳ—*without God*, or rather, *Atheists in the world*. We had, by nature, no knowledge of God, no acquaintance with Him. It is true, as soon as we came to the use of reason, we learned 'the invisible things of God, even His eternal power and Godhead, from the things that are made.' From the things that are seen we inferred the existence of an eternal, powerful Being, that is not seen. But still, although we acknowledged His being, we had no acquaintance with Him. As we know there is an Emperor of China, whom yet we do not know; so we knew there was a King of all the earth, yet we knew Him not. Indeed we could not by any of our natural faculties. By none of these could we attain the knowledge of God. We could no more perceive Him by our natural understanding, than we could see Him with our eyes. For 'no one knoweth the Father but the Son, and he to whom the Son willeth to reveal Him. And no one knoweth the Son but the Father, and he to whom the Father revealeth Him.'

4. We read of an ancient king who, being desirous to know what was the *natural language* of men, in order to bring the matter to a certain issue, made the following experiment: he ordered two infants, as soon as they were born, to be conveyed to a place prepared for them, where they were brought up without any instruction at all, and without ever hearing a human voice. And what was the event? Why, that when they were at length brought out of their confinement, they spake no language at all; they uttered only inarticulate sounds, like those of other animals. Were two infants in like manner to be brought up from the womb without being instructed in any religion, there is little room to doubt but (unless the grace of God interposed) the event would be just the same. They would have no religion at all: they would have no more knowledge of God than the beasts of the field, than the wild ass's colt. Such is natural religion, abstracted from traditional, and from the influences of God's Spirit.

5. And having no knowledge, we can have no love of God: we cannot love Him we know not. Most men *talk* indeed of loving God, and perhaps imagine they do; at least, few will acknowledge they do not love Him: but the fact is too plain to be denied. No man loves God by nature, any more than he does a stone, or the earth he treads upon. What we love we delight in: but no man has naturally any delight in God. In our natural state we cannot conceive how any one should delight in Him. We take no pleasure in Him at all; He is utterly tasteless to us. To love God! it is far above, out of our sight. We cannot, naturally, attain unto it.

6. We have by nature, not only no love, but no fear of God. It is allowed, indeed, that most men have, sooner or later, a kind of senseless, irrational fear, properly called 'superstition'; though the blundering Epicureans gave it the name of 'religion.' Yet even this is not natural, but acquired; chiefly by conversation or from example. By nature 'God is not in all our thoughts': we leave Him to manage His own affairs, to sit quietly, as we imagine, in heaven, and leave us on earth to manage ours; so that we have no more of the fear of God before our eyes, than of the love of God in our hearts.

7. Thus are all men 'Atheists in the world.' But Atheism itself does not screen us from idolatry. In his natural state, every man born into the world is a rank idolater. Perhaps, indeed, we may not be such in the vulgar sense of the word. We do not, like the idolatrous Heathens, worship molten or graven images. We do not bow down to the stock of a tree, to the work of our own hands. We do not pray to the angels or saints in heaven, any more than to the saints that are upon the earth. But what then? We have set up our idols in our hearts; and to these we bow down, and worship them: we worship ourselves, when we pay that honour to ourselves which is due to God only. Therefore, all pride is idolatry; it is ascribing to ourselves what is due to God alone. And although pride was not made for man, yet where is the man that is born without it? But hereby we rob God of His unalienable right, and idolatrously usurp His glory.

8. But pride is not the only sort of idolatry which we are all by nature guilty of. Satan has stamped his own image on our heart in self-will also. 'I will,' said he, before he was cast out of heaven, 'I will sit upon the sides of the north': I will do my own will and pleasure, independently on that of my Creator. The same does every man born into the world say, and that in a thousand instances; nay, and avow it too, without ever blushing upon the account, without either fear or shame. Ask the man, 'Why did you do this?' He answers, 'Because I had a mind to it.' What is this but, 'Because it was my will'; that is, in effect, because the devil and I are agreed; because Satan and I govern our actions by one and the same principle. The will of God, meantime, is not in his thoughts, is not considered in the least degree; anthough it be the supreme rule of every intelligent creature, whether in heaven or earth, resulting from the essential, unalterable relation which all creatures bear to their Creator.

9. So far we bear the image of the devil, and tread in his steps. But at the next step we leave Satan behind; we run into an idolatry whereof he is not guilty: I mean, love of the world; which is now as natural to every man, as to love his own will. What is more natural to us than to seek happiness in the creature, instead of the Creator—to seek that satisfaction

in the works of His hands, which can be found in God only? What more natural than 'the desire of the flesh'? that is, of the pleasure of sense in every kind? Men indeed talk magnificently of despising these low pleasures, particularly men of learning and education. They affect to sit loose to the gratification of those appetites wherein they stand on a level with the beasts that perish. But it is mere affectation! for every man is conscious to himself, that in this respect he is, by nature, a very beast. Sensual appetites, even those of the lowest kind, have, more or less, the dominion over him. They lead him captive; they drag him to and fro, in spite of his boasted reason. The man, with all his good breeding, and other accomplishments, has no pre-eminence over the goat: nay, it is much to be doubted, whether the beast has not the pre-eminence over him. Certainly he has, if we may hearken to one of their modern oracles, who very decently tell us,

> Once in a season beasts too taste of love;
> Only the beast of reason is its slave,
> And in that folly drudges all the year.

A considerable difference indeed, it must be allowed, there is between man and man, arising (beside that wrought by preventing grace) from difference of constitution and of education. But, notwithstanding this, who, that is not utterly ignorant of himself, can here cast the first stone at another? Who can abide the test of our blessed Lord's comment on the Seventh Commandment—'He that looketh on a woman to lust after her hath committed adultery with her already in his heart'? So that one knows not which to wonder at most, the ignorance or the insolence of those men who speak with such disdain of them that are overcome by desires which every man has felt in his own breast; the desire of every pleasure of sense, innocent or not, being natural to every child of man.

10. And so is 'the desire of the eye': the desire of the pleasures of the imagination. These arise either from great, or beautiful, or uncommon objects—if the two former do not coincide with the latter; for perhaps it would appear, upon a diligent inquiry, that neither grand nor beautiful objects please any longer than

they are new; that when the novelty of them is over, the greatest part, at least, of the pleasure they give is over; and in the same proportion as they become familiar, they become flat and insipid. But let us experience this ever so often, the same desire will remain still. The inbred thirst continues fixed in the soul; nay, the more it is indulged, the more it increases, and incites us to follow after another, and yet another object; although we leave every one with an abortive hope, and a deluded expectation Yea,

> The hoary fool, who many days
>   Has struggled with continued sorrow,
> Renews his hope, and fondly lays
>   The desperate bet upon to-morrow!
>
> To-morrow comes! 'Tis noon! 'Tis night!
>   This day, like all the former, flies:
> Yet on he goes, to seek delight
>   To-morrow, till to-night he dies!

11. A third symptom of this fatal disease—the love of the world, which is so deeply rooted in our nature—is 'the pride of life'; the desire of praise, of the honour that cometh of men. This the greatest admirers of human nature allow to be strictly natural; as natural as the sight, or hearing, or any other of the external senses. And are they ashamed of it, even men of letters, men of refined and improved understanding? So far from it, that they glory therein! They applaud themselves for their love of applause! Yea, eminent Christians, so called, make no difficulty of adopting the saying of the old, vain Heathen, '*Animi dissoluti est et nequam negligere quid de se homines sentiant:*' 'Not to regard what men think of us is the mark of a wicked and abandoned mind.' So that to go calm and unmoved through honour and dishonour, through evil report and good report, is with them a sign of one that is, indeed, not fit to live: 'away with such a fellow from the earth!' But would one imagine that these men had ever heard of Jesus Christ or His Apostles; or that they knew who it was that said, 'How can ye believe who receive honour one of another, and seek not the honour which cometh of God only?' But if this be really so, if it be impossible to believe, and

consequently to please God, so long as we receive or seek honour one of another, and seek not the honour which cometh of God only; then in what a condition are all mankind! the Christians as well as Heathens! since they all seek honour one of another! since it is as natural for them so to do, themselves being the judges, as it is to see the light which strikes upon their eye, or to hear the sound which enters their ear; yea, since they account it a sign of a virtuous mind, to seek the praise of men, and of a vicious one to be content with the honour that cometh of God only!

III. 1. I proceed to draw a few inferences from what has been said. And, first, from hence we may learn one grand fundamental difference between Christianity, considered as a system of doctrines, and the most refined Heathensim. Many of the ancient Heathens have largely described the vices of particular men. They have spoken much against their covetousness, or cruelty; their luxury, or prodigality. Some have dared to say, that 'no man is born without vices of one kind or another.' But still, as none of them were apprised of the fall of man, so none of them knew of his total corruption. They knew not that all men were empty of all good, and filled with all manner of evil. They were wholly ignorant of the entire depravation of the whole human nature, of every man born into the world, in every faculty of his soul, not so much by those particular vices which reign in particular persons, as by the general flood of Atheism and idolatry, of pride, self-will, and love of the world. This, therefore, is the first grand distinguishing point between Heathenism and Christianity. The one acknowledges that many men are infected with many vices, and even born with a proneness to them; but supposes withal, that in some the natural good much over-balances the evil: the other declares that all men are 'conceived in sin.' and 'shapen in wickedness'—that hence there is in every man a 'carnal mind which is enmity against God; which is not, cannot be, subject to' His 'law'; and which so infects the whole soul, that 'there dwelleth in' him, 'in his flesh,' in his natural state, 'no good thing'; but 'every imagination of the thoughts of his heart is evil,' only evil, and that 'continually.'

2. Hence we may, secondly, learn, that all who deny this, call it 'original sin,' or by any other title, are but Heathens still, in the fundamental point which differences Heathenism from Christianity. They may, indeed, allow, that men have many vices; that some are born with us; and that, consequently, we are not born altogether so wise or so virtuous as we should be; there being few that will roundly affirm, 'We are born with as much propensity to good as to evil, and that every man is, by nature, as virtuous and wise as Adam was at his creation.' But here is the *shibboleth*: Is man by nature filled with all manner of evil? Is he void of all good? Is he wholly fallen? Is his soul totally corrupted? Or, to come back to the text, is 'every imagination of the thoughts of his heart only evil continually'? Allow this, and you are so far a Christian. Deny it, and you are but an Heathen still.

3. We may learn from hence, in the third place, what is the proper nature of religion, of the religion of Jesus Christ. It is θεραπεία ψυχῆς—God's method of *healing a soul* which is thus diseased. Hereby the great Physician of souls applies medicines to heal this sickness; to restore human nature, totally corrupted in all its faculties. God heals all our Atheism by the knowledge of Himself, and of Jesus Christ whom He hath sent; by giving us faith, a divine evidence and conviction of God, and of the things of God—in particular, of this important truth, 'Christ loved *me*, and gave Himself for *me*.' By repentance and lowliness of heart, the deadly disease of pride is healed; that of self-will by resignation, a meek and thankful submission to the will of God; and for the love of the world in all its branches, the love of God is the sovereign remedy. Now, this is properly religion, 'faith' thus 'working by love': working the genuine meek humility, entire deadness to the world, with a loving, thankful acquiescence in, and conformity to, the whole will and word of God.

4. Indeed, if man were not thus fallen, there would be no need of all this. There would be no occasion for this work in the heart, this renewal in the spirit of our mind. The super-fluity of godliness would then be a more proper expression than the 'superfluity of naughtiness.' For an outside religion, without

any godliness at all, would suffice to all rational intents and purposes. It does, accordingly, suffice, in the judgement of those who deny this corruption of our nature. They make very little more of religion than the famous Mr. Hobbes did of reason. According to him, reason is only 'a well-ordered train of words': according to them, religion is only a well-ordered train of words and actions. And they speak consistently with themselves; for if the inside be not full of wickedness, if this be clean already, what remains, but to 'cleanse the outside of the cup'? Outward reformation, if their supposition be just, is indeed the one thing needful.

5. But ye have not so learned the oracles of God. Ye know that He who seeth what is in man gives a far different account both of nature and grace, of our fall and our recovery. Ye know that the great end of religion is, to renew our hearts in the image of God, to repair that total loss of righteousness and true holiness which we sustained by the sin of our first parent. Ye know that all religion which does not answer this end, all that stops short of this, the renewal of our soul in the image of God, after the likeness of Him that created it, is no other than a poor farce, and a mere mockery of God, to the destruction of our own soul. O beware of all those teachers of lies, who would palm this upon you for Christianity! Regard them not, although they should come unto you with all the deceiveableness of unrighteousness; with all smoothness of language, all decency, yea, beauty and elegance of expression, all professions of earnest good-will to you, and reverence for the holy Scriptures. Keep to the plain, old faith, 'once delivered to the saints,' and delivered by the Spirit of God to our hearts. Know your disease! Know your cure! Ye were born in sin: therefore, 'ye must be born again,' born of God. By nature ye are wholly corrupted: by grace ye shall be wholly renewed. In Adam ye all died: in the second Adam, in Christ, ye all are made alive. 'You that were dead in sins hath He quickened': He hath already given you a principle of life, even faith in Him who loved you and gave Himself for you! Now, 'go on from faith to faith,' until your whole sickness be healed, and all that 'mind be in you which was also in Christ Jesus'!

SERMON XXXIX

THE NEW BIRTH

Ye must be born again.—JOHN iii. 7.

IF any doctrines within the whole compass of Christianity may be properly termed 'fundamental,' they are doubtless these two,—the doctrine of justification, and that of the new birth: the former relating to that great work which God does *for us*, in forgiving our sins; the latter, to the great work which God does *in us*, in renewing our fallen nature. In order of *time*, neither of these is before the other; in the moment we are justified by the grace of God, through the redemption that is in Jesus, we are also 'born of the Spirit'; but in order of *thinking*, as it is termed, justification precedes the new birth. We first conceive His wrath to be turned away, and then His Spirit to work in our hearts.

2. How great importance then must it be of, to every child of man, throughly to understand these fundamental doctrines! From a full conviction of this, many excellent men have wrote very largely concerning justification, explaining every point relating thereto, and opening the scriptures which treat upon it. Many likewise have wrote on the new birth: and some of them largely enough; but yet not so clearly as might have been desired, nor so deeply and accurately; having either given a dark, abstruse account of it, or a slight and superficial one. Therefore a full, and at the same time a clear, account of the new birth seems to be wanting still; such as may enable us to give a satisfactory answer to these three questions: first, Why must we be born again—what is the foundation of this doctrine of the new birth? secondly, How must we be born again—what is the nature of the new birth? and, thirdly, Wherefore must we be born again—to what end is it necessary? These questions, by the assistance of God, I shall briefly and plainly answer; and then subjoin a few inferences which will naturally follow.

I. 1. And, first, Why must we be born again? What is the foundation of this doctrine? The foundation of it lies near as deep as the creation of the world; in the scriptural account whereof we read, 'And God,' the three-one God, 'said, Let us make man in our image, after our likeness. So God created man in His own image, in the image of God created He him' (Gen. i. 26, 27):—not barely in his *natural image*, a picture of His own immortality; a spiritual being, endued with understanding, freedom of will, and various affections; nor merely in his *political image*, the governor of this lower world, having 'dominion over the fishes of the sea, and over all the earth': but chiefly in his *moral image*; which, according to the Apostle, is 'righteousness and true holiness' (Eph. iv. 24). In this image of God was man made. 'God is love'; accordingly, man at his creation was full of love; which was the sole principle of all his tempers, thoughts, words, and actions. God is full of justice, mercy, and truth; so was man as he came from the hands of his Creator. God is spotless purity; and so man was in the beginning pure from every sinful blot; otherwise God could not have pronounced him, as well as all the other works of His hands, 'very good' (Gen. i. 31). This he could not have been, had he not been pure from sin, and filled with righteousness and true holiness. For there is no medium: if we suppose an intelligent creature not to love God, not to be righteous and holy, we necessarily suppose him not to be good at all; much less to be 'very good.'

2. But, although man was made in the image of God, yet he was not made immutable. This would have been inconsistent with that state of trial in which God was pleased to place him. He was therefore created able to stand, and yet liable to fall. And this God Himself apprised him of, and gave him a solemn warning against it. Nevertheless, man did not abide in honour: he fell from his high estate. He 'ate of the tree whereof the Lord had commanded him, Thou shalt not eat thereof.' By this wilful act of disobedience to his Creator, this flat rebellion against his Sovereign, he openly declared that he would no longer have God to rule over him; that he would be governed by his own will, and not the will of Him that created him; and

that he would not seek his happiness in God, but in the world, in the works of his hands. Now, God had told him before, 'In the day that thou eatest' of that fruit, 'thou shalt surely die.' And the word of the Lord cannot be broken. Accordingly, in that day he did die; he died to God—the most dreadful of all deaths. He lost the life of God: he was separated from Him, in union with whom his spiritual life consisted. The body dies when it is separated from the soul; the soul, when it is separated from God. But this separation from God, Adam sustained in the day, the hour, he ate of the forbidden fruit. And of this he gave immediate proof; presently showing by his behaviour, that the love of God was extinguished in his soul, which was now 'alienated from the life of God.' Instead of this, he was now under the power of servile fear, so that he fled from the presence of the Lord. Yea, so little did he retain even of the knowledge of Him who filleth heaven and earth, that he endeavoured to 'hide himself from the Lord God among the trees of the garden' (Gen. iii. 8); so had he lost both the knowledge and the love of God, without which the image of God could not subsist. Of this, therefore, he was deprived at the same time, and became unholy as well as unhappy. In the room of this, he had sunk into pride and self-will, the very image of the devil; and into sensual appetites and desires, the image of the beasts that perish.

3. If it be said, 'Nay, but that threatening, "In the day that thou eatest thereof, thou shalt surely die," refers to temporal death, and that alone, to the death of the body only'; the answer; is plain; to affirm this is flatly and palpably to make God a liar; to aver that the God of truth positively affirmed a thing contrary to truth. For it is evident Adam did not *die* in this sense, 'in the day that he ate thereof.' He lived, in the sense opposite to this death, above nine hundred years after. So that this cannot possibly be understood of the death of the body, without impeaching the veracity of God. It must therefore be understood of spiritual death, the loss of the life and image of God.

4. And in Adam all died, all human kind, all the children of men who were then in Adams' loins. The natural consequence of this is, that every one descended from him comes into the world spiritually dead, dead to God, wholly dead in sin; entirely

void of the life of God; void of the image of God, of all that righteousness and holiness wherein Adam was created. Instead of this, every man born into the world now bears the image of the devil, in pride and self-will; the image of the beast, in sensual appetites and desires. This, then, is the foundation of the new birth,—the entire corruption of our nature. Hence it is, that, being born in sin, we must be 'born again.' Hence every one that is born of a woman must be born of the Spirit of God.

II. 1. But how must a man be born again? What is the nature of the new birth? This is the second question. And a question it is of the highest moment that can be conceived. We ought not, therefore, in so weighty a concern, to be content with a slight inquiry; but to examine it with all possible care, and to ponder it in our hearts, till we fully understand this important point, and clearly see how we are to be born again.

2. Not that we are to expect any minute, philosophical account of the manner how this is done. Our Lord sufficiently guards us against any such expectation, by the words immediately following the text; wherein He reminds Nicodemus of as indisputable a fact as any in the whole compass of nature, which, notwithstanding, the wisest man under the sun is not able fully to explain. 'The wind bloweth where it listeth,' —not by thy power or wisdom; 'and thou hearest the sound thereof,'—thou art absolutely assured, beyond all doubt, that it doth blow; 'but thou canst not tell whence it cometh, nor whither it goeth,'—the precise manner how it begins and ends, rises and falls, no man can tell. 'So is every one that is born of the Spirit': thou mayest be as absolutely assured of the fact, as of the blowing of the wind; but the precise manner how it is done, how the Holy Spirit works this in the soul, neither thou nor the wisest of the children of men is able to explain.

3. However, it suffices for every rational and Christian purpose, that, without descending into curious, critical inquiries, we can give a plain scriptural account of the nature of the new birth. This will satisfy every reasonable man, who desires only the salvation of his soul. The expression, 'being born again,' was not first used by our Lord in His conversation with Nico-

demus: it was well known before that time, and was in common use among the Jews when our Saviour appeared among them. When an adult Heathen was convinced that the Jewish religion was of God, and desired to join therein, it was the custom to baptize him first before he was admitted to circumcision. And when he was baptized, he was said to be born again; by which they meant, that he who was before a child of the devil was now adopted into the family of God, and accounted one of His children. This expression, therefore, which Nicodemus, being 'a teacher in Israel,' ought to have understood well, our Lord uses in conversing with him; only in a stronger sense than he was accustomed to. And this might be the reason of his asking, 'How can these things be?' They cannot be literally: a man cannot 'enter a second time into his mother's womb, and be born': but they may, spiritually: a man may be born from above, born of God, born of the Spirit, in a manner which bears a very near analogy to the natural birth.

4. Before a child is born into the world he has eyes, but sees not; he has ears, but does not hear. He has a very imperfect use of any other sense. He has no knowledge of any of the things of the world, or any natural understanding. To that manner of existence which he then has, we do not even give the name of life. It is then only when a man is born, that we say he begins to live. For as soon as he is born, he begins to see the light, and the various objects with which he is encompassed. His ears are then opened, and he hears the sounds which successively strike upon them. At the same time, all the other organs of sense begin to be exercised upon their proper objects. He likewise breathes, and lives in a manner wholly different from what he did before. How exactly doth the parallel hold in all these instances! While a man is in a mere natural state, before he is born of God, he has, in a spiritual sense, eyes and sees not; a thick impenetrable veil lies upon them: he has ears, but hears not; he is utterly deaf to what he is most of all concerned to hear. His other spiritual senses are all locked up: he is in the same condition as if he had them not. Hence he has no knowledge of God; no intercourse with Him; he is not at all aquainted with Him. He has no true knowledge of the things of God,

either of spiritual or eternal things; therefore, though he is a living man, he is a dead Christian. But as soon as he is born of God, there is a total change in all these particulars. The 'eyes of his understanding are opened' (such is the language of the great Apostle); and, He who of old 'commanded light to shine out of darkness shining on his heart, he sees the light of the glory of God,' His glorious love, 'in the face of Jesus Christ.' His ears being opened, he is now capable of hearing the inward voice of God, saying, 'Be of good cheer; thy sins are forgiven thee'; 'Go and sin no more.' This is the purport of what God speaks to his heart; although perhaps not in these very words. He is now ready to hear whatsoever 'He that teacheth man knowledge' is pleased, from time to time to reveal to him. He 'feels in his heart,' to use the language of our Church, 'the mighty working of the Spirit of God'; not in a gross, carnal sense, as the men of the world stupidly and wilfully misunderstand the expression; though they have been told again and again, we mean thereby neither more nor less than this: he feels, is inwardly sensible of, the graces which the Spirit of God works in his heart. He feels, he is conscious of, a 'peace which passeth all understanding.' He many times feels such a joy in God as is 'unspeakable, and full of glory.' He feels 'the love of God shed abroad in his heart by the Holy Ghost which is given unto him'; and all his spiritual senses are then exercised to discern spiritual good and evil. By the use of these, he is daily increasing in the knowledge of God, of Jesus Christ whom He hath sent, and of all the things pertaining to His inward kingdom. And now he may be properly said to live: God having quickened him by His Spirit, he is alive to God through Jesus Christ. He lives a life which the world knoweth not of, a 'life which is hid with Christ in God.' God is continually breathing, as it were, upon the soul; and his soul is breathing unto God. Grace is descending into his heart; and prayer and praise ascending to heaven; and by this intercourse between God and man, this fellowship with the Father and the Son, as by a kind of spiritual respiration, the life of God in the soul is sustained; and the child of God grows up, till he comes to the 'full measure of the stature of Christ.'

5. From hence it manifestly appears, what is the nature

of the new birth. It is that great change which God works in the soul when He brings it into life; when He raises it from the death of sin to the life of righteousness. It is the change wrought in the whole soul by the almighty Spirit of God when it is 'created anew in Christ Jesus'; when it is 'renewed after the image of God in righteousness and true holiness'; when the love of the world is changed into the love of God; pride into humility; passion into meekness; hatred, envy, malice, into a sincere, tender, disinterested love for all mankind. In a word, it is that change whereby the earthly, sensual, devilish mind is turned into the 'mind which was in Christ Jesus.' This is the nature of the new birth: 'so is every one that is born of the Spirit.'

III. 1. It is not difficult for any who has considered these things, to see the necessity of the new birth, and to answer the third question, Wherefore, to what end, is it necessary that we should be born again? It is very easily discerned, that this is necessary, first, in order to holiness. For what is holiness according to the oracles of God? Not a bare external religion, a round of outward duties, how many soever they be, and how exactly soever performed. No: gospel holiness is no less than the image of God stamped upon the heart; it is no other than the whole mind which was in Christ Jesus; it consists of all heavenly affections and tempers mingled together in one. It implies such a continual, thankful love to Him who hath not withheld from us His Son, His only Son, as makes it natural, and in a manner necessary to us, to love every child of man; as fills us 'with bowels of mercies, kindness, gentleness, long-suffering.' It is such a love of God as teaches us to be blameless in all manner of conversation; as enables us to present our souls and bodies, all we are and all we have, all our thoughts, words, and actions, a continual sacrifice to God, acceptable through Christ Jesus. Now, this holiness can have no existence till we are renewed in the image of our mind. It cannot commence in the soul till that change be wrought; till, by the power of the Highest overshadowing us, we are 'brought from darkness to light, from the power of Satan unto God'; that is, till we are born again; which, therefore, is absolutely necessary in order to holiness.

2. But 'without holiness no man shall see the Lord,' shall see the face of God in glory. Of consequence, the new birth is absolutely necessary in order to eternal salvation. Men may indeed flatter themselves (so desperately wicked and so deceitful is the heart of man!) that they may live in their sins till they come to the last gasp, and yet afterwards live with God; and thousands do really believe, that they have found a broad way which leadeth not to destruction. 'What danger,' say they, 'can a woman be in that is so *harmless* and so *virtuous*? What fear is there that so *honest* a man, one of so strict *morality*, should miss of heaven; especially, if, over and above all this, they constantly attend on church and sacrament?' One of these will ask with all assurance, 'What! shall not I do as well as my neighbours?' Yes, as well as your unholy neighbours; as well as your neighbours that die in their sins! For you will all drop into the pit together, into the nethermost hell! You will all lie together in the lake of fire; 'the lake of fire burning with brimstone.' Then, at length, you will see (but God grant you may see it before!) the necessity of holiness in order to glory; and, consequently, of the new birth, since none can be holy, except he be born again.

3. For the same reason, except he be born again, none can be happy even in this world. For it is not possible, in the nature of things, that a man should be happy who is not holy. Even the poor, ungodly poet could tell us, *Nemo malus felix*: 'No wicked man is happy.' The reason is plain: all unholy tempers are uneasy tempers: not only malice, hatred, envy, jealousy, revenge, create a present hell in the breast; but even the softer passions, if not kept within due bounds, give a thousand times more pain than pleasure. Even 'hope,' when 'deferred' (and how often must this be the case!) 'maketh the heart sick': and every desire which is not according to the will of God is liable to 'pierce' us 'through with many sorrows': and all those general sources of sin—pride, self-will, and idolatry—are, in the same proportion as they prevail, general sources of misery. Therefore, as long as these reign in any soul, happiness has no place there. But they must reign till the bent of our nature is changed, that is, till we are born again; consequently, the new birth is abso-

lutely necessary in order to happiness in this world, as well as in the world to come.

IV. I proposed in the last place to subjoin a few inferences, which naturally follow from the preceding observations.

1. And, first it follows, that baptism is not the new birth: they are not one and the same thing. Many indeed seem to imagine that they are just the same; at least, they speak as if they thought so; but I do not know that this opinion is publicly avowed by any denomination of Christians whatever. Certainly it is not by any within these kingdoms, whether of the established Church, or dissenting from it. The judgement of the latter is clearly declared in their large Catechism[1]: Q. 'What are the parts of a sacrament? A. The parts of a sacrament are two: the one an outward and sensible sign; the other, an inward and spiritual grace, thereby signified. Q. What is baptism? A. Baptism is a sacrament, wherein Christ hath ordained the washing with water, to be a sign and seal of regeneration by His Spirit.' Here it is manifest, baptism, the sign, is spoken of as distinct from regeneration, the thing signified.

In the Church Catechism likewise, the judgement of our Church is declared with the utmost clearness: 'What meanest thou by this word, sacrament? A. I mean an outward and visible sign of an inward and spiritual grace. Q. What is the outward part or form in baptism? A. Water, wherein the person is baptized, in the name of the Father, Son, and Holy Ghost. Q. What is the inward part, or thing signified? A. A death unto sin, and a new birth unto righteousness.' Nothing, therefore, is plainer, than that, according to the Church of England, baptism is not the new birth.

But indeed the reason of the thing is so clear and evident, as not to need any other authority. For what can be more plain, than that the one is an external, the other an internal, work; that the one is a visible, the other an invisible thing, and therefore wholly different from each other?—the one being an act of man, purifying the body; the other a change wrought by God in the soul: so that the former is just as distinguishable from the

[1] Q. 163 165.

latter, as the soul from the body, or water from the Holy Ghost.

2. From the preceding reflections we may, secondly, observe, that as the new birth is not the same thing with baptism, so it does not always accompany baptism: they do not constantly go together. A man may possibly be 'born of water,' and yet not be 'born of the Spirit.' There may sometimes be the outward sign, where there is not the inward grace. I do not now speak with regard to infants: it is certain our Church supposes that all who are baptized in their infancy are at the same time born again; and it is allowed that the whole Office for the Baptism of Infants proceeds upon this supposition. Nor is it an objection of any weight against this, that we cannot comprehend how this work can be wrought in infants. For neither can we comprehend how it is wrought in a person of riper years. But whatever be the case with infants, it is sure all of riper years who are baptized are not at the same time born again. 'The tree is known by its fruits.' And hereby it appears too plain to be denied, that divers of those who were children of the devil before they were baptized continue the same after baptism; 'for the works of their father they do': they continue servants of sin, without any pretence either to inward or outward holiness.

3. A third inference which we may draw from what has been observed is that the new birth is not the same with sanctification. This is indeed taken for granted by many; particularly by an eminent writer in his late treatise on the nature and grounds of Christian Regeneration.[1] To waive several other weighty objections which might be made to that tract, this is a palpable one: it all along speaks of regeneration as a progressive work, carried on in the soul by slow degrees, from the time of our first turning to God. This is undeniably true of sanctification; but of regeneration, the new birth, it is not true. This is a part of sanctification, not the whole; it is the gate to it, the entrance into it. When we are born again, then our sanctification, our inward and outward holiness begins; and thenceforward we are gradually to 'grow up in Him who is our Head.' This expression of the Apostle admirably illustrates the difference

[1] Law's *Grounds and Reasons of Christian Regeneration*, published in 1739.

between one and the other, and farther points out the exact analogy there is between natural and spiritual things. A child is born of a woman in a moment, or at least in a very short time: afterward he gradually and slowly grows, till he attains to the stature of a man. In like manner, a child is born of God in a short time, if not in a moment. But it is by slow degrees that he afterward grows up to the measure of the full stature of Christ. The same relation, therefore, which there is between our natural birth and our growth, there is also between our new birth and our sanctification.

4. One point more we may learn from the preceding observations. But it is a point of so great importance, as may excuse the considering it the more carefully, and prosecuting it at some length. What must one who loves the souls of men, and is grieved that any of them should perish, say to one whom he sees living in Sabbath-breaking, drunkenness, or any other wilful sin? What can he say, if the foregoing observations are true, but 'You must be born again'? 'No,' says a zealous man, 'that cannot be: how can you talk so uncharitably to the man? Has he not been baptized already? He cannot be born again now.' Can he not be born again? Do you affirm this? Then he cannot be saved. Though he be as old as Nicodemus was, yet 'except he be born again, he cannot see the kingdom of God.' Therefore in saying, 'He cannot be born again,' you in effect deliver him over to damnation. And where lies the uncharitableness now? on my side, or on yours? I say, he may be born again, and so become an heir of salvation. You say, 'He cannot be born again': and if so, he must inevitably perish! So you utterly block up his way to salvation, and send him to hell, out of mere charity!

But perhaps the sinner himself, to whom in real charity we say, 'You must be born again,' has been taught to say, 'I defy your new doctrine; I need not be born again: I was born again when I was baptized. What! would you have me deny my baptism?' I answer, first, there is nothing under heaven which can excuse a lie; otherwise I should say to an open sinner, 'If you have been baptized, do not own it. For how highly does this aggravate your guilt! How will it increase your damnation!

Was you devoted to God at eight days old, and have you been all these years devoting yourself to the devil? Was you, even before you had the use of reason, consecrated to God the Father, the Son, and the Holy Ghost? And have you, ever since you had the use of it, been flying in the face of God, and consecrating yourself to Satan? Does the abomination of desolation—the love of the world, pride, anger, lust, foolish desire, and a whole train of vile affections—stand where it ought not? Have you set up all these accursed things in that soul which was once a temple of the Holy Ghost; set apart for an "habitation of God, through the Spirit" yea, solemnly given up to Him? And do you glory in this, that you once belonged to God? O be ashamed! blush! hide yourself in the earth! Never boast more of what ought to fill you with confusion, to make you ashamed before God and man'! I answer, secondly, you have already denied your baptism; and that in the most effectual manner. You have denied it a thousand and a thousand times; and you do so still, day by day. For in your baptism you renounced the devil and all his works. Whenever, therefore, you give place to him again, whenever you do any of the works of the devil, then you deny your baptism. Therefore you deny it by every wilful sin; by every act of uncleanness, drunkenness, or revenge; by every obscene or profane word; by every oath that comes out of your mouth. Every time you profane the day of the Lord, you thereby deny your baptism; yea, every time you do anything to another which you would not he should do to you. I answer, thirdly, be you baptized or unbaptized, 'you must be born again'; otherwise it is not possible you should be inwardly holy: and without inward as well as outward holiness, you cannot be happy, even in this world, much less in the world to come. Do you say, 'Nay, but I do no harm to any man; I am honest and just in all my dealings; I do not curse, or take the Lord's name in vain; I do not profane the Lord's day; I am no drunkard; I do not slander my neighbour, nor live in any wilful sin'? If this be so, it were much to be wished that all men went as far as you do. But you must go farther yet, or you cannot be saved: still 'you must be born again.' Do you add, 'I do go farther yet; for I not only do no harm, but do all the good I can'? I doubt that fact:

I fear you have had a thousand opportunities of doing good
which you have suffered to pass by unimproved, and for which
therefore you are accountable to God. But if you had improved them all, if you really had done all the good you possibly
could to all men, yet this does not at all alter the case; still 'you
must be born again.' Without this nothing will do any good to
your poor, sinful, polluted soul. 'Nay, but I constantly attend
all the ordinances of God: I keep to my church and sacrament.'
It is well you do: but all this will not keep you from hell, except
you be born again. Go to church twice a day; go to the Lord's
table every week; say ever so many prayers in private; hear
ever so many good sermons; read ever so many good books;
still 'you must be born again': none of these things will stand in
the place of the new birth; no, nor anything under heaven. Let
this, therefore, if you have not already experienced this inward
work of God, be your continual prayer: 'Lord, add this to all
Thy blessings,—let me be born again! Deny whatever Thou
pleasest, but deny not this; let me be "born from above"! Take
away whatsoever seemeth Thee good—reputation, fortune,
friends, health—only give me this, to be born of the Spirit,
to be received among the children of God! Let me be born,
"not of corruptible seed, but incorruptible, by the word of God,
which liveth and abideth for ever"; and then let me daily "grow
in grace, and in the knowledge of our Lord and Saviour Jesus
Christ"!'

SERMON XL

THE WILDERNESS STATE

*Ye now have sorrow: but I will see you again, and your heart shall rejoice,
and your joy no man taketh from you.*—JOHN xvi. 22.

AFTER God had wrought a great deliverance for Israel, by
bringing them out of the house of bondage, they did not
immediately enter into the land which He had promised to their

fathers; but 'wandered out of the way in the wilderness,' and were variously tempted and distressed. In like manner, after God has delivered them that fear Him from the bondage of sin and Satan, after they are 'justified freely by His grace, through the redemption that is in Jesus,' yet not many of them immediately enter into 'the rest which remaineth for the people of God.' The greater part of them wander, more or less, out of the good way into which He hath brought them. They come, as it were, into a 'waste and howling desert,' where they are variously tempted and tormented: and this, some, in allusion to the case of the Israelites, have termed 'a wilderness state.'

2. Certain it is, that the condition wherein these are has a right to the tenderest compassion. They labour under an evil and sore disease; though one that is not commonly understood; and for this very reason it is the more difficult for them to find a remedy. Being in darkness themselves, they cannot be supposed to understand the nature of their own disorder; and few of their brethren, nay, perhaps, of their teachers, know either what their sickness is, or how to heal it. So much the more need there is to inquire, first, what is the nature of this disease? secondly, what is the cause? and, thirdly, what is the cure of it?

I. 1. And, first, what is the nature of this disease, into which so many fall after they have believed? Wherein does it properly consist? and what are the genuine symptoms of it? It properly consists in the loss of that faith which God once wrought in their heart. They that are *in the wilderness* have not now that divine 'evidence,' that satisfactory conviction, 'of things not seen,' which they once enjoyed. They have not now that inward demonstration of the Spirit which before enabled each of them to say, 'The life I live, I live by faith in the Son of God, who loved me, and gave Himself for me.' The light of heaven does not now 'shine in their hearts,' neither do they 'see Him that is invisible'; but darkness is again on the face of their souls, and blindness on the eyes of their understanding. The Spirit no longer 'witnesses with their spirits, that they are the children of God': neither does He continue as the Spirit of adoption, 'crying' in their hearts, 'Abba, Father.' They have not now a sure trust in His love, and a liberty of approaching Him with holy boldness. 'Though He slay me, yet will I trust in Him,' is no more the language of their heart; but they are shorn of their strength, and become weak and feeble-minded, even as other men.

2. Hence, secondly, proceeds the loss of love; which cannot but rise or fall, at the same time, and in the same proportion, with true, living faith. Accordingly, they that are deprived of their faith, are deprived of the love of God also. They cannot now say, 'Lord, Thou knowest all things, Thou knowest that I love Thee.' They are not now happy in God, as every one is that truly loves Him. They do not delight in Him as in time past, and 'smell the odour of His ointments.' Once, all their 'desire was unto Him, and to the remembrance of His name'; but now even their desires are cold and dead, if not utterly extinguished. And as their love of God is waxed cold, so is also their love of their neighbour. They have not now that zeal for the souls of men, that longing after their welfare, that fervent, restless, active desire of their being reconciled to God. They do not feel those 'bowels of mercies' for the sheep that are lost, that tender 'compassion for the ignorant, and them that are out of the way.' Once they were 'gentle toward all men,' meekly instructing such as opposed the truth; and, 'if any was overtaken in a fault, restoring such an one in the spirit of meekness': but, after a suspense, perhaps of many days, anger begins to regain its power; yea, peevishness and impatience thrust sore at them that they may fall; and it is well if they are not sometimes driven, even to 'render evil for evil, and railing for railing.'

3. In consequence of the loss of faith and love, follows, thirdly, loss of joy in the Holy Ghost. For if the loving consciousness of pardon be no more, the joy resulting therefrom cannot remain. If the Spirit does not witness with our spirit that we are the children of God, the joy that flowed from the inward witness must also be at an end. And, in like manner, they who once 'rejoiced with joy unspeakable,' 'in hope of the glory of God,' now they are deprived of that 'hope full of immortality,' are deprived of the joy it occasioned; as also of that which resulted from a consciousness of 'the love of God,' then 'shed abroad in their hearts.' For the cause being removed,

so is the effect; the fountain being dammed up, those living waters spring no more to refresh the thirsty soul.

4. With loss of faith, and love, and joy, there is also joined, fourthly, the loss of that 'peace which' once passed 'all understanding.' That sweet tranquillity of mind, that composure of spirit, is gone. Painful doubt returns; doubt, whether we ever did, and perhaps whether we ever shall, believe. We begin to doubt, whether we ever did find in our hearts the real testimony of the Spirit; whether we did not rather deceive our own souls, and mistake the voice of nature for the voice of God; nay, and perhaps, whether we shall ever hear His voice, and find favour in His sight. And these doubts are again joined with servile fear, with that fear which hath torment. We fear the wrath of God, even as before we believed: we fear, lest we should be cast out of His presence; and thence sink again into that fear of death, from which we were before wholly delivered.

5. But even this is not all; for loss of peace is accompanied with loss of power. We know every one who has peace with God, through Jesus Christ, has power over all sin. But whenever he loses the peace of God, he loses also the power over sin. While that peace remained, power also remained, even over the besetting sin, whether it were the sin of his nature, of his constitution, of his education, or his profession; yea, and over those evil tempers and desires which, till then, he could not conquer. Sin had then no more dominion over him; but he hath now no more dominion over sin. He may struggle, indeed, but he cannot overcome; the crown is fallen from his head. His enemies again prevail over him, and, more or less, bring him into bondage. The glory is departed from him, even the kingdom of God which was in his heart. He is dispossessed of righteousness, as well as of peace and joy in the Holy Ghost.

II. 1. Such is the nature of what many have termed, and not improperly, 'the wilderness state.' But the nature of it may be more fully understood by inquiring, secondly, What are the causes of it? These, indeed, are various. But I dare not rank among these the bare, arbitrary, sovereign will of God. He 'rejoiceth in the prosperity of His servants: He delighteth not to afflict or grieve the children of men.' His invariable will is our sanctification, attended with 'peace and joy in the Holy Ghost.' These are His own free gifts; and we are assured 'the gifts of God are,' on His part, 'without repentance.' He never repenteth of what He hath given, or desires to withdraw them from us. Therefore He never *deserts* us, as some speak: it is we only that *desert* Him.

(i.) 2. The most usual cause of inward darkness is *sin*, of one kind or another. This it is which generally occasions what is often a complication of sin and misery. And, first, sin of commission. This may frequently be observed to darken the soul in a moment; especially if it be a known, a wilful, or presumptuous sin. If, for instance, a person, who is now walking in the clear light of God's countenance should be any way prevailed on to commit a single act of drunkenness, or uncleanness, it would be no wonder if in that very hour he fell into utter darkness. It is true there have been some very rare cases, wherein God has prevented this, by an extraordinary display of His pardoning mercy, almost in the very instant. But in general, such an abuse of the goodness of God, so gross an insult on His love, occasions an immediate estrangement from God, and a 'darkness that may be felt.'

3. But it may be hoped this case is not very frequent; that there are not many who so despise the riches of His goodness as, while they walk in His light, so grossly and presumptuously to rebel against Him. That light is much more frequently lost by giving way to sins of omission. This, indeed, does not immediately quench the Spirit, but gradually and slowly. The former may be compared to pouring water upon a fire; the latter, to withdrawing the fuel from it. And many times will that loving Spirit reprove our neglect, before He departs from us. Many are the inward checks, the secret notices, He gives, before His influences are withdrawn. So that only a train of omissions, wilfully persisted in, can bring us into utter darkness.

4. Perhaps no sin of omission more frequently occasions this than the neglect of private prayer; the want whereof cannot be supplied by any other ordinance whatever. Nothing can be more plain, than that the life of God in the soul does not con-

tinue, much less increase, unless we use all opportunities of communion with God, and pouring out our hearts before Him. If, therefore, we are negligent of this, if we suffer business, company, or any avocation whatever, to prevent these secret exercises of the soul (or, which comes to the same thing, to make us hurry them over in a slight and careless manner), that life will surely decay. And if we long or frequently intermit them, it will gradually die away.

5. Another sin of omission, which frequently brings the soul of a believer into darkness, is the neglect of what was so strongly enjoined, even under the Jewish dispensation: 'Thou shalt, in any wise, rebuke thy neighbour, and not suffer sin upon him: thou shalt not hate thy brother in thy heart.' Now, if we do hate our brother in our heart, if we do not rebuke him when we see him in a fault, but suffer sin upon him, this will soon bring leanness into our own soul; seeing hereby we are partakers of his sin. By neglecting to reprove our neighbour, we make his sin our own: we become accountable for it to God: we saw his danger, and gave him no warning: so, 'if he perish in his iniquity,' God may justly require 'his blood at our hands.' No wonder then, if by thus grieving the Spirit, we lose the light of His countenance.

6. A third cause of our losing this is, the giving way to some kind of inward sin. For example: we know, every one that is 'proud in heart is an abomination to the Lord'; and that, although this pride of heart should not appear in the outward conversation. Now, how easily may a soul filled with peace and joy fall into this snare of the devil! How natural is it for him to imagine that he has more grace, more wisdom or strength, than he really has! to 'think more highly of himself than he ought to think'! How natural to glory in something he has received, as if he had not received it! But seeing God continually 'resisteth the proud, and giveth grace' only 'to the humble,' this must certainly obscure, if not wholly destroy, the light which before shone on his heart.

7. The same effect may be produced by giving place to anger, whatever the provocation or occasion be; yea, though it were coloured over with the name of 'zeal for the truth,' or 'for the glory of God.' Indeed, all zeal which is any other than the flame

of love is 'earthly, animal, and devilish.' It is the flame of wrath: it is flat, sinful anger, neither better nor worse. And nothing is a greater enemy to the mild, gentle love of God than this: they never did, they never can, subsist together to one breast. In the same proportion as this prevails, love and joy in the Holy Ghost decrease. This is particularly observable in the case of *offence*; I mean, anger at any of our brethren, at any of those who are united with us either by civil or religious ties. If we give way to the spirit of offence but one hour, we lose the sweet influences of the Holy Spirit; so that, instead of amending them, we destroy ourselves, and become an easy prey to any enemy that assaults us.

8. But suppose we are aware of this snare of the devil, we may be attacked from another quarter. When fierceness and anger are asleep, and love alone is waking, we may be no less endangered by desire, which equally tends to darken the soul This is the sure effect of any foolish desire, any vain or inordinate affection. If we set our affection on things of the earth, on any person or thing under the sun; if we desire any thing but God, and what tends to God; if we seek happiness in any creature; the jealous God will surely contend with us, for He can admit of no rival. And if we will not hear His warning voice, and return unto Him with our whole soul, if we continue to grieve Him with our idols, and running after other gods, we shall soon be cold, barren, and dry; and the god of this world will blind and darken our hearts.

9. But this he frequently does, even when we do not give way to any positive sin. It is enough, it gives him sufficient advantage, if we do not 'stir up the gift of God which is in us'; if we do not agonize continually 'to enter in at the strait gate'; if we do not earnestly 'strive for the mastery,' and 'take the kingdom of heaven by violence.' There needs no more than not to fight, and we are sure to be conquered. Let us only be careless or 'faint in our mind,' let us be easy and indolent, and our natural darkness will soon return, and overspread our soul. It is enough, therefore, if we give way to spiritual sloth; this will effectually darken the soul: it will as surely destroy the light of God, if not so swiftly, as murder or adultery.

10. But it is well to be observed, that the cause of our darkness (whatsoever it be, whether omission or commission, whether inward or outward sin) is not always nigh at hand. Sometimes the sin which occasioned the present distress may lie at a considerable distance. It might be committed days, or weeks, or months before. And that God now withdraws His light and peace on account of what was done so long ago, is not (as one might at first imagine) an instance of His severity, but rather a proof of His long-suffering and tender mercy. He waited all this time, if haply we would see, acknowledge, and correct what was amiss; and, in default of this, He at length shows His displeasure, if thus, at last He may bring us to repentance.

(ii.) 1. Another general cause of this darkness is *ignorance*; which is likewise of various kinds If men know not the Scriptures, if they imagine there are passages either in the Old or New Testament which assert, that all believers, without exception, *must* sometimes be in darkness; this ignorance will naturally bring upon them the darkness which they expect. And how common a case has this been among us! How few are there that do not expect it! And no wonder, seeing they are taught to expect it; seeing their guides lead them into this way. Not only the mystic writers of the Romish Church, but many of the most spiritual and experimental in our own (very few of the last century excepted), lay it down with all assurance, as a plain, unquestionable scripture doctrine, and cite many texts to prove it.

2. Ignorance also of the work of God in the soul frequently occasions this darkness. Men imagine (because so they have been taught, particularly by writers of the Romish communion, whose plausible assertions too many Protestants have received without due examination) that they are not always to walk in *luminous faith*; that this is only a *lower dispensation*; that as they rise higher, they are to leave those *sensible comforts*, and to live by *naked faith* (naked, indeed, if it be stripped both of love, and peace, and joy in the Holy Ghost!); that a state of light and joy is good, but a state of darkness and dryness is better; that it is by these alone we can be purified from pride, love of the world, and inordinate self-love; and that, therefore, we ought neither

35

to expect nor desire to walk in the light always. Hence it is (though other reasons may concur), that the main body of pious men in the Romish Church generally walk in a dark uncomfortable way, and if ever they receive soon lose the light of God.

(iii.) 1. A third general cause of this darkness is *temptation*. When the candle of the Lord first shines on our head, temptation fequently flees away, and totally disappears. All is calm within, perhaps without too, while God makes our enemies to be at peace with us. It is then very natural to suppose that we shall not see war any more. And there are instances wherein this calm has continued, not only for weeks, but for months or years. But commonly it is otherwise: in a short time 'the winds blow, the rains descend, and the floods arise' anew. They who know not either the Son or the Father, and consequently hate His children, when God slackens the bridle which is in their teeth, will show that hatred in various instances. As of old, 'he that was born after the flesh persecuted him that was born after the Spirit, even so it is now'; the same cause still producing the same effect. The evil which yet remains in the heart will then also move afresh; anger, and many other roots of bitterness, will endeavour to spring up. At the same time Satan will not be wanting to cast in his fiery darts; and the soul will have to wrestle, not only with the world, not only 'with flesh and blood, but with principalities and powers, with the rulers of the darkness of this world, with wicked spirits in high places.' Now, when so various assaults are made at once, and perhaps with the utmost violence, it is not strange if it should occasion, not only heaviness, but even darkness in a weak believer — more especially, if he was not watching; if these assaults are made in an hour when he looked not for them; if he expected nothing less, but had fondly told himself the day of evil would return no more.

2. The force of those temptations which arise from within will be exceedingly heightened if we before thought too highly of ourselves, as if we had been cleansed from all sin. And how naturally do we imagine this during the warmth of our first love! How ready are we to believe that God has 'fulfilled in us

the' whole 'work of faith with power'; that because we *feel* no sin, we *have* none in us; but the soul is all love! And well may a sharp attack from an enemy whom we supposed to be not only conquered but slain, throw us into much heaviness of soul; yea, sometimes, into utter darkness: particularly when we *reason* with this enemy, instead of instantly calling upon God, and casting ourselves upon Him, by simple faith, who 'alone knoweth to deliver'·His 'out of temptation.'

III. These are the usual causes of this second darkness. Inquire we, thirdly, what is the cure of it!

1. To suppose that this is one and the same in all cases, is a great and fatal mistake; and yet extremely common, even among many who pass for experienced Christians, yea, perhaps, take upon them to be teachers in Israel, to be the guides of other souls. Accordingly, they know and use but one medicine, whatever be the cause of the distemper. They begin immediately to apply the promises; to *preach the gospel*, as they call it. To give comfort, is the single point at which they aim; in order to which they say many soft and tender things, concerning the love of God to poor, helpless sinners, and the efficacy of the blood of Christ. Now this is *quackery* indeed, and that of the worst sort, as it tends, if not to kill men's bodies, yet, without the peculiar mercy of God, 'to destroy both their bodies and souls in hell.' It is hard to speak of these 'daubers with untempered mortar,' these promise-mongers, as they deserve. They well deserve the title, which has been ignorantly given to others: they are *spiritual mountebanks*. They do, in effect, make 'the blood of the covenant an unholy·thing.' They vilely prostitute the promises of God, by thus applying them to all without distinction. Whereas, indeed, the cure of spiritual, as of bodily, diseases must be as various as are the causes of them. The first thing, therefore, is, to find out the cause; and this will naturally point out the cure.

2. For instance: is it sin which occasions darkness? What sin? Is it outward sin of any kind? Does your conscience accuse you of committing any sin, whereby you grieve the Holy Spirit of God? Is it on this account that He is departed from you, and

that joy and peace are departed with Him? And how can you expect they should return, till you put away the accursed thing? Let the wicked forsake his way'; 'cleanse your hands, ye sinners'; 'put away the evil of your doings'; so shall your 'light break out of obscurity'; the Lord will return and 'abundantly pardon.'

3. If, upon the closest search, you can find no sin of commission which causes the cloud upon your soul, inquire next, if there be not some sin of omission which separates between God and you. Do you 'not suffer sin upon your brother'? Do you reprove them that sin in your sight? Do you walk in all the ordinances of God? in public, family, private prayer? If not, if you habitually neglect any one of these known duties, how can you expect that the light of His countenance should continue to shine upon you? Make haste to 'strengthen the things that remain'; then your soul shall live. 'To-day, if ye will hear His voice,' by His grace supply what is lacking. When you hear a voice behind you saying, 'This is the way, walk thou in it,' harden not your heart; be no more 'disobedient to the heavenly calling.' Till the sin, whether of omission or commission, be removed, all comfort is false and deceitful. It is only skinning the wound over, which still festers and rankles beneath. Look for no peace within, till you are at peace with God; which cannot be without 'fruits meet for repentance.'

4. But perhaps you are not conscious of even any sin of omission which impairs your peace and joy in the Holy Ghost. Is there not, then, some inward sin, which, as a root of bitterness, springs up in your heart to trouble you? Is not your dryness and barrenness of soul occasioned by your heart's 'departing from the living God'? Has not 'the foot of pride come against' you? Have you not thought of yourself 'more highly than you ought to think'? Have you not, in any respect, 'sacrificed to your own net, and burned incense to your own drag'? Have you not ascribed your success in any undertaking to your own courage, or strength, or wisdom? Have you not boasted of something 'you have received, as though you had not received it'? Have you not gloried in anything, 'save in the cross of our Lord Jesus Christ'? Have you not sought after or desired the praise of men? Have you not taken pleasure in it? If so, you see the way you are

to take. If you have fallen by pride, 'humble yourself under the mighty hand of God, and He will exalt you in due time.' Have not you forced Him to depart from you, by giving place to anger? Have not you 'fretted yourself because of the ungodly'? or 'been envious against the evil-doers'? Have you not been offended at any of your brethren, looking at their (real or imagined) sin, so as to sin yourself against the great law of love, by estranging your heart from them? Then look unto the Lord, that you may renew your strength; that all this sharpness and coldness may be done away; that love, and peace, and joy may return together, and you may be invariably kind to each other, and 'tender-hearted, forgiving one another, even as God for Christ's sake hath forgiven you.' Have not you given way to any foolish desire? to any kind or degree of inordinate affection? How then can the love of God have place in your heart, till you put away your idols? 'Be not deceived: God is not mocked': He will not dwell in a divided heart. As long, therefore, as you cherish Delilah in your bosom, He has no place there. It is vain to hope for a recovery of His light, till you pluck out the right eye, and cast it from you. O let there be no longer delay! Cry to Him, that He may enable you so to do! Bewail your own impotence and helplessness; and, the Lord being your helper, enter in at the strait gate: take the kingdom of heaven by violence! Cast out every idol from His sanctuary, and the glory of the Lord shall soon appear.

5. Perhaps it is this very thing, the want of striving, spiritual sloth, which keeps your soul in darkness. You dwell at ease in the land; there is no war in your coasts; and so you are quiet and unconcerned. You go on in the same even track of outward duties, and are content there to abide. And do you wonder, meantime, that your soul is dead? O stir yourself up before the Lord! Arise, and shake yourself from the dust; wrestle with God for the mighty blessing; pour out your soul unto God in prayer and continue therein with all perseverance! Watch! Awake out of sleep; and keep awake!—otherwise there is nothing to be expected, but that you will be alienated more and more from the light and life of God.

6. If, upon the fullest and most impartial examination of

yourself, you cannot discern that you at present give way either
to spiritual sloth, or any other inward or outward sin, then call
to mind the time that is past. Consider your former tempers,
words, and actions. Have these been right before the Lord?
'Commune with Him in your chamber, and be still'; and desire
of Him to try the ground of your heart, and bring to your
remembrance whatever has at any time offended the eyes of His
glory. If the guilt of any unrepented sin remain on your soul, it
cannot be but you will remain in darkness, till, having been
renewed by repentance, you are again washed by faith in 'the
fountain opened for sin and uncleanness.'

7. Entirely different will be the manner of the cure, if the
cause of the disease be not sin, but ignorance. It may be ignorance of the meaning of Scripture; perhaps occasioned by ignorant
commentators—ignorant, at least, in this respect, however knowing and learned they may be in other particulars. And, in this
case, that ignorance must be removed before we can remove the
darkness arising from it. We must show the true meaning of
those texts which have been misunderstood. My design does
not permit me to consider all the passages of Scripture which
have been pressed into this service. I shall just mention two or
three, which are frequently brought to prove, that all believers
must, sooner or later, 'walk in darkness.'

8. One of these is Isa. l. 10: 'Who is among you that feareth
the Lord, that obeyeth the voice of His servant, that walketh in
darkness, and hath no light? let him trust in the name of the
Lord, and stay upon his God.' But how does it appear, either from
the text or context, that the person here spoken of ever had
light? One who is convinced of sin 'feareth the Lord, and obeyeth the voice of His servant.' And him we should advise, though
he was still dark of soul, and had never seen the light of God's
countenance, yet to 'trust in the name of the Lord, and stay upon
his God.' This text, therefore, proves nothing less than that a
believer in Christ 'must sometimes *walk in darkness.*'

9. Another text which has been supposed to speak the same
doctrine, is Hos. ii. 14: 'I will allure her, and bring her into the
wilderness, and speak comfortably unto her.' Hence it has been
inferred, that God will bring every believer *into the wilderness,*

into a state of deadness and darkness. But it is certain, the text speaks no such thing; for it does not appear that it speaks of particular believers at all: it manifestly refers to the Jewish nation; and, perhaps, to that only. But if it be applicable to particular persons, the plain meaning of it is this: I will draw him by love; I will next convince him of sin; and then comfort him by My pardoning mercy.

10. A third scripture, from whence the same inference has been drawn, is that above recited, 'Ye now have sorrow: but I will see you again, and your heart shall rejoice, and your joy no man taketh from you.' This has been supposed to imply, that God would, after a time, withdraw Himself from all believers; and that they could not, till after they had thus sorrowed, have the joy which no man could take from them. But the whole context shows, that our Lord is here speaking personally to the Apostles, and no others; and that He is speaking concerning those particular events, His own death and resurrection. 'A little while,' says He, 'and ye shall not see Me,' namely, whilst I am in the grave: 'and again, a little while, and ye shall see Me'; when I am risen from the dead. 'Ye will weep and lament, and the world will rejoice: but your sorrow shall be turned into joy.' 'Ye now have sorrow,' because I am about to be taken from your head; 'but I will see you again,' after My resurrection, 'and your heart shall rejoice; and your joy,' which I will then give you, 'no man taketh from you.' All this we know was literally fulfilled in the particular case of the Apostles. But no inference can be drawn from hence with regard to God's dealings with believers in general.

11. A fourth text (to mention no more), which has been frequently cited in proof of the same doctrine, is 1 Pet. iv. 12: 'Beloved, think it not strange concerning the fiery trial which is to try you.' But this is full as foreign to the point as the preceding. The text, literally rendered, runs thus: 'Beloved, wonder not at the burning which is among you, which is for your trial.' Now, however, this may be accommodated to inward trials, in a secondary sense; yet, primarily, it doubtless refers to martyrdom, and the sufferings connected with it. Neither, therefore, is this text anything at all to the purpose for which it is cited. And we

may challenge all men to bring one text, either from the Old or New Testament, which is any more to the purpose than this.

12. 'But is not darkness much more profitable for the soul than light? Is not the work of God in the heart most swiftly and effectually carried on during a state of inward suffering? Is not a believer more swiftly and throughly purified by sorrow than by joy?—by anguish, and pain, and distress, and spiritual martyrdoms, than by continual peace?' So the Mystics teach; so it is written in their books; but not in the oracles of God. The Scripture nowhere says that the absence of God best perfects His work in the heart! Rather, His presence, and a clear communion with the Father and the Son: a strong consciousness of this will do more in an hour, than His absence in an age. Joy in the Holy Ghost will far more effectually purify the soul, than the want of that joy; and the peace of God is the best means of refining the soul from the dross of earthly affections. Away then with the idle conceit, that the kingdom of God is divided against itself, that the peace of God, and joy in the Holy Ghost, are obstructive of righteousness; and that we are saved, not by faith, but by unbelief; not by hope, but by despair!

13. So long as men dream thus, they may well 'walk in darkness': nor can the effect cease, till the cause is removed. But yet we must not imagine it will immediately cease, even when the cause is no more. When either ignorance or sin has caused darkness, one or the other may be removed, and yet the light which was obstructed thereby may not immediately return. As it is the free gift of God, He may restore it, sooner or later, as it pleases Him. In the case of sin, we cannot reasonably expect that it should immediately return. The sin began before the punishment, which may, therefore, justly remain after the sin is at an end. And even in the natural course of things, though a wound cannot be healed while the dart is sticking in the flesh; yet neither is it healed as soon as that is drawn out, but soreness and pain may remain long after.

14. Lastly. If darkness be occasioned by manifold and heavy and unexpected temptations, the best way of removing and preventing this is, to teach believers always to expect temptation, seeing they dwell in an evil world among wicked, subtle,

malicious spirits, and have an heart capable of all evil. Convince them that the whole work of sanctification is not, as they imagined, wrought at once; that when they first believe they are but as new-born babes, who are gradually to grow up, and may expect many storms before they come to the full stature of Christ. Above all, let them be instructed, when the storm is upon them, not to reason with the devil, but to pray; to pour out their souls before God, and show Him of their trouble. And these are the persons unto whom, chiefly, we are to apply the great and precious promises; not to the ignorant, till the ignorance is removed, much less to the impenitent sinner. To these we may largely and affectionately declare the loving-kindness of God our Saviour, and expatiate upon His tender mercies which have been ever of old. Here we may dwell upon the faithfulness of God, whose 'word is tried to the uttermost'; and upon the virtue of that blood which was shed for us, to 'cleanse us from all sin': and God will then bear witness to His word, and bring their souls out of trouble. He will say, 'Arise, shine; for thy light is come, and the glory of the Lord is risen upon thee.' Yea, and that light, if thou walk humbly and closely with God, will 'shine more and more unto the perfect day.'

SERMON XLI

HEAVINESS THROUGH MANIFOLD TEMPTATIONS

Now for a season, if need be, ye are in heaviness through manifold temptations.
—I Pet. i. 6.

IN the preceding discourse I have particularly spoken of that darkness of mind into which those are often observed to fall who once walked in the light of God's countenance. Nearly related to this is the heaviness of soul which is still more common, even among believers. Indeed, almost all the children of God experience this, in an higher or lower degree. And so great is the resemblance between one and the other, that they are frequently confounded together; and we are apt to say, indifferently, 'Such an one is in darkness,' or, 'Such an one is in heaviness'; as if they were equivalent terms, one of which implied no more than the other. But they are far, very far, from it. Darkness is one thing; heaviness is another. There is a difference, yea, a wide and essential difference, between the former and the latter. And such a difference it is, as all the children of God are deeply concerned to understand: otherwise, nothing will be more easy than for them to slide out of heaviness into darkness. In order to prevent this, I will endeavour to show,—

I. WHAT MANNER OF PERSONS THOSE WERE TO WHOM THE APOSTLE SAYS, 'YE ARE IN HEAVINESS'!

II. WHAT KIND OF HEAVINESS THEY WERE IN:

III. WHAT WERE THE CAUSES: AND,

IV. WHAT WERE THE ENDS OF IT. I SHALL CONCLUDE WITH SOME INFERENCES.

I. 1. I am, in the first place, to show what manner of persons those were to whom the Apostle says, 'Ye are in heaviness.' And, first, it is beyond all dispute, that they were believers at the time the Apostle thus addressed them: for so he expressly says (verse 5), 'Ye who are kept by the power of God through faith unto salvation.' Again (verse 7), he mentions 'the trial of their faith, much more precious than that of gold which perisheth.' And yet again (verse 9), he speaks of their 'receiving the end of their faith, the salvation of their souls.' At the same time, therefore, that they were 'in heaviness,' they were possessed of living faith. Their heaviness did not destroy their faith: they still 'endured, as seeing Him that is invisible.'

2. Neither did their heaviness destroy their peace; the peace which passeth all understanding'; which is inseparable from true, living faith. This we may easily gather from the second verse, wherein the Apostle prays, not that grace and *peace* may be *given* them, but only that it may 'be *multiplied* unto' them: that the blessing which they already enjoyed might be more abundantly bestowed upon them.

3. The persons to whom the Apostle here speaks were also full of a living hope For thus he speaks (verse 3), 'Blessed be

the God and Father of our Lord Jesus Christ, who according to His abundant mercy hath begotten us again'—me and you, all of us who are 'sanctified by the Spirit,' and enjoy the 'sprinkling of the blood of Jesus Christ'—'unto a living hope, unto an inheritance,' that is, unto a living hope of an inheritance, 'incorruptible, undefiled, and that fadeth not away.' So that, notwithstanding their heaviness, they still retained an hope full of immortality.

4. And they still 'rejoiced in hope of the glory of God.' They were filled with joy in the Holy Ghost. So (verse 8), the Apostle having just mentioned the final 'revelation of Jesus Christ' (namely, when He cometh to judge the world), immediately adds, 'In whom, though now ye see Him not,' not with your bodily eyes, 'yet believing, ye rejoice with joy unspeakable: and full of glory.' Their heaviness, therefore, was not only consistent with living hope, but also with joy unspeakable: at the same time they were thus heavy, they nevertheless rejoiced with joy full of glory.

5. In the midst of their heaviness they likewise still enjoyed the love of God, which had been shed abroad in their hearts; 'whom,' says the Apostle, 'having not seen, ye love.' Though ye have not seen Him face to face; yet, knowing Him by faith, ye have obeyed His word, 'My son, give Me thy heart.' He is your God, and your love, the desire of your eyes, and your 'exceeding great reward.' Ye have sought and found happiness in Him: ye 'delight in the Lord,' and He hath given you your 'hearts' desire.'

6. Once more: though they were heavy, yet were they holy; they retained the same power over sin. They were still 'kept' from this, 'by the power of God'; they were 'obedient children, not fashioned according to their former desires'; but 'as He that had called them is holy,' so were they 'holy in all manner of conversation.' Knowing they were 'redeemed by the precious blood of Christ, as a lamb without spot, and without blemish, they had, through the faith and hope, which they had in God, 'purified their souls by the Spirit.' So that, upon the whole, their heaviness well consisted with faith, with hope, with love of God and man, with the peace of God, with joy in the Holy

Ghost, with inward and outward holiness. It did no way impair, much less destroy, any part of the work of God in their hearts. It did not at all interfere with that 'sanctification of the Spirit' which is the root of all true obedience; neither with the happiness which must needs result from grace and peace reigning in the heart.

II. 1. Hence we may easily learn what kind of heaviness they were in,—the second thing which I shall endeavour to show. The word, in the original, is λυπηθέντες—*made sorry, grieved*: from λύπη—*grief*, or *sorrow*. This is the constant, literal meaning of the word: and, this being observed, there is no ambiguity in the expression, nor any difficulty in understanding it. The persons spoken of here were *grieved*: the heaviness they were in was neither more nor less than *sorrow*, or *grief*,—a passion which every child of man is well acquainted with.

2. It is probable our translators rendered it *heaviness* (though a less common word), to denote two things: first, the degree, and next, the continuance of it. It does indeed seem, that it is not a slight or inconsiderable degree of grief which is here spoken of; but such as makes a strong impression upon, and sinks deep into, the soul. Neither does this appear to be a transient sorrow, such as passes away in an hour; but rather, such as, having taken fast hold of the heart, is not presently shaken off, but continues for some time, as a settled temper, rather than a passion, even in them that have living faith in Christ, and the genuine love of God in their hearts.

3. Even in these, this heaviness may sometimes be so deep, as to overshadow the whole soul; to give a colour, as it were, to all the affections; such as will appear in the whole behaviour. It may likewise have an influence over the body; particularly in those that are either of a naturally weak constitution, or weakened by some accidental disorder, especially of the nervous kind. In many cases, we find 'the corruptible body presses down the soul': in this, the soul rather presses down the body, and weakens it more and more. Nay, I will not say that deep and lasting sorrow of heart may not sometimes weaken a strong constitution, and lay the foundation of such bodily disorders as

are not easily removed: and yet, all this may consist with a measure of that faith which still worketh by love.

4. This may well be termed a 'fiery trial'; and though it is not the same with that the Apostle speaks of in the fourth chapter, yet many of the expressions there used concerning outward sufferings may be accommodated to this inward affliction. They cannot, indeed, with any propriety, be applied to them that are in darkness. These do not, cannot rejoice; neither is it true, that 'the spirit of glory and of God resteth upon' them. But He frequently doth on those that are in heaviness; so that, though sorrowful, yet are they always rejoicing.

III. 1. But to proceed to the third point: what are the causes of such sorrow or heaviness in a true believer? The Apostle tells us clearly: 'Ye are in heaviness,' says he, 'through manifold temptations'; ποικίλοις—*manifold*, not only many in number, but of many kinds. They may be varied and diversified a thousand ways, by the change or addition of numberless circumstances. And this very diversity and variety make it more difficult to guard against them. Among these we may rank all bodily disorders; particularly acute diseases, and violent pain of every kind, whether affecting the whole body, or the smallest part of it. It is true, some who have enjoyed uninterrupted health, and have felt none of these, may make light of them, and wonder that sickness, or pain of body, should bring heaviness upon the mind. And perhaps one in a thousand is of so peculiar a constitution as not to feel pain like other men. So hath it pleased God to show His almighty power, by producing some of these prodigies of nature, who have seemed not to regard pain at all, though of the severest kind; if that contempt of pain was not owing partly to the force of education, partly to a preternatural cause—to the power either of good or evil spirits, who raised those men above the state of mere nature. But, abstracting from these particular cases, it is, in general, a just observation, that

> Pain is perfect misery, and extreme
> Quite overturns all patience.

And even where this is prevented by the grace of God, where men do 'possess their souls in patience,' it may, nevertheless, occasion much inward heaviness: the soul sympathizing with the body.

2. All diseases of long continuance, though less painful, are apt to produce the same effect. When God appoints over us consumption, or the chilling and burning ague, if it be not speedily removed, it will not only 'consume the eyes,' but 'cause sorrow of heart.' This is eminently the case with regard to all those which are termed *nervous disorders*. And faith does not overturn the course of nature: natural causes still produce natural effects. Faith no more hinders the *sinking of the spirit* (as it is called) in an hysteric illness, than the rising of the pulse in a fever.

3. Again: when 'calamity cometh as a whirlwind, and poverty as an armed man'; is this a little temptation? Is it strange if it occasion sorrow and heaviness? Although this also may appear but a small thing to those that stand at a distance, or who look, and 'pass by on the other side'; yet it is otherwise to them that feel it. 'Having food and raiment' (indeed the latter word, σκεπάσματα, implies *lodging* as well as *apparel*), we may, if the love of God is in our hearts, 'be therewith content.' But what shall they do who have none of these? who, as it were, 'embrace the rock for a shelter'? who have only the earth to lie upon and only the sky to cover them? who have not a dry, or warm, much less a clean, abode for themselves and their little ones? no, nor clothing to keep themselves, or those they love next themselves, from pinching cold, either by day or night? I laugh at the stupid Heathen crying out,

> *Nil habet infelix paupertas durius in se,*
> *Quàm quod ridiculos homines facit!*

Has poverty nothing worse in it that this, that it *makes men liable to be laughed at*? It is a sign this idle poet talked by rote of the things which he knew not. Is not want of food something worse than this? God pronounced it as a curse upon man, that he should earn it 'by the sweat of his brow.' But how many are there in this Christian country, that toil, and labour, and sweat, and have it not at last, but struggle with weariness and hunger together? Is it not worse for one, after a hard day's labour, to come back to a poor, cold, dirty, uncomfortable lodging, and to find there not even the food which is needful to repair his wasted strength? You that live at ease in the earth, that want nothing but eyes to see, ears to hear, and hearts to understand how well God hath dwelt with you, is it not worse to seek bread day by day, and find none? perhaps to find the comfort also of five or six children crying for what he has not to give! Were it not that he is restrained by an unseen hand, would he not soon 'curse God and die'? O want of bread! want of bread! Who can tell what this means, unless he hath felt it himself? I am astonished it occasions no more than heaviness even in them that believe.

4. Perhaps, next to this, we may place the death of those who were near and dear unto us; of a tender parent, and one not much declined into the vale of years; of a beloved child, just rising into life, and clasping about our heart of a friend that was as our own soul—next the grace of God, the last, best gift of Heaven. And a thousand circumstances may enhance the distress. Perhaps the child, the friend, died in our embrace!—perhaps, was snatched away when we looked not for it! flourishing, cut down like a flower. In all these cases, we not only may, but ought to, be affected: it is the design of God that we should. He would not have us stocks and stones. He would have our affections regulated, not extinguished. Therefore, 'nature unreproved may drop a tear.' There may be sorrow without sin.

5. A still deeper sorrow we may feel for those who are dead while they live; on account of the unkindness, ingratitude, apostasy, of those who were united to us in the closest ties. Who can express what a lover of souls may feel for a friend, a brother, dead to God? for an husband, a wife, a parent, a child rushing into sin, as an horse into the battle; and, in spite of all arguments and persuasions, hasting to work out his own damnation. And this anguish of spirit may be heightened to an inconceivable degree, by the consideration, that he who is now posting to destruction once ran well in the way of life. Whatever

he was in time past serves now to no other purpose than to make our reflections on what he is more piercing and afflictive.

6. In all these circumstances, we may be assured, our great adversary will not be wanting to improve his opportunity. He, who is always 'walking about, seeking whom he may devour,' will then, especially, use all his power, all his skill, if haply he may gain any advantage over the soul that is already cast down. He will not be sparing of his fiery darts, such as are most likely to find an entrance, and to fix most deeply in the heart, by their suitableness to the temptation that assaults it. He will labour to inject unbelieving, or blasphemous, or repining thoughts. He will suggest that God does not regard, does not govern, the earth; or, at least, that he does not govern it aright, not by the rules of justice and mercy. He will endeavour to stir up the heart against God, to renew our natural enmity against Him. And if we attempt to fight him with his own weapons, if we begin to reason with him, more and more heaviness will undoubtedly ensue, if not utter darkness.

7. It has been frequently supposed, that there is another cause, if not of darkness, at least, of heaviness; namely, God's withdrawing Himself from the soul, because it is His sovereign will. Certainly He will do this, if we grieve His Holy Spirit, either by outward or inward sin; either by doing evil, or neglecting to do good; by giving way either to pride or anger, to spiritual sloth, to foolish desire, or inordinate affecton. But that He ever withdraws Himself *because he will*, merely because it is His good pleasure, I absolutely deny. There is no text in all the Bible which gives any colour for such a supposition Nay, it is a supposition, contrary, not only to many particular texts, but to the whole tenor of Scripture. It is repugnant to the very nature of God: it is utterly beneath His majesty and wisdom (as an eminent writer strongly expresses it), 'to play at bo-peep with His creatures.' It is inconsistent both with His justice and mercy, and with the sound experience of all His children.

8. One more cause of heaviness is mentioned by many of those who were termed 'mystic authors.' And the notion has crept in, I know not how, even among plain people who have no acquaintance with them. I cannot better explain this, than

in the words of a late writer, who relates this as her own experience: 'I continued so happy in my Beloved, that, although I should have been forced to live a vagabond in a desert, I should have found no difficulty in it. This state had not lasted long, when, in effect, I found myself led into a desert. I found myself in a forlorn condition, altogether poor, wretched, and miserable. The proper source of this grief is, the knowledge of ourselves; by which we find that there is an extreme unlikeness between God and us. We see ourselves most opposite to Him; and that our inmost soul is entirely corrupted, depraved, and full of all kind of evil and malignity, of the world and the flesh, and all sorts of abominations.'—From hence it has been inferred, that the knowledge of ourselves, without which we should perish everlastingly, must, even after we have attained justifying faith, occasion the deepest heaviness.

9. But upon this I would observe, (1) In the preceding paragraph, this writer says, 'Hearing I had not a true faith in Christ, I offered myself up to God, and immediately felt His love.' It may be so; and yet it does not appear that this was justification. It is more probable, it was no more than what are usually termed, the 'drawings of the Father.' And if so, the heaviness and darkness which followed was no other than conviction of sin; which, in the nature of things, must precede that faith whereby we are justified. (2) Suppose she was justified almost the same moment she was convinced of wanting faith, there was then no time for that gradually-increasing self-knowledge which uses to precede justification; in this case, therefore, it came after, and was probably the more severe, the less it was expected. (3) It is allowed there will be a far deeper, a far clearer and fuller knowledge of our inbred sin, of our total corruption by nature, after justification, than ever there was before it. But this need not occasion darkness of soul: I will not say, that it *must* bring us into heaviness. Were it so, the Apostle would not have used that expression, *if need be*; for there would be an absolute, indispensable need of it for all that would know themselves; that is, in effect, for all that would know the perfect love of God, and be thereby 'made meet to be partakers of the inheritance of the saints in light.' But this

is by no means the case. On the contrary, God may increase the knowledge of ourselves to any degree, and increase, in the same proportion, the knowledge of Himself and the experience of His love. And in this case there would be no 'desert' no 'misery' no 'forlorn condition'; but love, and peace, and joy, gradually springing up into everlasting life.

IV. 1. For what ends, then (which was the fourth thing to be considered), does God permit heaviness to befall so many of His children? The Apostle gives us a plain and direct answer to this important question: 'that the trial of their faith, which is much more precious than gold that perisheth, though it be tried by fire, may be found unto praise, and honour, and glory, at the revelation of Jesus Christ' (verse 7). There may be an allusion to this, in that well-known passage of the fourth chapter (although it primarily relates to quite another thing, as has been already observed): 'Think it not strange concerning the fiery trial which is to try you: but rejoice that ye are partakers of the sufferings of Christ; that, when His glory shall be revealed, ye may likewise rejoice with exceeding great joy' (verse 12, &c.).

2. Hence we learn, that the first and great end of God's permitting the temptations which bring heaviness on His children, is the trial of their faith, which is tried by these, even as gold by the fire. Now we know, gold tried in the fire is purified thereby; is separated from its dross. And so is faith in the fire of temptation; the more it is tried, the more it is purified; yea, and not only purified, but also strengthened, confirmed, increased abundantly, by so many more proofs of the wisdom and power, the love and faithfulness of God. This, then—to increase our faith—is one gracious end of God's permitting those manifold temptations.

3. They serve to try, to purify, to confirm, and increase that living hope also, whereunto 'the God and Father of our Lord Jesus Christ hath begotten us again of His abundant mercy.' Indeed our hope cannot but increase in the same proportion with our faith. On this foundation it stands: believing in His name, living by faith in the Son of God, we hope for, we have

a confident expectation of, the glory which shall be revealed; and, consequently, whatever strengthens our faith, increases our hope also. At the same time it increases our joy in the Lord, which cannot but attend a hope full of immortality. In this view the Apostle exhorts believers in the other chapter: 'Rejoice that ye are partakers of the sufferings of Christ.' On this very account, 'happy are you; for the Spirit of glory and of God resteth upon you': and hereby ye are enabled, even in the midst of sufferings, to 'rejoice with joy unspeakable and full of glory.'

4. They rejoice the more, because the trials which increase their faith and hope increase their love also; both their gratitude to God for all His mercies, and their good-will to all mankind. Accordingly, the more deeply sensible they are of the loving-kindness of God their Saviour, the more is their heart inflamed with love to Him who 'first loved us.' The clearer and stronger evidence they have of the glory that shall be revealed, the more do they love Him who hath purchased it for them, and 'given them the earnest' thereof 'in their hearts.' And this, the increase of their love, is another end of the temptations permitted to come upon them.

5. Yet another is, their advance in holiness; holiness of heart, and holiness of conversation,—the latter naturally resulting from the former; for a good tree will bring forth good fruit. And all inward holiness is the immediate fruit of the faith that worketh by love. By this the blessed Spirit purifies the heart from pride, self-will, passion; from love of the world, from foolish and hurtful desires, from vile and vain affections. Beside that, sanctified afflictions have, through the grace of God, an immediate and direct tendency to holiness. Through the operation of His Spirit, they humble, more and more, and abase the soul before God. They calm and meeken our turbulent spirit, tame the fierceness of our nature, soften our obstinacy and self-will, crucify us to the world, and bring us to expect all our strength from, and to seek all our happiness in, God.

6. And all these terminate in that great end, that our faith, hope, love, and holiness 'may be found,' if it doth not yet appear, 'unto praise' from God Himself, 'and honour' from men and angels, 'and glory,' assigned by the great Judge to all

that have endured unto the end. And this will be assigned in that awful day to every man, 'according to his works'; according to the work which God had wrought in his heart, and the outward works which he has wrought for God; and likewise according to what he had suffered: so that all these trials are unspeakable gain. So many ways do these 'light afflictions, which are but for a moment, work out for us a far more exceeding and eternal weight of glory'!

7. Add to this the advantage which others may receive by seeing our behaviour under affliction We find by experience, example frequently makes a deeper impression upon us than precept. And what examples have a stronger influence, not only on those who are partakers of like precious faith, but even on them who have not known God, than that of a soul calm and serene in the midst of storms; sorrowful, yet always rejoicing; meekly accepting whatever is the will of God, however grievous it may be to nature; saying, in sickness and pain, 'The cup which my Father hath given me, shall I not drink it?'—in loss or want, 'The Lord gave; the Lord hath taken away; blessed be the name of the Lord!'

V. 1. I am to conclude with some inferences. And, first, how wide is the difference between darkness of soul, and heaviness; which, nevertheless, are so generally confounded with each other, even by experienced Christians! Darkness, or the wilderness state, implies a total loss of joy in the Holy Ghost: heaviness does not; in the midst of this we may 'rejoice with joy unspeakable.' They that are in darkness have lost the peace of God: they that are in heaviness have not; so far from it, that at the very time 'peace,' as well as 'grace,' may 'be multiplied' unto them. In the former, the love of God is waxed cold, if it be not utterly extinguished; in the latter, it retains its full force, or, rather, increases daily. In these, faith itself, if not totally lost, is, however, grievously decayed: their evidence and conviction of things not seen, particularly of the pardoning love of God, is not so clear or strong as in time past; and their trust in Him is proportionably weakened: those, though they see Him not, yet have a clear, unshaken confidence in God, and an abiding evidence of that love whereby all their sins are blotted out. So that as long as we can distinguish faith from unbelief, hope from despair, peace from war, the love of God from the love of the world, we may infallibly distinguish heaviness from darkness!

2. We may learn from hence, secondly, that there may be need of heaviness, but there can be no need of darkness. There may be need of our being in 'heaviness for a season,' in order to the ends above recited; at least, in this sense, as it is a natural result of those 'manifold temptations,' which are needful to try and increase our faith, to confirm and enlarge our hope, to purify our heart from all unholy tempers, and to perfect us in love. And, by consequence, they are needful in order to brighten our crown, and add to our eternal weight of glory. But we cannot say, that darkness is needful in order to any of these ends. It is no way conducive to them: the loss of faith, hope, love, is surely neither conducive to holiness, nor to the increase of that reward in heaven which will be in proportion to our holiness on earth.

3. From the Apostle's manner of speaking we may gather, thirdly, that even heaviness is not *always* needful. 'Now, for a season, if need be': so it is not needful for *all persons*; nor for any person at *all times*. God is able, He has both power and wisdom, to work, when He pleases, the same work of grace in any soul by other means. And in some instances He does so; He causes those whom it pleaseth Him to go on from strength to strength, even till they 'perfect holiness in His fear,' with scarce any heaviness at all; as having an absolute power over the heart of man, and moving all the springs of it at His pleasure. But these cases are rare: God generally sees good to try 'acceptable men in the furnace of affliction.' So that manifold temptations, and heaviness, more or less, are usually the portion of His dearest children

4. We ought, therefore, lastly, to watch and pray, and use our utmost endeavours to avoid falling into darkness. But we need not be solicitous how to avoid, so much as how to improve by, heaviness. Our great care should be, so to behave ourselves under it, so to wait upon the Lord therein, that it may fully answer all the design of His love, in permitting it to come

upon us; that it may be a means of increasing our faith, of confirming our hope, of perfecting us in alll holiness. Whenever it comes, let us have an eye to those gracious ends for which it is permitted, and use all diligence that we may not make void the counsel of God against ourselves. Let us earnestly work together with Him, by the grace which He is continually giving us, in 'purifying ourselves from all pollution, both of flesh and spirit,' and daily growing in the grace of our Lord Jesus Christ, till we are received into His everlasting kingdom!

SERMON XLII

SELF-DENIAL

And He said to them all, If any man will come after Me, let him deny himself, and take up his cross daily, and follow Me.—LUKE ix. 23.

IT has been frequently imagined, that the direction here given related chiefly, if not wholly, to the Apostles; at least, to the Christians of the first ages, or those in a state of persecution. But this is a grievous mistake: for although our blessed Lord is here directing His discourse more immediately to His Apostles, and those other disciples who attended Him in the days of His flesh: yet, in them He speaks to us, and to all mankind, without any exception or limitation. The very reason of the thing puts it beyond dispute, that the duty which is here enjoined is not peculiar to them, or to the Christians of the early ages. It no more regards any particular order of men, or particular time, than any particular country. No: it is of the most universal nature, respecting all times, and all persons, yea, and all things; not meats and drinks only, and things pertaining to the senses The meaning is, 'If any man,' of whatever rank, station, circumstances, in any nation, in any age of the world, 'will' effectually 'come after Me, let him deny himself' in all things; let him 'take up his cross,' of whatever kind; yea, and that 'daily; and follow Me.'

2. The *denying* ourselves, and the *taking up our cross*, in the full extent of the expression, is not a thing of small concern:

it is not expedient only, as are some of the circumstantials of religion; but it is absolutely, indispensably necessary, either to our becoming or continuing His disciples. It is absolutely necessary, in the very nature of the thing, to our coming after Him, and following Him; insomuch that, as far as we do not practise it, we are not His disciples. If we do not continually deny ourselves, we do not learn of Him. but of other masters. If we do not take up our cross daily, we do not come after Him, but after the world, or the prince of the world, or our own fleshly mind. If we are not walking in the way of the cross, we are not following Him; we are not treading in His steps; but going back from, or at least wide of, Him.

3. It is for this reason, that so many ministers of Christ, in almost every age and nation, particularly since the Reformation of the church from the innovations and corruptions gradually crept into it, have wrote and spoke so largely on this important duty, both in their public discourses and private exhortations. This induced them to disperse abroad many tracts upon the subject; and some in our own nation. They knew, both from the oracles of God and from the testimony of their own experience, how impossible it was not to deny our Master, unless we will deny ourselves; and how vainly we attempt to follow Him that was crucified, unless we take up our own cross daily.

4. But may not this very consideration make it reasonable to inquire, If so much has been said and wrote on the subject already, what need is there to say or write any more? I answer, there are no inconsiderable numbers, even of people fearing God, who have not had the opportunity either of hearing what has been spoke, or reading what has been wrote, upon it. And perhaps, if they had read much of what has been written, they would not have been much profited. Many who have wrote (some of them large volumes), do by no means appear to have understood the subject. Either they had imperfect views of the very nature of it (and then they could never explain it to theres), or they were unacquainted with the due extent of it; they did not see how exceeding broad this command is; or they were not sensible of the absolute, the indispensable necessity of

it. Others speak of it in so dark, so perplexed, so intricate, so
mystical a manner, as if they designed rather to conceal it from
the vulgar, than to explain it to common readers. Others speak
admirably well, with great clearness and strength, on the necessity of self-denial; but then they deal in generals only, without
coming to particular instances, and so are of little use to the
bulk of mankind, to men of ordinary capacity and education.
And if some of them do descend to particulars, it is to those
particulars only which do not affect the generality of men,
since they seldom, if ever, occur in common life; such as the
enduring imprisonment, or tortures—the giving up, in a literal
sense, their houses or lands, their husbands or wives, children,
or life itself; to none of which we are called, nor are likely to be,
unless God should permit times of public persecution to return.
In the meantime, I know of no writer in the English tongue
who has described the nature of self-denial in plain and intelligible terms, such as lie level with common understandings,
and applied it to those little particulars which daily occur in
common life. A discourse of this kind is wanted still; and it is
wanted the more, because in every stage of the spiritual life,
although there is a variety of particular hindrances of our
attaining grace or growing therein, yet are all resolvable into
these general ones,—either we do not deny ourselves, or we do
not take up our cross.

In order to supply this defect in some degree, I shall endeavour to show, first, what it is for a man to deny himself,
and what to take up his cross; and, secondly, that if a man be not
fully Christ's disciple, it is always owing to the want of this.

I. 1. I shall, first, endeavour to show, what it is for a man
to 'deny himself, and take up his cross daily.' This is a point
which is, of all others, most necessary to be considered and
throughly understood, even on this account, that it is, of all
others, most opposed by numerous and powerful enemies.
All our nature must certainly rise up against this, even in its
own defence; the world, consequently, the men who take nature,
not grace, for their guide, abhor the very sound of it. And the
great enemy of our souls, well knowing its importance, cannot

but move every stone against it. But this is not all: even those who have in some measure shaken off the yoke of the devil, who have experienced, especially of late years, a real work of grace in their hearts, yet are no friends to this grand doctrine of Christianity, though it is so peculiarly insisted on by their Master. Some of them are as deeply and totally ingnorant concerning it, as if there was not one word about it in the Bible. Others are farther off still, having unawares imbibed strong prejudices against it. These they have received partly from outside Christians, men of a fair speech and behaviour, who want nothing of godliness but the power, nothing of religion but the spirit; and partly from those who did once, if they do not now, 'taste of the powers of the world to come.' But are there any of these who do not both practise self-denial themselves, and recommend it to others? You are little acquainted with mankind, if you doubt of this. There are whole bodies of men who only do not declare war against it. To go no farther than London: look upon the whole body of Predestinarians, who by the free mercy of God have lately been called out of the darkness of nature into the light of faith. Are they patterns of self-denial? How few of them even profess to practise it at all! How few of them recommend it themselves, or are pleased with them that do! Rather, do they not continually represent it in the most odious colours, as if it were seeking 'salvation by works,' or seeking 'to establish our own righteousness'? And how readily do Antinomians of all kinds, from the smooth Moravian, to the boisterous, foul-mouthed Ranter, join the cry, with their silly, unmeaning cant of *legality*, and *preaching the law*! Therefore you are in constant danger of being wheedled, hectored, or ridiculed out of this important gospel doctrine, either by false teachers, or false brethren (more or less beguiled from the simplicity of the gospel), if you are not deeply grounded therein. Let fervent prayer, then, go before, accompany, and follow what you are now about to read, that it may be written in your heart by the finger of God, so as never to be erased.

2. But what is self-denial? Wherein are we to deny ourselves? And whence does the necessity of this arise? I answer, the will of God is the supreme, unalterable rule for every intelligent

creature; equally binding every angel in heaven, and every man upon earth. Nor can it be otherwise: this is the natural, necessary result of the relation between creatures and their Creator. But if the will of God be our one rule of action in everything, great and small, it follows, by undeniable consequence, that we are not to do our own will in anything. Here, therefore, we see at once the nature, with the ground and reason, of self-denial. We see the nature of self-denial; it is the denying or refusing to follow our own will, from a conviction that the will of God is the only rule of action to us. And we see the reason thereof, because we are creatures; because 'it is He that hath made us, and not we ourselves.'

3. This reason for self-denial must hold, even with regard to the angels of God in heaven; and with regard to man, innocent and holy, as he came out of the hands of his Creator. But a farther reason for it arises from the condition wherein all men are since the fall. We are all now 'shapen in wickedness, and in sin did our mother conceive us.' Our nature is altogether corrupt in every power and faculty. And our will, depraved equally with the rest, is wholly bent to indulge our natural corruption. On the other hand, it is the will of God that we resist and counteract that corruption, not at some times or in some things only, but at all times and in all things. Here, therefore, is a farther ground for constant and universal self-denial.

4. To illustrate this a little further: the will of God is a path leading straight to God. The will of man, which once ran parallel with it, is now another path, not only different from it, but, in our present state, directly contrary to it: it leads from God. If, therefore, we walk in the one, we must necessarily quit the other. We cannot walk in both. Indeed, a man *of faint heart and feeble hands* may *go in two ways*, one after the other. But he cannot walk in two ways at the same time: he cannot, at one and the same time, follow his own will, and follow the will of God: he must choose the one or the other; denying God's will, to follow his own; or denying himself, to follow the will of God.

5. Now, it is undoubtedly pleasing, for the time, to follow our own will, by indulging, in any instance that offers, the

corruption of our nature: but by following it in anything, we so far strengthen the perverseness of our will; and by indulging it, we continually increase the corruption of our nature. So, by the food which is agreeable to the palate, we often increase a bodily disease: it gratifies the taste, but it inflames the disorder; it brings pleasure, but it also brings death.

6. On the whole, then, to deny ourselves, is, to deny our own will, where it does not fall in with the will of God; and that however pleasing it may be. It is, to deny ourselves any pleasure which does not spring from, and lead to, God; that is, in effect, to refuse going out of our way, though into a pleasant, flowery path; to refuse what we know to be deadly poison, though agreeable to the taste.

7. And every one that would follow Christ, that would be His real disciple, must not only deny himself, but take up his cross also. A cross is anything contrary to our will, anything displeasing to our nature. So that taking up our cross goes a little farther than denying ourselves; it rises a little higher, and is a more difficult task to flesh and blood; it being more easy to forgo pleasure, than to endure pain.

8. Now, in running 'the race that is set before us,' according to the will of God, there is often a cross lying in the way; that is, something which is not only not joyous, but grievous; something which is contrary to our will, which is displeasing to our nature. What, then, is to be done? The choice is plain: either we must take up our cross, or we must turn aside from the way of God, 'from the holy commandment delivered to us'; if we do not stop altogether, or turn back to everlasting perdition!

9. In order to the healing of that corruption, that evil disease, which every man brings with him into the world, it is often needful to pluck out, as it were, a right eye, to cut off a right hand,—so painful is either the thing itself which must be done, or the only means of doing it; the parting, suppose, with a foolish desire, with an inordinate affection; or a separation from the object of it, without which it can never be extinguished. In the former kind, the tearing away such a desire or affection, when it is deeply rooted in the soul, is often like the piercing of a sword, yea, like 'the dividing asunder of the soul and

spirit, the joints and marrow.' The Lord then sits upon the soul as a refiner's fire, to burn up all the dross thereof. And this is a cross indeed; it is essentially painful; it must be so, in the very nature of the thing. The soul cannot be thus torn asunder, it cannot pass through the fire, without pain.

10. In the latter kind, the means to heal a sin-sick soul, to cure a foolish desire, an inordinate affection, are often painful, not in the nature of the thing, but from the nature of the disease. So when our Lord said to the rich young man, 'Go, sell that thou hast, and give to the poor' (as well knowing, this was the only means of healing his covetousness), the very thought of it gave him so much pain, that 'he went away sorrowful'; choosing rather to part with his hope of heaven, than his possessions on earth. This was a burden he could not consent to lift, a cross he would not take up. And in the one kind or the other, every follower of Christ will surely have need to 'take up his cross daily.'

11. The 'taking up' differs a little from 'bearing his cross.' We are then properly said to 'bear our cross,' when we endure what is laid upon us without our choice, with meekness and resignation. Whereas, we do not properly 'take up our cross,' but when we voluntarily suffer what it is in our power to avoid; when we willingly embrace the will of God, though contrary to our own; when we choose what is painful, because it is the will of our wise and gracious Creator.

12. And thus it behoves every disciple of Christ to take up, as well as to bear, his cross. Indeed, in one sense, it is not *his* alone; it is common to him, and many others; seeing there is no temptation befalls any man, εἰ μὴ ἀνθρώπινος,—'but such as is common to men': such as is incident and adapted to their common nature and situation in the present world. But in another sense, as it is considered with all its circumstances, it is his; peculiar to himself: it is prepared of God for him; it is given by God to him, as a token of His love. And if he receives it as such, and, after using such means to remove the pressure as Christian wisdom directs, lies as clay in the potter's hand; it is disposed and ordered by God for his good, both with regard to the quality of it, and in respect to its quantity and degree, its duration, and every other circumstance.

13. In all this, we may easily conceive our blessed Lord to act as the Physician of our souls, not merely 'for His own pleasure, but for our profit, that we may be partakers of His holiness.' If, in searching our wounds, He puts us to pain, it is only in order to heal them. He cuts away what is putrefied or unsound, in order to preserve the sound part. And if we freely choose the loss of a limb, rather than the whole body should perish; how much more should we choose, figuratively, to cut off a right hand, rather than the whole soul should be cast into hell!

14. We see plainly, then, both the nature and ground of taking up our cross. It does not imply the *disciplining ourselves* (as some speak); the literally tearing our own flesh; the wearing hair-cloth, or iron girdles, or anything else that would impair our bodily health (although we know not what allowance God may make for those who act thus through involuntary ignorance) but the embracing the will of God, though contrary to our own; the choosing wholesome, though bitter, medicines; the freely accepting temporary pain, of whatever kind, and in whatever degree, when it is either essentially or accidentally necessary to eternal pleasure.

II. 1. I am, secondly, to show, that it is always owing to the want either of self-denial, or taking up his cross, that any man does not throughly follow Him, is not fully a disciple of Christ.

It is true, this may be partly owing, in some cases, to the want of the means of grace: of hearing the true word of God spoken with power; of the sacraments, or of Christian fellowship. But where none of these is wanting, the great hindrance of our receiving or growing in the grace of God is always the want of denying ourselves, or taking up our cross.

2. A few instances will make this plain. A man hears the word which is able to save his soul: he is well pleased with what he hears, acknowledges the truth, and is a little affected by it; yet he remains 'dead in trespasses and sins,' senseless and unawakened. Why is this? Because he will not part with his bosom sin, though he now knows it is an abomination to the Lord. He came to hear, full of lust and unholy desire; and he will

not part with them. Therefore no deep impression is made upon him, but his foolish heart is still hardened: that is, he is still senseless and unawakened, because he will not deny himself.

3. Suppose he [begins to awake out of sleep, and his eyes are a little opened, why are they so quickly closed again? Why does he again sink into the sleep of death? Because he again yields to his bosom sin; he drinks again of the pleasing poison. Therefore it is impossible that any lasting impression should be made upon his heart; that is, he relapses into his fatal insensibility, because he will not deny himself.

4. But this is not the case with all. We have many instances of those who when once awakened sleep no more. The impressions once received do not wear away: they are not only deep, but lasting. And yet, many of these have not found what they seek: they mourn, and yet are not comforted. Now, why is this? It is because they do not 'bring forth fruits meet for repentance'; because they do not, according to the grace they have received, 'cease from evil, and do good.' They do not cease from the easily besetting sin, the sin of their constitution, of their education, or of their profession; or they omit doing the good they may, and know they ought to do, because of some disagreeable circumstances attending it: that is, they do not attain faith, because they will not 'deny themselves,' or 'take up their cross.'

5. But this man did receive 'the heavenly gift'; he did 'taste of the powers of the world to come'; he saw 'the light of the glory of God in the face of Jesus Christ'; the 'peace which passeth all understanding' did rule his heart and mind; and 'the love of God was shed abroad' therein, 'by the Holy Ghost which was given unto him.' Yet he is now weak as another man; he again relishes the things of earth, and has more taste for the things which are seen than for those which are not seen; the eye of his understanding is closed again, so that he cannot 'see Him that is invisible'; his love is waxed cold, and the peace of God no longer rules in his heart. And no marvel; for he has again given place to the devil, and grieved the Holy Spirit of God. He has turned again unto folly, to some pleasing sin, if not in outward act, yet in heart. He has given place to pride, or anger,

or desire, to self-will or stubbornness. Or he did not stir up the gift of God which was in him; he gave way to spiritual sloth, and would not be at the pains of 'praying always, and watching thereunto with all perseverance': that is, he made shipwreck of the faith, for want of self-denial, and taking up his cross daily

6. But perhaps he has not made shipwreck of the faith: he has still a measure of the Spirit of adoption, which continues to witness with his spirit that he is a child of God. However, he is not 'going on to perfection'; he is not, as once, hungering and thirsting after righteousness, panting after the whole image and full enjoyment of God, as the hart after the waterbrook. Rather he is weary and faint in his mind, and, as it were, hovering between life and death. And why is he thus, but because he hath forgotten the word of God, 'By works is faith made perfect'? He does not use all diligence in working the works of God He does not 'continue instant in prayer,' private as well as public; in communicating, hearing, meditation, fasting, and religious conference. If he does not wholly neglect some of these means, at least he does not use them all with his might. Or he is not zealous of works of charity, as well as works of piety He is not merciful after his power, with the full ability which God giveth. He does not fervently serve the Lord by doing good to men, in every kind and in every degree he can, to their souls as well as their bodies. And why does he not continue in prayer? Because in times of dryness it is pain and grief unto him. He does not continue in hearing at all opportunities, because sleep is sweet; or it is cold, or dark, or rainy. But why does he not continue in works of mercy? Because he cannot feed the hungry, or clothe the naked, unless he retrench the expense of his own apparel, or use cheaper and less pleasing food Beside which, the visiting the sick, or those that are in prison, is attended with many disagreeable circumstances. And so are most works of spiritual mercy; reproof in particular. He *would* reprove his neighbour; but sometimes shame, sometimes fear, comes between; for he may expose himself, not only to ridicule, but to heavier inconveniences too. Upon these and the like considerations he omits one or more, if not all, works of mercy and piety. Therefore, his faith is not made perfect, neither

can he grow in grace; namely, because he will not deny himself, and take up his daily cross.

7. It manifestly follows, that it is always owing to the want either of self-denial, or taking up his cross, that a man does not throughly follow his Lord, that he is not fully a disciple of Christ. It is owing to this, that he who is dead in sin does not awake, though the trumpet be blown; that he who begins to awake out of sleep, yet has no deep or lasting conviction; that he who is deeply and lastingly convinced of sin does not attain remission of sins; that some who have received this heavenly gift retain it not, but make shipwreck of the faith; and that others, if they do not draw back to perdition, yet are weary and faint in their mind, and do not reach the mark of the prize of the high calling of God in Christ Jesus.

III. 1. How easily may we learn hence, that they know neither the Scripture nor the power of God, who directly or indirectly, in public or in private, oppose the doctrine of self-denial and the daily cross! How totally ignorant are these men of an hundred particular texts, as well as of the general tenor of the whole oracles of God! And how entirely unacquainted must they be with true, genuine, Christian experience—of the manner wherein the Holy Spirit ever did, and does at this day, work in the souls of men! They may talk, indeed, very loudly and confidently (a natural fruit of ignorance), as though they were the only men who understood either the Word of God, or the experience of His children; but their words are, in every sense, *vain words*; they are weighed in the balance, and found wanting.

2. We may learn from hence, secondly, the real cause why not only many particular persons, but even bodies of men, who were once burning and shining lights, have now lost both their light and heat. If they did not hate and oppose they at least lightly esteemed, this precious gospel doctrine. If they did not boldly say, '*Abnegationem omnem proculcamus, internecioni damus*'; 'We trample all self-denial under foot, we devote it to destruction'; yet they neither valued it according to its high importance, nor took any pains in practising it. '*Hanc mystici docent,*' said that great, bad man: 'the *mystic* writers

teach self-denial.' No; the *inspired* writers! And God teaches it to every soul who is willing to hear His voice!

3. We may learn from hence, thirdly, that it is not enough for a minister of the gospel not to oppose the doctrine of self-denial, to say nothing concerning it. Nay, he cannot satisfy his duty by saying a little in favour of it. If he would, indeed, be pure from the blood of all men, he must speak of it frequently and largely; he must inculcate the necessity of it in the clearest and strongest manner; he must press it with his might, on all persons, at all times, and in all places; laying 'line upon line, line upon line, precept upon precept, precept upon precept': so shall he have a conscience void of offence; so shall he save his own soul and those that hear him.

4. Lastly: see that you apply this, every one of you, to your own soul. Meditate upon it when you are in secret: ponder it in your heart! Take care not only to understand it throughly but to remember it to your lives' end! Cry unto the Strong for strength, that you may no sooner understand, than enter upon the practice of it! Delay not the time, but practise it immediately, from this very hour! Practise it universally, on every one of the thousand occasions which occur in all circumstances of life! Practise it daily, without intermission, from the hour you first set your hand to the plough, and enduring therein, to the end, till your spirit returns to God!

SERMON XLIII

THE CURE OF EVIL-SPEAKING

If thy brother shall trespass against thee, go and tell him his fault between thee and him alone: if he shall hear thee, thou hast gained thy brother.

But if he will not hear thee, then take with thee one or two more, that in the mouth of two or three witnesses every word may be established.

And if he shall neglect to hear them, tell it unto the church: but if he neglect to hear the church, let him be unto thee as an heathen man and a publican.—
—MATT. xviii. 15-17.

'SPEAK evil of no man,' says the great Apostle: as plain a command as, 'Thou shalt do no murder.' But who even among

Christians, regards this command? Yea, how few are there that
so much as understand it! What is evil-speaking? It is not, as
some suppose, the same with lying or slandering. All a man says
may be as true as the Bible; and yet the saying of it is evil-
speaking. For evil-speaking is neither more nor less than speaking
evil of an absent person; relating something evil, which was
really done or said by one that is not present when it is related.
Suppose, having seen a man drunk, or heard him curse or
swear, I tell this when he is absent; it is evil-speaking. In our
language this is also, by an extremely proper name, termed
'backbiting.' Nor is there any material difference between this
and what we usually style 'tale-bearing.' If the tale be delivered
in a soft and quiet manner (perhaps with expressions of good-
will to the person, and of hope that things may not be quite so
bad), then we call it 'whispering.' But in whatever manner it
be done, the thing is the same; the same in substance, if not in
circumstance. Still it is evil-speaking; still this command,
'Speak evil of no man,' is trampled under foot; if we relate to
another the fault of a third person, when he is not present to
answer for himself.

2. And how extremely common is this sin, among all orders
and degrees of men! How do high and low, rich and poor, wise
and foolish, learned and unlearned, run into it continually!
Persons who differ from each other in all things else, nevertheless
agree in this. How few are there that can testify before God, 'I
am clear in this matter; I have always set a watch before my
mouth, and kept the door of my lips'! What conversation do
you hear, of any considerable length, whereof evil-speaking
is not one ingredient? and that even among persons who, in the
general, have the fear of God before their eyes, and do really
desire to have a conscience void of offence toward God and
toward man.

3. And the very commonness of this sin makes it difficult
to be avoided. As we are encompassed with it on very side,
so, if we are not deeply sensible of the danger, and continually
guarding against it, we are liable to be carried away by the
torrent. In this instance, almost the whole of mankind is, as
it were, in a conspiracy against us. And their example steals

upon us, we know not how; so that we insensibly slide into the imitation of it. Besides, it is recommended from within, as well as from without. There is scarce any wrong temper in the mind of man, which may not be occasionally gratified by it, and consequently incline us to it. It gratifies our pride, to relate those faults of others whereof we think ourselves not to be guilty. Anger, resentment, and all unkind tempers, are indulged by speaking against those with whom we are displeased; and, in many cases, by reciting the sins of their neighbours, men indulge their own foolish and hurtful desires.

4. Evil-speaking is the more difficult to be avoided, because it frequently attacks us in disguise. We speak thus out of a noble, generous (it is well if we do not say), holy indignation, against these vile creatures! We commit sin from mere hatred of sin! We serve the devil out of pure zeal for God! It is merely in order to punish the wicked that we run into this wickedness. 'So do the passions' (as one speaks) 'all justify themselves,' and palm sin upon us under the veil of holiness!

5. But is there no way to avoid the snare? Unquestionably there is. Our blessed Lord has marked out a plain way for His followers, in the words above recited None, who warily and steadily walk in this path, will ever fall into evil-speaking. This rule is either an infallible preventive, or a certain cure of it. In the preceding verses, our Lord had said, 'Woe to the world, because of offences,'—unspeakable misery will arise in the world from this baleful fountain (*offences* are all things whereby any one is turned out of, or hindered in, the ways of God): 'For it must be that offences come,'—such is the nature of things; such the wickedness, folly, and weakness of mankind: 'but woe to that man,'—miserable is that man, 'by whom the offence cometh.' 'Wherefore, if thy hand, thy foot, thine eye, cause thee to offend,'—if the most dear enjoyment, the most beloved and useful person, turn thee out of or hinder thee in the way, 'pluck it out,'—cut them off, and cast them from thee. But how can we avoid giving offence to some, and being offended at others? especially, suppose they are quite in the wrong, and we see it with our own eyes? Our Lord here teaches us how: He lays down a sure method of avoiding offences and evil-

speaking together. 'If thy brother shall trespass against thee, go and tell him of his fault between thee and him alone: if he shall hear thee, thou hast gained thy brother. But if he will not hear thee, then take with thee one or two more, that in the mouth of two or three witnesses every word may be established. And if he shall neglect to hear them, tell it unto the church: but if he neglect to hear the church, let him be unto thee as an heathen man and a publican.'

I. 1. First. 'If thy brother shall sin against thee, go and tell him of his fault between thee and him alone.' The most literal way of following this first rule, where it is practicable, is the best: therefore, if thou seest with thine own eyes a brother, a fellow Christian, commit undeniable sin, or hearest it with thine own ears, so that it is impossible for thee to doubt the fact, then thy part is plain: take the very first opportunity of going to him; and, if thou canst have access, 'tell him of his fault between thee and him alone.' Indeed, great care is to be taken that this is done in a right spirit, and in a right manner. The success of a reproof greatly depends on the spirit wherein it is given. Be not, therefore, wanting in earnest prayer to God, that it may be given in a lowly spirit; with a deep, piercing conviction, that it is God alone who maketh thee to differ; and that if any good be done by what is now spoken, God doeth it Himself. Pray that He would guard thy heart, enlighten thy mind, and direct thy tongue to such words as He may please to bless. See that thou speak in a meek as well as a lowly spirit; for the 'wrath of man worketh not the righteousness of God.' If he be 'overtaken in a fault,' he can no otherwise be restored, than 'in the spirit of meekness.' If he opposes the truth, yet he cannot be brought to the knowledge thereof, but by gentleness. Still speak in a spirit of tender love, 'which many waters cannot quench.' If love is not conquered, it conquers all things. Who can tell the force of love?

> Love can bow down the stubborn neck,
>   The stone to flesh convert;
> Soften, and melt, and pierce, and break
>   An adamantine heart.

Confirm, then, your love toward him, and you will thereby 'heap coals of fire upon his head.'

2. But see that the manner also wherein you speak be according to the gospel of Christ. Avoid everything in look, gesture, word, and tone of voice, that savours of pride or self-sufficiency. Studiously avoid everything magisterial or dogmatical, everything that looks like arrogance or assuming. Beware of the most distant approach to disdain, overbearing, or contempt. With equal care avoid all appearance of anger; and though you use great plainness of speech, yet let there be no reproach, no railing accusation, no token of any warmth, but that of love. Above all, let there be no shadow of hate or ill-will, no bitterness or sourness of expression; but use the air and language of sweetness as well as gentleness, that all may appear to flow from love in the heart. And yet this sweetness need not hinder your speaking in the most serious and solemn manner; as far as may be, in the very words of the oracles of God (for there are none like them), and as under the eye of Him who is coming to judge the quick and dead.

3. If you have not an opportunity of speaking to him in person, or cannot have access, you may do it by a messenger; by a common friend, in whose prudence, as well as uprightness, you can throughly confide. Such a person, speaking in your name, and in the spirit and manner above described, may answer the same end, and, in a good degree, supply your lack of service. Only beware you do not feign the want of opportunity, in order to shun the cross; neither take it for granted that you cannot have access, without ever making the trial. Whenever you can speak in your own person, it is far better. But you should rather do it by another, than not at all: this way is better than none.

4. But what, if you can neither speak yourself, nor find such a messenger as you can confide in? If this be really the case, it then only remains to write. And there may be some circumstances which make this the most advisable way of speaking. One of these circumstances is, when the person with whom we have to do is of so warm and impetuous a temper as does not easily bear reproof, especially from an equal or inferior. But

it may be so introduced and softened in writing as to make it far more tolerable. Besides, many will read the very same words, which they could not bear to hear. It does not give so violent a shock to their pride, nor so sensibly touch their honour. And suppose it makes little impression at first, they will, perhaps, give it a second reading, and, upon farther consideration, lay to heart what before they disregarded. If you add your name, this is nearly the same thing as going to him, and speaking in person. And this should always be done, unless it be rendered improper by some very particular reason.

5. It should be well observed, not only that this is a step which our Lord absolutely commands us to take, but that He commands us to take this step first, before we attempt any other. No alternative is allowed, no choice of anything else: this is the way; walk thou in it. It is true, He enjoins us, if need require, to take two other steps; but they are to be taken successively after this step, and neither of them before it: much less are we to take any other step, either before or beside this. To do anything else, or not to do this, is, therefore, equally inexcusable.

6. Do not think to excuse yourself for taking an entirely different step, by saying, 'Why, I did not speak to any one, till I was so burdened that I could not refrain.' You was burdened! It was no wonder you should, unless your conscience was seared; for you was under the guilt of sin, of disobeying a plain commandment of God! You ought immediately to have gone, and told 'your brother of his fault between you and him alone.' If you did not, how should you be other than burdened (unless your heart was utterly hardened), while you was trampling the command of God under foot, and 'hating your brother in your heart'? And what a way you have found to unburden yourself! God reproves you for a sin of omission, for not telling your brother of his fault; and you comfort yourself under His reproof by a sin of commission, by telling your brother's fault to another person! Ease bought by sin is a dear purchase! I trust in God, you will have no ease, but will be burdened so much the more, till you 'go to your brother and tell him,' and no one else.

7. I know but of one exception to this rule: there may be

a peculiar case, wherein it is necessary to accuse the guilty, though absent, in order to preserve the innocent. For instance: you are acquainted with the design which a man has against the property or life of his neighbour. Now, the case may be so circumstanced, that there is no other way of hindering that design from taking effect, but the making it known, without delay, to him against whom it is laid. In this case, therefore, this rule is set aside, as is that of the Apostle, 'Speak evil of no man': and it is lawful, yea, it is our bounden duty, to speak evil of an absent person, in order to prevent his doing evil to others and himself at the same time. But remember, meanwhile, that all evil-speaking is, in its own nature, deadly poison. Therefore if you are sometimes constrained to use it as a medicine, yet use it with fear and trembling; seeing it is so dangerous a medicine, that nothing but absolute necessity can excuse your using it at all. Accordingly, use it as seldom as possible; never but when there is such a necessity: and even then use as little of it as is possible; only so much as is necessary for the end proposed. At all other times, 'go and tell him of his fault between thee and him alone.'

II. 1. But what, 'if he will not hear'? if he repay evil for good? if he be enraged rather than convinced? What, if he hear to no purpose, and go on still in the evil of his way? We must expect this will frequently be the case; the mildest and tenderest reproof will have no effect; but the blessing we wished for another will return into our own bosom. And what are we to do then? Our Lord has given us a clear and full direction. Then 'take with thee one or two more': this is the second step. Take one or two whom you know to be of a loving spirit, lovers of God and of their neighbour. See, likewise, that they be of a lowly spirit, and 'clothed with humility.' Let them also be such as are meek and gentle, patient and long-suffering; not apt to 'return evil for evil, or railing for railing, but contrariwise blessing.' Let them be men of understanding, such as are endued with wisdom from above; and men unbiassed, free from partiality, free from prejudice of any kind. Care should likewise be taken, that both the persons and their characters be well known to him: and let those that are acceptable to him be chosen preferable to any others.

2. Love will dictate the manner wherein they should proceed, according to the nature of the case. Nor can any one particular manner be prescribed for all cases. But perhaps, in general, one might advise, before they enter upon the thing itself, let them mildly and affectionately declare that they have no anger or prejudice toward him, and that it is merely from a principle of good-will that they now come, or at all concern themselves with his affairs. To make this the more apparent, they might then calmly attend to your repetition of your former conversation with him, and to what he said in his own defence, before they attempted to determine anything. After this they would be better able to judge in what manner to proceed, 'that by the mouth of two or three witnesses every word might be established'; that whatever you have said may have its full force by the additional weight of their authority.

3. In order to this, may they not, (1) Briefly repeat what you spoke, and what he answered? (2) Enlarge upon, open, and confirm the reasons which you had given? (3) Give weight to your reproof, showing how just, how kind, and how seasonable it was? And, lastly, enforce the advices and persuasions which you had annexed to it? And these may likewise hereafter, if need should require, bear witness of what was spoken.

4. With regard to this, as well as the preceding rule, we may observe, that our Lord gives us no choice, leaves us no alternative, but expressly commands us to do this, and nothing else in the place of it. He likewise directs us when to do this; neither sooner nor later; namely, *after* we have taken the first, and *before* we have taken the third step. It is then only that we are authorized to relate the evil another has done, to those whom we desire to bear a part with us in this great instance of brotherly love. But let us have a care how we relate it to any other person, till both these steps have been taken. If we neglect to take these, of if we take any others, what wonder if we are burdened still? For we are sinners against God, and against our neighbour; and how fairly soever we may colour it, yet, if we have any conscience, our sin will find us out, and bring a burden upon our soul.

III. 1. That we may be throughly instructed in this weighty affair, our Lord has given us a still farther direction: 'If he will not hear them,' then, and not till then, 'tell it to the church.' This is the third step. All the question is, how this word, 'the church,' is here to be understood. But the very nature of the thing will determine this beyond all reasonable doubt. You cannot tell it to the national Church, the whole body of men termed 'the Church of England.' Neither would it answer any Christian end if you could: this, therefore, is not the meaning of the word. Neither can you tell it to that whole body of people in England with whom you have a more immediate connexion. Nor, indeed, would this answer any good end: the word, therefore, is not to be understood thus. It would not answer any valuable end to tell the faults of every particular member to the church (if you would so term it), the congregation or society, united together in London. It remains that you tell it to the elder or elders of the church, to those who are overseers of that flock of Christ to which you both belong, who watch over yours and his soul, 'as they that must give account.' And this should be done, if it conveniently can, in the presence of the person concerned, and, though plainly, yet with all the tenderness and love which the nature of the thing will admit. It properly belongs to their office, to determine concerning the behaviour of those under their care, and to rebuke, according to the demerit of the offence, 'with all authority.' When, therefore, you have done this, you have done all which the Word of God, or the law of love, requireth of you: you are not now partaker of his sin: but if he perish, his blood is on his own head.

2. Here, also, let it be observed, that this, and no other, is the third step which we are to take; and that we are to take it in its order after the other two; not before the second, much less the first, unless in some very particular circumstance. Indeed, in one case, the second step may coincide with this: they may be, in a manner, one and the same. The elder or elders of the church may be so connected with the offending brother, that they may set aside the necessity, and supply the place, of the one or two witnesses; so that it may suffice to tell it to them, after you have told it to your brother, 'between you and him alone.'

3. When you have done this, you have delivered your own soul. 'If he will not hear the church,' if he persist in his sin, 'let him be to thee as an heathen man and a publican.' You are under no obligation to think of him any more; only when you commend him to God in prayer. You need not speak of him any more, but leave him to his own Master. Indeed, you still owe to him, as to all other Heathens, earnest, tender good-will. You owe him courtesy, and, as occasion offers, all the offices of humanity. But have no friendship, no familiarity with him; no other intercourse than with an open Heathen.

4. But if this be the rule by which Christians walk, which is the land where the Christians live? A few you may possibly find scattered up and down, who made a conscience of observing it. But how very few! How thinly scattered upon the face of the earth! And where is there any body of men that universally walk thereby? Can we find them in Europe? or, to go no farther, in Great Britain or Ireland? I fear not: I fear we may search these kingdoms throughout, and yet search in vain. Alas for the Christian world! Alas for Protestants, for Reformed Christians! Oh, 'who will rise up with me against the wicked?' 'Who will take God's part' against the evil-speakers? Art thou the man? By the grace of God, wilt thou be one who art not carried away by the torrent? Art thou fully determined, God being thy helper, from this very hour to set a watch, a continual 'watch, before thy mouth, and keep the door of thy lips'? From this hour wilt thou walk by this rule, 'Speaking evil of no man'? If thou seest thy brother do evil, wilt thou 'tell him of his fault between thee and him alone'? afterwards, 'take one or two' witnesses, and then only 'tell it to the church'? If this be the full purpose of thy heart, then learn one lesson well, 'Hear evil of no man.' If there were no hearers, there would be no speakers, of evil. And is not (according to the vulgar proverb) the receiver as bad as the thief? If, then, any begin to speak evil in thy hearing, check him immediately. Refuse to hear the voice of the charmer, charm he never so sweetly; let him use ever so soft a manner, so mild an accent, ever so many pro-fessions of good-will for him whom he is stabbing in the dark, whom he smiteth under the fifth rib! Resolutely refuse to hear.

though the whisperer complain of being 'burdened till he speak'
Burdened! thou fool! dost thou travail with thy cursed secret,
as a woman travaileth with child? Go, then, and be delivered
of thy burden in the way the Lord hath ordained! First, 'go
and tell thy brother of his fault between thee and him alone':
next, 'take with thee one or two' common friends, and tell him
in their presence: if neither of these steps take effect, then 'tell
it to the church.' But, at the peril of thy soul, tell it to no one
else, either before or after, unless in that one exempt case, when
it is absolutely needful to preserve the innocent! Why shouldest
thou burden another as well as thyself, by making him partaker
of thy sin?

5. Oh that all you who bear the reproach of Christ, who are
in derision called Methodists, would set an example to the
Christian world, so called, at least in this one instance! Put ye
away evil-speaking, tale-bearing, whispering: let none of them
proceed out of your mouth! See that you 'speak evil of no man';
of the absent, nothing but good. If ye must be distinguished,
whether ye will or no, let this be the distinguishing mark of a
Methodist: 'He censures no man behind his back: by this fruit
ye may know him.' What a blessed effect of this self-denial
should we quickly feel in our hearts! How would our 'peace
flow as a river,' when we thus 'followed peace with all men'!
How would the love of God abound in our own souls, while
we thus confirmed our love to our brethren! And wht an
effect would it have on all that were united together in the name
of the Lord Jesus! How would brotherly love continually
increase, when this grand hindrance of it was removed! All
the members of Christ's mystical body would then naturally
care for each other. 'If one member suffered, all would suffer
with it'; 'if one was honoured, all would rejoice with it'; and
every one would love his brother 'with a pure heart fervently.'
Nor is this all: but what an effect might this have, even on the
wild unthinking world! How soon would they descry in us,
what they could not find among all the thousands of their
brethren, and cry (as Julian the apostate to his heathen courtiers),
'See how these Christians love one another!' By this chiefly
would God convince the world, and prepare them also for His

kingdom; as we may easily learn from those remarkable words in our Lord's last, solemn prayer: 'I pray for them who shall believe in Me, that they may be one, as Thou, Father, art in Me, and I in Thee, . . . that the world may believe that Thou hast sent Me.' The Lord hasten the time! The Lord enable us thus to love one another, not only 'in word and in tongue, but in deed and in truth,' even as Christ hath loved us!

SERMON XLIV

THE USE OF MONEY

I say unto you, Make to yourselves friends of the mammon of unrighteousness; that, when ye fail, they may receive you into everlasting habitations.—
Luke xvi. 9.

Our Lord, having finished the beautiful parable of the Prodigal Son, which He had particularly addressed to those who murmured at His receiving publicans and sinners, adds another relation of a different kind, addresssed rather to the children of God. 'He said unto His disciiples'—not so much to the Scribes and Pharisees, to whom He had been speaking before—'There was a certain rich man, who had a steward, and he was accused to him of wasting his goods. And calling him, he said, Give an account of thy stewardship for thou canst be no longer steward' (verses 1, 2). After reciting the method which the bad steward used to provide against the day of necessity, our Saviour adds, 'His lord commended the unjust steward'; namely, in this respect, that he used timely precaution; and subjoins this weighty reflection, 'The children of this world are wiser in their generation than the children of light' (verse 8): those who seek no other portion than this world 'are wiser' (not absolutely; for they are, one and all, the veriest fools, the most egregious madmen under heaven; but, 'in their generation,' in their own way; they are more consistent with themselves; they are truer to their acknowledged principles; they more steadily pursue their end) 'than the children of light,'—than they who see 'the light of the glory of God in the face of Jesus Christ.' Then follow the words above recited: 'And I'—the only-begotten Son of God, the Creator, Lord, and possessor of heaven and earth, and all that is therein; the Judge of all, to whom ye are to 'give an account of your stewardship,' when ye 'can be no longer stewards'; 'I say unto you'—learn in this respect, even of the unjust steward —'make yourselves friends,' by wise, timely precaution, 'of the mammon of unrighteousness.' 'Mammon' means riches, or money. It is termed 'the mammon of unrighteousness,' because of the unrighteous manner wherein it is frequently procured, and wherein even that which was honestly procured is generally employed. 'Make yourself friends' of this, by doing all possible good, particularly to the children of God; 'that, when ye fail'— when ye return to dust, when ye have no more place under the sun—those of them who are gone before 'may receive you,' may welcome you, into the 'everlasting habitations.'

2. An excellent branch of Christian wisdom is here inculcated by our Lord on all His followers, namely, the right use of money,—a subject largely spoken of, after their manner, by men of the world; but not sufficiently considered by those whom God hath chosen out of the world. These, generally, do not consider, as the importance of the subject requires, the use of this excellent talent. Neither do they understand how to employ it to the greatest advantage; the introduction of which into the world is one admirable instance of the wise and gracious providence of God. It has, indeed, been the manner of poets, orators, and philosophers, in almost all ages and nations, to rail at this, as the grand corrupter of the world, the bane of virtue, the pest of human society. Hence, nothing so commonly heard, as

> *Nocens ferrum, ferroque nocentius aurum:*
> (And gold, more mischievous than keenest steel.)

Hence the lamentable complaint,

> *Effodiuntur opes, irritamenta malorum.*
> (Wealth is dug up, incentive to all ill.)

Nay, one celebrated writer gravely exhorts his countrymen, in order to banish all vice at once, to 'throw all their money into the sea':

> *In mare proximum:*
> *Summi materiem mali!*

But is not all this mere empty rant? Is there any solid reason therein? By no means. For, let the world be as corrupt as it will, is gold or silver to blame? 'The love of money,' we know, 'is the root of all evil'; but not the thing itself. The fault does not lie in the money, but in them that use it. It may be used ill: and what may not? But it may likewise be used well: it is full as applicable to the best, as to the worst uses. It is of unspeakable service to all civilized nations, in all the common affairs of life: it is a most compendious instrument of transacting all manner of business, and (if we use it according to Christian wisdom) of doing all manner of good. It is true, were man in a state of innocence, or were all men 'filled with the Holy Ghost,' so that, like the infant church at Jerusalem, 'no man counted anything he had his own,' but 'distribution was made to every one as he had need,' the use of it would be superseded; as we cannot conceive there is anything of the kind among the inhabitants of heaven. But, in the present state of mankind, it is an excellent gift of God, answering the noblest ends. In the hands of His children, it is food for the hungry, drink for the thirsty, raiment for the naked: it gives to the traveller and the stranger where to lay his head. By it we may supply the place of an husband to the widow, and of a father to the fatherless. We may be a defence for the oppressed, a means of health to the sick, of ease to them that are in pain; it may be as eyes to the blind, as feet to the lame; yea, a lifter up from the gates of death.

3. It is, therefore, of the highest concern, that all who fear God know how to employ this valuable talent; that they be instructed how it may answer these glorious ends, and in the highest degree. And, perhaps, all the instructions which are necessary for this may be reduced to three plain rules, by the exact observance whereof we may approve ourselves faithful stewards of 'the mammon of unrighteousness.'

I. 1. The first of these is (he that heareth, let him understand!) 'Gain all you can.' Here we may speak like the children of the world: we meet them on their own ground. And it is our bounden duty to do this: we ought to gain all we can gain, without buying gold too dear, without paying more for it than it is worth. But this it is certain we ought not to do; we ought not to gain money at the expense of life, nor (which is in effect the same thing) at the expense of our health. Therefore, no gain whatsoever should induce us to enter into, or to continue in, any employ, which is of such a kind, or is attended with so hard or so long labour, as to impair our constitution. Neither should we begin or continue in any business which necessarily deprives us of proper seasons for food and sleep, in such a proportion as our nature requires. Indeed, there is a great difference here. Some employments are absolutely and totally unhealthy; as those which imply the dealing much with arsenic, or other equally hurtful minerals, or the breathing an air tainted with streams of melting lead, which must at length destroy the firmest constitution. Others may not be absolutely unhealthy, but only to persons of a weak constitution. Such are those which require many hours to be spent in writing; especially if a person write sitting, and lean upon his stomach, or remain long in an uneasy posture. But whatever it is which reason or experience shows to be destructive of health or strength, that we may not submit to; seeing 'the life is more' valuable 'than meat, and the body than raiment': and, if we are already engaged in such an employ, we should exchange it, as soon as possible, for some which, if it lessen our gain, will, however, not lessen our health

2. We are, secondly, to gain all we can without hurting our mind, any more than our body. For neither may we hurt this: we must preserve, at all events, the spirit of an healthful mind. Therefore, we may not engage or continue in any sinful trade; any that is contrary to the law of God, or of our country. Such are all that necessarily imply our robbing or defrauding the king of his lawful customs. For it is, at least, as sinful to defraud the king of his right, as to rob our fellow subjects: and the king has full as much right to his customs as we have to our houses and apparel Other businesses there are which, however

innocent in themselves, cannot be followed with innocence now; at least not in England; such, for instance, as will not afford a competent maintenance without cheating or lying, or conformity to some custom which is not consistent with a good conscience: these, likewise, are sacredly to be avoided, whatever gain they may be attended with, provided we follow the custom of the trade; for, to gain money, we must not lose our souls. There are yet others which many pursue with perfect innocence, without hurting either their body or mind; and yet, perhaps, you cannot; either they may entangle you in that company which would destroy your soul; and by repeated experiments it may appear that you cannot separate the one from the other; or there may be an idiosyncrasy—a peculiarity in your constitution of soul (as there is in the bodily constitution of many), by reason whereof that employment is deadly to you, which another may safely follow. So I am convinced, from many experiments, I could not study, to any degree of perfection, either mathematics, arithmetic, or algebra, without being a Deist, if not an Atheist: and yet others may study them all their lives without sustaining any inconvenience. None, therefore, can here determine for another; but every man must judge for himself, and abstain from whatever he in particular finds to be hurtful to his soul.

3. We are, thirdly, to gain all we can, without hurting our neighbour. But this we may not, cannot do, if we love our neighbour as ourselves. We cannot, if we love every one as ourselves, hurt any one *in his substance*. We cannot devour the increase of his lands, and perhaps the lands and houses themselves, by gaming, by overgrown bills (whether on account of physic, or law, or anything else), or by requiring or taking such interest as even the laws of our country forbid. Hereby all pawnbroking is excluded: seeing, whatever good we might do thereby, all unprejudiced men see with grief to be abundantly overbalanced by the evil. And if it were otherwise, yet we are not allowed to 'do evil that good may come.' We cannot, consistent with brotherly love, sell our goods below the market price; we cannot study to ruin our neighbour's trade, in order to advance our own; much less can we entice away, or receive,

any of his servants or workmen whom he has need of. None can gain by swallowing up his neighbour's substance, without gaining the damnation of hell!

4. Neither may we gain by hurting our neighbour *in his body*. Therefore we may not sell anything which tends to impair health. Such is, eminently, all that liquid fire, commonly called drams, or spirituous liquors. It is true, these may have a place in medicine; they may be of use in some bodily disorders; although there would rarely be occasion for them, were it not for the unskilfulness of the practitioner. Therefore, such as prepare and sell them only for this end may keep their conscience clear. But who are they? Who prepare them only for this end? Do you know ten such distillers in England? Then excuse these. But all who sell them in the common way, to any that will buy, are poisoners general. They murder His Majesty's subjects by wholesale, neither does their eye pity or spare. They drive them to hell, like sheep. And what is their gain? Is it not the blood of these men? Who then would envy their large estates and sumptuous palaces? A curse is in the midst of them: the curse of God cleaves to the stones, the timber, the furniture of them! The curse of God is in their gardens, their walks, their groves; a fire that burns to the nethermost hell! Blood, blood is there: the foundation, the floor, the walls, the roof, are stained with blood! And canst thou hope, O thou man of blood, though thou art 'clothed in scarlet and fine linen, and farest sumptuously every day'; canst thou hope to deliver down thy *fields of blood* to the third generation? Not so; for there is a God in heaven: therefore, thy name shall soon be rooted out. Like as those whom thou hast destroyed, body and soul, 'thy memorial shall perish with thee!'

5. And are not they partakers of the same guilt, though in a lower degree, whether surgeons, apothecaries, or physicians, who play with the lives or health of men, to enlarge their own gain? who purposely lengthen the pain or disease, which they are able to remove speedily? who protract the cure of their patient's body, in order to plunder his substance? Can any man be clear before God, who does not shorten every disorder 'as much as he can,' and remove all sickness and pain

38

'as soon as he can'? He cannot: for nothing can be more clear, than that he does not 'love his neighbour as himself'; than that he does not 'do unto others, as he would they should do unto himself.'

6. This is dear-bought gain. And so is whatever is procured by hurting our neighbour *in his soul*; by ministering, suppose, either directly or indirectly, to his unchastity or intemperance; which certainly none can do who has any fear of God, or any real desire of pleasing Him. It nearly concerns all those to consider this, who have anything to do with taverns, victualling-houses, opera-houses, play-houses, or any other places of public fashionable diversion. If these profit the souls of men, you are clear; your employment is good, and your gain innocent; but if they are either sinful in themselves, or natural inlets to sin of various kinds, then, it is to be feared, you have a sad account to make. O beware, lest God say in that day, 'These have perished in their iniquity, but their blood do I require at thy hands!'

7. These cautions and restrictions being observed, it is the bounden duty of all who are engaged in worldly business to observe that first and great rule of Christian wisdom, with respect to money, 'Gain all you can.' Gain all you can by honest industry. Use all possible diligence in your calling. Lose no time. If you understand yourself, and your relation to God and man, you know you have none to spare. If you understand your particular calling, as you ought, you will have no time that hangs upon your hands. Every business will afford some employment sufficient for every day and every hour. That wherein you are placed, if you follow it in earnest, will leave you no leisure for silly, unprofitable diversions. You have always something better to do, something that will profit you, more or less. And 'whatsoever thy hand findeth to do, do it with thy might.' Do it as soon as possible: no delay! No putting off from day to day, or from hour to hour! Never leave anything till to-morrow, which you can do to-day. And do it as well as possible. Do not sleep or yawn over it: put your whole strength to the work. Spare no pains. Let nothing be done by halves, or in a slight and careless manner. Let nothing in your business be left undone, if it can be done by labour or patience.

8. Gain all you can, by common sense, by using in your

business all the understanding which God has given you. It is amazing to observe, how few do this; how men run on in the same dull track with their forefathers. But whatever they do who know not God, this is no rule for you. It is a shame for a Christian not to improve upon *them* in whatever he takes in hand. You should be continually learning, from the experience of others, or from your own experience, reading, and reflection, to do everything you have to do better to-day than you did yesterday. And see that you practise whatever you learn, that you may make the best of all that is in your hands.

II. 1. Having gained all you can, by honest wisdom, and unwearied diligence, the second rule of Christian prudence is, 'Save all you can.' Do not throw the precious talent into the sea: leave that folly to heathen philosophers. Do not throw it away in idle expenses, which is just the same as throwing it into the sea. Expend no part of it merely to gratify the desire of the flesh, the desire of the eye, or the pride of life.

2. Do not waste any part of so precious a talent, merely in gratifying the desires of the flesh; in procuring the pleasures of sense, of whatever kind; particularly, in enlarging the pleasure of tasting. I do not mean, avoid gluttony and drunkenness only: an honest Heathen would condemn these. But there is a regular, reputable kind of sensuality, an elegant epicurism, which does not immediately disorder the stomach, nor (sensibly at least) impair the understanding; and yet (to mention no other effects of it now) it cannot be maintained without considerable expense. Cut off all this expense! Despise delicacy and variety, and be content with what plain nature requires.

3. Do not waste any part of so precious a talent, merely in gratifying the desire of the eye, by superfluous or expensive apparel, or by needless ornaments. Waste no part of it in curiously adorning your houses; in superfluous or expensive furniture; in costly pictures, painting, gilding, books; in elegant rather than useful gardens. Let your neighbours, who know nothing better, do this: 'let the dead bury their dead.' But 'what is that to thee?' says our Lord: 'follow thou Me.' Are you willing? Then you are able so to do!

4. Lay out nothing to gratify the pride of life, to gain the admiration or praise of men. This motive of expense is frequently interwoven with one or both of the former. Men are expensive in diet, or apparel, or furniture, not barely to please their appetite, or to gratify their eye, or their imagination, but their vanity too. 'So long as thou doest well unto thyself, men will speak good of thee.' So long as thou art 'clothed in purple and fine linen, and farest sumptuously every day,' no doubt many will applaud thy elegance of taste, thy generosity and hospitality. But do not buy their applause so dear. Rather be content with the honour that cometh from God.

5. Who would expend anything in gratifying these desires, if he considered, that to gratify them is to increase them? Nothing can be more certain than this: daily experience shows the more they are indulged, they increase the more. Whenever, therefore, you expend anything to please your taste or other senses, you pay so much for sensuality. When you lay out money to please your eye, you give so much for an increase of curiosity—for a stronger attachment to these pleasures which perish in the using. While you are purchasing anything which men use to applaud, you are purchasing more vanity. Had you not then enough of vanity, sensuality, curiosity, before? Was there need of any addition? And would you pay for it too? What manner of wisdom is this? Would not the literally throwing your money into the sea be a less mischievous folly?

6. And why should you throw away money upon your children, any more than upon yourself, in delicate food, in gay or costly apparel, in superfluities of any kind? Why should you purchase for them more pride or lust, more vanity, or foolish and hurtful desires? They do not want any more; they have enough already; nature has made ample provision for them: why should you be at farther expense to increase their temptations and snares, and to pierce them through with more sorrows?

7. Do not leave it to them to throw away. If you have good reason to believe they would waste what is now in your possession, in gratifying, and thereby increasing, the desire of the flesh, the desire of the eye, or the pride of life; at the peril of

theirs and your own soul, do not set these traps in their way. Do not offer your sons or your daughters unto Belial, any more than unto Moloch. Have pity upon them, and remove out of their way what you may easily foresee would increase their sins, and consequently plunge them deeper into everlasting perdition! How amazing, then, is the infatuation of those parents who think they can never leave their children enough! What! cannot you leave them enough of arrows, firebrands, and death? not enough of foolish and hurtful desires? not enough of pride, lust, ambition, vanity? not enough of everlasting burnings? Poor wretch! thou fearest where no fear is. Surely both thou and they, when ye are lifting up your eyes in hell, will have enough both of 'the worm that never dieth,' and of 'the fire that never shall be quenched'!

8. 'What then would you do, if you was in my case? if you had a considerable fortune to leave?' Whether I *would* do it or no, I know what I *ought* to do: this will admit of no reasonable question. If I had one child, elder or younger, who knew the value of money, one who, I believed, would put it to the true use, I should think it my absolute, indispensable duty to leave that child the bulk of my fortune; and to the rest just so much as would enable them to live in the manner they had been accustomed to do. 'But what, if all your children were equally ignorant of the true use of money?' I ought then (hard saying! who can hear it?) to give each what would keep him above want; and to bestow all the rest in such a manner as I judged would be most for the glory of God.

III. 1. But let not any man imagine that he has done anything, barely by going thus far, by 'gaining and saving all he can,' if he were to stop here. All this is nothing, if a man go not forward, if he does not point all this at a farther end. Nor, indeed, can a man properly be said to save anything, if he only lays it up. You may as well throw your money into the sea, as bury it in the earth. And you may as well bury it in the earth, as in your chest, or in the Bank of England. Not to use, is effectually to throw it away. If, therefore, you would indeed 'make yourselves friends of the mammon of unrighteousness,' add the third rule to the two preceding. Having, first, gained all you can, and, secondly, saved all you can, then 'give all you can.'

2. In order to see the ground and reason of this, consider, when the Possessor of heaven and earth brought you into being, and placed you in this world, He placed you here, not as a proprietor, but a steward: as such He entrusted you, for a season, with goods of various kinds; but the sole property of these still rests in Him, nor can ever be alienated from Him. As you yourself are not your own, but His, such is, likewise, all that you enjoy. Such is your soul and your body, not your own, but God's. And so is your substance in particular. And He has told you, in the most clear and express terms, how you are to employ it for Him, in such a manner, that it may be all an holy sacrifice, acceptable through Christ Jesus. And this light, easy service, He hath promised to reward with an eternal weight of glory.

3. The directions which God has given us, touching the use of our worldly substance, may be comprised in the following particulars. If you desire to be a faithful and a wise steward, out of that portion of your Lord's goods which He has for the present lodged in your hands, but with the right of resuming whenever it pleases him, first, provide things needful for yourself; food to eat, raiment to put on, whatever nature moderately requires for preserving the body in health and strength. Secondly provide these for your wife, your children, your servants, or any others who pertain to your household. If, when this is done, there be an overplus left, then "do good to them that are of the household of faith.' If there be an overplus still, "as you have opportunity, do good unto all men." In so doing, you give all you can; nay, in a sound sense, all you have: for all that is laid out in this manner is really given to God. You "render unto God the things that are God's," not only by what you give to the poor, but also by that which you expend in providing things needful for yourself and your household.

4. If, then, a doubt should at any time arise in your mind concerning what you are going to expend, either on yourself or any part of your family, you have an easy way to remove

it. Calmly and seriously inquire, "(1.) In expending this, am I acting according to my character? Am I acting herein, not as a proprietor, but as a steward of my Lord's goods? (2.) Am I doing this in obedience to his word? In what scripture does he require me so to do? (3.) Can I offer up this action, this expense, as a sacrifice to God through Jesus Christ? (4.) Have I reason to believe, that for this very work I shall have a reward at the resurrection of the just?" You will seldom need anything more to remove any doubt which arises on this head; but, by this four-fold consideration, you will receive clear light as to the way wherein you should go.

5. If any doubt still remain, you may farther examine yourself by prayer, according to those heads of inquiry. Try whether you can say to the Searcher of hearts, your conscience not condemning you, "Lord, thou seest I am going to expend this sum on that food, apparel, furniture. And thou knowest, I act therein with a single eye, as a steward of thy goods, expending this portion of them thus, in pursuance of the design thou hadst in entrusting me with them. Thou knowest I do this in obedience to thy word, as thou commandest, and because thou commandest it. Let this, I beseech thee, be an holy sacrifice, acceptable through Jesus Christ! And give me a witness in myself, that for this labour of love I shall have a recompence when thou rewardest every man according to his works." Now, if your conscience bear you witness in the Holy Ghost, that this prayer is well-pleasing to God, then have you no reason to doubt but that expense is right and good, and such as will never make you ashamed.

6. You see, then, what it is to "make yourselves friends of the mammon of unrighteousness," and by what means you may procure, "that when ye fail, they may receive you into the everlasting habitations." You see the nature and extent of truly Christian prudence, so far as it relates to the use of that great talent, money. Gain all you can, without hurting either yourself or your neighbour, in soul or body, by applying hereto with unintermitted diligence, and with all the understanding which God has given you; —save all you can, by cutting off every expense which serves only to indulge foolish desire; to gratify

either the desire of the flesh, the desire of the eye, or the pride
of life; waste nothing, living or dying, on sin or folly, whether
for yourself or your children;—and then give all you can, or,
in other words, give all you have to God. Do not stint yourself,
like a Jew rather than a Christian, to this or that proportion.
Render unto God, not a tenth, not a third, not half, but all
that is God's, be it more or less; by employing all on yourself,
your household, the household of faith, and all mankind, in
such a manner, that you may give a good account of your
stewardship, when ye can be no longer stewards; in such a
manner as the oracles of God direct, both by general and particular precepts; in such a manner, that whatever ye do may be
"a sacrifice of a sweet-smelling savour to God," and that every
act may be rewarded in that day, when the Lord cometh with
all his saints.

7. Brethren, can we be either wise or faithful stewards unless
we thus manage our Lord's goods? We cannot, as not only the
oracles of God, but our own conscience, beareth witness. Then
why should we delay? Why should we confer any longer with
flesh and blood, or men of the world? Our kingdom, our
wisdom, is not of this world: heathen custom is nothing to us.
We follow no men any farther than they are followers of Christ.
Hear ye him: yea, to-day, while it is called to-day, hear and
obey his voice! At this hour, and from this hour, do his will:
fulfil his word, in this and in all things! I entreat you, in the
name of the Lord Jesus, act up to the dignity of your calling!
No more sloth! Whatsoever your hand findeth to do, do it
with your might! No more waste! Cut off every expense
which fashion caprice, or flesh and blood demand! No more
covetousness! But employ whatever God has entrusted you
with, in doing good, all possible good, in every possible kind
and degree, to the household of faith, to all men! This is no
small part of "the wisdom of the just." Give all ye have, as well
as all ye are, a spiritual sacrifice to Him who withheld not from
you His Son, His only Son: so "laying up in store for yourselves a good foundation against the time to come, that ye
may attain eternal life!"

THE END

INDEX